FOAL

"YOU'LL NEVER KNOW"

by C. Tyler

"COLLATERAL DAMAGE"

THE U.S. DEPARTMENT OF DEFENSE DEFINES COLLATERAL DAMAGE AS 'UNINTENTIONAL OR INCIDENTAL INJURY OR DAMAGE TO PERSONS OR OBJECTS THAT WOULD NOT BE LAWFUL MILITARY TARGETS.

OTHER BOOKS BY C. TYLER

THE JOB THING (FANTAGRAPHICS BOOKS, 1993)
LATE BLOOMER (FANTAGRAPHICS BOOKS, 2005)
YOU'LL NEVER KNOW BOOK I: A GOOD and
    DECENT MAN (FANTAGRAPHICS BOOKS, 2009)

FANTAGRAPHICS BOOKS
7563 LAKE CITY WAY NE
SEATTLE, WA 98115

DESIGNED BY C. TYLER AND J. COVEY
PRODUCTION BY PAUL BARESH
EDITED BY KIM THOMPSON
ASSOCIATE PUBLISHER: ERIC REYNOLDS
PUBLISHED BY GARY GROTH AND KIM THOMPSON

TO RECEIVE A FREE CATALOGUE OF COMICS, CALL 1-800-657-1100, OR
VISIT THE FANTAGRAPHICS WEBSITE: www.fantagraphics.com.

DISTRIBUTED IN THE U.S. BY W.W. NORTON AND COMPANY, INC. (212-354-5500)
DISTRIBUTED IN CANADA BY CANADIAN MANDA GROUP (416-516-0911)
DISTRIBUTED IN THE UNITED KINGDOM BY TURNAROUND DISTRIBUTION (208-829-3009)

C. TYLER WEBSITE: www.bloomerland.com
FACEBOOK: CAROL TYLER

FIRST PRINTING: July 2010

ISBN: 978-1-60699-418-4

PRINTED IN SINGAPORE

C. TYLER PERSONAL THANKS TO:
MOM AND DAD. GINIA AND HER FAMILY. ALL OTHER TYLERS.
JUSTIN GREEN, JULIA and ALLEN, THREE DOGS. GOOD FOLKS
AND NEIGHBORS, ARTS AND COMICS PEOPLE. FRIENDS AND
ASSOCIATES AT UC'S DAAP SCHOOL OF ART AND THE CGC.
M.B. REILLY. STUDENTS. CAREGIVERS WHO GOT ME THROUGH
THE SURGERY. KIM AND THE FANTA TEAM. LOTS OF OTHER
COOL PEOPLE AND FORCES THAT CHALLENGE and DELIGHT.
GIANT THANKS TO THE U.S. ARMY SIGNAL CORPS FOR THE
PHOTO DOCUMENTATION OF WWII. HOW COULD ANYONE
DOUBT THE HISTORICAL RECORD? — I WANT TO
ACKNOWLEDGE THE FAMILIES THAT, BECAUSE OF YNK,
HAVE BEGUN LONG OVERDUE CONVERSATIONS. —
AND FINALLY, TO MY SISTER ANN: THANK YOU FOR
GUIDING ME EVERY STEP OF THE WAY.

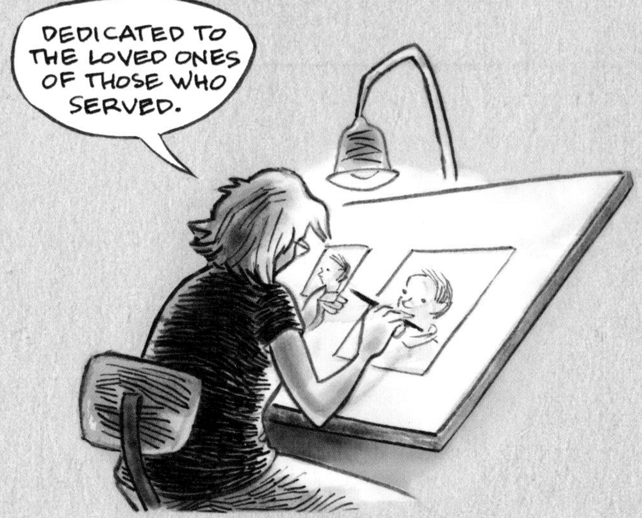
DEDICATED TO THE LOVED ONES OF THOSE WHO SERVED.

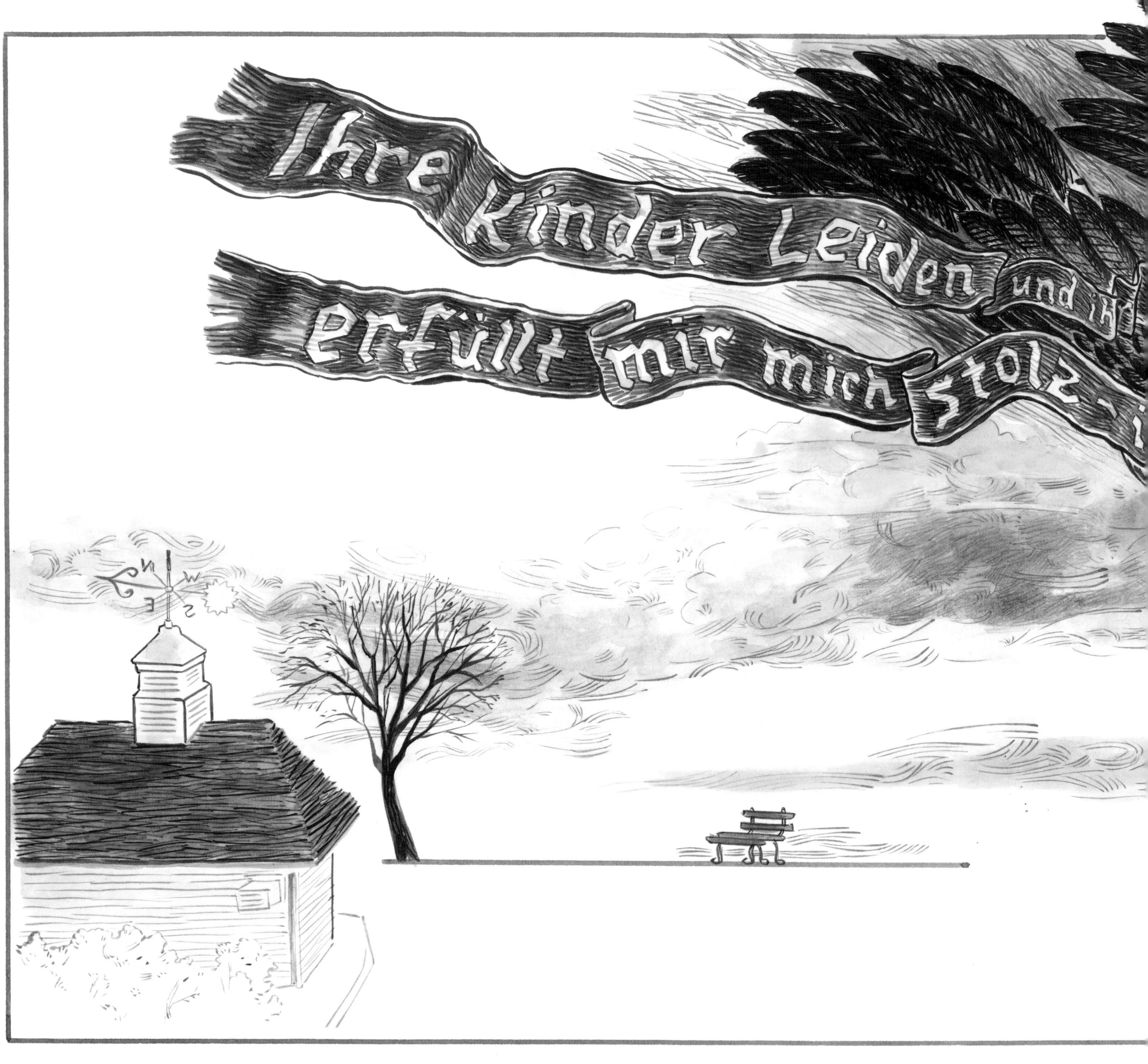
Ihre Kinder Leiden und ih
erfüllt mir mich stolz -
N
W
E
S

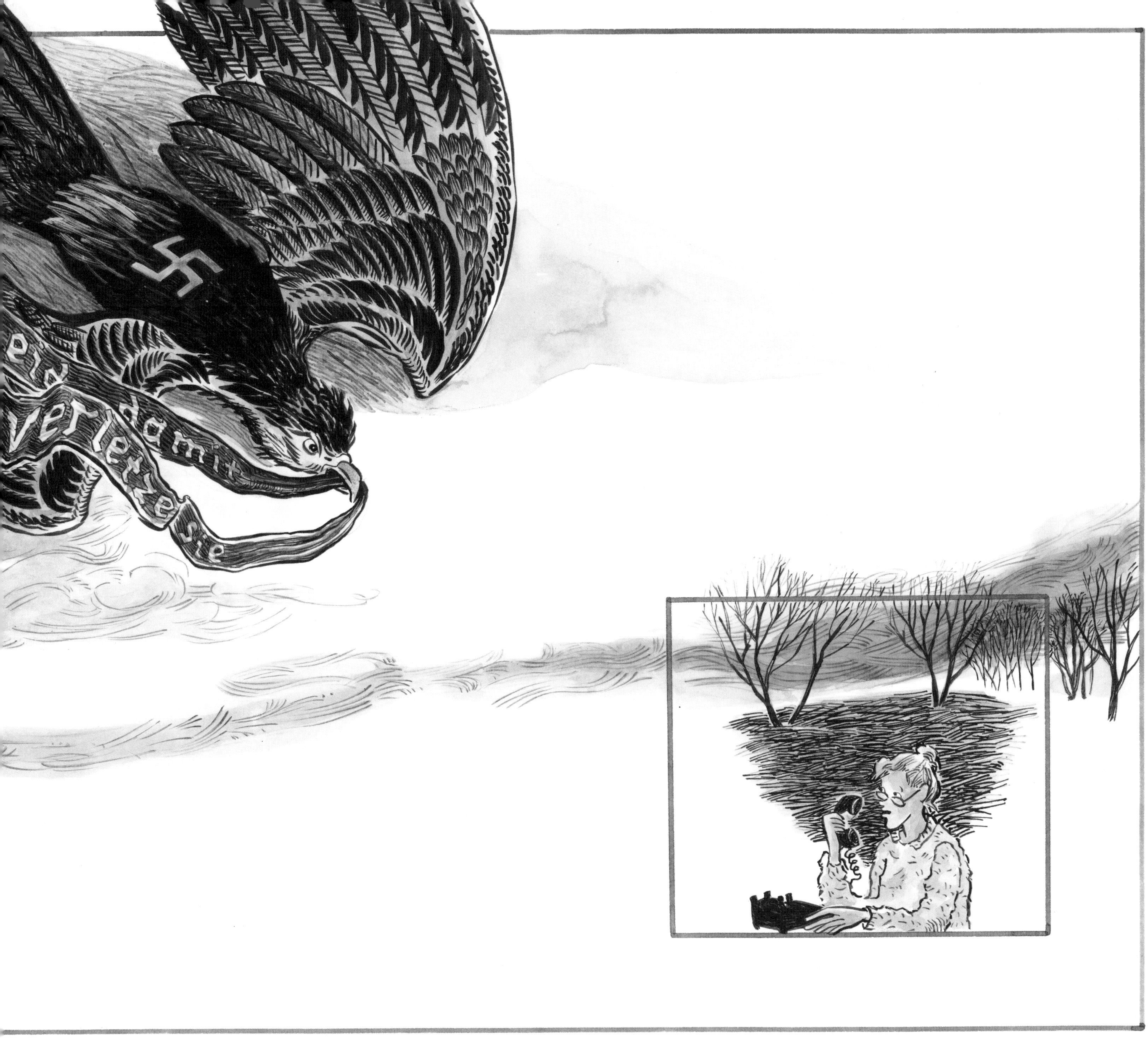
damit
verletze sie

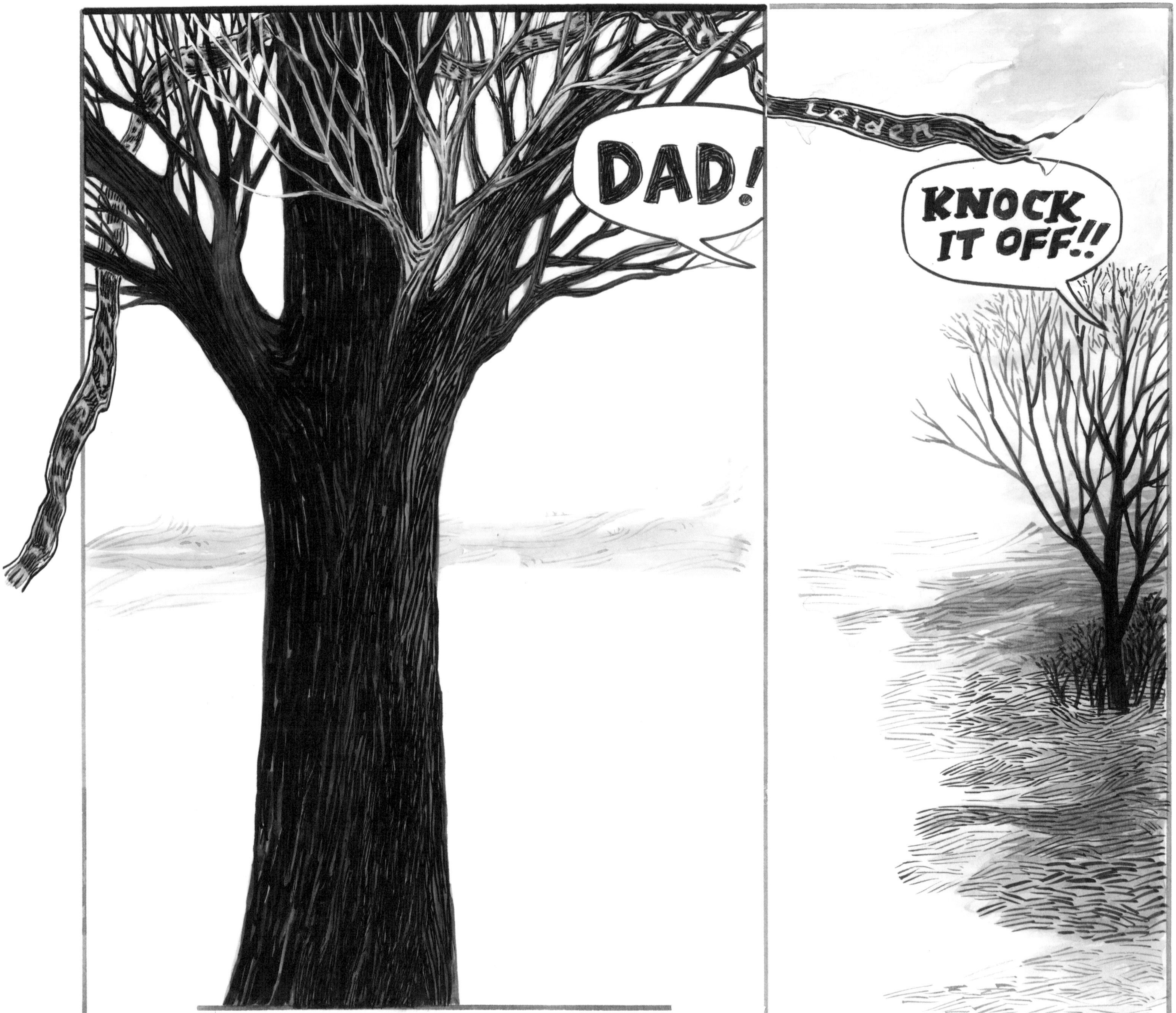
DAD!
KNOCK IT OFF!!

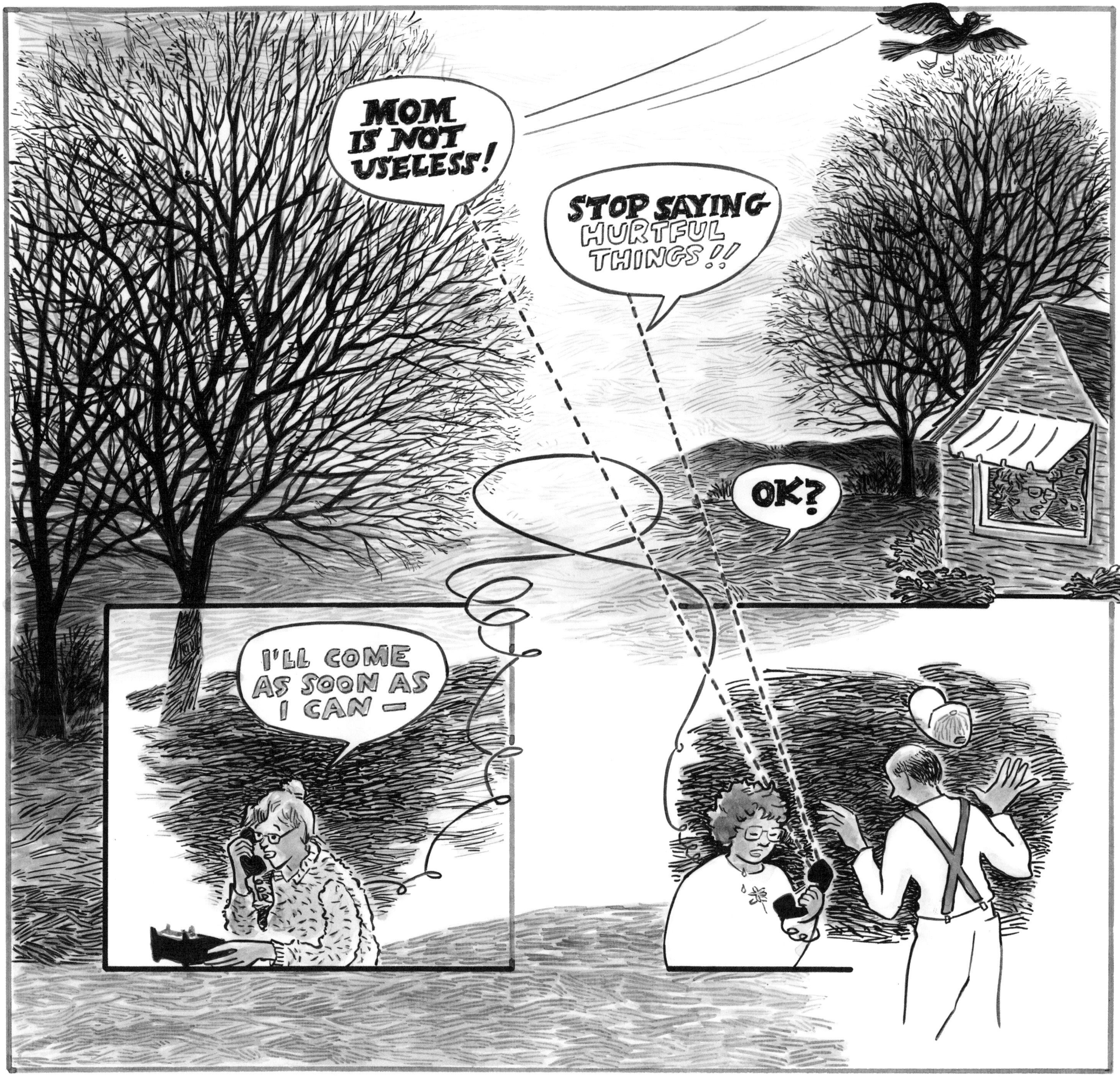
MOM IS NOT USELESS!
STOP SAYING HURTFUL THINGS!!
OK?
I'LL COME AS SOON AS I CAN –

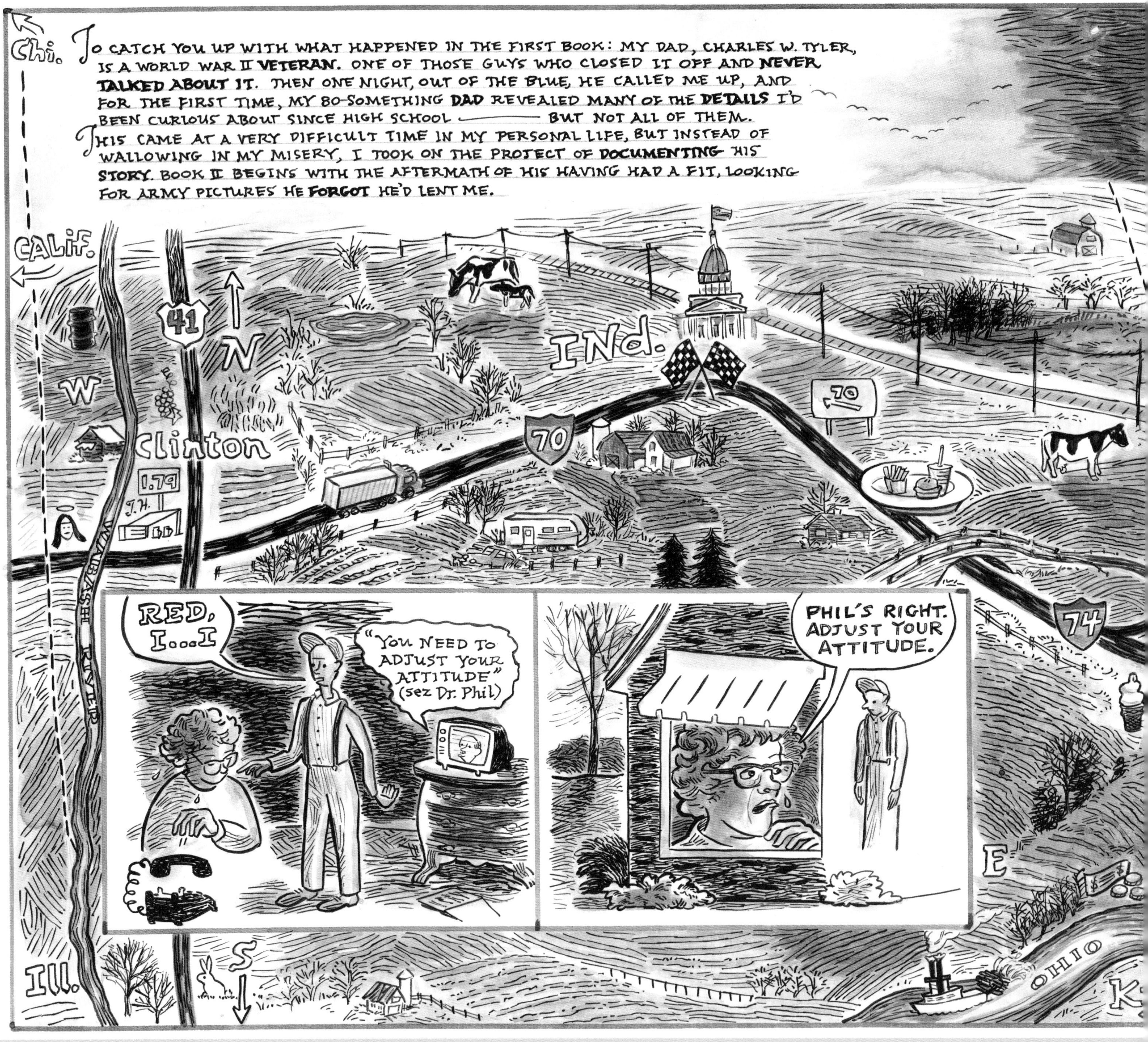
TO CATCH YOU UP WITH WHAT HAPPENED IN THE FIRST BOOK: MY DAD, CHARLES W. TYLER, IS A WORLD WAR II **VETERAN**. ONE OF THOSE GUYS WHO CLOSED IT OFF AND **NEVER TALKED ABOUT IT**. THEN ONE NIGHT, OUT OF THE BLUE, HE CALLED ME UP, AND FOR THE FIRST TIME, MY 80-SOMETHING **DAD** REVEALED MANY OF THE **DETAILS** I'D BEEN CURIOUS ABOUT SINCE HIGH SCHOOL —— BUT NOT ALL OF THEM.
THIS CAME AT A VERY DIFFICULT TIME IN MY PERSONAL LIFE, BUT INSTEAD OF WALLOWING IN MY MISERY, I TOOK ON THE PROJECT OF **DOCUMENTING** HIS **STORY**. BOOK II BEGINS WITH THE AFTERMATH OF HIS HAVING HAD A FIT, LOOKING FOR ARMY PICTURES HE **FORGOT** HE'D LENT ME.
Chi.
CALIF.
41
N
W
IND.
70
Clinton
1.79
J.H.
WABASH RIVER
74
RED, I...I
"YOU NEED TO ADJUST YOUR ATTITUDE" (sez Dr. Phil)
PHIL'S RIGHT. ADJUST YOUR ATTITUDE.
E
OHIO
S
Ill.
K

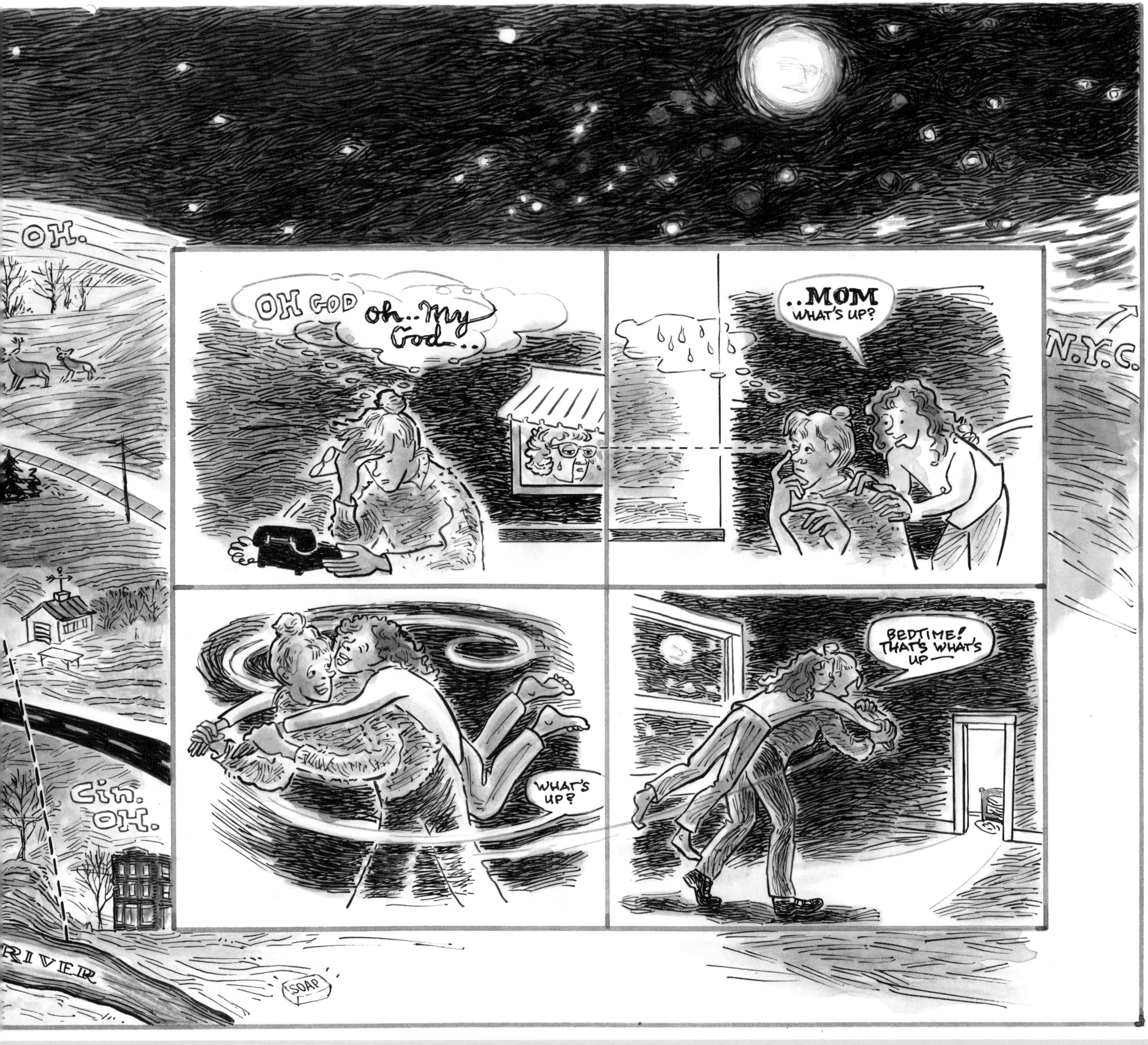

OH.
N.Y.C.
OH GOD oh... My God...
..MOM WHAT'S UP?
WHAT'S UP?
BEDTIME! THAT'S WHAT'S UP—
Cin. OH.
RIVER
SOAP

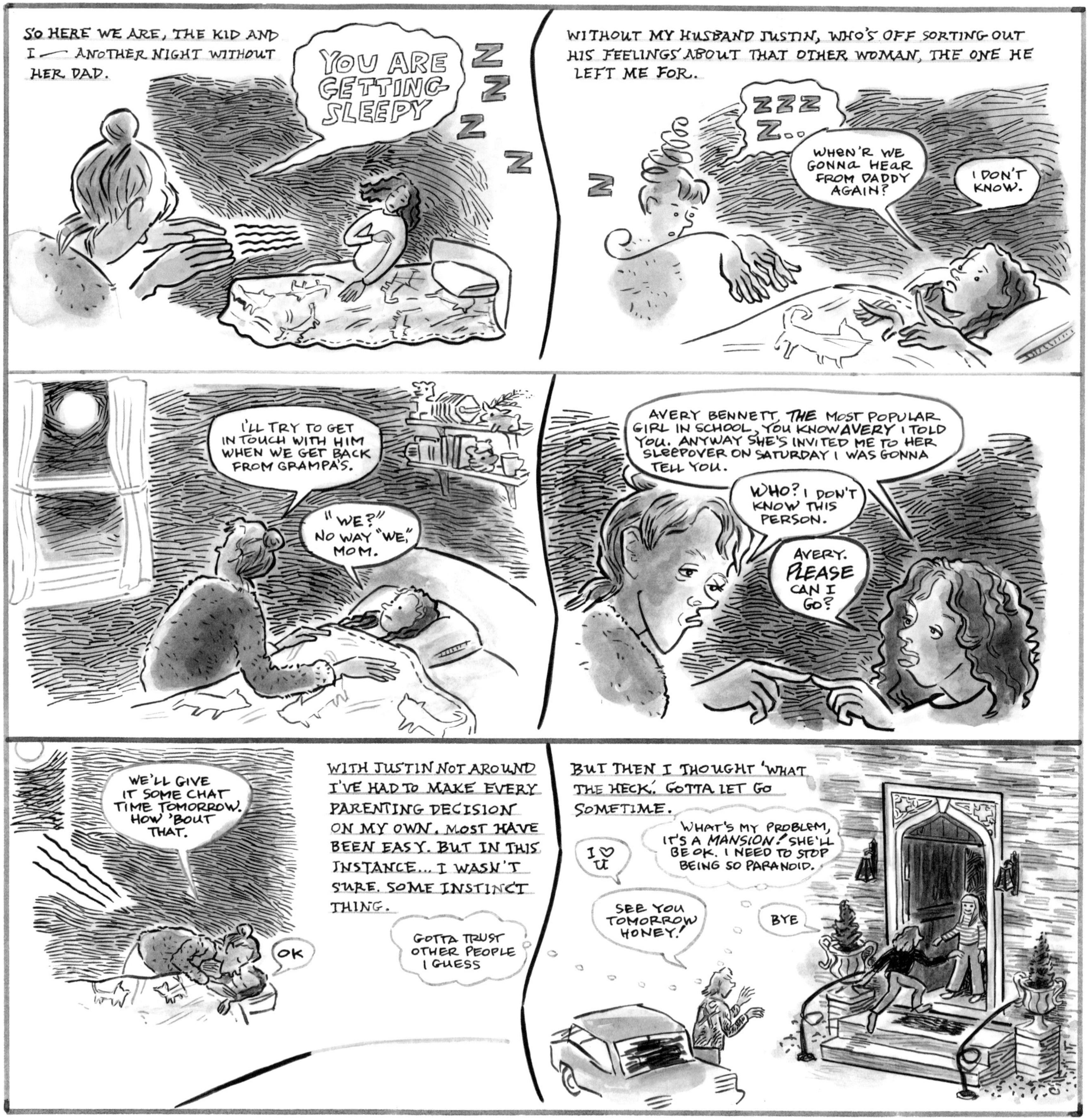
SO HERE WE ARE, THE KID AND I — ANOTHER NIGHT WITHOUT HER DAD.
YOU ARE GETTING SLEEPY
Z Z Z Z
WITHOUT MY HUSBAND JUSTIN, WHO'S OFF SORTING OUT HIS 'FEELINGS' ABOUT THAT OTHER WOMAN, THE ONE HE LEFT ME FOR.
ZZZ Z..
Z
WHEN'R WE GONNA HEAR FROM DADDY AGAIN?
I DON'T KNOW.
I'LL TRY TO GET IN TOUCH WITH HIM WHEN WE GET BACK FROM GRAMPA'S.
"WE?" NO WAY "WE," MOM.
AVERY BENNETT, THE MOST POPULAR GIRL IN SCHOOL, YOU KNOW AVERY I TOLD YOU. ANYWAY SHE'S INVITED ME TO HER SLEEPOVER ON SATURDAY I WAS GONNA TELL YOU.
WHO? I DON'T KNOW THIS PERSON.
AVERY. PLEASE CAN I GO?
WE'LL GIVE IT SOME CHAT TIME TOMORROW. HOW 'BOUT THAT.
OK
WITH JUSTIN NOT AROUND I'VE HAD TO MAKE EVERY PARENTING DECISION ON MY OWN. MOST HAVE BEEN EASY. BUT IN THIS INSTANCE... I WASN'T SURE. SOME INSTINCT THING.
GOTTA TRUST OTHER PEOPLE I GUESS
BUT THEN I THOUGHT 'WHAT THE HECK.' GOTTA LET GO SOMETIME.
WHAT'S MY PROBLEM, IT'S A MANSION! SHE'LL BE OK. I NEED TO STOP BEING SO PARANOID.
I ♡ U
SEE YOU TOMORROW HONEY!
BYE

PEOPLE YOU NEED TO KNOW

Before Going Any Further. Just to be Clear.

THESE ARE THE **5** MAIN CHARACTERS OF THIS STORY, OR MAYBE I SHOULD SAY **TRILOGY** SINCE THIS IS BOOK II OF MY EFFORT KNOWN AS **"YOU'LL NEVER KNOW"**. MY NAME IS C. TYLER AND I AM THE NARRATOR, ARTIST AND WRITER. SEE MY LOOK EXPLAINED IN #5 BELOW. MY **DAD**, #1, IS THE MAIN SUBJECT. MOTHER, **HANNAH**, IS LISTED SECOND. SHE HAS A STORY TO TELL IN THIS BOOK. **JULIA** IS MY DAUGHTER, TWIRLING INTO HER TEENS. HER DAD IS MY HUSBAND **JUSTIN**, WHO IN BOOK I HAD GONE OFF TO SOUL SEARCH, LEAVING ME TO RAISE OUR KID. —— I'M SEEKING HAPPY SOLUTIONS, BUT SO MANY UNRESOLVED ISSUES DEMAND ATTENTION...

1. Soldier Boy · Busy · Never Idle · **CHUCK**

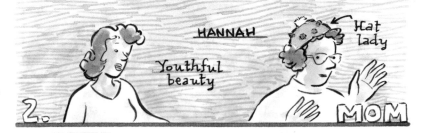

2. HANNAH · Youthful beauty · Hat lady · **MOM**

WHEN IN DOUBT GO BACK AND CHECK/REFER TO BOOK I.

3. Joyful energy · **JULIA**

4. Perennially in plaid · **JUD** OR **JUSTIN**

MY HAIR STYLES REVEAL:

5. Eggbeater curls → Innocent · Capable Mom · Pony tail → · Seeker · Wild Wolf → · Traveler. · Nut. · Top knot → · Wise and Mature? · (we'll see...) · C.T.

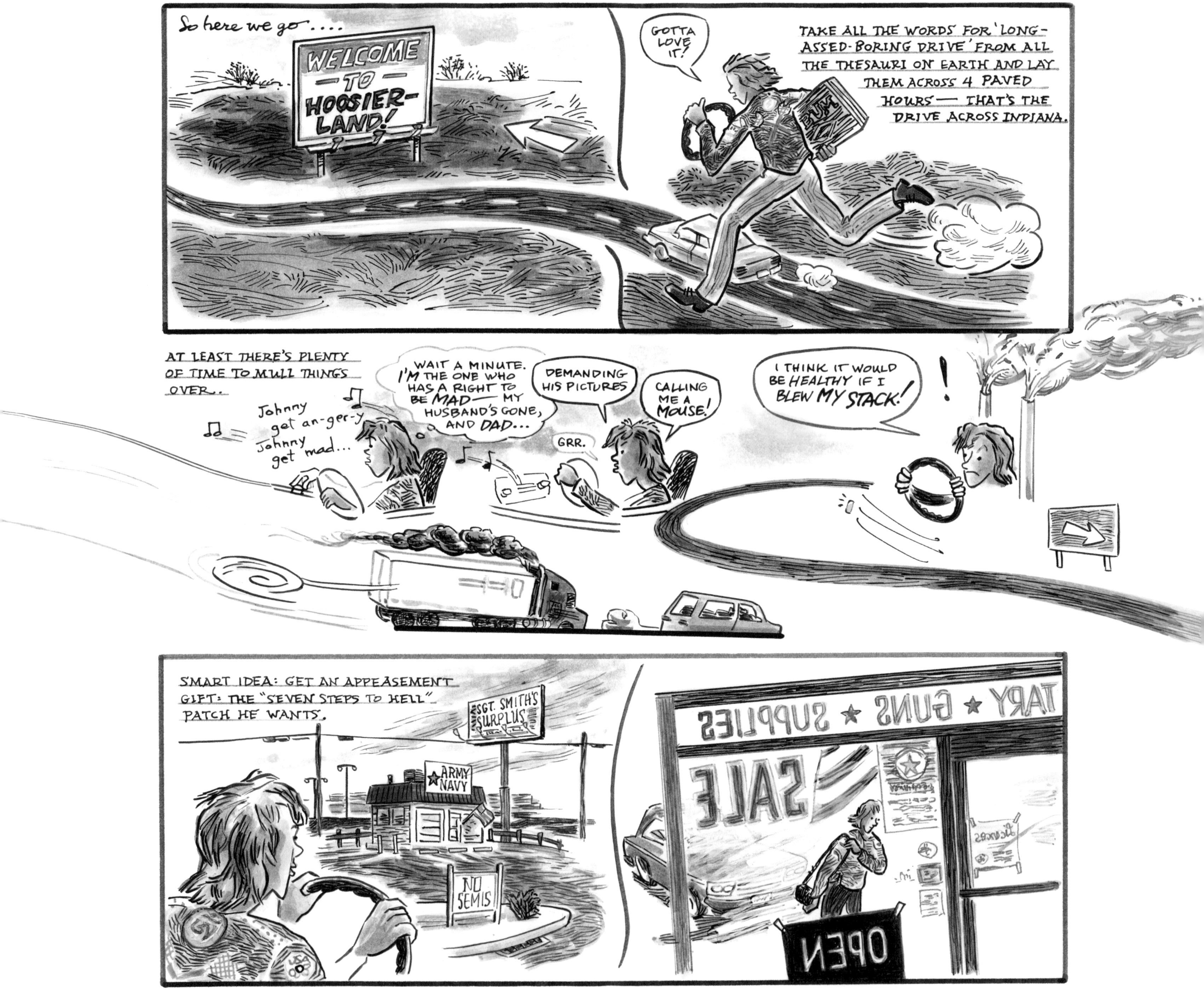
So here we go....
WELCOME TO HOOSIER-LAND!
GOTTA LOVE IT!
TAKE ALL THE WORDS FOR 'LONG-ASSED-BORING DRIVE' FROM ALL THE THESAURI ON EARTH AND LAY THEM ACROSS 4 PAVED HOURS— THAT'S THE DRIVE ACROSS INDIANA.
AT LEAST THERE'S PLENTY OF TIME TO MULL THINGS OVER.
Johnny get an-ger-y Johnny get mad...
WAIT A MINUTE. I'M THE ONE WHO HAS A RIGHT TO BE MAD— MY HUSBAND'S GONE, AND DAD...
GRR.
DEMANDING HIS PICTURES
CALLING ME A MOUSE!
I THINK IT WOULD BE HEALTHY IF I BLEW MY STACK!
!
SMART IDEA: GET AN APPEASEMENT GIFT: THE "SEVEN STEPS TO HELL" PATCH HE WANTS.
SGT. SMITH'S SURPLUS
ARMY NAVY
NO SEMIS
TARY ★ GUNS ★ SUPPLIES
SALE
OPEN

SGT. SMITH'S IS AN OLD TEXACO STATION WITH BUZZING FLUORESCENTS AND FEW CUSTOMERS. IT'S AN ODDLY CALMING PLACE.

POW·MIA

I'M AMAZED AT HOW MUCH MILITARY HISTORY AND ARMY TRIVIA I'VE COME TO KNOW.

ANZIO

WHERE?

IT LOOKS LIKE I-RAK

THUNDERBIRD. 45 INFANTRY. THAT'S MAULDIN'S OUTFIT.

WELL IF THEY'S ANYONE C-N GIT SADDAM, IT'S YOUR BOY.

YOU'RE RIGHT ABOUT THAT.

NO CHECKS

ANOTHER SMART IDEA: KEEP MY ANTI-WAR SENTIMENTS TO MYSELF.

SAY..

THAT'S AN M-43 LINER YOU GOT ON.

I GUESS. IT WAS MY DAD'S. WWII.

I KNOW I'VE ADDED STUFF TO IT, BUT THIS "SEVEN STEPS" PATCH IS FOR HIM.

ARMY

I'VE ALREADY GOT A "SEVEN STEPS" PATCH, ALONG WITH A TIBETAN FLAG...

QUILTED

FOR YOUR DAD?

THEN IT'S ON ME.

I LOVE THOSE OLD GUYS.

I LIKE WHAT YER DOIN' WITH THE JACKET.

I DO TOO.

THANKS. IT'S A WORK IN PROGRESS.

I'LL BE BACK

ARMY

"THE JACKET"

THANK YOU

CLUSTERS

FLORALS

A BUDDHIST PEACE SYMBOL AND A RED CRISS-CROSS LIKE DAD'S SUSPENDERS.

OLYMPIC TEAM PATCH (MY BRO'S), CALIFORNIA FLAG, WWII SERVICE STAR

THE BIG RED 1 FOUND ON STREET

THE *REAL* DEAL WOULD BE An "IKE" JACKET

MADE POPULAR IN 1943-44 BY GENERAL EISENHOWER ("IKE") DURING HIS COMMAND OF THE "ETO", EUROPEAN THEATER OF OPERATIONS.

A stylish addition to the Olive-Drab Collection!

THE IKE JACKET WAS A MOST COVETED ISSUE FOR THE FIELD WEARY DOG-FACES WHO HAD SUFFERED IN THE SEVERELY UTILITARIAN AND MARKEDLY UN-SEXY M-43 JACKET.

This is what my liner is from

M-43

NOW DAT'S SUMPIN' I GOTTA HAVE.

DITTO.

YOU COULD ONLY GET AN 'IKE' IF YOU WERE AN AIRMAN OR HAD BEEN OVERSEAS.

HOWEVER, DAD'S WAS DESTROYED IN A HOUSE FIRE SOON AFTER HIS DISCHARGE. FEB. 1946. AT HIS PARENT'S' HOUSE.

THEY WERE LUCKY TO GET OUT WITH THEIR LIVES! HIS JACKET HUNG IN A DOWNSTAIRS CLOSET NEAR TO WHERE THE BOILER BLEW.

BUT THE HUMBLE LINER, THE ONE I WEAR, HAD BEEN IN A TRUNK IN THE GARAGE.

I REALLY DO LOVE MY DAD AND I AM *SO* PROUD OF HIM. BUT HE CAN BE SUCH A *SHIT!*

I arrived to find an immaculate house with two peaceful senior citizens.

Everything was as it should be.

MOM   DAD   THE DOG   THE T.V.

So calm —

YOU WOULD NEVER KNOW THAT THERE HAD BEEN YELLING, THAT THERE HAD BEEN AN UNSETTLING CYCLONE BLOW THROUGH HERE.

WHAT!

WHADDYA MEAN YOU DON'T NEED 'EM. I DROVE ALL THE WAY OVER HERE —

— IT'S MY STUFF, THAT'S ALL.

DAMN IF I DIDN'T TAKE THE BAIT. AGAIN!!

HERE'S YER SEVENTH PATCH —

YOU GOT MOM ALL UPSET. AND ME...

SHE'S FINE, ARENCHA, RED —

UM

CONFUSIONS   SHIFTS.

JUST LIKE WHEN I WAS

A KID.

Pencil feels good on flat paint

In our home, there were two distinct tones:

JOLLY AND Mad.

AS IN CRABBY AND EXHAUSTED

the 1950s

Much of the time, both of them seemed like they were mad.

WHO DID THIS.

SCRIBBLING ON THE WALL!

HaHa YOU'RE IN TRUB-BL

I GUESS I'M GONNA HAVE TO GO OUT IN THE YARD AND GET ME A PEPPER STICK!

GIVE 'EM ALL A SPANKIN'

I DUNNO

NOT ME.

MOM

DAD

GUILTY

Working hard and dealing with kids can make you mad.

Of course, I took it personally.

Boy, could they wrangle! And when they did, I felt invisible.

and I felt small, small, so very small, living in a TINY place. Just a fleck, really, in:

Jolly? Nothin' jolly about callous jokes...

Nothin' jolly about still living out of a duffel bag...

...or sudden acrobatics when a passing vehicle would backfire.

That was very disconcerting to witness.

Or how about the time he choked Mom —

You see, one night, she came into bed late and when she bent down to kiss him, he went for her throat. "Don't sneak up on me"

Random turbulence — who needs it!

I never knew what to expect.

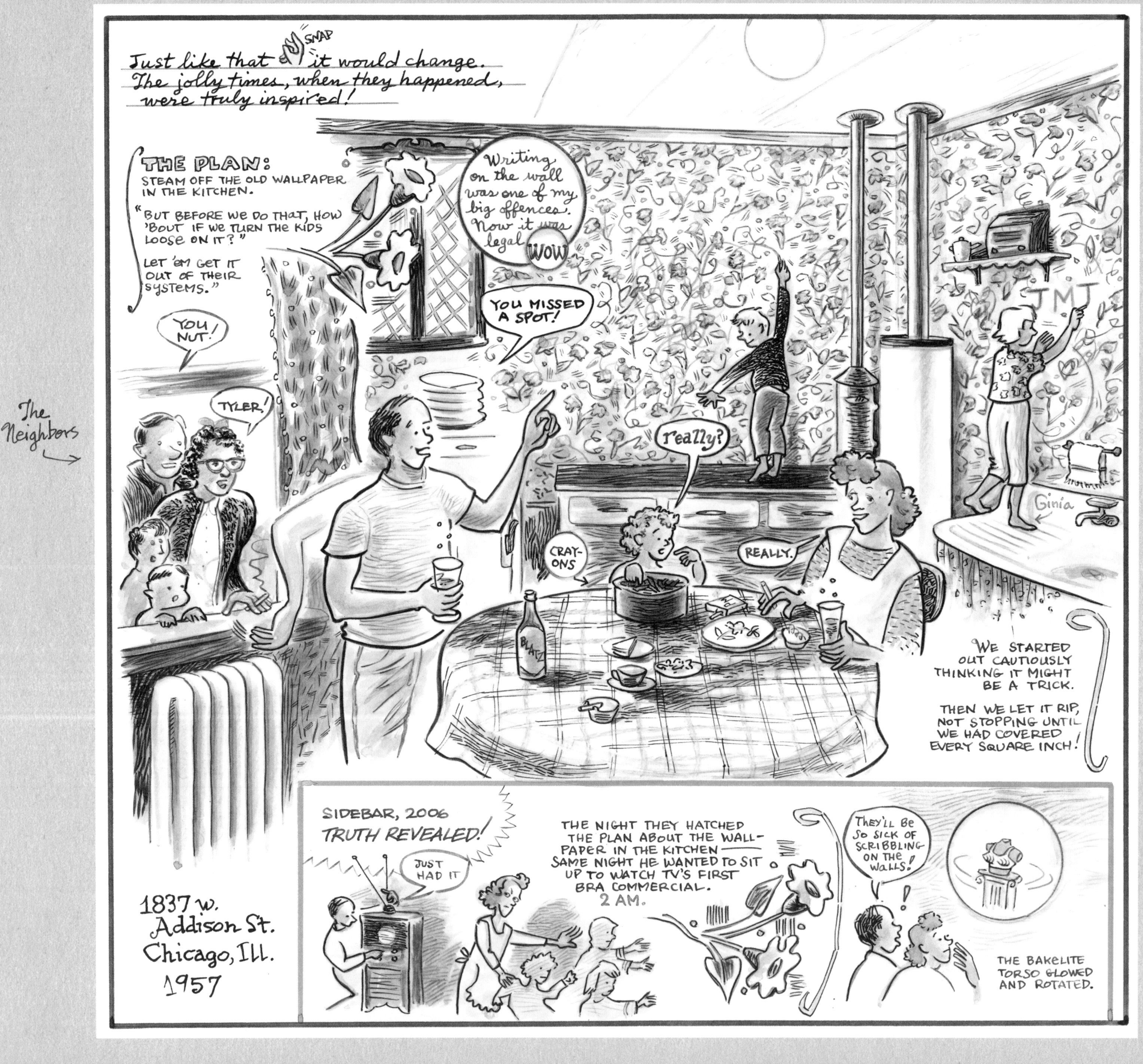

Just like that SNAP it would change.
The jolly times, when they happened, were truly inspired!
THE PLAN:
STEAM OFF THE OLD WALLPAPER IN THE KITCHEN.
"BUT BEFORE WE DO THAT, HOW 'BOUT IF WE TURN THE KIDS LOOSE ON IT?"
LET 'EM GET IT OUT OF THEIR SYSTEMS."
Writing on the wall was one of my big offences. Now it was legal. WOW
YOU NUT!
YOU MISSED A SPOT!
The Neighbors
TYLER!
really?
CRAYONS
REALLY.
JMT
Ginia
BLATZ
WE STARTED OUT CAUTIOUSLY THINKING IT MIGHT BE A TRICK.
THEN WE LET IT RIP, NOT STOPPING UNTIL WE HAD COVERED EVERY SQUARE INCH!
1837 W. Addison St. Chicago, Ill. 1957
SIDEBAR, 2006
TRUTH REVEALED!
JUST HAD IT
THE NIGHT THEY HATCHED THE PLAN ABOUT THE WALLPAPER IN THE KITCHEN — SAME NIGHT HE WANTED TO SIT UP TO WATCH TV'S FIRST BRA COMMERCIAL. 2 AM.
They'll Be So sick of SCRIBBLING ON THE WALLS!
THE BAKELITE TORSO GLOWED AND ROTATED.

HOW I EARNED A LABEL by Miss La Dee Da.

That's their neighbors and best friends, Gordy & Wilma (in the window) with their kids.

Wilma and Mom pre-dated Betty and Wilma on the Flintstones!

Same for Dad and Gordy. It was kind of like the Honeymooners.

Chicago in the 1950s — Kids could play outside without supervision.

There were parameters, but mostly we were free to do whatever.

Before I got old enough to roam, the big kids stuck me in the yard.

As the runt, they considered me a drag.

It was during this time that us Tyler kids acquired our life-long labels.

So anyway, Dad and Gordy had their stuff out to do this little cement job.

What's a kid to do, stuck in the yard all alone?

And so this label was now mine: "La Dee Da." Thanks a lot Gordy!

Set in cement. It's how my Dad saw me for the next 50 years!!

Later
BACK IN REAL TIME. IN THE 'RENTS' KITCHEN.
So La Dee Da sez:
How 'bout if I fix us some eats?
AAK!
MOUSE DROPPINGS. OH MY GOD THEY'RE EV'RY-WHERE!
GODDAMM IT! —HE'S BACK.
LITTLE S.O.B.
BACK?
HERE.
FEED THE TRASH CAN.
DON'T TAKE ANY CHANCES.
This mouse situation—NOT like it was when I was small.
HERE.
WOULD YOU CALL THIS BOLD
OR DESPERATE?
SUR-VIVAL.
CHEWED THROUGH TUPPERWARE
Mom woulda been on top of it.
I'VE SEEN THEM PRY THE LID OFF A CANISTER.
VERMIN.
POUR SOME BLEACH IN THAT WATER
PHEW!

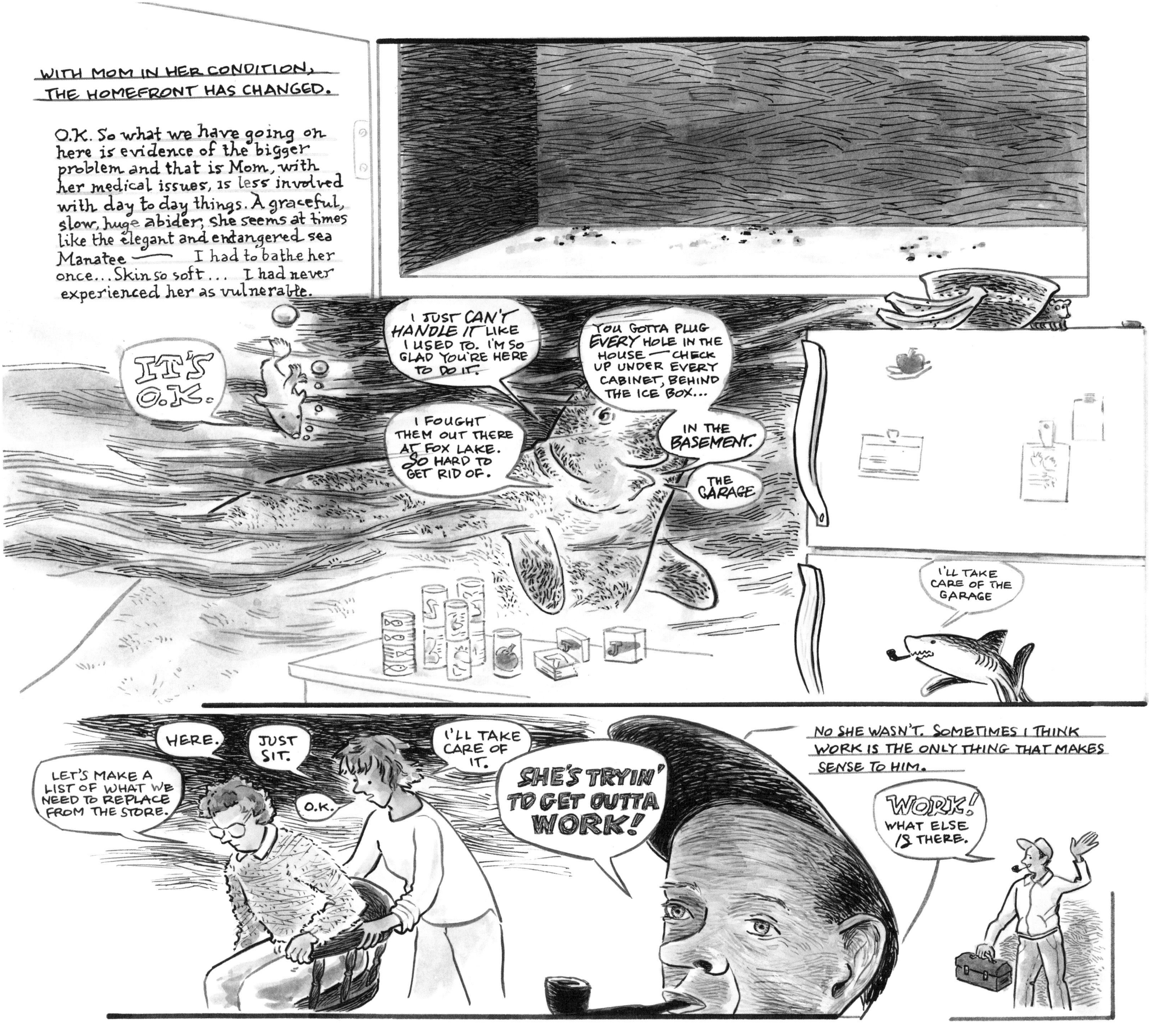
WITH MOM IN HER CONDITION, THE HOMEFRONT HAS CHANGED.
O.K. So what we have going on here is evidence of the bigger problem and that is Mom, with her medical issues, is less involved with day to day things. A graceful, slow, huge abider, she seems at times like the elegant and entangered sea Manatee — I had to bathe her once... Skin so soft... I had never experienced her as vulnerable.
IT'S O.K.
I JUST CAN'T HANDLE IT LIKE I USED TO. I'M SO GLAD YOU'RE HERE TO DO IT.
I FOUGHT THEM OUT THERE AT FOX LAKE. SO HARD TO GET RID OF.
YOU GOTTA PLUG EVERY HOLE IN THE HOUSE — CHECK UP UNDER EVERY CABINET, BEHIND THE ICE BOX...
IN THE BASEMENT.
THE GARAGE
I'LL TAKE CARE OF THE GARAGE
LET'S MAKE A LIST OF WHAT WE NEED TO REPLACE FROM THE STORE.
HERE.
JUST SIT.
O.K.
I'LL TAKE CARE OF IT.
SHE'S TRYIN' TO GET OUTTA WORK!
NO SHE WASN'T. SOMETIMES I THINK WORK IS THE ONLY THING THAT MAKES SENSE TO HIM.
WORK! WHAT ELSE IS THERE.

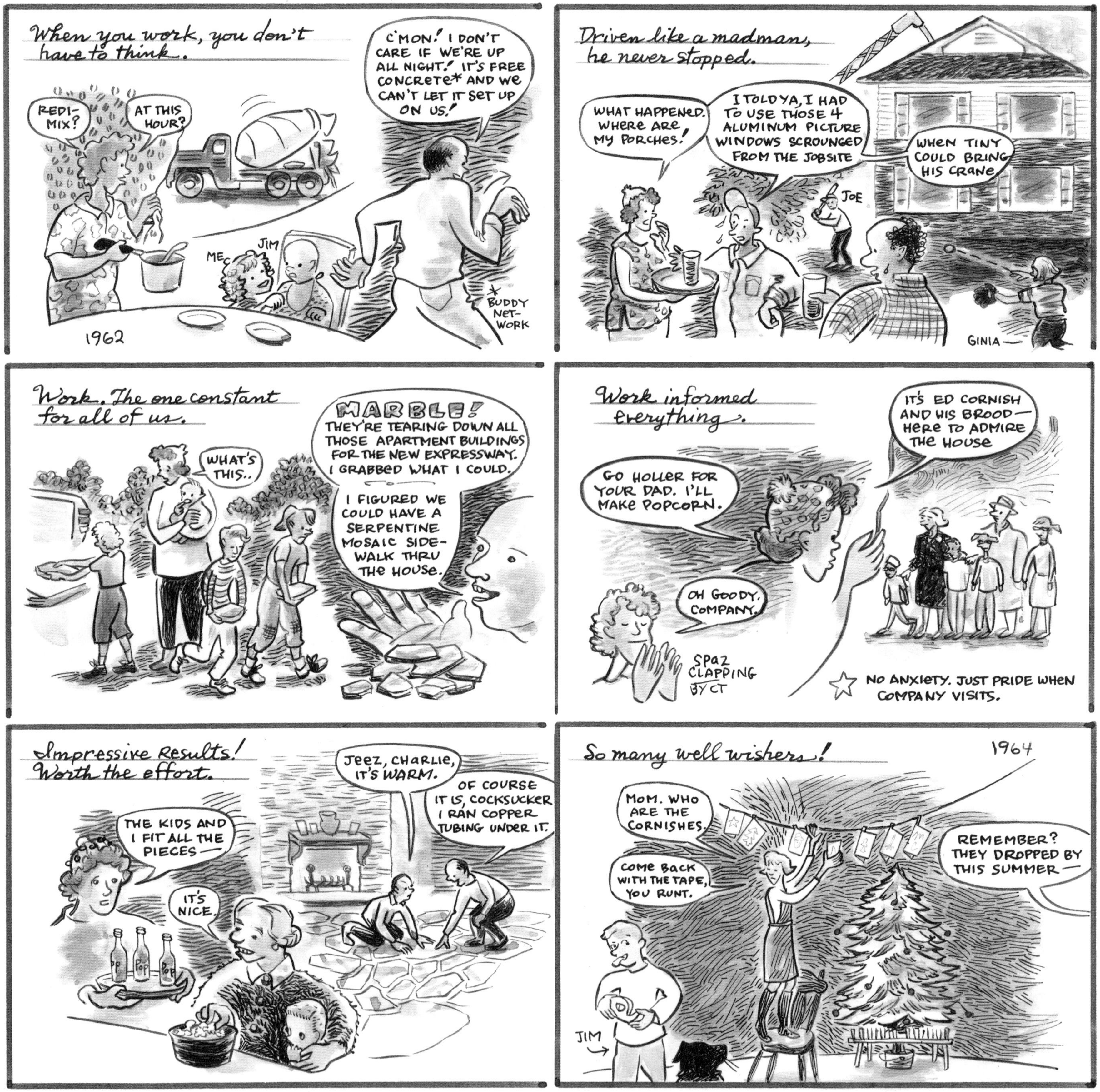
When you work, you don't have to think.
REDI-MIX?
AT THIS HOUR?
C'MON! I DON'T CARE IF WE'RE UP ALL NIGHT! IT'S FREE CONCRETE* AND WE CAN'T LET IT SET UP ON US!
ME
JIM
* BUDDY NET-WORK
1962
Driven like a madman, he never stopped.
WHAT HAPPENED. WHERE ARE MY PORCHES!
I TOLDYA, I HAD TO USE THOSE 4 ALUMINUM PICTURE WINDOWS SCROUNGED FROM THE JOBSITE
WHEN TINY COULD BRING HIS CRANE
JOE
GINIA—
Work. The one constant for all of us.
WHAT'S THIS..
MARBLE! THEY'RE TEARING DOWN ALL THOSE APARTMENT BUILDINGS FOR THE NEW EXPRESSWAY. I GRABBED WHAT I COULD.
I FIGURED WE COULD HAVE A SERPENTINE MOSAIC SIDE-WALK THRU THE HOUSE.
Work informed everything.
GO HOLLER FOR YOUR DAD. I'LL MAKE POPCORN.
IT'S ED CORNISH AND HIS BROOD— HERE TO ADMIRE THE HOUSE
OH GOODY. COMPANY.
SPAZ CLAPPING BY CT
☆ NO ANXIETY. JUST PRIDE WHEN COMPANY VISITS.
Impressive Results! Worth the effort.
THE KIDS AND I FIT ALL THE PIECES—
IT'S NICE.
JEEZ, CHARLIE, IT'S WARM.
OF COURSE IT IS, COCKSUCKER I RAN COPPER TUBING UNDER IT.
POP
POP
POP
So many well wishers!
1964
MOM. WHO ARE THE CORNISHES.
COME BACK WITH THE TAPE, YOU RUNT.
REMEMBER? THEY DROPPED BY THIS SUMMER—
JIM

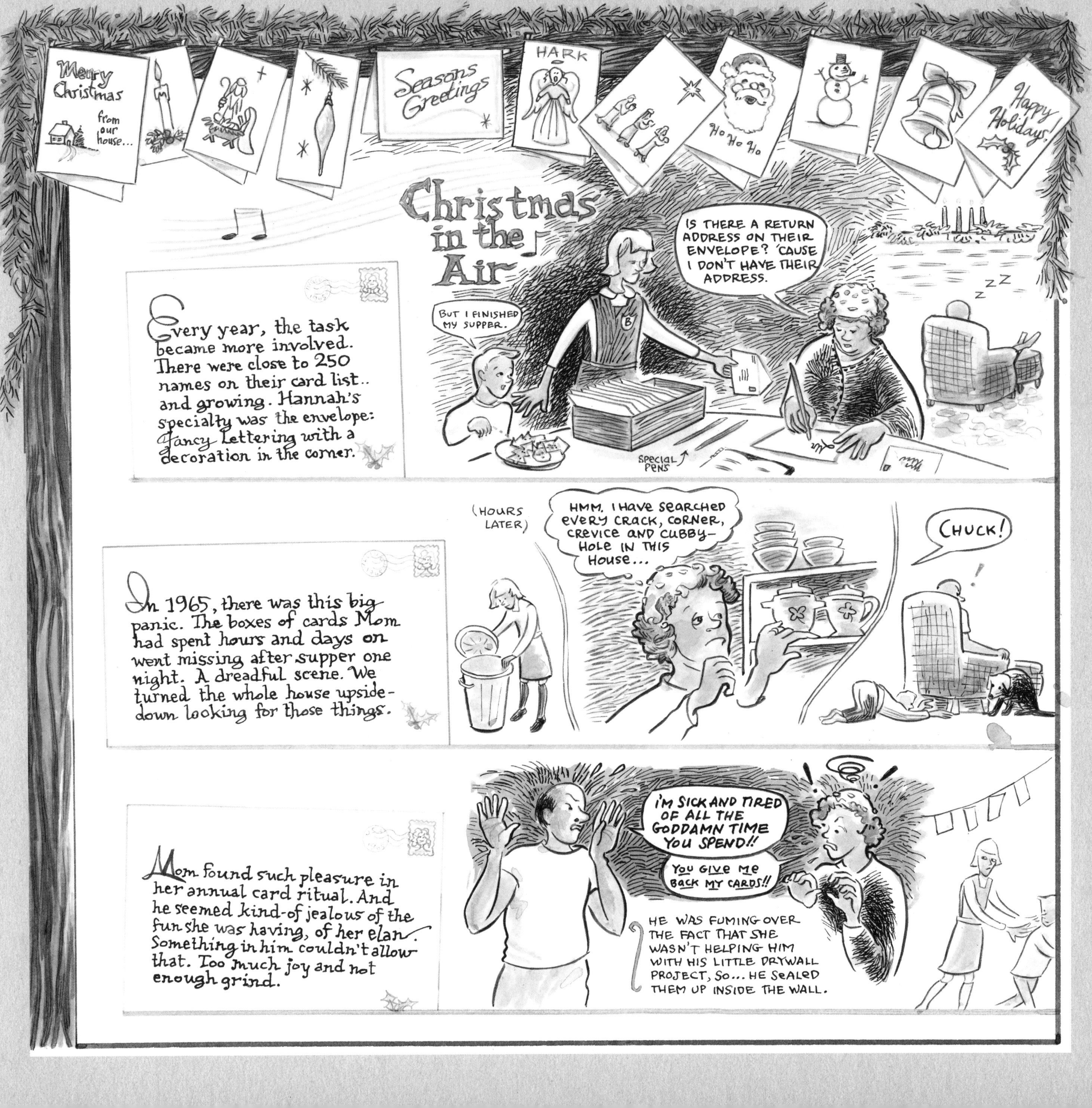

Merry Christmas
from our house...
HARK
Seasons Greetings
Ho Ho Ho
Happy Holidays!
Christmas in the Air
Every year, the task became more involved. There were close to 250 names on their card list.. and growing. Hannah's specialty was the envelope: fancy Lettering with a decoration in the corner.
BUT I FINISHED MY SUPPER.
IS THERE A RETURN ADDRESS ON THEIR ENVELOPE? 'CAUSE I DON'T HAVE THEIR ADDRESS.
ZZZ
SPECIAL PENS
In 1965, there was this big panic. The boxes of cards Mom had spent hours and days on went missing after supper one night. A dreadful scene. We turned the whole house upside-down looking for those things.
(HOURS LATER)
HMM. I HAVE SEARCHED EVERY CRACK, CORNER, CREVICE AND CUBBY-HOLE IN THIS HOUSE...
CHUCK!
Mom found such pleasure in her annual card ritual. And he seemed kind-of jealous of the fun she was having, of her elan. Something in him couldn't allow that. Too much joy and not enough grind.
I'M SICK AND TIRED OF ALL THE GODDAMN TIME YOU SPEND!!
YOU GIVE ME BACK MY CARDS!!
HE WAS FUMING OVER THE FACT THAT SHE WASN'T HELPING HIM WITH HIS LITTLE DRYWALL PROJECT, SO... HE SEALED THEM UP INSIDE THE WALL.

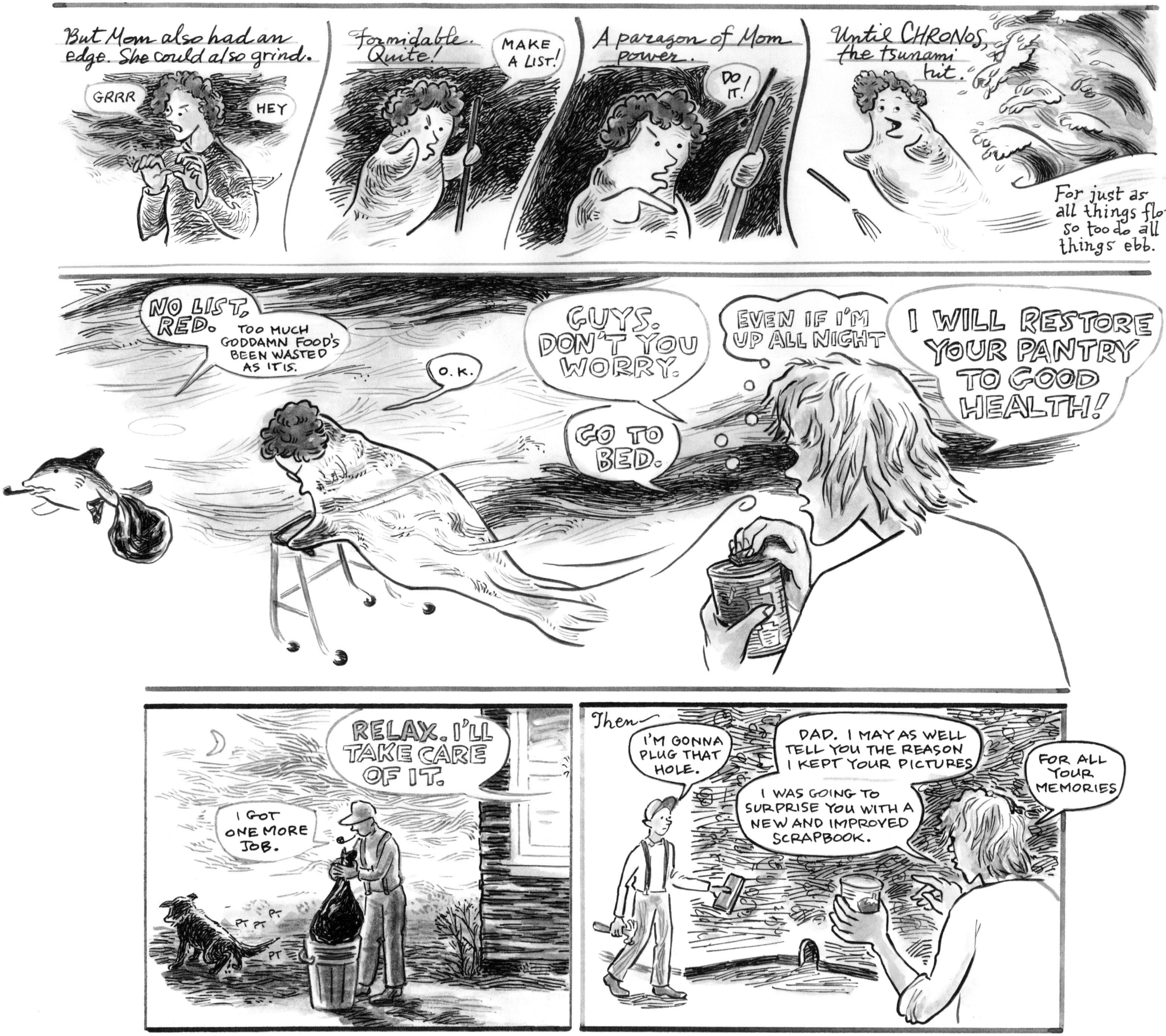

But Mom also had an edge. She could also grind.
GRRR
HEY
Formidable. Quite!
MAKE A LIST!
A paragon of Mom power.
DO IT!
Until CHRONOS, the tsunami hit.
For just as all things flow, so too do all things ebb.
NO LIST, RED.
TOO MUCH GODDAMN FOOD'S BEEN WASTED AS IT IS.
O.K.
GUYS. DON'T YOU WORRY.
GO TO BED.
EVEN IF I'M UP ALL NIGHT
I WILL RESTORE YOUR PANTRY TO GOOD HEALTH!
RELAX. I'LL TAKE CARE OF IT.
I GOT ONE MORE JOB.
PT PT PT
PT
Then—
I'M GONNA PLUG THAT HOLE.
DAD. I MAY AS WELL TELL YOU THE REASON I KEPT YOUR PICTURES
I WAS GOING TO SURPRISE YOU WITH A NEW AND IMPROVED SCRAPBOOK.
FOR ALL YOUR MEMORIES

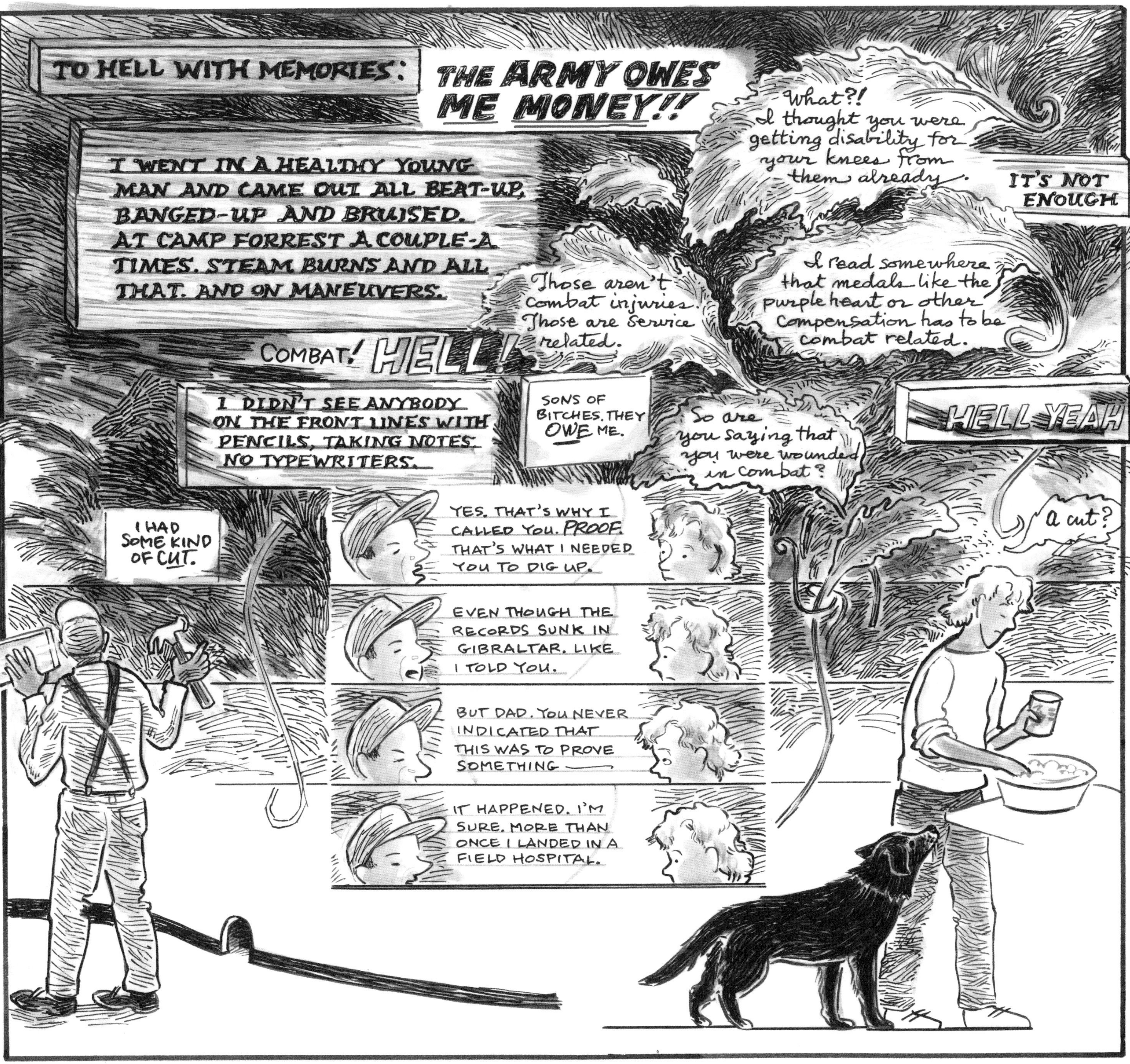
TO HELL WITH MEMORIES:
THE ARMY OWES ME MONEY!!
I WENT IN A HEALTHY YOUNG MAN AND CAME OUT ALL BEAT-UP, BANGED-UP AND BRUISED. AT CAMP FORREST A COUPLE-A TIMES. STEAM BURNS AND ALL THAT. AND ON MANEUVERS.
What?! I thought you were getting disability for your knees from them already.
IT'S NOT ENOUGH
Those aren't combat injuries. Those are Service related.
I read somewhere that medals like the purple heart or other Compensation has to be combat related.
COMBAT! HELL!
I DIDN'T SEE ANYBODY ON THE FRONT LINES WITH PENCILS, TAKING NOTES. NO TYPEWRITERS.
SONS OF BITCHES. THEY OWE ME.
So are you saying that you were wounded in combat?
HELL YEAH
I HAD SOME KIND OF CUT.
a cut?
YES. THAT'S WHY I CALLED YOU. PROOF. THAT'S WHAT I NEEDED YOU TO DIG UP.
EVEN THOUGH THE RECORDS SUNK IN GIBRALTAR. LIKE I TOLD YOU.
BUT DAD. YOU NEVER INDICATED THAT THIS WAS TO PROVE SOMETHING —
IT HAPPENED. I'M SURE. MORE THAN ONCE I LANDED IN A FIELD HOSPITAL.

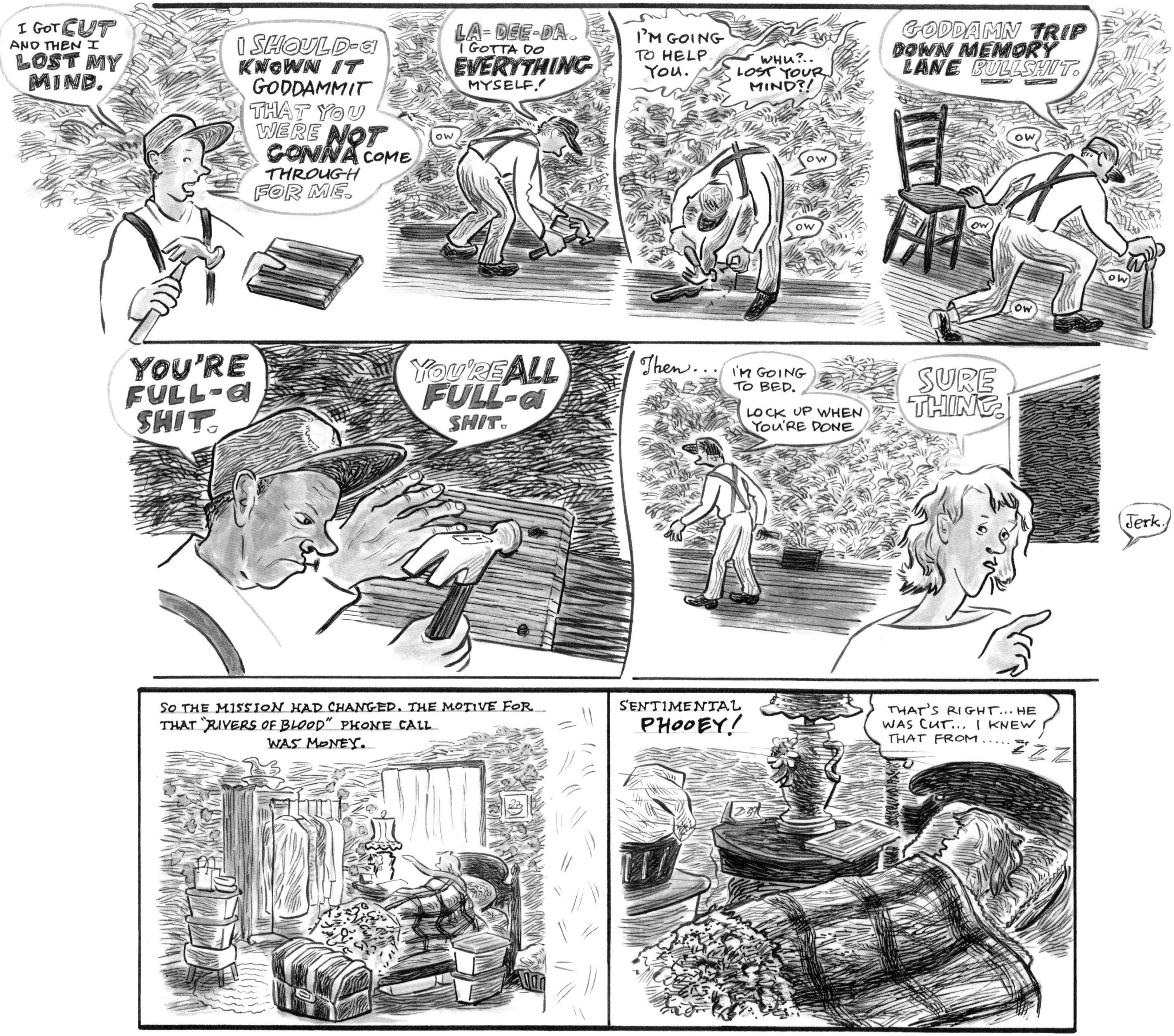

I GOT CUT AND THEN I LOST MY MIND.
I SHOULD-a KNOWN IT GODDAMMIT THAT YOU WERE NOT GONNA COME THROUGH FOR ME.
LA-DEE-DA. I GOTTA DO EVERYTHING MYSELF!
OW
I'M GOING TO HELP YOU.
WHU?.. LOST YOUR MIND?!
OW
OW
GODDAMN TRIP DOWN MEMORY LANE BULLSHIT.
OW
OW
OW
OW
YOU'RE FULL-a SHIT.
YOU'RE ALL FULL-a SHIT.
Then...
I'M GOING TO BED.
LOCK UP WHEN YOU'RE DONE
SURE THING.
Jerk.
SO THE MISSION HAD CHANGED. THE MOTIVE FOR THAT "RIVERS OF BLOOD" PHONE CALL WAS MONEY.
SENTIMENTAL PHOOEY!
THAT'S RIGHT... HE WAS CUT... I KNEW THAT FROM..... ZZZ

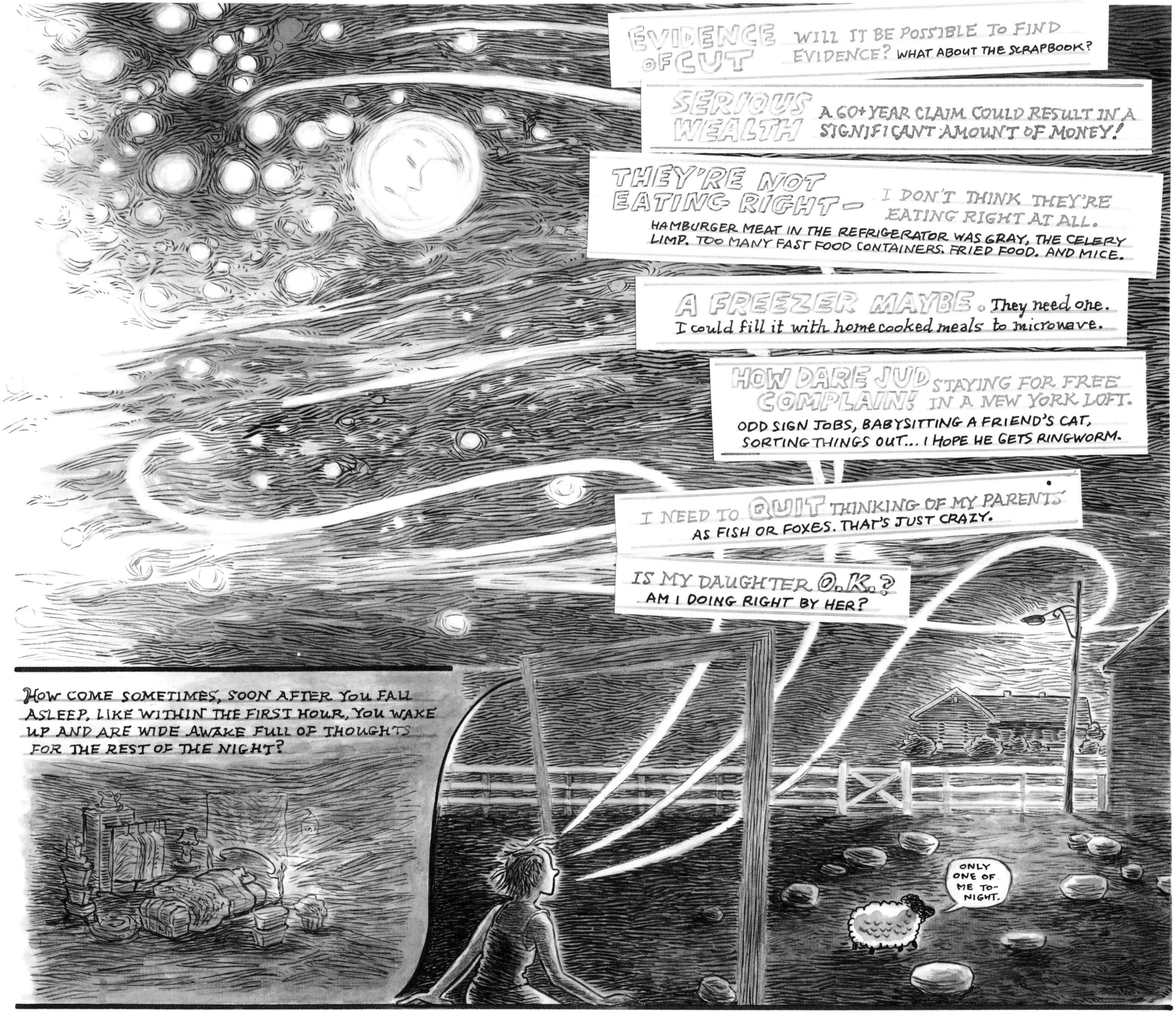
EVIDENCE OF CUT
WILL IT BE POSSIBLE TO FIND EVIDENCE? WHAT ABOUT THE SCRAPBOOK?
SERIOUS WEALTH
A 60+ YEAR CLAIM COULD RESULT IN A SIGNIFICANT AMOUNT OF MONEY!
THEY'RE NOT EATING RIGHT - I DON'T THINK THEY'RE EATING RIGHT AT ALL.
HAMBURGER MEAT IN THE REFRIGERATOR WAS GRAY, THE CELERY LIMP. TOO MANY FAST FOOD CONTAINERS. FRIED FOOD. AND MICE.
A FREEZER MAYBE. They need one. I could fill it with home cooked meals to microwave.
HOW DARE JUD COMPLAIN! STAYING FOR FREE IN A NEW YORK LOFT.
ODD SIGN JOBS, BABYSITTING A FRIEND'S CAT, SORTING THINGS OUT... I HOPE HE GETS RINGWORM.
I NEED TO QUIT THINKING OF MY PARENTS AS FISH OR FOXES. THAT'S JUST CRAZY.
IS MY DAUGHTER O.K.? AM I DOING RIGHT BY HER?
HOW COME SOMETIMES, SOON AFTER YOU FALL ASLEEP, LIKE WITHIN THE FIRST HOUR, YOU WAKE UP AND ARE WIDE AWAKE FULL OF THOUGHTS FOR THE REST OF THE NIGHT?
ONLY ONE OF ME TO-NIGHT.

Next Morning

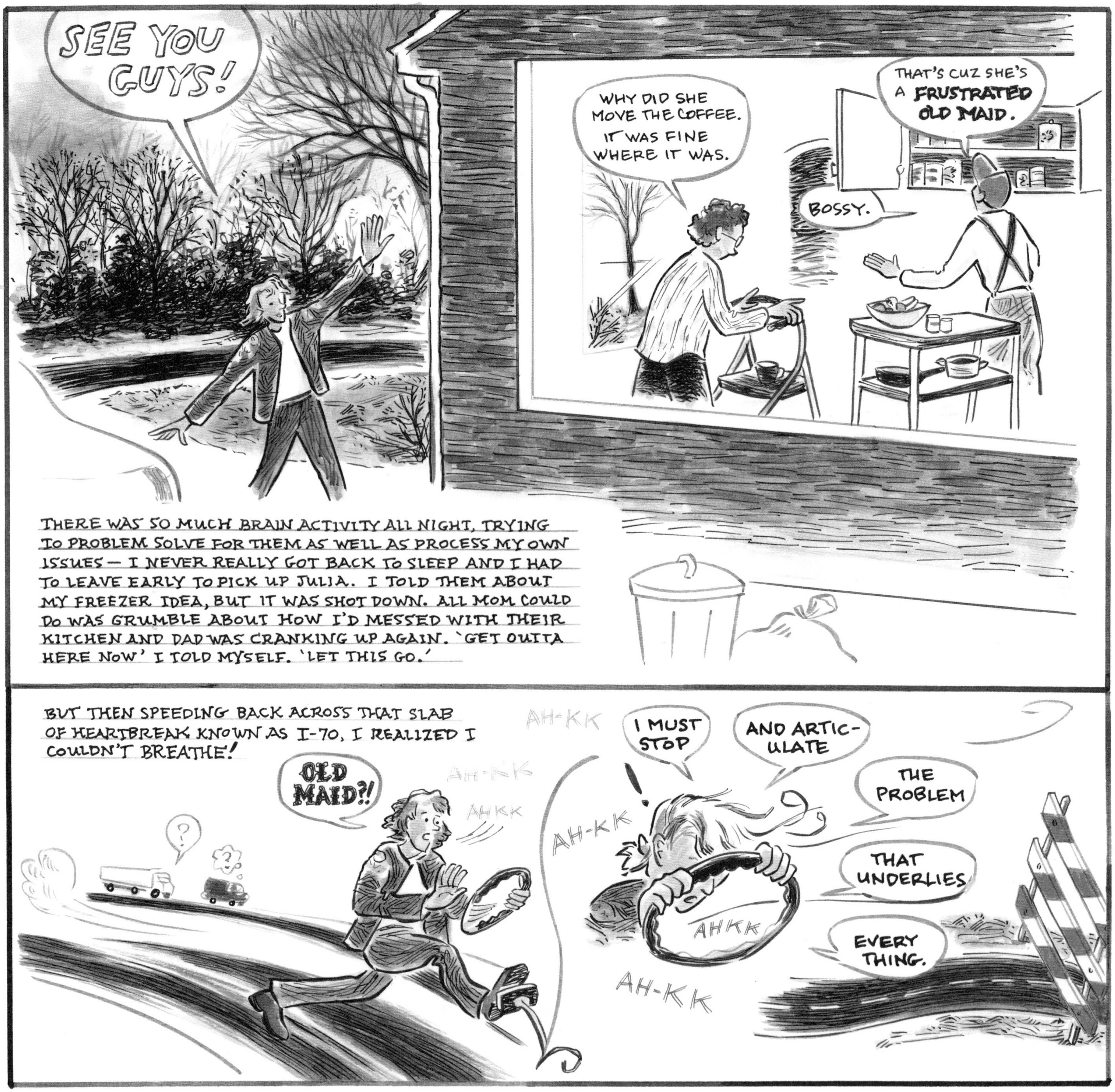

SEE YOU GUYS!
WHY DID SHE MOVE THE COFFEE. IT WAS FINE WHERE IT WAS.
THAT'S CUZ SHE'S A FRUSTRATED OLD MAID.
BOSSY.
THERE WAS SO MUCH BRAIN ACTIVITY ALL NIGHT, TRYING TO PROBLEM SOLVE FOR THEM AS WELL AS PROCESS MY OWN ISSUES — I NEVER REALLY GOT BACK TO SLEEP AND I HAD TO LEAVE EARLY TO PICK UP JULIA. I TOLD THEM ABOUT MY FREEZER IDEA, BUT IT WAS SHOT DOWN. ALL MOM COULD DO WAS GRUMBLE ABOUT HOW I'D MESSED WITH THEIR KITCHEN AND DAD WAS CRANKING UP AGAIN. 'GET OUTTA HERE NOW' I TOLD MYSELF. 'LET THIS GO.'
BUT THEN SPEEDING BACK ACROSS THAT SLAB OF HEARTBREAK KNOWN AS I-70, I REALIZED I COULDN'T BREATHE!
OLD MAID?!
AH-KK
AH-KK
AHKK
AH-KK
I MUST STOP
AND ARTIC-ULATE
THE PROBLEM
THAT UNDERLIES
EVERY THING.
AHKK
AH-KK

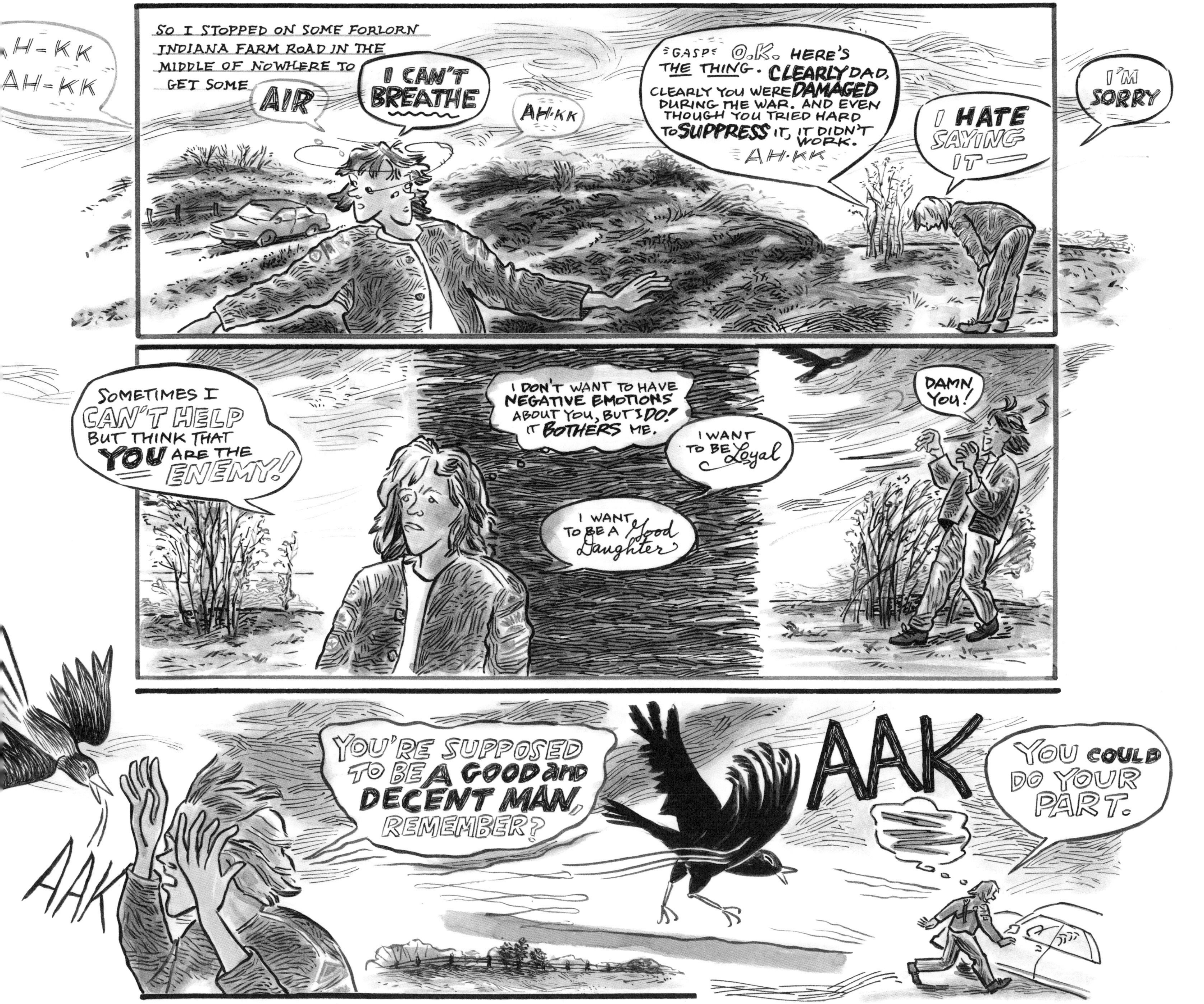
AH-KK
AH-KK
SO I STOPPED ON SOME FORLORN INDIANA FARM ROAD IN THE MIDDLE OF NOWHERE TO GET SOME
AIR
I CAN'T BREATHE
AH-KK
GASP O.K. HERE'S THE THING. CLEARLY DAD, CLEARLY YOU WERE DAMAGED DURING THE WAR. AND EVEN THOUGH YOU TRIED HARD TO SUPPRESS IT, IT DIDN'T WORK.
AH-KK
I HATE SAYING IT—
I'M SORRY
SOMETIMES I CAN'T HELP BUT THINK THAT YOU ARE THE ENEMY!
I DON'T WANT TO HAVE NEGATIVE EMOTIONS ABOUT YOU, BUT I DO! IT BOTHERS ME.
I WANT TO BE Loyal
I WANT TO BE A Good Daughter
DAMN YOU!
AAK
YOU'RE SUPPOSED TO BE A GOOD and DECENT MAN, REMEMBER?
AAK
YOU COULD DO YOUR PART.

Remember how I explained my bent-out-of-shape-ness? Caused by a too-busy Dad? Well, it was more than that...
FORGIVE ME. THIS FEELS LIKE BLASPHEMY!
THE 5 UNTENABLE TRANSGRESSIONS OF DEAR OL' DAD
Which in truth don't seem like such a big deal, but the accumulation over time for a fragile and sensitive little girl...
#1
No Time For Me
FROM DAY ONE. I SHOWED THIS IN BOOK I AS A BENT TREE.
#2 Many little cuts - verbal
— I don't give a damn what you think
— you're just a pip-squeak
— can't expect you to do anything right
— I'll tell you when you're tired
— aren't you the little actress
— etc.
CONTAGIOUS TO SIBLINGS. BECAME THE NORM.
#3 Constantly Denying Reality
A.
MY TUMMY HURTS
NO IT DOESN'T
YOU'RE JUST TRYIN' TO GET ATTENTION THAT'S ALL.
National Foods
IKE OUSTS SELF
B.
WHAT THE HELL'S THE MATTER WITH YOU!
EAT
#4 Those Jolly-Mad Mood Swings
fueled by alcohol, demons and exhaustion.
WENT OVER THAT.
Before getting to Number 5, a sudden, vivid memory of an old transgression of my very own — about a mouse.
YOW
I WAS A KILLER
by C. Tyler
Fox Lake, IL. 1959
All this bullying and bickering
SHAD-DAP!
But it's mine. I caught it.
One day my brother Joe caught a mouse.
Get it out.
O.K.
HERE
And then I was given the power to...
Let 'im go
Yeah You.
Lord over him.
Cute.
Fate in my hands.
OOPS! Come back!
Try to escape, will ya!
Gotcha
PINNED UNDER EDGE
The one thing I had control over. Botched.
I hid the crime from everyone.
Here
Gone?
Yup
Corpse laid there all summer. Like jerky.

Completely mortified by my heinous act...

ever heard of LAZARUS?

I became convinced, if they knew I was a KILLER

the lousy treatment would increase.

HEH HEH

So I kept everyone distracted...

HELL! HELL! HELL!

Accepted bad treatment graciously

That's where you're going, Spaz

HELL

And prayed for a miracle.

C'MON LADY.

Then, that day with the house in the air...

as seen in Book I

I was struck not only by the unbelieve-ableness of the act...

How did he Do that!

But also because in one swoop of the backhoe...

Dad had obliterated the crimescene!!!

Hooray!

Major Relief!

Miracle

And a realization:

we're even

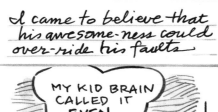

I came to believe that his awesome-ness could over-ride his faults

MY KID BRAIN CALLED IT EVEN.

ALL WAS FORGIVEN

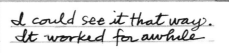

I could see it that way. It worked for awhile

♪♪ oh My PaPa ♪♪

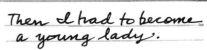

Then I had to become a young lady.

D'YA THINK I'M PRETTY?

AW FER CRYIN' OUT LOUD!

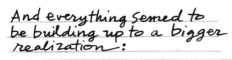

And everything seemed to be building up to a bigger realization:

No. #5

The question of love and self-worth.

LIFETIME CONFUSION.

Let's start with Mom. Lady Manatee. What was her role?

MOM:
• A.K.A. THE HAT LADY
• A LITTLE STAND-OFF-ISH AS WELL
• HOME, KIDS AND PART-TIME JOB
• DEFINITELY ON CHUCK'S TEAM

Here's how that went:

I'LL EXPLAIN NUMBER 5...

A girl looks to her Mom for clues about how to be.

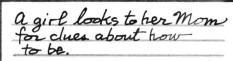

And I had 2 versions to choose from: the Doll in the pictures...

or the Hat Lady? (She started the hat thing in my teen years.)

Or forget the Hat Lady and go with the British Invasion.

Then in High School, there were two paths to choose from

Back then, 'secretarial' was considered to be a dead-end.

Imagine my joy: a way out of here!

But when I made my announcement at dinner:

He leveled my dreams like a bulldozer.

I still prepared for college, but in secret.

My covert college prep activities only got me in trouble.

Then Dad got it in his head that I was about to go "wild".

Like the daughter of a contractor pal of his, Charlene Woolsey:

Char's long-suffering parents considered her to be uncontrollable and bad.

They tried everything, reform school, the convent. Nothing worked.

She got 'knocked-up' and then, a botched back room procedure left her sterile.

Her dad was creepy. I know. I had to sit on his lap once. Poor Charlene!

But Dad couldn't express his concerns to me directly.

Instead, I had to hear it from the Hat Lady, his hired gun...

Whom by this time, I also despised. All those years of emotional distancing...

Didn't they know that eventually it would come home to roost!

So I left home to face the future not knowing myself very well..

feeling a bit lost as to what I would become..

especially with those UNTENABLES hanging over me.

Glad to be on my own, nevertheless.

Ready to believe anything to get affection.

You saw me around. We may have met.

The eager, love-starved hippie chick....

or maybe the drunken babe at the frat house.

Were you in on the pass-around in the back seat?

I was just a "give-in" gal for awhile there.

Mom had reminded me many times:

But this girl needed to hear it from the source.

So she wouldn't have had to ask each guy:

So here's your Number 5 — the enormous cardiac void, a primal deficit, unfulfilled...

..rooted in that early disconnection.

All my life, I've met the same guy over and over, it seems.

Although each time he's wearing a different face —

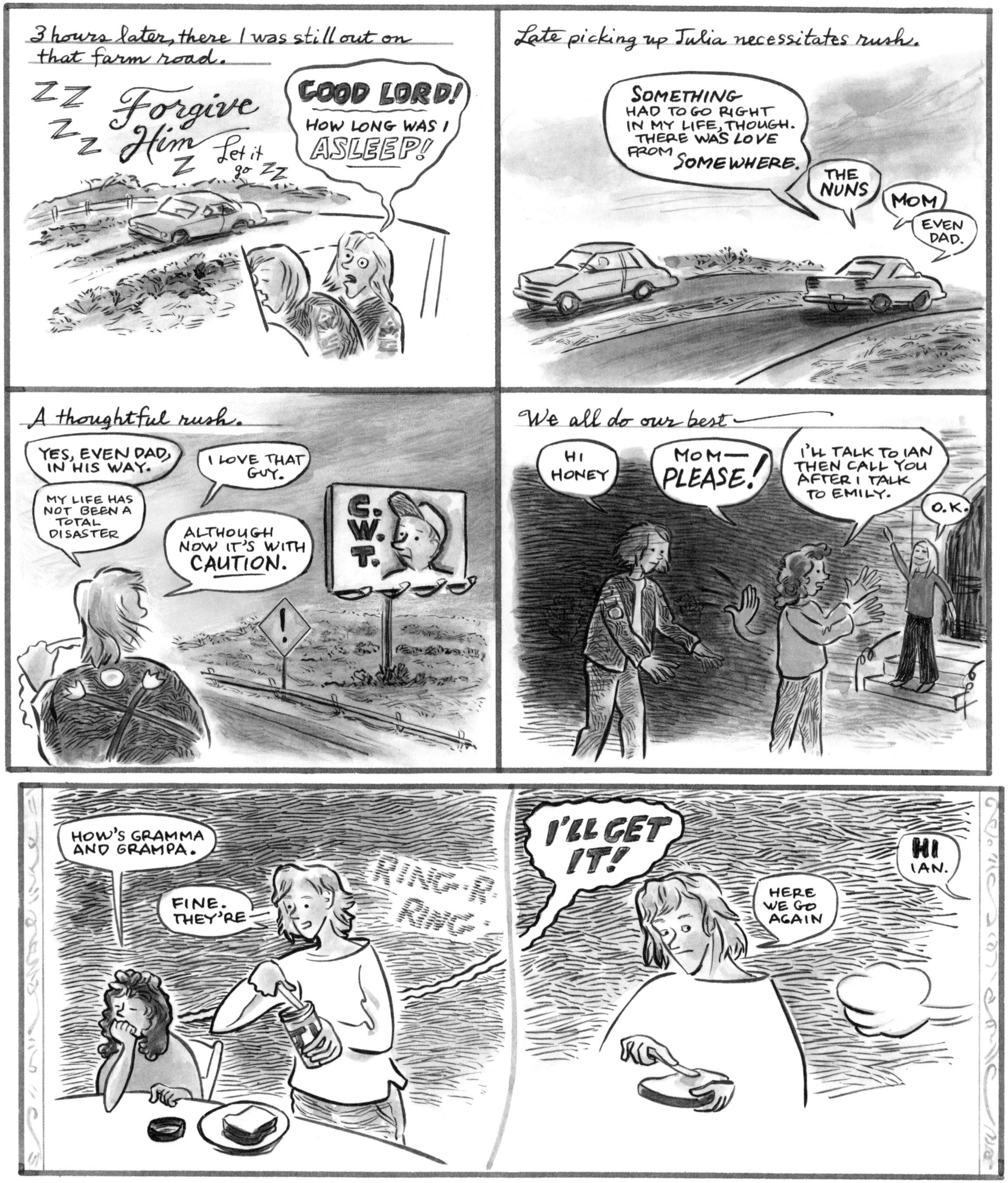

3 hours later, there I was still out on that farm road.
ZZ Forgive Him ZZ Let it go ZZ
GOOD LORD! HOW LONG WAS I ASLEEP!
Late picking up Julia necessitates rush.
SOMETHING HAD TO GO RIGHT IN MY LIFE, THOUGH. THERE WAS LOVE FROM SOMEWHERE.
THE NUNS
MOM
EVEN DAD.
A thoughtful rush.
YES, EVEN DAD, IN HIS WAY.
I LOVE THAT GUY.
MY LIFE HAS NOT BEEN A TOTAL DISASTER
ALTHOUGH NOW IT'S WITH CAUTION.
C. W. T.
We all do our best
HI HONEY
MOM— PLEASE!
I'LL TALK TO IAN THEN CALL YOU AFTER I TALK TO EMILY.
O.K.
HOW'S GRAMMA AND GRAMPA.
FINE. THEY'RE—
RING-R-RING
I'LL GET IT!
HERE WE GO AGAIN
HI IAN.

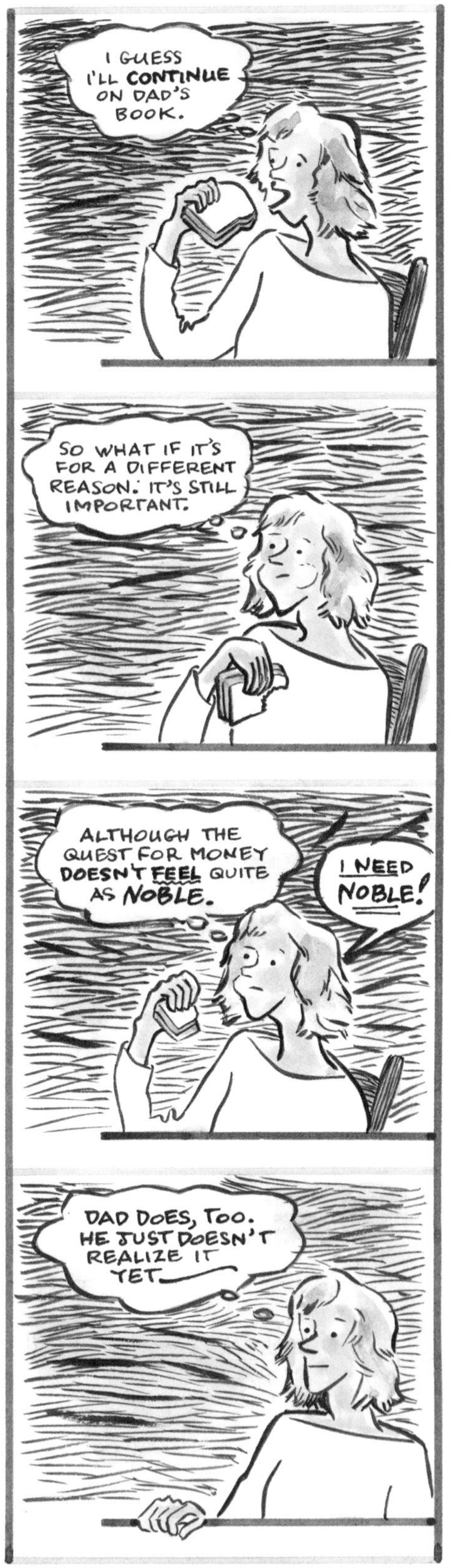

I GUESS I'LL CONTINUE ON DAD'S BOOK.
SO WHAT IF IT'S FOR A DIFFERENT REASON. IT'S STILL IMPORTANT.
ALTHOUGH THE QUEST FOR MONEY DOESN'T FEEL QUITE AS NOBLE.
I NEED NOBLE!
DAD DOES, TOO. HE JUST DOESN'T REALIZE IT YET.

Update on the Personal Workspace

NO MATTER WHAT'S GOING ON WITH YOUR LIFE, ALWAYS SET ASIDE A SEPARATE, SPECIAL PLACE.

2929 Markbreit Avenue

A Room With a Muse.

It's Affordable and Safe

STILL DRAWING ON A PLANK AND SLEEPING ON A PIECE OF FOAM

ñ ARF

View from the top floor: traffic and the seasons passing. People walking their dogs. My window on the world, where 'Life Goes On' seems possible.

P.U.

I MISS MY DOG

Vivian lives below us. Been here 17 years. Married to cigarettes. Hole in her lung. When she lights up, her smoke wafts up and comes out of my electric outlets!

SSSH!   HE'S SINGLE   HMM

Veterinarian Jim on the bottom floor in what was once a storefront. He always wears a blue shirt and always slams the door on his walk to the office nearby.

GIT TO WERK

ALTHOUGH I DON'T HAVE A WORKSPACE AS GRAND AS DAD'S, I DO HAVE THE PLANK. AND IF THIS PROJECT WASN'T ON THE PLANK, I BELIEVE I'D WALK IT INTO A SEA OF DESPAIR

POOR OLD SOULS

Middlew

Meow   what the PUCK

ONWARD TO THE CHAPTER ON ITALY! But first, let me describe the basement: Must and centipedes. Vivian's defunct old appliances. Evidence of the good times, left by former tenants. And Jim the Vet stores hundreds and hundreds of obsolete x-rays in boxes marked canine/feline deceased.

DAD'S ARMY SCRAPBOOK
AND
TOUR OF DUTY HIGHLIGHTS

PART III

~ ITALY ~

JULY 1944 – OCTOBER 1944

Only THIS time,
I'm looking for
EVIDENCE.

Knee Deep

"On the boat over to Italy, all the talk was about Normandy. Rumor had it that the war wouldn't last very much longer. Just a little mopping up, that's all. With Jerry on the run, victory was at hand.

"Going past Sicily, we saw people coming out in their little boats to greet us. So we got excited and threw our bars of soap to them. A funny thing happened: they started eating the soap thinking they were candy bars.

"Naples — big harbor. That's where we docked."

JUL 15 1944

"Hurry up and wait, with a little shot of SNAFU. This was Naples. *Napoli*. Right away when I figured out, it wasn't plumbing they needed me for... I was on hold in a 'Repple Depple'." (Short for Personnel Replacement Depot — a system to replace casualties, the wounded and the dead.) "We were fresh meat."

"Your life ain't worth a damn. We were there waiting while they were digging trenches for the poor bastards that didn't make it. Our turn was coming so the vino was flowing. We drank like there was no tomorrow."

39

"Liquor — now *THAT* was something else. Vino was cheap, beer too. But liquor — that was the way to go alright.

"Next thing 'What's this?' 'Get up there Jack* we want you driving us.' It turns out that the officers needed my truck to sneak their cases of liquor off of the Navy ships. That's how I had access to the good stuff. Of course. So I slipped off a case or two of my own and sold it on the black market. That's how you did it. Everybody did it. Us hunks of meat had to make some extra money somehow."

*everyone calls everyone else 'Jack'.

40

"This buddy I met in the Repple Depple — SNOOSE I called him. From Red Lake, Minnesota. Well, we decided we needed something to keep the booze cold. So we went back to the Navy ship — as a construction foreman, I had access. And the truck they gave me. I lied like a son-of-a-bitch to get what we needed.

"They gave us blocks of ice and we stole wood from the quartermaster. We built this giant ice house, there in Naples, Italy — in the middle of summer. 12" thick walls. Hoo hoo, two boys from the midwest. I imagine it's still there."

41

"Somebody had set up three blankets for hookers out in a field — one each for a blonde, a brunette and a redhead. Guys would stand in line and when it was their turn, they'd put their bills down on the blanket. This had nothing to do with love. Strictly wartime survival for the dames.

"Snoose and I, we were married men, but that didn't keep us from snatching up a few stray bills while those broads weren't lookin'. That's how we paid the Navy guys for all that ice."

42

"There in Naples, picking up ammo for a dump — 3 shells in a pack piled up there as high as you could throw it onto a 6×6 (truck) 9' high and a block square.

"We put a couple of Italians to watch it one night. See, they used to be our enemies, but now they were on our side. So one of those guys shot at somebody, hit the dump and up it went! Boy, we had the wildest bunch of fireworks you'd ever seen! Next thing I know, I'm under Mark Clark headed up to what was called the 'Purple Heart Valley.'"

43

"I had a speedboat up there supposedly for hunting mines. Just goofing off, that's all.

"I asked this guy I'd met in Africa — he was in real estate — to get me a boat. Every fence post or building we nicked or banged up, he took note of it and I guess the United States paid for it. We paid in full.

"So I asked this guy could he get me a casa. Wouldn't you know next thing I've got a nice house with a boat on a river in Italy. Wow. Who it belonged to, I'll never know."

44

"There we were for a few days at my casa. How about a nice dinner before moving on? A little fish with your vino? Except that fishing in Italy wasn't like fishing at home. We decided to throw a grenade into the water and then catch the fish as they came flying out. Great idea, except that some son-of-a-bitch happened to toss in a shrapnel grenade. Holy shit we ran for cover!

"We were just a bunch of crazy kids having a blast over there."

45

By mid-August, three Army infantry Divisions were pulled out of Italy for the invasion of Southern France, and left behind were the smaller rag-tag repple units and far fewer resources. Their mission was to push past the Arno River, up into the impossible terrain of the Apennines Mountains and drive the Nazis off the cliffs and into hell.

A miserable landscape: craggy hills and passes and countless unnamed creeks that could in an instant after a downpour become raging torrents. Fall starts the rainy season.

46

Certainly more than one of these creeks ran red with blood, and which one Chuck encountered, we'll never know.

"The Germans... we couldn't get them out. Shooting the shit out of us from the hills. We crossed the river with fixed bayonets. (a blade at the end of a rifle, which means close contact with the enemy). Krauts: they hated bayonets.

"The river turnt red. I'll never forget that."

"You never knew if you were gonna catch a bullet or get stung by a bee. Hunched over in the rain, I bit into a marmalade sandwich and got stung in the mouth 4 times. My whole face swelled up and I landed over in the sickbay.

"No rest there. Circus Sally kept strafing the hospital *Roop Roop Roop* with his machine gun. You could hear him coming. I didn't like being a sitting duck, but being laid up gave me a chance to catch up on my mail."

"Soon enough, I was back in a truck, hauling artillery up to the front in a blackout. In a convoy, following the little 1"x2" teardrop tail lights all night while fighting the god-dam mud in my 12 wheel vehicle, sinking up to the axles. They were always moving the road because of mud holes that could swallow up a truck in no time.

"I kept a pistol on my lap, not a rifle — not handy in the cab of a truck. And if I needed bullets, I could get 'em off a dead guy. The bodies were everywhere."

49

"Mud. Knee deep. So much mud that the legs of our cots were on planks. Couldn't wiggle or it would slide off and you'd be up to your neck, wet and filthy. A little stream ran up through the middle of our tent and that's where to aim while peeing off the side of a cot." As long as it runs downhill...

"Laid up there, we couldn't move off the cots so we used our little pill cups as ships to send messages back and forth on the stream. 'Fuck you' the notes would say. 'Kilroy was here' and all that."

50

"The people buried everything to keep the enemy from getting it: cars, jewelry, sugar. They hid up in the hills until the Germans left and then they would come down waving a flag of whatever country, loyal to whomever just to survive. They were disappointed with us a bit. We were the beat-and-tired grunts rolling in after driving all night, after the stateside commandos had come through there handing out chocolates ahead of us. You know, those desk jockeys in clean uniforms who zip in on a Jeep after the enemy leaves. We had no such treats."

51

"I noticed while driving that the men made the women walk out in front. Was this some custom or *Kaboom* land mines. 30-40 paces behind, the men stayed.

"So many people out on the roads! They wouldn't get out of the way! We'd honk and they'd just stand there, so we had to knock 'em over. 'Hey, here's some butter, now *MOVE*' but they'd just grease their axles with it so their wagons wouldn't squeak. No stopping the army convoy. We must have knocked over a hundred guys. They didn't listen to us. Things of war, I guess."

52

Civilians were getting it as bad as the soldiers. Worse, because women and children were involved. Families. Old people. Animals. Rotting dead animals everywhere — This was their homes, roads, villages. This was their land being trampled upon. People caught between armies, coming and going.

"Pretty soon I got word that my bunch was due to leave Italy. Being sent to France to do what, I didn't know. All I could think was that nothing could be worse than this god-forsaken mud hole!"

OCT 16

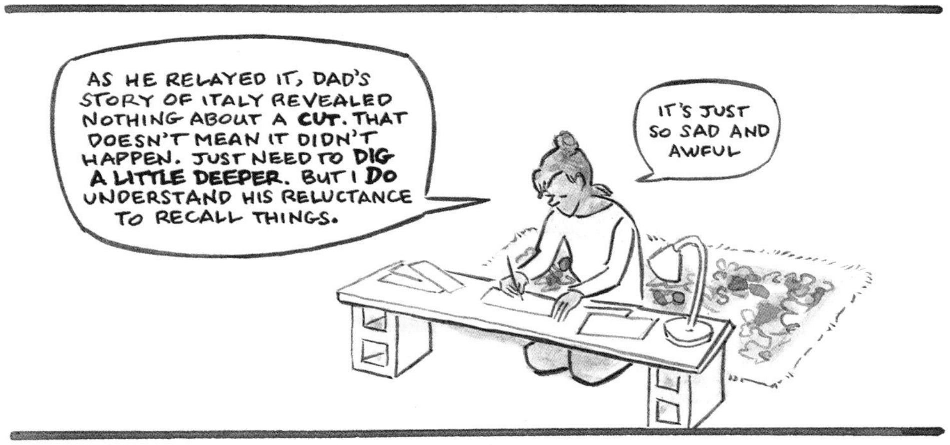
AS HE RELAYED IT, DAD'S STORY OF ITALY REVEALED NOTHING ABOUT A **CUT**. THAT DOESN'T MEAN IT DIDN'T HAPPEN. JUST NEED TO **DIG A LITTLE DEEPER**. BUT I **DO** UNDERSTAND HIS RELUCTANCE TO RECALL THINGS.
IT'S JUST SO SAD AND AWFUL

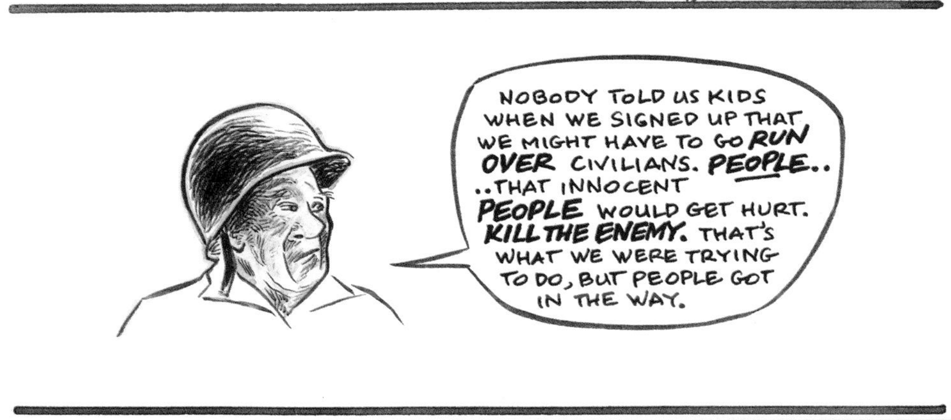
NOBODY TOLD US KIDS WHEN WE SIGNED UP THAT WE MIGHT HAVE TO GO **RUN OVER** CIVILIANS. **PEOPLE**.. ..THAT INNOCENT **PEOPLE** WOULD GET HURT. **KILL THE ENEMY.** THAT'S WHAT WE WERE TRYING TO DO, BUT PEOPLE GOT IN THE WAY.

Some Days I Just Feel Like Cryin' — GRIEF IS A BUCKET THAT MUST BE EMPTIED.

My apt. bldg. is directly across the street from the back of a funeral parlor. From my windows, I see the service entrance, an empty parking lot and a perfectly centered wooden bench, where often I park my tearful mind.

I don't want to carry on in front of the kid...

So I empty the bucket by watchin' the bench.

The families, when they come... it's a working class place.

I'm sad

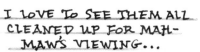

I love to see them all cleaned up for Mah-Maw's viewing...

Me, too

For Uncle So-and-So's wake.

We's all sad

I love it when a trucker puts on a clean vest.

O.K.

CALM ABIDING. STEADFAST CALM. THAT'S WHAT GETS ONE THROUGH THE HARD TIMES.

I SHOULD'VE NEVER GOTTEN INTO IT THIS MORNING WITH JUSTIN.

THE WORST THING IS, JULIA HEARD ME SHOUTING AT HER DAD ON THE PHONE.

IN THESE BATTLES, THE INNOCENT OFTEN GET HURT.

"I Had a Classroom" by Ms. Tyler

After years of subbing, I finally got my very own self-contained classroom. First grade. 15 students. A honey of a gig. How do you spell 'I love this'?

As a sub, I had picked up many teacher tricks. Add to that all I had learned as a volunteer at my daughter's magnet school-of-the-arts and the sum total was one creative and mucho-ly effective learning ~~ptase~~ place.

Most of my students were the children of immigrants from Thailand, Laos, Vietnam, Samoa, Mexico. Many Hmong. No English spoken at home. I had to prepare homework packets in 5 languages, working during my own time with interpreters. Many of the kids were from a single parent home. Or there was a drug or a gang situation. I came to realize after awhile how rough life was for them off campus. So I decided to make my classroom the safest, most wonderful place on earth. A zone of sanity, stability and fun.

By February, they were reading (ahead of the other first grades) and were Number 1 in Math. And then Justin walked out on me. Hit me like a rock.

Needless to say, teaching was no longer a passion, merely a job. Obsessively, I poured my energies into grief and the Justin re-education effort (don't do this other woman!). This led to insomnia and anorexic-level weight loss. By mid-April I had become non-functional to the point where I didn't trust myself as a parent, and sent our kid back east to live with my brothers for awhile.

Then came the Incident, one Sunday night. Justin and I, out on a sidewalk in front of an odd building arguing for hours and hours. Turns out it was an illegal sweatshop full of Asian ladies, trapped there listening to our off hour cadences — nasty and swarming. In the wee-hours they tumbled out into an awaiting van. As they passed me, they shot warning looks, a universal 'help yourself, sister' coming right at me. No translation needed.

It was the hour where I had to either go A. home and try to get 2 hours of sleep before entering my now completely dysfunctional classroom or B. board a train and never look back on the sorry mess my life had become.

I heard the children wailed for weeks at my departure. I loved them, precious. I hurt them, terribly. So very sorry I am. Unforgivable. But it was die or start over. And I missed my girl.

I ALSO HAD TO GET COLD AND GET RID OF OUR FAMILY DOG — MAKES ME SHUDDER TO THINK ABOUT IT. — WILL ATONEMENT FOR THESE CRIMES EVER BE POSSIBLE?

Perfectly Trained

Shep/Lab Mix

BONNIE

BONNIE

SNIF

ON THIS DAY, THE ARGUMENT AND THE MEMORIES GOT TO US. WE STAYED HOME.

Mama

SNIF

SNIF

I KNOW. I'M SORRY TOO.

C'MON

LET'S SIT

"*School Age Child*" by Julia's mom.

I asked a lot of her. Pulling her from her classroom before the year was complete. I'd worked so hard getting her into the arts magnet program, and 6TH grade was the best year yet. The theme: Ancient civilizations. All about Egypt, Greece and Rome. At the time she left they were on the Spartans, which she didn't care for at all. So in her mind, it was the perfect time to leave. Egypt was her favorite. She even re-named herself JULIAMAYHET GREENATIRI.

Her California school classmates were like siblings and she missed them terribly, having gone through everything with them since "K". Now she was starting over with a new crop of less forgiving kids, and at that awkward age where looks can cut, cliques are vicious, bullies rule and the weak become desperate. Such is Junior High. Cinti, OH.

Everything had changed in her world. No palm trees, mild winters or liberal attitudes here. Rust-bucket Ohio is a jerky chew of tall brick structures and sub-zero temps. But my amazing little Julia seems to be transitioning quite well. She likes snow and is making new friends. I'm blessed with the bright spirit of my school age child. The one thing I don't have to worry about.

DRAWN BY JULIA MAY GREEN

A LITTLE LATER
Mom
What
HOW 'BOUT MAKE AN ARMY BOOK ABOUT JOHNNY.*
DAD WOULD LIKE IT
* JOHNNY IS JUSTIN'S DAD
WOAH HONEY
THAT'S A TALL ORDER
John C. Green ANOTHER WWII VETERAN WHO DIDN'T TALK ABOUT HIS SERVICE... IN THE ARMY AIR CORPS.
Best Years of My Life
1909-1970
A FEW DETAILS SHARED WITH HIS BROTHERS, BUT NEVER WITH JUSTIN, HIS SON
POP?
HE'S ANOTHER ONE OF THOSE DISTANT DADS THAT DEFINED THAT GENERATION.
HEY!
POP!
HMM.. INSIGHT INTO JUSTIN.
IF I WAS DAMAGED BY A WAR-TORN FATHER, THEN JUSTIN...
Y'KNOW WHAT, MISS JULIA
I think YOU can do that booklet someday?

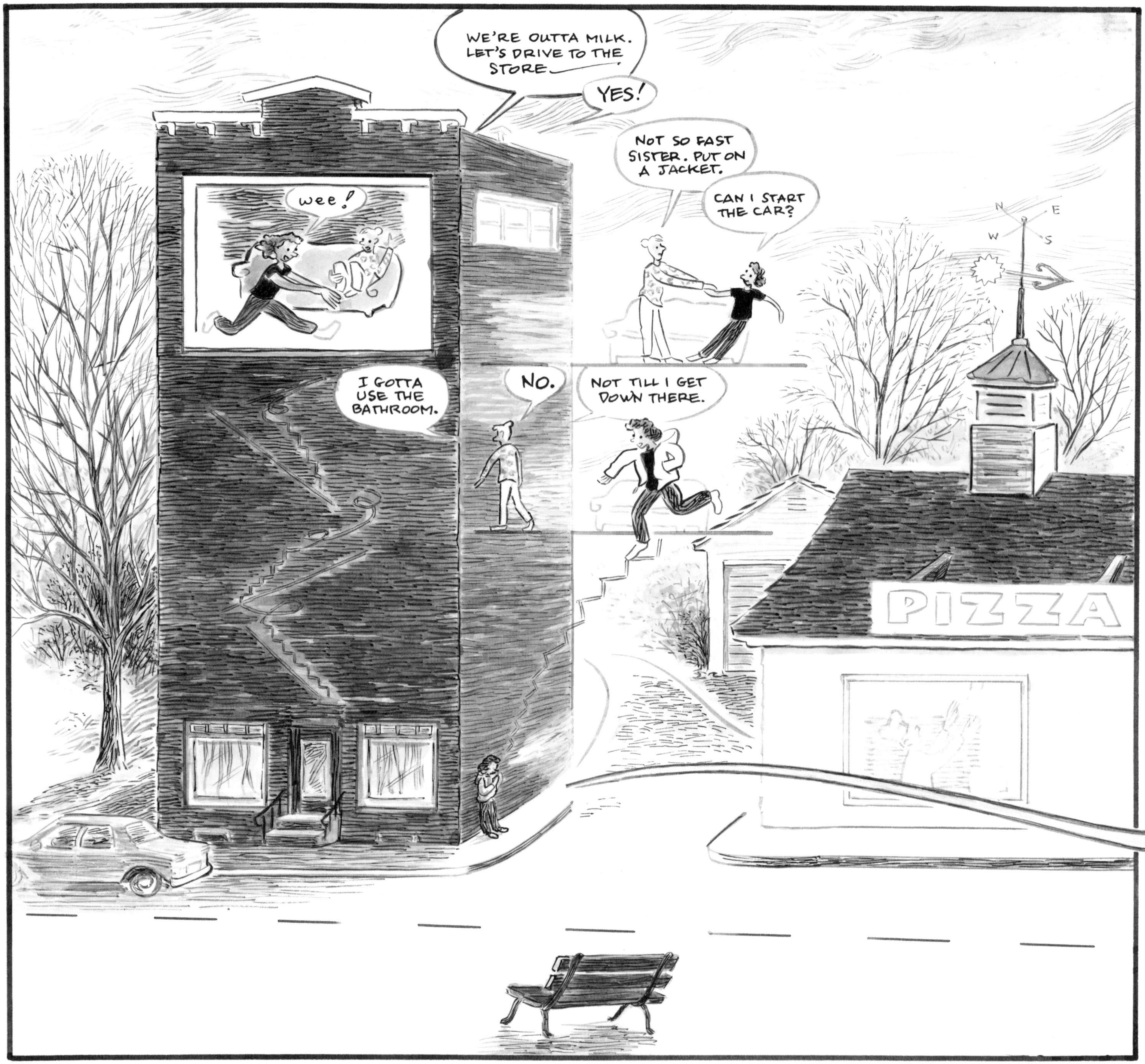
WE'RE OUTTA MILK. LET'S DRIVE TO THE STORE
YES!
wee!
NOT SO FAST SISTER. PUT ON A JACKET.
CAN I START THE CAR?
N
E
W
S
I GOTTA USE THE BATHROOM.
NO.
NOT TILL I GET DOWN THERE.
PIZZA

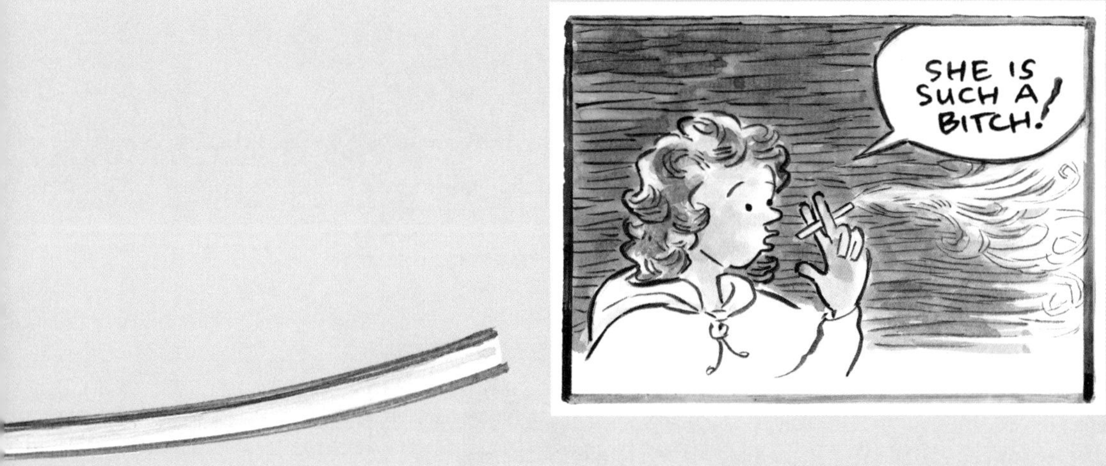
SHE IS SUCH A BITCH!

THIS NEXT SECTION: A BACKSTORY.

FLASHING BACK TO THE 1990s

HOW CHUCK CAME TO **BY WAY OF ILLNESS**
KNOW ABOUT HIS CUT AT CAMP CHEMO
AND THE EVENTS THAT CIRCUITOUSLY
LED TO HIS EVENTUALLY SHARING
HIS ARMY STORY. **BEGINNING IN 2002**
WITH THAT PHONE CALL

A Helpful TIMELINE and MAP:

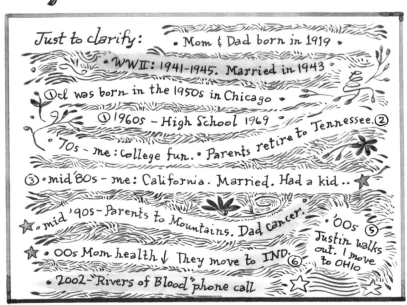

Just to clarify: • Mom & Dad born in 1919 •
• WWII: 1941-1945. Married in 1943 •
① I was born in the 1950s in Chicago •
① 1960s - High School 1969
• '70s - me: College fun. • Parents retire to Tennessee. ②
③ • mid '80s - me: California. Married. Had a kid ..
• mid '90s - Parents to Mountains. Dad cancer. • '00s ⑤
Justin walks
out. I move
• 00s Mom health ↓ They move to IND. ⑥ to OHIO
• 2002 - "Rivers of Blood" phone call

The next 19 pages

THIS COLOR INDICATES WHEN CHUCK'S ARMY EXPERIENCES, THOUGHTS, AND ACTIVE MEMORIES OCCURRED.

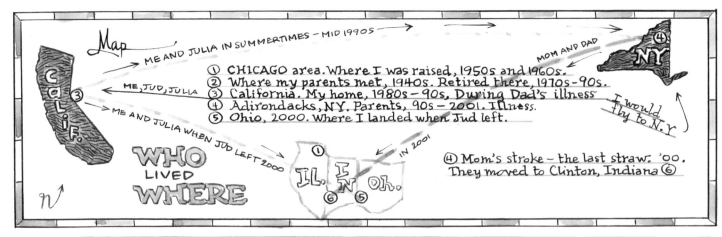

Map

ME AND JULIA IN SUMMERTIMES - MID 1990s →

MOM AND DAD

NY ④

ME, JUD, JULIA

ME AND JULIA WHEN JUD LEFT 2000

Calif. ③

① CHICAGO area. Where I was raised, 1950s and 1960s.
② Where my parents met, 1940s. Retired there, 1970s-90s.
③ California. My home, 1980s-90s. During Dad's illness
④ Adirondacks, N.Y. Parents, 90s-2001. Illness.
⑤ Ohio, 2000. Where I landed when Jud left.

I would fly to N.Y.

WHO LIVED WHERE

① IN 2001
Il. I Oh.
N
⑥ ⑤

④ Mom's stroke - the last straw. '00.
They moved to Clinton, Indiana ⑥

Though a continent apart, my sister and I planned a pure gold family gala for their 50TH anniversary. Surprise!

Celebrating 50 Years!

-1943-

-1993-

WE FILLED TWO BASKETS!!

HERE WAS OUR COOL IDEA: WE SENT A FLIER (THAT KIND OF LOOKED LIKE THIS PAGE) TO EVERY NAME ON THEIR CHRISTMAS CARD LIST. IT SAID:

"We envision a huge basket in the center of the table overflowing with cards, photos, anecdotes and special wishes from friends like you. We decided that greetings from your heart are what they'll treasure most."

We were right! ☺

The celebration of their five decades together included a Mass followed by a festive dinner. In attendance: The children, Virginia from McHenry, IL, Joe and Jim, both from Saranac Lake NY, and Carol from Sacramento, CA. Spouses and Grandchildren, too.

We figured they had enough blenders.

MARVELOUS!

OH GIRLS!

OH HERE'S A GOOD ONE: "I'll never forget the time that Charlie gave us that shrimp wrapped in newspaper to put in the freezer. At least I thought it was shrimp until I unwrapped it at supper one night and found it was all shells! HA HA and Congrats." —the Cornishes.

HUH HUH

HA HA!

Then Chuck launched his big announcement:

PSST. CAROL. WHO ARE THE CORNISHES.

HA!

I NEED YOU KIDS TO HELP.

I THINK I'D LIKE TO BUILD A NEW HOUSE FROM SCRATCH.

We had our concerns. Starting with his being 74 years old.

UH

SURE

I GUESS

FOR MY DREAM GIRL.

But this is Chuck Tyler...

I WANT TO BUILD IT UP IN NEW YORK, NEAR MY SONS—

LIVE NEAR MY BOYS.

A CABIN IN THE WOODS

DREAMGIRL. OK. I GET THAT OK, CABIN IN THE WOODS, I GET THAT. LIVE NEAR THE SONS— CORNY LOGIC. WHAT ABOUT THE DAUGHTERS?

WHAT ABOUT US GIRLS?

GIRLS DON'T MATTER. IT'S THE SONS— THAT'S WHAT MATTERS.

AAK! DON'T TALK LIKE THAT.

☆ THEY HAD RETIRED TO TENNESSEE TO A NICE TOWN NEAR WHERE THEY MET. WE THOUGHT THEY WERE SET.

There would be no stopping this testosterone affirming adventure.

LET'S DO IT!

WELL

ARE YOU OK WITH THIS, MOM?

The two decades in Tennessee had been good ones. Especially for Hannah.

I'LL BE FINE. DON'T PAY ANY ATTENTION TO WHAT YOUR FATHER SAID.

I'M READY

The Women's Prayer Circle had helped her process her life's saddest chapter. *

..TO EASE THE PAIN SHE STILL FEELS

A-men

GOOD SHEPHERD CHURCH • DECHERD, TENNESSEE   1992

* which appears later in this book

So they sold their house in Tenn, and bought 2 acres in the heart of the Adirondack Mountains, N.Y.

WHEREVER THIS ROCK LANDS 'LL BE THE CENTER OF MY HOUSE.

SO MUCH FOR THE SURVEYOR!

JIM

JOE

"THE SONS"

Basement poured, walls up, roof on, windows, water and sewer. Just needs finishing.

IT'S JUST MY EAR I'M TELLIN' YA.

FEELS LIKE THERE'S A BUMBLE BEE DOWN IN THERE —

JOE

Next, I get a call from my brother: Stage II Dukes B colon carcinoma. Us siblings come up with a plan —

JOE AND I WILL COVER SURGERY

OK AND I'LL BE UP THERE IN A MONTH WHEN SCHOOL'S OUT, FOR THE ENTIRE SUMMER. I'LL COVER CHEMO.

GINIA WILL BE UP, TOO, WHEN HER SCHOOL IS OUT.

I could not think of a day when my Dad was ever sick.

WOW-WEE LOOK AT ALL THOSE LAKES!

... even the time when he lopped off the end of his finger, when he hit it with the sledge-hammer, while putting in the pier on Stanton Point. Wrapped a rag around it and finished the job.

I CAN'T WAIT TO GO SWIMMING WITH THE COUSINS!

Being down... I just don't associate him with illness.

NOW LISTEN. WE ARE NOT HERE FOR FUN AND GAMES — GRAMPA IS VERY VERY SICK

3A

But I didn't expect this:

HAND ME A LEVEL

DAD!

GRAMPA, I THOUGHT YOU'RE SPOSTA HAVE CANCER

HE DON'T STOP FOR NOTHIN'.

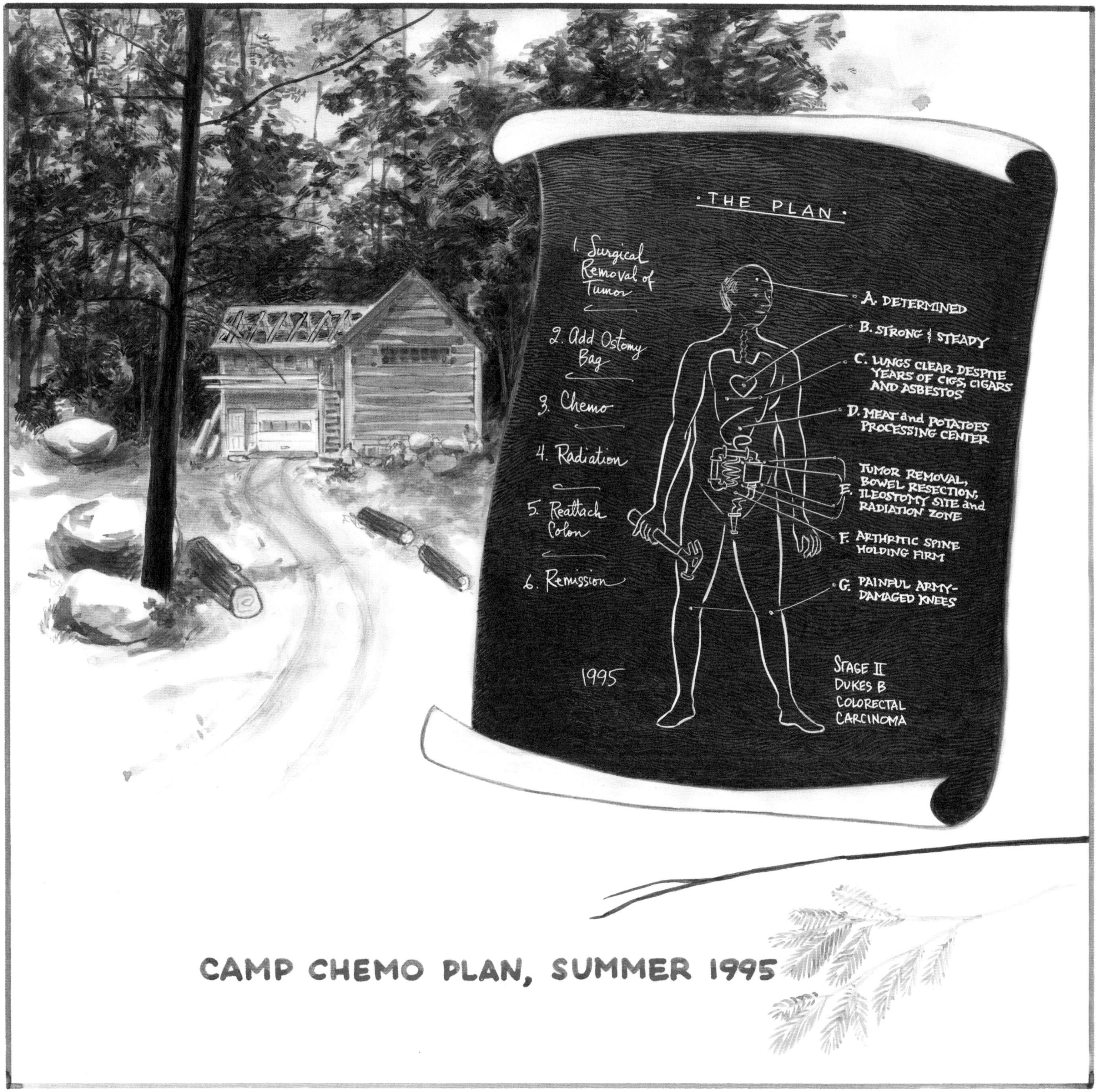
·THE PLAN·
1. Surgical Removal of Tumor
2. Add Ostomy Bag
3. Chemo
4. Radiation
5. Reattach Colon
6. Remission
A. DETERMINED
B. STRONG & STEADY
C. LUNGS CLEAR DESPITE YEARS OF CIGS, CIGARS AND ASBESTOS
D. MEAT and POTATOES PROCESSING CENTER
E. TUMOR REMOVAL, BOWEL RESECTION, ILEOSTOMY SITE and RADIATION ZONE
F. ARTHRITIC SPINE HOLDING FIRM
G. PAINFUL ARMY-DAMAGED KNEES
1995
STAGE II DUKES B COLORECTAL CARCINOMA

CAMP CHEMO PLAN, SUMMER 1995

Over the next few months, it kinda went like this: go for some chemo, then come home and get busy with some drywall. Few days later, go for another treatment, come home and get busy again. He simply stayed focused on the house. Certainly no reason to focus on hair loss.

This was the deal at Camp Chemo.

He sure didn't act sick, although if he felt bad, he sure wouldn't have told me about it. It's possible to gauge how somebody's feeling by how they look, but he just looked like a 75 year old. Another way to tell would be the activity level, and well... hey. This is Chuck Tyler. One of Georgie's boys (Patton that is). That means he's unstoppable.

So I set up a card table and worked on my comics, there, under the 'floor to ceiling' windows of the "great room." The windows that mother insisted we cover with drapes, so she didn't feel so all exposed out there in the woods (?). I mainly played a supportive role and helped whenever they'd let me. (For some reason, I wasn't allowed to drive the car!)!

A patch of illness can mark a time of vulnerability, when people step in to help and show their love. But Chuck had that invisible brick wall, and while heroically coping with the side effects of his treatment, it was very difficult to deal with the raging, pissy stalwart he had become. He did let the medical people in — a pussycat with the nurses ..

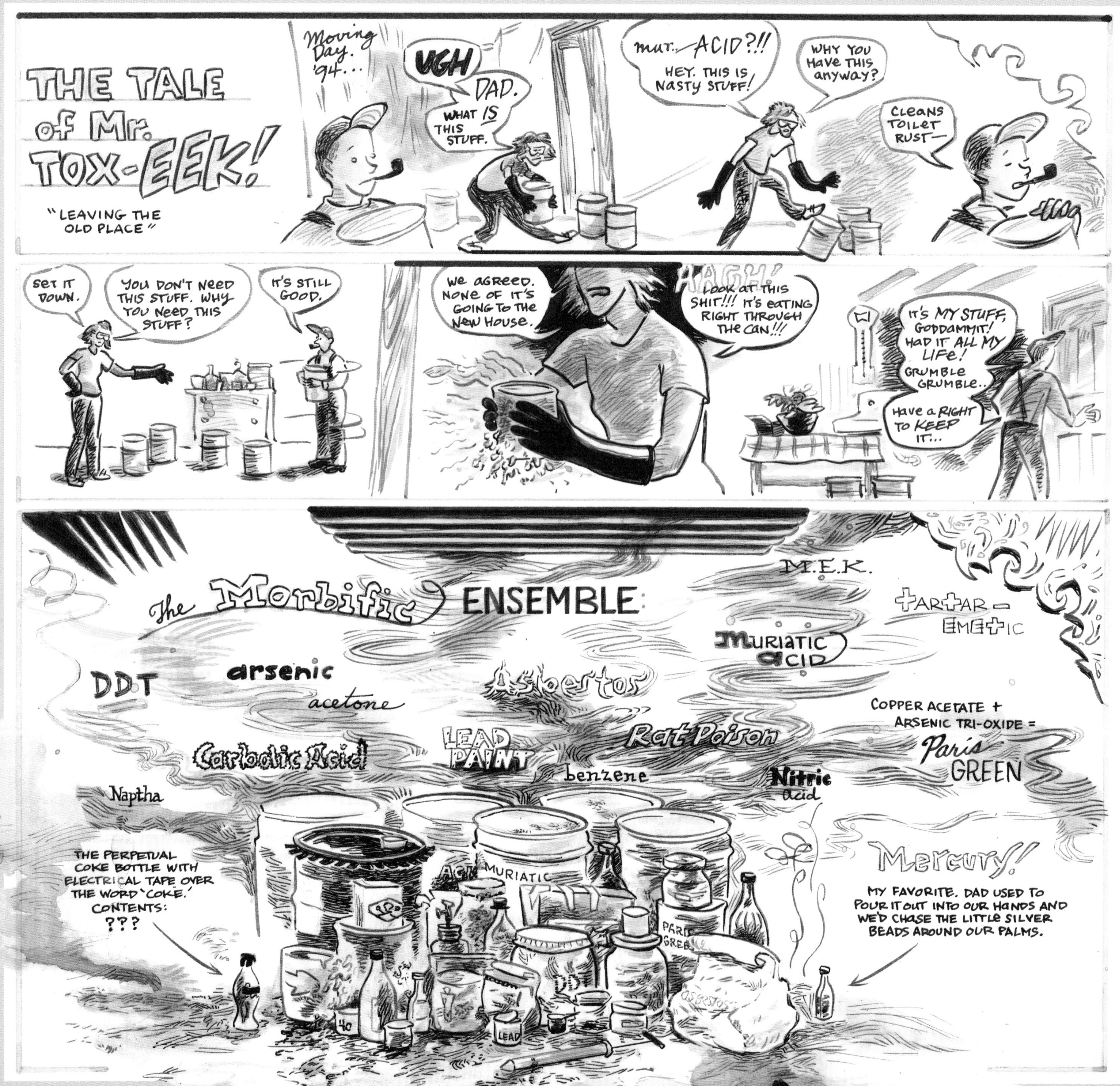

THE TALE of Mr. TOX-EEK!
"LEAVING THE OLD PLACE"
Moving Day. '94...
UGH
DAD.
WHAT IS THIS STUFF.
mur. ACID?!!
HEY. THIS IS NASTY STUFF!
WHY YOU HAVE THIS ANYWAY?
CLEANS TOILET RUST—
SET IT DOWN.
YOU DON'T NEED THIS STUFF. WHY YOU NEED THIS STUFF?
IT'S STILL GOOD.
WE AGREED. NONE OF IT'S GOING TO THE NEW HOUSE.
AAGH!
LOOK AT THIS SHIT!!! IT'S EATING RIGHT THROUGH THE CAN!!!
IT'S MY STUFF, GODDAMMIT! HAD IT ALL MY LIFE!
GRUMBLE GRUMBLE..
HAVE A RIGHT TO KEEP IT...
The Morbific ENSEMBLE:
M.E.K.
TARTAR-EMETIC
MURIATIC ACID
DDT
arsenic
acetone
Asbestos
COPPER ACETATE + ARSENIC TRI-OXIDE = Paris GREEN
Carbolic Acid
LEAD PAINT
Rat Poison
benzene
Nitric Acid
Naptha
THE PERPETUAL COKE BOTTLE WITH ELECTRICAL TAPE OVER THE WORD 'COKE.' CONTENTS: ???
Mercury!
MY FAVORITE. DAD USED TO POUR IT OUT INTO OUR HANDS AND WE'D CHASE THE LITTLE SILVER BEADS AROUND OUR PALMS.
MURIATIC
PARIS GREEN
DDT
ASBESTOS
LEAD

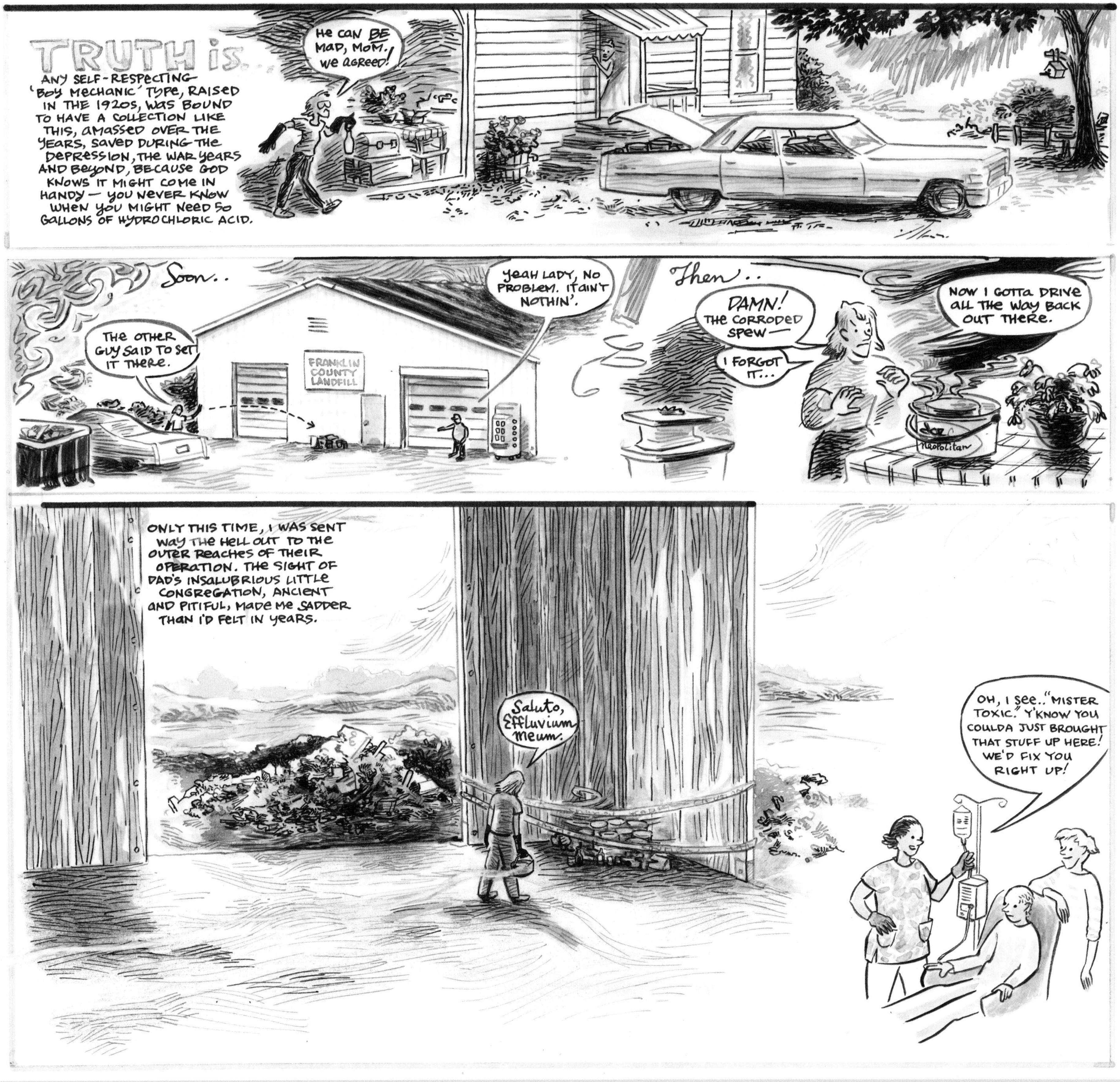
TRUTH is...
ANY SELF-RESPECTING 'BOY MECHANIC' TYPE, RAISED IN THE 1920S, WAS BOUND TO HAVE A COLLECTION LIKE THIS, AMASSED OVER THE YEARS, SAVED DURING THE DEPRESSION, THE WAR YEARS AND BEYOND, BECAUSE GOD KNOWS IT MIGHT COME IN HANDY — YOU NEVER KNOW WHEN YOU MIGHT NEED 50 GALLONS OF HYDROCHLORIC ACID.
He can BE MAD, MOM. We agreed!
Soon..
The other guy said to set it there.
FRANKLIN COUNTY LANDFILL
Yeah lady, no problem. It ain't nothin'.
Then..
DAMN! The corroded spew—
I forgot it...
Now I gotta drive all the way back out there.
ONLY THIS TIME, I WAS SENT WAY THE HELL OUT TO THE OUTER REACHES OF THEIR OPERATION. THE SIGHT OF DAD'S INSALUBRIOUS LITTLE CONGREGATION, ANCIENT AND PITIFUL, MADE ME SADDER THAN I'D FELT IN YEARS.
Saluto, Effluvium meum.
OH, I SEE.. "MISTER TOXIC." Y'KNOW YOU COULDA JUST BROUGHT THAT STUFF UP HERE! WE'D FIX YOU RIGHT UP!

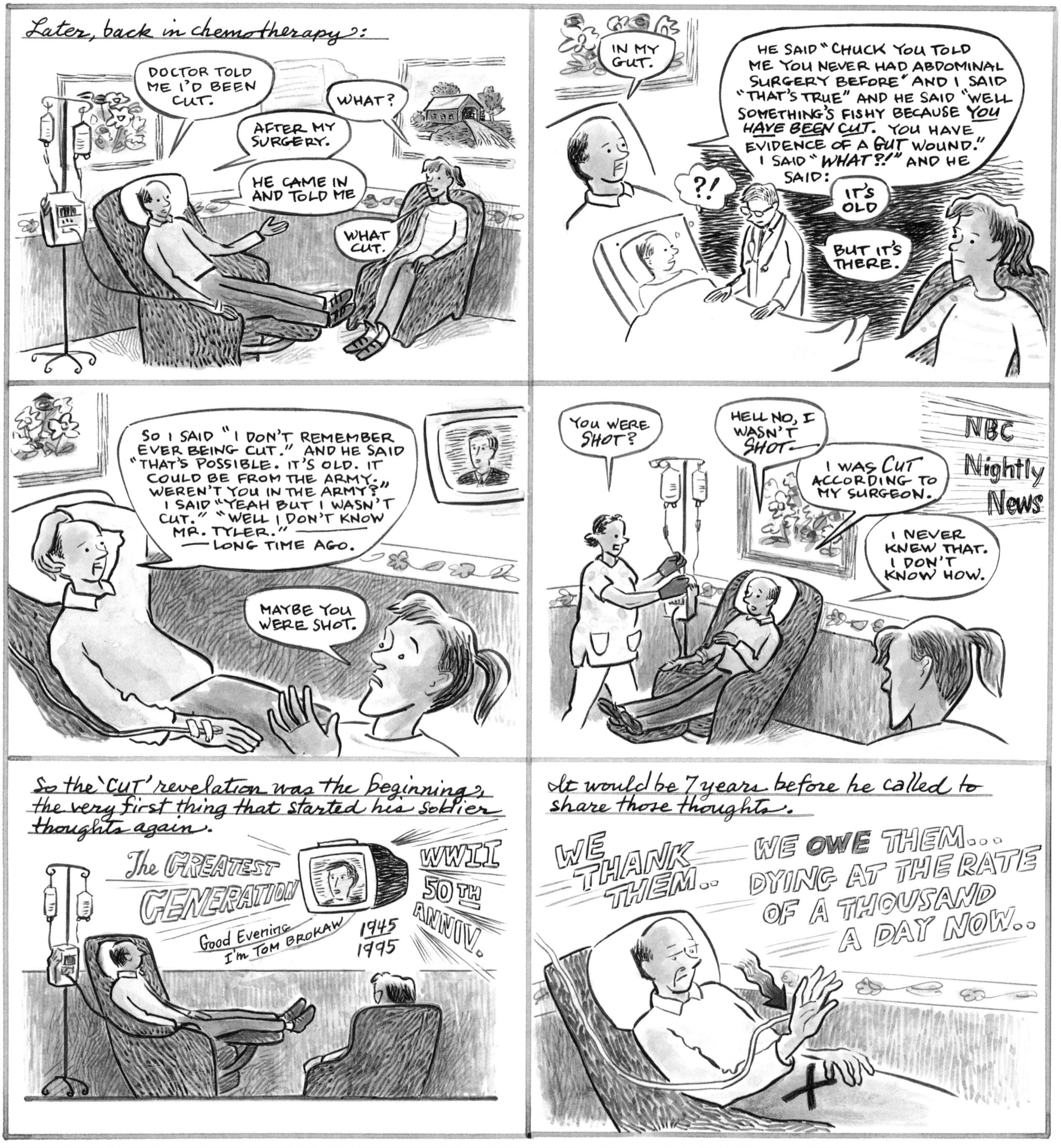

Later, back in chemotherapy:
DOCTOR TOLD ME I'D BEEN CUT.
WHAT?
AFTER MY SURGERY.
HE CAME IN AND TOLD ME
WHAT CUT.
IN MY GUT.
HE SAID "CHUCK YOU TOLD ME YOU NEVER HAD ABDOMINAL SURGERY BEFORE" AND I SAID "THAT'S TRUE" AND HE SAID "WELL SOMETHING'S FISHY BECAUSE YOU HAVE BEEN CUT. YOU HAVE EVIDENCE OF A GUT WOUND." I SAID "WHAT?!" AND HE SAID:
?!
IT'S OLD
BUT IT'S THERE.
SO I SAID "I DON'T REMEMBER EVER BEING CUT." AND HE SAID "THAT'S POSSIBLE. IT'S OLD. IT COULD BE FROM THE ARMY." WEREN'T YOU IN THE ARMY?" I SAID "YEAH BUT I WASN'T CUT." "WELL I DON'T KNOW MR. TYLER." — LONG TIME AGO.
MAYBE YOU WERE SHOT.
YOU WERE SHOT?
HELL NO, I WASN'T SHOT.
I WAS CUT ACCORDING TO MY SURGEON.
NBC Nightly News
I NEVER KNEW THAT. I DON'T KNOW HOW.
So the 'CUT' revelation was the beginning, the very first thing that started his soldier thoughts again.
The GREATEST GENERATION
Good Evening I'm TOM BROKAW
WWII 50TH ANNIV.
1945 1995
It would be 7 years before he called to share those thoughts.
WE THANK THEM..
WE OWE THEM... DYING AT THE RATE OF A THOUSAND A DAY NOW..

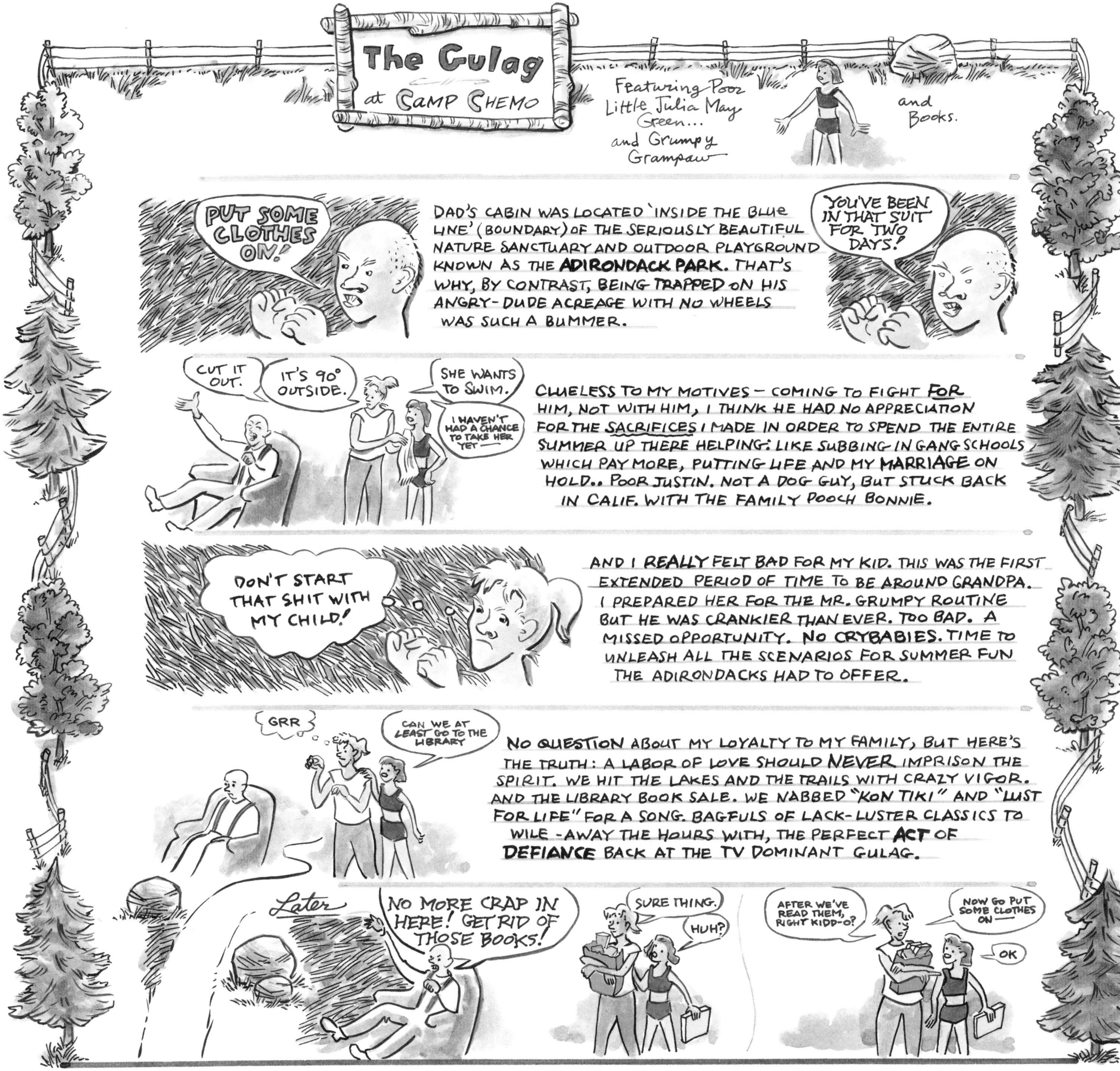
The Gulag
at Camp Chemo
Featuring Poor Little Julia May Green... and Grumpy Grampaw
and Books.
PUT SOME CLOTHES ON!
DAD'S CABIN WAS LOCATED 'INSIDE THE BLUE LINE' (BOUNDARY) OF THE SERIOUSLY BEAUTIFUL NATURE SANCTUARY AND OUTDOOR PLAYGROUND KNOWN AS THE ADIRONDACK PARK. THAT'S WHY, BY CONTRAST, BEING TRAPPED ON HIS ANGRY-DUDE ACREAGE WITH NO WHEELS WAS SUCH A BUMMER.
YOU'VE BEEN IN THAT SUIT FOR TWO DAYS!
CUT IT OUT.
IT'S 90° OUTSIDE.
SHE WANTS TO SWIM.
I HAVEN'T HAD A CHANCE TO TAKE HER YET —
CLUELESS TO MY MOTIVES — COMING TO FIGHT FOR HIM, NOT WITH HIM, I THINK HE HAD NO APPRECIATION FOR THE SACRIFICES I MADE IN ORDER TO SPEND THE ENTIRE SUMMER UP THERE HELPING: LIKE SUBBING IN GANG SCHOOLS WHICH PAY MORE, PUTTING LIFE AND MY MARRIAGE ON HOLD.. POOR JUSTIN. NOT A DOG GUY, BUT STUCK BACK IN CALIF. WITH THE FAMILY POOCH BONNIE.
DON'T START THAT SHIT WITH MY CHILD!
AND I REALLY FELT BAD FOR MY KID. THIS WAS THE FIRST EXTENDED PERIOD OF TIME TO BE AROUND GRANDPA. I PREPARED HER FOR THE MR. GRUMPY ROUTINE BUT HE WAS CRANKIER THAN EVER. TOO BAD. A MISSED OPPORTUNITY. NO CRYBABIES. TIME TO UNLEASH ALL THE SCENARIOS FOR SUMMER FUN THE ADIRONDACKS HAD TO OFFER.
GRR
CAN WE AT LEAST GO TO THE LIBRARY
NO QUESTION ABOUT MY LOYALTY TO MY FAMILY, BUT HERE'S THE TRUTH: A LABOR OF LOVE SHOULD NEVER IMPRISON THE SPIRIT. WE HIT THE LAKES AND THE TRAILS WITH CRAZY VIGOR. AND THE LIBRARY BOOK SALE. WE NABBED "KON TIKI" AND "LUST FOR LIFE" FOR A SONG. BAGFULS OF LACK-LUSTER CLASSICS TO WILE-AWAY THE HOURS WITH, THE PERFECT ACT OF DEFIANCE BACK AT THE TV DOMINANT GULAG.
Later
NO MORE CRAP IN HERE! GET RID OF THOSE BOOKS!
SURE THING.
HUH?
AFTER WE'VE READ THEM, RIGHT KIDD-O?
NOW GO PUT SOME CLOTHES ON —
OK

Clarion at the Camp

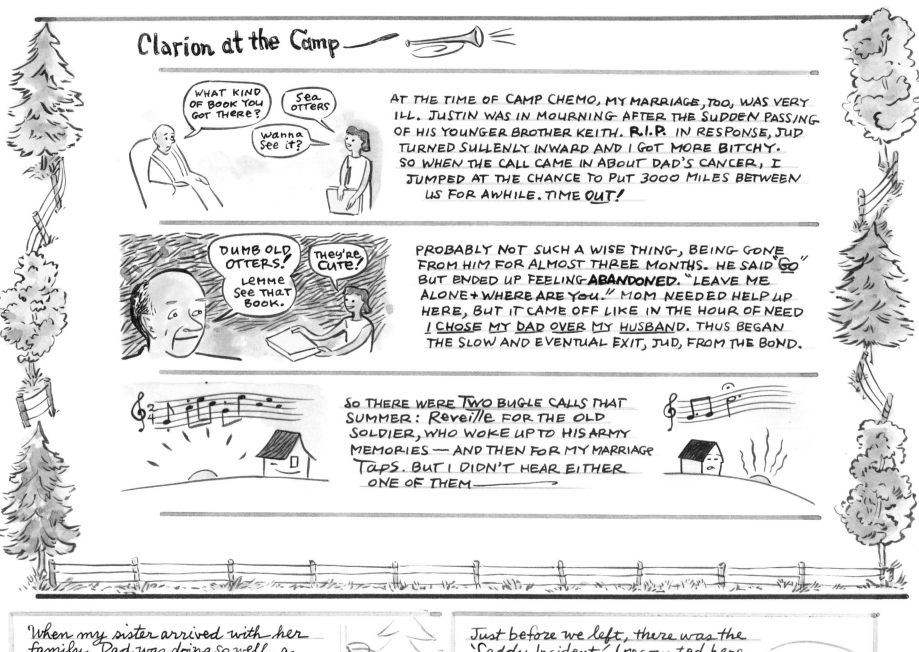

"WHAT KIND OF BOOK YOU GOT THERE?"

"SEA OTTERS"

"WANNA SEE IT?"

AT THE TIME OF CAMP CHEMO, MY MARRIAGE, TOO, WAS VERY ILL. JUSTIN WAS IN MOURNING AFTER THE SUDDEN PASSING OF HIS YOUNGER BROTHER KEITH. **R.I.P.** IN RESPONSE, JUD TURNED SULLENLY INWARD AND I GOT MORE BITCHY. SO WHEN THE CALL CAME IN ABOUT DAD'S CANCER, I JUMPED AT THE CHANCE TO PUT 3000 MILES BETWEEN US FOR AWHILE. TIME <u>OUT</u>!

"DUMB OLD OTTERS! LEMME SEE THAT BOOK."

"THEY'RE CUTE!"

PROBABLY NOT SUCH A WISE THING, BEING GONE FROM HIM FOR ALMOST THREE MONTHS. HE SAID "<u>GO</u>" BUT ENDED UP FEELING **ABANDONED**. "LEAVE ME ALONE + WHERE ARE YOU." MOM NEEDED HELP UP HERE, BUT IT CAME OFF LIKE IN THE HOUR OF NEED <u>I CHOSE MY DAD OVER MY HUSBAND</u>. THUS BEGAN THE SLOW AND EVENTUAL EXIT, JUD, FROM THE BOND.

SO THERE WERE <u>TWO</u> BUGLE CALLS THAT SUMMER: *Reveille* FOR THE OLD SOLDIER, WHO WOKE UP TO HIS ARMY MEMORIES — AND THEN FOR MY MARRIAGE *Taps*. BUT I DIDN'T HEAR EITHER ONE OF THEM

When my sister arrived with her family, Dad was doing so well, a festive atmosphere took hold.

"GRAMPA'S NOT DEAD YET FROM CANCER SO WE'RE HAVING A CAKE, RIGHT?"

"SHH"

"HOW COME GRAMPA IS IN HIS CHAIR. YOU SAID HE WAS ON DEATH'S DOOR-STOP."

JOY!

"THAT'S NOT AN APPROPRIATE THING TO SAY? I CAN THINK IT TO MYSELF, RIGHT? BUT I DON'T HAVE TO SAY IT?"

JOY'S AUTISM LOGIC

WE ALL NEEDED TO LAUGH.

HA HA HA HA HA HA

Just before we left, there was the 'Caddy Incident' (recounted here in 2009).

"...WHAT FOR?"

"C'MON, MOM. 6 BOXES OF RIBBON?!"

"OH."

"LET'S TOSS 'EM"

"KEEP ONE."

"I WAS PART OF THE RESCUE TEAM THAT CAME LATER. HELP ME REMEMBER WHAT HAPPENED TO THE CAR."

2009. TRYING TO RECALL

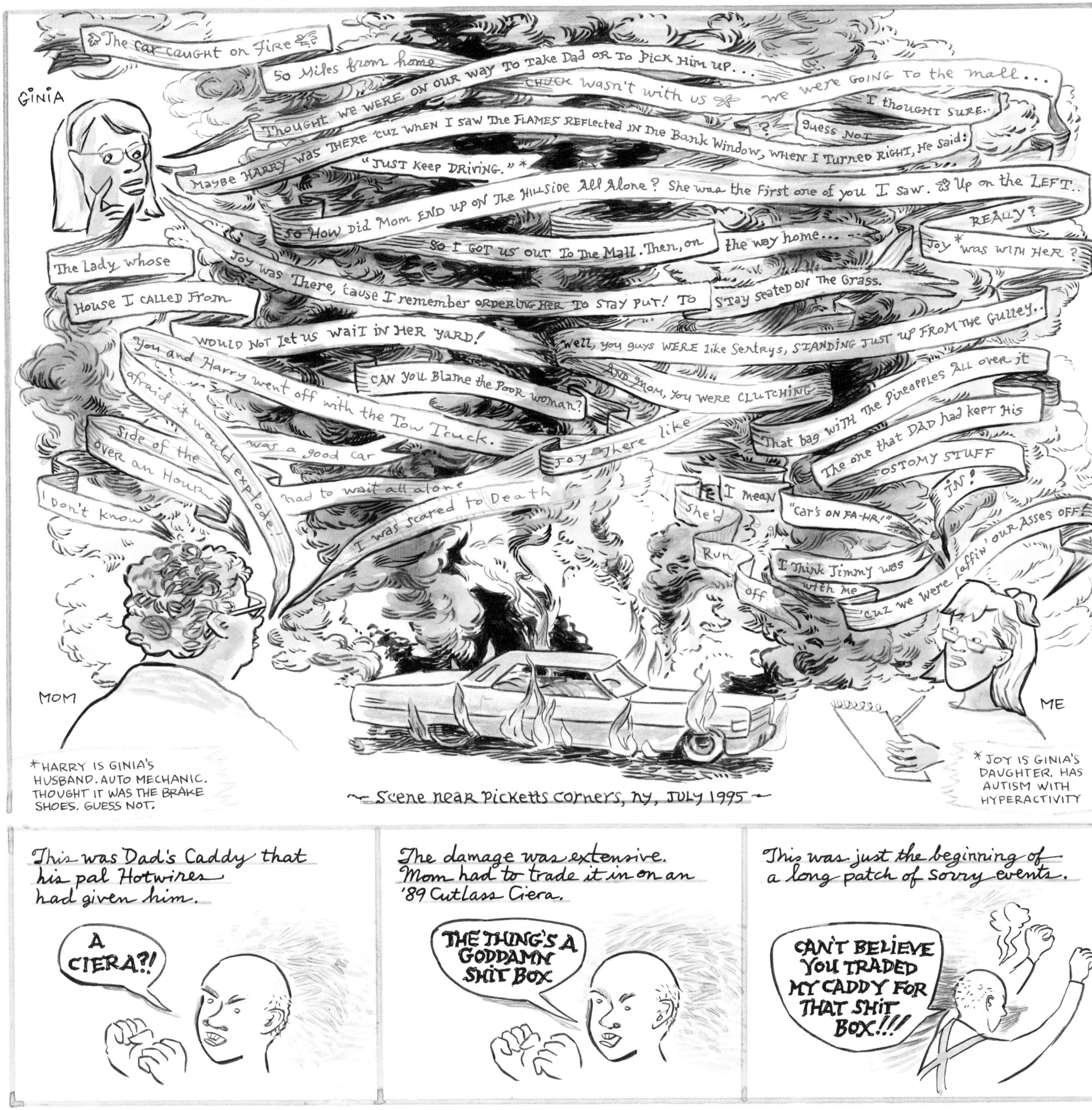

GINIA
The car caught on Fire
50 Miles from home
So Miles from home
So we were on our way to take Dad or to pick him up...
Chuck wasn't with us
we were going to the mall...
I thought sure..
Guess Not
Thought we were there 'cuz when I saw the flames reflected in the Bank Window, when I turned right, He said:
Maybe Harry was there
"Just keep driving." *
So how did Mom end up on the hillside all alone? She was the first one of you I saw. Up on the LEFT..
REALLY?
So I got us out to the Mall. Then, on the way home...
Joy * was with her?
The lady whose House I called From
would not let us wait in her yard!
Joy was there, 'cause I remember ordering her to stay put! To stay seated on the grass.
Well, you guys were like Sentrys, standing just up from the Gulley..
And Mom, you were clutching
that bag with the pineapples all over it
The one that Dad had kept his ostomy stuff in!
Can you blame the poor woman?
You and Harry went off with the Tow Truck.
afraid it would explode!
was a good car
Joy there like
Side of the
over an Hour
I Don't know
had to wait all alone
I was scared to Death
She'd
I mean
"Car's on fa-hr."
Run
off
I think Jimmy was with me
'cuz we were laffin' our asses off!
MOM
ME
* Harry is Ginia's husband. Auto mechanic. Thought it was the brake shoes. Guess not.
~ Scene near Picketts Corners, NY, July 1995 ~
* Joy is Ginia's daughter, has autism with hyperactivity
This was Dad's Caddy that his pal Hotwires had given him.
A CIERA?!
The damage was extensive. Mom had to trade it in on an '89 Cutlass Ciera.
THE THING'S A GODDAMN SHIT BOX
This was just the beginning of a long patch of sorry events.
CAN'T BELIEVE YOU TRADED MY CADDY FOR THAT SHIT BOX!!!

The Dog Days. In the months after I left, things hit rock bottom.

Mini is Jim's dog. He brought her to the house/job-site every single day.

A lifetime dog lover, Dad had been without a dog for ten years. He adored Mini.

Throughout his illness, he had Mini at his side. That is until SHE got sick.

Convinced Mini had "taken" his cancer, Dad built her a St. Francis shrine. But then:

Jim thought a new puppy would cheer him up. Till she knocked him over—

Radiation had weakened his bones. The hip had shattered.

As soon as he could, in defiance of doctor's orders, he was back at it.

About a month after the hip healed, while busy with rock placement...

Tore the muscles clean away from the spine. This time it was all winter in bed on opiates.

Spring. Mom took over dolling up the yard. Until OOPS! she tripped on loose gravel..

..and hit the back of her head on a rock.

She came to — then went about her chores. But the next morning:

Dad (who was doing much better) — his reaction was to give her an aspirin...

...and then help her get up and dressed for the big grandkid birthday party.

Staccato responses. A torpid affect. Everyone noticed she was not herself.

A swarm of tests at the ER ruled out everything. They sent her home.

Next morning, she couldn't get up. She couldn't move her left side at all.

Then, I get a call from my brother: serious stroke. Time for another sibling plan:

Because Mom said things, and her eyes blinked, everyone felt hopeful.

But then the doctor delivered his sobering assessment: brain damage.

She was shuttled off to a therapy place immediately with Dad by her side.

Good thing Ginia brought her camper so Dad could stay right there near rehab.

And I cared for kids, cousins and canines at the cabin.

ALWAYS STAY BUSY SO YOU DON'T HAVE TO THINK. Somehow, through all of this, the cabin was completed.

As far as that 'living near the sons' notion: Not the best outcome. They had busy lives with families and jobs.

...SAID THEY'D BE HERE AFTER TRICK-OR-TREAT.

My sister and I came up as often as possible — which for school teachers meant Christmas and summers.

...SAID THEY'D CALL WHEN THE PLANE LANDED.

With Mom in slow motion, Dad craved activity. He joined the V.F.W.

WHERE IN FRANCE?

DIJON

The V.F.W.: supportive and helpful. A perfect environment to wonder openly about that cut.

R-RE-ED! LOOK HERE WHAT MY NEW PAL ART SENT OVER!

HUH?

But mostly, Mom and Dad were isolated, unsure of what would come next.

WHADDYA THINK, RED?

I'M NOT THINKING

I'M JUST SITTING HERE.

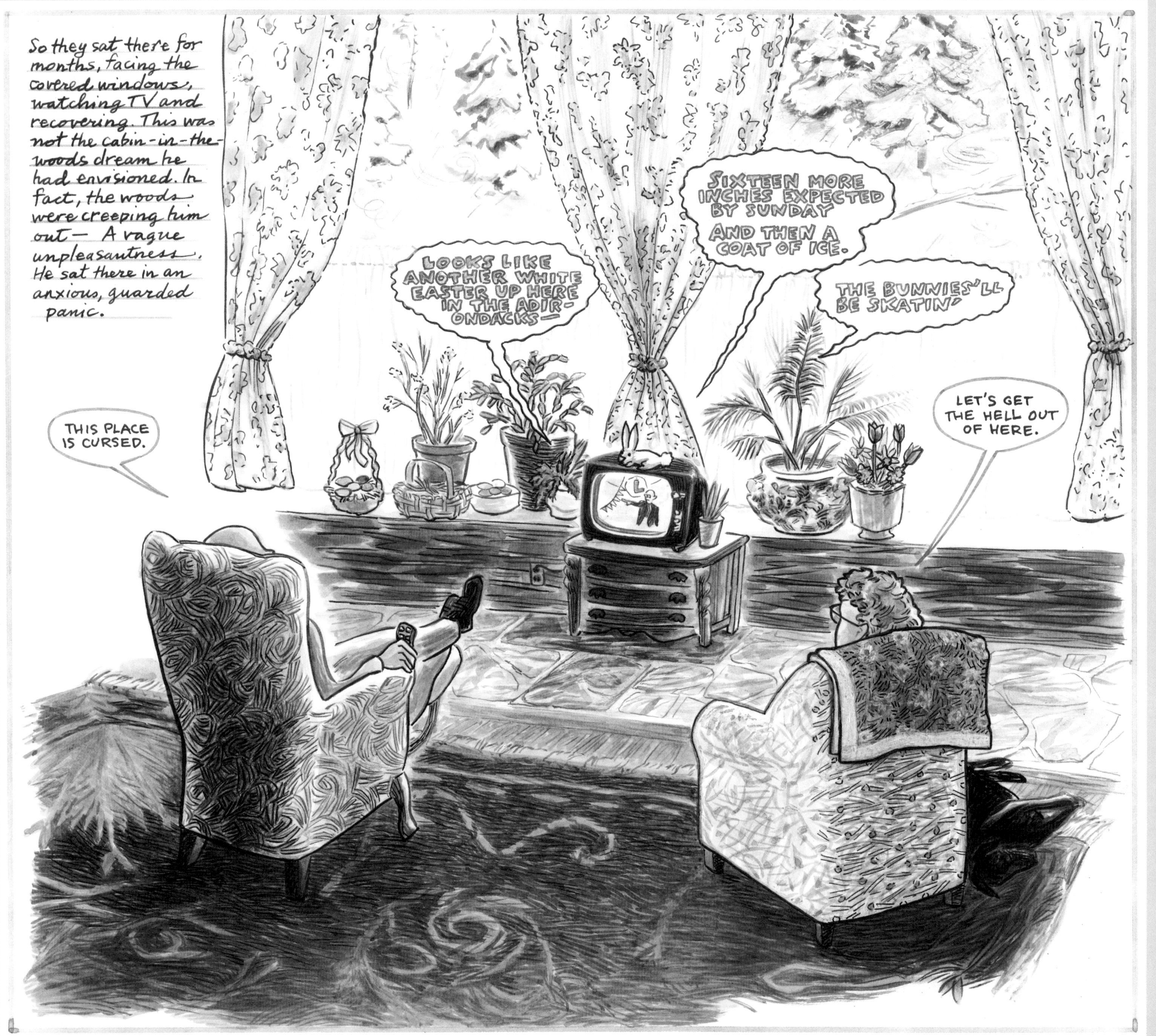
So they sat there for months, facing the covered windows, watching TV and recovering. This was not the cabin-in-the-woods dream he had envisioned. In fact, the woods were creeping him out— A vague unpleasantness. He sat there in an anxious, guarded panic.
LOOKS LIKE ANOTHER WHITE EASTER UP HERE IN THE ADIR-ONDACKS—
SIXTEEN MORE INCHES EXPECTED BY SUNDAY
AND THEN A COAT OF ICE.
THE BUNNIES'LL BE SKATIN'
THIS PLACE IS CURSED.
LET'S GET THE HELL OUT OF HERE.

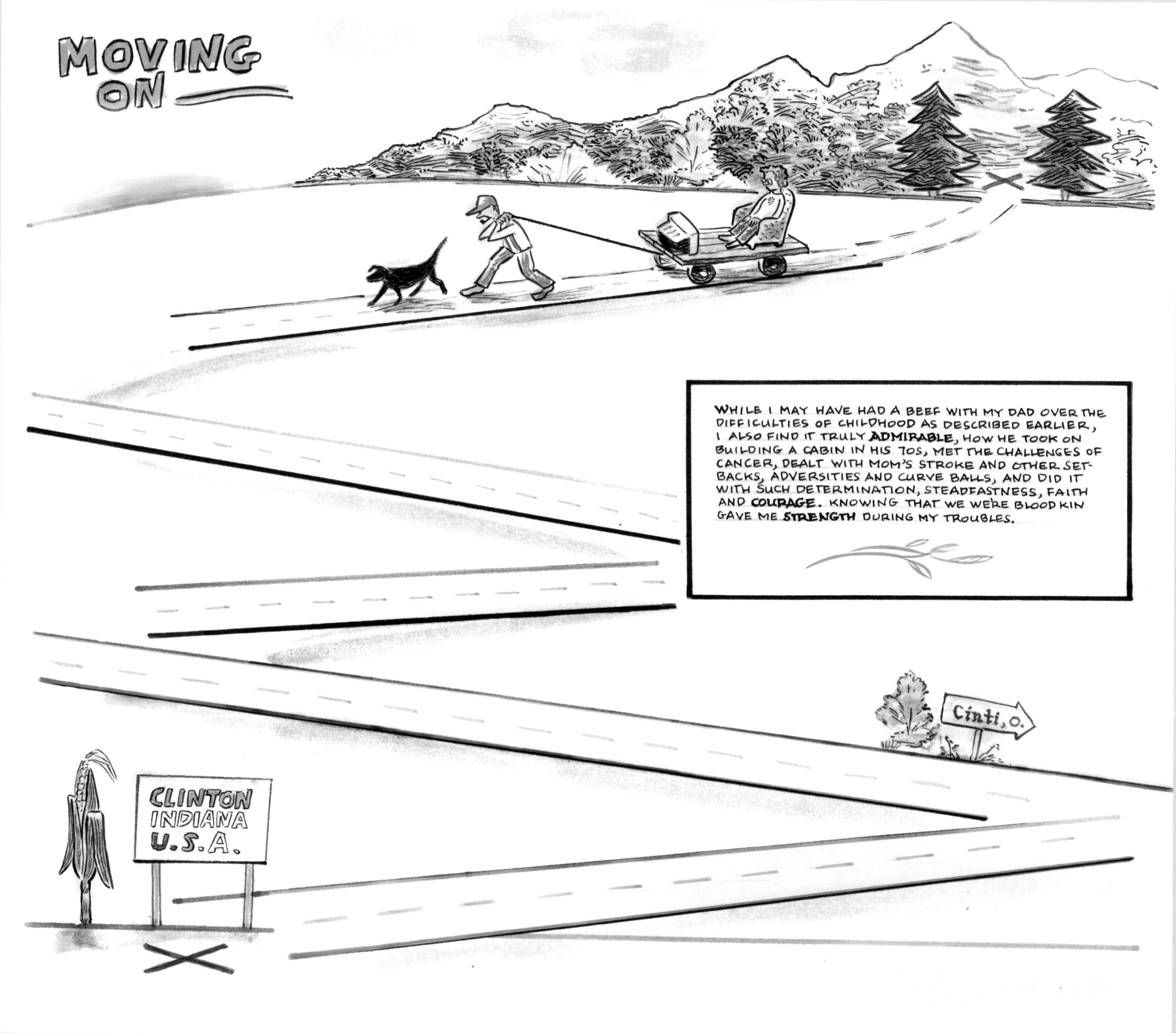
MOVING ON
WHILE I MAY HAVE HAD A BEEF WITH MY DAD OVER THE DIFFICULTIES OF CHILDHOOD AS DESCRIBED EARLIER, I ALSO FIND IT TRULY ADMIRABLE, HOW HE TOOK ON BUILDING A CABIN IN HIS 70S, MET THE CHALLENGES OF CANCER, DEALT WITH MOM'S STROKE AND OTHER SET-BACKS, ADVERSITIES AND CURVE BALLS, AND DID IT WITH SUCH DETERMINATION, STEADFASTNESS, FAITH AND COURAGE. KNOWING THAT WE WE'RE BLOOD KIN GAVE ME STRENGTH DURING MY TROUBLES.
Cinti, O.
CLINTON INDIANA U.S.A.

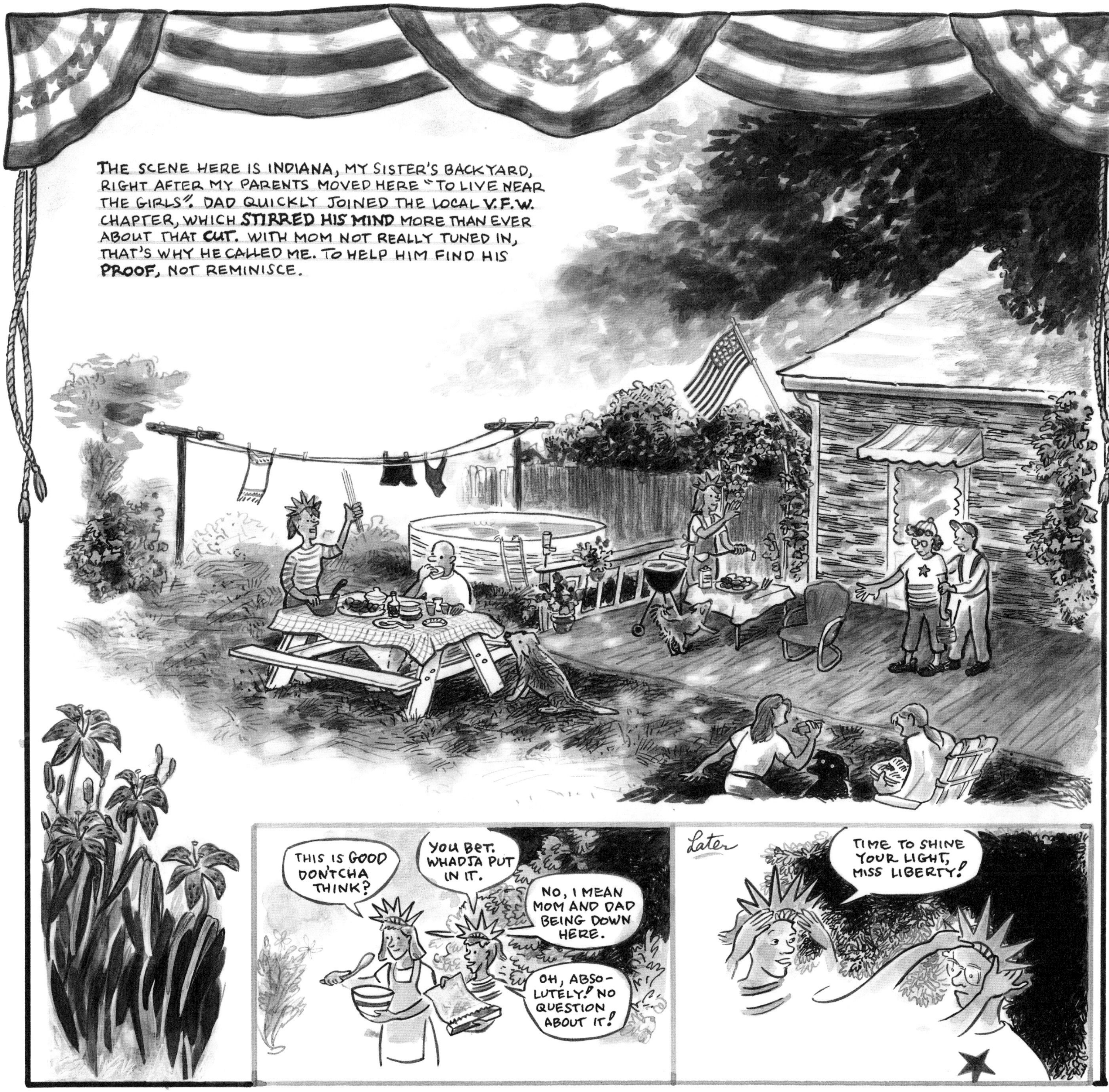
THE SCENE HERE IS INDIANA, MY SISTER'S BACKYARD, RIGHT AFTER MY PARENTS MOVED HERE "TO LIVE NEAR THE GIRLS". DAD QUICKLY JOINED THE LOCAL V.F.W. CHAPTER, WHICH STIRRED HIS MIND MORE THAN EVER ABOUT THAT CUT. WITH MOM NOT REALLY TUNED IN, THAT'S WHY HE CALLED ME. TO HELP HIM FIND HIS PROOF, NOT REMINISCE.
THIS IS GOOD DON'TCHA THINK?
YOU BET. WHADJA PUT IN IT.
NO, I MEAN MOM AND DAD BEING DOWN HERE.
OH, ABSO-LUTELY! NO QUESTION ABOUT IT!
Later
TIME TO SHINE YOUR LIGHT, MISS LIBERTY!

Everyone knows about that miracle inside our heads, the transcendent gray matter known as the brain.

But it took only one fully loaded clot to expunge a most precious area of Mother's mind, her "Sweet Spot."

Gone were many intangibles like modesty, the ability to relish evanescence, or to declare "I'm tickled pink!" and really mean it.

She could tell you the bank balance or work a crossword puzzle, but the sizzle had fizzled.

Nobody wanted to consider her condition irreversible or accept her as being tethered to an inevitable decline.

Especially Chuck. Not going to go for no sour grapes, no boo-hooing or enabling a poor, pitiful situation.

So he poked at her, he pestered and cajoled..

.. he prodded and insisted. He never let up.

At times it seemed kinda cruel,

but everything was at stake.

He believed, as we all did, that she was going to recover, by God! That she could, she would be her old self again ... eventually.

Through sheer force of his will, perhaps, and through heart work, mostly. Through heart.

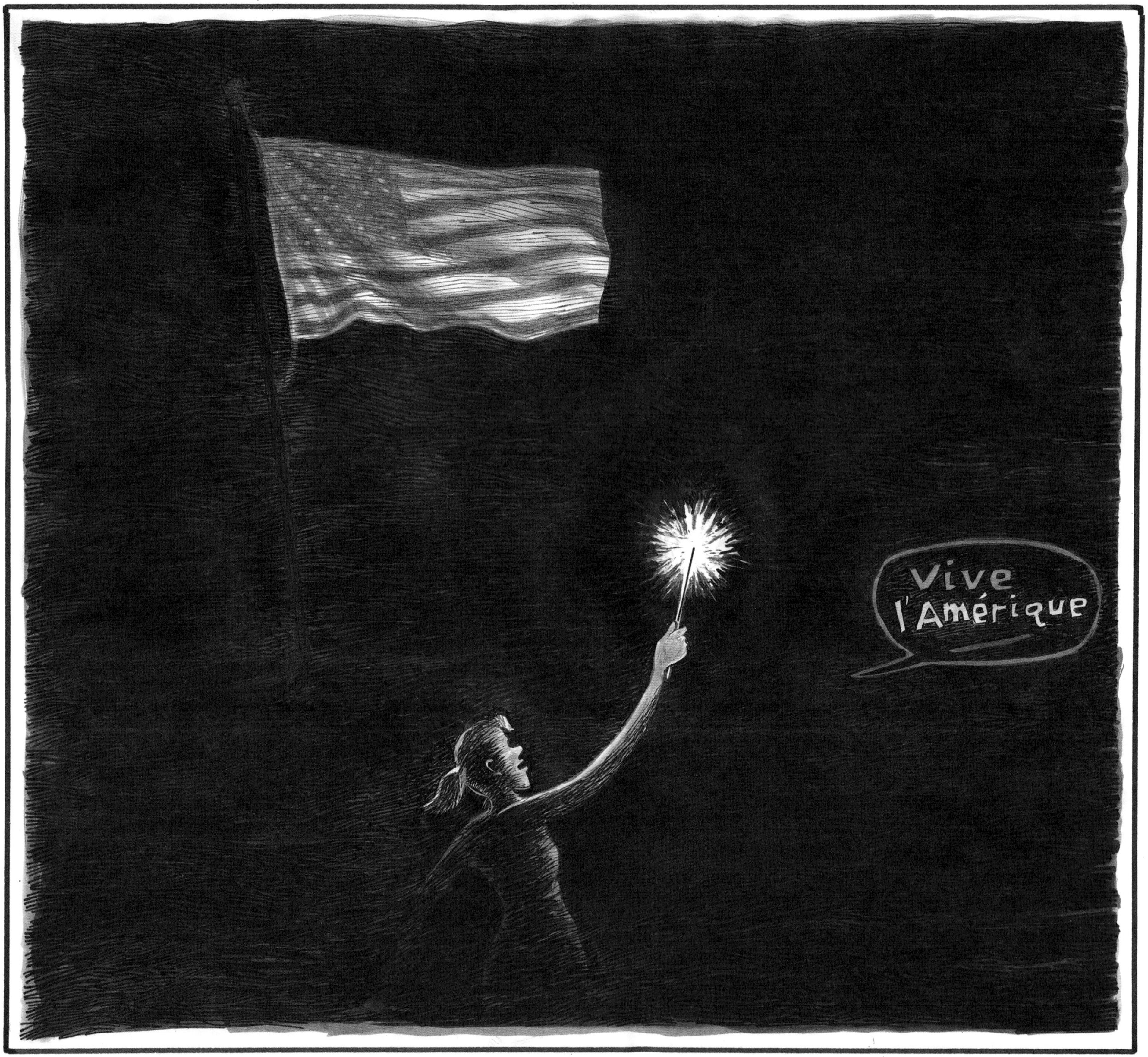
Vive l'Amérique

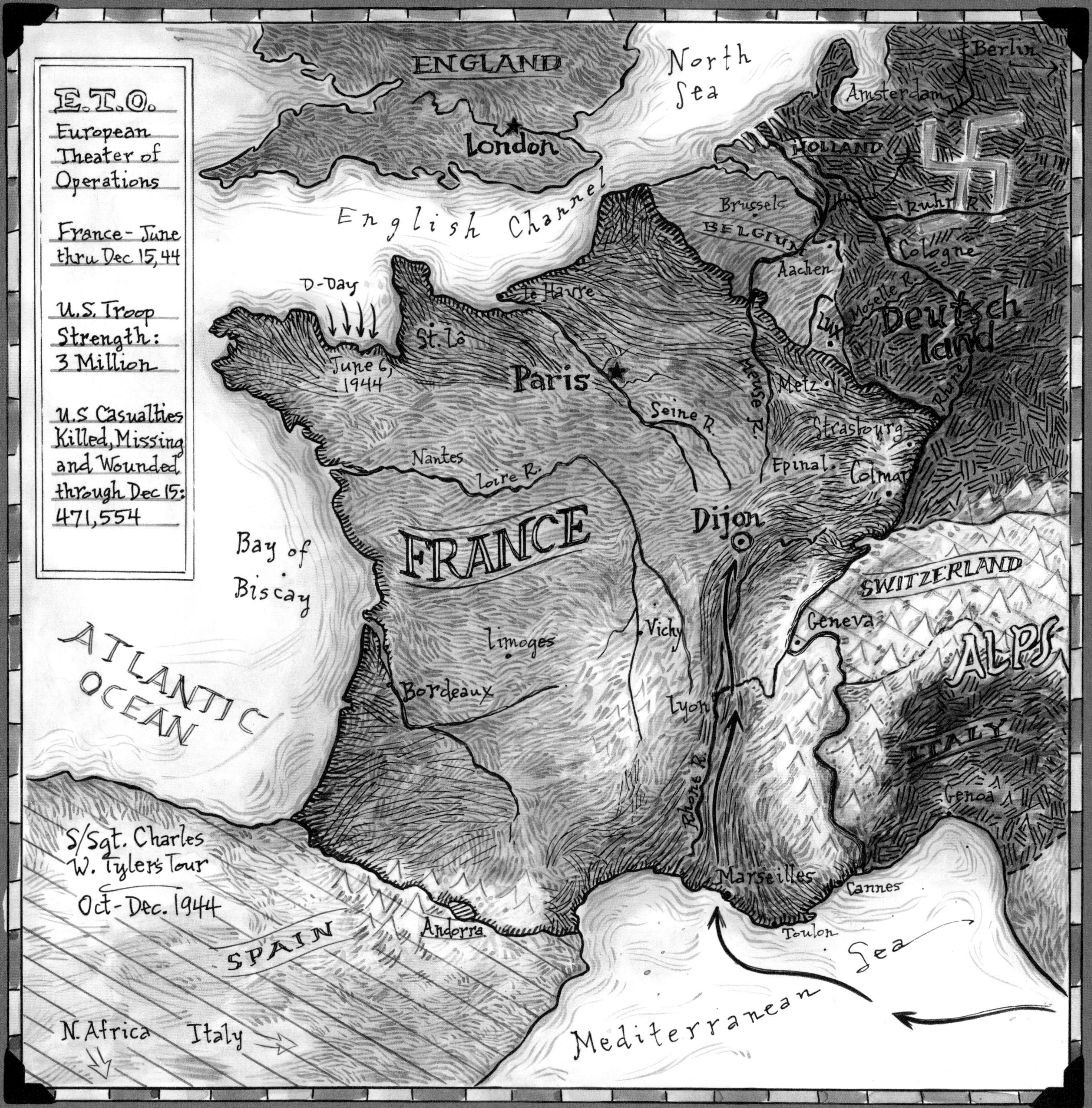

E.T.O.
European Theater of Operations
France - June thru Dec 15, 44
U.S. Troop Strength: 3 Million
U.S Casualties Killed, Missing and Wounded through Dec 15: 471,554
S/Sgt. Charles W. Tyler's Tour Oct-Dec. 1944
ENGLAND
London
North Sea
Amsterdam
Berlin
HOLLAND
Brussels
BELGIUM
Ruhr R.
Cologne
Aachen
Moselle R.
Deutschland
LUX
English Channel
D-Day
June 6, 1944
Le Havre
St. Lô
Paris
Seine R.
Meuse R.
Metz
Rhine
Strasbourg
Epinal
Colmar
Nantes
Loire R.
FRANCE
Dijon
Bay of Biscay
SWITZERLAND
Geneva
Vichy
Limoges
ALPS
ATLANTIC OCEAN
Bordeaux
Lyon
ITALY
Rhone R.
Genoa
Marseilles
Cannes
Toulon
Andorra
SPAIN
Mediterranean Sea
N. Africa
Italy

DAD'S ARMY SCRAPBOOK
AND
TOUR OF DUTY HIGHLIGHTS

PART IV

FRANCE

OCTOBER 1944 – DECEMBER 1944

Still looking for PROOF!

Hi-Hi-Hee

"Going from Italy to Southern France, we were on one of the big English ships. It wasn't the Queen, but it was a big one, tho. Real delicacy—— they're gonna treat us extra nice and so they give us fish eyes and fish eggs. Sour. Pickled. For *BREAKFAST!* We threw that shit all over that ship and had to stay in that mess for 3 days. Stink! Flies! Oh you never _seen_ such a mess!"

"The only thing that kept me going through all this was Red. If it wasn't for her, I don't know what I woulda done."

OCT 17 1944

54

"Got off the boat in Marseilles. And lo and behold, that real estate guy hollers at me, 'Hey Chuck.'Come with me. You c'n catch up to your unit later.' Bivouacked up a short way.' He had a Jeep with a 55 gallon drum of gas in the back. We drove up to the right some place on some road, met some guy and sold the Jeep and the 55 gallons of gas. Gas was more valuable than anything.

"So there I was, not 2 minutes in France and in the black market again, right off the bat, without even asking for it."

OCT 19

55

"Held up in Marseilles for a couple-a days because our guys were still clearing the Rhone valley. Our staging area was an old armory type building that had the roof blown away. Barrels here and there for fires. The place was full of the walking wounded. The sergeant there says to me, 'It's a bit chilly, so when you go out, bring some firewood home.'

"Later, I got all hepped-up on champagne blanc and drove a streetcar into an ammo truck. I went through the windshield."

56

"On the way back to the armory, I'm thinkin' 'Oh boy. I gotta bring some firewood for the walking wounded.' So I drug back some 2×4s, some 12-15' long with sticks on them. Like it must've been somebody's fence post I got a hold of. I was drunk. It was dark.

"Before I go to sleep, I pack the barrels good with this stuff and the next thing I know, the barrels are flaming up, burning straight up like wild, sparks falling on these poor bastards, sick and they're burning up — oh we had a hell of an awful time that night."

57

"Up the Rhone from Marseilles — total destruction. Our job was to pick up ammo on the side of the road. We didn't have such an easy time of it. What a mangled mess! Tanks, Renaults, carts. Our Air Force had strafed it bad. And what we didn't destroy, the Germans, when they left, tore everything to pieces. Then everything was bulldozed off onto the shoulders by our engineers. This went on for miles, a hundred miles. I thought Italy was a mess. Frying pan to the fire."

58

"I wound up at the American Standard Factory, where they put me in charge of repairing blown out tires. In Dijon. With POW labor. I had 509 Germans, 200 some Italians and 169 Hungarians. Every 2 weeks or so we'd send a cab-over engine truck to Heidelberg maybe to get beer. We had it on tap, 24/7. They all drank it. The Germans would sing and march *MACH SCHNELL!* The Hungarians were cryin' all the time and the I-talians were f**ing through the fence."

59

"This buddy of mine says, 'Chuck, you don't want to stay with the prisoners. Stay off the post.' So he got me a 22 room hotel for my little gang. I think there were 8 soldiers, 8 of us. We each had our own private room and I was in charge of the place.

"I run a good depot. We fixed 100,000 tires in 6 weeks. I know 'cause I made note of that. They promoted me to Master Sgt., but I didn't like the extra paperwork. I'm not a pencil-pusher, so they dropped me back down to Staff Sergeant."

60

" I took up smoking cigars in France because I could make money selling my cigarettes. Everybody wanted our U.S. smokes, but no interest in cigars. So I made money that way. And when I went out, I would sell my spare tire because I could always come back to the depot for another one. I guess I could still get in trouble for that. —— We got paid with invasion money, not the Yankee dollar. All deals were done with it, even on the black market. We'd take it to a tavern to exchange it at whatever percentage because local money, the Lira or the Franc, were better to have. "

61

"I took a 3 day leave to see Paris. I drove around. It wasn't nothin'. The Eiffel Tower— closed. Sent post cards. Never felt so lonely as I did in Paris. — So I come home early to find my hotel in shambles! Across the street was the medical station for all the whores in town and apparently my guys had invited them over to our hotel. They were eating all our food, drinking, tore everything to hell. Biggest whore house you ever seen! I run everybody out, made 'em buy all new dishes and got the Germans to clean up."

62

"I guess one night I had a little too much to drink and passed out in the Tire Depot. I'll never forget the German officers. They had a lot of respect for me. They knew I was fair. So they cleaned me up, washed me, polished my boots without being asked... never used being drunk against me, never mentioned it as far as I knew.

"I had a lot of respect for them, too. They kept clean and busy. Hard to think of them sometimes as the enemy. But I never forgot that they were."

63

"'Killer Kane', this guy I knew, comes to see me. 'Let's go to Lausanne, Switzerland for a few days. R&R.' He had a couple of girls in the car—but I was a married man. But I wanted to go for a ride. See something nice besides tires and prisoners. So we're going around these mountain switchbacks. He's a little sauced and takes a curve too fast. Next thing I know, we're teetering on a cliff. And then he starts to go psycho, just like in combat. I wasn't gonna die like this. Because Red would have thought I was cheating on her when really, I was just out ridin'."

NOV 17

64

"Around Thanksgiving, here come 2 Frogs in a Renault (French officers) with a couple of gals. Headed for the Riviera. They needed gas.

"There was this great big bottle with wicker around it on top of their car. I really wanted that bottle. 'No. No' Finally, I filled his tank and gave him 2 5 gallon jerry cans extra. Not what I wanted but whatever, you know, hoping, bartering—He gave me that bottle. Then I discovered it was full of cognac! We drank that up in one day."

NOV 20

65

"Around this time, I got word from home. From Red. We had been out of touch for so long with the mail being crossed up and all. I couldn't for the life of me figure out her message. Finally one of the guys said it looked to him like a stork notice. That 'she' looked like me. Congrats and all that. I sipped my cognac, convinced that since now I was a daddy and the war was just about over, they'd ship me home for the holidays. But — no such luck. Funny thing, though: That picture I lost in Africa, of Red — It got sent to me in Dijon."

66

However, he was not getting shipped home any time soon. In fact, just the opposite. "You see, those Frogs with the cognac, they said they seen piles of our uniforms and ammo up on the front lines for I guess our final big push up into Germany after our G.I.s finished their Christmas R and R. Our line was skimpy and the Germans knew it. Next thing I know, I'm dumping gas for Patton, around the clock, out the back of a truck convoy. I pretty much gave up on sleep or the idea I was ever gonna get any rest."

DEC 19 1944

The Dreadful Reality — DEC. 16, 1944. THE GERMAN ARMY ASSAULTED OUR SKIMPY FRONT LINES IN A DESPERATE PUSH TO REGAIN CONTROL OF EUROPE. THIS CAMPAIGN CAME TO BE KNOWN AS THE "BATTLE OF THE BULGE." — IT CLAIMED 89,500 U.S. CASUALTIES.

60 YEARS LATER, LET'S ADD ONE MORE CASUALTY TO THAT LIST, BECAUSE IT WAS AN EXHAUSTED STAFF SGT. C. TYLER WHO WAS EVENTUALLY CALLED BACK INTO COMBAT, WITH IMAGES OF BLOODY RIVERS, MUD TINGED WITH THE HORRIFIC AND THOSE CIVILIANS STILL IN HIS HEAD.

AND THEN THERE WAS FRANCE, TORN ALL TO SHREDS. DAY AFTER DAY HE TRIED TO CALM HIS MIND, BUT THE BLOWN TIRES KEPT COMING IN, AND THE HOOKERS KEPT HOOKIN' AND THE PLANE ENGINES BEGAN IN EARNEST, SO TOO, THE MADNESS OF WAR...

I WISH I COULD SAY IT WAS THE FIRST TIME I'D GOTTEN A CALL FROM MY CHILD'S SCHOOL. SEEMS LIKE ONCE OR TWICE A WEEK LATELY——EVERYTHING FROM SASSING THE TEACHER TO SKIPPING CLASS. AND IT'S BEEN GOING ON EVER SINCE SHE STARTED HANGING AROUND WITH THAT AVERY BENNETT. I KNEW SHE WAS TROUBLE. FROM THAT VERY FIRST TIME JULIA WENT OVER THERE.

THOSE OTHER CALLS: AGE APPROPRIATE. BUT THIS TIME SHE WENT TOO FAR. SHE TRIPPED THE CIRCUIT BREAKER FOR THE ENTIRE SCHOOL. ON A DARE. SO NOW SHE'S BEEN SUSPENDED FOR A WEEK.—— I MADE MY APOLOGIES TO THE VICE PRINCIPAL (AGAIN) AND WAS ALL SET TO TAKE HER HOME. JUST ONE LITTLE PROBLEM: SHE WAS IN THE RESTROOM VOMITING ——APPARENTLY MY LITTLE DARLING WAS PLASTERED.

BEING DRUNK WASN'T THE *HALF* OF IT! WHEN I GOT HER IN THE CAR, I DEMANDED SHE SPILL OUT THE CONTENTS OF HER BACK-PACK: OH MY GOD, REEFER, CONDOMS, RAZOR BLADES, CIGARETTES, PURPLE HAIR DYE AND A HALF EMPTY PINT OF JACK-IN-THE-BLACK THAT SHE *CLAIMS* HAD BEEN PARKED THERE BY AVERY (WHOSE MOM WOULD KILL HER IF SHE FOUND OUT SO COULD I *PLEASE* NOT SAY ANYTHING.)

AS IF I WAS GOING TO COVER FOR THAT LITTLE *BRAT!* SO I READ MISS JULIA THE RIOT ACT BETWEEN EVERY STOP-AND-OPEN-THE-DOOR-SO-SHE-CAN-VOMIT STOP ON THE WAY HOME. IT'S A SHOCKER TO BE SURE, SEEING YOUR KID IN SUCH A SORRY STATE. I'M NOT SURE WHAT GOOD IT DOES TO CURSE THE "EX" (IF HE IS MY "EX"), BUT DOING SO, EVEN IN MY MIND ONLY, SEEMED TO HELP MY DRIVING.

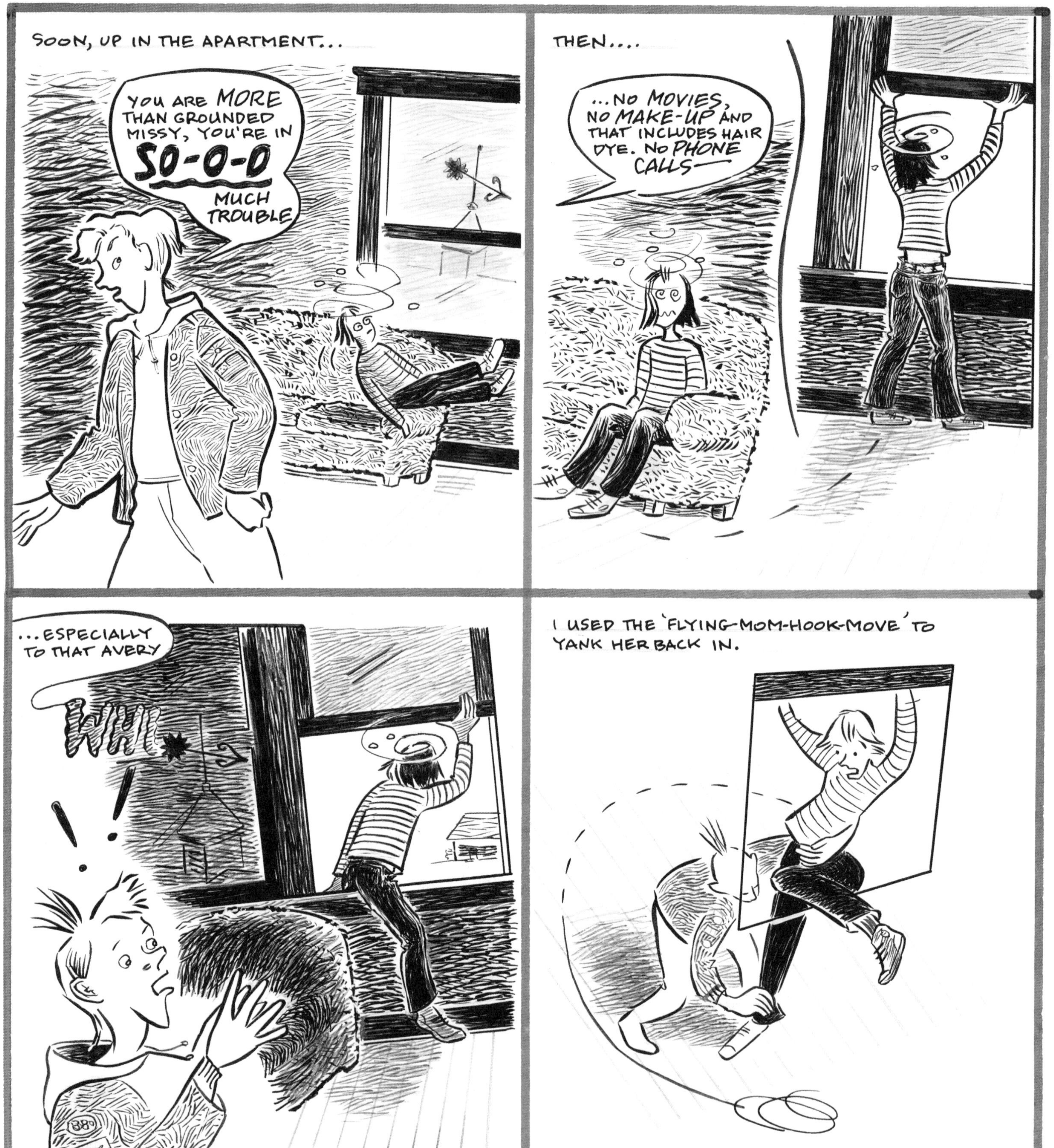
SOON, UP IN THE APARTMENT...
YOU ARE MORE THAN GROUNDED MISSY, YOU'RE IN SO-O-O MUCH TROUBLE
THEN....
...NO MOVIES, NO MAKE-UP AND THAT INCLUDES HAIR DYE. NO PHONE CALLS—
...ESPECIALLY TO THAT AVERY
WHI
I USED THE 'FLYING-MOM-HOOK-MOVE' TO YANK HER BACK IN.

AFTER WE CAUGHT OUR BREATH AND SHE THREW UP ON ME, I MADE HER SPILL IT OVER WHAT THE HELL WAS GOING ON. `I NEED AIR` SHE WHINED BUT I WASN'T BUYING IT. SO IT CAME DOWN TO THE MOST CHILLING REVELATION. "I'M NOT SUPPOSED TO TELL YOU BECAUSE HE'LL GET MAD AT ME." & OH YEAH? WHO'S THAT?" HER RUEFUL RETORT "THE BIRD MAN INSIDE MY HEAD. THE ONE WHO TOLD ME TO SUCK IN AIR BY JUMPING."

NEEDLESS TO SAY, I RAN HER TO THE ER IMMEDIATELY. SAT THERE IN SHOCK. WAITED AND WAITED AND WAITED. SAT THERE AND WAITED. NURSE COMES IN, TAKES NOTES AND VITALS, GOES OUT. COMES BACK IN TO CHECK. GOES BACK OUT. IT'S CHIPPER HERE, FOR THE KIDS' SAKE. EVERYONE'S CHIPPER, AS OPPOSED TO *WEIGHTY*, WHICH IS WHAT THE REAL SITUATION IS.

HOW COULD SHE BE HEARING A *VOICE*? IT'S JUST NOT *TRUE*! I KNOW MY CHILD. IT'S THE *BOOZE* MOST LIKELY. OR THE WEED. OR LORD KNOWS WHATEVER ELSE SHE'S UP TO ⸺ I AM *REALLY* GOING AFTER THAT AVERY. TRACK DOWN HER MOTHER IN EUROPE SOMEWHERE… STEP-MOM MAYBE? STAFF? DAMMIT, I WANT A DIAGNOSIS *NOW* SO WE CAN GET OUT OF HERE. I NEED TO SUCK IN AIR…. NEAR A TREE-TRUNK.

FINALLY, THE DOCTOR COMES IN. MORE TESTS NEED TO RULE OUT THIS AND THAT. WHAT'S CAUSING HER BEHAVIOR CHANGES. ORDERED A COMPLETE PSYCH EVALUATION TO FIGURE OUT THE VOICE. DEPRESSION? ANXIETY? HE CAN'T SAY. SO, SHE'S BEING ADMITTED FOR A FEW DAYS IN A 24 HOUR SECURITY WATCH UNIT DUE TO THE WINDOW INCIDENT. I'M WELCOME TO STAY….

IN ALL THE CHAOS, I HAD INADVERTENTLY PUT THE KEYS TO THE APARTMENT INTO JULIA'S BACKPACK, WHICH IS NOW **LOCKED UP** WITH HER, OVER AT CHILDREN'S HOSPITAL. SO I CALLED THE LANDLORD. HE'LL BE OVER SOON. AND AS SOON AS I GET UP THERE, I'LL CALL HER DAD. — I FEEL **TERRIBLE** LEAVING HER AT THE HOSPITAL ALONE. SHE MUST BE FRIGHTENED. IF MY CLOTHES WEREN'T COATED WITH THROW-UP, I'D-A NEVER LEFT. GOTTA GET RIGHT BACK.

I CAN'T HELP THINKING ABOUT MY **SISTER** AT THIS TIME, AND THE **STORY** MOM HAD TOLD. BEFORE HER STROKE.

The Hannah STORY

THE HANNah STORY

Hannah E. Yates Tyler revealed her darkest chapter in 1994. I wrote it down then. Here is that story. By C. Tyler.

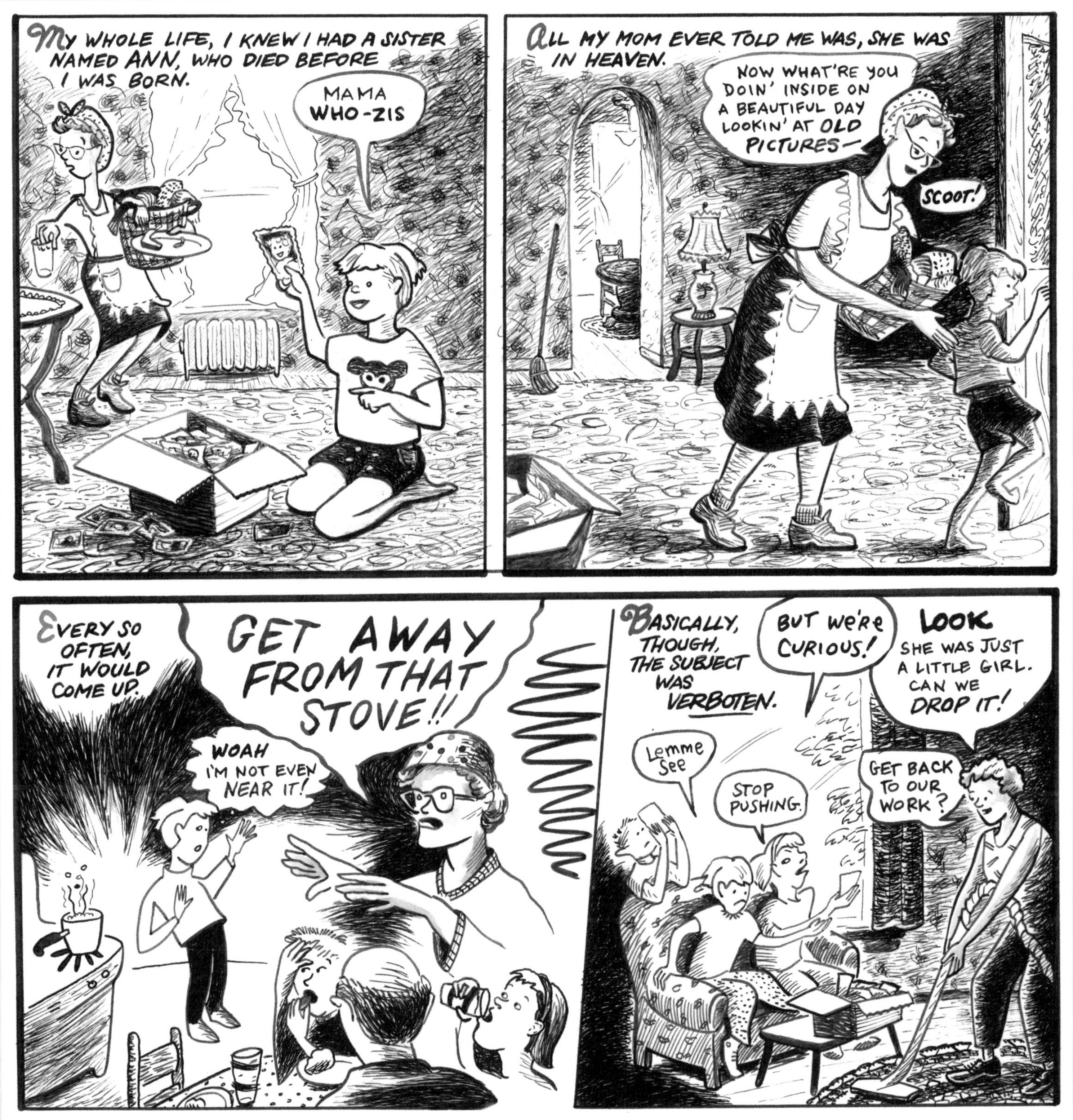
My whole life, I knew I had a sister named ANN, who died before I was born.
MAMA WHO-ZIS
All my mom ever told me was, she was in heaven.
NOW WHAT'RE YOU DOIN' INSIDE ON A BEAUTIFUL DAY LOOKIN' AT OLD PICTURES—
SCOOT!
Every so often, it would come up.
GET AWAY FROM THAT STOVE!!
WOAH I'M NOT EVEN NEAR IT!
Basically, though, the subject was VERBOTEN.
BUT WE're CURIOUS!
LOOK SHE WAS JUST A LITTLE GIRL. CAN WE DROP IT!
Lemme See
STOP PUSHING.
GET BACK TO OUR WORK?

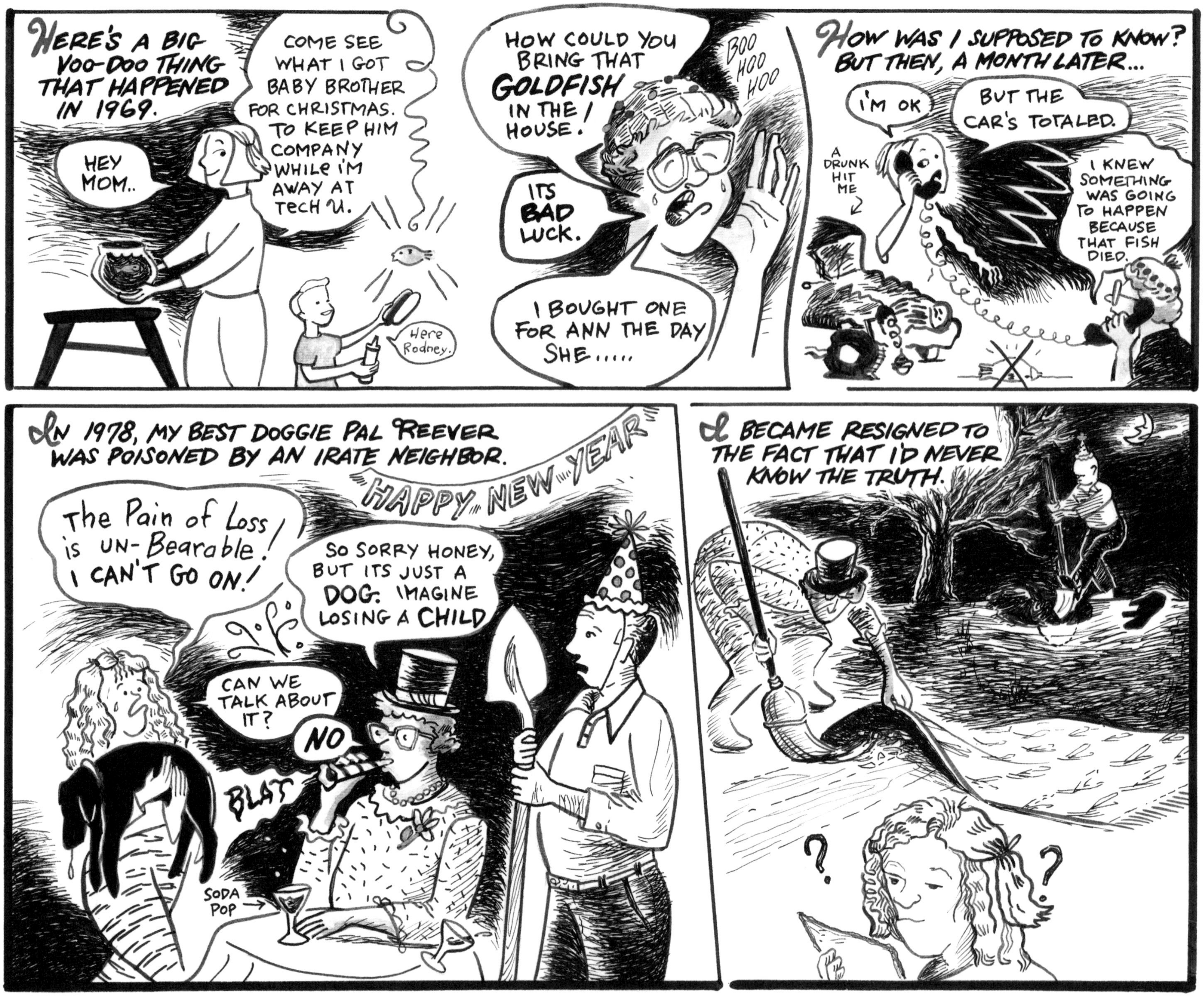

HERE'S A BIG VOO-DOO THING THAT HAPPENED IN 1969.
HEY MOM..
COME SEE WHAT I GOT BABY BROTHER FOR CHRISTMAS. TO KEEP HIM COMPANY WHILE I'M AWAY AT TECH U.
Here Rodney.
HOW COULD YOU BRING THAT GOLDFISH IN THE HOUSE!
BOO HOO HOO
ITS BAD LUCK.
I BOUGHT ONE FOR ANN THE DAY SHE.....
HOW WAS I SUPPOSED TO KNOW? BUT THEN, A MONTH LATER...
I'M OK
BUT THE CAR'S TOTALED.
A DRUNK HIT ME
I KNEW SOMETHING WAS GOING TO HAPPEN BECAUSE THAT FISH DIED.
IN 1978, MY BEST DOGGIE PAL REEVER WAS POISONED BY AN IRATE NEIGHBOR.
HAPPY NEW YEAR
The Pain of Loss is UN-Bearable! I CAN'T GO ON!
SO SORRY HONEY, BUT ITS JUST A DOG. IMAGINE LOSING A CHILD
CAN WE TALK ABOUT IT?
NO
BLAT
SODA POP
I BECAME RESIGNED TO THE FACT THAT I'D NEVER KNOW THE TRUTH.
? ?

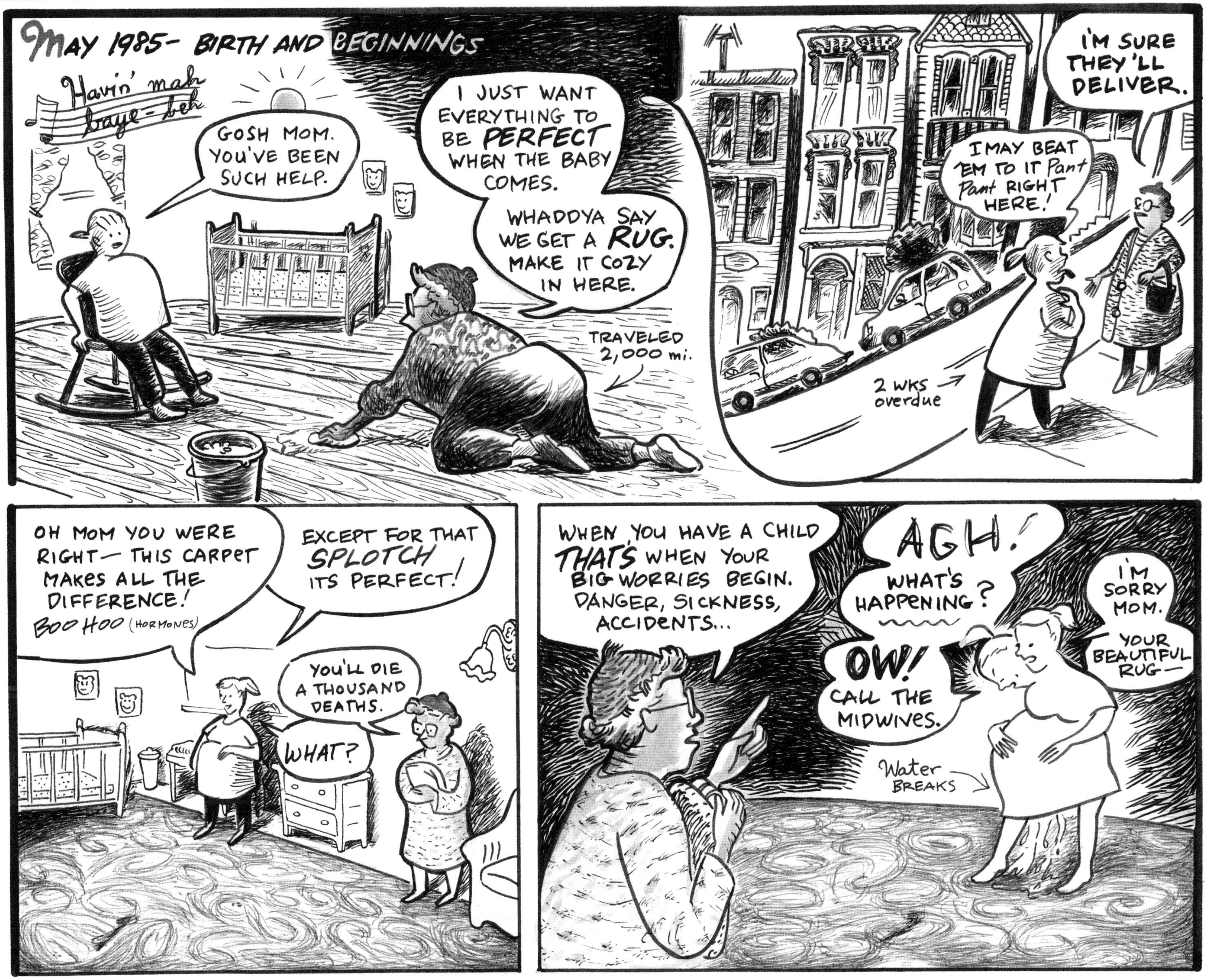
MAY 1985- BIRTH AND BEGINNINGS
Havin' mah baye-beh
GOSH MOM. YOU'VE BEEN SUCH HELP.
I JUST WANT EVERYTHING TO BE PERFECT WHEN THE BABY COMES.
WHADDYA SAY WE GET A RUG. MAKE IT COZY IN HERE.
TRAVELED 2,000 mi.
I'M SURE THEY'LL DELIVER.
I MAY BEAT 'EM TO IT Pant Pant RIGHT HERE!
2 WKS overdue
OH MOM YOU WERE RIGHT— THIS CARPET MAKES ALL THE DIFFERENCE! BOO HOO (HORMONES)
EXCEPT FOR THAT SPLOTCH ITS PERFECT!
YOU'LL DIE A THOUSAND DEATHS.
WHAT?
WHEN YOU HAVE A CHILD THAT'S WHEN YOUR BIG WORRIES BEGIN. DANGER, SICKNESS, ACCIDENTS...
AGH! WHAT'S HAPPENING?
OW! CALL THE MIDWIVES.
I'M SORRY MOM.
YOUR BEAUTIFUL RUG—
Water BREAKS

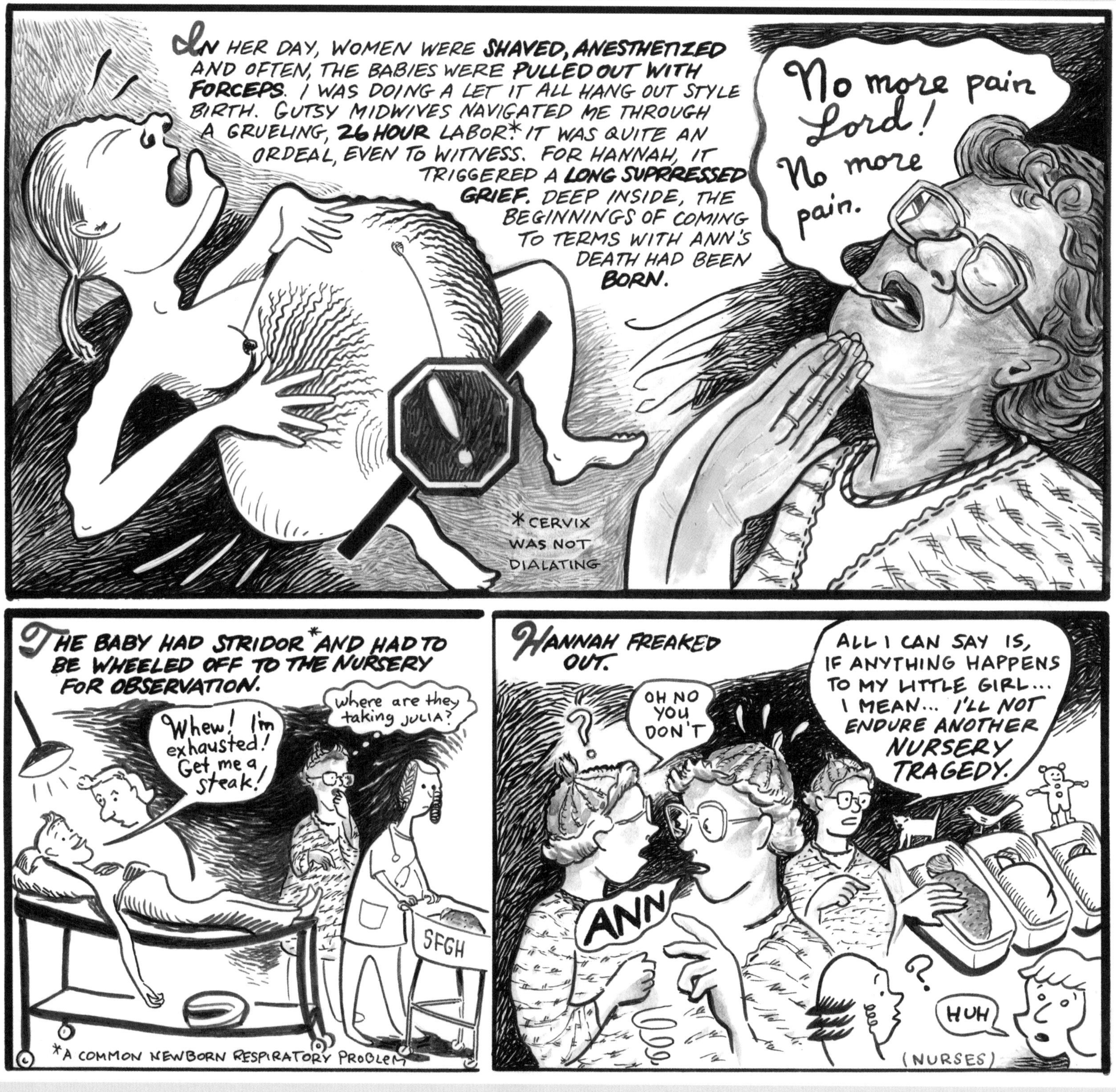
IN HER DAY, WOMEN WERE SHAVED, ANESTHETIZED AND OFTEN, THE BABIES WERE PULLED OUT WITH FORCEPS. I WAS DOING A LET IT ALL HANG OUT STYLE BIRTH. GUTSY MIDWIVES NAVIGATED ME THROUGH A GRUELING, 26 HOUR LABOR.* IT WAS QUITE AN ORDEAL, EVEN TO WITNESS. FOR HANNAH, IT TRIGGERED A LONG SUPPRESSED GRIEF. DEEP INSIDE, THE BEGINNINGS OF COMING TO TERMS WITH ANN'S DEATH HAD BEEN BORN.
No more pain Lord! No more pain.
*CERVIX WAS NOT DIALATING
THE BABY HAD STRIDOR* AND HAD TO BE WHEELED OFF TO THE NURSERY FOR OBSERVATION.
Whew! I'm exhausted! Get me a steak!
where are they taking JULIA?
SFGH
*A COMMON NEWBORN RESPIRATORY PROBLEM
HANNAH FREAKED OUT.
OH NO YOU DON'T
ALL I CAN SAY IS, IF ANYTHING HAPPENS TO MY LITTLE GIRL... I MEAN... I'LL NOT ENDURE ANOTHER NURSERY TRAGEDY.
ANN
HUH
(NURSES)

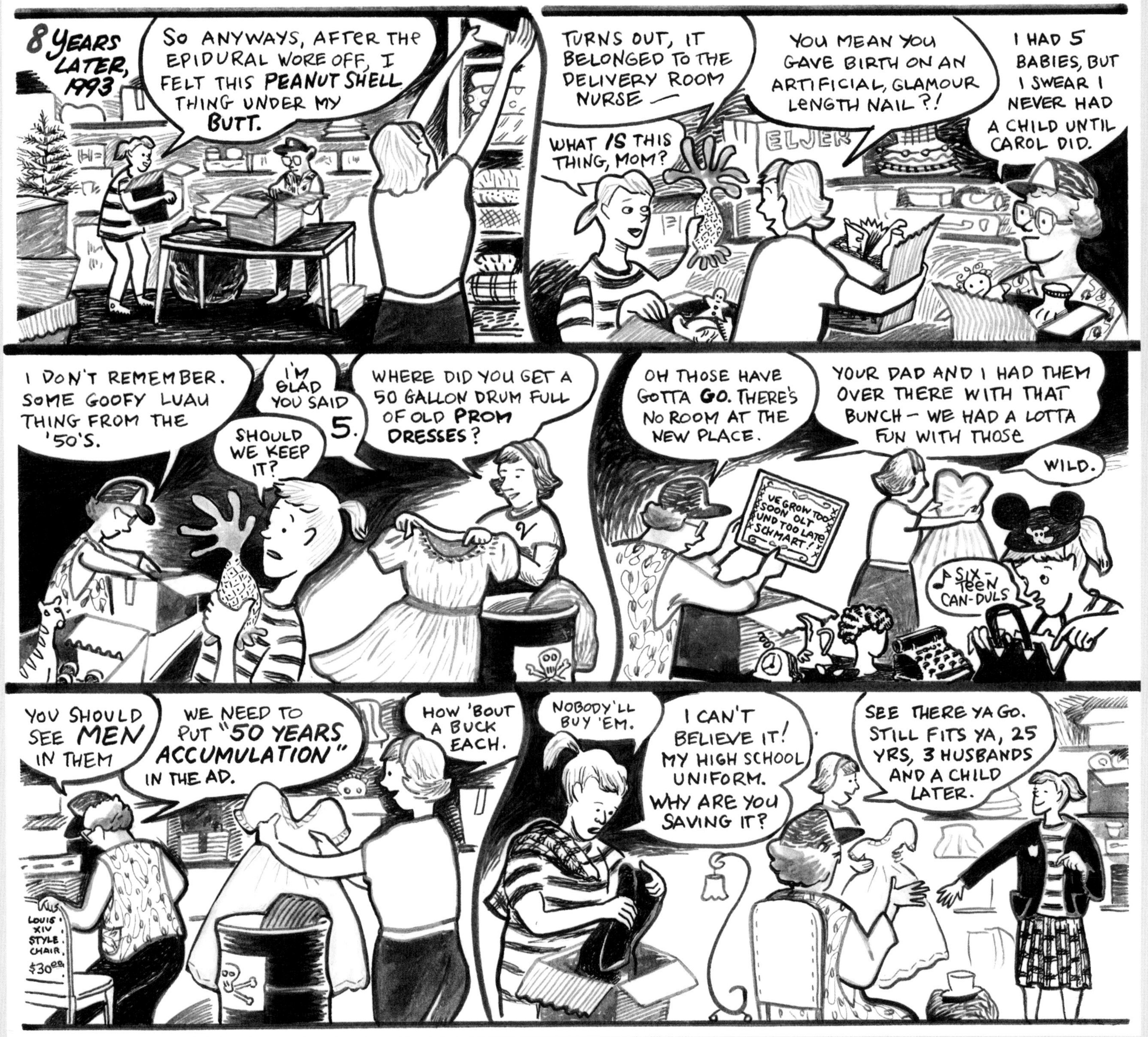

8 YEARS LATER, 1993
SO ANYWAYS, AFTER THE EPIDURAL WORE OFF, I FELT THIS PEANUT SHELL THING UNDER MY BUTT.
TURNS OUT, IT BELONGED TO THE DELIVERY ROOM NURSE —
WHAT IS THIS THING, MOM?
YOU MEAN YOU GAVE BIRTH ON AN ARTIFICIAL, GLAMOUR LENGTH NAIL?!
ELJER
I HAD 5 BABIES, BUT I SWEAR I NEVER HAD A CHILD UNTIL CAROL DID.
I DON'T REMEMBER. SOME GOOFY LUAU THING FROM THE '50'S.
I'M GLAD YOU SAID 5.
SHOULD WE KEEP IT?
WHERE DID YOU GET A 50 GALLON DRUM FULL OF OLD PROM DRESSES?
OH THOSE HAVE GOTTA GO. THERE'S NO ROOM AT THE NEW PLACE.
VE GROW TOO SOON OLT UND TOO LATE SCHMART!
YOUR DAD AND I HAD THEM OVER THERE WITH THAT BUNCH — WE HAD A LOTTA FUN WITH THOSE
WILD.
♪ SIX-TEEN CAN-DULS
YOU SHOULD SEE MEN IN THEM
WE NEED TO PUT "50 YEARS ACCUMULATION" IN THE AD.
HOW 'BOUT A BUCK EACH.
LOUIS XIV STYLE CHAIR. $30.00
NOBODY'LL BUY 'EM.
I CAN'T BELIEVE IT! MY HIGH SCHOOL UNIFORM. WHY ARE YOU SAVING IT?
SEE THERE YA GO. STILL FITS YA, 25 YRS, 3 HUSBANDS AND A CHILD LATER.

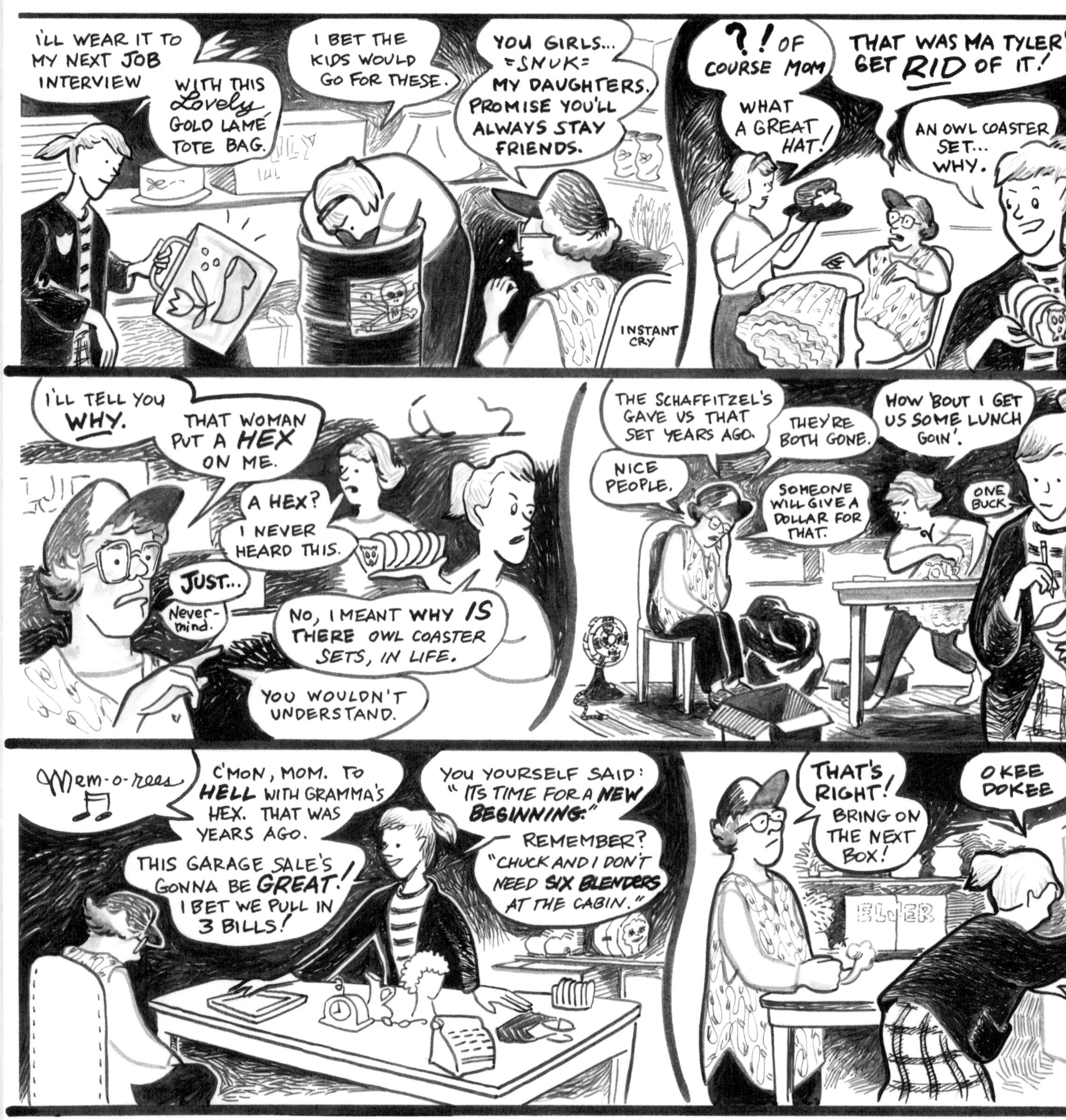

I'LL WEAR IT TO MY NEXT JOB INTERVIEW
WITH THIS Lovely GOLD LAMÉ TOTE BAG.
I BET THE KIDS WOULD GO FOR THESE.
YOU GIRLS... =SNUK= MY DAUGHTERS. PROMISE YOU'LL ALWAYS STAY FRIENDS.
INSTANT CRY
?! OF COURSE MOM
WHAT A GREAT HAT!
THAT WAS MA TYLER'S. GET RID OF IT!
AN OWL COASTER SET... WHY.
I'LL TELL YOU WHY.
THAT WOMAN PUT A HEX ON ME.
A HEX?
I NEVER HEARD THIS.
JUST...
Never-mind.
NO, I MEANT WHY IS THERE OWL COASTER SETS, IN LIFE.
YOU WOULDN'T UNDERSTAND.
THE SCHAFFITZEL'S GAVE US THAT SET YEARS AGO.
NICE PEOPLE.
THEY'RE BOTH GONE.
SOMEONE WILL GIVE A DOLLAR FOR THAT.
HOW 'BOUT I GET US SOME LUNCH GOIN'.
ONE BUCK
Mem-o-rees
C'MON, MOM. TO HELL WITH GRAMMA'S HEX. THAT WAS YEARS AGO.
THIS GARAGE SALE'S GONNA BE GREAT! I BET WE PULL IN 3 BILLS!
YOU YOURSELF SAID: "ITS TIME FOR A NEW BEGINNING."
REMEMBER? "CHUCK AND I DON'T NEED SIX BLENDERS AT THE CABIN."
THAT'S RIGHT! BRING ON THE NEXT BOX!
OKEE DOKEE

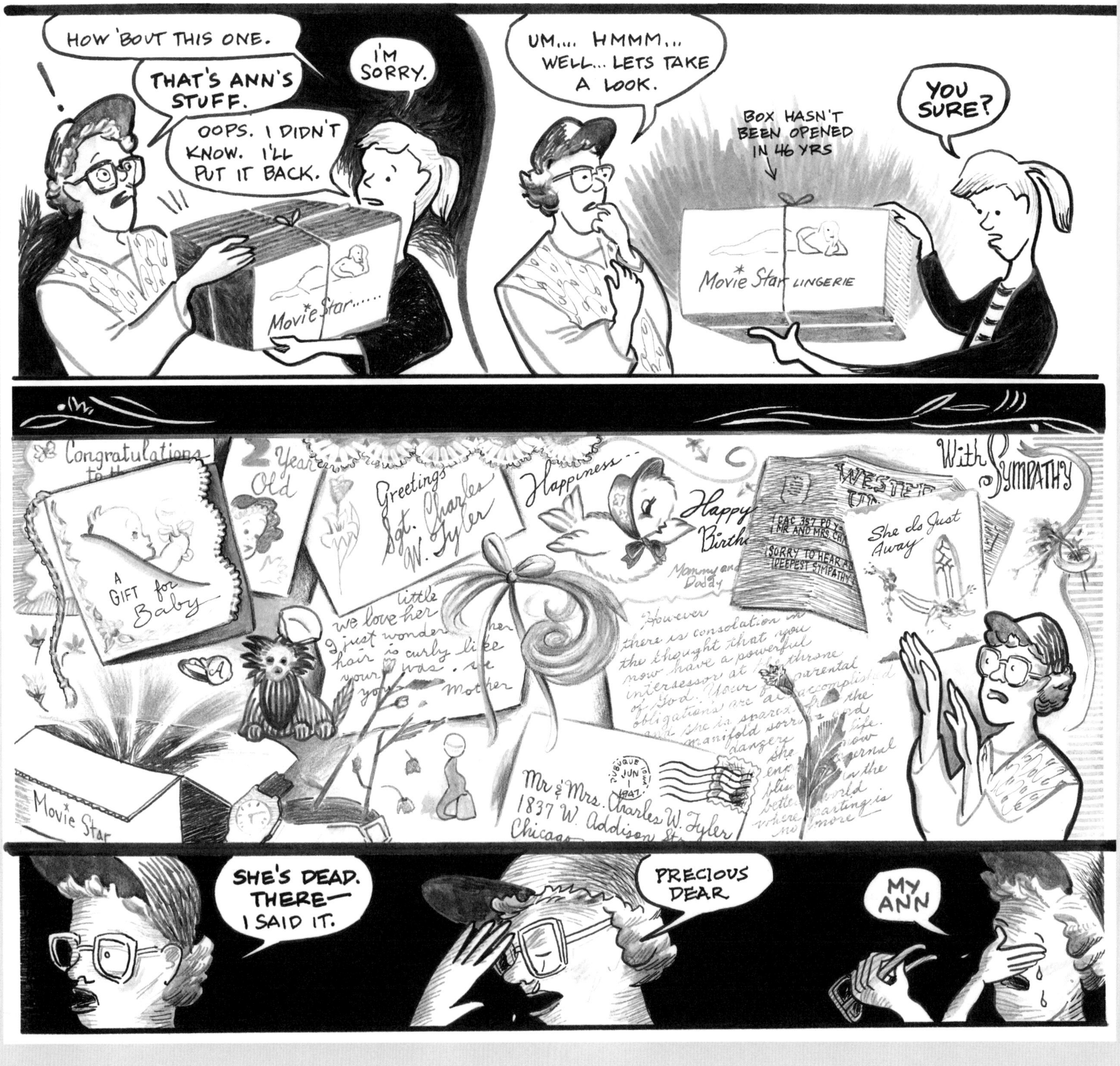
HOW 'BOUT THIS ONE.
!
THAT'S ANN'S STUFF.
OOPS. I DIDN'T KNOW. I'LL PUT IT BACK.
I'M SORRY.
Movie Star......
UM.... HMMM... WELL... LETS TAKE A LOOK.
BOX HASN'T BEEN OPENED IN 46 YRS
Movie Star LINGERIE
YOU SURE?
Congratulations
A GIFT for Baby
Old
Greetings Sgt. Charles W. Tyler
Happiness...
Mommy and Daddy
With Sympathy
She is Just Away
SORRY TO HEAR
DEEPEST SYMPATHY
we love her
Mother
However there is consolation in the thought that you now have a powerful intercessor at the throne of God.
Movie Star
Mr & Mrs. Charles W. Tyler
1837 W. Addison St.
Chicago
SHE'S DEAD. THERE— I SAID IT.
PRECIOUS DEAR
MY ANN

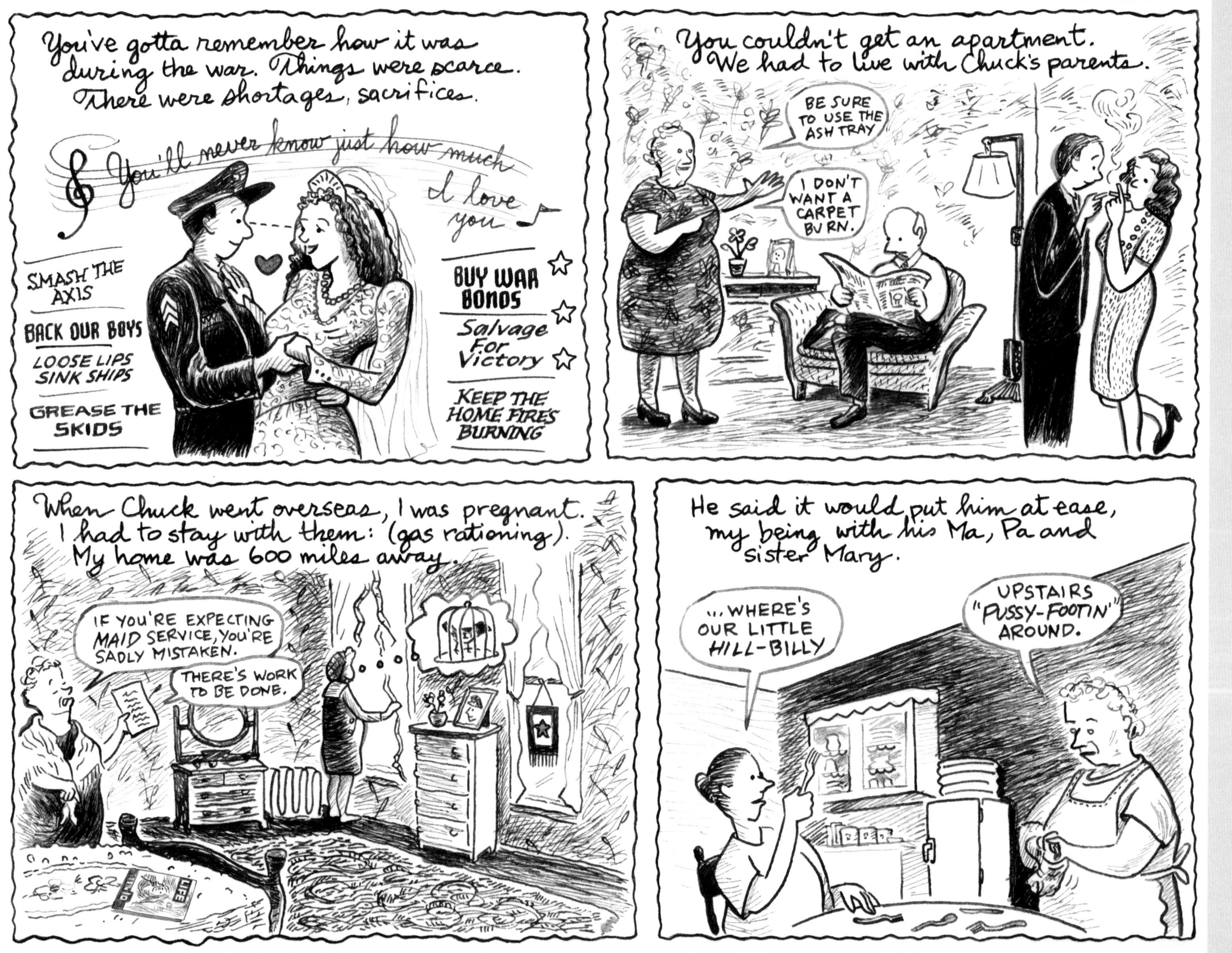
You've gotta remember how it was during the war. Things were scarce. There were shortages, sacrifices.
You'll never know just how much I love you
SMASH THE AXIS
BACK OUR BOYS
LOOSE LIPS SINK SHIPS
GREASE THE SKIDS
BUY WAR BONDS
Salvage For Victory
KEEP THE HOME FIRES BURNING
You couldn't get an apartment. We had to live with Chuck's parents.
BE SURE TO USE THE ASH TRAY
I DON'T WANT A CARPET BURN.
When Chuck went overseas, I was pregnant. I had to stay with them: (gas rationing). My home was 600 miles away.
IF YOU'RE EXPECTING MAID SERVICE, YOU'RE SADLY MISTAKEN.
THERE'S WORK TO BE DONE.
He said it would put him at ease, my being with his Ma, Pa and sister Mary.
...WHERE'S OUR LITTLE HILL-BILLY
UPSTAIRS "PUSSY-FOOTIN" AROUND.

Before marriage, I was so independent! I had my own style, my own life. A working woman—head of personnel at Camp Forrest.

But I loved Chuck so much, I was willing to put up with anything for awhile.

Ann was my refuge.

A link to my beloved, in that Hell known as Paulina St.

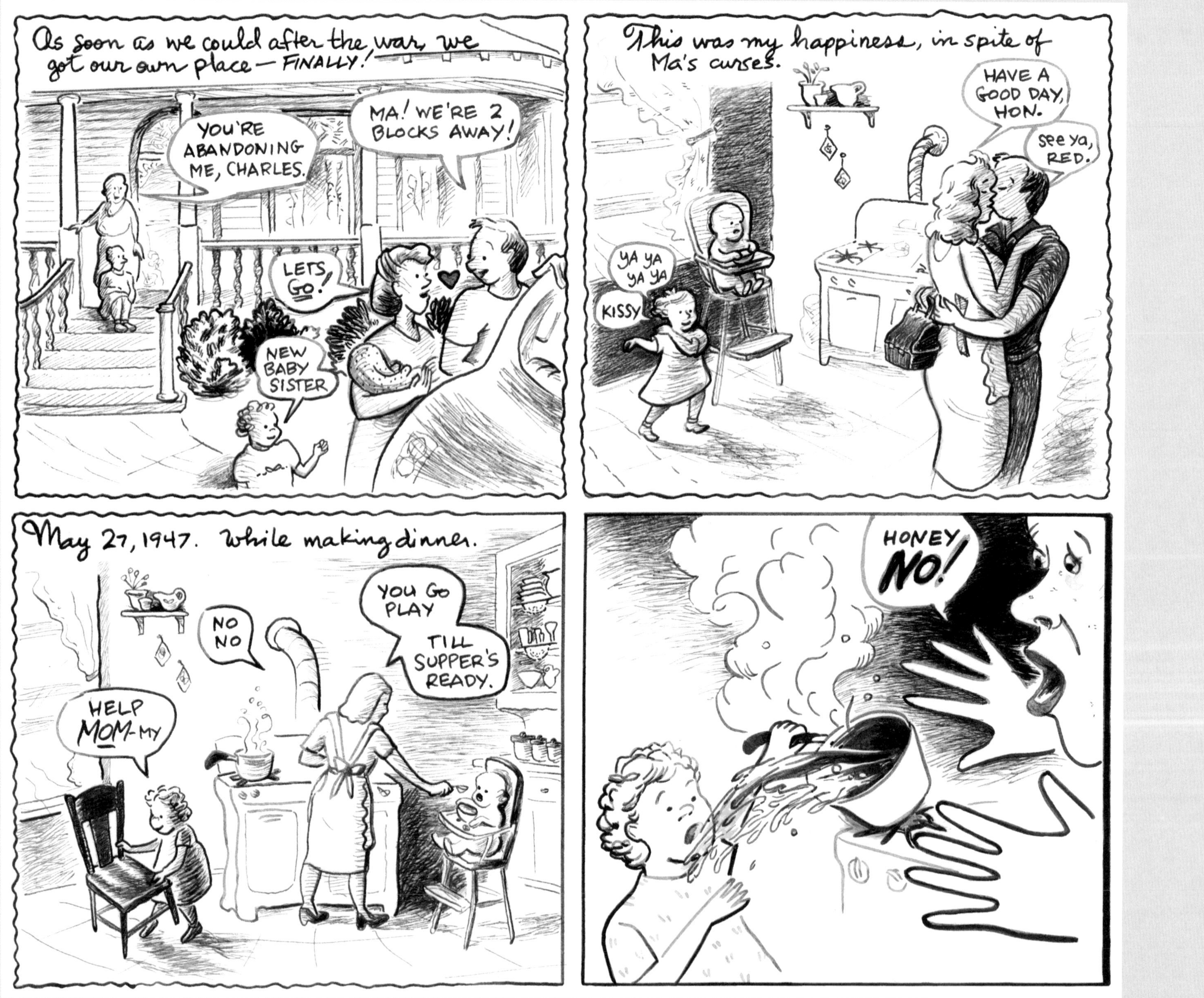

As soon as we could after the war, we got our own place—FINALLY!
YOU'RE ABANDONING ME, CHARLES.
MA! WE'RE 2 BLOCKS AWAY!
LETS GO!
NEW BABY SISTER
This was my happiness, in spite of Ma's curses.
HAVE A GOOD DAY, HON.
SEE YA, RED.
YA YA YA YA
KISSY
May 27, 1947. While making dinner.
NO NO
YOU GO PLAY
TILL SUPPER'S READY.
HELP MOM-MY
HONEY NO!

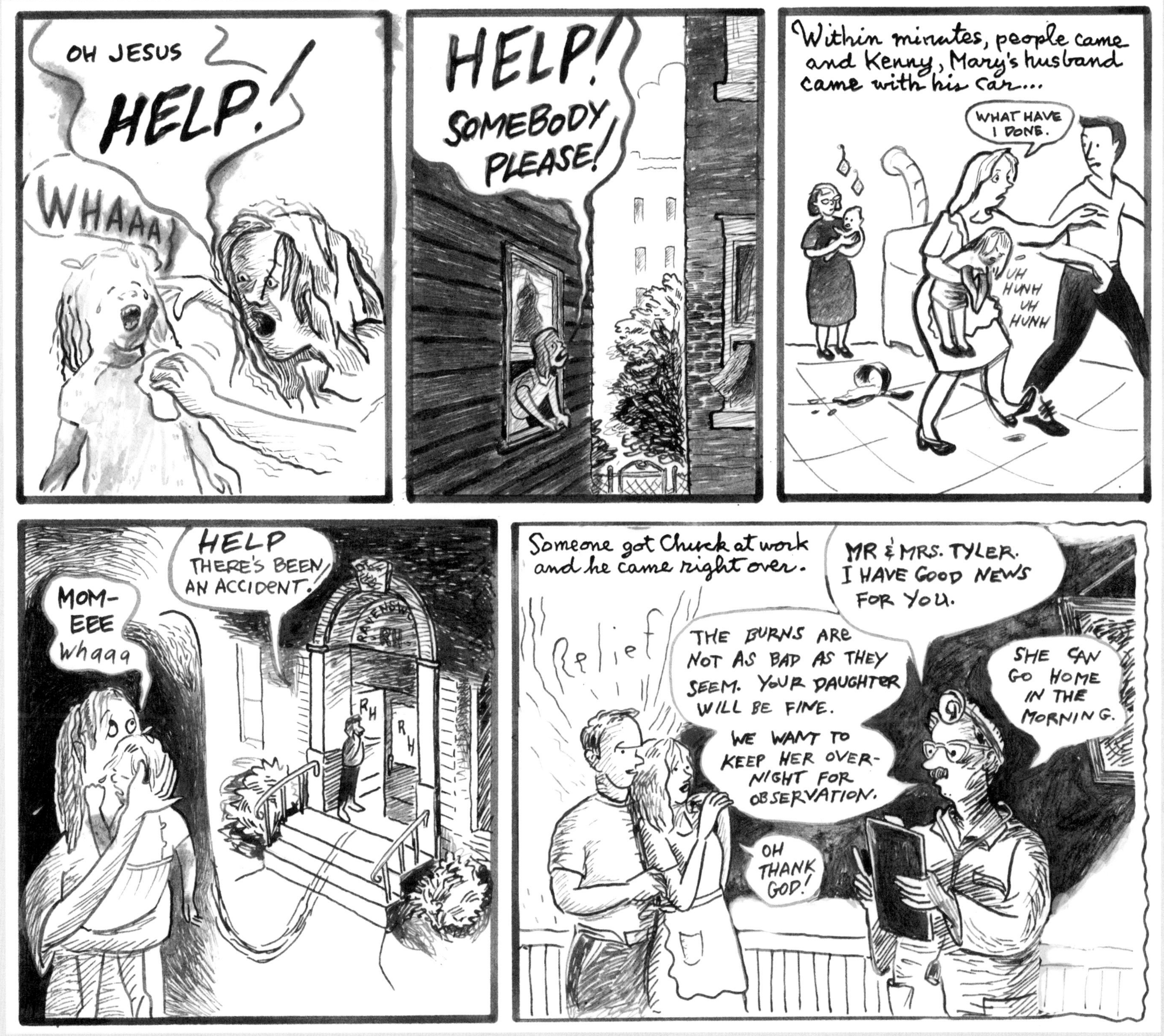
OH JESUS
HELP!
WHAAA!
HELP!
SOMEBODY PLEASE!
Within minutes, people came and Kenny, Mary's husband came with his car....
WHAT HAVE I DONE.
UH HUNH UH HUNH
HELP THERE'S BEEN AN ACCIDENT!
MOM-EEE whaaa
Someone got Chuck at work and he came right over.
MR & MRS. TYLER. I HAVE GOOD NEWS FOR YOU.
Relief
THE BURNS ARE NOT AS BAD AS THEY SEEM. YOUR DAUGHTER WILL BE FINE.
WE WANT TO KEEP HER OVER-NIGHT FOR OBSERVATION.
SHE CAN GO HOME IN THE MORNING.
OH THANK GOD!

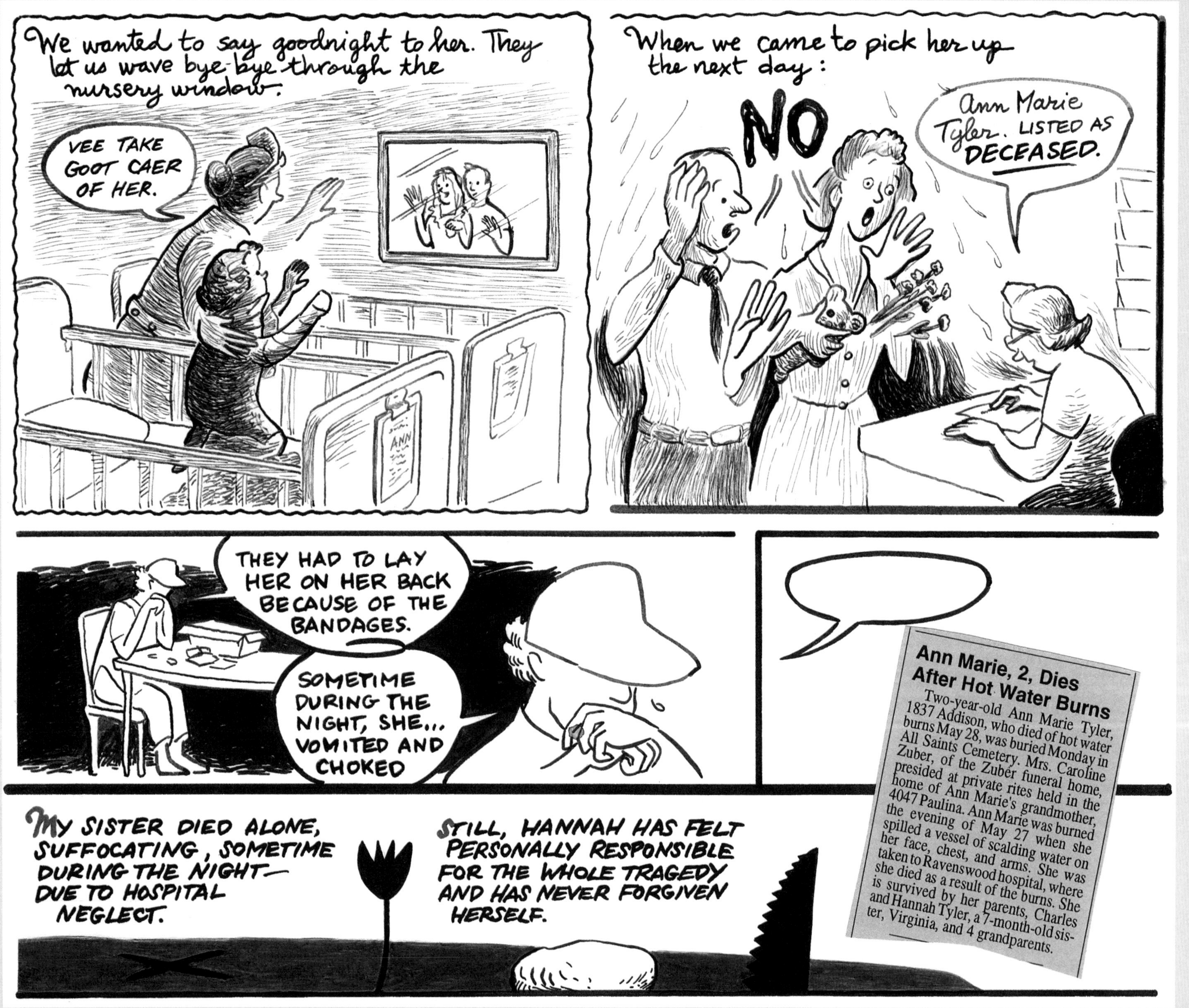
We wanted to say goodnight to her. They let us wave bye-bye through the nursery window.
VEE TAKE GOOT CAER OF HER.
ANN
When we came to pick her up the next day:
NO
Ann Marie Tyler. LISTED AS DECEASED.
THEY HAD TO LAY HER ON HER BACK BECAUSE OF THE BANDAGES.
SOMETIME DURING THE NIGHT, SHE... VOMITED AND CHOKED
Ann Marie, 2, Dies After Hot Water Burns
Two-year-old Ann Marie Tyler, 1837 Addison, who died of hot water burns May 28, was buried Monday in All Saints Cemetery. Mrs. Caroline Zuber, of the Zuber funeral home, presided at private rites held in the home of Ann Marie's grandmother, 4047 Paulina. Ann Marie was burned the evening of May 27 when she spilled a vessel of scalding water on her face, chest, and arms. She was taken to Ravenswood hospital, where she died as a result of the burns. She is survived by her parents, Charles and Hannah Tyler, a 7-month-old sister, Virginia, and 4 grandparents.
MY SISTER DIED ALONE, SUFFOCATING, SOMETIME DURING THE NIGHT— DUE TO HOSPITAL NEGLECT.
STILL, HANNAH HAS FELT PERSONALLY RESPONSIBLE FOR THE WHOLE TRAGEDY AND HAS NEVER FORGIVEN HERSELF.

My mother came up - her first trip ever away from home (not even to my wedding). She came to Ann's funeral and fainted.

For the rest of her life, Ma made it her business to torture us because we wouldn't sue. We refused to profit from her death.

I felt so worn out, I could barely function. Soon found out I was expecting baby #3.

I dreaded Sundays at Ma's. The dining room ajoined the little alcove where Ann was laid out (a Victorian custom — at Ma's insistence.)

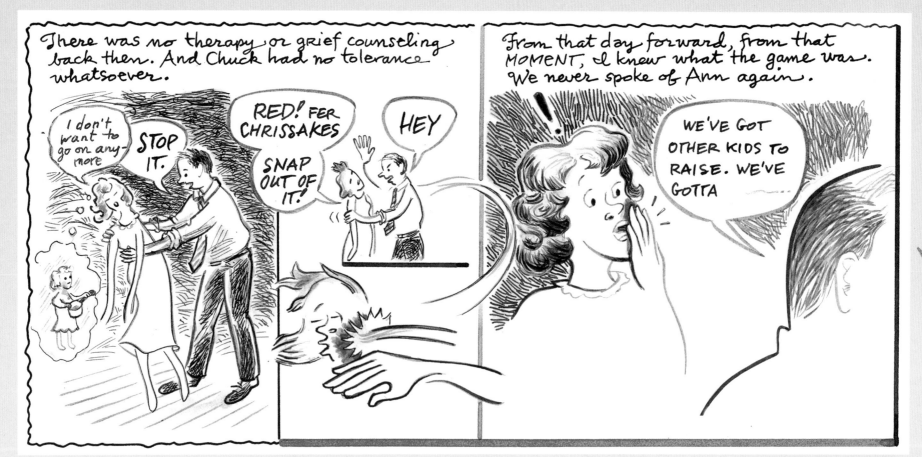

There was no therapy or grief counseling back then. And Chuck had no tolerance whatsoever.

From that day forward, from that MOMENT, I knew what the game was. We never spoke of Ann again.

FORGET.

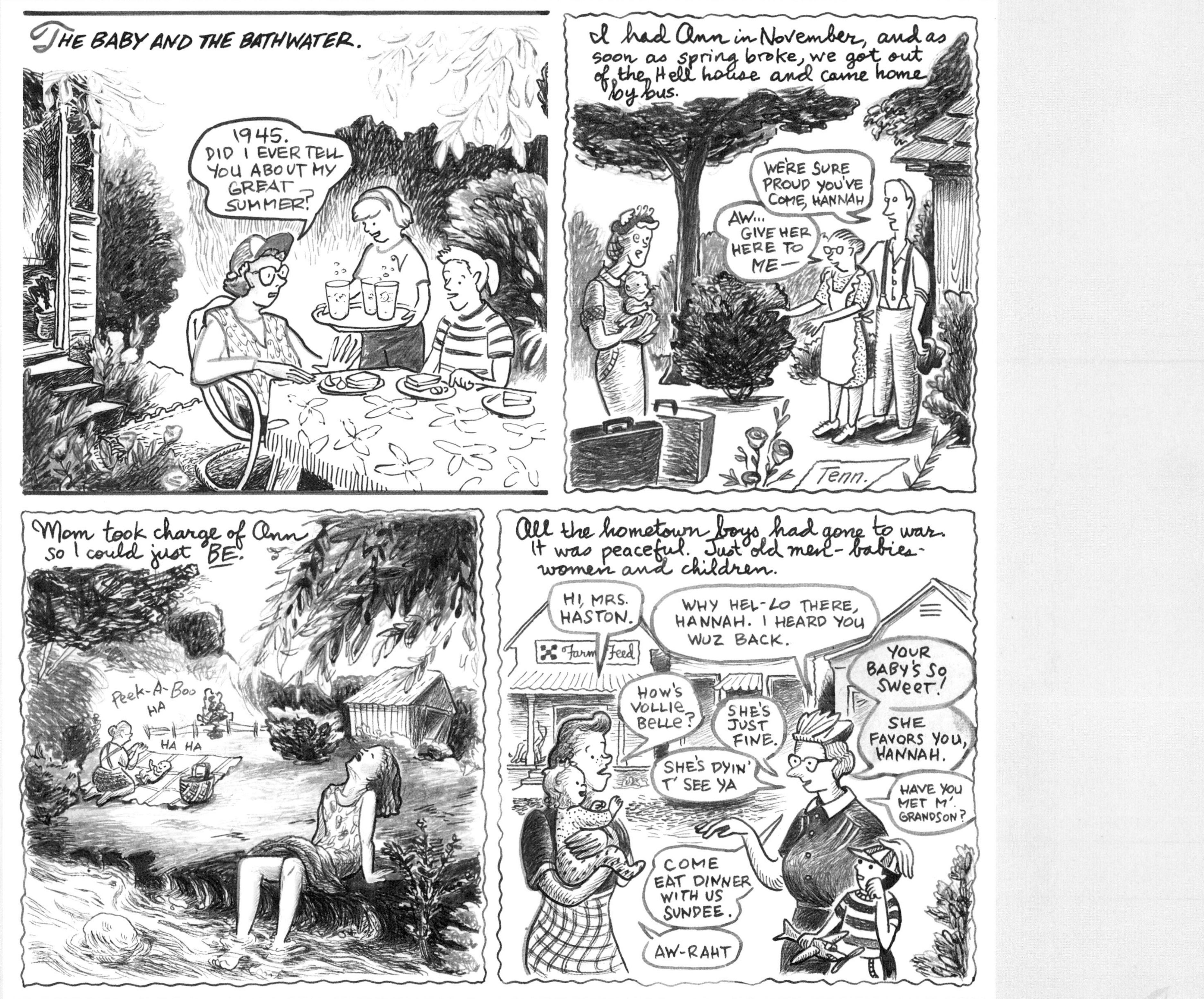
THE BABY AND THE BATHWATER.
1945. DID I EVER TELL YOU ABOUT MY GREAT SUMMER?
I had Ann in November, and as soon as spring broke, we got out of the Hell house and came home by bus.
WE'RE SURE PROUD YOU'VE COME, HANNAH
AW... GIVE HER HERE TO ME—
Tenn.
Mom took charge of Ann so I could just BE.
Peek-A-Boo
HA
HA HA
All the hometown boys had gone to war. It was peaceful. Just old men-babies-women and children.
HI, MRS. HASTON.
WHY HEL-LO THERE, HANNAH. I HEARD YOU WUZ BACK.
Farm Feed
YOUR BABY'S SO SWEET!
SHE FAVORS YOU, HANNAH.
HOW'S VOLLIE BELLE?
SHE'S JUST FINE.
SHE'S DYIN' T' SEE YA
HAVE YOU MET M' GRANDSON?
COME EAT DINNER WITH US SUNDEE.
AW-RAHT

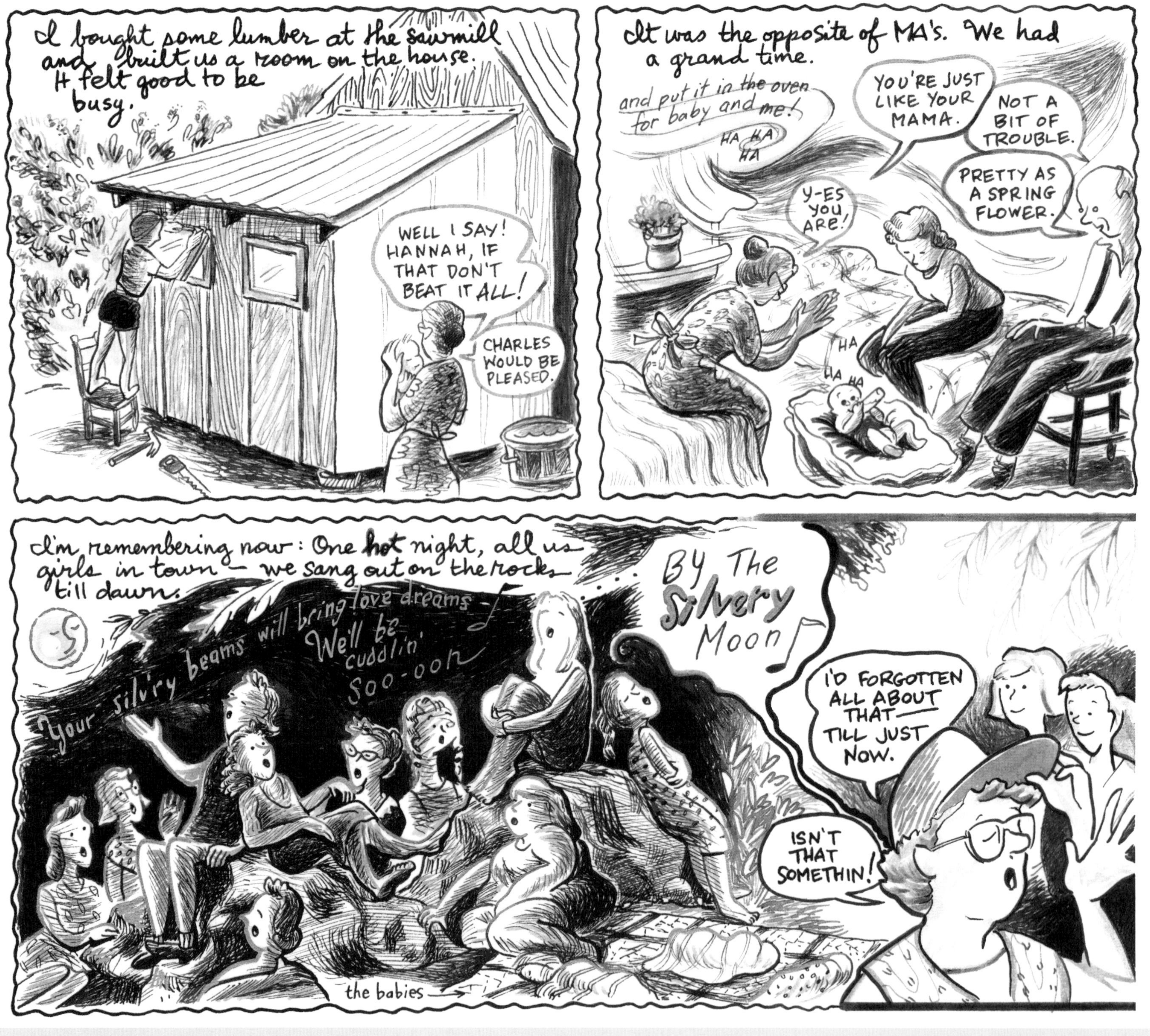
I bought some lumber at the sawmill and built us a room on the house. It felt good to be busy.
WELL I SAY! HANNAH, IF THAT DON'T BEAT IT ALL!
CHARLES WOULD BE PLEASED.
It was the opposite of MA's. We had a grand time.
and put it in the oven for baby and me!
HA HA HA
YOU'RE JUST LIKE YOUR MAMA.
NOT A BIT OF TROUBLE.
PRETTY AS A SPRING FLOWER.
Y-ES YOU ARE!
HA
HA HA
I'm remembering now: One hot night, all us girls in town — we sang out on the rocks till dawn.
Your silvery beams will bring love dreams
We'll be cuddlin' soo-oon
By The Silvery Moon
I'D FORGOTTEN ALL ABOUT THAT— TILL JUST NOW.
ISN'T THAT SOMETHIN!
the babies

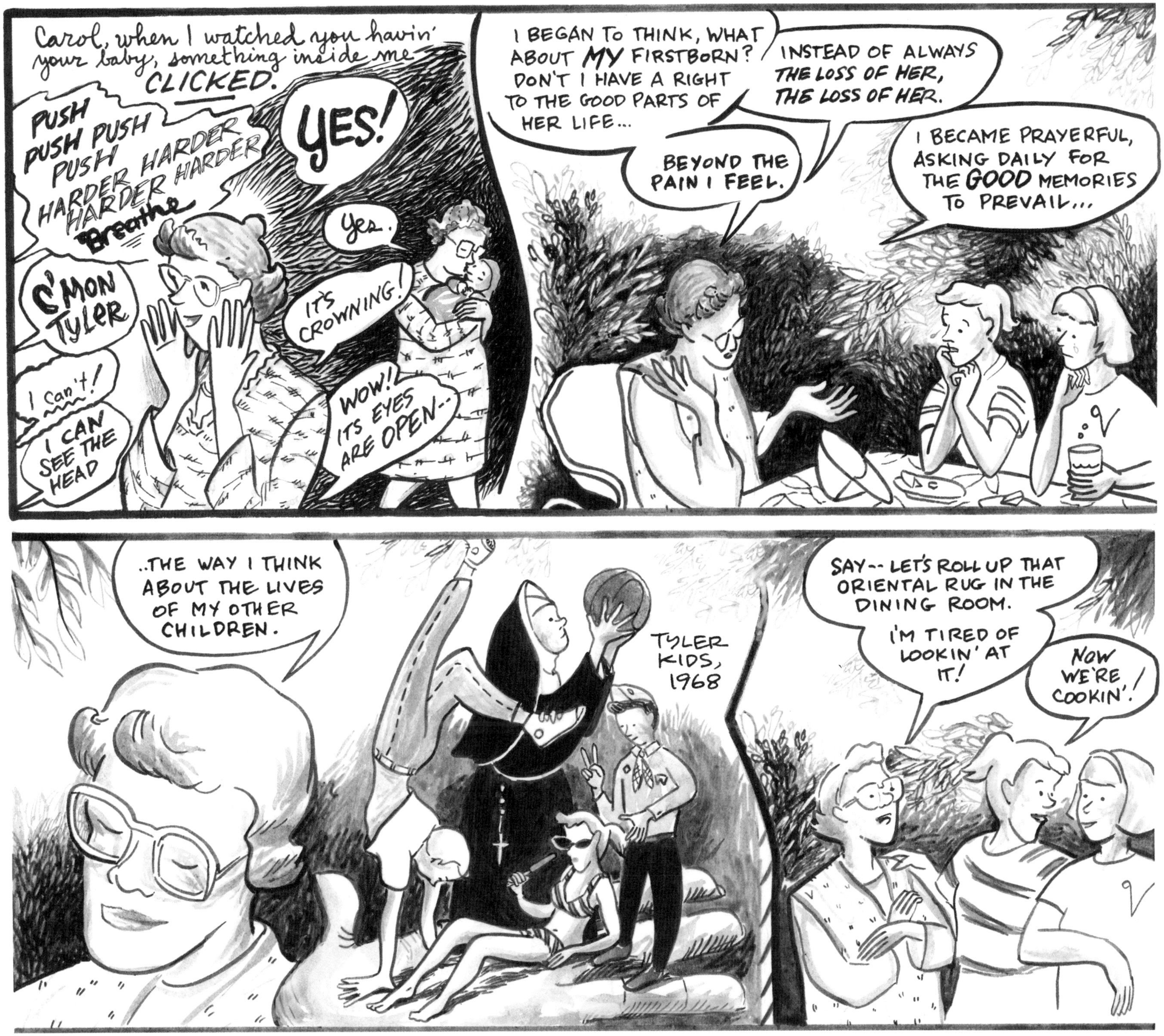
Carol, when I watched you havin' your baby, something inside me CLICKED.
PUSH PUSH PUSH PUSH
HARDER HARDER HARDER HARDER
Breathe
YES!
Yes.
C'MON TYLER
IT'S CROWNING!
I can't!
I CAN SEE THE HEAD
WOW! ITS EYES ARE OPEN..
I BEGAN TO THINK, WHAT ABOUT MY FIRSTBORN? DON'T I HAVE A RIGHT TO THE GOOD PARTS OF HER LIFE...
INSTEAD OF ALWAYS THE LOSS OF HER, THE LOSS OF HER.
BEYOND THE PAIN I FEEL.
I BECAME PRAYERFUL, ASKING DAILY FOR THE GOOD MEMORIES TO PREVAIL...
..THE WAY I THINK ABOUT THE LIVES OF MY OTHER CHILDREN.
TYLER KIDS, 1968
SAY-- LET'S ROLL UP THAT ORIENTAL RUG IN THE DINING ROOM.
I'M TIRED OF LOOKIN' AT IT!
NOW WE'RE COOKIN'!

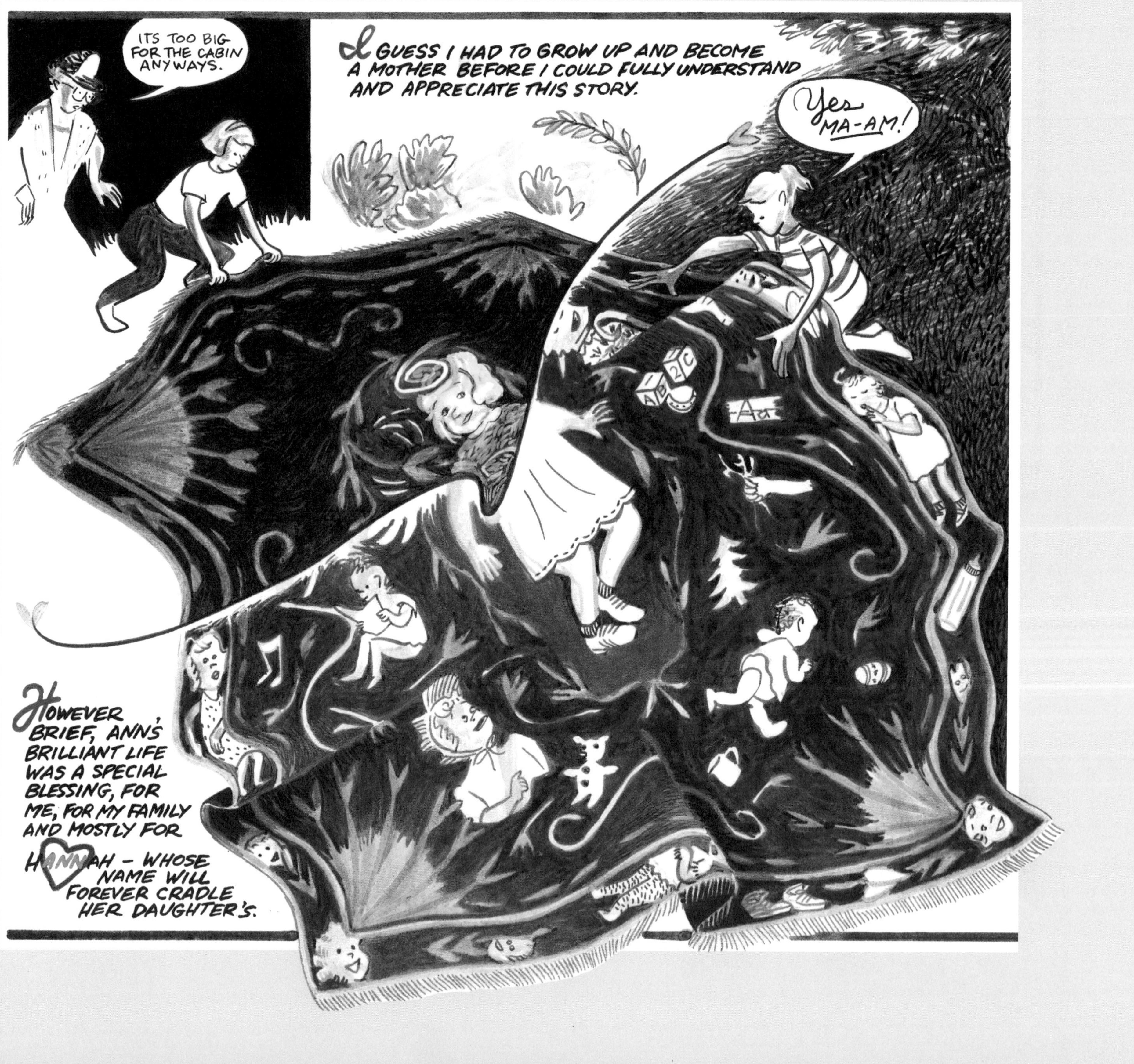
ITS TOO BIG FOR THE CABIN ANYWAYS.
I GUESS I HAD TO GROW UP AND BECOME A MOTHER BEFORE I COULD FULLY UNDERSTAND AND APPRECIATE THIS STORY.
Yes MA-AM!
HOWEVER BRIEF, ANN'S BRILLIANT LIFE WAS A SPECIAL BLESSING, FOR ME, FOR MY FAMILY AND MOSTLY FOR HANNAH - WHOSE NAME WILL FOREVER CRADLE HER DAUGHTER'S.

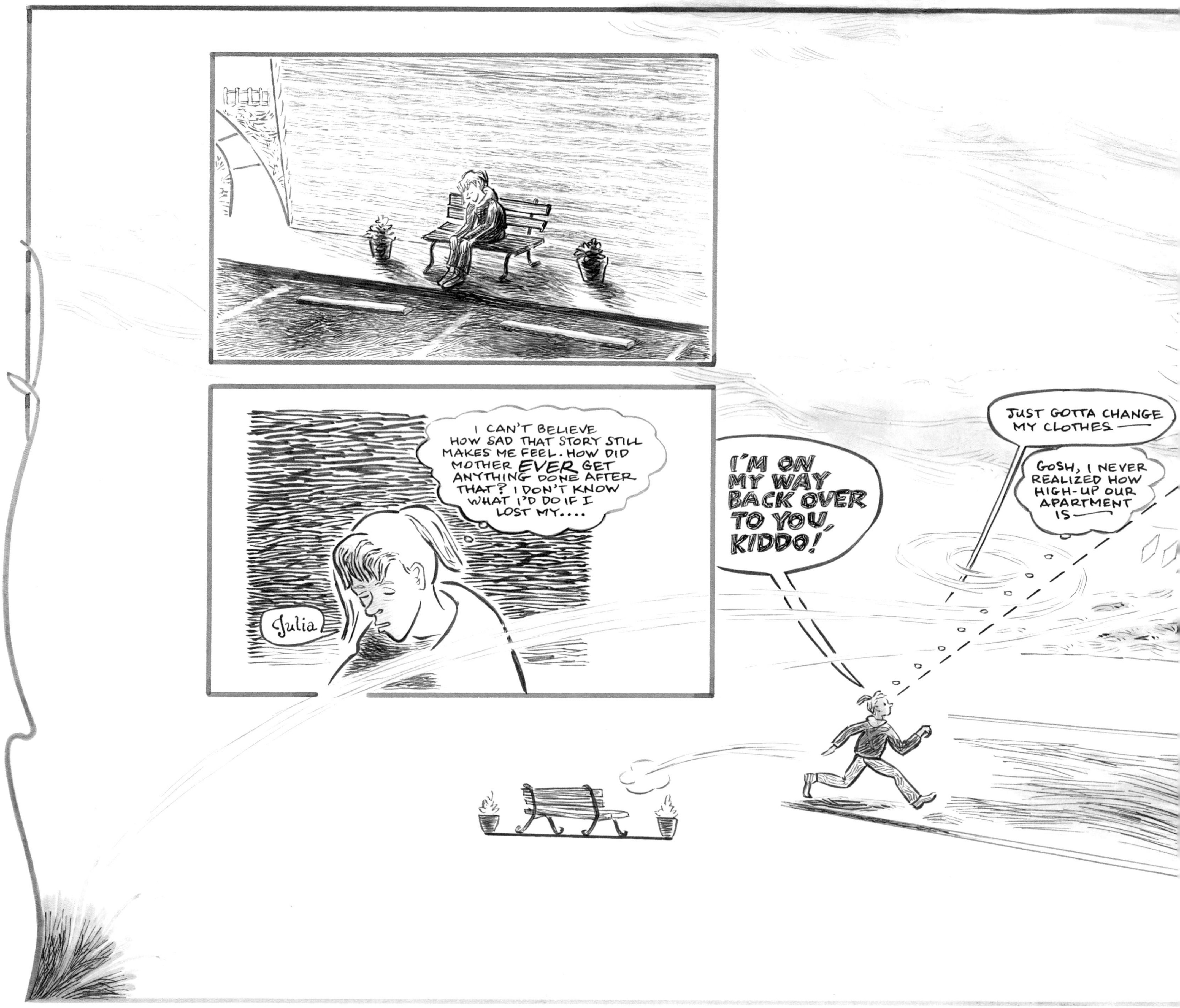
I CAN'T BELIEVE HOW SAD THAT STORY STILL MAKES ME FEEL. HOW DID MOTHER EVER GET ANYTHING DONE AFTER THAT? I DON'T KNOW WHAT I'D DO IF I LOST MY....
Julia
I'M ON MY WAY BACK OVER TO YOU, KIDDO!
JUST GOTTA CHANGE MY CLOTHES—
GOSH, I NEVER REALIZED HOW HIGH-UP OUR APARTMENT IS—

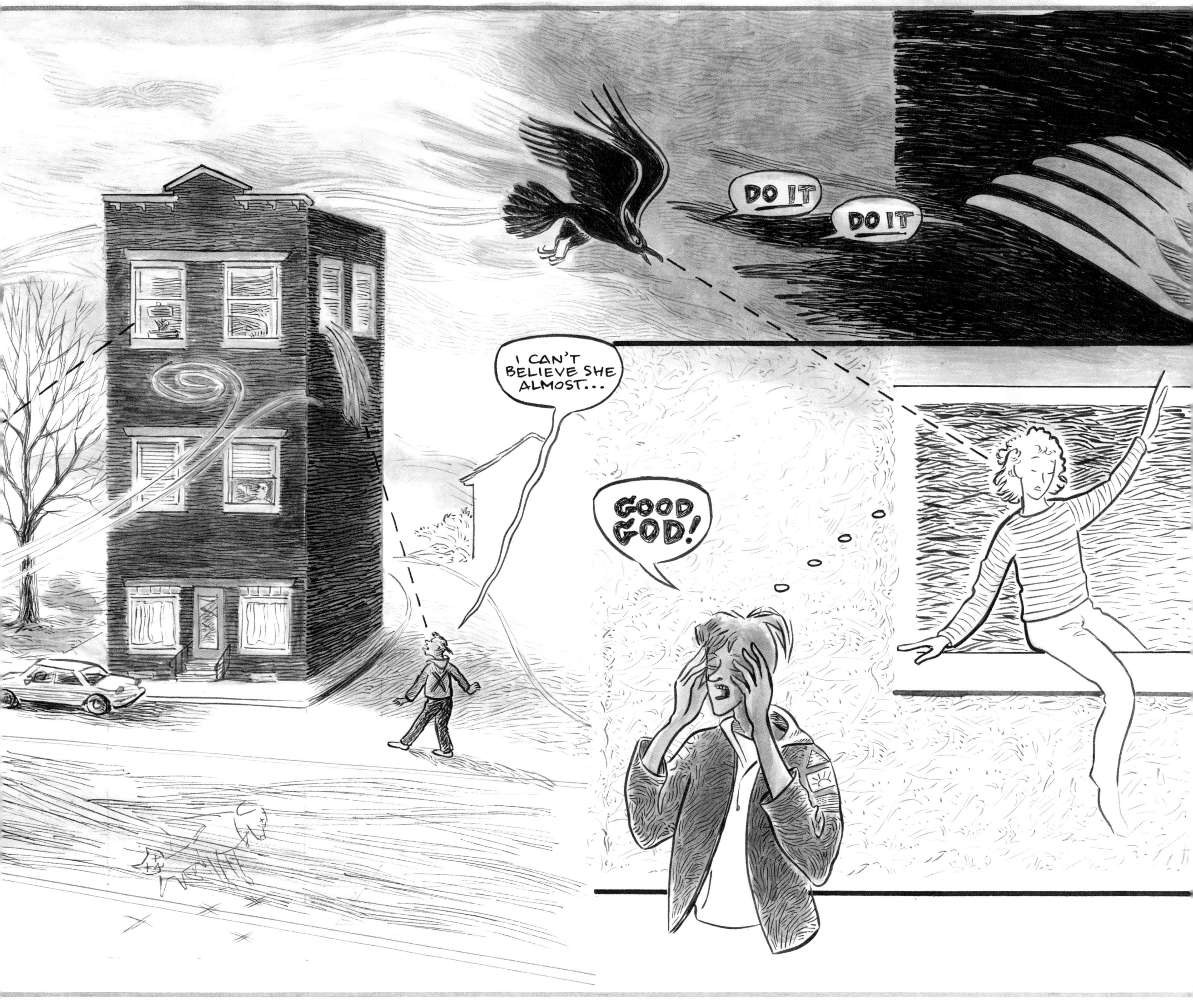

DO IT
DO IT
I CAN'T BELIEVE SHE ALMOST...
GOOD GOD!

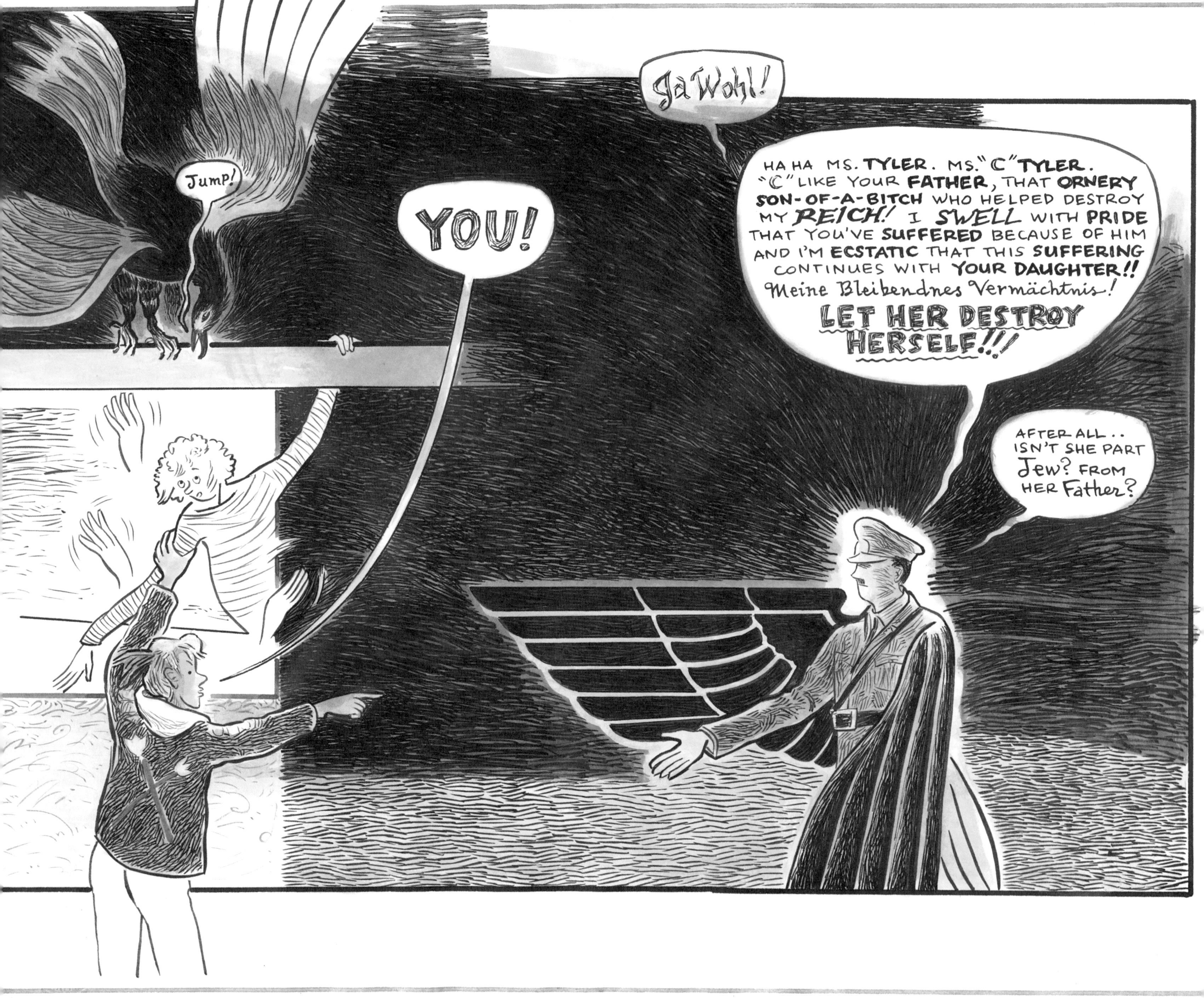
Jump!
YOU!
Ja Wohl!
HA HA MS. TYLER. MS. "C" TYLER. "C" LIKE YOUR FATHER, THAT ORNERY SON-OF-A-BITCH WHO HELPED DESTROY MY REICH! I SWELL WITH PRIDE THAT YOU'VE SUFFERED BECAUSE OF HIM AND I'M ECSTATIC THAT THIS SUFFERING CONTINUES WITH YOUR DAUGHTER!! Meine Bleibendnes Vermächtnis! LET HER DESTROY HERSELF!!!
AFTER ALL.. ISN'T SHE PART Jew? FROM HER Father?

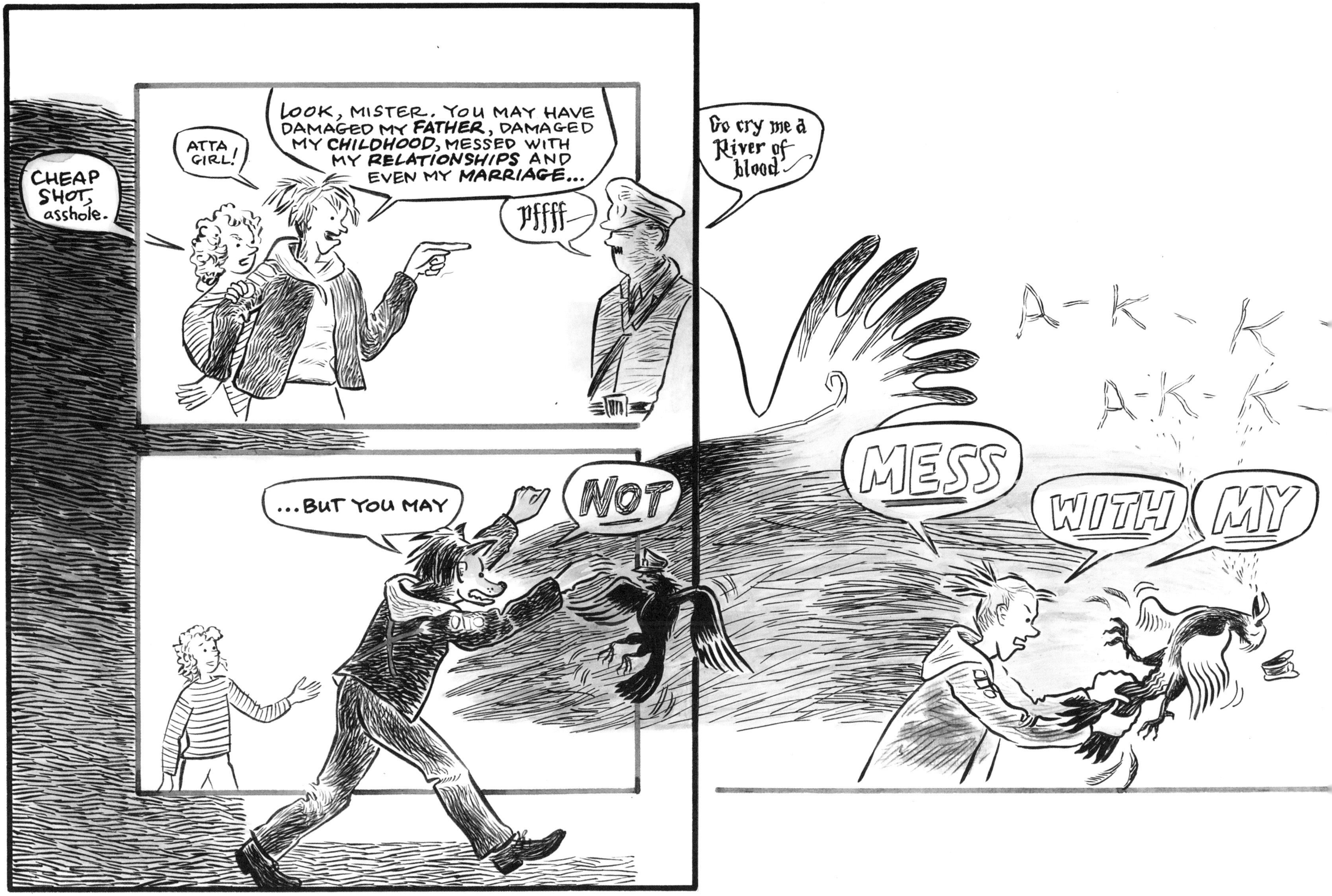

CHEAP SHOT, asshole.
ATTA GIRL!
LOOK, MISTER. YOU MAY HAVE DAMAGED MY **FATHER**, DAMAGED MY **CHILDHOOD**, MESSED WITH MY **RELATIONSHIPS** AND EVEN MY **MARRIAGE**...
pffff—
Go cry me a River of blood.
...BUT YOU MAY
NOT
MESS
WITH
MY
A-K-K-
A-K-K-

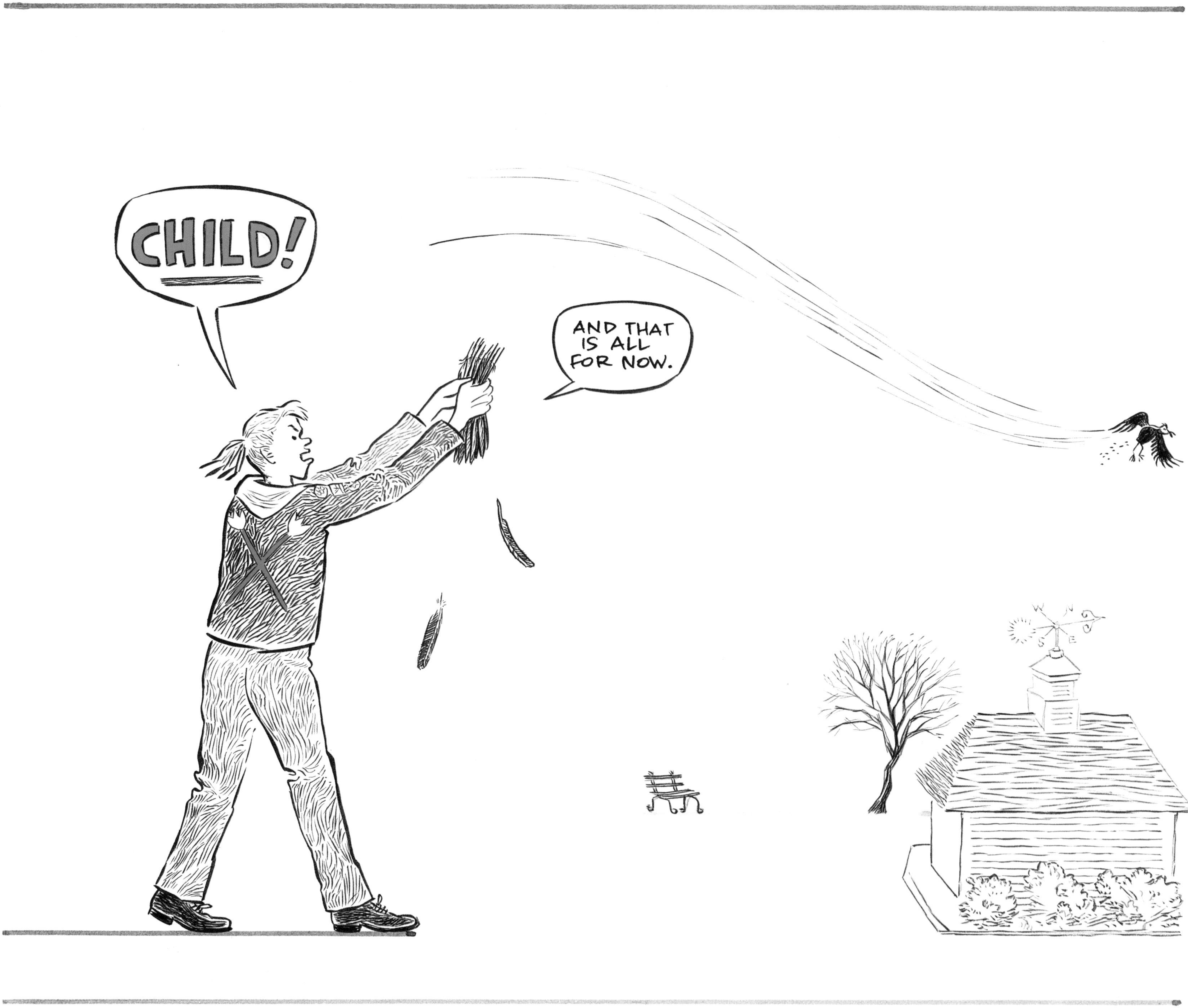
CHILD!
AND THAT IS ALL FOR NOW.

Rodger E. Farley

3/22/84

The Design of the Aeroplane

Frontispiece The gannet knows it without reading books. Body cambered and tail down to reduce speed increases lift, and the nose-down pitching moment. To trim wings move forward to displace centre of pressure ahead of centre of gravity. Airflow begins to separate near wing trailing edges as speed is reduced, causing soft feathers to ruffle upwards, turbulating the boundary layer, delaying further separation and stall. *Alula* (bastard wing) acts as a slat by extending at the leading edge, inboard of the primary (pinion) feathers, to delay stall by keeping flow attached. Landing gear coming down to increase drag, before rolling (wings half folded) into an evasive dive. (*DMT Ettlinger via Shell Aviation News, UK*)

THE DESIGN OF
THE AEROPLANE

... Which describes Common-sense mechanics
of design as they affect the flying qualities of
aeroplanes needing only one pilot.

DARROL STINTON

MBE, CEng, MIMechE, FRAeS, RAF(Ret)

VAN NOSTRAND REINHOLD COMPANY
NEW YORK CINCINNATI TORONTO LONDON MELBOURNE

For my gentle, encouraging wife Jacqueline, and
children Julian, Caroline, Terry, Matthew and
Penelope

Copyright © 1983 by Darrol Stinton

Library of Congress Catalog Card Number 82–13635

ISBN 0–442–28249–4

Printed in Great Britain

Published in the United States in 1983
by Van Nostrand Reinhold Company Inc.
135 West 50th Street
New York, NY 10020, U.S.A.

First published in Great Britain by Granada Publishing 1983 under the title
'The Design of The Aeroplane'
Frogmore, St Albans, Herts AL2 2NF
and
36 Golden Square, London W1R 4AH

16 15 14 13 12 11 10 9 8 7 6 5 4 3 2 1

Library of Congress Cataloging in Publication Data

Stinton, Darrol, 1927–
   The design of the airplane.

   British ed. has title: The design of the aeroplane.
   Includes index.
   1. Airplanes—Design and construction.   I. Title.
TL671.2.S773   1983   629.134'1   82–13635
ISBN 0–442–28249–4

Foreword

Professor L. F. Crabtree, BSc, DIC, PhD, CEng, AFAIAA, FRAeS;
*Sir George White Professor of Aeronautics, University of Bristol and
Past President of the Royal Aeronautical Society.*

Almost every line of this book shows the author's experience in aeroplane design, in flying and testing, as a pilot in the Royal Air Force and a test pilot at Farnborough, as a test pilot-surveyor for the Civil Aviation Authority, in teaching others the fascinating details of performance, stability and control, and in relating these to flying qualities – although this latter subject is to be developed more fully in the author's next book.

For those who want to design and build their own small aeroplanes, this book takes them step-by-step through the aerodynamic and weight calculations required. It not only tells how, but also gives a well-balanced treatment of the theoretical background. The reader is given a very clear physical picture of the fluid dynamic processes involved in all aspects of flight, and whereas the equations are given in rigorous form, only an elementary knowledge of mathematics is needed to make full use of the text, for the author's own physical insight is transmitted to the reader in the simplest and clearest terms.

Students of aeronautical engineering on even the most advanced courses will also find the book of great value throughout their studies, especially for the treatment of aircraft stability and control.

The author has some new insights on these subjects which will greatly assist such students to understand the ideas involved and methods used in the analysis of stability and control problems. In many formal textbooks these are presented in a more complicated and difficult way than is really necessary.

A feature of the book is the last chapter where forty examples of particular project design problems are presented and used to illustrate points made in the preceding chapters. Students will find themselves referring to the book throughout the whole of their subsequent careers, and it can be recommended to all who are interested in aeroplane design, whether it be as a hobby or a full-time career.

Preface

'Grasp the leading praecognita of all things –
grasp the trunk hard only, and you will shake
all the branches.'

Cornelius Ford's advice to Samuel Johnson
(1709–84)

Aeroplane design is both an art and a science. The most successful designers are those
with an instinct for the nature of air and the way it wants to behave when disturbed. If
aircraft are shaped in ways which help the air to adjust to their passage, instead of
forcing it aside, less energy is expended, less noise is created and less fuel is consumed.
Therefore, good design favours protection of the environment.

This is a trunk shaking book within the spirit of Cornelius Ford's advice, dealing
with aeroplanes at the lighter end of the spectrum. In many ways we have reached a
critical stage in the development of light aviation. Design has to change in the pursuit
of greater efficiency. The environment can no longer be ignored. There are some
people around who say that the design and development of smaller aircraft has got
stuck because there is nowhere for it to go. Others like Burt Rutan in Mojave have
different ideas and plough new furrows with tail first and even stranger shapes. But
even though shapes of aeroplanes may vary widely, especially in their arrangements of
lifting surfaces, they are all governed by the same fundamental principles and the way
in which air wants to move.

There is much rich ground for anyone to dig simply by going back and looking
around at the ideas of earlier designers. For example, a modern tail first or Canard
aeroplane, shaped to fly efficiently on low power, employs that configuration for much
the same reason as the Wright Brothers chose it for their gliders in 1901 and their Flyer
of 1903: the lift forces from both surfaces worked in the same direction and this
achieved economy of effort in lifting a given weight into the air. When the tail is at the
back its lift works downwards, in opposition to wing lift, when rotating the aircraft
into the attitude needed to lift off the ground.

Microlight and other minimum aeroplanes which have been developed from hang-
gliders no longer reflect the delta membrane Rogallo wing designs of a few years ago.
There has been a new twist given: development has not just gone full circle so that the
aeroplane has been re-invented, it has moved onwards in a spiral.

Although this book is concerned with aeroplanes for single-pilot operations the net
is wide between the microlight and the upper limit of 12 500 lb (5 670 kg). Agricultural

aircraft will exceed this limit in future, while many could be microlight. All the aeroplanes for single pilot operation are in General Aviation which involves everything civil that flies, other than airlines, and accounts for around 96 per cent of the civil aeroplanes in the Western World, 80 per cent of all civil flying time (50 million hours or more) and more than one half of the passengers carried.

The stimulus for writing *The Design of the Aeroplane* has come from two directions. I have managed to combine design engineering with test flying – something easier to accomplish in the USA or Germany than in the UK. Some years ago I wrote a physical text book called *The Anatomy of the Aeroplane* in which I sought to combine both disciplines. The way in which it sold into universities, colleges and the industry around the world, and into the flying training organisations of the Services, showed that it fulfilled a need. This book takes steps beyond *The Anatomy* into mechanics of the subject as a creative entity, combining design and test flying as two sides of one coin.

The second impulse has been given by the *Air Registration Board* (later *Airworthiness Division of the Civil Aviation Authority*) which I joined as a design surveyor–test pilot in 1969. ARB and CAA have sent me since 1970 to the *Experimental Aircraft Association* Fly-in at Oshkosh, in Wisconsin. At that Convention, among the grassroots of aviation and aircraft which can be shaped by one mind instead of teams and committees (a camel is defined as a horse designed by a committee), 14 000 aircraft fly in and out of a county airport at the rate of one movement every three seconds without accident caused by such rates. There too can be found the beginning and restatement of all knowledge leading ultimately to Concorde, Airbus, a plethora of big jets, and even the moon. In the *EAA* are people who talk design and fly. On my first visit I left one week later with predilections and prejudices kicked awry, lighter in weight, wiser and older, with seventeen utterly different types of aeroplane in my log book – and a number of enduring friendships which have expanded professional life and pleasure ever since.

As a result this book is intended to be what I can only describe as the book I needed to tell me things when my own ideas were being formed. It is about bedrock and direction in the design of aeroplanes to be flown by a single pilot. It covers the whole range of civil aeroplanes with which I am concerned. These stretch from microlight and minimum aeroplanes to heavyweight agricultural and aerial work machines, by way of aeroplanes for amateur builders (scale replicas, tourers, racers and aerobatic aircraft) to those mass-produced by industry for the General Aviation market. In writing it I have borne in mind the advice to test pilots of David P. Davies, past Head of *Flight Department* and Chief Test Pilot of the *ARB* (later, *Airworthiness Division of the Civil Aviation Authority*), which richly deserves wider appreciation.

> 'Don't believe other people, prove it for yourself.
> Stick to what you have proved believable.
> Don't be overawed by other more senior people.
> Don't ignore the feelings in your bones.'

What is within these pages I have found to be true for all of my practical purposes (although I am quite prepared to listen to anyone else's constructive experience which might oppose it).

I make no apology for the text leaning initially in the direction of British certification. Our light aircraft industry has declined badly and most of the aeroplanes flying here have been built abroad. If any reader wishes to build an aeroplane in the

UK, or to buy one from abroad, or to sell to a buyer for operation on the British Register, the Civil Aviation Authority must be dealt with, because it has the task of interpreting and administering the law.

The law here is not the same as it is in France, or Germany, or Italy, and the Authority does not operate as the *Federal Aviation Administration* in the USA, where the laws too are different. Some people find the Authority a hurdle, others a challenge, many both. It is not paid for out of Federal taxes but has to make its own charges, which are based upon man hours. One of the causes of difficulty that I have found repeatedly with applicants is that they leave too much homework to be done by the Authority. If some of the material here helps to ease their problems, it will have served a useful purpose.

Aircraft design is about people every bit as much as machines, which is why I introduce quotations. The things said by people reflect their experience. I have cast my net wide, because after more than 30 years flying and nearly 40 years with and around design organisations, I believe that advice given by Sir George Cayley, the Wright Brothers and many others since is as true today as ever. In this subject history must never be ignored.

What I say here, proved to my satisfaction by my own experience, are my own views. They do not reflect either the policy or the opinion of the Civil Aviation Authority, the Royal Air Force, or any branch of Her Majesty's Government involved with aviation.

Most of the people with whom I am concerned and for whom this book is written manage to remain enthusiastic, even when confronted by unsympathetic bureaucracy and often stark economic reality. Nevertheless, their world of aeroplanes dealt with in this book continues to expand at a rate around 7 to 10 per cent per annum (in the UK) in spite of recession. Unfortunately the word enthusiast is sometimes used disdainfully, certainly on this side of the Atlantic.

The inversion and reversal of meanings of words is common in aeronautics: *sophisticated* is an all too frequent example which shows sloppy thinking and limited vocabulary, neither of which we can afford. Enthusiast comes from one of those delightful Greek words full of dancing letters (with which our subject is liberally sprinkled): $\epsilon\nu\theta o\upsilon\sigma\iota\alpha\sigma\tau\eta s$, which means possessing a god within. The people who carry aviation forwards and who, from the beginning, stamped it with the uniqueness of their characters, were enthusiasts. Out of deference to the ancient Greeks without whose elegance this book could not have been produced, I also stick to the lovely word aeroplane: $'\alpha\epsilon\rho o\pi\lambda\alpha\nu os$, air-wandering because it captures most accurately the spirit of almost everyone who has shaped me as a flying-man and author of this textbook. I believe that all of us who care about aviation and who have either been fortunate enough to learn to fly, or who would like to be able to do so, contain something of the same spirit and fire. As Paul Poberezny, President of the *Experimental Aircraft Assocation*, was reported as saying in the December 1980 *Air Progress*: '... enthusiasm coupled with experience is an unbeatable formula for success ...'

If you have a mind like mine it will go blank and the brain will stall at the first sight of a page of mathematics. Unfortunately, though, mathematics cannot be avoided, because we are concerned with shapes, proportions, sizes, weights and power required. Even though there are mathematics here, all has been kept as simple as possible. Take heart, mathematics eluded me when young and I had to teach it to myself from scratch long after I left school and got into aeronautics. Thus I can only echo what Sylvanus P. Thompson said in his book *Calculus Made Easy* (Macmillan and Co, Limited, London) which first appeared in 1910:

'Being myself a remarkably stupid fellow, I have had to unteach
myself the difficulties, and now beg to present to my fellow
fools the parts that are not hard. Master these thoroughly,
and the rest will follow. What one fool can do, another can.'

Choice of units was a problem. The trend is towards metrication with the younger
generation in schools and colleges, not to mention Europe. But vast numbers of older
people in the English speaking world still work in the foot/pound/second Rankine
system. Therefore I have written in FPSR primary units with metric in brackets.
Extensive conversion tables are included to please everyone – especially slower witted,
older people like me, who have no real idea what a Newton looks or feels like (beyond it
being the weight of one small apple – ten of which make a deca Newton, or kilogram).

I hope that you get out of *The Design of the Aeroplane* as much as you can, because I
know of few subjects comparable with this, in which beauty of line and aesthetic
satisfaction of flight blend so precisely with the special elegance of reason.

                                                            D. Stinton

List of Plates

List of Symbols

Symbol	Meaning	Symbol	Meaning
A	Area (also of cross-section)	ac_T	Aerodynamic centre of top plane
A	Aspect ratio	$(a_1)_\beta$	Lift slope of fin with angle of yaw, β
A	Moment of inertia in roll (about O-X axis)	$(a_2)_\zeta$	Lift slope due to rudder deflection, ζ
A	Nozzle area of jet engine		
A	Weight of air in a given volume swallowed by jet engine	B	Moment of inertia in pitch (about O-Y axis)
A_c, A_{cmax}	Areas of cross-section of body generating mainly form drag	B	Term used in measurement of stick free static margin
Ae	Effective aspect ratio	b	Wingspan
A_f	Geometric aspect ratio	b_f	Effective semi span of fin-plus-rudder
A_g	Equivalent aspect ratio of wing in ground effect	b_f	Flap span
		b_o	Hinge moment coefficient due to camber of surface ahead of control surface
A_{nose}	Aspect ratio of nose forward of wing aerodynamic centre	b_1	Rate of change of elevator hinge moment coefficient with change in stabiliser angle of attack
A_p	Area of flat plate normal to airflow		
A_s	Aspect ratio of stabiliser		
A_w	Parasite wetted area	b_1	Span of longer plane of a biplane
A_{wf}	Fuselage surface area	b_2	Rate of change of elevator hinge moment coefficient with elevator deflection span of shorter plane of a biplane
A_π	Relevant area for estimating parasite drag		
$\overline{A}$	$(a_2 \eta_s \overline{V}_s)$ Slope of trim curve	b_3	Rate of change of elevator hinge moment coefficient with tab deflector
a	Acceleration, deceleration		
a	Horizontal distance between centre of gravity and main wheel axle	₵	Centre-line
		C	Constant
a	Lift slope, $dC_L/d\alpha$	C	Modulus of rigidity of a section
a	Speed of sound	C	Moment of inertia in yaw (about O-Z axis)
a_A	Lift slope of surface of aspect ratio A		
a_w	Wing weight factor	C_D	Total three dimensional drag coefficient D/qs
a_f	Fin lift slope based upon its geometry ie, of fin-plus-rudder, fixed		
		C_{DF}	Zero lift drag coefficient
a_f	Lift slope of foreplane (canard)	C_{DL}	Lift dependent drag coefficient
a_{fe}	Fin lift slope with wing, body and tailplane effects	C_{DO}	Zero-lift drag coefficient, profile drag coefficient
a_g	Lift slope in ground effect	C_{DX}	Intercept on C_D axis, $\approx C_{Dp}$
a_{nose}	Lift slope due to nose of body	C_{Dform}	Form drag coefficient
a_o	Two dimensional lift slope ie when aspect is infinity	C_{Dfric}	Friction drag coefficient
		C_{Di}	Induced drag coefficient
a_r	Lift slope of rearplane	C_{Dmin}	Minimum drag coefficient
a^1	Lift slope ratio a_g/a	C_{Dp}	Parasite drag coefficient Dp/qs
a^1	Propeller inflow factor	$C_{D\pi}$	Drag coefficient based on a relevant area A_π other than wing area
a_1	Lift slope of tail stabiliser		
$\overline{a}_1$	Equivalent lift slope of stabiliser when elevator moves (ie, floats or trails)	C_F	Thrust coefficient
		C_H	Hinge moment coefficient
a_2	Lift slope due to elevator deflection	C_L	Lift coefficient three dimensional
a_3	Lift slope due to tab deflection	C_{LA}	Lift coefficient of a wing of aspect ratio A
ac	Aerodynamic centre	C_{Lf}	Lift coefficient of foreplane
ac_B	Aerodynamic centre of bottom plane		

Symbol	Meaning	Symbol	Meaning
C_{Lmax}	Maximum lift coefficient	$\bar{\bar{c}}$	Aerodynamic mean chord MAC
C_{Lr}	Lift coefficient of rearplane		
C_{Ls}	Lift coefficient of stabilator	D	Available distance in which to take off
C_{Lto}	Lift coefficient in take off configuration	D	Average diameter of fuselage or body
C_M	Pitching moment coefficient	D	Depth of float
C_{MCG}	Pitching moment coefficient about centre of gravity	D	Moment arm of tab centre of pressure about main control hinge (can be measured to tab centroid in practice)
C_{MD}	Moment coefficient about CG of drag resultant	D	Total drag
C_{MF}	Moment coefficient about CG of thrust	D_F	Zero lift drag
C_{Mfus}	Moment coefficient due to fuselage	D_{fric}	Frictional drag usually of wing
C_{Mo}	Moment coefficient of zero lift	D_{form}	Form drag usually of wing
$C_{Mo(wing + body)}$	Moment coefficient of zero lift for wing plus body combination	D_L	Lift dependent drag
C_{MOfus}	Moment coefficient of fuselage	D_{min}	Minimum drag
C_{Ms}	Tab moment coefficient about hinge of stabilator	D_b	Parasite drag of body
		D_d	Duct drag
C_{Mac}	Pitching moment coefficient about aerodynamic centre	D_e	Parasite extraneous drag
		D_{fw}	Zero lift wave drag
C_{MacB}	Pitching moment coefficient about aerodynamic centre of bottom plane of biplane	D_{lw}	Lift wave drag
		D_i	Induced drag
		D_p	Parasite drag
C_{MacT}	Pitching coefficient about aerodynamic centre of top plane of biplane	D_o	Zero lift (profile) drag of wing
		D_1	Diameter of circle having same cross sectional area of float
C_{Macf}	Pitching moment coefficient about aerodynamic centre of foreplane	d	Depth of fuselage at fin quarter chord intercept with top line (of skin)
C_{Macr}	Pitching moment coefficient about aerodynamic centre of rearplane	d	Diameter
$C_{p\,lower}$	Pressure coefficient for lower surface of aerofoil section	d	Moment arm of flap (control) centre of pressure about hinge axis
$C_{p\,upper}$	Pressure coefficient for upper surface of aerofoil section	d	Propeller diameter
		d_{duct}	Diameter of fan duct
C_p	Pressure coefficient	d_g	Height of aerodynamic centre of wing above ground
C_R	Crossforce coefficient		
C^1	Rudder power coefficient to prevent incipient spin	$\bar{d}$	Wake displacement from O–X plane of wing aerodynamic centre
c	Capacity (of engine)	E	Effectiveness of power plant
c	Wing (aerofoil surface) chord	E	Young's modulus of elasticity, stress/strain
$c_{balance}$	Chord of aerodynamic balance ahead of hinge line	e	Oswalds' efficiency factor
c_{flap}	Chord of flap control behind hinge line	e	Strain (change in length/original length)
c_{do}	Section profile drag coefficient		
c_d	Duct chord (propulsor)	F	Froude number
c_d	Section drag coefficient (two dimensional)	F	Force
		F	Propeller } thrust Jet engine }
c_{dx}	Intercept of parabolic polar on c_d axis when $c_l=0$	F	Weight of fuel in a given mixture/volume swallowed by engine
c_{lmax}	Maximum section lift coefficient	F_A	Factor for adjusting flap lift slope to that for another aspect ratio, from a wing of $A=6$
c_f	Flapchord		
c_l	Section lift coefficient (two dimensional)		
c_r	Chord length at aerofoil root (or in plane of symmetry)	F_F	Fuselage weight factor
c_t	Chord length at aerofoil tip	F_p	Engine installation (weight) factor
c_η	Local chord of control surface section (eg elevator, but see Table 2–7 for other suffices, eg c_ξ for aileron)	F_T	(Weight per area of tail surface)/(weight per area of equivalent cantilever monoplane surface)
c'	Mean chord of flapped portion of wing	F_w	Structural weight factor
c'	Power specific fuel consumption (piston engine)	F_w	(Weight per aerofoil surface)/(weight per equivalent cantilever monoplane surface)
c_1	Chord of longer plane of a biplane		
c_2	Chord of shorter plane of a biplane	F_f	Factor changing zero lift angle of attack of a three dimensional wing
$\bar{c}$	SMC: standard mean chord		
$\bar{c}_B$	Mean chord of bottom plane of a biplane	F_p	Powerplant installation factor
$\bar{c}_T$	Mean chord of top plane of a biplane	f	Compressive or tensile stress
$\bar{c}_f$	Mean chord of foreplane	f	Frequency of sound
$\bar{c}_r$	Mean chord of rearplane	f	Total equivalent parasite area = a function of f_b
$\bar{c}_\eta$	Standard mean chord of control surface (see Table 2.7 for other suffices eg, c_ξ for aileron)	f_{Af}	Factor affecting effective aspect ratio of fin and rudder, due to stabiliser

Symbol	Meaning	Symbol	Meaning
f_b	Basic parasite area of an aeroplane	K_{XX}, K_{YY}	Radii of gyration (about X-X and Y-Y axes
f_J	Efficiency factor accounting for propeller operating off-design	K'_n	Static margin (stick-free)
f_w	Planform factor modifying lift slope	K'	Induced drag factor of real wing with rest of aeroplane attached
f_t	Diameter of fan	k	Constant
f_η	Factor of propulsive efficiency changing with true airspeed	k	Factor measuring cruise efficiency
$f_1, 2, 3 \ldots$	Elements of parasite area	k	Factor of proportionality measuring minimum power for flight
f	Fuel consumption rate, df/dt	k	Munk's span factor
G	Biplane gap	k	Radius of gyration
G	Fuel capacity. Imp gal	k_{XX}	Radius of gyration about O-X axis
g	Gravitational acceleration, constant 32.2 ft/sec²	k_{YY}	Radius of gyration about O-Y axis
H_{mech}	Hinge moment due to mechanical arrangement of control system	L	Available landing distance
H_m	Manoeuvre margin (stick fixed)	L	Length of torsional axis of a member being twisted
H_n	CG margin (stick fixed)	L	Length of body (element)
H_o	Hinge moment due to camber of main aerofoil surface	L	Lift (three dimensional)
H^1m	Manoeuvre margin (stick free)	L	Rolling moment (about O-X axis)
H^1n	CG margin (stick free)	L_B	Lift of bottom plane
$H\alpha$	Hinge moment due to incidence on angle of attack	L_T	Lift of top plane of biplane
$H\beta$	Hinge moment due to tab movement	L_o	Local component of lift
$H\eta$	Hinge moment due to elevator movement	L_s	Stabiliser lift (when necessary to make a distinction)
h	Fraction of the standard mean chord, SMC, which locates the centre of gravity	L_w	Lift of wing (when necessary to make a distinction)
$\pm h$	Height of tail stabiliser above or below mean line of wake	L_l	Fuselage length from firewall to tip of tail cone
h	Nominal height of fin and rudder	L_β	Lift increment due to tab (trimmer) deflection$=a_3\Delta\beta$
h	Vertical height of CG above ground	L_η or L_ξ	Lift increment due to flap (control) deflection $=a_2\Delta\eta$
h_m	Manoeuvre point (stick fixed) on SMC	$L_p, L_r, L_v,$ L_ξ, L_ζ	Rolling moment derivatives
h^1m	Manoeuvre point (stick-free) on SMC	$(L/D)_R$	Lift drag ratio for longest range
h_n	Neutral point (stick-fixed) on SMC	$(L/D)_{max}$	Maximum lift/drag ratio
h^1n	Neutral point (stick-free) on SMC	l	Litre
h_o	Location of aerodynamic centre of wing-plus fuselage on SMC	l	Distance downstream of wing aerodynamic centre
$-\Delta h_o$	Forward shift of aerodynamic centre of wing-plus-fuselage along SMC	l	Local lift force (on a two dimensional section)
I	Moment of inertia (second moment of area of a section)	l_{flap}	Moment arm of flap on control surface centroid, actually centre of pressure, about hinge
I_{XX}	Moment of inertia about O-X axis $=A$	l_{horn}	Moment arm of control horn centroid, actually centre of pressure about hinge
I_{YY}	Moment of inertia about O-Y axis $=B$		
I_{ZZ}	Moment of inertia about O-Z axis $=C$	l_{nose}	Length of fuselage nose ahead of wing **ac**
$I_{O'X'}, I_{O'Y'},$ $I_{O'Z'}$	Corresponding moments of inertia about axes parallel with O-X, O-Y, O-Z	l_f	Moment arm of aerodynamic centre of fin plus rudder about CG
		l_f	Moment arm of foreplane **ac** about CG
i_s	Tail stabiliser incidence	l_r	Moment arm of centroid of unshielded area of rudder about CG
i_w	Wing incidence		
		l_r	Moment arm of rear plane **ac** about CG
J	Joule	l_s	Distance to aerodynamic centre of stabiliser from **ac** of wing
J	Polar moment of inertia (polar second moment of area of a section)	l'_s	Distance between **ac** of aeroplane and **ac** of wing
J	Propeller advance ratio	$\bar{l}_{pb}, \bar{l}_{pw}, \bar{l}_\zeta$	Rolling moment coefficients in a spin
K	Control response factor	$l_p, l_r, l_v, l_\zeta, l_\xi$	Rolling moment coefficient derivatives
K	Induced (vortex) drag factor $1/e$		
K	(Maximum stress in skin)/(Hoop stress due to cut out)	M	Mach number
		M_{crit}	Critical Mach number
K	Overturning coefficient	M_c	Cruise Mach number
KE_{bit}	Increment of kinetic energy	M_t	Mach number of propeller blade tip
K_n	Static margin (stick-fixed)	MP	Manoeuvre point stick fixed
K_p	Factor of increased dynamic pressure q_p/q	MP¹	Manoeuvre point stick free
		M	Bending moment

Symbol	Meaning	Symbol	Meaning
M	Momentum	p	Rate of roll about O-X axis
M	Pitching moment (usually about O-X axis	p	Section form factor
		p	Static pressure at nozzle of jet engine
M	Total mass of a body, w/g	p	Stress
Mac	Pitching moment about aerodynamic centre	$p_{average}$	Average static pressure
		p_{peak}	Peak static pressure
$MacB$	Moment coefficient about **ac** of bottom of biplane	p_{ref}	Reference pressure (of sound)
		p_a	Atmospheric pressure
$MacT$	Moment coefficient about **ac** of top plane of biplane	p_o	Total pressure
		p_1, p_2	Different related static pressures
$Macf$	Pitching moment about **ac** of foreplane	P_∞	Free stream static pressure (far from a body)
$Macr$	Pitching moment about **ac** of rearplane		
$Macs$	Pitching moment about **ac** of stabiliser	$\bar{p}$	Specific weight (jet engine)
$Macw$	Pitching moment about **ac** of wing when it is necessary to make a distinction	Q	Magnitude of gyroscopic couple due to propeller
M_{CG}	Pitching moment about centre of gravity	q	Dynamic pressure
m	Metre	q	Pitch rate about O-X axis
m	Form factor for body profile in elevation	q	Shear stress at some radius from torsional axis of a section
m	Mass element		
m	Slope of a tangent to C_D/C_L^2 curve	q_s	Dynamic pressure at stabiliser (tail)
m	Trail, horizontal distance between **CG** and main wheel axle	q_w	Dynamic pressure in wake at some point w, displaced from mean line of wake
m_a	Mass of air		
$\dot{m}_a$	dm_a/dt, air mass flow rate	q_{wm}	Mean line dynamic pressure within wake
m_b	Mass of control surface mass balance	q_{ws}	Dynamic pressure at leading edge of stabiliser (tail), bathed in wake
m_e	Elevation gear ratio		
m_t	Trim tab gear ratio	q_∞	Free stream dynamic pressure (far from a body)
m_w	Mass of wing		
m_η	Mass of control surface (eg, elevator) while m_ξ applies to aileron, (see Table 2-7 for other suffices)	R	Reynolds number
		R	Braking force
		R	Gas constant
Δm	Increment of mass	R	Radius of curvature of neutral axis of a structural member
N	Newton		
NP	Neutral point	R	Radius of path around which circulation is measured
NP	Neutral point (stick fixed)		
NP[1]	Neutral point (stick free)	R	Reacting force
N	Number of primary feathers for constant spanwise lift coefficient along a bird's wing	R	Range
		R	Resultant crossforce
		R	Structural resistance (reaction) to aerodynamic input
N	Number of propeller blades		
N	Ultimate load factor	R	Hydrodynamic resistance
N	Yawing moment about O-Z axis	R	Tangential (braking) force between wheel and ground
$Np, Nr, Nv, N_\zeta, N_\xi$	Yawing moment derivatives		
		R_A	Ratio of stabiliser aspect ratio to wing aspect ratio, As/A
n	Factor by which equivalent parasite area f_b is multiplied to account for effect of landing gear		
		$\bar{R}$	Specific air range
		r	Radius
n	Factor indicating the increase in take off distance due to surface condition	r	Radius of centre of pressure of propeller blade about shaft centre line
n	Factor measuring the effect of configuration upon service ceiling	r	Radius of a stressed fibre element from torsional axis of a section
n	Normal load factor (gust and manoeuvre)	r	Yaw rate (about O-Z axis)
n	Service ceiling factor	r_d	Duct radius (propulsor)
n	Propeller revolutions per minute		
n	Wheel base	SMC	Standard mean chord, $\bar{c}$
n_a	Applied centripetal acceleration	S	Area of a propeller blade
$n_p, n_r, n_v, n_\zeta, n_\xi$	Yawing moment coefficient derivatives	S	Wing area
		S_{flap}	Area of flap (control) surface aft of hinge
n_1, n_2, n_3	Load factors	S_{horn}	Area of control horn balance
P	Power, rated power	S_{het}	Wing planform area outside line of body
P	Stick force	S_{nose}	Area of nose of fuselage ahead of wing **ac**
$Pmin$	Minimum power	S_B	Area of bottom plane of biplane
Pe	Power expressed in FPSR units	S_T	Area of top plane of biplane
$Pe(climb)$	Power for climb in FPSR units	S_T	Crude sum of total area of vertical and horizontal tail services
Pt	Thrust horsepower, THP		
p	Body section form factor	S_d	Projected area of duct (propulsor)
p	(Lift coefficient of top plane)/(Lift coefficient of bottom plane), C_{LT}/C_{LB}	S_f	Area of fin-plus-rudder
		S_f	Area of foreplane

Symbol	Meaning	Symbol	Meaning
S_r	Area of rearplane	V_1	Decision speed on take off
S_r	Unshielded area of rudder alone	V_2	Take off safety speed
S_s	Stabiliser area	V	True airspeed velocity
S_s	Unshielded area of rudder (fin) and rear fuselage	Va	Aquaplaning speed
S_w	Wing area when it is necessary to make a distinction	Vi	Indicated airspeed
		$Vimd$	IAS for minimum drag
		$Vimp$	IAS for minimum power
S_η	Area of elevator aft of hinge line	$Vimax(v/d)$	TAS for max speed/drag ratio
S_ξ	Aileron area aft of hinge line.	$Vimax(v/p)$	TAS for max speed/power ratio
s	Semi span of a wing surface, $b/2$	V_J	Jet velocity relative to engine
s	Take off distance, TOD	Vmd	TAS for minimum drag
s_F	Landing distance from 50 ft (15 m) screen	Vmp	TAS for minimum power
s_G	Deceleration distance on ground	Vp	Final propeller wash velocity
s_1	Ground run on take off	V_∞	Velocity of free stream (far from a body)
s_2	Transition distance on take off	$\bar{V}_f$	Volume coefficient of foreplane
s_3	Distance over ground covered in initial climb to defined screen (obstacle)	$\bar{V}_f$	Sometimes used as another form of fin volume coefficient where $\bar{V}_f = \frac{1}{2}\bar{V}_\zeta$
s_{50}	Distance between 50 ft (15 m) screen and touchdown	$\bar{V}_r$	Rearplane volume coefficient (usually the same as Vs)
		$\bar{V}_s$	Stabiliser (tail) volume coefficient
T	Temperature	$\bar{V}_v$	Vee-tail volume coefficient
T	Time (dimensional analysis)	$\bar{V}_\zeta$	Fin (and rudder) volume coefficient
T	Torque	$\bar{V}_\xi$	Aileron volume coefficient
t	Thickness, of an aerofoil section ('structural' thickness)	v	Impulsive velocity imparted to air mass by a propeller
t	Time usually in seconds	v	Increased incremental velocity imparted to air by propeller
t/c	Thickness ratio of root section	v	Linear velocity (also along O-Y axis)
t_1, t_2 etc	Different, related, ambient temperatures	v	Maximum velocity of descent (impact with ground)
u, ui	Airspeed of vertical gust (used by some other sources)	v	Sideslip velocity
u	Linear velocity (along O-X axis)	v	Velocity along O-Y axis
		v_c	Rate of climb
V	Target threshold (over the hedge) speed	v_d	Rate of descent in FPSR units
V_A	Design manoeuvring speed	v_1, v_2 etc	Different related gas volumes
V_{ATO}	Target threshold speed all engines working		
V_{AT_1}	Target threshold speed, one engine inoperative (and so on for V_{AT_2})	W	Watt
		W	Weight (of aircraft)
V_{app}	Approach speed	W_a	Weight of airflow
V_B	Design speed for maximum gust intensity	W_{DI}	De-icing system weight
V_C	Design cruising speed	W_E	Weight of engine
V_D	Design diving speed	W_E	Zero fuel weight (useable fuel gone)
V_{DF}	Demonstrated flight during speed	W_{ES}	Weight of electrical system
V_F	Flap limiting speed	W_{Fuel}	Fuel weight
V_{FE}	Maximum flap extended speed	W_F	Fuselage (and hull) weight
V_{LE}	Maximum landing gear extend speed	W_{FC}	Flying control system weight
V_{LO}	Maximum landing gear operating speed	W_{FE}	Weight of fixed equipment
V_{MCA}	Minimum control speed in flight	W_{FEI}	Weight of flight and engine instruments
V_{MCG}	Minimum control speed on ground	W_{FO}	Weight of fuel-plus-oil systems
V_{MO}	Maximum operating speed	W_{FP}	Weight of fuel pumps, cocks, pipes
V_{NE}	Never exceed speed	W_{FS}	Weight of fuel system alone
V_{NO}	Maximum structural cruising speed	W_{HP}	Weight of hydraulic and pneumatic systems
V_R	Rotation speed when incidence is increased for lift off	W_{Misc}	Miscellaneous weight
V_{REF}	An American term more or less the same as VAT	W_{Nac}	Nacelle weight
		W_{Nc}	Nav/comm equipment weight
V_{RMS}	Root mean speed during take-off run	W_n	Load on nose wheel
V_S	Stall speed	W_n	Weight of any component, n
V_{S_1}	Stall speed for a particular configuration	W_{oil}	Weight of oil
V_{S_0}	Stall or minimum flight speed in landing configuration	W_o	Gross or all up weight
		W_{Pay}	Payload weight
V_{SSE}	Intentional one engine inoperative speed	W_p	Powerplant weight
V_{US}	Unstick speed (seaplane) but exchangeable with lift off speed (V_{LO}) if preferred	W_{PF}	Weight of paint and finish
		W_{PFC}	Weight of powered flying controls
V_X	Best angle of climb speed	W_{RE}	Weight of removeable equipment
V_Y	Best rate of climb speed	W_{Sys}	Toal weight of systems
V_{YSE}	Best rate of climb speed with engine failure	W_{Tank}	Fuel tank weight
		W_T	Weight of tail surfaces

Symbol	Meaning	Symbol	Meaning
W_u	Undercarriage (landing gear) weight	α	Geometric angle of attack of wing
W_w	Wing group weight	α	Propeller blade angle of attack
W_η	Weight of control surface (eg, elevator, but see Table 2-7 for other suffixes)	α_{eff}	Effective angle of attack
$\dot{W}_a$	dWa/dt, rate at which a given weight of air, Wa is flowing	α_i	Induced angle of attack
		α_l, α_r	Angles of attack of left and right wing
w	Maximum width of fuselage nose ahead of wing ac	α_s	Stabiliser angle of attack
w	Linear velocity (along O-Z axis), downwash velocity	α_{si}	Stabiliser setting angle
		$\Delta\alpha_{sw}$	Tail damping contribution due to change in angle of attack when pitching
w	Semi thickness of wake	$\Delta\alpha_{s\eta}$	Change in effective angle of attack of stabiliser with elevator deflected
w	Wing loading		
w	Velocity along O-Z axis (eg gust)	α_w	Wing angle of attack when it is necessary to make a distinction from α
w_{ac}	Downwash at aerodynamic centre of wing	α_{zl}	Zero lift angle of attack
		α_o	Angle of attack for infinite aspect ratio
$\overline{w}$	Specific weight of piston or turbo-prop engine	α_{09}	Angle of attack for 0.9 C_{Lmax}
		β	Angle of attack of fin
X	Force in direction O-X	β	Deadrise angle
X_ξ	Aileron drag	β	Propeller pitch angle
x	Distance measured horizontally or along the O-X axis	β	Tab deflection
		β_o	Tab datum setting
x	Unknown quantity		
x_n	Moment arm of component, n, about CG	Γ	Average or general strength of circulation
x_s	Distance from hinge (pivot) to ac of stabilator	Γ_o	Theoretical maximum circulation in the plane of symmetry
$x_{1.2....n}$	Distances from O-X axis	$\pm\gamma$	Angle of flight path to horizontal climb (positive), glide (negative)
x	Moment arm of centre of gravity about O-Z or O'-Z' axis	γ	Dihedral angle of tailplane
$\overline{x}$	Moment arm of lift about CG	γ	Helix angle of flight path in a spin
		γ	Ratio of specific heats at constant pressure and volume
Y	Force in direction O-Y		
Y	Height of equivalent plane of biplane above bottom plane	γ_{min}	Minimum angle of glide
$Yp, Yr, Yv,$		Δ	An increment change in a quantity (eg, $\Delta C_L, \Delta\alpha$)
Y_ζ, Y_ξ	Side force derivatives		
y	Distance of element (of mass) measured normal to the plane of symmetry	δ	Correction factor for induced drag due to wing planform
y	Distance of stressed element from neutral axis of a section	δ	Total deflection of tyre and shock absorber
y	Height of tailplane above fin-fuselage junction at the fin ¼ chord (see also Z)	δ	Trim angle of seaplane hull
		δ_{leg}	Deflection of undercarriage shock absorber leg
y_n	Lateral moment arm of component, n, offset from CG	δ_{tyre}	Deflection of tyre
$y_p, y_r, y_v,$		δ_c	Profile drag factor for (flapchord)/(wing + flap) chord
y_ζ, y_ξ	Sideforce coefficient derivatives		
y_ξ	Moment arm of aileron centroid about CG	δ_s	Profile drag factor for (flapped wing area)/(total wing area)
$\overline{v}$	Moment arm of centre of gravity about O-X axis	δ_β	Profile drag factor for flap deflection
		ϵ	Angle of downwash
ZLL	Zero lift line	ϵ	Damping coefficient in a spin
Z	Force in direction O-Z	ϵ_f	Angle of upwash at foreplane due to rearplane
Z	Roll damping force		
Z	Height of tailplane above, or below, fuselage-fin junction (see also y)	ϵ_p	Angle of downwash in propwash (slipstream)
Z_D	Moment arm of drag about CG	ϵ_t	Angle of downwash at tailplane (or rearplane) due to wing or foreplane
Z_F	Moment arm of thrust about CG		
$Z_p, Z_r, Z_v,$			
Z_ζ, Z_ξ	Force derivatives in direction O-Z	ζ	Rudder deflection
z	Distance measured in direction O-Z		
z	Length of semi-minor axis of ellipse	η	Efficiency of a process
z_D	Moment arm of drag about CG	η	Efficiency of propeller
z_F	Moment of thrust about CG	η	Efficiency of undercarriage leg plus tyre as a shock absorber
z_n	Moment arm of component, n, above or below CG	η	Elevator deflection
$z_p, z_r, z_v, z_\zeta z_\xi$	Normal force coefficient derivatives	η_{leg}	Efficiency of undercarriage leg as a shock absorber
z	Vertical moment arm of centre of gravity about O-X or O'-X' axis	η_{tyre}	Efficiency of tyre as a shock absorber

Symbol	Meaning	Symbol	Meaning
η_{max}	Theoretical maximum efficiency of propeller	ν	Coefficient of kinematic viscosity, μ/ρ
η_f	Foreplane (canard) efficiency	ν_0	Coefficient of kinematic viscosity at sea level, ISA
η_m	Efficiency of a mechanical process (eg, mechanical efficiency of engine)	ξ	Aileron deflection
η_p	Overall propulsive efficiency		
η_s	Stabiliser (tail) efficiency	π	(Circumference/diameter) of a circle $\approx 3.141593\ldots$
η_t	'Internal' thermal efficiency of engine		
$\bar{\eta}$	'Ideal' Froude efficiency		
θ	Angle of pitch	ρ	Ambient density of air
θ	Angle of rake of landing gear	ρ_0	Density of air at sea level, ISA
θ	Angle of twist of an element, or a section due to an applied torque	σ	Relative density, ρ/ρ_0
θ	Half-vertex angle of a cone	σ	Increment in downwash angle for a biplane compared with a monoplane
θ_v	Angle of wing tilt in a spin		
κ	$\Delta C_{Hmech}/\Delta C_L$: a factor of proportionality	τ	Aerofoil section thickness ratio
		τ	Correction factor for induced angle of attack due to wing planform
$()_\kappa$	Term affected by $\Delta C_{Hmech}/\Delta C_L$	τ	Time for one acoustic (pressure) cycle
Λ	Angle of wing sweep		
λ	Rotational term contributing to anti-spin moment coefficient	ϕ	Angle of bank
		ϕ	Included angle of bevelled trailing edge
λ	1/Scale	ϕ	Propeller helix angle
λ	Taper ratio: (tip chord/root chord)		
λ	Term used when calculating effect of body in a spin	χ_1	A variable function affecting the static margin, stick-free, $H^1{}_n$
λ	Wave length		
λ_b	Flap span factor	ψ	Angle of yaw (general notation)
λ_c	Flap chord factor	ψ_1	A variable function affecting the static margin, stick-fixed, H_n
λ_β	Flap deflection factor		
μ	Braking coefficient	Ω	Rate of rotation about spin axis
μ	Coefficient of rolling friction	Ω_1	Rate of propeller rotation
μ	Dynamic viscosity	Ω_2	Rate of pitch or yaw of propeller disc
μ	(Shorter span)/(longer span) of biplane		
μ^1	Thrust specific fuel consumption	ω	Angular velocity (or rate) of rotation
μ_1	Longitudinal relative aircraft density		

Equivalent Anglo-American terms

English	American
accelerate-stop	— RTO (rejected takeoff)
aerobatics	— acrobatics
aeroplane	— airplane
airworthiness requirements BCAR	— FAR
allowable deficiency	— no-go item, despatch deviation or
	— minimum equipment item
amateur-built	— homebuilt
boost pressure	— manifold pressure
coaming	— glareshield
clamshells	— buckets
compressor	— spool
EAS	— CAS (at sea level only)
engine acceleration	— spool-up
flick roll	— snap roll
inter-com	— inter-phone
Mach trimmer	— pitch-trim compensator
maximum continuous	— METO (maximum except take-off; piston
	— engines only
microlight (or minimum aircraft)	— ultralight
relight	— flight start
spectacles	— yoke
tailplane	— stabiliser
throttle	— thrust lever
undercarriage	— gear
unstick	— lift-off
V_{AT}	— Vref

A comprehensive source of terms is to be found in: Gunston, W. (1980) *Jane's Aerospace Dictionary*. London: Jane's Publishing Company Limited.

Acknowledgements

I am indebted to a large number of people who, either personally or through organisations, have given me guidance, advice, photographs, information and connections, or who have helped by kicking ideas around. Among them are: the late Andy J. Coombe, also Desmond Norman, Managing Director, and Terence Boughton, *NDN Aircraft Limited*; Newton F. Harrison DSO AFC; Harold Best-Devereux; Gus A. Limbach; Professor L. F. Crabtree, past President, *Royal Aeronautical Society*; Professors Dennis Howe and John J. Spillman, *College of Aeronautics*, Cranfield; Professor Luigi Pascale, *Partenavia*; Dr James Henderson; T. H. Kerr, Director, *Royal Aircraft Establishment*, Farnborough, for advice on spinning; Dr Bruce J. Holmes, *National Aeronautics and Space Administration*, Langley, for advice on spinning and agricultural aviation research; H. H. B. M. Thomas, for advice on controls; Dr R. K. Nangia and Jim Fletcher, for advice on forward swept wings; Hanno Fischer, Technical Director, *Rhein Flugzeugbau GmbH*; J. Lynn Helms (qualified test pilot), Administrator, *Federal Aviation Administration*; John A. Bagley, *Imperial Science Museum*, London; Arnold W. L. Nayler, Librarian, and G. R. (Tim) Wrixon, *Royal Aeronautical Society*; Dennis Goode, Chief Librarian, and Brian Kervell, *Royal Aircraft Establishment*, Farnborough; Norman Grossman, Chairman, *Fairchild Republic Company*; Dieter König; Noel Penny and Bob W. Chevis, *Noel Penny Turbines Limited*; David Lockspeiser; John Monnett; A. J. Greenhalgh; David P. Davies, past Head of Flight Department, and Gordon Corps, past Chief Test Pilot, Paul White, John R. W. Smith, R. A. Nesbitt-Dufort, Les Bramhall, Graham Skillen, Bob Page, Bill Horsley, W. H. Winyard, the late Dave Morgan, Airworthiness Division, *Civil Aviation Authority*; Dr Pawez Kumar; Don I. Burns; Tony Bianchi; Peter D. Chappell, David J. Mitchell, both of *Engineering Sciences Data Unit*; Mike Ramsden, Editor-in-Chief, Roger Bacon, Cliff Barnett and Ian Parker of *Flight International*; Vivian H. Bellamy (professional builder of replica aircraft); Ian Senior, Chairman, and Philip Meeson, *British Aerobatic Association*; Pat Miller, Bill Bowker and Ladislav C. Marmol, for advice on agricultural aviation; A. J. E. Perkins; Peter J. Bish; Harald Penrose; Lloyd R. Jenkinson; Rolf H. Wild; Martin Simons; Freddy To; Dennis Fowler; Bob Cleary; Mike J. Searle; Spencer Flack; Alain Ernoult; Bill Bonner; Charles A. Mendenhall; T. C. Warren; John Hall; Dennis W. Stevens and George E. Woodley, *Ciba-Geigy*; Steve Wittman (veteran racing pilot and designer extraordinary); Ray Hegy (veteran propeller craftsman); Len Houston; Eric Barker; R. Frost; Bob Wilson and Peter Ward, *Pilatus Britten-*

Norman Limited; Peter E. Peck and Marion J. Dees Jr, *Piper Aircraft Corporation*; Norman Hall-Warren; Ernest E. Stott; John Fricker; George Robson, European Manager, *Garrett International SA*; Paul H. Poberezny, President, and Jack Cox, *Experimental Aircraft Association*; Howard Levy; John W. R. Taylor, Editor, *Jane's All the World's Aircraft*; James Gilbert, Editor, *Pilot Magazine*; Hugh Scanlan, past Editor, *Shell Aviation News*; Professor E. F. Blick; Gordon Bain; Guido F. Pessotti and José Ximenes of *Embraer*; W. B. Silvestri; Mike Archer; C. S. H. Sawyers; George Wrzesien; Gordon Swanborough; John Hall; D. M. T. Ettlinger; David Ogilvy; David Rendel; Steven Dalton; John Barlee; Bill Gunston; John Tweddel; Squadron Leader M. C. Johnson RAF; Jim Bede; Burt Rutan; L. Waters; J. L. Haney; Jack Hulsey; Ed J. Gray; Frank Irving, *Imperial College*, London; three ex RAF Polish pilots Eric Wardzinski, W. L. 'Spud' Potocki DFC, Czesław M. Głowczinski; and retired test pilot Frank Bullen (whose early instruction has saved my neck more than once); two booksellers Jack Beaumont, *Aviation Bookshop*, London, and Dennis A. Collett of *Old House Bookshop, Farnham*; also E. S. Mallett, Director, and H. H. Pearcey, *National Maritime Institute*; and the late Charles Gibbs-Smith, of the Victoria and Albert Museum, and L. E. Schweizer.

I am also grateful to the following organisations: College of Aeronautics, Cranfield; University of Bristol; University of Bath; University of Technology, Loughborough; Partenavia Costruzioni Aeronautiche SpA; Rhein Flugzeugbau; Piper Aircraft Corporation; Pratt & Whitney Aircraft Corporation; Flight International; Imperial Science Museum; Air Replicas International; British Aerobatic Association; British Aerospace; Noel Penny Turbines Limited; National Maritime Institute; Civil Aviation Authority; Federal Aviation Administration; Engineering Sciences Data Unit; National Aeronautics and Space Administration; Royal Aeronautical Society; Experimental Aircraft Association; Personal Plane Services; Lockspeiser Aircraft Limited; Cessna Aircraft Company; Shuttleworth Collection; Natural History Photographic Agency; Imperial College, Department of Aeronautics, London; Bowker Air Services Limited; Miller Aerial Spraying Limited; A. D. S. Aerial Limited; Wytwórnia Sprzętu Komunikacyjnego; Monnet Experimental Aircraft Inc; Lockheed Aircraft Corporation; König Motorenbau KG; Aero Bonner Company Limited; Empresa Brasileira de Aeronautica SA; Thunder Engines Inc; London Express News; The Times; Ayres Corporation; Her Majesty's Stationery Office; Shin Meiwa Industry Co. Ltd; Fairchild Republic Company; NDN Aircraft Limited; Air Touring Services Limited; Viking Aircraft; Ciba-Geigy Plastics and Additives Company; Pilatus Britten-Norman Limited; British Aerobatic Association; Thunder Wings; Rolls-Royce (UK) Limited; Avco Lycoming; Teledyne Continental; Alcor Aviation Limited; Dowty Rotol Limited; Garrett Corporation; Schweizer Aircraft Corporation; Hang Gliding; Dover Publications Inc; Westland Aircraft Limited; Pilot Magazine.

Finally, I must thank Sally Jones, June Hay and my wife Jacqueline, without whose efforts this book would not have come together.

SECTION I

INTRODUCTION

CHAPTER 1

Airworthiness the Object

'Safety begins in the mind of an aircraft designer.'
Quoted by J. M. Ramsden in *The Safe Airline*.

'Safe=airworthy=meeting the requirements.'
David P. Davies, formerly Chief Test Pilot, Airworthiness Division of the Civil Aviation
Authority.

Whether we want to buy an aeroplane, or design and build one of our own (which is
one reason for picking this book off the shelf), we cannot simply leap into the air when
the time comes, and take flight. Certain tough formalities must be observed which flow
from and are backed by the law, not least of which is the matter of determining the
airworthiness of the aircraft in some degree.

Clearly airworthiness implies a certain level of safety, like saying that a ship is
seaworthy, and it takes little forethought to realise that there must be some yardstick
against which airworthiness can be assessed. We might start with a general, all-
embracing design requirement: 'An aeroplane shall be designed and built to fly safely.'
Unfortunately we cannot then dust our hands and get on with the job, believing that in
one swipe we have got rid of government and other official interference and struck a
blow for freedom. Our trouble has only just begun.

Think, for one moment, about the legal questions that might follow such a bald
statement after a subsequent accident. It needs expanding, ideally to leave no
questions.

Another attempt leaves questions too – and notice qualifying, conditional words
creeping in:

'An aeroplane shall be demonstrated to be able to take off, climb, fly a given distance
and manoeuvre while carrying a specified load, within a previously defined airspace,
by an appropriately licensed pilot, without becoming uncontrollable, or unduly tiring
to fly. The probability of catastrophic failure due to structural or mechanical causes
shall be significantly less than once in ten million (1 in 10^7) flights.'

Some of the questions raised are:

☐ What is the type of load and is it private or commercial (i.e. carried for hire and
reward)?
☐ What is the type of flight, eg, visual or instrument, by day or by night?
Is the aircraft to operate from land, water, or both?

☐ What are the required minimum take-off and landing distances and at what altitudes and ambient temperatures (changes in which affect achieved performance)?

☐ How shall the climb be specified: as a rate or as a gradient (to avoid obstacles), and at what weight, altitude and ambient temperature?

☐ What headwind, tailwind and crosswind conditions must be met?

☐ What are the manoeuvre criteria?

☐ What are the control criteria?

☐ What provisions must be made to enable the pilot to release the controls in flight without consequent loss of control?

☐ If the aircraft is to fly a specified distance, at what speed should it fly and what fuel reserves are needed?

☐ What departures in speed and deviations from flight path might be tolerated, in all phases of flight, without undue risk of structural and mechanical failure?

To answer such questions we need airworthiness requirements of various kinds, some governing performance, others, control, stability, trimmability, structural and mechanical design, minimum equipment, minimum crew and a host of other things. What is more, our answers will involve the introduction of more qualifying and conditional weasel-words to satisfy lawyers; and the questions will continue to proliferate.

What is airworthiness?

According to *The Oxford English Dictionary*, **worthy** corresponds with the worth of, i.e., appropriateness, suitability, or fitness for use (in flight, within our context, which starts and ends on the ground: from chock to chock). So an aircraft that is airworthy is one fit for use in the way it was designed and built to fly. This brings up the most difficult question: 'What if there is an accident – how then shall airworthiness be *shown* to have been proved?' That is no academic question. It might become necessary to prove one day that a design was safe when it was certificated, or that it conformed with its type in series production or after maintenance had been carried out. It is the worry of everyone who, having had some say in the decision to underwrite the airworthiness of an aircraft, later has to justify the action, possibly on oath in court. The question is not eased by increasing experience and modern technology. One has only to look at the aftermath of a flying accident to appreciate the value of proving airworthiness in the eyes of the lawyer's 'reasonable man' (i.e., a no-nonsense chap sitting on top of a Clapham bus). Product liability (which determines what compensation must be given to victims when something we have produced fails) and its associated legislation has an increasing influence upon our lives. A claim for contributory negligence in the United States can be devastating (more easily so than in Britain, where the courts appear to require greater proof of negligence). Early in 1976 an American aviation attorney, Harry A. Wilson, was reported as saying that manufacturers have a duty to ensure that their customers are competent to handle their products. It would follow that provision of such assured competence could cause manufacturers' legal defence costs to rise from around six to fifteen per cent or more in future, increasing considerably the cost of an aircraft to be passed on to the customer.

There is no relaxation of standards in sight, and anyone concerned with flying has to appreciate that the law and regulation is here to stay. One reason for this chapter is to tell you how to fit in with the system to your own advantage, instead of bucking it, which is counter-productive.

The matter of airworthiness is rather like the filling in a sandwich; the law on one side, the owner/operator on the other. It is rarely appreciated that the process of certification, which causes so much grief (especially for many British applicants who have to pay money when seeking certificates of airworthiness for their aircraft), is both a buffer for them and a shield against law which is weighty and sharp-edged.

With certain exceptions, covered by procedures that need not be mentioned yet, no civil aircraft is allowed to fly over the United Kingdom unless it holds a valid certificate of airworthiness issued by the country of its registration. British law is stated in the *Air Navigation Order 1976* (ref. 1.1), which is a statute of parliament, administered (and sometimes changed by) the Civil Aviation Authority (the powers of which are bestowed by the Civil Aviation Act 1971). It says: 'An aircraft shall not fly unless there is in force in respect thereof a certificate of airworthiness duly issued or rendered valid under the law of the country in which the aircraft is registered, and any conditions subject to which the certificate was issued or rendered valid are complied with.' In short, a certificate of airworthiness (generally called a C of A) is a form of passport to sovereign airspace. Without one flight is illegal unless certain other conditions have been complied with. Illegal flight without a C of A might invalidate insurance cover in the event of an accident.

A certificate of airworthiness does not give us the right to fly in the airspace of other countries without their consent. A C of A must be issued by a member state of the International Civil Aviation Organisation (ICAO), in compliance with Annex 8 to the Chicago Convention, before it can be assumed that it will be acceptable to other member states for flight in their airspace.

To be awarded a certificate of airworthiness an aircraft must be demonstrated to be airworthy. Airworthiness can be defined as 'the contribution made by the aircraft itself to the safety of the flight when the pilot has been removed from the man–machine loop'. It is concerned with those aspects of design, construction, maintenance and the provision of all related limitations and essential information which together determine fitness for flight. Thus, a C of A is awarded to an aircraft and its equipment, although under certain circumstances the award may also be conditional upon the aircraft being operated under the control of certain named persons or perhaps just one individual.

Airworthiness is directly proportional to the safety inherent in an aircraft and its equipment, and to the accuracy of the supporting information and limitations given to the pilot who has the job of managing the flight. Safety can never be 100 per cent. For example, in the early 1950s the fatal accident rate for public transport aeroplanes was about 1 in 50000 flights (ref. 1.2). In the late 1970s it was one twentieth of that figure. So, using airworthiness terminology, the passenger can be told that the risk of being involved is one in one million, or 10^{-6} (which is the shorthand way of writing one divided by ten multiplied by itself six times). Other ways of expressing risk are in terms of fatal accidents per 100000 flying hours. A survey carried out in 1978 showed that in General Aviation, which is that part of aviation other than the civil airlines and military, the fatality rates were: Australia, about 1.7 per 100000 hours; New Zealand, 2.4 per 100000 hours; Britain, 3 per 100000 hours; and the USA, 2.1 per 100000 hours. The Australians flew double the British hours but had half their fatality rate. The Americans flew fifty-five times more than the British but had two thirds of the British fatality rate.

An aeroplane does not have to be 100 per cent safe to be airworthy. The acceptable rate is commensurate with its job. One expects a wide-body airliner to be safer than a crop-sprayer. The definition of an acceptable level of risk for each operation has been a matter of subjective judgement for a long time. It is related to what the public, excited by the press and broadcasting, can stand. Thus, the loss of a big jet with all of nearly three hundred passengers is no more nor less disturbing in the late 1970s than was the loss of the airship Hindenburg in the early 1930s in which two thirds of the relatively small number of passengers survived (although this is rarely mentioned).

The effort put into the manufacture of an aircraft takes time and skill to make it safe, and both are expensive. In Britain the applicant for a certificate of airworthiness has to pay the cost. In the rest of the world, without exception known to the author, the cost of certification is borne out of public funds. The British have to thank Winston Churchill (doyen of national pride and enterprise) for that state of affairs. The British industry regulates itself and pays the price of self-regulation because Winston Churchill said during a debate in parliament on the air estimates, around 1919, that aviation had come of age and should 'fly by itself'.

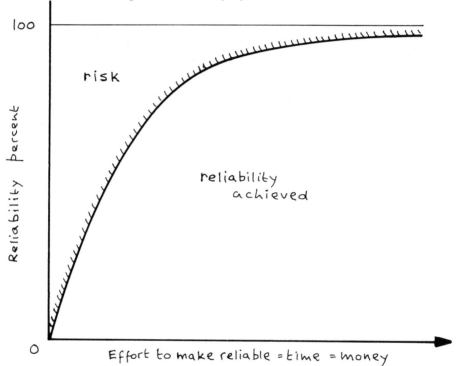

Fig. 1.1   Reliability in terms of effort, its cost and the Law of Diminishing Returns.

Effort is subject to the law of diminishing returns, as shown in fig. 1.1 in which reliability is taken as a measure of airworthiness. No matter how hard we try, we never quite reach 100 per cent reliability and zero risk. As a practical indication of this, since 1973 the author has kept statistics of the number of British light aeroplanes found to be fit for renewals of Cs of A when the engineers who had worked on them for repairs and maintenance considered them to be so. The result over seven years has been one in nine. This is not the fault of the engineers; there are many factors, and engineers are only one. This result is a consequence of what can be afforded.

If we redraw fig. 1.1 to show risk against effort we obtain fig. 1.2. At each end of the curve we may draw regions of financial reality. Too little effort = too low reliability = exceptionally high insurance premium (if a company can be found to provide cover). Too much costly effort and the applicant goes out of business or turns his attention to ways of ducking his legal obligations.

British certification (ref. 1.3)

As long as an aircraft does not weigh more than 12 500 lb (5 700 kg) it may be operated as a public transport by one pilot. In this book we concentrate upon such one-pilot aeroplanes, even though a second pilot's seat may have been provided. If there is no intention to carry passengers, certain aircraft heavier than 12 500 lb may be certificated for operation by one pilot.

A certificate of airworthiness is *not* needed for flights beginning and ending in Britain (and avoiding foreign airspace) if they involve:

☐ A glider, not operating as a public transport.
☐ A balloon, not operating as a public transport.
☐ A kite.

An aircraft flying under the following (ref. 1.1):
'*A' Conditions*, which allow an aircraft, which has no valid C of A, to fly to qualify for the issue or renewal of the certificate, or for approval of modifications, or of anything else needed to make the machine fit for certification;
'*B' Conditions*, which cover flights made under the supervision of an organisation approved for certification purposes by the Civil Aviation Authority.
An aircraft flying in accordance with the conditions of a *Permit to Fly*, issued by the Civil Aviation Authority.

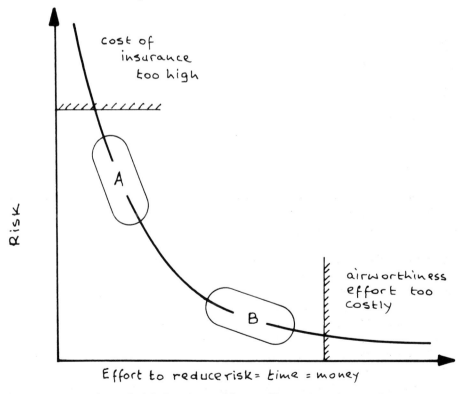

Fig. 1.2   Reduction of risk by airworthiness effort takes time and costs money. Amateur-built aircraft, A, although involving higher risk than public transport aircraft, B, are acceptable as long as they are limited by the conditions of the certificate of airworthiness, or permit to fly, to flight over less populated areas.

Categories of certificate

Every aircraft with a C of A is categorised, those grossing less than 6000 lb (2730 kg) being replaced in one of the following:

☐ *Transport* (valid for three years): any purpose.
☐ *Aerial work* (valid for three years): aerial work only (e.g., agricultural use).
☐ *Private* (valid for three years): any purpose other than the above.
☐ *Special* (valid for one year): any purpose other than public transport/aerial work, but excluding passenger-carrying unless expressly permitted.

A Permit to Fly (which carries no burden of airworthiness, but which implies that the level of risk is acceptable) is issued annually and normally is given to homebuilts, or military and vintage aircraft for which there are flight-time and utilisation limits, more often than not. The Special Category applies to 'odd' aircraft such as those not built to internationally agreed airworthiness standards and some embodying glued timber. Any privately owned aeroplane that does not meet Permit to Fly or Special Category crtiteria has to be certificated in the Transport, Aerial Work or Private categories.

Maintenance schedules

Aircraft operating in the Transport, Aerial Work and Private categories have to be maintained to a schedule approved by the Civil Aviation Authority (CAA). Two have been produced by the CAA, one for aeroplanes and the other for rotary-winged machines. The Authority is prepared to approve independently submitted schedules. The following intervals for checks have been set for each airworthiness category:

☐ *Transport and Aerial Work:*
    Check A: To be carried out before the first flight of every day.
    50 hour: At periods not exceeding fifty hour flying or sixty-two days, whichever is the sooner, and to be signed for by an appropriately licensed engineer.
    100 hour: No calendar time limits. To be signed for as above.
    Annual: No limitations to flying time. It can be anticipated by up to sixty-two days without affecting the next yearly check date. To be signed for as above.
☐ *Private:* The schedule is broadly similar to the Transport and Aerial work categories, with an important and useful exception: a fifty hour check may be carried out by an owner or an operator of an aircraft who is a licensed pilot.
☐ *Special Category and Permit to Fly:* Maintenance to an approved schedule is not required, but owners have to show that their aircraft are maintained in airworthy condition. Revised logbooks have been introduced by the CAA and checks must be recorded. A Certificate of Compliance is needed whenever mandatory inspections, overhauls, repairs and replacements have been carried out.

Renewal procedures

For Transport, Aerial work and Private Category Cs of A the renewal is based upon a review of the aircraft and its maintenance records during a *Star Inspection* by a nominated person in a suitably approved organisation. The amount of work involved depends on the standard of maintenance kept up during the life of the C of A.

    Renewal of the C of A in the Special Category involves a package of work agreed after an inspection by a licensed engineer or CAA-approved organisation, supported by an examination by a CAA surveyor.

For a Permit to Fly a survey of the aircraft is carried out either by a CAA surveyor or one of the approved organisations.

Gliders operated at British Gliding Association (BGA) sites fly with certificates or permits issued after recommendations have been made by an inspector of the BGA. Motor gliders which fit the *Redhill Definition (1969)* shown in table 1-1 are treated as gliders. Those which do not are regarded as aeroplanes and as such are subject to the categorisation and procedures given above. Glider tugs operated by clubs fly with Private Cs of A.

At a count taken in 1980 there were about 4 800 light aircraft under 6 000 lb (2 730 kg) gross weight on the British Register – roughly 70 per cent of the total of 6 800 in the country. Nearly 80 per cent of the aeroplanes on the Register, 5 300, weighed less than 12 500 lb (5 700 kg) and fit within the scope of this book. Around 700 of the aeroplanes were light twins. Amateur or homebuilt aircraft totalled some 450, with perhaps another 300 in various stages of construction. Throughout the recession the number of aircraft coming on to the Register has continued to grow around six to seven per cent per year, although other estimates put growth nearer eleven per cent – and more for turbopropeller twins.

TABLE 1–1

Self-Launching Motor Glider – Redhill Definition (1969)

Maximum Weight	1 650 lb (750 kg)
Maximum Take-Off Distance	2 000 ft (600 m) to 50 ft (15 m) in zero wind
Maximum Rate of Climb	1 000 ft (300 m) in 4 minutes with zero wind
Maximum Stall Speed	40 knots (75 km/h) at maximum weight with Centre of Gravity forward
Minimum Normal Glide Ratio	20:1
Glide Ratio with Spoilers	8:1 or less at $1.4 \times$ stall speed in the relevant configuration
Minimum Wing Span	45 ft (14 m)
Maximum Seats	2
Minimum Power Loading	20 lb (9 kg) per Brake Horsepower
Maximum Fuel	8 Imperial gallons (36 litres) two seat
	6 Imperial gallons (27 litres) single seat

Airworthiness Division of the CAA has no British requirements for self-launching motor-gliders. When needed, resort is made to the airworthiness requirements of the *Organisation Scientifique et Technique du Vol à Voile, Section 5*; or the *Information on Design and Test Specifications* of the *Luftfahrt–Bundesamt*, the Federal German airworthiness authority.

Performance groups

Aeroplanes in the five airworthiness categories given above are further subdivided in terms of minimum required levels of performance:

☐ Group A: Aeroplanes which can continue a flight even though an engine might fail.
☐ Group B: Non-existent.

Plate 1–1 (Top) *Cessna Conquest* (*Garrett TPE 331* turbo-propeller) a miniature fuel-efficient airliner mainly found in Public Transport Category. (*Cessna Aircraft Company, USA*)

☐ Group C: Aeroplanes with a level of performance that enables them to continue a flight with a failed engine, but only after the take-off and initial climb are completed.

☐ Group D: Basically single-engined aeroplanes with no provision for performance if the engine should fail.

☐ Group E: Aeroplanes for which there is limited scheduling of performance. In reality the paperwork is simplified, but the required level of performance is raised in consequence to at least the levels of Groups C or D. For example, Group E aeroplanes are limited to a maximum or gross weight of 6 000 lb (2 730 kg).

Note: Limitations on the minimum speed at the stall are imposed upon Groups D and E aeroplanes, unlike those in other groups.

Most aeroplanes in this book would be in Group D or E, or have no minimum required performance at all, beyond a minimum rate of climb which varies with fixed and retractable landing gear.

Conditions to be satisfied

If we want to design and build an aeroplane for sale in the UK, we must take certain steps, the first and most obvious one being to get in touch with Airworthiness Division of the CAA, either at its headquarters in Redhill, or through the local Area Office under a Surveyor in Charge. If the aeroplane is not to be for sale but is for fun, say, the cheapest route is to approach the *Popular Flying Association* which is an approved organisation empowered to recommend the award of Permits to Fly to aircraft within the limitations of table 1–2. Various organisations exist to help the amateur, and these are listed at the end of this chapter.

Assuming that the aircraft is to be certificated:

☐ The design must be approved by the CAA.

☐ Construction must be of specified (usually 'released') materials, in conformity with the approved design and the workmanship must be to an acceptable inspection standard.

☐ The aeroplane must be fitted with prescribed instruments and equipment to minimum scales quoted in a Schedule of the Air Navigation Order (ref. 1.1).

☐ Engine(s), propeller(s), instruments, equipment and radio must be of approved type and their installations approved.

☐ The aircraft must be weighed, the centre of gravity calculated and the necessary loading information prepared to an approved standard.

☐ A satisfactory demonstration must be made during flight trials that the aircraft is safe for the purpose for which it is intended. The demonstration may also involve a confirmatory test flight by a CAA test pilot.

Plate 1–1 (Upper Middle)   French *Robin HR200/100* which may be found in either the Private or Public Transport categories. (*Author*)

Plate 1–1 (Lower Middle)   Veteran *Bristol F2B* (1916) (designed by F. S. Barnwell (1890–1938) which flies with the *Shuttleworth Collection* on a Permit to Fly). (*Shuttleworth Collection, UK*)

Plate 1–1 (Bottom)   A tricky ex-spoil-of-war lacking much technical information when first brought onto the British Register. Russian *Yakovlev YAK-II* with lively flying qualities – and a bite at the stall – which operates on a Permit to Fly. (*Author*)

A venture of such an enterprising kind usually involves setting up a manufacturing organisation. It will also be necessary to have the organisation approved by the CAA to keep its involvement and certification costs to a minimum. Approval is analogous to establishing credit worthiness with a bank. In this case the Authority satisfies itself that certain responsibilities for design, manufacture and inspection can be delegated within the organisation, so as to keep its own people out of the exercise as much as possible.

TABLE 1–2

Limitations to Popular Flying Association Aeroplanes

Maximum Weight	1 750 lb (800 kg)
Maximum Seats	2
Take-Off Power	125 Brake Horsepower
Maximum Stall Speed	60 mph (52 knots, 96 km/h) with a fully approved engine, or 50 mph (43 knots, 80 km/h) with an unapproved engine

TABLE 1–3

International Definition of a Microlight Aeroplane
(Federation Aeronautique Internationale)

Dry (empty) weight, W	$\triangleright$ 150 kg (330.7 lb)
Maximum seats	2
Wing area	$\triangleleft$ $(W/10)$ m² ($\triangleleft$ $(W\,\mathrm{lb}/2.05)$ ft²)

Relevant airworthiness requirements

Airworthiness standards are published as codes by a number of countries. The two major codes are *British Civil Airworthiness Requirements* (BCARs) published by the Civil Aviation Authority and the US *Federal Aviation Regulations* (FARs) of the Federal Aviation Administration (FAA), the American certificating authority. In general an aircraft designed to meet both codes can be certificated anywhere in the world, because of increasing alignment between them. The sections of British Civil Airworthiness Requirements covering aeroplane design are:

☐ *Section D* which was written originally for aeroplanes of all weights. It is now applicable to Performance Group A machines heavier than 12 500 lb (5 700 kg).

☐ *Section E* applies to gliders in all except the Special Category, and of maximum weight not exceeding 1 500 lb (682 kg). Certification in the Special Category, or for heavier weights, requires consultation between the applicant and the Authority.

☐ *Section K* was written originally for small aeroplanes not exceeding 6 000 lb (2 730 kg) which were simple in conception, design and construction. Its scope was widened later to cover similarly simple types with gross weights up to 12 500 lb (5 700 kg).

Additionally, Section A covers certification and approval procedures, Section C covers engines and propellers, Section J deals with electrical equipment, Section L with licensing, Section N noise and Section R radio equipment.

The Americans have differences of emphasis more than philosophy. Passenger transport is split into three levels: trunk airlines, local service airlines, and commuter and air-taxi. Federal Aviation Regulations (FAR) affecting general aviation are:

- ☐ FAR Part 23 which defines the airworthiness of private and air-taxi aeroplanes lighter than 12 500 lb (5 700 kg).
- ☐ FAR Part 25 defines the airworthiness of public-transport aeroplanes grossing more than 12 500 lb (5 700 kg).
- ☐ FAR Part 135 is the operating regulation laying down standards for air-taxis and commuters.
- ☐ FAR Part 121 specifies air-carrier operating standards.
- ☐ CAB Part 298 is the commercial standard set by the Civil Aeronautics Board (CAB) to govern non-certificated carriers, mainly commuters.

There are profound similarities between the American and British codes which make it attractive for critics to argue at a superficial level that Britain should hoist on board the Federal Aviation Regulations while discarding its own. Either from ignorance, or with deliberation, such critics pay no attention to the differences in the technical and operational experience, their different philosophies and differing laws of each country. While the laws of the United States are in certain respects the children of British laws, there are vast differences in the application of each, and the consequences flowing from them. For example, John V. Brennan, executive vice-president of United Aviation Underwriters Inc., speaking at a Flight Safety Foundation/Federal Bar Association meeting in Washington DC in October 1977 was quoted as saying: 'Product-liability litigation has a positive effect on aviation safety. Aircraft manufacturers today recognise the need to concern themselves with adequate warnings and safe design of their products ... federal regulations pertaining to aviation ... are minimum standards ... It is not necessary to enumerate here those accidents which would not have occurred had the regulatory process been operating as Congress had intended' (ref. 1.4). In Britain product-liability legislation has nothing like the same power through its application, perhaps because British lawyers and insurance underwriters are not yet as aggressive as their colleagues in the United States. British courts have not begun to handle anything like the enormous sums of money involved in damages that are commonplace in America. Instead, Airworthiness Division of the CAA (and the Air Registration Board before it) achieves good husbandry of safety though its own codes and practices with little recourse to law.

A major difference between the American and British systems, which has caused difficulties for applicants for British Cs of A in the past, has been in connection with public transport certification of certain American light aeroplanes. We have reciprocal agreements with the Americans (and with some other nations like the French) whereby we are able to accept many of their certification standards as our own. An exception has been the scheduling of performance needed to meet British air navigation regulations. The result was that many American Flight Manuals, while satisfying FAA regulations, failed to satisfy BCARs. So the Authority found it necessary to publish, for example, an Airworthiness Information Leaflet on the subject (ref. 1.5) telling people the minimum information to be supplied with an aeroplane for classification in Group E. Other sources of additional requirements are published by CAA and FAA (refs. 1.6 and 1.7). Such shortfall, which is a consequence of differences in laws, is being reduced and increasing numbers of American Flight Manuals now satisfy BCARs.

With the growth of the European Economic Community has come the need for a joint airworthiness code, called Joint Airworthiness Requirements (JARs). There is a considerable amount of work to be done and this draws heavily upon the marriage of FARs and BCARs because many European countries, France being a typical example, employ Federal Aviation Regulations as a national airworthiness code.

Cutting British certification and other costs

Anything which reduces the active involvement of Airworthiness Division staff in the certification process cuts its manhours and therefore its costs. Repeatedly, applicants bring increased charges upon their heads through not doing their homework. This book is concerned only with design for airworthy flying qualities, which embrace:

☐ Handling qualities of control, stability and trimmability.
☐ Performance.
Here, we shall not include a third:
☐ Functioning of automatic and other systems to achieve an acceptable level of safety by day or night, possibly in adverse weather conditions, in controlled and restricted airspace.

A pervading factor is the practical design of the cockpit layout, even though it cannot be seen to be an equal part with any of the above. Each factor embraced by the term flying qualities is covered by published requirements. But when dealing with applicants it is evident on too many occasions that they have not taken the trouble to see what lies between the covers of BCAR's. Even so they have the right to ask for the advice of the Authority, which is given free of charge and even that is not sought as often as might be wished.

Before drawing an aeroplane it is a good thing to have in mind exactly what it is to do. The operational realities influence the design. This in turn leads to the optimisation for greatest effect. There is a good rule in design:

KEEP IT SIMPLE.

The rule is hard to apply, especially during the initial stages. A second rule should be observed:

ONE INNOVATION AT A TIME.

Few innovations work straight off; they take time and money ironing out the bugs. If we try more than one at a time, a failure in one direction can spawn sympathetic failures among the others. The Americans, dealing with the most potently effective amateur-built aircraft movement the world has ever seen employ what they call the KISS system: Keep It Simple, Stupid!

The fuel crisis is upon us and it is essential to design clean economic aeroplanes. It takes power to haul airframe drag around the sky and power uses fuel. Therefore we have to look for economies in *payload* and *range*. Payload is that part of the load carried which makes money for the operator. Together with the weight of fuel, oil and movable furnishing and equipment directly associated with it, payload contributes to the *disposable load*, or *useful load*, so that the weight of an aeroplane is given by:

Gross (or all-up) weight   = empty weight + useful load
                                = standard empty weight + usable fuel
                                    + payload + crew + ballast   (1–1)

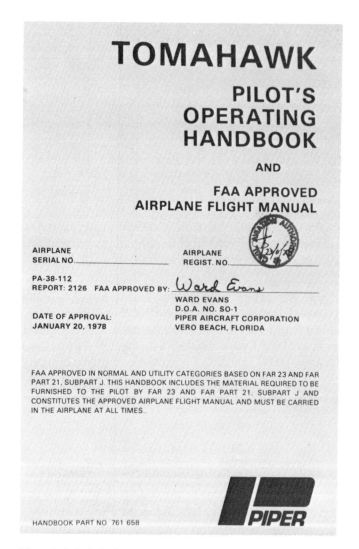

Plate 1–2 (left & right) Two versions of the same document for the same aeroplane. The one on the left has legal weight in the UK, because it has the stamp of Civil Aviation Authority approval, lacking on the other. (*Graham Skillen, UK*)

Where,

$$\text{Empty weight} = \text{powerplant weight} + \text{structure weight} \\ + \text{weight of controls} \\ + \text{weight of equipment and services} \qquad (1\text{--}2)$$

and

$$\text{Standard empty weight} = \text{weight of the standard aeroplane including unusable} \\ \text{fuel, full operating fluids and full oil} \qquad (1\text{--}2a)$$

TOMAHAWK

PILOT'S OPERATING HANDBOOK

AND

FAA APPROVED AIRPLANE FLIGHT MANUAL

AIRPLANE
SERIAL NO._____

AIRPLANE
REGIST. NO._____

PA-38-112
REPORT: 2126   FAA APPROVED BY: _Ward Evans_

WARD EVANS
D.O.A. NO. SO-1
PIPER AIRCRAFT CORPORATION
VERO BEACH, FLORIDA

DATE OF APPROVAL:
JANUARY 20, 1978

FAA APPROVED IN NORMAL AND UTILITY CATEGORIES BASED ON FAR 23 AND FAR PART 21, SUBPART J. THIS HANDBOOK INCLUDES THE MATERIAL REQUIRED TO BE FURNISHED TO THE PILOT ·BY FAR 23 AND FAR PART 21, SUBPART J AND CONSTITUTES THE APPROVED AIRPLANE FLIGHT MANUAL AND MUST BE CARRIED IN THE AIRPLANE AT ALL TIMES.

PIPER

HANDBOOK PART NO. 761 658

Plate 1–2 (right)

Weight is dealt with in chapter 14.

Sometimes payload and range are linked in the idea of *productivity* which draws upon the concepts of work and power in mechanics (see chapter 2). Work is force times distance, while power is the rate of doing work, i.e. force times speed. Productivity is approached through the economist's work-term:

$$\text{Payload-range} = \text{payload} \times \text{distance flown} \qquad (1\text{--}3)$$

which is usually given in ton-miles. From this comes the economist's power-term:

$$\begin{aligned} \text{Productivity} &= \text{payload ton-miles per hour} \\ &= \text{payload block speed.} \end{aligned} \qquad (1\text{--}4)$$

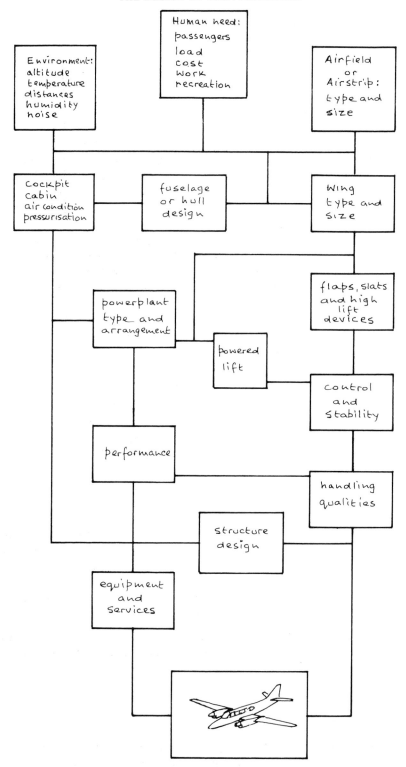

Fig. 1.3 Steps from initial operational needs to final shape of aircraft.

Block speed is the total distance from one airfield to another, divided by the block time from starting the engine(s) before take-off to shutting down again after landing. Power costs money and productivity is the way of making it.

Other useful yardsticks for judging whether or not one's design is in the right 'ballpark' are:

$$\text{Wing loading} = \text{gross weight} / \text{wing area} \qquad (1\text{-}5)$$

and,

$$\text{Power loading} = \text{gross weight} / \text{rated installed power.} \qquad (1\text{-}6)$$

As we shall see in chapter 6, Equation (6-31), an old fashioned rule of thumb for 'good' performance was that wing loading $\times$ power loading (i.e. W^2/SP) should lie between 90 and 135, when working in lb/ft^2 and lb/BHP. The sorts of aeroplanes to which the rule applied were strictly limited, as we shall see.

There is little excuse today for our not finding the information needed to design and build an aeroplane of our own. To make such excuses harder still, a considerable number of references has been given in this book. Advice given by the Civil Aviation Authority and by the Federal Aviation Administration is free. Publications, modestly priced by present standards are readily available telling us exactly what is needed to make our aircraft effective and socially acceptable (so that they do not reduce the quality of life of others who could not care less about flying).

We need every bit of documentation we can lay our hands on to verify, relevantly, the evidence upon which certification must be based. If the CAA has to do the digging instead the time taken will cost us money.

If we intend designing an aeroplane we must keep a *type record*, to include at least:

☐ A three-view general arrangement drawing of the aircraft.
☐ A list of the general arrangement drawings, including references to other drawings, which in association completely define the design of the aircraft.
☐ A summary of basic aerodynamic and other data used in the design.
☐ A summary of all design assumptions and calculations.
☐ A summary of details of the aircraft weight and centre of gravity.
☐ A list of reserve factors for ultimate loads for all critical parts of the aircraft structure.
☐ Copies of reports giving particulars and results of airworthiness acceptance tests.
☐ Particulars of any variations from the Civil Aviation Authority requirements that have been authorised with respect to the design, giving the reference number of the Authority document authorising the variations.
☐ Copies of subsidiary type records and Declarations of Design and Performance, prepared with respect to the components or equipment of the aircraft.

The list looks more formidable than it is, as long as we are methodical. A practical idea is to open a large day-book into which every idea, no matter how crude or inaccurate can be jotted by date and time – including notes of conversations and steps in the creative process.

Amateur-built aircraft in the USA

The American Federal Aviation Administration is financed by taxes out of the General Fund of the US Treasury and certification work is therefore paid for by the public instead of the applicant, unlike the case in Britain. The headquarters of the FAA is in

Washington DC and controls four Aircraft Certification Directorates, each containing a number of Manufacturing Inspection District Offices (MIDO) and General Aviation District Offices (GADO).

The amateur builder is encouraged to visit his local office before building an aircraft. Original certification is the responsibility of the FAA MIDOs, but in many parts of the country the responsibility has been delegated to the GADOs.

There are no prescribed design requirements for homebuilts in the United States; anything goes, but there are safeguards. A Maintenance Inspector of the Federal Aviation Administration (FAA) will require to vet drawings from which an aircraft is to be built. He may well criticise certain design features and can require them to be changed in the absence of evidence of safety. The Inspector needs to know the origins of materials used and these must be up to good commercial standards at least.

To qualify for certification in the Experimental/Amateur-Built Category, the bulk of the aircraft must have been constructed by the builder(s) for recreational or educational purposes. This is the FAAs '51 per cent rule'. To satisfy it, evidence including relevant invoices and shipping documents, is needed to substantiate that more than half of the aircraft was built for these purposes. Prototypes built for commercial purposes either by individuals or by companies are ineligible, as are aircraft used for research and development.

A permanent identification (data) plate must be attached to the aircraft. Registration marks must be carried and the word 'Experimental' must be marked near each entrance in letters 2 in (5 cm) high. A passenger warning placard must be displayed in the cockpit of single and multi-seat aircraft, in full view of the occupants, saying:

> 'Passenger Warning – This aircraft is amateur built and does not comply with federal safety regulations for standard aircraft.'

The aircraft should be fitted with instruments and equipment listed in FAR 91.33 appropriate to the flights that will be made, i.e. to Visual or Instrument Flight Rules (VFR or IFR). For VFR flights by day, for example, the aircraft should have an airspeed indicator, altimeter, magnetic direction-indicating compass, tachometer, oil pressure gauge, temperature gauge (for liquid-cooled engines), oil temperature gauge (air-cooled engines), manifold pressure gauge (altitude engine), fuel gauge indicating the quantity in each tank, a position indicator for retractable landing gear, and seat belts. Engine and flight instruments must be clearly marked with engine and airframe limitations. The builder has a duty to establish those limitations and to mark the instruments accordingly.

An FAA inspector looks at the aircraft before it is covered to see if good practices have been followed. The aircraft is inspected again before it is cleared for its first flight. Before the final inspection the aircraft must be weighed and the most aft and forward positions of the centre of gravity determined. This information is to be recorded and a copy kept in the aircraft. The FAA inspector reviews the information to check that the aircraft is loaded within the established limits. Before flight he has the right to check anything, including running the engine from idle to full power.

To qualify for the award of an 'Experimental Category C of A' the amateur builder has to prove the fitness of his aircraft by having it flown in a specified area where, if it falls to earth, it is unlikely to hurt innocent third parties. The test flying period, which amounts to proving the aircraft by usage, lasts for a minimum number of flying hours specified by the FAA. This was 75 hours for an aircraft fitted with an unapproved engine or 50 hours with one approved. Both of these figures have since been reduced.

That aspect of the American certification procedure has been adopted by the Airworthiness Division of the CAA for a number of American amateur designs built in Britain. Examples are the *Pitts S-1 Special* and the *Wittman Tailwind*. In each case there were no strength calculations available, so the Surveyor in Charge of the local office arranged for inspections as the work progressed. The aircraft were then test flown for appropriate periods at a local airfield, clear of towns and built-up areas. At the end of the test periods they were flown by an Airworthiness Division test pilot to verify the data being submitted by the applicants for issue of Cs of A.

Regulation of safety in Britain and America has a number of elements which fall broadly under the following common headings:

(fiscal constraints) + (enforcement constraints) = publicly acceptable level
$$\text{of safety} \qquad (1\text{--}7)$$

In America the equation breaks into:

(law enforcement) + (insurance regulations)
+ (ground inspection by, or required by, FAA)
+ (on-going education by FAA)   = publicly acceptable level
+ (positive monitoring by FAA)   of safety   (1–7a)

Contravention of any of the terms, or failure to comply, hits the pocket either directly or indirectly by: large court and attorney's fees, increased insurance premiums, product liability, error and omission (or other relevant insurances) and loss of inspection approval by the FAA of mechanics designated to carry out C of A inspections on behalf of the Administration – an accolade much sought after and highly prized.

In Britain we do not have the equivalent of on-going education. Instead the Airworthiness Division equation could be written in almost exactly the same way, except that the last three terms in brackets on the left hand side of eq(1–7a) might be replaced by:

(airworthiness division ground inspection + monitoring + flight test)   (1–7b)

These have been linked together because AD flight test is an airborne inspection, during which a stick is poked in an aeroplane's ear to find out if it has any dangerous features among other things.

Organisations to help enthusiasts

Quite apart from the Civil Aviation Authority and the Federal Aviation Administration, which can be asked for help and advice freely, here are some organisations which are able to give technical advice and support to people wanting to design, build and fly their own aeroplanes and gliders. The list is not exhaustive, but it will give us a start:

USA: *Experimental Aircraft Association International Inc (EAA)*, PO Box 229, Hales Corners, Wisconsin 53130, USA, is the premier non-profit making organisation catering for the needs of enthusiasts of all kinds. It is world-wide in scale and covers everything from amateur building to ownership of vintage and classic aircraft. The EAA is organised in Chapters, some of which are overseas, looking after their own national movements.

The Association does not have Civil Aviation Authority (Airworthiness Division) approval because its constitution would not equip it for meeting British legal requirements, but that is no disadvantage. The Association publishes a wide range of useful literature, including the magazine *Sport Aviation*.

UK: *Popular Flying Association (PFA)*, Terminal building, Shoreham Airport, Shoreham-by-Sea, Sussex BN4 5FF, England, is a CAA(AD) approved organisation which is the founding and representative body in Britain of amateur constructors and operators of ultra-light and group-operated aircraft. The PFA is organised into local groups called Struts, employs a full-time engineering officer and publishes the magazine *Popular Flying*.

France: *Reseau du Sport de l'Air (RSA)*, 39 Rue Sauffroy, 75017 Paris, France, is the French equivalent of EAA and PFA. It publishes the magazine *Les Cahiers du RSA*.

Germany: *Oskar Ursinus Vereinigung (OUV)* (Chapter 308, EAA), Tieckstrasse 3, 5000 Köln 30, West German Federal Republic.

UK: *British Gliding Assocation (BGA)*, Kimberley House, Vaughan Way, Leicester, England, is CAA(AD) approved to certify design and construction of privately built or imported gliders and self-launching motor gliders and to recommend their certification.

USA: *United States Hang Gliding Association (USHGA)*, PO Box 66306, Los Angeles, California 90066, USA, is a division of the National Aeronautical Association (NAA), which is the official representative of the Fédération Aéronautique Internationale (FAI), the world governing body of sport aviation. The Association publishes the magazine *Hang Gliding*.

UK: *British Hang Gliding Association (BHGA)*, 167A Cheddon Road, Taunton, Somerset TA2 7AH, England.

UK: *The Tiger Club*, Redhill Aerodrome, Redhill, Surrey, England.

UK: *Formula Air Racing Association (FARA)*, c/o The Tiger Club, Redhill Aerodrome, Redhill, Surrey, England.

UK: *The Historic Aircraft Association*, c/o Test Pilots Office, British Aerospace, Hatfield, Herts, AL10 9TL, England, registers pilots, engineers and technicians concerned with flight safety of historic aircraft in Britain, and includes representatives of all of the major collections.

U.K. *British Minimum Aircraft Association (BMAA)*, 80 St Georges Road, Aldershot, Hampshire, England.

New Zealand: *The Amateur Aircraft Constructors Association (AACA)* and *The Sport and Vintage Aviation Society (SVAS)* which share the *Sport Flying* magazine, PO Box 10058, Wellington, New Zealand.

Australia: *The Sport Aircraft Association of Australia*, National Membership Office, PO Box 193, Mentone, Victoria, 3194. Publishes the magazine *Airsport*.

Canada: *Director Airworthiness, Transport Canada*, Tower C, Place de Ville, Ottawa, Ontario K1A ON8. Telephone (613) 9921180.

The Authority is advised in certain areas of competence by:

Experimental Aircraft Association, Canada: Chairman, Technical Committee, EAAC, Suite 104, Rideau Park Towers, 1801 Riverside Drive, Ottawa, Ontario K1G OE7. Telephone (613) 998 3281.

South Africa: the Authority is *The Commissioner, Department of Civil Aviation*, Forum Building, Struben Street, Pretoria 0002. Telephone (12) 39111.

DCA is advised in areas of competence by selected members of:

Experimental Aircraft Association, South Africa, which consists of five chapters and is said to be the largest per capita outside the USA. Certificates of competence are awarded by DCA, on passing a written examination, for the inspection and certification of ultra light aircraft which operate with Permits to Fly (as against Certificates of Airworthiness). The Chairman of EAA South Africa, 26 Alro Court, Montclare, Durban, South Africa 4052. Telephone (424) 397.

Disabled pilots

Physical disability is not necessarily a bar to flying, provided that certain medical requirements can be satisfied, and the pilot plus aeroplane is shown to be a safe enough combination to the relevant Authority. Pilots without use of a hand or legs are flying. Some of them are famous.

To overcome the loss of use of a hand or leg(s), a prosthesis in the form of an artificial limb is often fitted which may be able to operate existing controls satisfactorily. Otherwise the controls must be adapted so that they can be operated in some other way from that normally intended, e.g. the rudder control may need to be operated by hand. Each mechanism must be especially designed for the particular need to be operated by hand. Airworthiness of such devices must then be demonstrated, treating them as mechanical extensions of the aircraft, rather than extensions of the pilot, and therefore subject to published airworthiness standards.

In the UK the Civil Aviation Authority has developed a procedure for helping disabled pilots. They should contact in the first instance:

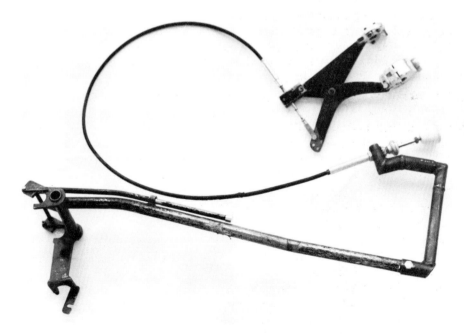

Plate 1-3   Rudder control with combined throttle control for operation by the left hand of a disabled pilot. The rudder control lever clips onto the rudder pedal of a *PA28 Cherokee(R. A. Nesbitt-Dufort, UK)*

Civil Aviation Authority (FCL3),
Aviation House,
129 Kingsway,
London, WC2N 6BQ.
Telephone (01) 405 6922
Telex 892 466

for initial guidance. For airworthiness advice and flight testing contact should be made with:

Civil Aviation Authority,
Airworthiness Division,
Brabazon House,
Redhill,
Surrey, RH1 1SQ.
Telephone Redhill (0737) 65966
Telex 27100

Disabled pilots in the USA are served by:

Wheelchair Pilots Association,
11018 102nd Avenue North,
Largo, Florida, 33540.
Telephone 393 3131

References

1.1 *Air Navigation Order and Regulations* (1976). Civil Aviation Authority.
1.2 Tye, W. (1977). '10⁶... And All That'. *Aircraft Engineering*.
1.3 CAP 396. *Airworthiness Certification*. Civil Aviation Authority.
1.4 Kreindler, L. S. (1977). Letter in *Flight International*.
1.5 AD/1L/0066/1–4 (1978). *Minimum Performance for Certification of Aircraft not exceeding 2730 kg max total weight authorised in UK Transport Category*. Civil Aviation Authority (Airworthiness Division).
1.6 VA Note 4 (Jan. 1975). *Additional Requirements on US Aeroplanes Designed to FAR Part 23 and Seeking UK Certification in the Public Transport Category*. Civil Aviation Authority (Airworthiness Division).
1.7 VA Note 5 (Jan. 1970). *FAA Additional Requirements for UK Airplanes (12500 lb or less maximum weight)*. Civil Aviation Authority (Airworthiness Division).

CHAPTER 2

Vocabulary of Design

'"When *I* use a word," Humpty Dumpty said in rather a scornful tone, "it means just what I choose it to mean – neither more nor less."'
Lewis Carroll, *Through the Looking Glass.*

The object of this chapter is to introduce the terms and constructions of the language of aircraft design. With these in hand we should then be able to break into the book at almost any point and pick up its threads. After all it is an unhelpful sort of textbook that checks enthusiasm by forcing us to begin at someone else's beginning.

The definitions are not meant to be academically pure. Aeronautics is a mixture of precise science, disciplined methods, consummate accuracy in telling it as it is after a test flight, gut-feeling and artistry. The last two may often seem to lack reason or explanation, but that makes them no less valid. In our subject it can be clearer at times to visualise and attempt to feel our way into a truth instead of approaching it by pure logic and mathematics. Mathematics is a handmaiden, a shorthand language. An aeroplane in flight is very much a living thing with a mind of its own, trying to do what *it* wants in response to an obdurate pilot and wilful air. The smaller the aeroplane the more it responds like a skittish horse to a rider than a machine to a man. There are reasons and this chapter is intended to give us a feeling for what goes on. In this way we might become more sensitive engineers, designers and pilots, with a sympathy for machinery.

Aerodynamics and aeroplane geometry

Aerodynamics is the scientific study of the way in which air moves, and reactions felt by surfaces to its motions.

Aerodynamic centre (ac). A point (about one quarter of the distance from the leading edge to the trailing edge of an aerofoil section) about which the resultant pitching moment of all aerodynamic forces acting upon it is constant – within the working range of angle of attack. It is also the point through which the resultant lift *increment* acts when there is a small change in angle of attack of the wing from its value in steady straight and level flight. Other tail and canard stabiliser surfaces have their own aerodynamic centres.

Aerodynamic force. A reaction felt by the surface of a body moving through air to changes in pressure and friction as the air slides past. It can be expressed as:

$$\text{pressure} \times \text{area over which it acts} = \text{force}$$
$$pA \text{ or } pS = F \tag{2-1}$$

General predictions of forces like lift and drag are made in terms of surface area, air density, airspeed and a pure number called, for example, *lift coefficient*, C_L and *drag coefficient*, C_D. The terms are tied together in the form of eq (2–1), by introducing *dynamic pressure*, q and *wing area*, S, where:

$$\text{gross wing area } = \text{ wingspan} \times \text{mean chord}$$
$$S = b\bar{c} \text{ (or } b\bar{\bar{c}}) \tag{2–2}$$

There are two mean chords which affect us. The one used more than any other in this book is:

Standard mean chord, SMC, $\bar{c}$, is the ratio of the gross wing area S divided by the wingspan b

i.e.
$$\bar{c} = \frac{S}{b} = \frac{\sum_{-b/2}^{+b/2} c\Delta y}{\sum_{-b/2}^{+b/2} \Delta y} \tag{2–2a}$$

Where $b/2$ is the semi-span also denoted S. For a straight tapered wing.

$$\bar{c} = \tfrac{1}{2}(\text{rootchord} + \text{tipchord})$$

The other is:

Aerodynamic mean chord, MAC, is a chord length $\bar{\bar{c}}$ in the plane of symmetry lying along the zero liftline of the wing, where

$$\bar{\bar{c}} = \frac{\sum_{-b/2}^{+b/2} c^2\,\Delta y}{\sum_{-b/2}^{+b/2} c\,\Delta y} = \frac{\sum_{-s}^{+s} c^2 \Delta y}{S} \tag{2–2b}$$

The mean aerodynamic chord is used as a datum length for calculating pitching moments and moment coefficient C_M. The mean aerodynamic chord is a datum to which the aerodynamic centre of the wing is referred.

For our essentially practical purposes we shall assume that $SMC \approx MAC$.

The dynamic pressure, q, is given by eq (2–9). Thus the forces

$$\text{lift, } L = C_L q S \tag{2–3a}$$
$$\text{drag, } D = C_D q S \tag{2–3b}$$

The term q is the force exerted per unit frontal area of the aircraft on impact with air of density ρ at speed V (*see* eq (2–9)).

Aerodynamic mean chord $\bar{\bar{c}}$. The equivalent chord of an aerofoil surface having the same span, area and aerodynamic properties as a wing or other relevant aerofoil of a real aeroplane, *see* eq (2–2b) above.

Aerofoil. A surface shaped to produce more lift than drag. Wings, tails and canard foreplanes, fins and rudders are all examples of such surfaces. The forces generated are the same whether the surface moves through the air, or the air flows past the surface.

Aerofoil section. The profile of an aerofoil when sliced from leading to trailing edge.

Aeroplane. A scholarly word from the Greek, meaning literally 'air-wandering' (*see* **Preface**) which is the neatest reason for not using the respectable, but less attractive, American word 'airplane'. The Oxford English Dictionary and the Glossary of Terms of the British Standards Institution conspire to define an aeroplane as a mechanically-driven heavier than air flying machine, with supporting surfaces fixed for flight.

Airbrake. A surface, or combination of high-drag surfaces, put out into the airflow to slow down.

Aircraft. A generic term used to describe all sorts of flying machines (ref. 1.1).

Airflow. The relative flow of air past any surface when we imagine the surface to remain fixed. The effect is the same if the eye moves with the surface.

Airspeed (see **Performance and operational terms**).

Angle of attack. The angle of a surface to the airflow, generally measured between the line of flight and the chord line of an aerofoil section, fig. 2.1.

Angle of incidence. The angle between the datum line of the aircraft from nose to tail, and the chord line of an aerofoil section.

Aspect ratio A. The way of describing how long the span is compared with the (mean) chord length of an aerofoil surface. The average distance between the leading and trailing edge is called the *standard mean chord* (SMC), denoted $\bar{c}$. If the wing is imagined to be a rectangular plank its aspect ratio is the ratio of span/SMC. But when it is not like a plank we resort to fig. 2.2 and the following:

$$\text{aspect ratio, } A \;=\; \text{wingspan/SMC} \qquad\qquad = \quad b/\bar{c}$$

and as area = span × chord in eq (2–2), SMC = area/span, so that:

$$\text{aspect ratio, } A \;=\; \text{wingspan}^2/\text{area} \qquad\qquad = \quad b^2/S \qquad (2\text{–}4)$$

Bernoulli's law. Although the law is usually ascribed to Daniel Bernoulli (1700–82) it was discovered by Leonard Euler (1707–83). We consider a small portion of air or liquid flow and ignore frictional effects. Then in our small quantity of flow, the sum of the *static pressure* and the *dynamic pressure* is constant along a streamline. The static pressure is equivalent to the weight of a column (or head) of air pressing down on unit area with a value equal to that measured at the streamline. Dynamic pressure is the force per unit area that would be exerted by the flow against a flat surface perpendicular to it. The pressures at any point in the flow are summed to give:

$$\text{total pressure} \qquad = \quad \text{static pressure} + \text{dynamic pressure}$$
$$p_0 \qquad\qquad = \quad p + q = \text{a constant } C \qquad (2\text{–}5)$$

A physical explanation is given in fig. 2.6.

Biplane. An aeroplane with one wing arranged more or less above the other (*see* also *gap* and *stagger*), fig. 2.3.

Boundary layer. The thin region of air next to the skin of an aircraft through which there is a change of relative airspeed, from zero at the skin to the full speed of the flow some way from it.

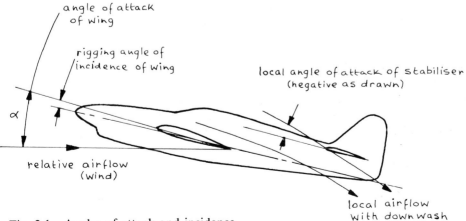

Fig. 2.1   Angles of attack and incidence.

Buffet. Shaking and thumping of the aircraft caused by turbulent lumps of agitated air left behind in the wake, usually at low speeds and large angles of attack. It can be caused by shock waves at high speed.

Buoyancy. The property of being able to float, either in air or water, the weight of fluid displaced being equal to the weight it supports (the Principle of Archimedes (287–212BC)).

Camber. Curvature of the geometric mean line of an aerofoil section, measured in terms of distance along and percentage of the chord line, *see* fig. 2.4.

Centre of pressure. The point at which the resultant pressure on a body is taken to act. The sum of the moments of all the pressure forces about the *CP* is zero.

Chord and chord line. The distance from leading to trailing edge of an aerofoil section, measured along the straight line joining them.

Circulation. Motion of air or water along a curved path. In such real flows, curved streamlines show that a flow is circulatory. Circulation produces lift.

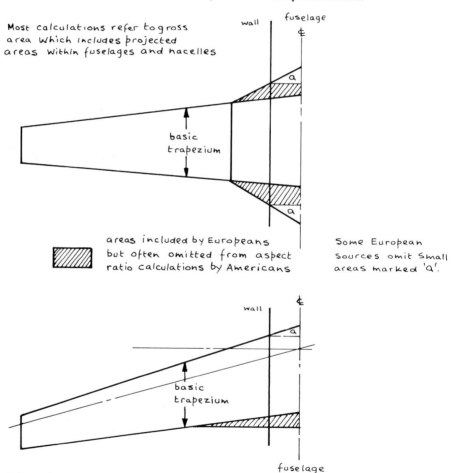

Fig. 2.2   Wing areas used in aspect ratio calculations. Some European measures of wing area can be larger than American. European measures can result in lower aspect ratios than those of the same wing in America. This is not a rigid rule. It follows that differences in such calculations can alter estimates of induced drag factors made on each side of the Atlantic.

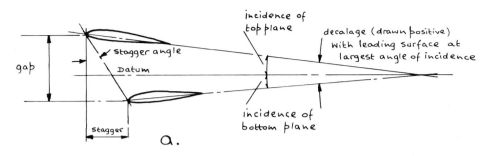

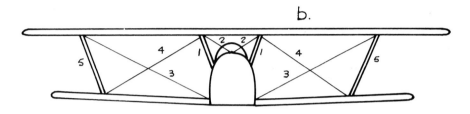

1. cabane struts 2. cabane bracing
3. lift bracing 4. landing wire bracing
5. interplane struts

Fig. 2.3   Basic rigging and bracing terms. In a, the term decalage may be used for the difference in incidence between wing and foreplane, or tailplane. Stagger may be defined as an angle or as a distance or as a percentage of the gap.

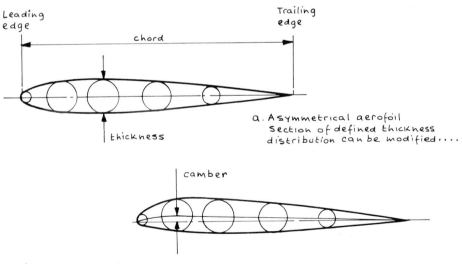

Fig. 2.4   Basic aerofoil geometry.

Coanda effect. The tendency of air or water to follow a curved surface is called after the discoverer of its importance, Henri Coanda (1886–1972), a Rumanian engineer. Coanda effect is demonstrated by running a tap and bringing the curved back of a spoon into contact with the water. The tip of the handle should be held lightly so that the spoon can swing freely. The spoon will be sucked sharply into the jet.

Compressibility. The ability of air to change volume (i.e. density) when squeezed (*see* chapter 3).

Compressibility effects. The formation of shock and expansion waves in a flow when air is forced to move faster than its natural limiting speed of sound. The speed at which shock waves are first apparent is the *critical Mach number*, M_{crit}.

Configuration. A term describing the geometry of an aeroplane, when various elements (flaps, landing gear) making up its shape have been rearranged for subsequent flight.

Datum (line). A straight line through a *datum point* from which measurements are made.

Decalage. The angle subtended between the chord lines of biplane wings, and between wings and stabiliser (*see* fig. 2.3). It is positive when the upper (or leading) surface is set at a larger angle of incidence than the other. In the case of wings and stabilisers, decalage is often called *longitudinal dihedral*, which must be positive for longitudinal stability.

Dihedral and anhedral (original cahedral). The rise of an aerofoil from root to tip is called dihedral; when the tip is lower than the root, anhedral.

Downwash. A downwards component of relative airflow normal to the direction of motion of the aircraft.

Drag, D (see also *aerodynamic force*, especially eq (2–3b)). The sum of the components of all aerodynamic forces acting on the aircraft, when resolved along the flight path. Such forces are caused by pressures normal (perpendicular) to the skin at any point, and by friction in the boundary layer of the air as it slides past. Drag represents lost energy and it has many sources. Two useful breaksdown are worth noting at this point, although drag is dealt with further in chapters 4 and 5.

☐ Drag as seen by the performance engineer, who splits it into 'lifting' and 'non-lifting' elements:

Lift-dependent drag, D_L induced drag, D_i. A pressure drag caused by surfaces forcing air around curved, circulatory paths so as to generate lift. At speeds low enough for air to behave incompressibly, it is convenient to use the term induced drag. But if air is displaced so fast that it achieves supersonic speed locally, it becomes compressible, and *wave drag* is caused by shocks and expansions additional to induced drag. Here we group that part of wave drag caused by the act of lifting, and induced drag, under the collective heading of lift-dependent drag.

Zero-lift, D_F or parasite drag, D_p. The group of drags which exist even though the aeroplane is diving straight downwards with the wings producing no lift. It therefore includes the profile drag of the wings, D_o (*see* eq (2.8)), which is present whether the wings are lifting or not.

Thus, when compressibility is present:

$$\text{total drag, } D \quad = \quad D_L + D_F \tag{2–6}$$

and when it is not:

$$D \quad = \quad D_i + D_p \tag{2–7}$$

☐ Drag as seen by the aerodynamicist: The main difference is that the drag of the wing is taken as a separate item from the remainder, the *extra-to-wing drag*.

Wing drag is the sum of the lift-dependent drag and the:

Profile (zero-lift) drag of the wing alone, D_o. The sum of the *form drag*, D_{form} (due to shape of the wing elbowing air aside) and the *skin friction drag*, D_{fric}, so that:

$$\text{profile drag, } D_o = D_{form} + D_{fric} \text{ of the wing} \qquad (2\text{--}8)$$

Extra-to-wing, or *parasite drag*. This may be thought of as the form drag of the remainder of the aircraft. It is precisely analogous to D_F or D_p above, minus the profile drag of the wing.

Dynamic pressure, q (*see* also chapter 3). The second term in eq (2–5), which is also the limit force felt per unit frontal area of an aeroplane (or any other shape). It may be shown that dynamic pressure is equivalent to the kinetic energy imparted to a unit volume of air by acceleration to the speed of flight, V, such that:

$$\text{dynamic pressure} = \tfrac{1}{2} \times \text{density of air} \times \text{relative true airspeed}^2$$
$$q = \tfrac{1}{2}\rho V^2 \qquad (2\text{--}9)$$

We say 'relative' because the pressure obtained is the same whether it is caused by the aircraft moving through the air, or by the air flowing past a stationary aircraft, as in a wind tunnel.

Flap. Part of the surface of an aerofoil that can be deflected to produce a change in effective camber and hence lifting pressure distribution.

Free stream. The condition of the relative airflow remote from the aircraft and so not influenced by its presence.

Gap. The vertical distance between the wings of a biplane.

Geometric mean chord (*see* standard mean chord, SMC, $\bar{c}$).

Hinge moment. The magnitude of the aerodynamic twisting effect exerted at the hinge line of a control or flap surface.

Incidence (*see* angle of incidence).

ISA (*see* Terms describing ambient conditions).

Lift, L. The component sum of all aerodynamic forces acting on an aircraft when resolved at right angles to the flight path. In steady straight and level flight the lift is equal and opposite to the weight of the machine.

Lift and drag coefficient C_L and C_D (*see also* eqs (2–3a) and (2–3b)). If we take the ratio of the wing loading (w, the *weight/wing area*) to the dynamic pressure q (eq (2–9)) we have a pure number which is a measure of the heaviness of the 'footprint' the aircraft can impose upon the air and usually reaches a maximum just before the stall. That ratio is called the lift coefficient, C_L. The higher the maximum lift coefficient, the slower the aeroplane can fly before the wing stalls. In a similar way, if we divide the total drag by the wing area, S, we convert it into a pressure term, like wing loading. If we then divide *drag/wing area* by the dynamic pressure, q, we have the drag coefficient of the aircraft, C_D, at a given speed. The various drag components: D_F, D_L, D_i, D_{form}, D_{fric}, for example, when divided by qS become C_{DF}, C_{DL}, C_{Di}, C_{Dform}, C_{Dfric} respectively.

Pitching moment. A torque, i.e. twisting effect applied by a system of forces acting in pitch about a chosen centre. The pitching moment on an aircraft is dealt with in exactly the same way as lift and drag, by turning it into a coefficient. Knowing that the *aerodynamic moment* is numerically equal to a *force* × a *lever arm*, for convenience we substitute the standard mean chord for the arm to give:

pitching moment = moment coefficient × dynamic pressure × wing area
                             ×standard mean chord

$$M = C_M q S c \qquad (2\text{--}10)$$

This is the general form. In practice we distinguish between the moments about the CG and ac and their respective coefficients by suffixes: $M_{CG}, M_{ac}, C_{MCG}, C_{Mac}$.

Pressure altitude (*see* under Terms describing ambient conditions).
Pressure coefficient. The ratio of the pressure (or pressure difference) at some point on a surface to the free-stream dynamic pressure. A pressure coefficient is negative when the local velocity is higher than the free-stream velocity.
Rake (of tips of wings and tails). Tips of surfaces are raked by cutting them at an angle of the line of flight, making the leading and the trailing edges of different lengths.
Reynolds number R. A pure number named after Osborne Reynolds, Professor of Engineering in the University of Manchester, who in 1883 carried out systematic experiments on the transition of flows from laminar (streamlined) to turbulent. Turbulent flows had already been analysed by a German engineer, Gotthilf Heinrich Ludwig Hagen (1797–1894) (ref. 2.1). Reynolds number is a measure of 'scale effect', which relates the various factors which cause the flow around a particular body to become turbulent with those which inhibit it (*see* chapter 3). Suffice it to say that if $\bar{c}$ is the standard mean chord, V the true airspeed, ρ the air density and μ its viscosity, then working in appropriate units:

Reynolds number = mean chord × true airspeed × density/viscosity
$$R \;\; = \;\; \bar{c}V\rho/\mu = \bar{c}V/\nu = \text{inertial force}/\text{viscous force} \qquad (2\text{--}11)$$

in which $\nu = \mu/\rho$ is called the *coefficient of kinematic viscosity* of the air. It is a useful measure, in its own right, of the ratio of 'quietness/excitability' of a given mass of molecules. As long as Reynolds number remains constant, then aerodynamic flow patterns remain geometrically similar and resulting forces directly proportional, regardless of the scale of the aircraft or aerofoils compared.
Scale effect (*see* Reynolds number).
Slat and slot. Sir Frederick Handley-Page (1885–1962) in Britain and Gustav V. Lachmann (1896–1966) when a German pilot in the First World War, both conceived the slat and slot independently, in 1919 and 1918 respectively (ref. 2.2). The slat is a small auxiliary aerofoil close to the leading edge of the main surface, which forms a slot between them. Slats are usually located on the upper surfaces near the tips of wings where they squeeze air through the slot, over the main wing, with increased airspeed, so that the aeroplane can fly slower without separation of the boundary layer and subsequent stall.
Slug. The unit of mass based upon the British Imperial system. Mass is the 'quantity of matter' contained within a body. When a force is applied to a mass, acceleration results, i.e. its speed or direction of motion will change. The relationship between force and acceleration was first correctly formulated by Sir Isaac Newton (1642–1727). His second law states:

force = mass × acceleration
$$F \;\; = \;\; ma \qquad (2\text{--}12)$$

(his first only says that no force means no acceleration).
   On the surface of the earth all masses are attracted by the force of gravity; the gravitational force attracting a body towards the earth is what we call *weight*. By eq

(2–12) this force produces an acceleration (which is the same for all bodies) and at the surface of the earth the acceleration due to gravity has the value $g = 32.2 \, \text{ft}/\text{s}^2 (9.8 \, \text{m}/\text{s}^2)$, which prevents masses flying away into space. All masses press down upon the ground with forces called *weight*. The density of air is $0.076474 \, \text{lb}/\text{ft}^3$ at sea level ISA (1.225 kg/m^3). Therefore, transposing eq (2–12) for mass, which is denoted ρ_o when dealing with air under sea level conditions, ISA:

$$\text{mass, } \rho_o \text{ per ft}^3 = \text{weight}/\text{'g'} = 0.76474/32.174$$
$$= 0.002377 \text{ slugs}/\text{ft}^3 \ (1.225 \text{ kg}/\text{m}^3) \text{ at sea level, ISA}$$
$$(2\text{–}13)$$

Looked at another way, a force of 1 lb will accelerate a mass of 1 slug at 1 ft/s².

Span. The distance between the tips of wings and similar surfaces, measured normal to the plane of symmetry of an aircraft.

Stagger. The amount by which one wing of a biplane is set ahead of the other (*see* fig. 2.3). Stagger is positive when the top wing is ahead of the bottom.

Stagnation point. A point on the skin of an aircraft where the local relative airflow is brought to rest.

Stall. Loss of lift caused by breakdown and separation of the flow over a wing (or other aerofoil surface) in the face of an adverse pressure gradient downstream (*see* chapter 3). Stalling is usually associated with large angles of attack.

Standard mean chord, SMC (also *geometric mean chord*). If an aerofoil surface of given span and area is replaced geometrically by an untapered parallel chord surface, with the same span and area, its chord is equivalent to the standard mean chord, $\bar{c}$. The geometric construction for finding the SMC is shown in fig. 2.5.

Static pressure p. The average force exerted upon unit area of surface by the bombardment due to random thermal motion of molecules of air (or any other fluid). See also Bernoulli's law, fig. 2.6 and eq (2–5).

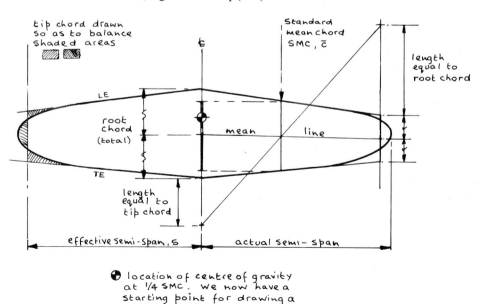

Fig. 2.5 The way to deal with planform and construction of standard mean chord for area and aspect ratio calculations (*see* eq (2–2)).

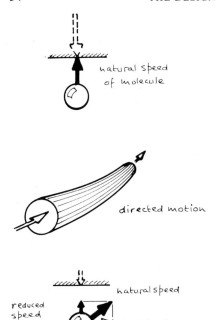

a. Molecules of air dancing around
in random motion at their
natural limiting speed (more
or less the speed of sound)
cause static pressure by impact
on a surface. Static pressure
is a maximum when molecular
motion is truly random, ie, when
the bulk of the air is 'at rest'

b. But when air is forced to move
and is directed we trace the
motion with streamlines, or
a filament of flow can be
formed by a streamtube formed
by streamlines, along which mass
flow is everywhere constant
(see Eq (2-14)).

c. The addition of a component of
directed motion cannot alter
the natural limiting speed (as
long as air temperature remains
unchanged), so that the impact
speed of a molecule against
a surface is now reduced,
and the static pressure falls
(Eq (2-5))

Fig. 2.6   This happens when air is caused to flow.

Streamline and streamtube (*see* fig. 2.6b). A *streamline* is an imaginary line marking the direction of a flow and by definition, there can be no flow across it. A *streamtube*, formed by a boundary of streamlines, contains a filament of flow. Because there is no gain or loss of flow through the walls of the tube, the mass flow per second past any cross section is constant, so that:

$$\text{cross sectional area} \times \text{true airspeed} \times \text{air density} = \text{constant}$$
$$A V \rho = C \qquad (2\text{–}14)$$

When the streamlines in a fluid are steady (i.e. successive imaginary snapshots look identical) the flow is called laminar. See also *turbulence*.

Subsonic and supersonic. The words mean slower and faster than the speed of sound.

Sweep, Λ. An aerofoil surface is said to be swept (usually backwards) in planform if any spanwise line between say, 15 per cent and 70 per cent of the chord back from the leading edge is *not* at right angles to the plane of symmetry of the aircraft.

Turbulence. The behaviour of air, or any other fluid, when it moves in a chopped up and lumpy way, with parcels of molecules tumbling over one another in disorderly fashion. In contrast with laminar flow, streamlines are not present in the fluid.

Vortex. Circulatory motion of a fluid about a centre, like water rotating as it flows down a drain hole in a bath.

Wing loading, w. The average weight of aircraft carried per unit wing area. In steady straight and level flight lift and weight are equal and opposite, so that the wing loading is then equal to the average lift per unit wing area.

Energy and other mechanical concepts

Aeronautics is mainly a mechanical subject. To fly, forces must be applied to cause action, and work is done. Energy, inertia, momentum, power, work and similar terms are of such fundamental importance that they must be swept under one common heading. For simplicity and ease of reading, speed is preferred to velocity when explaining something. Strictly speaking, velocity contains both direction and speed.

Centre of gravity (*see* under *Performance and operational terms*).

Energy and work. Energy is the capacity for doing work and it can adopt a variety of exchangeable forms when given the right conditions, i.e., mechanical, thermal (heat), chemical, electrical, atomic; and it seems impossible to destroy it. Even so, usable energy can be more easily lost than gained. Work is done when energy is expended by applying a force to a mass of any substance so as to make it move.

$$\text{work done} \ = \ \text{force applied} \times \text{distance moved} \qquad (2\text{--}15)$$

The types of energy in which we are interested are:

☐ *Kinetic energy (KE).* A result of motion. Imagine an aeroplane flying at a constant speed as measured between two fixed points on the ground. We know from eq (2–12) that as the aeroplane has accelerated at different rates from take-off, and as the mass of the machine has varied with fuel consumed, then the product of the *average* mass of the aeroplane $\times$ *average* acceleration gives the *average* force doing the work:

$$\text{force} \ = \ \text{mass of aircraft} \times \text{speed attained}/\text{time taken}$$

While: kinetic energy $=$ $\tfrac{1}{2} \times$ mass $\times$ speed^2

i.e. KE $=$ $\tfrac{1}{2} MV^2$ $\qquad (2\text{--}16)$

This equation should be compared with eq (2–9) which shows that the dynamic pressure on the nose of an aircraft, $q = \tfrac{1}{2}\rho V^2$, has exactly the same form, except that the symbol ρ is used for the mass per unit volume of air. Thus dynamic pressure q is a measure of the kinetic energy per unit volume of the air in motion.

Note: We can arrive at the same result using *dimensional analysis*, generally writing mass $= M$, distance $= L$ and time $= T$, so that:

force $= M(L/T)/T = ML/T^2$, where $L/T =$ speed, V

distance $= \tfrac{1}{2}(L/T)T = \tfrac{1}{2}L$

$KE = $ force $\times$ distance $= \tfrac{1}{2}(ML/T^2)L = \tfrac{1}{2}M(L/T^2) = \tfrac{1}{2}MV^2$ $\qquad (2\text{--}16a)$

See Appendix C.

☐ *Potential energy.* Is derived by virtue of position in space, raising the mass of a body through a change of height in a gravitational field. Thus, applying eq (2–15), if an aeroplane weighing 2200 lb (1000 kg) climbs 1000 ft (305 m) above the airfield:

potential energy gained $=$ 2200×1000

$=$ 2.2×10^6 ft lb (2.98×10^6 Nm or J)

which is obtained by burning fuel within the engine.

☐ *Thermal or heat energy.* This is a measure of the kinetic energy of molecules in a solid, liquid or gas by *specific heat*, i.e. the quantity of heat needed to raise the temperature of a defined mass of water by a given amount. Common units are: *British Thermal Unit, BTU.* The heat required to raise the temperature of 1 lb of water through 1°F is equivalent to 778 ft lbf work (1055 Nm or J) $\qquad (2\text{--}17a)$

Centigrade Heat Unit, CHU. The heat required to raise the temperature of 1 lb water through 1°C is equivalent to 1400 ft lbf work (1900 Nm or J)   (2–17b)

Joule, J. (after James Prescott Joule (1818–89) an English physicist). The unit of work in the SI system (table 2–5), when a force of one newton acts for one metre.

$$1 \text{ joule} = 0.736 \text{ BTU} \qquad (2\text{–}17c)$$

An important quantity in aerodynamics is:

$$\frac{\text{specific heat of air at constant pressure}}{\text{specific heat of air at constant volume}} = \gamma = 1.4 \qquad (2\text{–}18)$$

□*Pressure energy.* The capacity of a compressed gas to do work. When air is compressed within a cylinder by a piston the pressure rises directly with compression. The mean value of the pressure during the process is called the *mean effective pressure, MEP.* Consider the pressure energy during one stroke of a reciprocating engine:

$$\begin{aligned}
\text{pressure energy} &= \text{work done} = \text{force on piston} \times \text{distance moved} \\
&= \text{mean effective pressure} \times \text{piston area} \times \text{stroke} \\
&= MEP \times \text{swept volume (capacity) of cylinder} \qquad (2\text{–}19)
\end{aligned}$$

Efficiency. The effectiveness with which useful work is done for a given working input:

$$\begin{aligned}
\text{efficiency} &= \text{output of work/input of energy} \\
&= \text{output/input} \qquad (2\text{–}20)
\end{aligned}$$

Force and mass (*see slug* and eq (2–12)).

Inertia. A property possessed by all masses. If an aeroplane is at rest on the ground we have to push hard at first to make it move. Inertia of the mass resists the force, in an attempt to remain inertly in a state of rest. Once steady motion is established we have an equally hard job stopping it again. This time the inertia of the mass causes it to remain in uniform motion. Inertia therefore is experienced as resistance to a change of velocity..

Moment. If a force acts at a distance from a point to which it is connected by a lever, the moment of the force about the point is a measure of the *torque* applied:

$$\text{Moment} = \text{force} \times \text{length of lever} = \text{torque} \qquad (2\text{–}21)$$

To distinguish dimensionally between moment and work, a moment is measured in *lbf ft*, work in *ft lbf* in the FPSR system or Nm (joule) in the SI system (table 2–5).

Moment of inertia. A measure of the work that would be needed to impart kinetic energy of rotation to a body about an axis. The moment of inertia depends upon the shape and distribution of mass about the axis of rotation, fig. 2.7a. The clearest picture is that of a flywheel: when stationary it is in balance about its axis, regardless of angular position. But to make it rotate involves work and to stop it also requires work. Every little particle of the flywheel has a different mass Δm, the centre of gravity of which is located on a moment arm, r, from the axis of rotation. We know from eq (2–16) that, taking just one little bit of the flywheel,

$$\text{kinetic energy, } KE_{bit} = \tfrac{1}{2} \times \Delta m \times \text{linear speed}^2$$

where the linear speed of the bit, whirling around at ω radians per second is shown in fig. 2.7b and:

$$\text{linear velocity, } v = r_\omega \qquad (2\text{–}22)$$

so that $$KE_{bit} = (\Delta m r^2) \ \omega^2$$

and the kinetic energy of the whole, which is the work done in causing the total mass of the body M to rotate at a rate ω, is the sum of the individual kinetic energies of all of its bits:

$$KE_{whole} = \sum_0^M \left(\Delta mr^2 \right) \omega^2 \qquad (2\text{--}23)$$

Here $\sum_0^M$ uses the Greek letter sigma (Σ) to mean 'the sum of all of the little bits from 0 to total mass M'.

$$\text{moment of inertia of the whole, } I = \sum_0^M \Delta mr^2 \qquad (2\text{--}24)$$

Now, fig. 2.7a showed a body being rotated about two different axes. The total mass is the same, but the moment of inertia will be different depending upon which axis is used. We distinguish I_{XX} from I_{YY}, and imagine redistributing the total mass in the form of a spinning ring, a torus, with a *constant radius of gyration*, k, such that in the case of rotation about the X–X and Y–Y axes respectively:

$$\text{moment of inertia, } I_{XX} = Mk^2_{XX} \qquad (2\text{--}25a)$$
$$I_{YY} = Mk^2_{YY} \qquad (2\text{--}25b)$$

This is shown in fig. 2.7c.

Momentum. A fundamental property of a mass in motion, defined as:

$$\text{momentum} = \text{mass} \times \text{velocity}$$
$$M = mV \qquad (2\text{--}26)$$

The Newtonian system of dynamics is based upon three axioms called Newton's laws of motion:

(i) Every body continues in a state of rest or of uniform motion in a straight line unless it is compelled to change that state by the action of a force upon it.
(ii) The rate of change of momentum per unit time is proportional to the force causing it and its direction is the same as that of the force.
(iii) To every action there is an equal and opposite reaction.

If we look back to eq (2–12) and Newton's second law:

$$\text{force} = \text{rate of exchange of momentum} = \text{mass} \times \text{rate of change of}$$
$$\text{speed of time}$$
$$F = m \, dV/dt \qquad (2\text{--}27)$$

(where dV/dt is the ratio of a very small change in velocity ΔV with a small increment in time Δt, as the increments tend to zero).

But, *change of speed/time taken = acceleration*, a, which shows that eq (2–27) is identical to eq (2–12).

Power. The rate of doing work, which is the same as the rate at which energy is expended:

$$\text{power} = \text{force} \times \text{distance through which it is applied/time taken}$$
$$= \text{force} \times \text{velocity}$$
$$\text{i.e., } P = FV \qquad (2\text{--}28)$$

Conventionally power is measured in horsepower, or watts (1 watt = 1 joule per second) which are related by:

$$1 \text{ horsepower} = 550 \text{ ftlb/s } (33\,000 \text{ ftlb/min})$$
$$= 746 \text{ watts} \qquad (2\text{--}29)$$

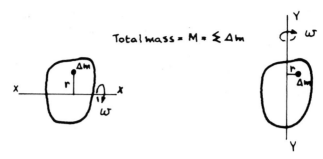

a. Moment of inertia about X-X axis, I_{xx}, is greater than moment of inertia of same body about Y-Y axis, I_{yy}.

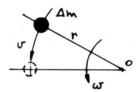

b Linear velocity v of particle, Δm rotating with angular velocity, ω, about an axis through instantaneous centre of rotation, O.

$$v = r\omega \qquad Eq (2-22)$$

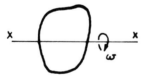 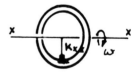

$$I_{xx} = M k_{xx}^2 \qquad Eq (2-25a)$$

c. Replacement of a body by a ring having same mass, M, and moment of inertia I_{xx}. The radius of gyration of such a ring is k_{xx}.

Fig. 2.7   Moment of inertia and radius of gyration.

For a piston engine we can apply eq (2–19) to calculate the *indicated horsepower*, IHP, as long as we know the capacity (total swept volume), the revolutions per minute, rpm, and the *indicated mean effective pressure*, IMEP, within the cylinders:

$$IHP = IMEP \times capacity \times rpm/33000 \qquad (2–30)$$

Mechanical losses prevent the theoretical IHP being realised. When all such losses are taken into account by using a dynamometer or a *prony brake* to measure the actual power transmitted by the engine drive shaft, we are measuring the *brake horsepower*, BHP (or *shaft brake horsepower*, SHP), where:

$$\text{BHP} = \text{engine mechanical efficiency, } \eta_m \times \text{IHP} \quad (2\text{-}31)$$

For a turbopropeller engine which produces shaft horsepower, plus residual jet thrust, then, in FPSR units:

$$\text{thrust equivalent horsepower} = \text{shaft horsepower} + \text{jet thrust} \times \text{true airspeed}/550$$
$$(2\text{-}32a)$$

in which the true airspeed, TAS, is really given in ft/s, so as to keep the units right. Under sea level static conditions 1 TEHP is produced by about 2.6 lbf jet thrust, so that:

$$\text{TEHP} \approx \text{SHP} + \text{jet thrust}/2.6 \quad (2\text{-}32b)$$

However, for practical (non-sales talk) purposes, the engineer counts only SHP. In each of these cases we assume that a propeller is used to produce the ultimate thrust horsepower, THP, and it is necessary to multiply the BHP in eq (2–31), or in eq (2–32b) by propeller efficiency. A wooden propeller has an efficiency around 70 per cent, while a metal propeller is about 80 per cent efficient so that, roughly:

$$\begin{aligned} \text{THP} &= \text{propeller efficiency, } \eta \times \text{BHP} \\ &= 0.7 \text{ to } 0.8 \text{ of the power available from the engine} \quad (2\text{-}33) \end{aligned}$$

under the actual conditions occurring in flight.

Slug (*see* under *Aerodynamics and Aeroplane Geometry*).
Specific heat (*see* under *Thermal*, or *heat energy*).

Engines and powerplants

Anti-detonants. A given mixture of air and fuel in the cylinders of a piston can be caused to explode prematurely (at, or just before the beginning of the firing stroke) by a critical combination of compression pressure and charge temperature.
Detonation or 'knocking' (as the phenomenon is called) causes loss of power and mechanical shocks that can cause engine failure.

There are two ways of making a fuel anti-knock. Both prevent excessively high temperatures and the undesirable burning characteristics which cause damage inside the cylinders. The first is to refine and blend fuels with high octane-ratings. The second is to add various substances which delay combustion to higher temperatures and pressures.
Octane-rating is the percentage of iso-octane in a blend of iso-octane and normal heptane (both of which are pure spirits) which has the same knock characteristics as the fuel being rated. Iso-octane has a very high anti-knock value, whereas heptane detonates readily in an engine. A mixture of both spirits has an intermediate value based upon their relative proportions.

The second method of delaying knock is by use of additives – substances which delay combustion. Ethyl fluid is one, containing tetraethyl lead, ethylene dibromide and aniline dye. Other additives are iso-octane, iso-pentane, ethyl alcohol, or benzol. The last two have certain attractions, but the alcohol does not have a good calorific value (work available per unit mass), and it has a marked affinity to water. Benzol raises the freezing point of the fuel excessively.

While 'leaded' fuels are commonest, some difficulties arise from fouling of spark plugs and corrosion of certain parts of the engine. Lead-based additives are now increasingly unpopular among conservationists, and people troubled about pollution of the atmosphere.

Bleed air. Compressed air from the main engine compressor drawn off for cabin pressurisation, heating and driving various services.

Boost pressure. Strictly, the increase of engine manifold pressure by supercharging (up to 20 lbf/in^2 (957.6 N/m^2) above atmospheric in some installations). The term is loosely used in general to define any measure of manifold pressure, usually in inches of mercury, Hg.

By-pass ratio. The ratio of the total air mass swallowed by a combination of jet engine plus fan, to the amount passing through the combustion chambers of the engine.

Carburettor and fuel injector. The function of the carburettor and the fuel injector is to supply the cylinders of an engine with an air/fuel mixture of the correct strength. There are three kinds of systems:

☐ *Float-type carburetter.* Which involves a float chamber. A negative-*g* unit is needed for inverted flight by specialised aerobatic aeroplanes.

☐ *Injection carburetter.* In which fuel is pumped into the eye of the supercharger inlet or intake valve ports.

☐ *Fuel injector system.* There is no choke: fuel is fed direct to the eye of the supercharger inlet, by way of an atomiser.

The last two types function in any position as long as the fuel supply from the tanks is maintained.

Critical engine. The engine, failure of which gives the most adverse effect on the flying characteristics of the aeroplane relative to the case immediately under consideration.

Ducted fan or propeller. A fan or propeller driven by the engine and working within a duct to reduce tip losses and noise, thus increasing propulsive efficiency.

Engine. A device for converting thermal energy, released by burning fuel, into propulsive work. For the purposes of this book we are interested in:

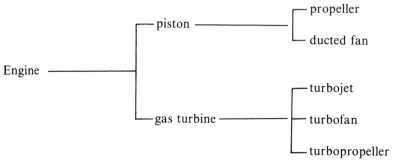

Exhaust gas temperature, EGT (also *jet pipe temperature, JPT*). The temperature used for control of the air/fuel ratio within efficient limits, so as to achieve the best power output, within the temperature limitations of the turbine and the tailpipe.

Feathering. Setting the blades of a stopped propeller at zero angle of attack, so as to reduce drag to the minimum by preventing windmilling, fig. 2.8.

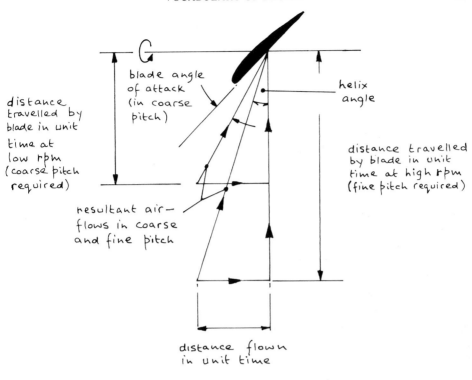

a. At lower rpm or higher airspeeds coarser pitch is needed for highest propeller efficiency

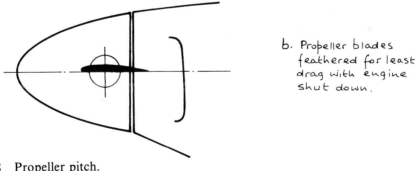

b. Propeller blades feathered for least drag with engine shut down.

Fig. 2.8 Propeller pitch.

Fuel. A liquid hydrocarbon, usually high octane (anti-knock) grade petrol or kerosene. Ultimately, the energy available in the fuel is released by burning with oxygen in air. The theoretically ideal (*stoichiometric*) ratio is 1 lb fuel to about 14 lb air. 1 lb petrol contains about 14.8×10^6 ft lbf energy (20.07 MJ) which, if all burned evenly in 1 minute with 100 per cent efficiency, would produce:

$$14\,800\,000/33\,000 = 448 \text{ hp (334.2 kW), using eq (2–29)} \qquad (2\text{–}34)$$

Losses in the process of converting thermal energy into mechanical work by a typical unsupercharged, i.e. normally aspirated piston engine, are shown in table 2–1:

TABLE 2-1

Percentage		Horsepower
100	Available in fuel	448
-2	heat lost in oil	-9
-11	heat loss to cooling air	-49
-5	heat lost to radiation	-22
-52	heat lost to exhaust	-234
---		---
30	Indicated horsepower	134
-5	mechanical losses	-22
---		---
25	Shaft brake horsepower	112

Thus, the brake thermal efficiency of the process is only about 25 per cent, so that the thermal output results in:

$$0.25 \times 448 \ = \ 112 \text{ hp (83.5 kW)} \tag{2-35}$$

This is the residual power left over for propulsion, before the propeller is bolted into place, with its own attendant losses.

Fuel consumption. The quantity of fuel burned in unit time. A more useful measure of fuel consumption for engineers is:

Specific fuel consumption (sfc), c'. The weight of fuel flowing to produce a given engine output. In the case of a piston-propeller engine, sfc is measured in fuel consumed per hour per brake horsepower (μg/J). For a jet, sfc is the weight of fuel consumed per hour per unit thrust, lb/h/lbf (mg/N/s).

Published figures necessarily refer to idealised standard conditions with no installation losses, so that specific fuel consumption is given in terms of rated power and thrust. In practice power and thrust are degraded by factors like propeller wear and tear, inlet losses, cowl drag, aerodynamic interference, scrubbing losses from accelerated propeller and fan washes, ram drag, pylon drag (and other sources of drag caused by the way in which an engine is mounted), bleed air, power absorbed by air conditioning and other services – all in addition to normal loss of air swallowed with changing ambient conditions. The general equation for sfc really involves the net, or 'stub' power or thrust, so that:

specific fuel consumption, c' = weight of fuel flow/net or 'stub 'power(piston) (2–36a)

μ' = weight of fuel flow/net or 'stub' thrust (jet)(2–36b)

The losses suffered inflate the actual sfc to 1.5 to 2 times more than the values given in brochures.

As a rough rule, in the case of simple piston engine like that given in table 2-1, to produce 112 BHP for 1 hour would require:

$$sfc, c' = 60 \times 1 \, \text{lb}/112 \, \text{hp} = \text{about } 0.5 \, \text{lb/h/hp} \; (85 \, \mu\text{g/J}) \qquad (2\text{–}37\text{a})$$

An equivalent value for a subsonic jet engine might be:

$$sfc, \mu' = 0.8 \text{ to } 0.9 \, \text{lb/h/lbf} \; (25 \text{ to } 28 \, \text{mg/N/s}) \qquad (2\text{–}37\text{b})$$

Fuel injector (*see carburetter*).

Humidity and relative humidity. Air is able to hold water vapour: the warmer the air the more vapour it can hold. When we feel the moisture in the air we say that it is humid. Air that can hold no more vapour is saturated. Humidity is measured in terms of relative humidity:

$$= \frac{\text{water vapour content of air}}{\text{water vapour content of saturated air at same temperature}} \qquad (2\text{–}38)$$

Humidity varies between air masses and with different meterological conditions in different parts of the world.

Indicated horsepower (*see power*, under **Energy and other mechanical concepts**).

Mixture control. A lever or knob which the pilot controls the ratio fuel/air for any given throttle setting. It can also be regarded as an altitude control by means of which the amount of fuel is reduced by the pilot as air density falls with height during a climb.

Pitch. The geometrical distance that a propeller would move forward in one revolution if the blades slid down an inclined plane, the angle of which is determined by the local pitch angle at a relevant section (*see* fig. 2.8):

$$\text{pitch angle} = \text{helix angle} + \text{blade angle of attack}$$
$$\beta = \phi + \alpha \qquad (2\text{–}39)$$

Propeller efficiency, η. The effectiveness of the propeller, expressed in terms of the ratio: *thrust horsepower/shaft horsepower*. Efficiencies vary, as we saw in eq (2–33).

Propwash. The airflow caused by the propeller alone.

Pusher and tractor propeller. A pusher propeller is arranged behind the engine (which points aft), while a tractor is in front of a forward pointing engine.

Slipstream. The relative airflow past an aircraft.

Specific weight, $\overline{p}$. A useful standard of design merit (as long as it can be accurately defined for a speed and height, both of which affect engine output):

$$\text{specific weight (pistons)} \; \overline{\omega} = \text{engine weight/net thrust horsepower}$$
$$\approx \text{engine weight/BHP} \qquad (2\text{–}40)$$

Strictly speaking the engine weight should also include the weight of the propeller.

$$\text{specific weight (jet)} \; \overline{p} = \text{engine weight/net thrust}$$
$$\approx \text{engine weight/rated thrust} \qquad (2\text{–}41)$$

Supercharger and turbo(super)charger. A form of pump which compresses the air supplied to the cylinders, to be mixed with fuel, so as to maintain power to higher altitudes. Whereas early superchargers were mechanically driven by gears, the modern turbosupercharger (*turbocharger*) is driven by the flow of exhaust gas through a turbine. A compressor is coupled to the turbine by a common shaft.

Throttle. The engine 'power' control by means of which the pilot varies the quantity of fuel/air mixture supplied to the combustion stage of the engine cycle and hence the power output.

Thrust, F. The force produced mainly by the propulsion system. A quick rule of thumb is that every brake horsepower generated by a piston-propeller engine produces at most about 3 lbf (13.44 N) thrust when the aircraft is lined up for take-off with the throttle wide open (a closer value is 2.6 lbf (11.5N), *see* eqs (2–32b) and (2–42)). Fig. 2.9 shows typical propwash velocity measured in knots for a light aeroplane with a 180 hp (134 kW) engine. With a standard condition propeller in fine pitch and the aeroplane stationary, propeller efficiency is about 0.7 and propwash is around 86 knots (145 ft/s (44.3 m/s)). Therefore, using eqs (2–28), (2–29) and (2–31):

$$\text{thrust, } F \times 145 = 0.7 \times \text{BHP} \times 550$$

which, on tranposing for thrust/brake horsepower, gives:

$$\text{F/BHP} \approx 2.6 \qquad\qquad (2\text{–}42)$$

This number is the same as that shown in eq (2–32b).

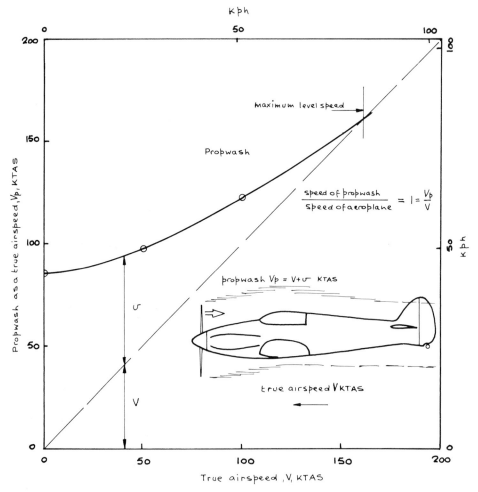

Fig. 2.9   Propwash velocity, Vp, as a function of true airspeed, V, for a typical 180BHP engine-propeller combination.

Flying controls, handling and stability

Control and *stability* are complementary. Control is needed to make an aircraft manoeuvrable. Stability is provided to make it behave during those moments when the control of the pilot is relaxed or diverted. However, control power is needed to overcome stability: the greater the inherent stability the more effort that is required. In the end, the degree of control required becomes a measure of aircraft stability.

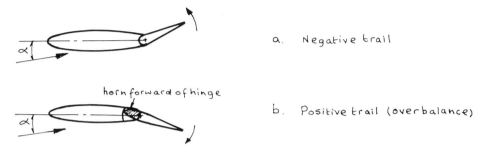

a. Negative trail

horn forward of hinge

b. Positive trail (overbalance)

Fig. 2.10 Control trail, or float.

Handling is another matter. An aeroplane may be stable and controllable, but unpleasant to fly. Another may be sheer delight for the pilot, even though stability may be almost non-existent. Assessment of handling and the associated terms is a disciplined way of attempting to describe subjective qualities, like sweetness and liveliness, in an objective way.

Control and control circuit behaviour

Aileron. A simple flap-like surface set at the outboard trailing edge of a wing, to provide control in roll.
Backlash. Free play in the cockpit control, i.e., any motion of a control which does not immediately deflect a control surface.
Breakout force. The force a pilot must apply to move a control from a given position. Such forces always involve circuit friction.
Elevator. The pitching control: usually a simple flap-like surface attached to the tailplane, or to a canard foreplane.
  The *monobloc elevator* is the continental name (used widely by the French) for the all-moving *stabilator*, which has no separate tailplane and elevator surfaces.
Float or trail. See fig. 2.10, is the tendency of a control surface to move with changes in the relative wind – either 'with' the wind, or 'against' it.
Friction. Control friction resists the pilot's effort to move a cockpit control.
Gearing. The relationship between control surface movement and the movement of the control in the cockpit.
Horn. Control horn balances are fitted to aileron, elevator and rudder surfaces, as required, so as to reduce the control forces felt by the pilot.
Hunting. Oscillation of a control surface about its trimmed position.
Locking. When a control surface moves to full deflection (due to overbalance or float) and it is difficult to centralise it using normal effort.
Monobloc stabiliser or elevator. An all-moving pitching control and stabiliser combined, with no separate tailplane and elevator.

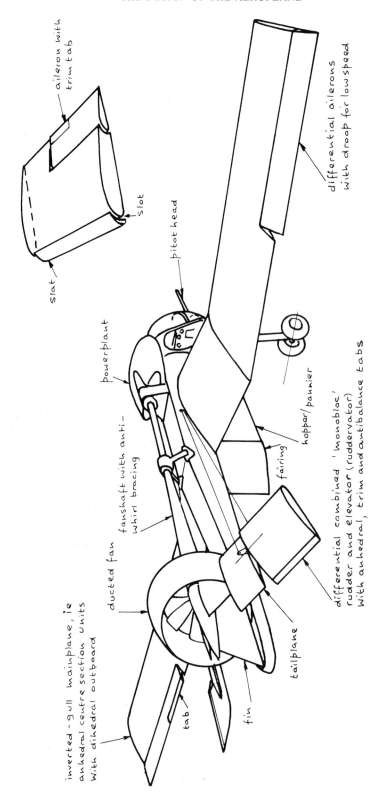

Fig. 2.11 Aerial-work aeroplane project illustrating some of the terms defined here.

Overbalance. The opposite of self-centring. A control is overbalanced when a force must be applied to prevent further deflection. If the force needed to deflect a control decreases with increasing deflection (but does not reverse), a *tendency to overbalance* exists.

Rudder. A simple flap-like surface attached to the fin, giving control in yaw. Certain aeroplanes employ monobloc fin and rudder surfaces.

Stabilator (see *Monobloc stabiliser*).

Tab. A minor elevator-like control surface attached to the trailing edge of the major elevator, aileron or rudder. Some tabs are used for *balance*, to reduce the force needed to deflect a control. Others are *anti-balance* tabs, used to increase control forces. *Geared* and *servo* tabs are special variants of the basic balance tab.

Trim tabs are used to reduce to zero the control force felt by the pilot. They fix the angle at which a control surface trails, or floats.

Trail (*see float*).

Handling terms

Control effectiveness. If deflection of a control produces the required response, then the control is effective. There are no degrees of effectiveness.

Feel. The subjective impression of the pilot to the response of the aircraft to control. That impression is correlated with the mechanical characteristics of the control system and the force gradients resulting from control deflection.

Harmonisation. Controls are said to be well harmonised when forces and deflections, and the response of the aircraft to them, are such that the pilot is not aware of having to use too much or too little effort. A rule passed down from the Second World War is that for sweet handling the *aileron: elevator: rudder* force needed to produce a common rate of response about each axis should be:

$$A:E:R = 1:2:4 \qquad (2\text{--}43)$$

Response. A term open to misuse. Response must be related to time. It is wrong to talk about 'control response', and accurate to say *aircraft response to control*. Responsiveness depends upon rotational inertia about an axis, aerodynamic damping and stability. Large aeroplanes tend to be sluggish. Very small aeroplanes tend to be as quick as cats.

Sensitivity. A sensitive control is one which produces a rapid response for the aircraft concerned, having due regard for smallness of control deflection, or control force, or both.

Spongy. A control is spongy when it feels as if it is connected to a spring, which must be compressed or extended before the control surface begins to move.

Response of aircraft

Dutch roll. A regular short period oscillation in yaw and roll.

Flutter. A high frequency oscillation usually caused by the inter-action of aerodynamic forces and the natural frequencies of control surfaces and structure.

Pilot induced oscillation, PIO. A driven oscillation, sometimes divergent, of the combination of the pilot and aircraft together. Aircraft response to control is so fast that slower corrective actions of the pilot get out of phase, sometimes disastrously.

Pitch up. A nose-up pitching motion which may be uncontrollable, and may be especially violent during steep turns at high Mach numbers.

Pitching. Angular motion about the lateral axis.

Porpoising. Fairly regular pitching oscillations of low frequency.

Post stall gyration, PSG. Uncontrolled motion(s) about one or more aircraft axes following departure from controlled flight. Large fluctuations in angle of attack are usually encountered.

Rocking. A lateral and directional oscillation, predominantly in roll.

Roll. Angular motion about the longitudinal axis.

Sideslip. Flight with a component of airflow from the side. *Skid* is sideslip towards the outside of a turn. *Slip* is sideslip into a turn.

Sinking. A marked increase in rate of descent with the aeroplane maintaining a more or less constant attitude, increasing the angle of attack. The condition is frequently met in the approach to the stall.

Skid (*see sideslip*).

Snaking. A lateral and directional oscillation, predominantly in *yaw*.

Tightening. With an aeroplane trimmed for level flight, tightening is the condition in a turn or a pull-out such that a push force is needed on the stick to hold constant 'g'.

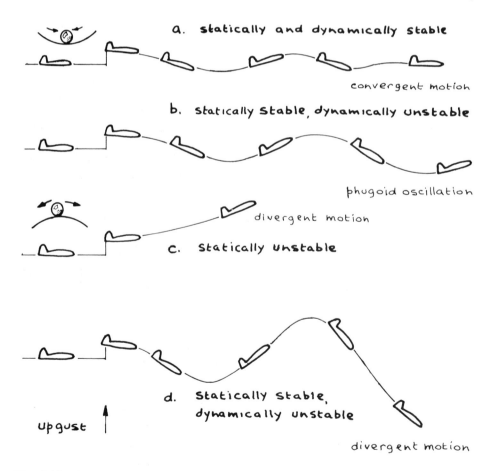

Fig. 2.12   Stable and unstable motions.

Vibration. A structural oscillation of high frequency, usually more than 1 cycle per second (1 Hz).

Wallowing. Uncommanded regular or irregular motion about all three axes at once.

Wandering. Slow and steady uncommanded changes of aircraft heading, not necessarily in the same direction.

Yawing. Angular motion about the normal axis (*see* table 2–7).

Stability and manoeuvrability

Assessment of stability. An aircraft is *stable* if, after disturbance, it tends to return to the trimmed condition.

measure of stability = magnitude of restoring moment/magnitude of disturbance   (2–44)

If the restoring moment is zero, stability is *neutral* and the aircraft remains in the disturbed state. A nose-up restoring moment is positive and nose-down, negative.

If, after disturbance, the aircraft departs still further from the trimmed condition it is *unstable*.

Fundamentally we are concerned with two kinds of stability:

☐ *Static stability*. This determines whether or not the aircraft will initially tend to return to its trimmed condition.

☐ *Dynamic stability*. This governs the subsequent behaviour after the initial response of the aircraft to the static restoring moment.

Both stabilities are affected in turn by the position of the control surfaces. If these are held rigidly by the pilot throughout the disturbance they are said to be *stick-fixed*, and the restoring moment has a related value. But if during the disturbance the control surfaces are allowed to trail or float, as when the pilot has let go of the stick (i.e., *stick-free*) then the stick-fixed restoring moment may be reduced or even increased, depending upon the control position when floating.

Centre of gravity (CG) margin H_n. The distance between the position of the CG and the *neutral point*, expressed as a percentage of the standard mean chord of the wing. The greater the CG margin the more stable the aircraft (*see* eq (2–46)).

Directional stability. 'Weathercock' stability in *yaw*.

Lateral stability. Stability in *roll*.

Longitudinal stability. Stability in *pitch*.

Magnitude of disturbance. A disturbance involves a change in angle of attack of a surface, $\Delta\alpha$, but this is useless in itself. A more useful measure within the working range of angle of attack is the corresponding change in lift coefficient, ΔC_L so that if the slope of the lift curve with angle of attack a is:

$$a = \Delta C_L/\Delta\alpha \qquad (2\text{–}45)$$

we may rewrite eq (2–44), placing a minus sign (–) in front of it to show that the restoring moment about the *CG* is against the disturbance when it is stable,

$-\Delta \mathrm{M}_{CG}$:

$$\text{measure of stability} = -\Delta\mathrm{M}_{CG}/\Delta\mathrm{C}_L \qquad (2\text{–}46)$$
$$= CG\ margin,\ H_n$$

$$\text{where measure of disturbance} = \Delta CL = a\ \Delta\alpha \qquad (2\text{–}47)$$

Manoeuvrability. The ability of an aircraft to change direction: the greater the change in a given time, the greater the manoeuvrability. Because a control movement by the pilot introduces an acceleration, 'g', normal to the flight path, we have two criteria:

$$\text{Stick-fixed manoeuvrability} = \text{stick movement}/\text{applied 'g'} \qquad (2\text{--}48)$$
$$\text{Stick-free manoeuvrability} = \text{stick force}/\text{applied 'g'} \qquad (2\text{--}49)$$

This is related to the 'feel' of the aircraft, because the stick force felt by the pilot is that needed to restrain the elevator from floating.

Manoeuvre margin. The distance between the centre of gravity and the *manoeuvre point*, expressed as a percentage of the standard mean chord, which gives a measure of manoeuvrability. The smaller the margin the 'twitchier' the response to control.

Manoeuvre points. The centre of gravity positions at which:

☐ Stick-fixed: *stick movement per 'g'* is zero.
☐ Stick-free: *stick force per 'g'* is zero.

Neutral points. The centre of gravity positions for neutral static stability where:

☐ Stick-fixed: *stick movement to trim a change of speed* is zero.
☐ Stick-free: *stick force to trim a change of speed* is zero.

Static margin, K_n. The real measure of static stability which is proportional to the CG margin, such that:

$$K_n = \psi_1 \, H_n \qquad (2\text{--}50)$$

The relationship ψ_1 tends to change with airspeed, bending and twisting of the airframe, propwash effects, and movements of passengers and crew (in larger aeroplanes).

Performance and operational terms

The following terms are intended to be of most use to pilots, although designers cannot afford to ignore them. Several quantities such as ambient temperature and airspeed cannot be measured directly by the instruments, but must be derived from instrument readings using theoretical relationships. In this section we assume that in all cases an 'instrument correction' is applied to our instruments to remove their inaccuracies.

Airspeed terms

CAS. Calibrated airspeed is the indicated speed of the aeroplane, corrected for position and instrument error. CAS is true airspeed, TAS, in the standard atmosphere at sea level.

EAS. Equivalent airspeed is CAS corrected for *scale altitude effect* (compressibility).

KCAS. Calibrated airspeed expressed in knots.

GS. Ground speed is the speed of an aeroplane relative to the ground.

IAS. Indicated airspeed is that shown on the airspeed indicator. Published IAS values assume zero instrument error, in exactly the same way as KCAS, KIAS and MIAS refer to IAS in knots and mph respectively.

M. Mach number (after Ernst Mach (1838–1916) the Austrian philosopher and physicist who first noted its significance). The ratio of the true airspeed, V, to the speed of sound, a, for the ambient conditions:

$$M = V/a \qquad (2\text{--}51)$$

TAS. True airspeed is the speed of an aeroplane relative to undisturbed air. It is related to calibrated airspeed corrected for altitude, temperature and compressibility, and to equivalent airspeed by the $\sqrt{}$ *relative density*, where:

$$\text{Relative air density, } \sigma = \rho/\rho_0 \qquad (2\text{--}52)$$
$$\text{and, TAS} = \text{EAS}/\sqrt{\sigma}$$
$$\text{or, } V = V_i/\sqrt{\sigma} \qquad (2\text{--}53)$$

When CAS and EAS are almost the same (say at low altitude) we have approximately $V = \text{CAS}/\sqrt{\sigma}$. Fig. 2.13 shows the relationship between KTAS and KEAS. Dynamic pressure, q, ISA, is given in fig. 2.14.

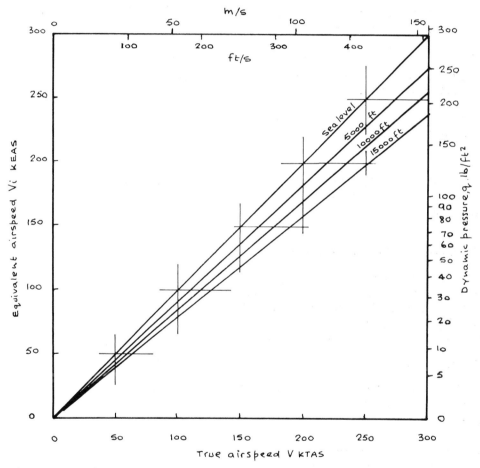

Fig. 2.13a   The relationship between true and equivalent airspeed and dynamic pressure (*see* eq (2–9)) in the International Standard Atmosphere.

The following airspeeds are EAS:

V_A. Design manoeuvring speed is the maximum speed at which application of full control will not overstress the aeroplane.

Vapp. Approach speed.

V_B. Design speed for maximum gust intensity.

V_C. Design cruising speed.

V_D. Design diving speed.

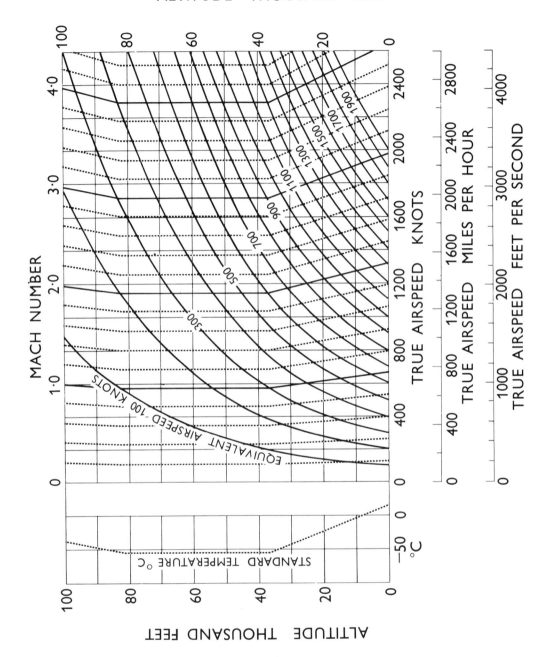

Fig. 2.13b   Theoretical relationship between airspeed Mach number.

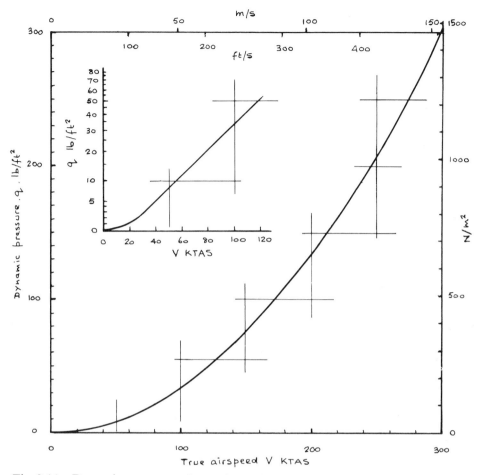

Fig. 2.14 Dynamic pressure and true airspeed at sealevel ISA. To find q at some other altitude multiply by the appropriate relative density (*see* fig. 3.1). The inset expands the ordinate logarithmically to make reading easier at low airspeed.

Non-aerobatic aeroplanes: the minimum value shall be at least equal to the greater of
$1.4 V_C$ and $V_C + 40$ KEAS.

Aerobatic aeroplanes: the minimum value of V_D shall be at least equal to 1.6 V_C.

V_{DF}. Demonstrated flight diving speed which, through various unexpected causes, may be less than V_D.

V_F. Flap limiting speed (when down).

V_{FE}. Maximum speed for actually extending or raising the flaps.

V_{LE}. Maximum speed with landing gear-extended.

V_{LO}. Maximum speed for lowering or retracting the undercarriage.

V_{MCA}. The minimum control speed in flight at which the aeroplane can be controlled directionally in accordance with Federal Aviation Regulations and British Civil Airworthiness Requirements. The prescribed conditions are: one engine inoperative and windmilling; not more than 5 deg. bank towards the live engine; take-off power on the live engine; landing gear up; flaps in the take-off position; and the most rearward centre of gravity.

V_{MCG}. Minimum control speed at which it is possible to maintain directional control during take-off when the engine fails and the wheels are still on the runway.

V_{MO}. Maximum operating speed.

V_{MU}. Minimum demonstrated unstick speed. At this speed it is possible to leave the ground with all engines operating and climb without undue hazard.

V_{NE} or M_{NE}. Never exceed speed or Mach number.

V_{NO}. Normal operating speed is the maximum structural cruising speed that should not be exceeded except in smooth air, and then only with caution.

V_{REF}. A term not used officially in the UK, which has originated in the USA. It is more or less the same as:

V_{AT}. The target threshold speed (i.e. the 'over the hedge speed', which is often shown on a graph of airspeed against weight.

V_{AT_0}. Target threshold speed, all engines working.

V_{AT_1}. Target threshold speed, one engine inoperative (and so on for V_{AT_2}).

V_S. Stalling speed or the minimum steady flight speed at which the aeroplane is controllable.

V_{SO}. Stalling speed or the minimum steady flight speed at which the aeroplane is controllable in the landing configuration.

V_{SSE}. Intentional one engine inoperative speed is a minimum speed selected by the manufacturer for intentionally rendering one engine inoperative in flight for pilot training. In Britain one engine should not be shut down intentionally for pilot training, or any reason other than an emergency, below 3 000 ft (910 m) above ground level (ref. 2.3).

V_X. Best angle-of-climb speed is the airspeed which delivers the greatest gain in altitude in the shortest possible horizontal distance (also called the best gradient-of-climb speed).

V_Y. Best rate-of-climb speed is the airspeed which delivers the greatest gain in altitude in the shortest possible time.

V_{YSE}. V_Y but with a failed engine on a twin.

V_1. Decision speed on take-off. Up to V_1, if an engine fails it should be possible to stop the aeroplane in the remaining runway length. Beyond V_1 the take-off must be continued.

V_R. Rotation speed at which the aeroplane is rotated in pitch into the take-off attitude, just before lift-off.

V_2. Take-off safety speed established by the manufacturer to add a safety margin to the minimum control speed, taking into account:

☐ Failure of the critical engine.
☐ Propeller windmilling on the failed engine.
☐ Full power on the live engine.
☐ Landing gear extended and flaps as recommended for take-off.
☐ Pilot of average strength and ability.
☐ Element of surprise.

Terms describing ambient conditions

ISA. International Standard Atmosphere based upon that of the International Civil Aviation Organisation, ICAO:

the air is a perfectly dry gas;
temperature at sea level 15° Celsius (59° Fahrenheit);
pressure at sea level 29.92 in Hg (1013.25 mb),

$$2\ 116\ lb/ft^2\ (1.01325 = 10^5\ N/m^2);$$

density at sea level, ρ_0, 0.00238 slugs/ft³, 0.0765 lb/ft³ (1.225 kg/m³);
temperature lapse rate 1.98°C/1000 ft (6.5°C/km) from sea level to the altitude at

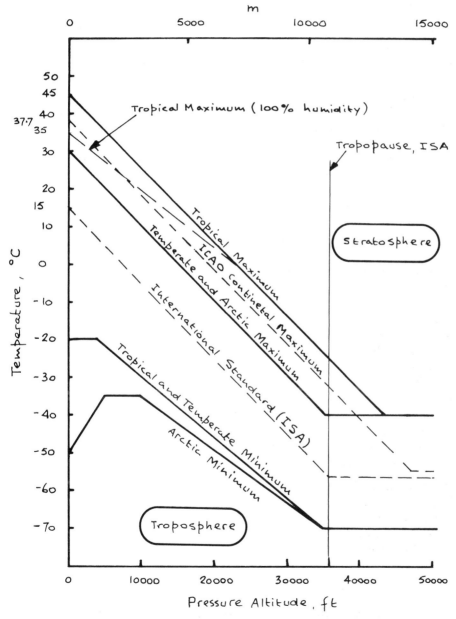

Fig. 2.15   Standard climates shown as envelopes for design purposes (ref. 2.4).

which temperature stabilises (in theory) at –56.5°C, i.e. 36090 ft (11000 m). That
point is called the *tropopause* (see fig. 2.15);
speed of sound at sea level 1116.4 ft/s (340.3 m/s);
kinematic viscosity, $\nu = \mu/\rho$, 1.5723×10^{-4} ft²/s (1.4606×10^{-5} m²/s);
ratio of specific heats, γ, 1.4.

OAT. Outside air temperature is the free air static (ambient) temperature obtained
either from in-flight temperature indications (adjusted for instrument error and
compressibility effects) or ground meteorological sources.
Density altitude. The height in the standard atmosphere at which the prevailing air
density occurs. Density altitude exceeds the *pressure altitude* (measured by the
altimeter) by roughly 110 ft/°C (33.5 m/°C) that the ambient temperature exceeds the
standard temperature for the altitude, and *vice versa*.
Indicated pressure altitude. The number actually read from an altimeter when the
barometric subscale has been set to 1013 mb, 29.92 in Hg.
Pressure altitude. Altitude measured from standard sea level pressure (1013 mb) by a
pressure or barometric altimeter. It is the indicated pressure altitude corrected for
position and instrument error. Here, altimeter instrument errors are assumed to be
zero.
Scale altitude (see Compressibility error under *Pressure error* in Terms used in flight
planning).
Station pressure. Actual atmospheric pressure at field elevation.

Terms describing power settings

Take-off power (TOP). Maximum power permissible for take-off.
Maximum continuous power (MCP). Maximum power permissible continuously in
flight.
Maximum climb power. Maximum power permissible during climb.
Maximum cruise power. Maximum power permissible during cruise.

Terms used in flight planning

Accelerate-stop distance. The distance needed to accelerate an aeroplane to a specified
speed and, assuming failure of an engine at the instant that speed is attained, to bring
the aircraft to a stop.
Ceiling. There are two ceilings:

☐ *Absolute ceiling.* The altitude at which the rate of climb is zero. Most normally
   aspirated piston engined aeroplanes seem to take about 45 minutes to reach
   somewhere near their absolute ceilings. Theoretically it cannot be attained.
☐ *Performance and service ceiling.* The *performance ceiling* (civil) is the altitude at
   which rate of climb is typically 150 ft/min (0.762 m/s). The military equivalent is the
   service ceiling where rate of climb is 100 ft/min (0.508 m/s).

Climb gradient. The demonstrated ratio of the change in height during a portion of a
climb in still air, to the horizontal distance traversed in the same time interval, usually
expressed as a percentage.
Climb rate (rate of climb). The demonstrated ratio of the change in height during a
portion of a climb in still air, to the time taken for that change:

rate, v_c = change in height/time, ft/min (m/s)

= change in height/horizontal distance × horizontal distance/time taken

= gradient × true airspeed   (2–54)

for aeroplanes of modest performance.

(Note: the same equation can be applied to rate of descent v_d)

Demonstrated crosswind velocity. The velocity of the crosswind component for which adequate control of the aeroplane during take-off and landing was actually demonstrated during certification tests.

MEA. Minimum *en route* instrument flight rule (IFR) altitude.

Minimum performance data (ref. 1.5). The information to be supplied with the aeroplane and made available to the Civil Aviation Authority for the aeroplane to be

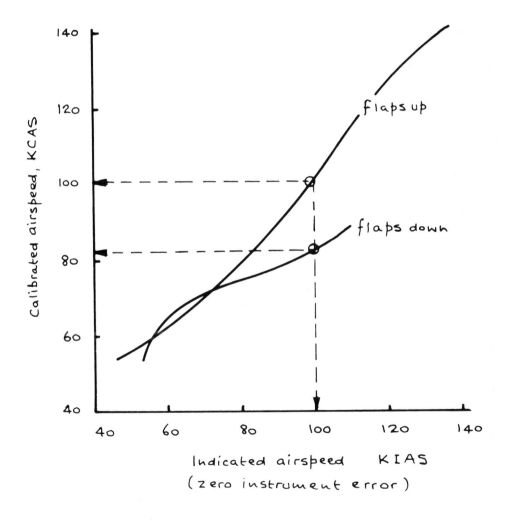

Fig. 2.16 Example of airspeed calibration.

certificated in the Performance Group E. Group E is the minimum clasification to qualify for certification in Britain in the Public Transport Category.

Pressure error. The pressure instruments which use the pitot-static sources suffer from:

☐ *Compressibility error.* At high speeds compressibility of the air increases its density, which adds an increment to the dynamic pressure. The airspeed indicator does not know this because it is calibrated on the assumption that air is incompressible, and over-reads in the same way that it would were the aeroplane to fly at the same true airspeed, but at a lower altitude. The error is therefore called *scale altitude effect*.

☐ *Position error* (PE). The error in readings caused by the position of the pitot head and static sources due to variations in the pressure field (streamline pattern) surrounding an aircraft. The field changes with airspeed and attitude to the flight path (angle of attack). In the absence of instrument error:

$$\text{calibrated airspeed} = \text{indicated airspeed} + \text{position error} \qquad (2\text{-}55)$$

Pressure errors are either presented as tables, or graphically, as shown in fig. 2.16. For most of our purposes equivalent airspeed, EAS, is equal to CAS (at sea level).

Route segment. A part of a route, each end of which is clearly identified by a geographical location, or a definite radio fix.

Screen height. The height above ground level at which a flight path pierces an imaginary erect screen on take-off and landing. Screen heights are 35 ft (10.7 m) and 50 ft (15.2 m), depending upon performance group and case.

WAT limits. Combinations of aeroplane *weight*, airfield *altitude* and outside air *temperature*, which together reduce the performance level to the airworthiness minima.

Noise. Sound that annoys.

Structural design terms

Aero-elasticity. Airloads on the skin distort the airframe, but the structure is said to be aero-elastic if it absorbs such loads without breakage and returns to its original shape when they are removed.

Bending relief. A technique used mainly to reduce the aero-elastic bending of wings, by spreading the weights of fuel, engines, and sometimes baggage loads, as far outboard as possible along the span.

Modulus of elasticity. A measure of material stiffness:

$$\text{Young's modulus of elasticity} = \text{stress}/\text{strain}$$
$$E = p/e \qquad (2\text{-}56)$$

Proof factor of safety. A measure of the ability of a structure to absorb the design limit load (i.e., maximum anticipated) without permanent distortion:

$$\text{proof factor of safety} = \text{proof load}/\text{limit load}$$
$$= \text{not less than } 1.0 \qquad (2\text{-}57)$$

Second moment of area. The moment of inertia of a section, the mass of which is unity.

Stiffness and specific stiffness. The ability of a material to resist distortion or strain. In aeronautics materials with high *specific stiffness* are needed for lightness:

specific stiffness = Young's modulus of elasticity/density of material (2–58)

Strain. Change of shape, particularly the major change resulting from a uniquely applied load. For example, strain occurs in tension, compression and shear, and it is expressed:

$$\text{strain} = \text{change in dimension}/\text{original dimension} \qquad (2\text{–}59)$$

Strain is caused by stress and *vice versa* (*see* fig. 2.17).
Strength and specific Strength:
  Proof strength. The strength needed to sustain the proof load:

$$\text{proof load} = \text{design limit load} \times \text{proof factor of safety} \qquad (2\text{–}60)$$

  Ultimate strength. The strength needed to sustain the ultimate load:

$$\begin{aligned}\text{ultimate load} &= \text{design limit load} \times \text{ultimate factor of safety} \\ &= 1.5 \times \text{design limit load} \qquad (2\text{–}61)\end{aligned}$$

in every case except certain specialised military applications.
  Specific strength. A useful basis for comparison of material strength:

$$\text{specific strength} = \text{ultimate strength}/\text{density of material} \qquad (2\text{–}62)$$

Stress. A description of the condition when a force is applied to a material over a given area:

$$\text{stress} = \text{force}/\text{area of application} \qquad (2\text{–}63)$$

The form of the equation shows stress to be analogous to pressure. Never think of stress in isolation, or of stress being the root cause of strain. Both stress and strain can cause each other.

Weight and balance terms

APS weight. Aircraft prepared for service weight: a fully equipped operational aeroplane, empty, i.e. without crew, fuel or payload.
Arm. The horizontal distance from the reference datum to the centre of gravity, **CG**, of an item.
AUW, W$_o$. All-up (gross) weight: the combination of empty weight and useful load (eq.(1–1)).
CG. Centre of gravity: the point at which an aeroplane would balance if suspended. Its distance from the reference datum is found by dividing the total moment by the total weight of the aircraft. Technically, at the **CG**:

the sum of all weight or force moments about the **CG** = 0

so that if the weight of any component is W_n and its distance from a datum is x_n, then

$$W\bar{x} - W_1x_1 - W_2x_2 \ldots - W_nx_n = 0 \qquad (2\text{–}64)$$

where W is the weight of the whole and $\bar{x}$ the distance of the **CG** from the datum.
CG *arm.* The arm obtained by adding the individual moments of all parts of an aeroplane about the reference datum, and dividing that sum by the total weight of the aircraft.
CG *limits.* The extreme locations of the centre of gravity within which the aeroplane must be operated at a given weight.

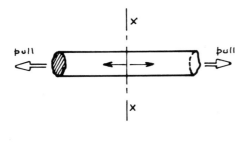

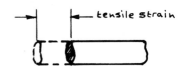

a. Tensile stress lengthens a member, and is measured by load ÷ cross sectional area at X–X.

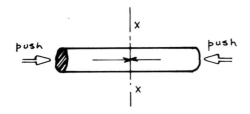

b. Compressive stress shortens a member, and is the opposite of a.

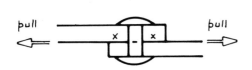

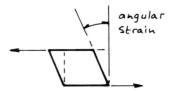

c. Shear stress causes strain measured as an angular displacement

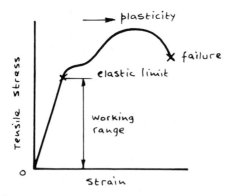

d. Behaviour of material when when stressed in tension. The object is to provide enough cross sectional area to keep within the working range of stress, ie, not to exceed the elastic limit.

Fig. 2.17   Basic stress, strain and elasticity.

Empty weights

☐ *Basic empty weight.* Standard empty weight plus optional equipment.
☐ *Standard empty weight.* Weight of a standard aeroplane including unusable fuel, full operating fluids and full oil (eq.(1–2a)).

Maximum weights

☐ *Maximum landing weight.* Maximum weight approved for touchdown on landing.
☐ *Maximum ramp weight.* Maximum weight approved for ground manoeuvre (it includes weight of fuel needed for start, taxi and run-up).
☐ *Maximum take-off weight.* Maximum weight approved for the start of the take-off run.
☐ *Maximum zero fuel weight.* Maximum weight excluding usable fuel.

Payload. Weight of occupants, cargo and baggage (eq (1–1)).
Structure weight W_s

$$\text{structure weight} = \text{weights of wing(s)} + \text{fuselage} + \text{engine nacelles} + \text{tail unit} + \text{landing gear} \tag{2–65}$$

Miscellaneous terms

Froude number, F. A dimensionless number used in hydrodynamics, named after William Froude (1810–79), which is a relative of *Reynolds number*, R, used mainly in aerodynamics. Whereas Reynolds number describes the conditions for dynamic similarity of flows in terms of intertial and viscous forces, *Froude number* describes similarity in terms of inertial and gravitational forces involved in wave-making. It may be shown that:

$$\text{speed of wave propagation} = \sqrt{(\text{wave length} \times g/2\pi)}$$
$$V = \sqrt{(\lambda g/2\pi)} \tag{2–66}$$

where g = gravitational constant, 32.2 ft/sec², the remainder being in FPSR units. It may be shown that if L is the waterline length of a hull (in the way that chord length, c, is a measure of size (scale) in Reynolds number), then for similarity of wave formation:

$$\text{Froude number, } F = \sqrt{(\lambda/2\pi L)} = V\sqrt{gL}$$
$$\text{or, for convenience } = V^2/gL = \text{inertial force}/\text{gravity force} \tag{2–67}$$

where V is speed through the water. Froude number applies at the surface where waves are made, and Reynolds number may also be applied in water when a body is submerged. Ideally a hull should be tested in such a way as to have the same Froude and Reynolds number simultaneously, which requires:

$$\text{Froude number} \times \text{Reynolds number} = (\text{speed of wave propagation})^3/(\text{kinematic viscosity} \times g)$$
$$FR = V^3/\nu g \tag{2–68}$$

This condition would involve use of different fluids of varying kinematic viscosities over the range of V^3, which is impracticable. Thus the scaling of hulls is beset with considerable difficulties. There are ways of overcoming them but they are beyond the scope of this book.
LCN. Load classification number: a numerical way of matching the 'footprint

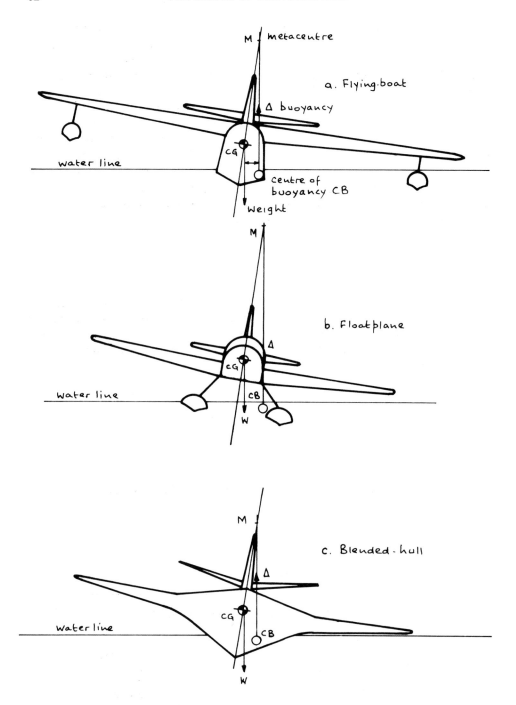

Fig. 2.18 The metacentre of the seaplane is above the centre of gravity, so that the couple of weight and buoyancy produce a positive righting moment. The larger the metacentric height (the height of the metacentre above the centre of buoyancy) the more powerful the righting moment.

'pressures' of aeroplane tyres to the strength and rigidity of 'flexible' pavements.

Metacentre. A term used in marine work and applied to seaplanes. If a seaplane heels to one side when afloat, the centre of buoyancy, **CB**, which is the centre of gravity of the displaced water, is displaced in the same direction. If now a vertical is drawn upwards through the **CB** as shown in fig. 2.18, it will be seen to intersect the plane of symmetry of the aeroplane at the metacentre. If the metacentre is above the centre of gravity of the aeroplane, it will right itself. If below, the seaplane will heel further over.

Metacentric height. The distance measured in the plane of symmetry between the metacentre and the centre of gravity of a seaplane (positive when above the **CG**, denoting positive stability). If the metacentric height is too great the craft will be too 'stiff' in the water, and it can be broken more easily by the waves.

Seaplane. Any waterborne aeroplane, including floatplanes and flying boats.

Undercarriage. (British) = *(landing) gear* (US).

Tables and conversion factors

One of the difficulties most of us have whenever we see a page with a scattering of mathematics is that the mind stops dead and the brain stalls. In this book mathematics cannot be avoided, because we are concerned with shapes, proportions, sizes and weights, not just principles. But, almost every equation consists of nothing more than statements like:

$$1 + 2 + 7 = 10$$
$$3 \times 10^{-4} = \frac{3}{10\,000} = 0.0003$$
$$\frac{1}{4} \times \frac{3}{7} = \frac{3}{28}$$

with the odd square root ($\sqrt{}$) or $\sqrt[4]{} = \sqrt{(\sqrt{})}$ thrown in here and there.

TABLE 2–1

Greek letters used as symbols

Capital	Small	English name	Capital	Small	English name
A	α	Alpha	N	ν	Nu
B	β	Beta	Ξ	ξ	Xi
Γ	γ	Gamma	O	o	Omikron
Δ	δ	Delta	Π	π	Pi
E	ϵ	Epsilon	P	ρ	Rho
Z	ζ	Zeta	Σ	σ	Sigma
H	η	Eta	T	τ	Tau
Θ	θ	Theta	Υ	υ	Upsilon
I	ι	Iota	Φ	ϕ	Phi
K	κ	Kappa	X	χ	Chi
Λ	λ	Lambda	Ψ	ψ	Psi
M	μ	Mu	Ω	ω	Omega

Because there are so many terms we have to give them mysterious looking symbols like x and y. Many terms belong to families and we denote them individually with suffixes. Thus, a family of drag terms is distinguished separately by D_L, D_{form}, D_{fric}, D_O, etc. A separate family of drag coefficients uses capital C to show what we are talking about, with C_{DL}, C_{Dform}, C_{Dfric}, C_{DO}, to make the necessary distinctions. When we run out of letters in the English alphabet we resort to Greek letters.

TABLE 2–2

Units in BCAR flight requirements

Quantity	Unit	Symbol	Remarks
Length	metre	m	Heights, altitudes and relatively
	foot	ft	short distances quoted in this unit.
Mass	kilogramme	kg	The term 'weight' has been retained
	pound	lb	when 'mass' is strictly correct. Equivalent existing unit not quoted where the weight represents a legal discriminant, e.g. 5 700 kg is maximum AUW for aeroplanes certificated to Section K.
Time	second	s	
Tempera-ture	degree Celsius	°C	The Kelvin scale is not used.
	degree Fahrenheit	°F	Equivalent temperature in °F is not quoted if it has always been the custom to use °C in the particular context.
Angle	degree	°	Radians are not used, even as equivalent.
Speed	kilometre per hour	km/h	Metres per second not used.
	knots	knots	The knot is the distance travelled in nautical miles per hour. The British nm is 6 080 ft (1 853.18 m). The International nm is 1 852 m exactly. Aviators tend to use 6 000 ft as a crude rule of thumb. Where it is necessary to be more accurate, we shall use the International nm, for which 1 kn = 0.514 m/s (whereas 1 kn (UK) = 0.514773 m/s).
Force	Newton	N	
	pounds force	lbf	
Rate of climb	metres per minute	m/min	
	feet per minute	ft/min	
Gradient of climb	per cent	%	Tangent of the climb angle expressed as a percentage.
Pressure (altimeter setting)	millibars	mbar	Newtons per square metre not used.

TABLE 2–3

Flight manual units

Quantity	Unit	Symbol	Remarks
Length (heights and altitudes)	foot	ft	Note conflict with BCAR primary unit.
Length (short horizontal, e.g. runway lengths)	metre	m	
(long horizontal)	nautical mile	—	
Length (depth, e.g. slush on runways)	millimetre inch	mm in	
Length (aircraft dimensions)	feet or inches	ft or in	
Mass	kilogramme pound	kg lb	The term 'weight' is commonly used. Equivalent not always quoted. Metric tons (tonne) not yet used but may be in the future.
Temperaature	degree Celsius	°C	
Angle	degree	°	
Speed	knot	kn	
Rate of climb	feet per minute	ft/min	
Gradient of climb	per cent	%	'ft/100 m' is also used in certain contexts.
Pressure	millibars	mbar	

TABLE 2–4

Prefixes

The following prefixes may be used to indicate decimal fractions or multiples of basic or derived metric SI units (*Système International d'Unités*, 1960) which employs the kilogramme, metre and second as the respective units of mass, length and time.

Fraction	Prefix	Symbol	Multiple	Prefix	Symbol
10^{-1}	deci	d	10	deca	da
10^{-2}	centi	c	10^2	hecto	h
10^{-3}	milli	m	10^3	kilo	k
10^{-6}	micro	μ	10^6	mega	M

TABLE 2–5

Conversion factors between the British FPSR (foot, pound, second, rankine) system and SI (Système International) units

Quantity	FPSR Units	Multiply by	To obtain SI Units	Multiply by	To obtain FPSR Units
Mass (M)	slug	1.459×10	kg	$6\text{-}852 \times 10^{-2}$	slug
Length (L)	ft	3.048×10^{-1}	m	3.281	ft
Density (ρ)	slug/ft³	5.155×10^2	kg/m³	1.940×10^{-3}	slug/ft³
Temperature (T)	°F + 460	5.56×10^{-1}	°C + 273	1.8	°F + 460
	°R		°K		°R
Velocity (V)	ft/sec	3.048×10^{-1}	m/sec	3.281	ft/sec
	mph	1.609	kph	6.214×10^{-1}	mph
	knot	1.853	kph	5.396×10^{-1}	knot
		0.515	m/sec	1.942	
Force (F)	lbf	4.448	N (newton)	2.248×10^{-1}	lbf
	slug ft/sec²		kg m/sec²		slug ft/sec²
Work	slug ft²/sec²	1.356	Nm	7.376×10^{-1}	slug ft²/sec²
Energy (J)	BTU		(joule)		BTU
Power (W)	slug ft²/sec³	1.356	Nm/sec	7.376×10^{-1}	slug ft²/sec³
	hp (550 ft lbf/sec)	7.456×10^2	(Watt)	1.341×10^{-3}	hp (550 ft lbf/sec)
Pressure (p)	slug/ft sec²	4.788×10	N/m²	2.088×10^{-2}	slug/ft sec²
	lbf/ft²		(pascal)		lbf/ft²
		4.788×10^{-4}	bar	2.088×10^3	
Specific Energy, etc	ft lbf/slug	9.290×10^{-2}	Nm/kg	1.076×10	ft lbf/slug
Gas Constant	ft lbf/slug° R	1.672×10^{-1}	Nm/kg° K	5.981	ft lbf/slug° R
Coef of Viscosity (μ)	slug/ft sec	4.788×10	kg/m sec	2.088×10^{-2}	slug/ft sec
Kinematic Viscosity (ν)	ft²/sec	9.290×10^{-2}	m²/sec	1.076×10	ft²/sec
Thermal Conductivity (k)	lbf/sec° R	8.007	N/sec° K	1.249×10^{-1}	lbf/sec° R
Heat Transfer Coefficient	lbf/ft sec° R	2.627×10	N/m sec° K	3.807×10^{-2}	lbf/ft sec° R
Frequency	c/sec	1.0	Hz (hertz)	1.0	c/sec

Footnote. Various derived units are named after eminent scientists and engineers. In addition to the *newton* (Sir Isaac Newton, see page 32), there are:
Celsius: Anders Celsius (1701–44), Swedish astronomer;
Hertz: H. R. Hertz (1857–94), German physicist;
Joule: James Prescott Joule (1818–89), English physicist;
Kelvin: Lord William Thomson Kelvin (1824–1907), Scottish physicist;
Pascal: Blaise Pascal (1623–62), French philosopher and scientist;
Rankine: William George Macquorn Rankine (1820–72), Scottish scientist and engineer:
Watt: James Watt (1736–1819), Scottish engineer who invented the first really efficient steam engine.

TABLE 2–6

Conversion Factors (mixed FPSR, metric and SI)

Multiply	By	To obtain
acres	0.4047	ha (= 10^3 m²)
	43 560	ft²
	0.0015625	mi²
standard atmospheres (atm)	76	cm Hg
	29.92	in Hg
	1.01325	bar (= 10^5 N/m²)
	1.033	kgf/cm²
	14.70	lbf/in²
	2116	lbf/ft²
	101 325	N/m²
bars (bar)	0.98692	atm
	14.5038	lbf/in²
British Thermal Unit (BTU)	0.5556	CHU
	1055	J
	0.2520	kcal (kilocalorie)
centimetres (cm)	0.3937	in
	0.032808	ft
centimetres of mercury at	0.01316	atm
0° C (cm Hg)	0.3937	in Hg
	0.1934	lbf/in²
	27.85	lbf/ft²
	135.95	kgf/m²
centimetres per second (cm/s)	0.032808	ft/s
	1.9685	ft/min
	0.02237	mph
cubic centimetres (cm³)	0.06102	in³
	3.531×10^{-5}	ft³
	0.001	litre
	2.642×10^{-4}	US gal
cubic feet (ft³)	28317	cm³
	0.028317	m³
	1728	in³
	0.037037	yd³
	7.481	US gal
	28.32	litre
cubic feet per minute (ft³/min)	0.472	litre/s
	0.028317	m³/min
cubic inches (in³)	16.39	cm³
	1.639×10^{-5}	m³
	5.787×10^{-4}	ft³
	0.5541	fl oz
	0.01639	litre
	4.329×10^{-3}	US gal
	0.01732	US qt
cubic metres (m³)	61024	in³
	1.308	yd³
	35.3147	ft³
	264.2	US gal

TABLE 2–6 – *continued*

Multiply	By	To obtain
cubic metres per minute (m³/min)	35.3147	ft³/min
cubic yards (yd³)	27	ft³
	0.7646	m³
	202	US gal
degrees (arc)	0.01745	radians
degrees per second (deg/s)	0.01745	radians/s
erg	1.0×10^{-7}	J
feet (ft)	30.48	cm
	0.3048	m
	12	in
	0.33333	yd
	0.0606061	rod
	1.894×10^{-4}	stm
	1.646×10^{-4}	nm (international)
feet per minute (ft/min)	0.01136	mph
	0.01829	km/h
	0.508	cm/s
	0.00508	m/s
feet per second (ft/s)	0.6818	mph
	1.097	km/h
	30.48	cm/s
	0.5925	knot (international)
foot–pounds (ft lbf)	0.138255	kgf m
	3.24×10^{-4}	kcal
	1.356	Nm (J)
foot-pounds per minute (ft lbf/min)	3.030×10^{-5}	hp
foot–pounds per second (ft lbf/s)	1.818×10^{-3}	hp
gallons, Imperial (Imp gal)	277.4	in³
	1.201	US gal
	4.546	litre
	153.707	fl oz
gallons, US dry (US gal dry)	268.8	in³
	1.556×10^{-1}	ft³
	1.164	US gal
	4.405	litre
gallons, US liquid (US gal)	231	in³
	0.1337	ft³
	4.951×10^{-3}	yd³
	3785.4	cm³
	3.785×10^{-3}	m³
	3.785	litre
	0.83267	Imp gal
	133.227	fl oz
US gallons per acre (gal/acre)	9.353	litre/ha
grams (g)	0.001	kg
	2.205×10^{-3}	lb
grams per centimetre (g/cm)	0.1	kg/m
	6.720×10^{-2}	lb/ft
	5.600×10^{-3}	lb/in
grams per cubic centimetre (g/cm³)	1000	kg/m³
	0.03613	lb/in³
	62.43	lb/ft³

TABLE 2–6 – *continued*

Multiply	By	To obtain
hectares (ha)	2.471	acres
	107 639	ft^2
	10 000	m^2
horsepower (hp)	33 000	ft lbf/min
	550	ft lbf/s
	0.7457	kW
	76.04	kgf m/s
	1.014	metric hp
	745.70	Nm/s (W)
horsepower, metric	75	kgf m/s
	0.9863	hp
inches (in)	25.40	mm
	2.540	cm
	0.0254	m
	0.08333	ft
	0.027777	yd
inches of mercury at 0° C	0.033421	atm
(in Hg)	0.4912	lb/in^2
	70.73	lb/ft^2
	345.3	kg/m^2
	2.540	cm Hg
	25.40	mm Hg
	3.386×10^3	N/m^2
inch–pounds (in lbf)	0.011521	kgf m
J (joule)	0.27778×10^{-6}	kWh
	1	Nm
	1	Ws
kilograms (kg)	2.204623	lb
	35.27	oz avdp
	1000	g
kilogram–calories (kcal)	3.9683	BTU
(kilocalories)	3088	ft lbf
	426.9	kgf m
kilogram–metre^2 (kg m^2)	3417	lb in^2
	23.729	lb ft^2
	0.7376	slug ft^2
kilograms per cubic metre	0.06243	lb/ft^3
(kg/m^3)	0.001	g/cm^3
kilograms per hectare (kg/ha)	0.892	lb/acre
kilograms per square centimetre	0.9678	atm
(kg/cm^2)	28.96	in Hg
	14.22	lbf/in^2
	2048	lbf/ft^2
kilograms per square metre	2.896×10^{-3}	in Hg
(kg/m^2)	1.422×10^{-3}	lb/in^2
	0.2048	lb/ft^2
kilometres (km)	1×10^5	cm
	3280.8	ft
	0.6214	stm
	0.53996	nm (international)
kilometers per hour (kph)	0.9113	ft/s
	58.68	ft/min

TABLE 2–6 – *continued*

Multiply	By	To obtain
	0.53996	knot (international)
	0.6214	mph
	0.27778	m/s
	16.67	m/min
kilowatt	1.34	hp
knots (knot) (international)	1	nm/h
	1.688	ft/s
	1.1508	mph
	1.852	km/h
	0.5144	m/s
litres (litre)	1000	cm^3
	61.02	in^3
	0.03531	ft^3
	33.814	fl oz
	0.2642	US gal
	0.2200	Imp gal
	1.0568	US qt
litres per hectare (litre/ha)	13.69	fl oz/acre
	0.107	US gal/acre
litres per second (litre/s)	2.12	ft^3/min
metres (m)	39.37	in
	3.280840	ft
	1.0936	yd
	0.198839	rod
	6.214×10^{-4}	stm
	5.3996×10^{-4}	nm (international)
metre–kilogram (kgf/m)	7.23301	ft lbf
	86.798	in lbf
metres per minute (m/min)	0.06	km/h
metres per second (m/sec)	3.280840	ft/s
	196.8504	ft/min
	2.237	mph
	3.6	km/h
microns	3.937×10^{-5}	in
miles (stm)	5280	ft
	1.6093	km
	1 609.3	m
	0.8690	nm (international)
miles per hour (mph)	44.704	cm/s
	0.4470	m/s
	1.467	ft/s
	88	ft/min
	1.6093	km/h
	0.8690	knot (international)
millibars	2.953×10^{-2}	in Hg
	0.1	kN/m^2
millimetres (mm)	0.03937	in
millimetres of mercury at 0°C (mm Hg)	0.03937	in Hg
international nautical miles (nm)	6076	ft
	1.1508	stm
	1852	m
	1.852	km

TABLE 2-6 – *continued*

Multiply	By	To obtain
Newton (N)	0.2248	lbf
ounces, fluid (fl oz)	8	dr fl
	29.57	cm^3
	1.805	in^3
	0.0296	litre
	0.0078	US gal
ounces, fluid per acre (fl oz/acre)	0.073	litre/ha
pounds (lb): mass	453.6	g
	0.453592	kg
	3.108×10^{-2}	slug
pounds force (lbf)	4.4482	N
	0.45359	kgf
pounds–feet (lbf ft)	1.356	Nm
pounds–feet^2 (lb ft^2)	0.421	kg m^2
	144	lb in^2
	0.0311	slug ft^2
pounds per acre (lb/acre)	1.121	kg/ha
pounds per cubic foot (lb/ft^3)	16.02	kg/m^3
pounds per cubic inch (lb/in^3)	1728	lb/ft^3
	27.68	g/cm^3
pounds per hour per pound force (lb/h/lbf)	28.3	mg/Ns
pounds per hour per horsepower (lb/h/hp)	169	μg/J
pounds-force per square foot (lbf/ft^2)	0.1414	in Hg
	4.88243	kgf/m^2
	4.725×10^{-4}	atm
	0.048	kN/m^2
pounds per square inch (psi or lbf/in^2)	5.1715	cm Hg
	2.036	in Hg
	0.06805	atm
	0.0689476	bar
	703.1	kg/m^2
	6.89476	kN/m^2
quart, US (qt)	0.94635	litre
	57.750	in^3
	3.342×10^{-2}	ft^3
radians	57.30	deg (arc)
	0.1592	rev
radians per second (radians/s)	57.296	deg/s
	0.1592	rev/s
	9.549	rpm
revolutions (rev)	6.283	radians
revolutions per minute (rpm or rev/min)	0.1047	radians/s
revolutions per second (rev/s)	6.283	radians/s
rod	16.5	ft
	5.5	yd
	5.0292	m
slug	14.594	kg
	32.174	lb
slug feet^2 (slug ft^2)	1.3559	kg m^2
	4633.1	lb in^2
	32.174	lb ft^2

TABLE 2–6 – *continued*

Multiply	By	To obtain
square centimetres (cm²)	0.1550	in²
	0.001076	ft²
square feet (ft²)	929.03	cm²
	0.092903	m²
	144	in²
	0.1111	yd²
	2.296×10^{-5}	acres
square inches (in²)	6.4516	cm²
	6.944×10^{-3}	ft²
square kilometres (km²)	0.3861	stm²
square metres (m²)	10.76391	ft²
	1.196	yd²
	0.0001	ha
square miles (mi²)	2.590	km²
	640	acres
square rods (rod²)	30.25	yd²
square yards (yd²)	0.8361	m²
	9	ft²
	0.0330579	rod²
ton	2240	lb
	1016	kg
	1.016	t (tonne)
ton-force (tonf)	9.964×10^3	N
tons per square foot (tonf/ft²)	107.252×10^3	kN/m²
watt (W)	1.34×10^{-3}	hp
	10^{-3}	kW
yards (yd)	0.9144	m
	3	ft
	36	in
	0.181818	rod

TABLE 2–7

General Notation*

Axes	OX	OY	OZ
Aerodynamic forces	X	Y	Z
Angular motions	ϕ (bank)	θ (pitch)	Ψ (yaw)
Linear velocities	u	v	w
Angular velocities	p	q	r
Moments of forces	L (roll)	M (pitch)	N (yaw)
Moments of inertia	A	B	C

(Note: $A \times B \approx C$)

* We do not use this notation exclusively in this book.

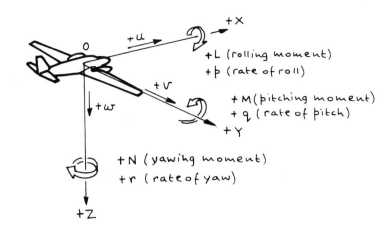

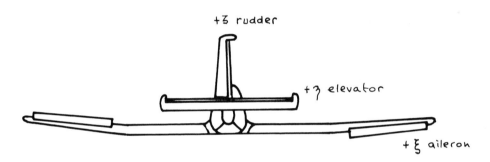

View in direction OX
showing notation for
control surfaces

See table 2–7.

References

2.1 von Kármán, T. (1957) *Aerodynamics*. New York: Cornell University Press.

2.2 Lachmann, G. V. ed. (1961) *Boundary Layer and Flow Control*. Oxford: Pergamon Press.

2.3 126/1972 *Aeronautical Information Circular*. Civil Aviation Authority.

2.4 Section K. *British Civil Airworthiness Requirements*. Civil Aviation Authority.

SECTION 2

AERODYNAMICS

CHAPTER 3

The Nature of Air

'An uninterrupted navigable ocean, that comes to the threshold of everyman's door, ought not to be neglected as a source of human gratification and advantage.'
Sir George Cayley (1816)
(from *Sir George Cayley's Aeronautics 1796–1855*, Charles H. Gibbs-Smith, Her Majesty's Stationery Office.)

Take a thin piece of plastic foil (such as that used for wrapping sandwiches) and press it smoothly against a window pane or mirror. If the air is squeezed evenly from between the film and the glass, the foil sticks to the surface. Why?

The foil is held there by air pressure acting in all directions due to the weight of a column of air rising above the foil to a height of some 450 nm or more (833 km). Air is a mixture of gases, chemically indifferent to one another. Roughly half the total weight of the atmosphere is accounted for in the first 18 000 ft (5 000 m) and another quarter in the next 18 000 ft. At very high altitude the heavier gases fail to rise until, around 45 nm (83 km) hydrogen and helium predominate. The pressure of oxygen needed falls rapidly with height until around 18 000 ft (5 500 m) the danger limit is reached, and oxygen must be fed mechanically to the pilot.

In temperate latitudes the first 36 000 ft (11 000 m) marks the extent of the *troposphere*, in which outside air temperature falls fairly steadily with height (as shown in fig. 2.15): this is known as the temperature lapse rate. However, the top of the troposphere is marked by a change in temperature lapse rate which is sharp enough for us to call its boundary the *tropopause*. Above the tropopause lies the *stratosphere*, the region of (almost) constant zero lapse rate. Farther out, other regions of change occur, but they do not affect the aircraft with which we are concerned.

Air 'at rest' is not so. Molecules dart around at random, exhibiting the classic undirected Brownian motion, first noticed in 1827 by the Scottish botanist Robert Brown (1773–1858), using very fine pollen grains suspended in water. In air, Brownian motion can be seen with fine particles of smoke. It provides direct evidence of the existence of molecules and support for the kinetic theory of their motions.

The speed at which molecules of air dash about is indicated by the ambient temperature of their mass (the parcel of molecules), thermal energy being a measure of kinetic energy, and *vice versa*. Sound is transmitted by pressure waves, the pulse of one molecule being transmitted to the next, and so on, at a rate proportional to their temperature. In short, the speed of sound rises with increasing outside air temperature. Cool the air and the reverse happens.

Significance of speed of sound

Molecules of air adjust to disturbances at a natural speed governed by their ambient temperature, which is not far removed from their speed of sound:

$$\text{average molecular speed}/\text{speed of sound} = 1.4 \qquad (3\text{--}1)$$

Pierre Simon de Laplace (1749–1827), French astronomer and mathematician, demonstrated that alternate compressions and rarefactions by which sound is carried throughout the air occur adiabatically, i.e. there is no heat transfer between fluid elements within the air and with its surroundings. The speed of sound is slower than molecular speed because of collisions, but it may be shown that:

$$\text{speed of sound} = \sqrt{(\text{ratio of specific heats} \times \text{static pressure}/\text{density})}$$

where $\qquad\qquad a = \sqrt{(\gamma p/\rho)} \qquad\qquad\qquad (3\text{--}2)$

Values of density and pressure are drawn separately against altitude in fig. 3.1a. Relative values have been used. In fig. 3.1b ambient temperature and speed of sound have been drawn, together with relative kinematic viscosity. The latter shows that as ν is the measure of placidity/ excitability of the molecules, they calm down rapidly because they thin out faster than the temperature falls.

Using sea level values, and $\gamma = 1.4$, in eq. (3–2):

$$a = 1\,117 \text{ ft/s} = 661 \text{ knot } (1\,225 \text{ km/h}) \qquad (3\text{--}3)$$

It may also be shown from eq. (2–51) that eq. (2–9) can be modified as follows, using eq. (3–2):

$$\text{dynamic pressure, } q = \tfrac{1}{2}\,\rho V^2 = \tfrac{1}{2}\,\gamma p \mathrm{M}^2$$
$$= 0.7\,p\mathrm{M}^2 \qquad (3\text{--}4)$$

Gas laws

Pressure, temperature, volume and density of any perfect gas are related by two famous laws named after Robert Boyle (1627–91), an Irish chemist, and Jacques Alexandre César Charles (1746–1823), a French physicist. Charles' law is sometimes attributed to Louis Gay-Lussac (1778–1850), another French physicist, who discovered it simultaneously:

□ *Boyle's law* states that when the temperature is constant:

$$\text{pressure}_1 \times \text{volume}_1 = \text{pressure}_2 \times \text{volume}_2$$

so that,

$$P_1/P_2 = v_2/v_1 = \text{constant} \qquad (3\text{--}5)$$

i.e. pressure and volume are inversely related.

□ *Charles' law* states that at constant pressure (and working in absolute temperature, K):

$$\text{temperature}_1/\text{temperature}_2 = \text{volume}_1/\text{volume}_2$$

i.e. $\qquad\qquad\qquad t_1/t_2 = v_1/v_2 = \text{constant} \qquad (3\text{--}6)$

and volume is proportional to temperature.

Now, as mass/volume = density $\qquad\qquad\qquad\qquad\qquad (3\text{--}7)$
we may combine Boyle's and Charles' laws as follows:

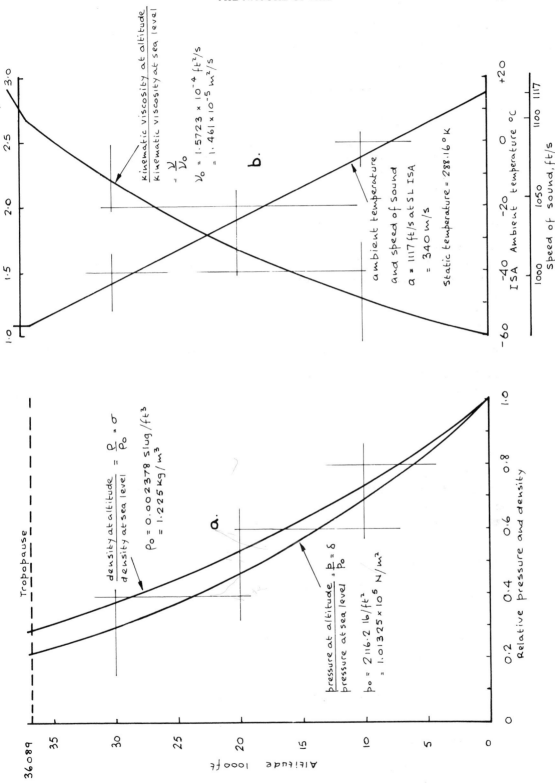

Fig. 3.1 Properties of the lower international standard atmosphere.

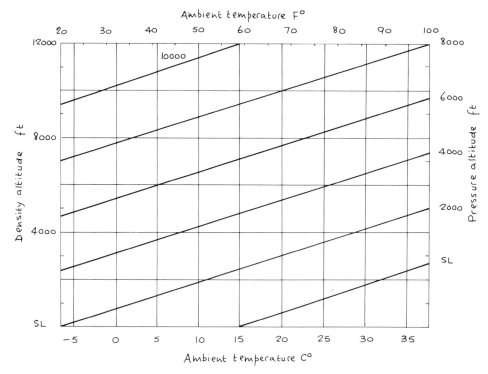

Fig. 3.1c   Pressure and density altitudes at constant sealevel static pressure.

$$p_1 v_1 / t_1 = p_2 v_2 / t_2 \qquad (3\text{–}8)$$

and,

$$p_1 / \rho_1 t_1 = p_2 / \rho_2 t_2 \qquad (3\text{–}9)$$

or, generally

$$p = \rho R t \qquad (3\text{–}10)$$

where R is a constant.

Air in slow motion (subsonic)

Hold out a piece of paper and let it fall. Its motions will be quite slow and it will probably rock and twist during its descent. The motions are the result of the interplay between aerodynamic forces and the dynamics of the paper, displacing molecules as it wafts downwards. The forces acting upon the paper are:

☐ gravity;
☐ pressure forces acting normal to its surfaces;
☐ frictional forces between the air and the surfaces of the paper, caused by viscosity;
while behind the paper is left:
☐ a wake in which viscosity causes particles of air to be dragged along to a certain
   extent, producing a momentum loss.

Viscosity is the property that makes a fluid 'real', as against mathematically 'ideal', and it only becomes important when fluids are set in motion. We could solve many problems if it could be disposed of, but we would banish lift as well. John William

Strutt, Lord Rayleigh (1842–1919), a great mathematical physicist, put matters succinctly in terms of hydrodynamics: 'On this theory the screw of a submerged boat would be useless but, on the other hand, its services would not be needed.' (ref. 3.1).

If we slide a film of fluid between finger and thumb it feels either 'thick' like syrup, or 'thin' like water. The sliding action shears the film, rather like spreading a pack of cards across a table. The shearing action causes a velocity gradient through the depth of film between finger and thumb, which is exactly the same as that caused at the skin of an aircraft passing through air initially at rest, fig. 3.2, the film in this case being the boundary layer. Viscosity (properly, *dynamic* or *absolute viscosity*) is measured by:

$$\mu = \text{drag force per unit area of sheared surface/change in velocity per unit} \\ \text{depth of layer or film} \qquad (3\text{–}11)$$

In practice viscosity is measured by the rate at which small spheres sink through a fluid; or by the rate at which fluid at a given pressure can be forced through a calibrated tube.

Dynamic viscosity is fairly insensitive to changes in pressure, but temperature alters its value considerably. The colder air becomes, the more slippery it grows. Liquids are the reverse – the colder they become the more viscous they are. But in aeronautics dynamic viscosity is of secondary importance to kinematic viscosity, ν, where:

$$\text{kinematic viscosity} = \text{dynamic viscosity/density}$$
$$\nu = \mu/\rho \qquad (3\text{–}12)$$

Kinematic viscosity indicates the state of play in a game between opposing properties of the molecules making up a fluid:

☐ The diffusive effect of friction which damps disturbances by causing molecules to cling together and to adjacent surfaces, slowing their motions, making them placid.

☐ The dynamic consequence of density, the measure of crowding together of molecules, which causes the disturbance of one to jostle the remainder into an excited response.

Typical sea level values for the International Standard Atmosphere, ISA are:

air:
$$\nu = 1.57 \times 10^{-4} \text{ ft}^2/\text{s} \; (1.46 \times 10^{-5} \text{ m}^2/\text{s}) \Big\} \qquad (3\text{–}13)$$
$$\nu = 1.23 \times 10^{-5} \text{ ft}^2/\text{s} \; (1.14 \times 10^{-6} \text{ m}^2/\text{s}) \Big\}$$

water:

The greater the value of the kinematic viscosity the more easily can a flow be caused to follow the curvature of a surface without breaking down into irregularity and turbulence. Air for example follows a shape thirteen times better than water, according to the values given above.

Two other factors govern the spread of a disturbance throughout a fluid by the number of molecules disturbed in a given time: *size* (i.e. scale) of a body; and its *relative speed*. These are measured in the case of an aeroplane by lengths, i.e. the standard mean chord, $\bar{c}$ (and at a specific station the local chord length) of a wing; and true airspeed, V. Taken all together we can look at the ratio of:

$$\text{factors affecting inertia forces/factors affecting viscous forces}$$

in air (or a fluid), when seeking to achieve geometric and dynamic similarity in a flow.

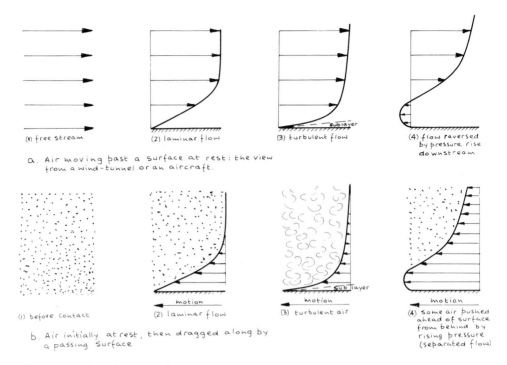

(1) free stream   (2) laminar flow   (3) turbulent flow   (4) flow reversed by pressure rise downstream

a. Air moving past a surface at rest: the view from a wind-tunnel or an aircraft.

(1) before contact   (2) laminar flow   (3) turbulent air   (4) some air pushed ahead of surface from behind by rising pressure (separated flow)

b. Air initially at rest, then dragged along by a passing surface

Fig. 3.2   Viscosity is a molecular resistance that causes marked changes in relative speed and hence velocity profile in the boundary layer adjacent to a surface. A profile in row (b) is identical to that in row (a).

We saw in eq. (2–11) that the measure of such proportionality is Reynolds number, R, where (using the above ratio):

R = size of aircraft in terms of chord length × TAS × air density/
dynamic viscosity of the air

i.e. $R = \bar{c}V\rho/\mu = \bar{c}V/\nu$ (2–11)

Fig. 3.3 shows five different flow regimes, each marked by a different Reynolds number. When R is less than 1, viscosity dominates the scene. When greater than 1, inertia effects predominate. The pictures represent changes of orders of magnitude, from as low as 10^{-2} to 10^6 (one hundredth to one million), give or take a bit.

A simplified formula for Reynolds number at sea level, working in V knots (KTAS), kinematic viscosity, ISA, and wing chord $\bar{c}$ ft, gives:

$$R = 1.075 \times 10^4 \, \bar{c}V \qquad (3–14)$$

Fig. 3.4 shows a curve of optimum thickness/chord ratio for a minimum drag streamlined aerofoil section plotted against Reynolds number (based upon ref. 3.2). Instead of chord, $\bar{c}$, in eq. (3–14) we may also substitute body–length (as long as it is in the streamwise direction) so as to use fig. 3.4 for any streamlined body.

An important thing to notice in figs 3.2 and 3.3 is the tripping of laminar flow into turbulence. This is accompanied by thickening of the boundary layer, which is impossible to draw to scale here, because a turbulent layer can be around ten times

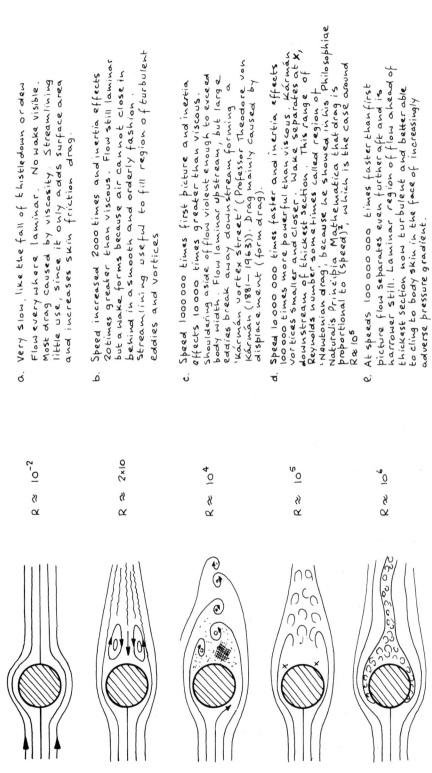

a. $R \approx 10^{-2}$

Very slow, like the fall of thistledown or dew. Flow everywhere laminar. No wake visible. Most drag caused by viscosity. Streamlining little use, since it only adds surface area and increases skin friction drag.

b. $R \approx 2 \times 10$

Speed increased 2000 times and inertia effects 20 times greater than viscous. Flow still laminar but a wake forms because air cannot close in behind in a smooth and orderly fashion. Streamlining useful to fill region of turbulent eddies and vortices.

c. $R \approx 10^4$

Speed 1 000 000 times first picture and inertia effects 10 000 times greater than viscous. Shouldering aside of flow violent enough to exceed body width. Flow laminar upstream, but large eddies break away downstream forming a 'Kármán vortex street' (Professor Theodore von Kármán (1881–1963)). Drag mainly caused by displacement (form drag).

d. $R \approx 10^5$

Speed 10 000 000 times faster and inertia effects 100 000 times more powerful than viscous. Kármán vortices smaller and closer. Wake separates at X, downstream of thickest section. This range of Reynolds number sometimes called region of 'Newtonian drag', because he showed in his Philosophiae Naturalis Principia Mathematica that drag is proportional to (speed)^2, which is the case around $R \approx 10^5$

e. $R \approx 10^6$

At speeds 100 000 000 times faster than first picture flow separates even further aft and its narrower still. Laminar region of flow ahead of thickest section now turbulent and better able to cling to body skin in the face of increasingly adverse pressure gradient.

Fig. 3.3　Flow patterns at different speeds shown in terms of Reynolds number, R = inertia effects / viscous effects (see eq (2–11)).

deeper than a laminar. Drag is increased, but turbulence acts like an energy-pump, sweeping relatively high speed air inwards to the surface of the skin, pushing outwards and away sluggish air in the boundary layer. In this way turbulence inhibits stagnation, balancing to a certain extent the difference in energy between the clinging boundary layer and the free stream.

Curved flow and circulation: basic (two dimensional) aerofoil theory

Paradoxically, efficient flight depends upon our ability to make a flow of air follow a curve. We can gain some idea why by spreading a thin layer of sand or salt on a table. Cut an arc out of a piece of card to make a flat-bottomed lens section, like that shown in fig. 3.5 view 1, and then slide it along through the grains at an angle α deg. as shown. Repeat the experiment with a concave lens section like that in fig. 3.5b. Grains are displaced as molecules of air would be, but the experiment fixes them by preventing their readjustment. Three distinct regions appear: A, B and C.

On the inside of the undersurface, A, grains crowd together and become more heaped the closer they are to the section. They are also forced to flow downwards from leading to trailing edge, accumulating at B. On the upper surface, C, a gap is left where they have been swept away. The regions where grains accumulate produce highest pressures. A region from which grains are swept is one of reduced pressure. (In practice such low speed sections do not work with sharp leading edges, because infinite changes in velocity occur, which cause immediate separation and a stall. Therefore real sections have rounded leading edges to encourage flows to follow the profile in a smooth manner, enabling the *Coanda* effect to work for as long as possible.)

In fig. 3.5(a and b) grains are deflected centripetally, especially so with undercamber. The forces felt by each section are centifugal reactions to the inertia of the grains which, when resolved into two force components, one at right angles to and the other parallel with motion of the sections, represent very crude lift and drag forces.

Of course, we must now take the next step and imagine the grains behaving like

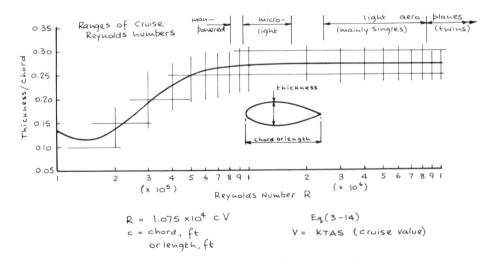

Fig. 3.4 Optimum thickness ratio (thickness/length or chord) generating least profile drag when fairing a given frontal area. (based upon ref. 3.2).

molecules of air, which detest a vacuum. Region C could not exist because air would rush around the leading edge to fill it, and it would attempt to negotiate the trailing edge at B. If we could see what happens we would notice two *circulatory* (vortex) motions like those sketched in fig. 3.5d. Conventional explanations of lift make no mention of the tight little vortex at the trailing edge, pushing air against the wind, as it were, carrying it along with the section from the first moment of the minutest motion. That little vortex is the trick card up Nature's sleeve. It can be detected on a real wing in

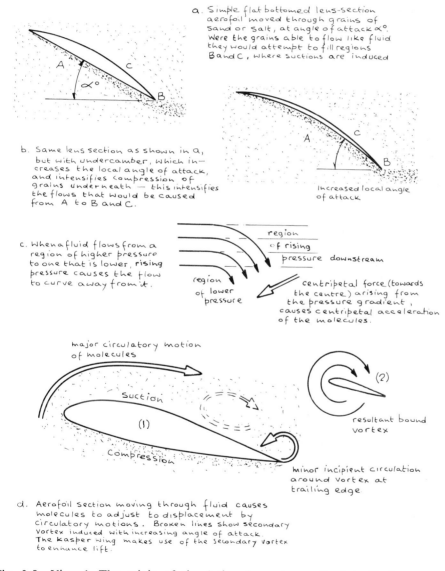

a. Simple flat bottomed lens-section aerofoil moved through grains of sand or salt, at angle of attack α°. Were the grains able to flow like fluid they would attempt to fill regions B and C, where suctions are induced

Increased local angle of attack

b. Same lens section as shown in a, but with undercamber, which increases the local angle of attack, and intensifies compression of grains underneath — this intensifies the flows that would be caused from A to B and C.

c. When a fluid flows from a region of higher pressure to one that is lower, rising pressure causes the flow to curve away from it.

region of rising pressure downstream

region of lower pressure

centripetal force (towards the centre) arising from the pressure gradient, causes centripetal acceleration of the molecules.

major circulatory motion of molecules

Suction

(1)

Compression

(2)

resultant bound vortex

minor incipient circulation around vortex at trailing edge

d. Aerofoil section moving through fluid causes molecules to adjust to displacement by circulatory motions. Broken lines show secondary vortex induced with increasing angle of attack. The Kasper wing makes use of the secondary vortex to enhance lift.

Fig. 3.5 View 1. The origin of circulation (a vortex motion) is displacement of molecules and particles of the medium through which specially shaped bodies pass. Pressure gradients are caused and flows are induced which are the response of the fluid medium to regain the *status quo* in some measure. This explanation comes close to satisfying the impact theory of lift enunciated by Sir Isaac Newton.

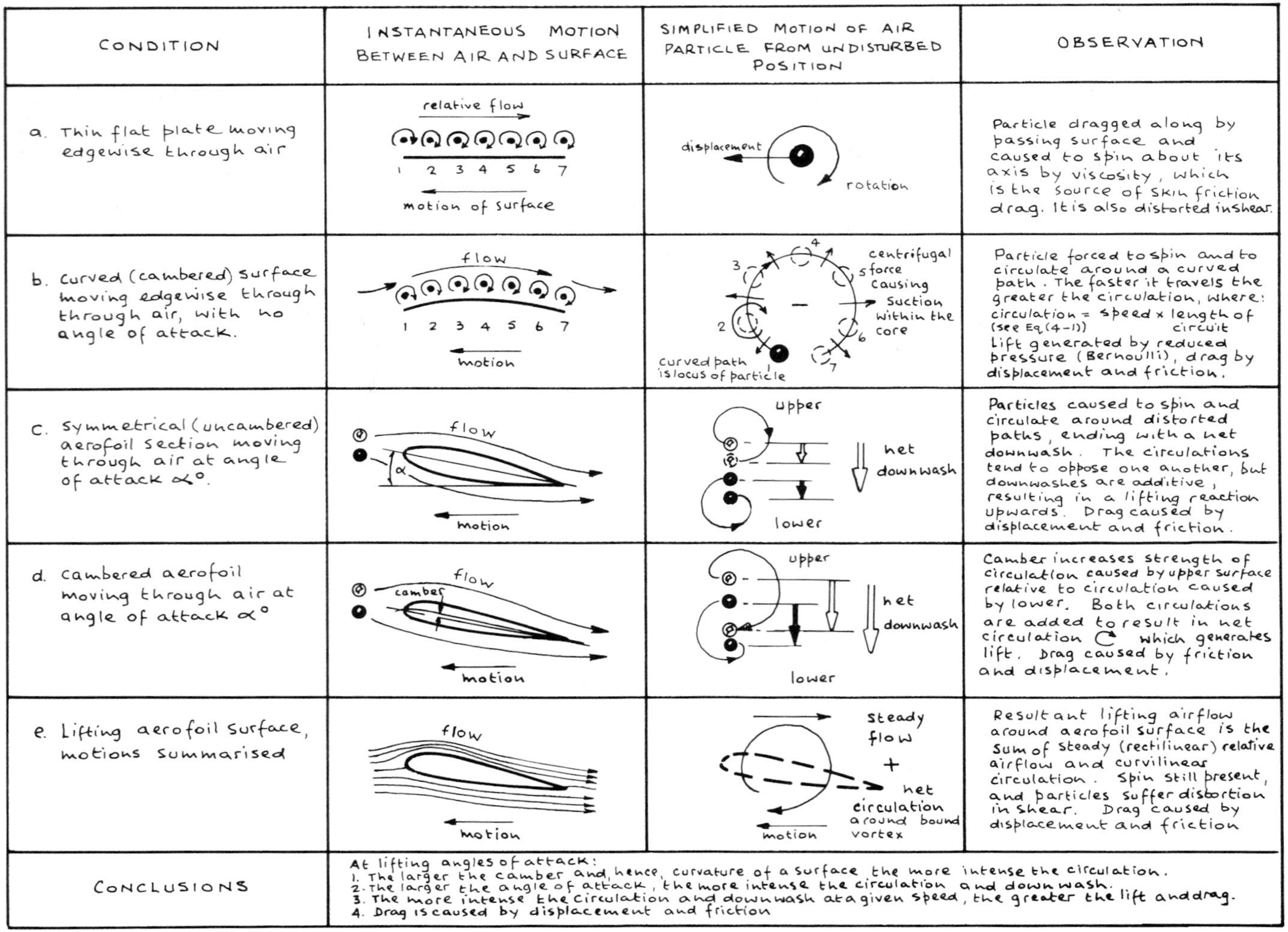

CONDITION	INSTANTANEOUS MOTION BETWEEN AIR AND SURFACE	SIMPLIFIED MOTION OF AIR PARTICLE FROM UNDISTURBED POSITION	OBSERVATION
a. Thin flat plate moving edgewise through air	relative flow — 1 2 3 4 5 6 7 — motion of surface	displacement / rotation	Particle dragged along by passing surface and caused to spin about its axis by viscosity, which is the source of skin friction drag. It is also distorted in shear.
b. Curved (cambered) surface moving edgewise through air, with no angle of attack.	flow — 1 2 3 4 5 6 7 — motion	centrifugal force causing suction within the core / curved path is locus of particle	Particle forced to spin and to circulate around a curved path. The faster it travels the greater the circulation, where: circulation = speed × length of circuit (see Eq (4-1)) Lift generated by reduced pressure (Bernoulli), drag by displacement and friction.
c. Symmetrical (uncambered) aerofoil section moving through air at angle of attack α.	flow / α / motion	upper / lower / net downwash	Particles caused to spin and circulate around distorted paths, ending with a net downwash. The circulations tend to oppose one another, but downwashes are additive, resulting in a lifting reaction upwards. Drag caused by displacement and friction.
d. Cambered aerofoil moving through air at angle of attack $\alpha°$	flow / camber / motion	upper / lower / net downwash	Camber increases strength of circulation caused by upper surface relative to circulation caused by lower. Both circulations are added to result in net circulation C which generates lift. Drag caused by friction and displacement.
e. Lifting aerofoil surface, motions summarised	flow / motion	steady flow + net circulation around bound vortex / motion	Resultant lifting airflow around aerofoil surface is the sum of steady (rectilinear) relative airflow and curvilinear circulation. Spin still present, circulation. Spin still present, and particles suffer distortion in shear. Drag caused by displacement and friction.
CONCLUSIONS	At lifting angles of attack: 1. The larger the camber and, hence, curvature of a surface the more intense the circulation. 2. The larger the angle of attack, the more intense the circulation and downwash. 3. The more intense the circulation and downwash at a given speed, the greater the lift and drag. 4. Drag is caused by displacement and friction.		

Fig. 3.5 View 2, circulation seen microscopically.

flight with wool tufts near the trailing edge. If the angle of attack is increased slightly, or the aileron is deflected downwards slightly, the wool tufts reverse direction and point forwards. The same effect can be seen in the feathers of birds at low speed.

From such a simple experiment two things can be said:

☐ *A curved flow always has the lowest pressure on the inside of the bend, towards the instantaneous centre of rotation*, as shown in fig. 3.5c. Pressure rises as we move radially outwards, away from the instantaneous centre.

☐ *If a region of rising pressure is caused downstream, the flow bends away from it.*

The description of the way in which lift is started by establishing a circulation in the flow does not invalidate other explanations involving, for example, Bernoulli's law. The other explanations are complementary in the sense shown in fig. 3.6, in which a free-stream flow has had a circulatory flow added. Addition of the two vectors at any point results in the conventional streamline motion of the air, the flow travelling fastest over the upper surface. Applying Bernoulli we know that where the flow is fastest, static pressure is least, and the difference in static pressure top and bottom results in an aerodynamic crossforce, with its components of lift and drag.

However, note that at subsonic speeds there is a clearly discernible total circulation of the air about an instantaneous centre of rotation, travelling with the aerofoil surface. That circulation forms a bound vortex across the span of strength Γ. A torque has been applied to the air in establishing the pressure distribution associated with circulation and, as Newton tells us that every action has an equal and opposite reaction, the air attempts to force the aerofoil surface to rotate in the opposite direction, nose-down. That reaction is called a *pitching moment*, which is always present in some degree. It has to be resisted (balanced) by an equal and opposite nose-up torque from the stabiliser for trimmed straight and level flight (as anyone who has ever built a model aeroplane knows).

Increasing and decreasing the angle of attack in fig. 3.5 raises and lowers the height of the leading edge of the section above the trailing edge, altering the swept volume and hence the mass of air acted upon in a given time. Therefore circulation, lift and drag increase and decrease with larger or smaller angle of attack, within the working range of the surface. That working range of angles of attack is from about −2 deg to +12 deg for a normal cambered aerofoil.

Camber causes circulation geometrically, and the lift generated by the cambered section in fig. 3.5b is even greater than that in a, for the same overall angle of attack. But the angle of zero lift of any cambered section is negative. Zero lift is a condition of a zero *total* circulation – but there remain *local* regions of quite intense circulation and pressure difference which, although cancelling out so as to produce no lift, nevertheless have additive circulations which cause a nose-down pitching moment (and drag) as we can see in the top portion of fig. 3.7.

The resultant aerodynamic crossforce, R, acts through the centre of pressure of an aerofoil, wandering backwards and forwards with changing angles of attack. At shallow angles, the centre of pressure is aft near the mid chord. As angle of attack is increased, the centre of pressure moves forwards towards the leading edge; while circulation, lift and pitching moment also increase. The combination of moving centre of pressure and varying pitching moment seems daunting when we have to balance the aircraft.

Fortuitously, it is possible to find a point of balance which is, in effect, the centre of all of the aerodynamic forces acting upon an aerofoil. That point is called the

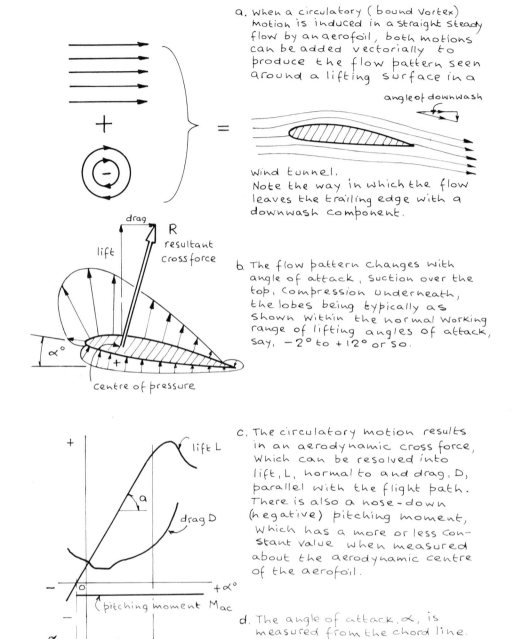

a. When a circulatory (bound vortex) motion is induced in a straight steady flow by an aerofoil, both motions can be added vectorially to produce the flow pattern seen around a lifting surface in a

angle of downwash

wind tunnel.
Note the way in which the flow leaves the trailing edge with a downwash component.

b. The flow pattern changes with angle of attack, suction over the top, compression underneath, the lobes being typically as shown within the normal working range of lifting angles of attack, say, $-2°$ to $+12°$ or so.

c. The circulatory motion results in an aerodynamic cross force, which can be resolved into lift, L, normal to and drag, D, parallel with the flight path. There is also a nose-down (negative) pitching moment, which has a more or less constant value when measured about the aerodynamic centre of the aerofoil.

d. The angle of attack, α, is measured from the chord line. When an aerofoil is cambered it has an additional angle at which lift is zero, α_{ZL}. This increases the effective angle of attack, α_{eff}.

Fig. 3.6 The way in which lift, drag and pitching moment are caused by a conventional aerofoil at subsonic speeds.

aerodynamic centre, **ac**, which lies very close to $\frac{1}{4}$ chord back from the leading edge, as shown in fig. 3.7b. Moments have been taken about four chordwise stations, each moment being the product of the lift force times the distance between the centre of pressure of the lift and the chordwise station, at four angles of attack. Drag has been neglected in our picture, because its effect is negligible. To have introduced it would have complicated the issue. When each set of moments is plotted we see that only one remains constant with changing angle of attack: that taken about the aerodynamic centre and this is denoted by M_{ac}. M_{ac} is negative which means that the centre of pressure is behind the aerodynamic centre. What is more, since the force increases with angle of attack and M_{ac} is constant, it must mean that the centre of pressure moves forwards, towards the aerodynamic centre, as angle of attack is increased.

It follows that the aerodynamic centre is more or less the best place to locate the centre of gravity of the aeroplane, because the nose-down pitching moment can then be countered economically with a modestly sized stabiliser, control and trimming surfaces. Place the CG anywhere else and a larger, heavier, costlier stabiliser is needed. Later, in chapter 11, we shall also see that the *ac* of the aeroplane is the point from which measurements are made for calculating stabiliser volume and longitudinal stability.

The magnitude of the nose-down moment coefficient, C_{Mac} (found by dividing moment M_{ac} by $qS\bar{c}$, as in eq. (2–10)) can be critical. A number of early monoplane wing failures were caused by the moment when designers reduced the height of the cabane bracing above the wings, so as to reduce drag. It was thought wrongly that the cabane bracing only prevented the wings from falling off downwards on landing. Instead a few wings twisted off leading edge downwards in high speed flight. One consequence was that the British Air Ministry stuck to the stronger biplane perhaps longer than was necessary.

Separation and stall

The working range of angles of attack corresponds with the straight line portion of the lift curve, where:

$$\text{lift slope, } a = \Delta L/\Delta\alpha = dC_L/d\alpha = \text{constant} \tag{3–15}$$

In order to calculate the lift coefficient of an aerofoil it is necessary to multiply the lift slope by the effective (or absolute) angle of attack α_{eff}, measured from the zero lift line such that, in fig. 3.6c we have:

$$C_L = a\ \alpha_{eff} \tag{3–15a}$$

and
$$\alpha_{eff} = \alpha - \alpha_{ZL} \tag{3–15b}$$

There is no anomaly when we think about the way in which aerofoil sections are developed from streamlined shapes which are initially symmetrical about the chord line, from which angle of attack is measured. The introduction of camber then causes sections to generate lift at relatively small negative angles of attack – which continue to be measured from the chord line of the original section. At larger angles of attack there is a breakdown of lifting circulation. Breakdown is rarely complete, but it is often abrupt enough to be marked by buffet and a sharp change in pitching moment and aircraft attitude accompanied by a 'g-break', detectable as a reduction in g measured by an accelerometer. The point of breakdown is the stall (the French, with picturesque clarity, say *décrocher*, to unhook) and an asymmetric stall, where one wing is more stalled than the other, is most dangerous. The pressure distributions sketched at the

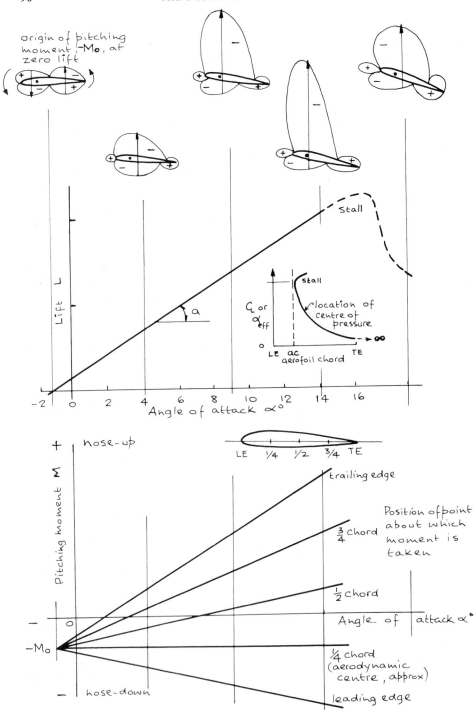

Fig. 3.7   Physical determination of aerodynamic centre by taking moments about various points along the wing chord. Drag is neglected and speed is constant. Note that the pitching moment $-M_o$ at zerolift is constant, regardless of the point about which it is taken.

top of fig. 3.7 show that even beyond the stall there may still be a powerful suction to contend with over a surface (suctions are high in flight, fabric and skin has to be fastened securely to prevent it lifting away from the ribs).

Wing sections and other aerofoils exhibit more than one type of stall, and these are clearly described in ref. 2.2, and in Appendix A, Item 66034.

☐ *Thin aerofoil stall.* Thin wings are often sharply curved just behind the leading edge, so that a steep adverse pressure gradient is established, even at shallow angles of attack. The flow cannot negotiate the bend without laminar separation. In separating, the flow becomes turbulent and, if it has the energy, turbulent re-attachment follows (fig. 3.8a), trapping a small *separation bubble* of air containing its own mini-circulation, which is then carried along with the aircraft. Bubble size varies from a small fraction of the chord to as much as the chord length. On a thin wing such a bubble may spread aft to the trailing edge with increasing angle of attack, until the wing is stalled.

☐ *Leading edge stall.* On a thicker wing, but still with plenty of curvature well forward so that a separation bubble forms, increasing angle of attack is accompanied by a chordwise shortening of the bubble. Eventually the pressure rise downstream becomes so steep that the bubble breaks down. An abrupt leading edge stall follows.

☐ *Rear stall.* Thicker modern sections with gentler curves forward and camber and maximum thickness further aft suffer primary, turbulent, separation of flow at the trailing edge. A separation bubble with turbulent re-attachment might still form just behind the leading edge with increasing angle of attack, but the dominant feature is the trailing edge vortex in fig. 3.5d, developed as shown in fig. 3.8c. A second vortex is induced further forwards, just downstream of the point of maximum thickness. The flow within the secondary trailing edge vortex bears a family resemblance to the flow within a leading edge separation bubble, being in the same sense. As angle of attack is further increased, the secondary vortex becomes so strong that its presence is sensed by the air upstream, which begins to show signs of agitation. Air ahead of the wing starts to vibrate just before the secondary vortex levers the boundary layer in front of it away from the surface of the wing, with a powerfully reversed flow. The development of the stall has been from the trailing edge this time, causing loss of lift behind the centre of gravity, while those portions of the wing ahead of the CG have continued to lift. The resulting stall often takes the form of an indeterminate longitudinal nodding motion, coupled with a full back stick minimum flying speed which, unlike the sharp nose-drop of the classic stall, may be hard to determine accurately.

A simple measure of aircraft efficiency is the ratio of maximum level speed/minimum speed (V_C/V_{SO}). The key to making the speed ratio large lies in avoiding flow separations for as long as possible. But, because inertia and eventual separation is natural to any flow, we have to resort to tricks and devices for making air behave itself over the widest range of angles of attack.

Ways of working air harder

Lift comes from circulation, which speeds up the flow over a wing while slowing the flow underneath so as to cause a differential pressure between them. There are three ways of making air work harder:

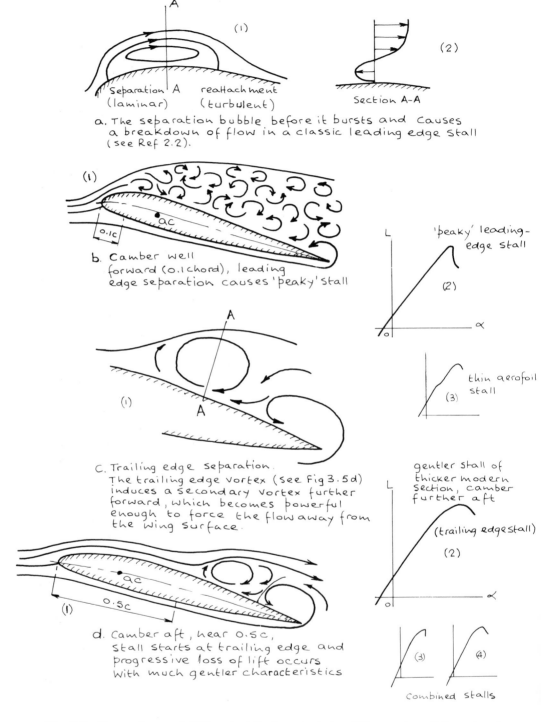

(1)

(2)

Separation A   reattachment
(laminar)   (turbulent)

Section A-A

a. The separation bubble before it bursts and causes
   a breakdown of flow in a classic leading edge stall
   (see Ref 2.2).

(1)

0.1c   ac

b. Camber well
   forward (0.1 chord), leading
   edge separation causes 'peaky' stall

L   'peaky' leading-
        edge stall

        (2)

                    α

A

(1)   A

        thin aerofoil
        stall
   (3)

C. Trailing edge separation.
   The trailing edge vortex (see Fig 3.5d)
   induces a secondary vortex further
   forward, which becomes powerful
   enough to force the flow away from
   the wing surface.

L   gentler stall of
        thicker modern
        section, camber
        further aft

        (trailing edge stall)

        (2)

                    α

ac

(1)   0.5c

d. Camber aft, near 0.5c,
   stall starts at trailing edge and
   progressive loss of lift occurs
   with much gentler characteristics

   (3)   (4)

        Combined stalls

Fig. 3.8 Separation and different stall characteristics. When an aerofoil section is
thin, the separation bubble in a may gradually extend the whole length of the chord
with increasing angle of attack, causing a 'thin aerofoil' stall.

☐ Infusion of energy into a flow by controlled turbulence: using turbulators and vortex generators.

☐ Variation of aerofoil sections and planforms by means of geometry, in the form of slats, slots, and area and camber-changing flaps.

Both methods might be thought of as passive, because no additional power is involved. A third way introduces power for active boundary layer control:

☐ Suction and blowing, both of which use more fuel to fly slowly and are too elaborate and uneconomic for our purposes here.

Boundary layer control (by vortices and turbulence)

Paradoxically turbulence and vortices which make a flow remain attached longer are in direct opposition to the need for low drag. But while a laminar flow causes less drag than any other, it is so delicately balanced and easily tripped into turbulence that it is usually more trouble than it is worth. Once a laminar flow has broken down and prematurely separated, the aerofoil loses more lift and suffers from higher drag than it would have done if the boundary layer had been turbulent and remained attached. Laminar separation occurs when the local speed of flow falls to about 94 per cent of the maximum achieved over the crest of a surface, although that value might range from 87 to 95 per cent, depending upon the steepness of the adverse gradient downstream. A turbulent layer, on the other hand, has been observed to separate much later, when the local speed of flow has dropped to about two thirds the peak value over the crest.

When a body is relatively blunt, a roughened surface which turbulates the boundary layer can cause less drag than a smooth one. That is said to be the reason why golf balls are dimpled, so that they fly further. Fig. 3.9a shows the difference in drag between a rough and smooth surface at a given speed and therefore Reynolds number.

Laminar flow is hard to maintain, but much time, effort and money has been spent trying to achieve it. Were it possible to generate a stable and durable laminar flow it would be the end of many problems for aerodynamicists and performance engineers. Unfortunately, the larger the Reynolds number the harder it is to maintain such a smooth and disciplined flow. Turbulence is generated by irregularities, like flies, raindrops, hoar frost (which has caused fatal accidents), dents, rivet heads, sharp or rough edges, even areas of scuffed paint. One motor glider with water drops on its highly polished, smooth wings had its take-off run doubled, and with its engine at full power was still firmly on the ground ten knots above the stall speed. Furthermore, stall characteristics can worsen dangerously.

There is a very thin laminar sublayer sandwiched between the main boundary layer and the skin (fig. 3.2a(3)), in which the change in airspeed is a straight line. The sublayer is there even when the main boundary layer is turbulent. A surface is said to be aerodynamically smooth as long as surface roughness and waviness lie completely within the laminar sublayer. When such imperfections protrude through the sublayer, as in the case of the raindrops on the wings of the motorglider, then laminar flow becomes turbulent.

Frost has been a notorious cause of many accidents because of its effect upon flows. Never attempt to fly with frost on the wings. Beware of dented leading edges, and cowlings of wing-mounted engines too, they have been known to cause bad stall characteristics.

Narrow wing chords, like those found on highly tapered wings and small scale aeroplanes, do not have the same aerodynamic characteristics as broader chord

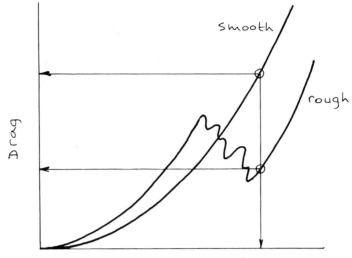

a. The effect of roughening the surface of a ball upon drag. While this shows why a dimpled golf ball flies further than one that is smooth, the same principle applies to other bodies of fairly blunt form.

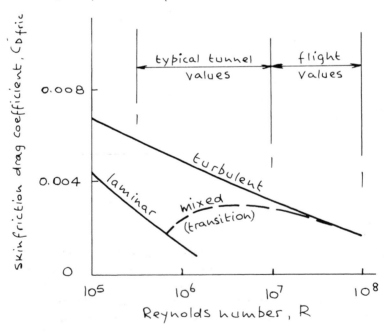

b. The effect of Reynolds number upon skin friction drag coefficient, showing why it is hard to achieve in flight.

Fig. 3.9   The effect of Reynolds number on skin friction drag of rough and smooth surfaces.

versions with the same aerofoil sections. Fig. 3.10 shows the differences in lift and drag coefficients that occur with Reynolds number with the same aerofoil section. Thus, a narrow chord can cause a 'peaky' lift curve, with a sudden hard stall; but increase the chord and the stall characteristics are softened. Furthermore, at a given angle of attack a broader chord can generate a higher lift/drag, bringing with it better cruise efficiency.

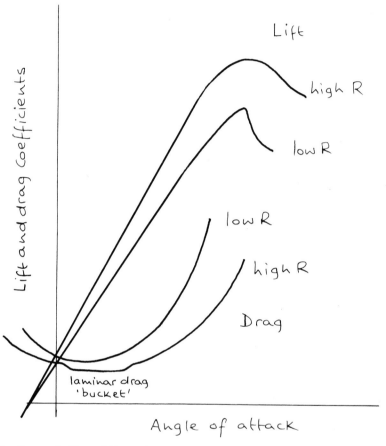

Fig. 3.10   General effect of Reynolds number upon lift and drag characteristics of the same aerofoil surface.

The disadvantages of narrow chords can be alleviated somewhat by the introduction of controlled turbulence, and vortices. Fig. 3.11a and c show vortex generators at a flap knuckle, to delay separation, and a vibrating rubber band in front of the leading edge of the wing of a model sailplane, to generate turbulence, so improving the flow.

Roughened surfaces are used in Nature to improve flying qualities. The barn owl, for example, has feathers with vortex-generating spiked vanes forming a serrated leading edge. The wing trailing edges are soft downy surfaces. The combination enables the owl to fly silently by delaying transition noise in the boundary layer, a thing quite impossible when the wings are lacquered. The noise is caused by fluctuating changes of pressure as the flow oscillates between laminar and turbulent at the point of transition on the wing chord.

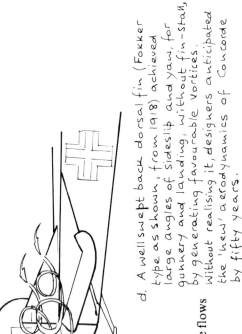

b The wings of insects (like the honey bee) are often laced with fine blood vessels which are dilated when warmed up and turbulate the flow as well as stiffening the thin membrane

(moths and butterflies have wings covered with fine hairs, and powder, which also act as turbulators).

d. A well swept back dorsal fin (Fokker type as shown, from 1918) achieved large angles of sideslip and yaw, for gunnery and landing, without fin-stall, by generating favourable vortices. Without realising it, designers anticipated the 'new' aerodynamics of Concorde by fifty years.

a. Vortex generators at flap or control surface knuckles can help to delay separation

c. A vibrating elastic turbulator in front of the leading edge of the wing of a model sailplane

Fig. 3.11 Some forms of turbulence and vortex generators, all of which make flows stick longer to lifting surfaces than would be the case without them.

Bats and many insects have thin membrane wings that are not efficient devices in themselves. But such wings contain networks of fine blood vessels, or are covered with tiny hairs, which appear to cause favourable roughening at the Reynolds numbers involved, enabling the creatures to fly better and more efficiently than would otherwise be the case. The bee, which has membrane wings, has to vibrate them before the first flight of the day to warm them up, increasing blood flow. The bumble bee, in spite of a high and seemingly inefficient wing loading, nevertheless carries nearly half of its weight as payload through such natural boundary layer control.

Table 3–1 compares the lift coefficients of a number of wings (based upon ref. 3.3) with those of aeroplanes. Birds flapping their wings generate lift more efficiently than many aeroplanes employing advanced high-lift devices.

TABLE 3–1

Maximum Lift Coefficients of Animal and Aeroplane Wings
(based upon ref. 3.3)

	Maximum C_L
Isolated locust forewing	1.3
Gliding birds	1.5 to 1.6
Gliding bats	1.5
Flapping birds	up to 2.8
Basic aeroplane	1.3 to 1.6

The Frontispiece shows clearly a number of aerodynamic features discussed in this chapter. The gannet was photographed while flying slowly. A reversal of flow by the trailing edge vortex has lifted the downy feathers near the trailing edge of its wings to delay further separation. The process is automatic. The body of the bird is well cambered with tail and feet slowing the air underneath, increasing local pressure and lift, while also trimming out the nose-up pitching caused by the wings being swept forwards, which brings the lift ahead of the centre of gravity (a change of geometry which delays tip-stall by causing the boundary layer to drift towards the root, which is thus caused to stall first). A small slat, called the *alula* (bastard wing) lying like a thumb along the leading edge of the wing at the structural wrist, has opened to deflect high pressure air from beneath the leading edge into the flow over the upper surface, again delaying separation.

Just as *down* ruffles the airflow over the wing of the bird, causing favourable turbulence, so too are vortex generators attached to wings and other surfaces to draw in free stream air and wash away stagnating air carried along with the aircraft. A vortex generator is a small plate aerofoil surface set at an angle of attack to the local flow, with its tip far enough away from the skin to protrude through the boundary layer. An intense tip vortex is established with suction in its core, in an area of adversely rising pressure. Each suction source opposes the stagnation of the flow, marked by rising static pressure, and acts like a broom which lifts air clinging to the skin to deposit it away in the free stream.

Vortex generators are used in areas of messy flows: bad junctions, flap and control surface knuckles, and in areas just forward of quite sharp curves which the air would be unable to follow, especially at large angles of attack. Examples are wing leading edges, humped canopy fairings, and some tail and rear fuselage surfaces.

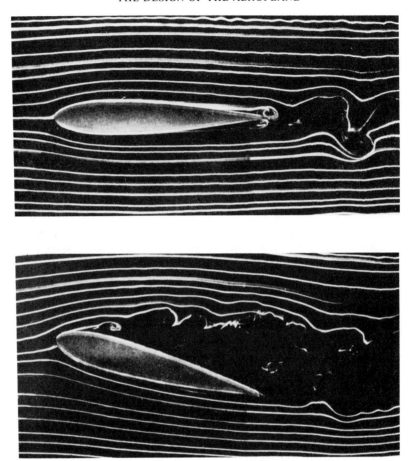

Plate 3–1 Streamlined flow breaking down into eddies and vortices: (Top) at zero angle of attack (note the stagnation streamline at the leading edge): (Bottom) at the stall (note the way in which the stagnation streamline has migrated to a point below and behind the leading edge). (*National Maritime Institute, UK*)

Related by function if not form are dorsal fillets, fuselage, tailplane and other strakes. Their quite highly swept leading edges, which must be relatively sharp-edged, generate favourable vortices which increase tail and fuselage damping, or which re-attach separating flows, at large angles of pitch and yaw (as when sideslipping and spinning).

Slats, slots and flaps

A slat is a small, cambered, aerofoil surface near the leading edge of a bigger one, arranged so as to form a slot. Air flows through the slot from a region of higher pressure to one of lower, infusing kinetic energy and delaying separation. The slat provides a high local C_L because of favourable suction from the main surface behind it which keeps the flow over it attached. However, suction and lift of the main surface are reduced somewhat by the presence of the slat at the leading edge. The *Handley Page* slot is one of the best known. The lift curve is extended to larger angles of attack, while the increment gain in lift depends upon slat chord/wing chord (one of 30 per cent more or less doubles C_{Lmax}).

All flaps are camber-changing devices of one form or another, although some also increase wing area. Camber change is harder to visualise with a split flap, but it serves the purpose by pushing air downwards, increasing the pressure underneath, intensifying the circulatory component of flow around the wing leading edge. The nose flap behaves very much like a slat, by introducing a strong camber near the leading edge. The leading edge suction peak is reduced at large angles of attack, boundary layer is thinned and stall angle of attack is increased.

Trailing edge flaps are the most obvious camber-increasing devices. The increased slope of the top surface, towards the trailing edge (seen most clearly with the geometry of the plain flap in table 3–2) increases the potential swept volume to be filled by the surrounding air. Large lift coefficients are achieved, but separation is hastened. The flap increases the angle of attack of the basic section (an approximate truth which can be seen by drawing a straight line between the leading edge of the wing and the trailing edge of the flap). Many and varied flap forms are to be found, some employing slats and slots, so as to delay separation.

Normal flying control surfaces are plain flaps (*see* chapter 12).

Plate 3–2 Wind-tunnel model of author's Warren-winged *S31–3*, which needed roughened leading edges to cause representative attached flow at test Reynolds numbers. It was impossible to induce a conventional stall and *g*-break with this wing, based on the work of Norman Hall-Warren. (*Shell Aviation News, UK*)

Aerofoil section families

There have been many aerofoil sections designed in many countries. Some of the more important have been grouped in rational families and series (usually having common thickness distributions, but with variations of their mean lines and relative

TABLE 3–2
Flap and slat characteristics

Description	Profile	C_{Lmax}	$\alpha°$ at C_{Lmax}	L/D at C_{Lmax}	C_{Mac}	Reference
Basic aerofoil Clark Y		1.29	15	7.5	−0.085	NACA TN 459
0.3c Plain flap deflected 45°		1.95	12	4.0	—	NACA TR 427
0.3c Slotted flap deflected 45°		1.98	12	4.0	—	NACA TR 427
0.3c Split flap deflected 45°		2.16	14	4.3	−0.250	NACA TN 422
0.3c, hinged at 0.8c Split (Zap) flap deflected 45°		2.26	13	4.43	−0.300	NACA TN 422
0.3c, hinged at 0.9c Split (Zap) flap deflected 45°		2.32	12.5	4.45	−0.385	NACA TN 422
0.3c Fowler flap deflected 40°		2.82	13	4.55	−0.660	NACA TR 534
0.4c Fowler flap deflected 40°		3.09	14	4.1	−0.860	NACA TR 534
0.3c Nose flap deflected 30° to 40° (best for sharp nosed sections with poor C_{Lmax})		2.09	28	4.0	—	Based upon Ref 3.10
Fixed slat forming a slot		1.77	24	5.35	—	NACA TR 427
Handley Page automatic Slat		1.84	28	4.1	—	NACA TN 459
Fixed slot and 0.3c plain flap deflected 45°		2.18	19	3.7	—	NACA TR 427
Fixed slot and 0.3c slotted flap deflected 45°		2.26	18	3.77	—	NACA TR 427
Handley Page slat and 0.4c Fowler flap deflected 40°		3.36	16	3.7	−0.740	NACA TN 459
0.1c Kruger flap (retracts backwards forming LE profile)		1.88	—	—	—	Estimates based on flight test results in Ref 3.11
0.1c Kruger flap 0.3c Fowler flap deflected 40°		3.41	—	—	—	

NACA References : aspect ratio 6, Reynolds number 609 000

thicknesses). Early families were those of Göttingen in Germany; RAF (Royal Aircraft Factory (but now Royal Aircraft Establishment)) in Britain; Coanda, Eiffel and St Cyr in France; Bambino, DGA and ISA in Italy; Clark and NACA (National Advisory Committee for Aeronautics (now NASA, National Aeronautics and Space

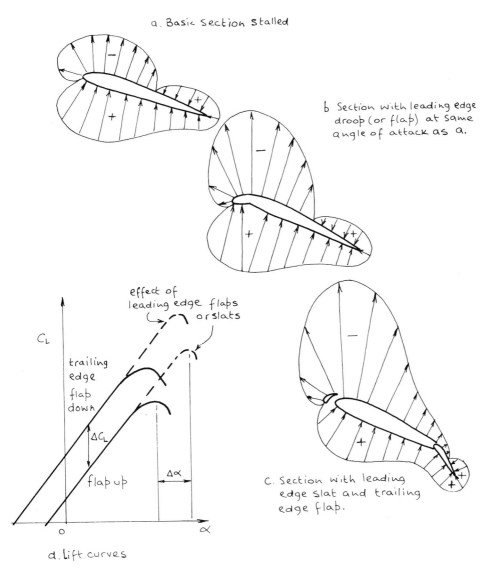

a. Basic Section Stalled

b Section with leading edge droop (or flap) at same angle of attack as a.

effect of leading edge flaps or slats

C_L

trailing edge flap down

ΔC_L

flap up

$\Delta \alpha$

o

α

d. lift curves

C. Section with leading edge slat and trailing edge flap.

Fig. 3.12   The effect of leading edge slat, flap and trailing edge flap upon lift and angle of attack of basic wing section.

Administration)) in the United States. NACA sections are perhaps the most universally known and well used.

Table 3–3 shows the salient characteristics of a number of useful sections, including the relatively new *GA(W)–1* and *GA(W)–2* profiles developed by NASA. These show very good lift/drag, but they tend to suffer from powerful pitching moments which tend to offset some other qualities. It is necessary to balance requirements for deep, light structures and good locations for spars; with good lift/drag; with ample lift at low speed and good stall characteristics; and with the size and weight of tail needed to cope with the pitching moments.

Air displaced faster than sound (supersonic)

At low airspeeds, around 100 knots at sea level (51.4 m/s), the dynamic pressure is only about 34 lbf/ft² (1630 N/m²) compared with the sea level static pressure of 2116 lbf/ft² (1.0132 × 10⁵ N/m²), ISA. But at speeds faster than M 0.3 or so, displacement of the air is accompanied by quite dramatic changes. Molecules are squeezed together. Their pressure and density increase. Calculations of dynamic pressure by means of eqs. (2–9) and (3–4) cannot be carried out by simply inserting whatever value is found from tables for air density, ρ. The change in density with compressibility causes us to add a percentage increment:

$$\text{percentage increase in dynamic pressure, } q = 25 \text{ per cent } M^2 + 2.5 \text{ per cent } M^4$$
$$= M^2/4 + M^2/40 \tag{3–16}$$

which is shown in fig. 3.13. Thus, at 66 knots the incompressible dynamic pressure is about the same as the compressible value, 10 lbf/ft² (480 N/m²). But at 400 knots, the incompressible value would be 542 lbf/ft² (26 016 N/m²), and the actual compressible value nearly 10 per cent more, at 596 lbf/ft² (28 608 N/m²). A change of this magnitude causes marked changes in lift, drag and pitching moment.

Very few light aeroplanes have been troubled by compressibility, because of inadequate engines. But modern materials which enable designers to achieve advanced, high quality, low drag profiles; automotive technology which provides cheap flap, gear and other systems; and the appearance of several small jet engines, may lead to a potent new breed of aircraft within reach of the amateur builder and private owner.

It is far easier to use lift, drag and pitching moment coefficients to describe the changes that occur with a wide range of operating speeds, altitudes and Reynolds numbers. By doing so units largely disappear and arithmetic becomes easier. We may add *pressure coefficient, C_p*, to this vocabulary, which enables us to describe the way in which pressures behave, in non-dimensional terms, with variations in airspeed and angle of attack.

Pressure coefficient is defined as:

$$C_p = \text{pressure difference/dynamic pressure} = (p - p_\infty)/q_\infty$$
$$= \Delta p/q_\infty \text{ (for static pressures)} \tag{3–17}$$
$$= (q - q_\infty)/q_\infty = -q/q_\infty \text{ (in terms of dynamic pressures)} \tag{3–17a}$$

and, knowing too that q varies as V^2, eq. (2–9), then at speeds too low for compressibility:

$$C_p = 1 - (V/V_\infty)^2 \text{ (in terms of airspeeds)} \tag{3–17b}$$

Now, look back to fig. 3.6b (or fig. 3.12) which shows suction and compression lobes around a wing. The same picture can be drawn more usefully by representing the chord as a straight line, and then plotting suction upwards and compression downwards, in terms of C_p, as shown in fig. 3.14. Eq (3–17b) demonstrates that peak suction marks maximum local airspeed; peak compression, minimum local airspeed.

If the local speed of flow reaches the speed of sound, the molecules of air are unable to adjust in time to changes in pressure brought about by the surface contours. Their behaviour is affected critically. We speak, therefore, of *subcritical* and *supercritical flows* and their associated aerodynamics.

Supercritical flows begin to occur when an aeroplane is flying at a speed around M

Derived characteristics of some NACA and NASA aerofoil sections

Aerofoil Section	Lift C_{Lmax} at (1) $R = 3 \times 10^6$	Section angle of attack° at C_{Lmax}	Moment about aerodynamic centre C_{Mac}	$R \times 6 \times 10^6$, Standard Roughness (2)			$\dfrac{\text{Thickness}}{\text{Chord}} \times 100$; Notes
				Best lift/drag C_L/C_{DO}	C_L at best C_L/C_{DO}	C_{DO} at best C_L/C_{DO}	
NACA 0009 (ref. 3.6)	1.25	13°	0	39	0.45	0.0115	9%, symmetrical; used for tail surfaces
NACA 4412 (ref. 3.6)	1.5	13°	−0.09	71	0.85	0.012	12%; docile stall; large pitching moment
NACA 23012 (ref. 3.6)	1.6	16°	−0.013	60	0.75	0.0125	12%; sharp stall
NACA 23015 (ref. 3.6)	1.5	15°	−0.008	52	0.65	0.0125	15%; sharp stall; small pitching moment
NACA 63_1–412 (ref. 3.6)	1.57	14°	−0.0075	67	0.8	0.012	12%, laminar; fair stall; small pitching moment
NACA 63_2-215 (ref. 3.6)	1.41	14°	−0.035	61	0.75	0.0123	15%, laminar; fair stall; moderate pitching moment
NACA 64_2-215 (ref. 3.6)	1.4	15°	−0.03	57	0.7	0.0122	15%, laminar; docile stall; moderate pitching moment
NACA 65_2-415 (ref. 3.6)	1.44	16°	−0.062	54	0.67	0.0123	15%, laminar; docile stall;marked pitching moment; *Piper Cherokee* wing
NASA GA(W)–1 (ref. 3.7)	1.7	16.5°	−0.09	69	1.27	0.0185	17%, new; docile stall; large pitching moment
NASA GA(W)–2 (ref. 3.8)	1.79	17°	−0.10	72	1.3	0.018	13%, new; docile stall; large pitching moment

(handwritten annotations: NACA 63_2-415 1.47 ; 14° ; −0.067 ; met small)

(1) Reynolds number calculations, see eqs. (2-11) and (3-14).
(2) These results are pessimistic because standard roughness prevents laminar flow and other theoretical benefits from being achieved. They are, therefore, closer to reality. The older NACA standard of roughness has been applied.

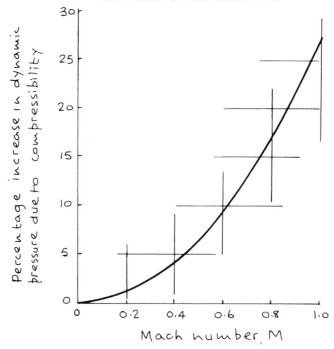

Fig. 3.13   Dynamic pressure is increased by compressibility of air, the percentage being approximately:

$$\frac{M^2}{4} + \frac{M^2}{40}$$ (eq (3–16))

(derived from ref. 3.5).

0.6. Although the aeroplane is flying subsonically the airflow has then reached sonic speed somewhere on the airframe (where C_p is most negative). As the aircraft approaches the speed of sound progressively large regions of local flow achieve supersonic speed. Other regions in which airflow is gathered up and carried along with the aircraft to a certain extent (making C_p positive) are subcritical, and these may still be found when the aeroplane has reached M 1.2 or even 1.4, depending upon the magnitude of the positive C_p peak.

We say, therefore, that the aeroplane is flying *transonically* as long as there is a jumble of mixed subcritical and supercritical flows somewhere on its skin.

When air is forced to supersonic speeds it objects, and tries to readjust to subsonic motion as quickly as possible. If able, it does so with a sharp deceleration, characterised by a *shock wave* which, under normal flight conditions, shows as a violent rise in static pressure taking place in a distance of a few thousandths of an inch. This is accompanied by an equally sharp rise in temperature. Shock waves can be heard on the skin of an aircraft by microphones inside the wing. Many readers will have heard the sonic bang of a supersonic aeroplane, when standing at a point on the ground where coalescing shock waves pass in the form of a strong pressure front.

As long as the air is prevented from decelerating after reaching the speed of sound locally on the airframe, Bernoulli's law holds and it can be caused to accelerate to even higher supersonic speeds through a series of *expansion waves* (expansion, because molecules are forced to move apart and their static pressure and density fall). An expansion wave is the opposite of a shock wave.

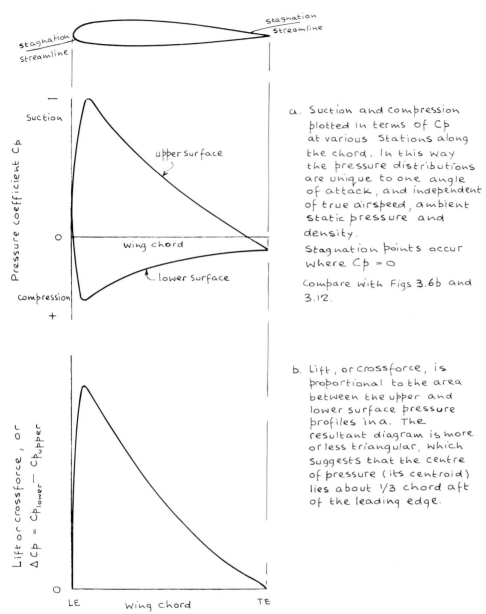

a. Suction and compression plotted in terms of Cp at various Stations along the chord. In this way the pressure distributions are unique to one angle of attack, and independent of true airspeed, ambient static pressure and density.

Stagnation points occur where Cp = 0

Compare with Figs 3.6b and 3.12.

b. Lift, or crossforce, is proportional to the area between the upper and lower surface pressure profiles in a. The resultant diagram is more or less triangular, which suggests that the centre of pressure (its centroid) lies about 1/3 chord aft of the leading edge.

Fig. 3.14 Conversion of pressure diagrams into lift distribution across chord (needed for structural design and stressing). These diagrams apply to an essentially slow-flying aeroplane with subcritical flow everywhere.

To see how it all works, imagine a streamlined solid of revolution like that shown in fig. 3.15, moving through the air like a javelin. At very low speeds the sharp point merely nudges molecules gently, so that they are able to transmit their warning pulses at the local speed of sound in all directions. Pressure waves radiate outwards in spherical ripples.

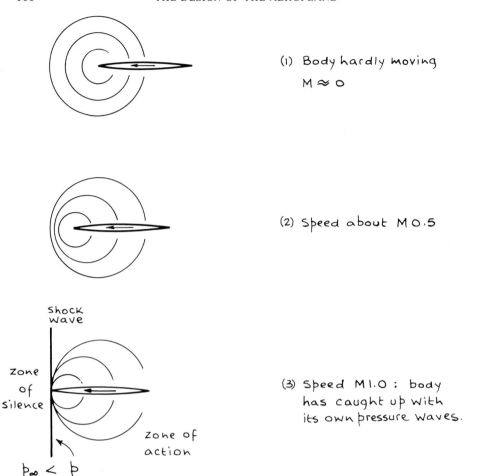

(1) Body hardly moving
    M ≈ 0

(2) Speed about M 0.5

(3) Speed M 1.0 : body
    has caught up with
    its own pressure waves.

Fig. 3.15a   Generation of a normal shockwave at high speed after von Kármán (ref. 2.1).

But as the solid body moves faster and faster, it gradually catches up with the pulses, crowding them together ahead of itself. When the body travels at the speed of sound (M 1.0) warning of its advance cannot be transmitted ahead, because it is travelling with its waves, which coalesce to form a normal shock wave at right angles to the line of flight. Ahead of the normal shock is an undisturbed region that von Kármán calls the 'zone of silence' (ref. 2.1). Behind it is his 'zone of action'. In front of the shock are the ambient conditions of the free stream. Behind the shock there has been a rise in pressure and temperature (kinetic heating), caused adiabatically by displacement, such that:

$$\text{temperature rise } \Delta T = (\text{true airspeed, mph}/100)^2 {}^\circ\text{C} \qquad (3\text{--}18)$$

to within three parts in 1 000. Alternatively, the temperature rise of the boundary layer is given by:

$$\Delta T = 75 \ M^2 {}^\circ F \qquad (3\text{--}18a)$$

under conditions found at high altitude.

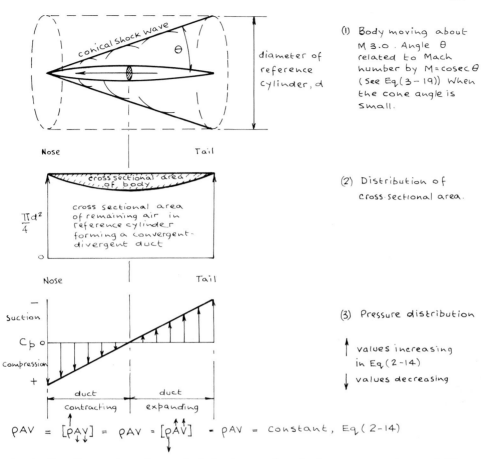

Fig. 3.15b Generation of a conical shock wave by a body at supersonic speed. The reference cylinder enables us to imagine the disturbance isolated from the remaining air. Note what is happening within eq (2–14).

At supersonic speeds the body travels faster than the pressure pulses, and a conical shock wave is formed (containing the zone of action). If the half-vertex angle of the cone subtends an angle θ deg it may be shown that when θ is small:

$$a/V = \sin \theta = 1/M \qquad \text{(from eq. (2–51))}$$
$$M = \csc \theta \qquad \text{(3–19)}$$

Now, if we draw a reference cylinder to just contain the shock cone and the body at any instant, we can see clearly that the air within it is squeezed by the passage of the body volume. The resulting pressure distribution is caused by:

☐ *Distribution of body volume* from nose to tail (i.e. distribution of the cross-sectional areas) which is intimately related to the changing *slope* of the body surface along its length.

☐ *Rate at which displacement of air by body volume occurs*: in short, the acceleration imparted to the air trapped within the cylinder drawn in fig. 3.15b by the local slope of the body surface (the steeper the slope the more rapid the acceleration).

As the slope of the surface, velocity and pressure distribution are all linked, for a given set of boundary layer conditions, the aerodynamicist has a powerful tool for calculating idealised shapes needed to produce best lift/drag at different design Mach numbers. This is the method of *area-ruling* an aircraft from nose to tail, so that the curve of total cross-sectional areas (i.e. including wings, tail surfaces, canopy, engine ducts and fairings) approximates to that of a solid of revolution generating minimum drag at the same speed.

There is an important difference between sub- and supercritical flows that is worth remembering. The key lies in eq. (2–14), which must hold for continuity because flow is neither lost nor gained, regardless of what is done to it during displacement. The changes in air density brought about by compressibility affect the exchange rate between cross-sectional area of a given streamtube and the flow velocity along it. In fig. 3.15d the cylinder is a gross streamtube, from which e and f are derived. Thus, subsonically:

$$\text{incompressible (constant density): } A \!\downarrow\, V\!\uparrow \, = A\!\uparrow \, V\!\downarrow$$

and we see that a contraction in cross-sectional area squeezes the flow to higher speed, and *vice versa*. But, when the air is compressible, as when supersonic, its density changes and the following situation occurs:

$$\text{compressible (density variable): } \rho\!\uparrow \, A\!\downarrow\, V\!\downarrow \, = \rho \, A\!\uparrow \, V\!\uparrow$$

so that a decrease in cross section chokes and slows the flow; and an opening out of the cross section expands and accelerates it.

The effect of such behaviour is shown in fig. 3.16, which represents pressure distributions over the upper surface of a wing at subsonic and supersonic speeds. In the transonic regime the wing would suffer an indeterminate mixture of the two.

The general speed range applicable to design data is:

low speed $M \leqslant 0.2$
subsonic $M = 0.2$ to 0.9
transonic $M = 0.7$ to 1.5
supersonic $M \geqslant 1.0$

Area-ruling

In recent years much work has been done to avoid the worst effects of mixed flows. In the 1950s Dr Richard T. Whitcomb of the (then) NACA Langley Research Centre in the USA developed his area-rule concept, by means of which he fattened and thinned fuselage cross sections from nose to tail, and added bulged fairings where required, to smooth the contours of the enclosed volume. The method is now part of design history, because of the dramatic change in performance bestowed on the *Convair YF–102*. Before area-ruling, the aeroplane generated too much drag to fly supersonically. After area-ruling, the aeroplane went supersonic in a climb.

Similar work proceeded towards the same ends in Britain, at the Royal Aircraft Establishment, Farnborough. There Professor Dietrich Küchemann (1911–1976), with others, approached the problem from a slightly different angle, but with much the same result.

Design of wing sections has followed a similar course. NASA has developed a supercritical wing from the original work of Whitcomb, and this has been paralleled by

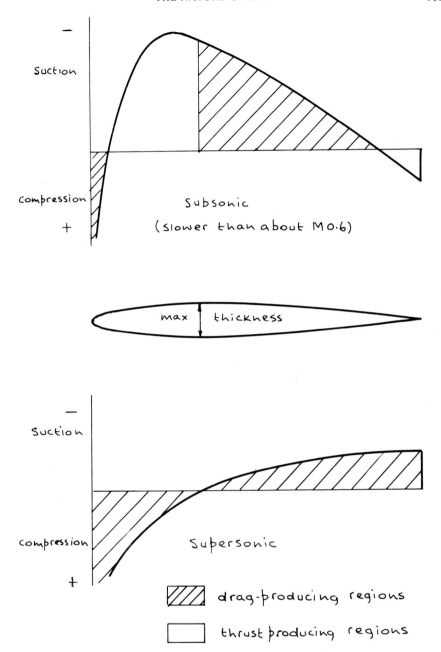

Fig. 3.16 Typical pressure distributions over an aerofoil at subsonic and supersonic speed.

special aerofoil sections evolved by RAE, and Hawker Siddeley Aviation (now part of British Aerospace), which have rear-loading and flat (roof-top) pressure distributions. Such sections have flatter curves on their upper surfaces, extending further aft, and deep curving bellies which sweep upwards and become concave towards the trailing

Plate 3–3   Natural control of lift and drag through control of the boundary layer is a feature of many creatures, including bats, owls, beetles, flies, moths. In the sea *cetaceans* (e.g., porpoises (often called dolphins)) can reduce drag by subtle changes of cross-sectional area to keep flows attached. (Top) Blood vessels in the wings of a worker bee stabilise the membranes and turbulate the flow. (Bottom) This *Small Elephant Hawk Moth* is covered with fine down and has dusty wing scales, which help to turbulate and attach the flow, aiding silent flight. (*Natural History Photographic Agency, UK*)

edge forming a cusp. Their profiles offload the forward portion of the wing, while the rearward part sustains a greater aerodynamic load. A smooth supersonic flow can be maintained further aft than is possible conventionally. The final shock, when it comes, is less intense than one formed further forwards with earlier sections. Overall an aeroplane with a rear-loaded, supercritical wing is able to cruise faster for a given power setting, or it can carry a heavier payload at the same speed. The critical Mach number, M_{crit}, at which the drag coefficient begins to rise significantly because of wave drag terms, is delayed to M 0.8 or 0.9.

Plate 3-3 (Bottom).

However, rear-loading moves the centre of lift of the wing about 10 per cent of the chord further aft, which causes the wing to be mounted further forwards on the fuselage. Furthermore larger, stronger and heavier elevators are needed to cope with the pitching moments. Loading of the rearward portion of such wings necessitates stronger structures toward the trailing edge, but as thicker wing sections of less area can be designed, this does not necessarily lead to heavier wings. There is often less room for fuel inside such smaller wings.

We have reached the end of a chapter that started by talking about the nature of air, and has ended by bringing us face to face with the much wider issue of arranging and shaping surfaces to make use of air in a disciplined and economical way.

This is the threshold of aeroplane design.

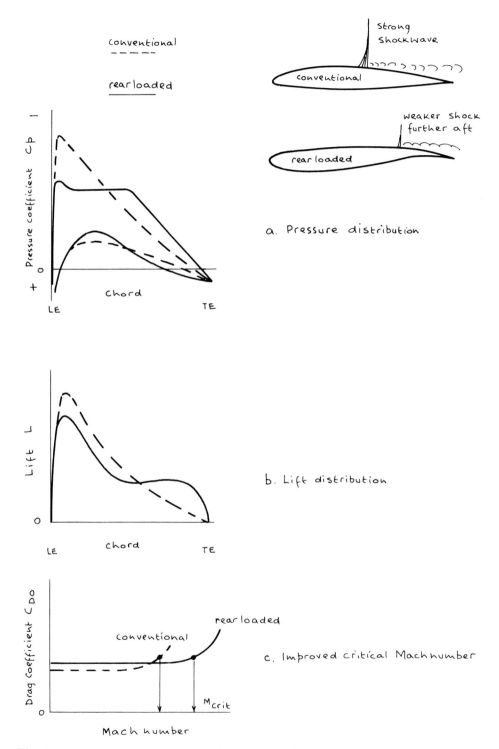

a. Pressure distribution

b. Lift distribution

c. Improved critical Mach number

Fig. 3.17 Comparison of conventional and rear-loaded (supercritical) aerofoil sections.

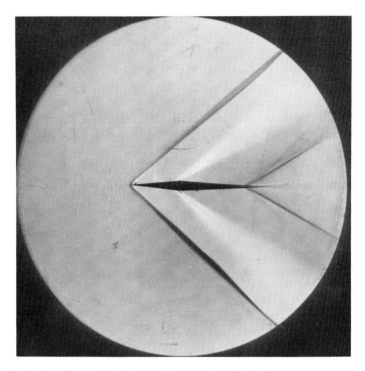

Plate 3–4 (Top)   Schlieren photograph of double wedge aerofoil section at Mach number 1.8, showing dark leading and trailing edge shock waves, with light coloured expansion waves at the crests in between. (*Imperial College, Department of Aeronautics, UK*)

Plate 3–4 (Bottom)   *Handley Page Victor* with 'Küchemann carrots' at wing trailing edges, to provide rudimentary favourable area-distribution, so reducing wave drag and unpleasant transonic side-effects. (*John Fricker, UK*)

Plate 3-5   *Rutan Model 72, Grizzly*, explores a more extreme tandem configuration (like a Warren-Wing with the foreplane reversed). The tail appears to bestow control authority in pitch which the *S31-3* lacked (see plate 3-2). *(Rutan Aircraft Factory, USA)*

References

3.1 Sutton, O. G. (1949) *The Science of Flight*. Harmondsworth, Middlesex: Penguin Books.

3.2 Bede Aircraft, Inc. Bede Design No 7 (Jan. 1971) *Sport Aviation,* Wisconsin: Experimental Aircraft Association International.

3.3 Pennycuick, C. J. (1972) *Animal Flight*. (*Studies in Biology No 33*). London: Arnold.

3.4 Perkins, C. D. and Hage, R. E. (1967) *Airplane Performance Stability and Control*. New York, London and Sydney: John Wiley & Sons, Inc.

3.5 Dommasch, D. O. Sherby, S. S. and Connolly, T. F. (1951) *Airplane Aerodynamics*. New York, Toronto and London: Pitman.

3.6 Abbott, I. A. and von Doenhoff, A. E. (1959) *Theory of Wing Sections, Including a Summary of Airfoil Data*. New York: Dover Publications Inc.

3.7 NASA TN D7428 (Dec. 1973) *Low Speed Aerodynamic Characteristics of a 17-Per cent-Thick Airfoil Section Designed for General Aviation*. National Aeronautics and Space Administration.

3.8 NASA TMX–72697 (1973) *Low Speed Aerodynamic Characteristics of a 13-Per cent Thick Airfoil Section Designed for General Aviation*. National Aeronautics and Space Administration.

3.9 Sunderland, L. D. (1977) 'What's New in Low Speed Airfoils?' *Sport Aviation*, Experimental Aircraft Association.

3.10 Lee, G. H. (1953) 'High Maximum Lift', *The Aeroplane*.

3.11 Kohlman, D. L. (1979) Flight Test Results for an Advanced Technology Light Airplane. *Journal of Aircraft* **16** (No 4), American Institute of Aeronautics and Astronautics.

CHAPTER 4

Arrangement of Surfaces

'There can be no doubt that the inclined plane, with a horizontal propelling apparatus, is the true principle of aerial navigation by mechanical means ... and there is nothing new in it, the principle has as yet remained dormant, for want of sufficient power.'
Sir George Cayley (1843).
(From *'Sir George Cayley's Aeronautics 1796–1855'*, Charles H. Gibbs-Smith, Her Majesty's Stationery Office.)

'We shall use results as long as they have not been refuted.'
Professor Dietrich Küchemann (ref. 4.1).

In the last chapter we looked at airflows moving essentially in two dimensions, in the plane of the paper. Here we consider them moving in three dimensions. Lift is derived from a cross-force on an aerofoil surface, and this in turn involves circulation, in the form of a major, bound vortex (fig. 3.5d(2)). The bound vortex lies along the span of the aerofoil, almost from tip to tip, although it is not of constant strength along its length. Near the tips the vortex bends around like a horseshoe and trails downstream in the wake of each, where it can sometimes be seen when air is moist, or heard in the hiss and whisper of collapsing vortices after a low-flying aeroplane has passed, plate 4.1.

Circulation along the span is hard to visualise unless helped by a camera. The closest the pilot comes to physical awareness of the presence of this strange phenomenon which both supports and retards him, is through changes in stick force needed to trim out the pitching moment from the lifting surfaces when flap is selected, or when attitude is changed. Even then the force is an amalgam of many other complicated pitching effects.

Strength of circulation is measured by the product of velocity and length of the curved path over which the velocity applies:

Γ = Tangential velocity $\times$ circumference of curve around which flow moves

which, for a purely rotational motion around a vortex core, at any radius outside the core, becomes:

$$\Gamma = 2\,\pi\,R\,v \text{ ft}^2/\text{s (m}^2/\text{s)} \qquad (4\text{--}1)$$

This equation tells us that when circulation is constant, the tangential velocity, v, varies inversely as R, the radius, as we move outwards from the core.

Wingspan: airflows in three dimensions

If we look up the wake of a rear-engined jet airliner that has passed overhead on its approach to land, we sometimes see a pattern of tip vortices and downwash traced in smoke, like that shown in fig. 4.1a. The spiral flows behind both tips, and the entrained downwash between them, are contained within an approximate cylinder of air which varies in diameter (depending upon how far it is behind the aeroplane), but which is more or less equal to the wingspan. Each tip vortex has a Rankine form (*see* footnote to table 2-5) consisting of a central core in which the rotational velocity increases with radius, like a wheel. Outside the core is a region in which velocity decreases as $1/R$, as we have just seen.

The cylinder represents the mass of air acted upon by the aeroplane in flight. Early ideas were that the mass of air was not cylindrical, but an ellipse, about 1.2 times wider than deep. But Frederick W. Lanchester (1878–1946), a profoundly original English

Plate 4–1   Tip vortices shed by a wing can contain such intense suction as to condense water vapour into cloud. The near-elliptic lift distribution along the span is also marked by vapour, and shows asymmetry caused by aileron deflection to reduce the angle of bank. (*John Tweddle, British Aerospace, Kingston, UK*)

Plate 4–2   Jim Bede in his *BD–5*, which is twice as long as the reclining pilot and is as quick reacting as a cat. It caused great excitement when it appeared but has suffered accidents through use of unsuitable engines by enthusiasts, as a result of several specified engines failing to materialise in time. The author found it an aeroplane to treat with caution and respect. (*Howard Levy*)

engineer, and Ludwig Prandtl (1875–1953), a German engineer at Göttingen, who brought incisive insight vision and analysis to fluid mechanics, assumed that a wing entrained a cylinder of air equal in diameter to the span. In fact, the mass of air appears to have a *vena contracta* form, sketched in fig. 4.1c, with a cylinder diameter $\sqrt{2}$ times the wingspan, at the wing; and a diameter somewhat less than the span some way behind in the wake. This is borne out by the way in which tip vortices draw themselves together in the wake, until they stabilise around wingspan/$\sqrt{2}$ to $\pi/4 \times$ wingspan (about $\frac{3}{4}$ of the span apart). Their form is shown by vapour trails behind high flying aeroplanes, or in smoke trailed from wing–mounted canisters.

Ahead of an aeroplane the air is sensibly unaffected. In the plane of the wing the cylinder, with a diameter $\sqrt{2}$ times the span, and length equal to the distance flown in one second, is given an impulse, a downwash velocity, w_w. Some way behind the wing the downwash has a final value, w. Now, by Newton's second law:

lift = rate of change of momentum of cylindrical mass of air of density, ρ

   = mass of cylinder $\times$ downwash velocity

   = $n \times$ weight of aircraft   (4–2)

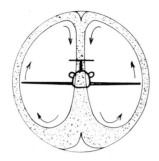

a. The mass of air worked on by a wing has a more or less circular cross-section with a diameter roughly equal to the span (see Eq (4-2). Each lobe contains a vortex skein from a wing tip. Between them is a region of downwash of entrained air. Outside them is a corresponding upwash. The energy in the motion of the air is proportional to the energy needed to sustain the weight of the aeroplane. Thus, the wake of a heavy transport, flying slowly, or a helicopter, is most dangerous to light aircraft.

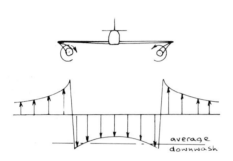

average downwash

b. Each trailing vortex has a Rankine form, giving a spanwise downwash distribution like that shown (only the rare elliptical lift distribution across the span gives constant downwash between the vortex cores). The average downwash velocity at the wing is about 5ft/s (1.5m/s) for a light aeroplane, and 16ft/s (5m/s) for a big jet transport. Downwash far downstream in the wake may have double these values.

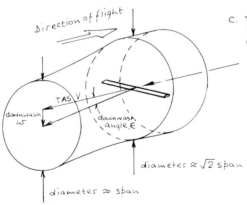

Direction of flight

TAS V

downwash w

downwash angle, ε

diameter ≈ √2 span

diameter ≈ span

Fig 4·1

c. The mass of air shown in a. resembles a cylinder in elevation with a vena contracta form

Fig. 4.1   The working mass of air acted upon by a wing in 1 second (after Lanchester and Prandtl)

(when lift is doing all of the work in sustaining the aircraft)
where n is the normal acceleration when manoeuvring. In straight and level flight $n=1$.

Thus, taking a cylinder of diameter equal to $\sqrt{2} \times$ span of the wing, b:

$$\text{lift, } L = (\pi/4)(\sqrt{2}b)^2 \rho Vw = nW \tag{4-2a}$$

and downwash velocity, $w = (2n/\pi\rho V)(W/b^2) = (2/\pi\rho V)(L/b^2)$ (4-3)

The angle of downwash, α_i in some notations ϵ in others, especially when we are concerned with the local flow at the tail, is the angle subtended by downwash velocity/TAS w/V, such that:

$$w/V = \tan \epsilon \text{ deg} \approx \epsilon \text{ radians} = (n/\pi q)(W/b^2) \tag{4-4}$$

or, knowing that $nW = \text{lift} = C_L qS$ (from eq. (2–3a)), we may also write:

$$\epsilon = C_L S/\pi b^2 = (1/\pi q)(L/b^2) \tag{4-4a}$$

And, as aspect ratio $A = b^2/S$ (from eq (2–4)):

$$\epsilon = C_L/\pi A \text{ radians} = \tan \epsilon \text{ deg} \tag{4-4b}$$

When multiplied by 57.3 we obtain the angle in degrees.

If we argue in exactly the same way about the downwash of a cylinder of air in the wake of the wing, of diameter equal to the wingspan, b instead of $\sqrt{2}b$, we find that the downwash velocity two to three wing chords behind at the tail is roughly doubled, to $2w$ (which is the theoretical value reached at infinity, although viscosity reduces it to zero long before that). The reason is that at the wing we have downwash caused in the main by the bound vortex, but behind in the wake there are the additional effects of the tip vortices, each providing their own impulses, fig. 4.2a, which increase the downwash angle by a further increment ϵ to 2ϵ.

Immediately ahead of the wing there is an upwash, as shown in fig. 4.2b, caused by the bound vortex. This must be taken into account when calculating local angle of attack of a surface lying forward of a wing.

The existence of downwash means that an aeroplane has to fly uphill aerodynamically, so as to maintain altitude. The shorter the span, the steeper the aerodynamic hill for a given wing area and weight. It follows that greater effort is required of the propulsion system to fly level, when a wing is short rather than long. Short spans are inefficient in these fuel-conscious times (in fact, we might say that they are positively antisocial within the context of most aircraft with which we are concerned). We only use short spans for special applications, like racing, which is quite a different matter from flying for range and fuel-efficiency. But one cannot extend the span of a wing indefinitely, because we run into the problem of its growing structural weight to resist bending, and the adverse effect upon the size of the fin and rudder, which must become larger and heavier in consequence of problems with directional stability and control.

Downwash reduces the geometric angle of attack as shown in fig. 4.2c, by the angle ϵ, such that:

$$\alpha_0 = \alpha - \epsilon \tag{4-5}$$

It also has the effect of bending backwards the lift vector through an angle ϵ, (or α_i), which introduces an induced component, D_i, which is also referred to as a vortex drag component by some sources. The downwash angle is usually small enough for us to be able to say:

$$\epsilon \text{ in radians} \approx \tan \epsilon \text{ deg} \approx \sin \epsilon \text{ deg} \tag{4-6}$$

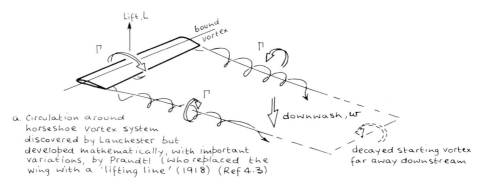

a. Circulation around horseshoe vortex system discovered by Lanchester but developed mathematically, with important variations, by Prandtl (who replaced the wing with a 'lifting line' (1918) (Ref 4.3)

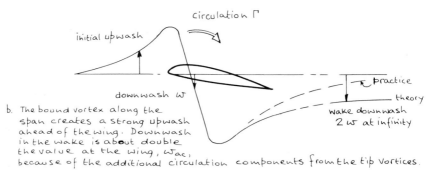

b. The bound vortex along the span creates a strong upwash ahead of the wing. Downwash in the wake is about double the value at the wing, w_{ac}, because of the additional circulation components from the tip vortices.

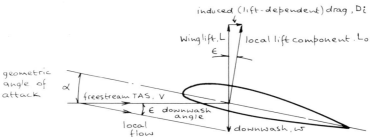

c. Downwash at the wing reduces the angle of attack, inducing an additional component of lift-dependent drag, D_i

Fig. 4.2   Downwash is the cause of induced drag.

so that we may use fig. 4.2(c) in conjunction with eqs. (4–4) and (4–4a) to state:

$$\text{induced drag, } D_i = L\epsilon = Lw/V$$
$$= (L/b)^2/\pi q = (W/b)^2 n^2/\pi q \qquad (4\text{–}7)$$

In straight and level flight the lift loading across the span. L/b, is equal to W/b, the weight of the aircraft divided by the wingspan. Both are referred to collectively as the *span loading*, so that we may say:

Induced drag varies with (*span loading*)^2

at any given speed (and, hence, dynamic pressure, q).

The term D_i can be converted into a drag coefficient, C_{Di}, by dividing through by qS. As lift $L = C_L qS$ the induced drag coefficient may be written:

$$C_{Di} = C_L^2/\pi A \qquad (4\text{-}8)$$

but this is only true when downwash is constant along the span, which condition requires an elliptical lift distribution. In practice a perfectly elliptic distribution is almost impossible to achieve, and the induced drag is increased in proportion to the deviation of the actual lift distribution from the ideal. Therefore, eq (4–8) must be rewritten in a form which takes account of planform effects, i.e.:

$$C_{Di} = C_L^2 (1 + \delta)/\pi A = C_L^2/\pi\, eA = KC_L^2/\pi\, A \qquad (4\text{-}9)$$

in which K is the induced drag factor, e is Oswald's efficiency factor, and:

$$K = (1 + \delta) = 1/e = \pi A/(C_L^2/C_{Di}) \qquad (4\text{-}9a)$$

Generally speaking $e = 0.7$ to 0.8, making the induced drag factor $K = 1.2$ to 1.4 for many light aeroplanes. The term δ is given in fig. 4.10b and c.

When wings and bodies are joined there is interference and local losses of lift over portions of the wingspan. The consequence is that the wing must be flown at an increased angle of attack to generate sufficient lift, which requires an increased lift coefficient. The increased lift coefficient increases the induced drag, and it is convenient to introduce a further distinction by using K' in place of K for the real aeroplane, such that: $\diagdown\quad w/b$

$$\text{actual (applied) induced drag coefficient } C_{Di} = (C_L^2/\pi)(K'/A) \qquad (4\text{-}9b)$$

The value of K is also dependent upon the shape of the drag polar, as we shall see in fig. 5.7, and this is a further reason for resorting to use of K' for the applied case, while reserving K for the theoretical wing alone.

The forms of eqs (4–8) to (4–9b) enable us to add that:

☐ The *induced drag coefficient* varies inversely with *aspect ratio*

for a given planform and lift distribution along the wingspan.

Spanwise lift distribution

The strength of the circulation of the bound vortex is not constant along the span, except when wingspan and aspect ratio are infinite. Fig. 4.3b shows the way in which higher pressure air underneath a wing leaks around the tips, decreasing the suction over the upper surfaces outboard, reducing lift. Lift is lost in the form of circulation shed in a family of trailing vortices behind the wing. Such leakage around the tips introduces a spanwise component of flow: outwards underneath the wing, inwards on top. The induced spanwise components rake the streamline outwards underneath the wings and inwards on their upper surfaces. The shorter the wingspan for a given wing area (i.e. the lower the aspect ratio) the greater the rake.

When the aspect ratio is about five, the angle of rake is 25 deg outwards from leading to trailing edge; while for $A = 6$ the rake reduces to 20 deg or so. For an infinitely long wing the rake is zero.

Lost circulation along the span is shed into the wake in the form of locally small vortices. These wind themselves up into two skeins, each forming a tip vortex, the

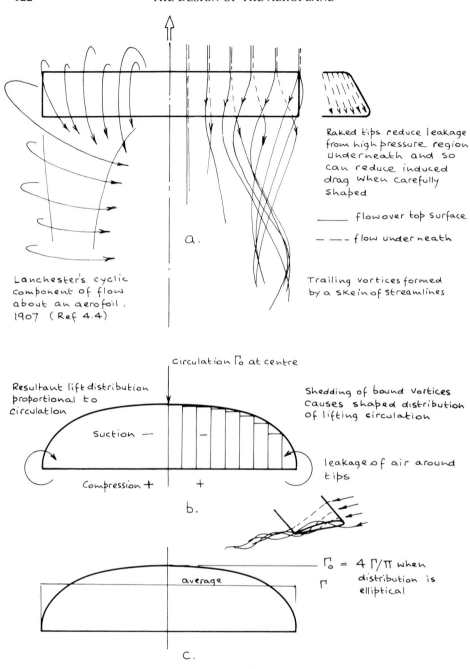

Raked tips reduce leakage from high pressure region underneath and so can reduce induced drag when carefully shaped

———— flow over top surface

— —·— flow underneath

a.

Lanchester's cyclic component of flow about an aerofoil, 1907 (Ref 4.4)

Trailing vortices formed by a skein of streamlines

Circulation Γ_0 at centre

Resultant lift distribution proportional to circulation

Shedding of bound vortices causes shaped distribution of lifting circulation

Suction —

Compression +

+

leakage of air around tips

b.

average

$\Gamma_0 = 4\,\Gamma/\pi$ when distribution is elliptical

Γ

c.

Fig. 4.3   Lift is directly proportional to circulation.

strength of which is equal to the circulation shed by the wing. Lanchester had the insight which gave the rest of the world knowledge of what happens to a wing of finite span, but his peers did not recognise it at the time. The concept is shown in fig. 4.3. The left hand side of (a) represents what he called 'the cyclic flow about an aerofoil'; while the right hand side develops the flow in accordance with the modern view. Both are the same. Prandtl had his own insights which were close to those of Lanchester. It was yet another of those coincidences of accordance in time, like the evolution of calculus from the fluxions of Newton and the integrals of one of the most brilliant German mathematicians and philsophers Gottfried Wilhelm Liebniz (1646–1716), which occurred simultaneously in two different parts of Europe.

Lift is directly proportional to circulation. A device which increases circulation also increases lift. The relationship between lift, L, and average circulation, Γ, is linked to eq (2–3a) by:

$$L = \Gamma \rho V b = C_L q S \qquad (4\text{–}10)$$

and, if lift distribution is elliptical, with a peak value at the centre line Γ_0:

$$\Gamma_0 = (4/\pi)\ \Gamma \qquad (4\text{–}10a)$$

Transposing for Γ and using eqs (2–4) and (2–9) for $b = S/c$ and $q = \frac{1}{2}\,\rho V^2$ respectively, we see that strength of circulation:

$$\Gamma = C_L c\ V/2 \text{ ft}^2/\text{s (m}^2/\text{s)} \qquad (4\text{–}11)$$

in appropriate units. We also saw that a cylinder of air with a diameter equal to the wingspan has a downwash twice that at the wing (where the cylinder is about $\sqrt{2}b$ diameter), such that:

$$L = (\pi/4)b^2\ \rho\ V(2w) \qquad (4\text{–}2b)$$

Thus, circulation and downwash are related and, by juggling with eq (4–10) to obtain span loading, L/b and nW/b:

$$\Gamma = (\pi/2)bw \qquad (4\text{–}12)$$
$$= (1/\rho V)(L/b) = (n/\rho V)(W/b) \qquad (4\text{–}13)$$

when n is the number of 'g units' of normal acceleration applied when manoeuvring at true airspeed V.

With such an elliptical distribution, the most intense circulation, Γ_0, is at the centre. This can be shown to be $4/\pi$ times larger than the average circulation, Γ, in eq (4–10). Thus, eq (4–13) can also be stated in terms of maximum circulation:

$$\Gamma_0 = (4/\pi\rho V)(L/b) = (4n/\pi\rho V)(W/b) \qquad (4\text{–}13a)$$

This gives the strength of each trailing vortex.

A useful way of approximating the span loading is known as the *Schrenk method* (Prof Dr Ing Oskar Schrenk (1901–   )) which relies on the fact that the distribution of lift across the span of an unswept wing does not differ much from elliptic, even for a highly non-elliptic planform. If a constant aerofoil section is used and there is no change of incidence in the form of wash-in (incidence in creasing from root to tip) or wash-out (incidence decreasing in the same direction), only the local chord affects the shape of the lift distribution. If we consider each unit of semi-span, the areas of the strip is $1 \times c$ (the local chord). If the local lift is l and the associated lift coefficient C_L then at any spanwise station:

$$l/q = C_L c \text{ per unit span} \qquad (4\text{–}14)$$

and we may construct the diagram of lift distribution as shown in fig. 4.4. The final

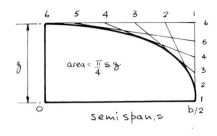

a. Draw an ellipse with the same area enclosed as the area under the curve of chord distribution shown in b, such that

$$\frac{\pi}{4} s z = \frac{s}{2}(c_r + c_t)$$

ie, $z = \frac{2}{\pi}(c_r + c_t)$

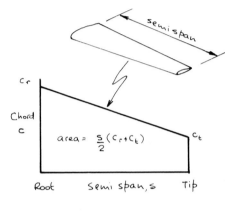

b. Chord distribution along semi-span of length $s = b/2$.

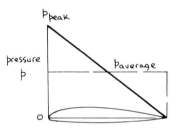

d. Chordwise pressure distribution and, hence lift-distribution

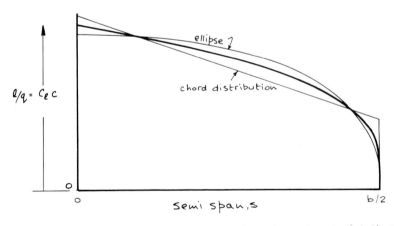

c. Lay the ellipse in a upon the chord distribution, b, and construct a mean line of lift distribution

Fig. 4.4   Schrenk's method of construction lift distribution for unswept wings.

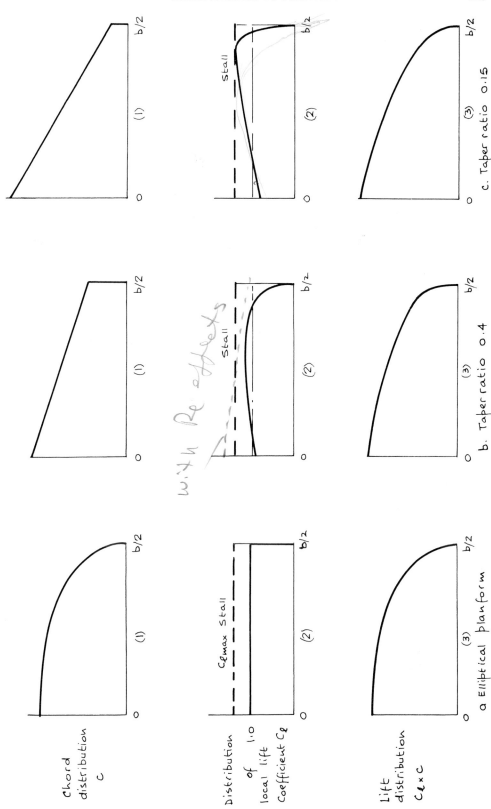

Fig. 4.5 (Semi-) spanwise lift distribution for three planforms. Note the way in which taper causes section lift coefficient to peak towards an early stall. Reduced Reynolds number towards the tip would make matters worse. In (c) washout towards the tip would reduce incidence and lift coefficient beneficially.

curve, midway between the elliptical distribution and the chord distribution is that of C_Lc at any station. Actual lift can be found by multiplying the local C_Lc by the dynamic pressure, q. If the values of C_Lc are divided by the local chord, c, we may plot the distribution of lift coefficient as shown in Figure 4.5a. The section C_{Lmax} is plotted on the same diagram. The point at which the C_L curve comes closest to the C_{Lmax} line shows where the stall is most likely to start. A rectangular wing stalls first at the root. The more tapered or swept back a wing becomes, the more the C_L curve becomes humped outboard, and the stall occurs first towards the tip. This is dangerous, because slight sideslip and asymmetries between each wing can cause one wing to stall before the other. A violent wing drop and roll may be the result of a stall, which can be exaggerated by use of corrective aileron. A spin might follow.

Ideally a wing must be encouraged to stall first at the root. Turbulence from the separating flow may then strike the tail, causing natural stall warning.

Fig. 4.4d shows the conventional approximation for the chordwise lift and pressure distribution, based upon fig. 3.14b. If we again take a strip of chord of unit width, the lift is proportional to the area under the triangle. By construction, the peak pressure in the vicinity of the leading edge is double the average across the chord:

$$\text{local lift, } L = \text{p}_{average}c = C_Lcq \qquad (4\text{-}15)$$
$$\text{pressure, } \text{p}_{peak} = 2\text{p}_{average} = 2\,C_lq \qquad (4\text{-}16)$$

Importance of low span loading

Once the planform of a wing is fixed the induced drag depends upon span loading and not aspect ratio. The longer the span the lower the span loading and the faster an aeroplane climbs and cruises. Span loading arises from the average pressure difference between the upper and lower surfaces. The lower the span loading, the smaller the pressure difference, and the further away the wing operates from those conditions where separation becomes critical.

Eq (4–7), which applies to elliptic distributions, becomes modified by reality in the same way as Eq (4–9), so that:

$$\text{induced drag, } D_i = (K'n^2/\pi q)(W/b)^2 = (K'/\pi q)(L/b)^2 \qquad (4\text{-}17)$$

When cruising straight and level, $n = 1$. Hence, the induced drag at a given speed and height varies as the induced drag factor of the wing planform, K', and the span loading, $(W/b)^2$. It follows that the induced drag changes with the weight of the aircraft as long as planform is unchanged by variable geometry, and greatest aerodynamic efficiency (as measured by K'/A) is achieved with aeroplane aspect ratios around 13 to 15 (fig. 4.10a).

Taper is only useful for reducing wing structure weight (which is increased by a long span). Too much taper provokes tip stalling. For practical purposes (and only if taper is needed), the ratio of tip chord/root chord should not be less than about 1/3, and not more than about 1/2 (ref. 4.5).

A span loading that is too high can be dangerous, because induced drag can delay take-off and result in a poor climb gradient. Les Berven, former test pilot of the *BD–5* is reported to have warned home-builders against flying the short-winged *A* version almost certainly for these reasons. Furthermore, short wings are usually lightning fast in roll. The author found the long-winged *B* version delightful to fly, tolerant of abuse but quick-reacting on the controls, making it easy to overcontrol initially. This is a tricky characteristic of all miniature aeroplanes, and one of their most important disadvantages.

Effect of reduced aspect ratio

Aspect ratio affects directly the slope of the lift curve, $a = dC_L/d\alpha$. The larger the aspect ratio, the more nearly does the lift slope approach the theoretical maximum for an infinitely long wing:

$$\text{i.e.} \qquad \text{ideal lift slope, } a_0 = 2\pi/\text{radian } (0.11/\text{deg}) \qquad (4\text{–}18)$$

But as aspect ratio is reduced, lift slope decreases by a factor $A/(A + 2)$, so that for aspect ratios less than infinity:

$$a_A = 2\pi A/(A + 2)$$
$$= a_0 A/(A + 2)/\text{radian in the normal range of values of } A \qquad (4\text{–}19a)$$

While for very low aspect ratios of 2 or less:

$$a_A = 2\pi(A/4) = a_0(A/4) \qquad (4\text{–}19b)$$

Fig. 4.6 shows the general effect of reducing aspect ratio upon the lift and drag curves; while fig. 4.7 shows the angle of attack needed for landing to achieve a typical $C_L = 1.0$, and highlights the constraint imposed by practical undercarriage length. Plate 4.3 shows the long legs of Charles H. Zimmerman's experimental *Chance Vought XF5U-1* of 1947, with an aspect ratio around $4/\pi$.

Increasing effective wingspan (vortex diffusion)

Long wings are efficient but cumbersome, and they can be heavy. Devices are being investigated which increase effective spans and aspect ratios without making spans physically larger. Birds did this first and have a message for us worth recounting.

Plate 4-3 Low aspect ratio wings operate at large angles of attack and need long legs for landing. Experimental *Chance Vought XF5 U-1*, 1948. (*Howard Levy USA*)

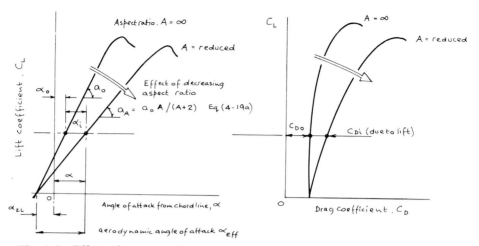

Fig. 4.6   Effect of aspect ratio, A, upon lift and drag characteristics.

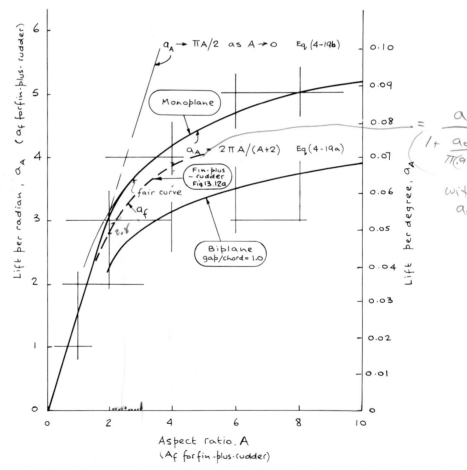

Fig. 4.6c   Effect of aspect ratio upon lift slope, a_A. This figure ignores the influence of form factor due to taper, eq (5–5) and fig. 5.5.

Plate 4–4 (Top)   Low aspect ratio winged *BAC Lightning* (aspect ratio 2.6) clawing at the air to fly alongside a *De Havilland Tiger Moth* (aspect ratio 7.2) which needs to do much less work on the air to remain airborne (*Squadron Leader MC Johnson, RAF*) (Bottom) Ingenuity of designer Reinholdt Platz (1886–1966) is shown in Fokker Dr1 triplane, with other D VII film replicas. Compact mass distribution, short span, deep under-cambered section and low wing loading of unbraced (propped-cantilever) planes, with ailerons on most efficient top surfaces, bestowed strength, stiffness and nimbleness. The round fin and rudder would not stall before about 30 deg deflection. With no fin or dihedral there was no weather cock or lateral stability to overcome, so that that marksmen like Werner Voss excelled at flat skidding turns for deflection shots (*loaned by Tony Bianchi*)

Soaring land and sea birds have broadly similar performance. They can climb in thermals, have flat glides and the ability to fly far. But land birds tend to have lower aspect ratios. For example albatrosses and frigate birds have pointed tips and aspect

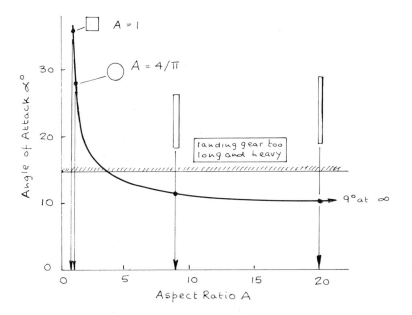

Fig. 4.7 Effect of aspect ratio on angle of attack to generate lift for landing ($C_L = 1.0$).

ratios approaching 18. Even common gulls have values of 10 or more. Pointed primary or pinion feathers twist leading edge down under load, providing natural washout, so that birds do not suffer stalls quite like rigid aeroplanes. Sea birds have almost unlimited distances in which to take off, and live on shores and cliffs, so that long spans are not detrimental.

Land birds have to contend with obstacles like bushes, trees, rocks and vegetation, and have to escape swiftly from predators. Birds of prey, which include vultures, eagles and condors, have plank-like wings with little taper. Primary feathers at the tips form five or more slots, and they are distinctly emarginated, having markedly narrowed chords at their outer ends. Wing aspect ratios are around 9.5 to 10 (over the whole spread), with slotted pinions occupying about 1/5 of the total span.

Why there should be such odd numbers of primary feathers is not known. However, the bird probably flies for minimum energy expenditure at $(L/D)_{max}$, which (for its wing section) occurs at an angle of attack around 3 degrees, say. A highly tapered wing has the tips operating near peak C_L, with α approximately 15 degrees. In the case of the bird each primary feather helps to diffuse the tip load, so that if there are N primaries, each shares something like C_L/N. Thus, with 5 feathers, each will operate around $C_L/5$ at an angle of attack for best L/D of $15/5 =$ approximately 3 degrees. A cursory look at a number of birds seems to show that the optimum number of primary feathers is around 5 to 7, which enables them to achieve almost constant spanwise C_L and elliptic lift distribution. This suggests a rough rule:

The number of primary feathers for constant spanwise lift coefficient along a bird's wing:

$N =$ approximately the angle of attack for $C_{Lmax}/$angle of attack
$$\text{for best } L/D. \qquad (4-20)$$

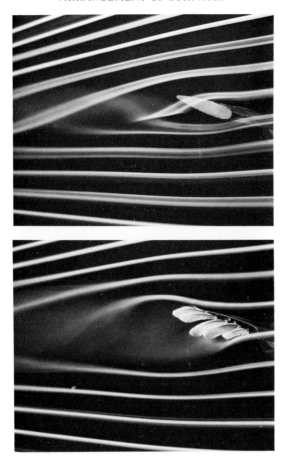

Plate 4–5 (Top) Trailing vortices shed by a plain wing tip.
(Middle) Diffusion of the tip vortex by the addition of five feathers
(like the primaries of a bird). (*Professor E. F. Blick (USA) via Shell
Aviation News, UK*) (Bottom) Spillman wing tip 'sails' fitted
experimentally to a *Piper PA25 Pawnee* of *Bowker Air Services
Ltd (UK). (Author)*

The differences between tips are shown in fig. 4.8. Those of land birds appear to suppress the tip vortices by the formation of a minor trailing vortex at the tip of each primary feather. The associated downwash, passing through the slot formed by the feather and the one following behind it, opposes leakage of air from the high pressure lower surface of the wing to the upper, low pressure surface. Thus the slotted tips of land birds act to 'unwind' tip vortices, diffusing them. Being weakened, induced drag is reduced in the same way as if the wings had been longer in span.

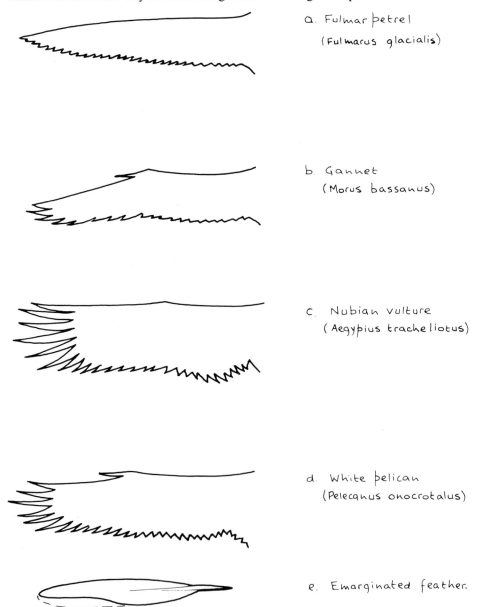

a. Fulmar petrel
   (Fulmarus glacialis)

b. Gannet
   (Morus bassanus)

c. Nubian vulture
   (Aegypius tracheliotus)

d. White pelican
   (Pelecanus onocrotalus)

e. Emarginated feather.

Fig. 4.8 Wings of seabirds (a and b) with aspect ratios around 12; and soaring land birds (c and d) with aspect ratios around 10, but with slots formed by emarginated pinion feathers. (Sketches not to scale.)

Tests carried out at the University of Oklahoma showed that the rotational speed of a piece of string held in the tip vortex of a plain wing was about 500 rpm. Behind a tip with slotted primaries the speed was reduced to only about 380 rpm, both at the same TAS and angle of attack (ref. 4.7).

Emarginated feathers twist aerodynamically about the resilient quill shaft, so that each adjusts to a best angle of attack to the local flow. A forward thrust component is generated, which reduces drag even more. Thus slotted pinions win on two counts, and quite rough calculations suggest that the reduction in induced drag is about 20 per cent. This is equivalent to a 25 per cent increase in Oswald's efficiency factor, e, or an increase in aspect ratio of the same amount (say, from 10 to 12.5).

Designers have also experimented with devices for suppressing tip vortices, and several are shown in fig. 4.9. End plates are among the oldest, and have the same effect as increasing wingspan by $4/5 \times$ total endplate height; but they are directionally destabilising, and must have a diameter equal to the wing chord at least, to be effective. They add wetted area, increasing parasitic drag, off-setting a large part of the reduction in lift dependent drag. Their efficiency can be improved by twisting them in opposition, above and below the wing (ref. 4.8).

Lying somewhere between the endplate, raked tip and lengthened span is the 'booster tip', fig. 4.9b. Theory suggests that they should be much bigger and therefore more unsightly than versions already fitted to several makes of light aeroplane. The author has not found such small booster tips to be of any measurable value – but they can be used by salesmen out to convince unwary customers.

A step beyond the endplate, towards the slotted pinion of a bird, is the Whitcomb 'winglet', fitted to the Rutan *VariEze* and *Long-EZ*. Both of the minor surfaces comprising the 'winglet' arrangement are cambered in the same sense as the wing, so that the vortex at each tip opposes the flow around the vortex from the main wing tip. Winglets work to unwind the main tip vortices, decreasing drag of the bare wing by about 14 per cent, it is claimed, but they can only be tailored for maximum efficiency at one speed. Whitcomb's general rule is that '*winglets give twice the increase in span efficiency as wingspan extension for the same increase in wing root bending moment*'.

Work has been done at the Cranfield Institute of Technology in England (ref. 4.9) and at NASA, Langley Aeronautical Systems Division, in the USA, on 'sails' and pinion-like wing tip extensions. These are cambered and twisted along their spans so as to operate at best local angles of attack. Three or four 'sails' per tip are said to increase Oswald's efficiency factor, e, by 10 to 20 per cent, decreasing K' in eq (4–17) by similar amounts. Like Whitcomb 'winglets' they can only be optimised for one speed.

Tip shape

The shape of a tip influences the path of a vortex leaving it and therefore the ultimate distance apart of the tip vortices, i.e. the span of the vortices forming a horsehoe system. Tip shape therefore affects directly the effective span and aspect ratio of the wing, increasing or decreasing the apparent diameter of the working cylinder of air visualised earlier in the chapter. The shorter the distance between the vortices downstream in the wake, the stronger the downwash and the greater the induced drag. It is very easy to observe the *vena contracta* shape of the tip vortices at air shows, where aerobatic aeroplanes often have smoke canisters at their wingtips.

Fig. 4.10 shows various influences of wing planform and tip shape upon the induced drag factor K (and K'). Fig. 4.10a shows typical values of K' and K'/A (which is

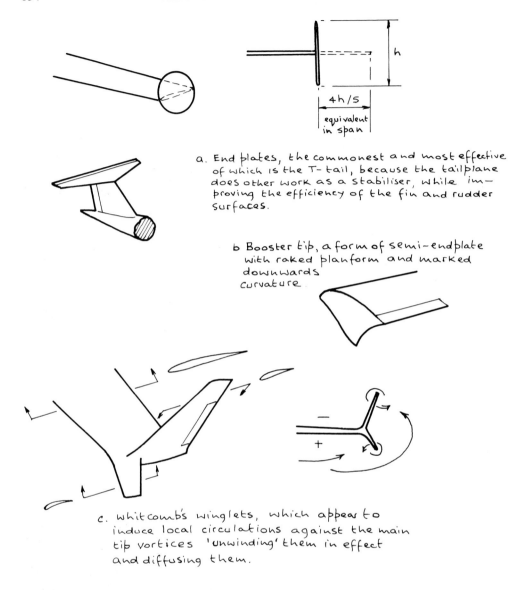

4h/5

equivalent in span

a. End plates, the commonest and most effective of which is the T-tail, because the tailplane does other work as a stabiliser, while improving the efficiency of the fin and rudder surfaces.

b Booster tip, a form of semi-endplate with raked planform and marked downwards curvature.

c. Whitcomb's winglets, which appear to induce local circulations against the main tip vortices 'unwinding' them in effect and diffusing them.

(Designed by JJ Spillman: now experimenting with five 'sails')

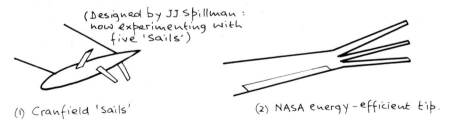

(1) Cranfield 'sails'   (2) NASA energy-efficient tip.

d. Tip modifications approaching the slotted wing tips of soaring land birds.

Fig. 4.9 Tip vortex diffusion to reduce induced drag.

Plate 4–6 (Top) Burt Rutan's canard *Model 33*, *Vari Eze* and Model 61, *Long EZ* have wrought a change in thinking which might have a profound influence in future. (*Author*) (Middle) Rutan's *Model 40 Defiant*, a push-pull canard with ventral rudder, ahead of the centre of gravity. (*Author*) (Bottom) *Piper PAT–1*, an experimental aeroplane from Pug Piper's 'Skunk-works' had a near tandem-wing arrangement. (*Cliff Barnett, Flight International, UK*)

Plate 4–6 (Bottom)

probably more important). This latter term is a minimum when aspect ratios of aeroplane wings are around 13 to 15, making induced drag a minimum. K'/A for gliders is a minimum when aspect ratio is 40 or more. But such high aspect ratios are impracticable structurally, being heavy with material needed to resist bending and torsional loads. The result is compromise, with aeroplane aspect ratios in the range 6 to 9, and gliders nearer 20 (plus or minus 4 or 5). The curves in this figure are empirical and include wing-body effects, in addition to taper – which is the reason for introducing K' in place of K.

The two graphs in fig. 4.10b are based upon Glauert (ref. 4.5, but see also ref. 3.4), who used correction factors τ and δ, such that in eq (4–5) we may work from eq (4–4b) to give:

$$\text{angle of attack, } \alpha = \alpha_0 + (C_L/\pi A)(1 + \tau) \qquad (4\text{–}21a)$$
$$= \alpha_0 + \epsilon' = \alpha_0 + (1 + \tau) \qquad (4\text{–}21b)$$
$$\text{where,} \qquad \epsilon' = \epsilon\,(1 + \tau) \qquad (4\text{–}21c)$$

The measure of planform efficiency is Oswald's efficiency factor, e, which was given in eqs (4–9) and (4–9a). Tip shape alters the value of e for a given surface and, therefore, contributes towards the magnitude of the induced drag factor K, and K'. Figure 4.10d shows e for several tips. Knowing that:

$$\text{Oswald's efficiency factor, } e, \text{ varies as } C_L{}^2/C_{Di} \qquad \text{from eq (4–9a)}$$

the steeper the slope of the line, the more efficient the planform for a given aspect ratio. The most efficient tip appears to be one that is raked, with the trailing edge of the wing longer than the leading edge. The angle of rake for greatest efficiency varies with aspect ratio (ref. 4.10), being around 20 to 25 deg when $A = 6$ to 5, respectively – reducing to 0 deg when aspect ratio is infinite. But work done by the author of ref. 4.4 suggests that

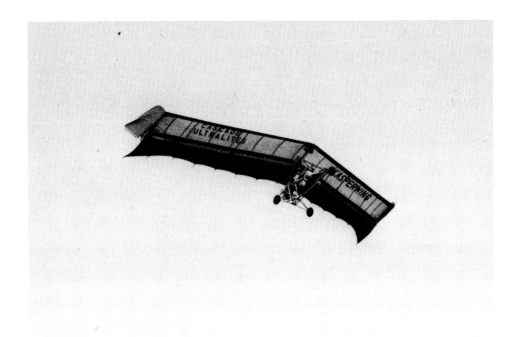

Plate 4–7 *Kasper-wing* tailless microlight which relies on weight
shift for control. (*Author*)

the angle of rake for best lift/drag is nearer 6 deg – although lift continues to increase
with rake. Hoerner shows that a sawn-off square tip gives excellent results, while a
raked tip is even better (ref. 4.8). His results do not appear to reveal a clear advantage
of the so-called 'Hoerner tip' over the raked or square-cut tip, although it has some
aesthetic advantage over the latter.

Three rules can be stated for tip shape:

☐ *Avoid tips with markedly cut away trailing corners* (towards the trailing edge).
☐ *Make trailing edges at least as long as leading edges.*
☐ *Sharpen the streamwise edges and the trailing edges of any tip, so that the flow
  creeping around it from underneath is forced to separate and so leave it cleanly as far
  outboard as possible.* This is the most important single factor.

Putting all three together we conclude that tips should be shaped in such a way as to
shed the tip vortices as far apart as possible. This is another way of saying that as the air
thrust downwards by the wing between the tip vortices does the work in generating lift,
the greater the distance between the vortices, the larger the mass of air acted upon by
the wing at a given speed and in a given time. The larger the working mass, the slower
the required downwash and the lower the induced drag. The closer the tip vortices, the
faster the downwash and the more energy that is wasted in producing the lift.

Aileron shape

When designing ailerons do not be tempted to extend them all of the way to the wing
tip, especially when the tip is raked. Peak suctions at aileron tips can cause high control
loads, and flutter may also result. On the other hand, if an aileron is set too far inboard,

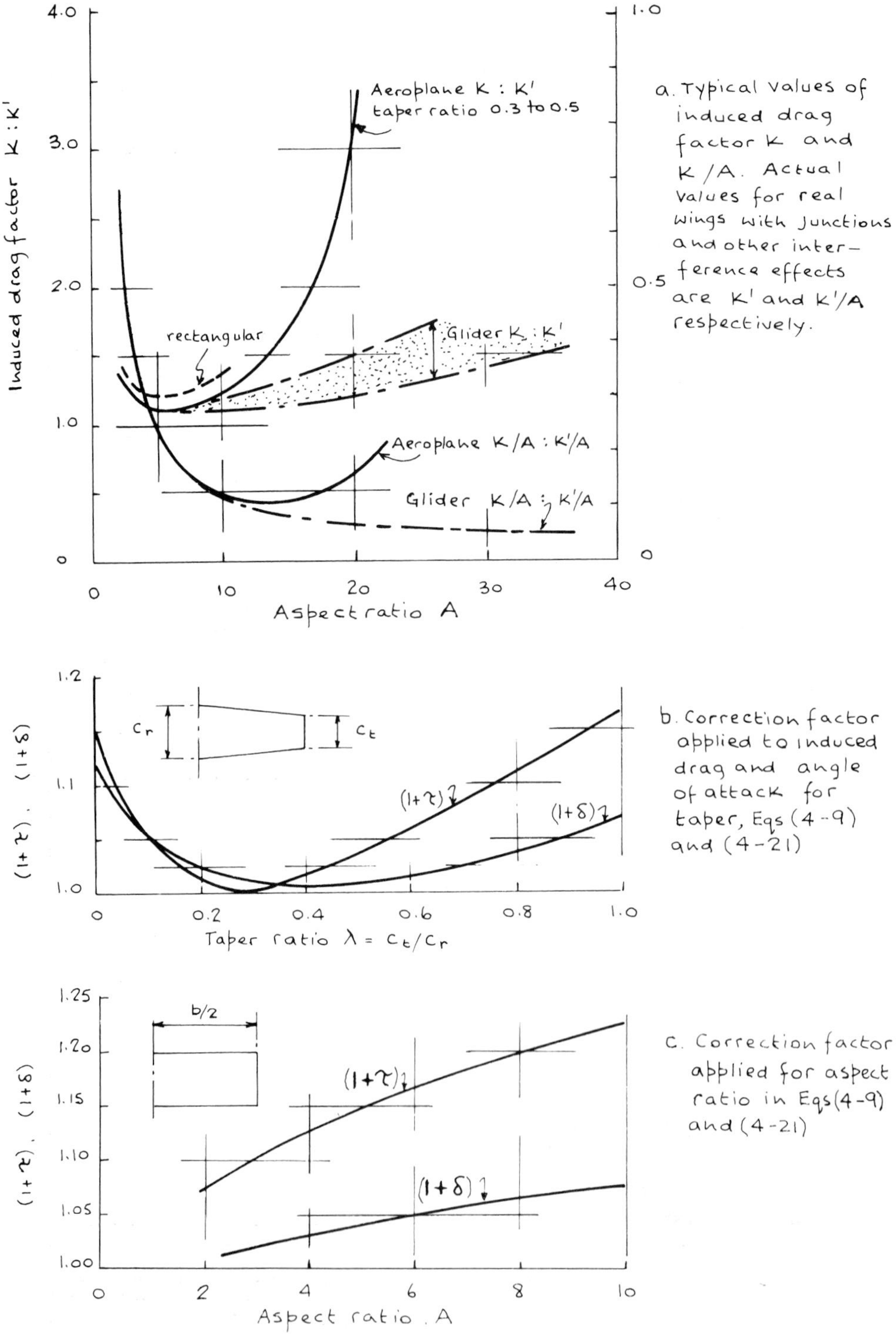

Fig. 4.10　Some factors affecting induced drag, wing tip and aileron shape (for b and c see ref. 3.4). (Continued next page.)

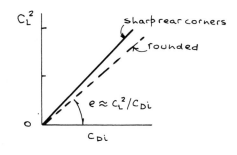

d. Some general results
and rules of wing tip
and aileron tip design

Tip Shape (calculated from Ref 4.8)	Oswald efficiency e percent	$K:K' = 1/e$ Eqs (4-9) and (4-9b)
'Hoerner' tip sharp rear corners	80	1.25
rounded (1) (2)	(1) 75 + (2) 75 −	about 1.33 with (1) slightly more efficient than (2)
Square with sharp edges	81	1.23
sharp rear corners Rake angle $\measuredangle$ = 0° for A = ∞ 20° for A = 6 25° for A = 1 to 5 } (Refs 4.10, 4.21)	82	1.22
Aileron chord 0.25c without flaps and 0.3c with	Most efficient region for aileron in terms of: rolling moment/hinge moment is 2/3 to 3/4 semispan outboard Ailerons on the top row are desirable, while those on the bottom row are undesirable because of the high control loads (hinge moments)	

Plate 4–8 *Rally 2B* microlight with a full set of control surfaces.
(*Author*)

rolling power will be reduced, so that larger ailerons are required – and this tends to reduce space available for flaps. In general, aileron chords should be a constant fraction of local wing chord.

Fins and rudders

Similar principles and strictures apply to the shaping of fins and rudders. Builders of World War 1 and other early replica aeroplanes will have noticed the predominantly squat, low aspect ratio profiles of vertical tail surfaces. These enabled pilots to use large angles of sideslip in combat, and on landing (they had no flaps to steepen the approach), without risk of fin stall or loss of directional control. The raked tips achieved (perhaps without realising it) the *non-linear lift* generated by vortices shed over the highly swept leading edges of supersonic slender wing forms at low speed and large angles of attack, that became familiar more than 50 years later (fig. 4.12c). Non-linear lift was explored with rectangular wings of low aspect ratio in the 1920s and 30s by Prandtl, among others. Küchemann gives an up to date account of its importance in modern aerodynamic practice (ref. 4.1).

One should avoid vertical surfaces with high aspect ratios, because they are prone to fin stalls at quite moderate angles of yaw. Whenever a fin has a dorsal fairing at its base, running forward into the top line of the fuselage, it is fairly safe to assume that the designer either had a problem, or anticipated one.

Tailless aeroplanes

The term *tailless* is something of a misnomer. Specifically, it means that the configuration has no separate (pitch) stabiliser. Nevertheless, longitudinal stability is achieved by building decalage into the wing, so that portions lying ahead of

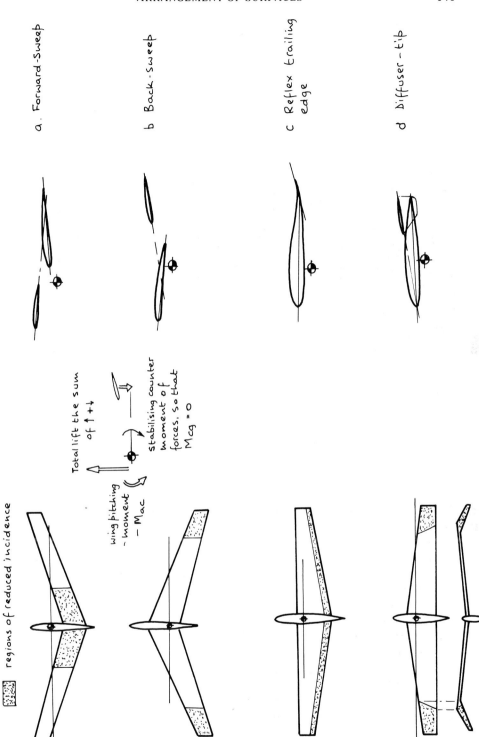

Fig. 4.11 Four possible tailless arrangements. Note that the incidence of surfaces behind the **CG** is less than that ahead.

the CG have larger angles of incidence than trailing portions following behind. In this way a nose-up moment is generated, equal and opposite to the normal nose-down pitching moment, M_{ac}.

Four possible arrangements of longitudinally stable tailless aircraft are shown in fig. 4.11 (longitudinal stability is discussed in chapter 11). Marske (ref. 4.12) describes a way of checking longitudinal stability of an aerofoil section, using a tub, or the kitchen sink. Cut a section out of 3/4 in (2 cm) board, with a chord about 10 in (25 cm), and add ballast so that it lies flat in the water, almost submerged. Give the section a gentle push forwards. If it follows a straight path it is neutrally stable. If it turns in the 'climb' direction with increasing speed, it is stable. But if it 'dives' it is unstable. The method was used to test sections with reflex camber towards the trailing edge. When the point of contraflexure of the camber line started 60 per cent back from the leading edge, the section was very stable. But when the reflex started at 85 per cent chord, the section was neutrally stable. Sections with marked undercamber, like the rear-loaded profiles described at the end of chapter 3, were very unstable.

The work of Marske, Fauvel and others shows that tailless aircraft do not necessarily need sweep. A reflex trailing edge to a section can give an unswept plank wing stable characteristics. But the centre of gravity position of an unswept tailless wing is limited in extent. Sweep, which effectively increases the chord of the wing, introduces a little more margin for mis-loading.

Sweep for high speed

There are three reasons for sweeping surfaces:

☐ Arranging the centre of gravity of the aeroplane and the aerodynamic centre of the wing to coincide more closely. Unusual change of sweep usually shows that a designer had a problem with the CG, after it was too late to hang the wing anywhere else.
☐ Providing longitudinal and directional stability for tailless aeroplanes.
☐ Improving high speed characteristics by delaying compressibility effects.

The use of sweep for high speed flight, to delay the onset of compressibility, was suggested by Dr-Ing Albert Betz (1886–1968) in 1939, after Prof Dr-Ing Adolf Busemann (1901–   ) had drawn attention to its advantages at the Volta Congress on high speed flight, in Rome in 1935. The theory of sweepback was said to have been discovered independently by Robert T. Jones in the United States, in 1945 (ref. 2.1).

Swept surfaces are sometimes described as yawed, or sheared. They work at high speeds because sweep lengthens geometrically the path between leading and trailing edges of a wing, as the secant of the angle of sweep. The slopes of surfaces facing the oncoming air grow less steep, acceleration of the air is slowed, velocity and pressure peaks are reduced. Wing sections are given greater fineness (chord length/maximum thickness), by sweep reducing geometrically the thickness/chord. Since:

$$\text{drag rise is roughly proportional to } (thickness/chord)^2 \qquad (4\text{--}22)$$

and as it may be shown that thickness/chord varies with cosine of the angle of sweep, critical Mach number is increased. Fig. 4.12 summarises several advantages of sweep, including the superiority of the delta wing in stowage volume and spar depth. Deltas have less favourable aerodynamics at subsonic speeds, which militate against their structural advantages among aircraft with which we are directly concerned.

Plate 4–9 If high speed and long range are not needed, biplanes are eminently sensible with their relatively low structure weight, high manoeuvrability, docility at low speed and the ability to operate from shorter strips than monoplanes. (Top) *Hegy Chuparosa* (12 ft 10 in (3.9 m) span, gap/span ≈ 1/4, and too twitchy for anyone but Ray Hegy to handle. (*Howard Levy, USA*) (Bottom) Polish *PZL M-15 Belphegor* agricultural jet biplane (72 ft (22 m) span, gap/span ≈ 1/8 – note hoppers between wings). (*Wytwórnia Sprzetu Komunikacyjnego, via Flight International UK*)

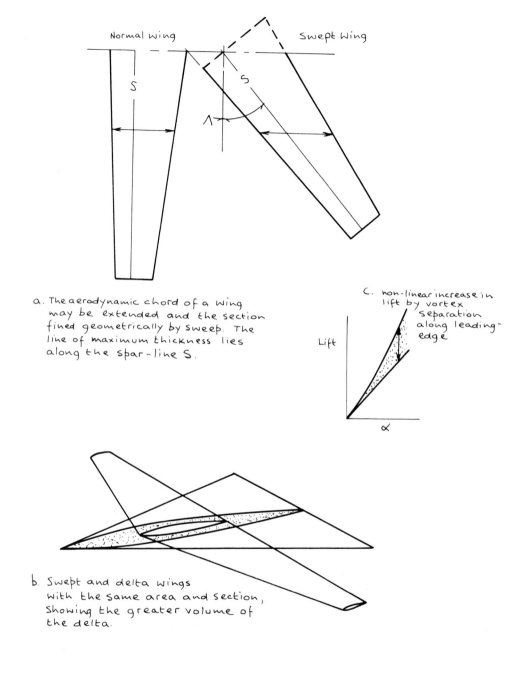

a. The aerodynamic chord of a wing
   may be extended and the section
   fined geometrically by sweep. The
   line of maximum thickness lies
   along the spar-line S.

c. non-linear increase in
   lift by vortex
   separation
   along leading-
   edge

b. Swept and delta wings
   with the same area and section,
   Showing the greater volume of
   the delta.

Fig. 4.12   Swept wings for high speed.

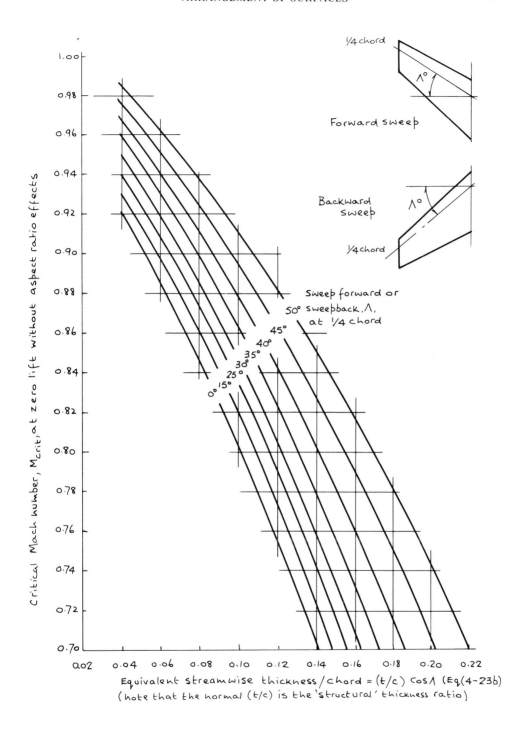

Fig. 4.12d   The effect of aerofoil sweep at the ¼ chord upon fineness and, hence, critical Mach number. For our practical purposes leading edge and ¼ chord sweep are more or less the same. Curves based upon ref. 4.13.

If we join points of equal static pressure on an aerofoil surface we obtain a pattern of isobars rather like that shown in fig. 4.13a. Isobar sweep more or less follows the leading edge at mid span, but it decreases towards tips and roots: because of the tendency for differential pressure to leak away at the tip, and because of friction and interference effects at the junction slowing the local flow. Thus, thickness ratio may be increased correspondingly at roots, without adversely affecting local critical Mach number, which enables wing structures to be lightened, and extra baggage or fuel stowed. Such thickened roots provide useful volume for landing gear units.

The component of flow normal to a wing leading edge should not exceed about M 0.7 for an orthodox subcritical wing section. Supercritical sections can work to higher values, as we saw in the last chapter. We can calculate the required sweep angle for the leading edge from the geometrical properties of sweep, i.e.

$$\text{Mach number normal to leading edge} = M \cos \Lambda \qquad (4\text{--}23a)$$

where M is the flight (streamwise) Mach number, and

$$\text{equivalent streamwise thickness/chord} = (t/c) \cos \Lambda \qquad (4\text{--}23b)$$

where (t/c) is the 'structural' thickness chord ratio measured normal to the wing leading edge. Thus, from eq (4–23a):

$$M_{crit} \cos \Lambda = 0.7$$
$$\text{or,} \qquad \Lambda = \sec^{-1} (1.45\ M_{crit}) \qquad (4\text{--}23c)$$

Comparison of backward and forward sweep

Swept back wings have two disadvantages at increased angles of attack and reduced speeds:

☐ Wing boundary layers tend to drift outboard, assisted by the spanwise component of flow in fig. 4.13a, which causes them to thicken and separate prematurely at the tips.
☐ Sweep staggers the vortices shed across the span, so that those shed inboard are ahead of those shed further out. This causes increased upwash ahead of the tip, with a corresponding increase in tip angle of attack, accompanied by premature peaking of the lift coefficient (fig. 4.14).

The overall result is that swept back wing tips stall before the root, while the root (which is ahead of the centre of gravity) continues to lift. Pitch-up follows, forcing a full stall, a rapid drag rise, and possible pitch-roll-yaw divergence. There may also occur degradation of control effectiveness, perhaps even control reversal in some cases.

Forward sweep avoids premature tip stall, because the root stalls first. Ailerons tend to remain effective, but pitch-up still occurs. However, forward sweep has an adverse effect upon directional stability, and larger fin area is needed than with sweepback.

Tandem aerofoils

Any aeroplane that is not tailless has tandem surfaces of one sort or another. A conventional arrangement with a tail is as much a tandem as a canard aeroplane with a foreplane – only proportions differ, and in differing proportions so differing interference.

Free-flight models of tandem winged aircraft with two planes of equal area do not fly

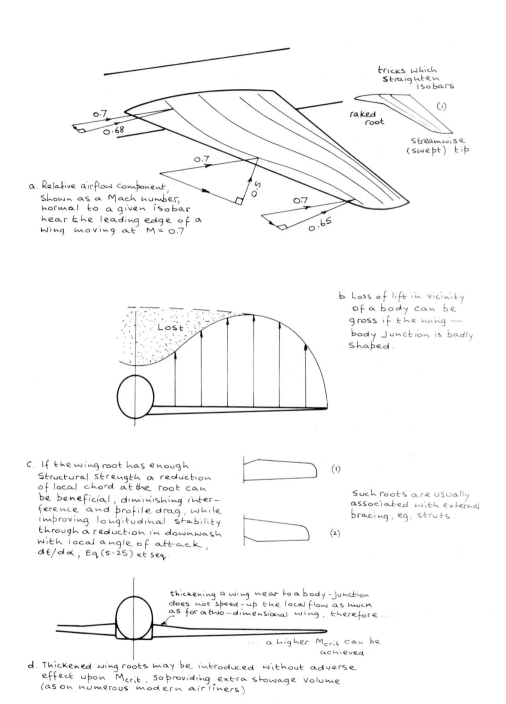

a. Relative airflow component, shown as a Mach number, normal to a given isobar near the leading edge of a wing moving at M = 0.7

tricks which straighten isobars

raked root

streamwise (swept) tip

b. Loss of lift in vicinity of a body can be gross if the wing — body junction is badly shaped.

c. If the wing root has enough structural strength a reduction of local chord at the root can be beneficial, diminishing interference and profile drag, while improving longitudinal stability through a reduction in downwash with local angle of attack, $d\epsilon/d\alpha$, Eq (5-25) et seq.

Such roots are usually associated with external bracing, eg, struts.

thickening a wing near to a body-junction does not speed-up the local flow as much as for a two-dimensional wing, therefore....

.... a higher M_{crit} can be achieved.

d. Thickened wing roots may be introduced without adverse effect upon M_{crit}, so providing extra stowage volume (as on numerous modern airliners)

Fig. 4.13   The effect of wing ends (roots and tips) upon isobar sweep, lift distribution and indirectly local lift/drag ratio.

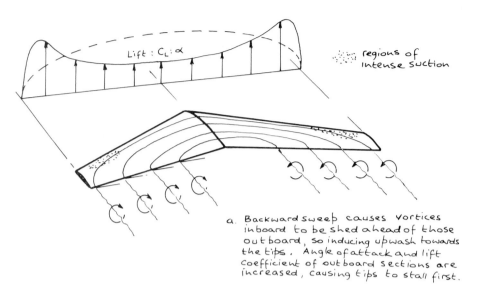

a. Backward sweep causes vortices inboard to be shed ahead of those outboard, so inducing upwash towards the tips. Angle of attack and lift coefficient of outboard sections are increased, causing tips to stall first.

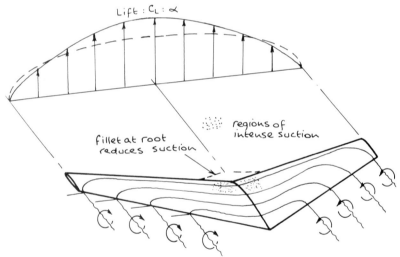

b. Forward sweep causes vortices outboard to be shed ahead of those inboard. The effect is the opposite of a: tip stalling is suppressed by off-loading outboard sections. The span-wise lift distribution of a forward-swept wing is nearly elliptic and further forward than for one swept back. This, with root losses, helps to shift the aerodynamic centre 7 percent to 10 percent further forward than for a sweptback wing

Fig. 4.14 a and b   Comparison between backward and forward sweep, assuming both wings are rigid and not affected by aero-elasticity.

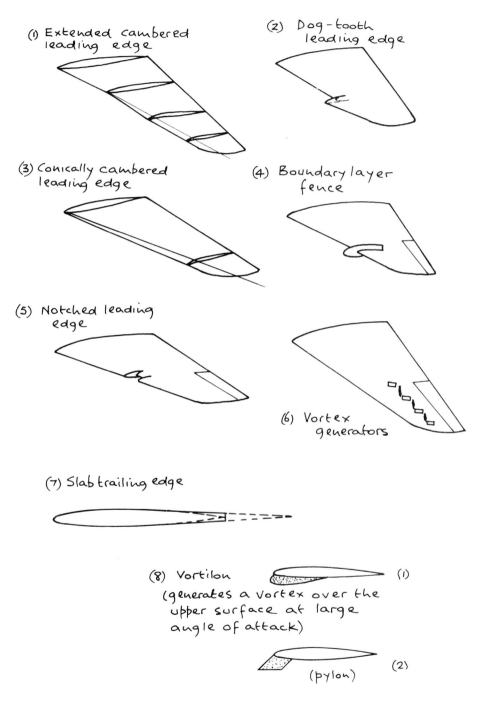

(1) Extended cambered leading edge

(2) Dog-tooth leading edge

(3) Conically cambered leading edge

(4) Boundary layer fence

(5) Notched leading edge

(6) Vortex generators

(7) Slab trailing edge

(8) Vortilon (generates a vortex over the upper surface at large angle of attack)

(1)

(pylon)

(2)

Fig. 4.14c Aerodynamic palliatives for improving local airflows over wings. (2), (4), (5) (6) and (8) generate controlled vortices which help to carry away stagnating boundary layers to the trailing edge, in a predictable manner. They are in a sense the vacuum cleaners of the aerodynamicist.

Plate 4–10 Arrangements of surfaces which involve both tandem wing and biplane characteristics (Top) French *Lederlin 380–L*, a development of Mignet's *Flying Flea* (fig. 4.22). (Bottom) French *Starck AS35A* which has ailerons on the surfaces boxing-in the wing tips. (*Harold Best–Devereux, UK*)

well. They cannot make up their minds which wing should dominate the other when disturbed in pitch. With the centre of gravity of the aeroplane mid-way between their aerodynamic centres, models can be coaxed to fly, hunting slowly in pitch, with a well-damped phugoid oscillation (chapter 2, Stability and Manoeuvrability). As the centre of gravity is moved forwards or aft, and the proportions of the planes are altered, so that eventually the ratio of the larger to the smaller is about 5/1, the oscillation dies away.

Stability is a complicated and vital matter. For safety an aircraft must be positively stable and comfortable to fly. There may be exceptions, as with highly specialised competition aerobatic aircraft. But suffice it to say at this point that positive longitudinal stability is achieved by making the foreplane (wing) loading and lift coefficient higher than those of the rearplane, regardless of which is the main wing. The leading surface must always stall first.

Canards have certain advantages which make them attractive for short field operation. Rotation into a flying attitude on take-off is achieved by a lift force from a canard foreplane, which is added to the lift of the wing. Rotation of an aeroplane with a tail is achieved with an anti-lift download, subtracted from the lift of the whole because it opposes the wing. A canard has a better get-up-and-go in a shorter distance than a conventional machine with the same weight, wing and power loadings.

There is also some evidence (ref. 4.14) that the induced drag of a pair of tandem aerofoils is less than that of a conventional wing-plus-tail. To achieve this condition the rearplane carries one half of the total lift and is set higher than the foreplane. For minimum drag the sum of the spanwise lift distributions must be elliptical.

However, canards can have disadvantages. They need more keel surface aft for directional stability, to cope with centres of gravity that are further aft (fig. 4.15). Tail

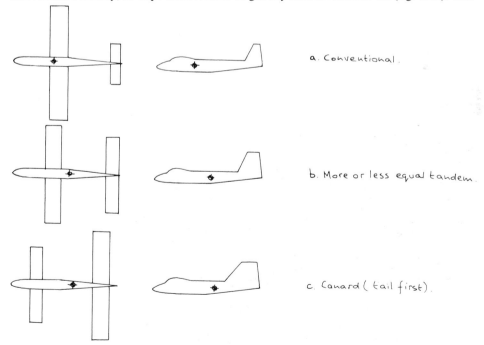

Fig. 4.15 Effect of redistributing lifting surfaces of an aeroplane upon **CG** position and vertical stabiliser area.

weight is increased, cancelling more often than not any advantage that might be gained in the way of smaller and lighter wing to achieve the same field performance.

However, Rutan has broken with the convention of placing the stabiliser behind the wing with his *Vari-Eze* and *Long-EZ*. The acid test of such vigorous thinking along old lines will probably come with the aircraft which must follow these unusual homebuilt machines – for example, during formal certification test flying of canards with commercial applications.

The Wright Brothers' *Flyer* of 1903 was a canard, like their gliders. Dr Paul MacReady's *Gossamer Condor* that won the *Kremer Prize* for manpowered flight in 1978 was a canard, and so was his manpowered *Gossamer Albatross* which flew across the Channel in 1979, on the 70th anniversary of Bleriot's crossing. In Britain *Lockspeiser Aircraft Limited* was formed to develop and market its *Land Development Aircraft*, a canard aeroplane for aerial work. The author has found the flying qualities of Lockspeiser's 7/10 scale *LDA–01* as refreshingly different from those of conventional machines as the delightfully docile *Rutan Long-EZ* (and the quicker reacting *Vari-Eze*).

There can be problems with tandem and canard wing arrangements. The trailing vortices from the foreplane, which must be more highly loaded than the rearplane for longitudinal stability, cause downwash which reduces, to a certain extent, the angle of attack of the rearplane. The rearplane induces an upwash ahead of it which increases somewhat the angle of attack of the foreplane. When such aeroplanes are yawed the rearplanes can be affected adversely by the trailing vortices from the foreplanes, and care is needed when locating the surfaces (fig. 4.16). Conventional aeroplanes have tails (which are usually less than 1/3 of the mainplane in area, and at least 2 1/2 wing chords behind it) which work well inside and away from the path of the wing tip vortices. The upwash from the smaller tail surface can usually be ignored in its effect upon the wing ahead of it.

Rigging of tandem wings and stabilisers

The setting angle of a stabiliser and the amount of 'longitudinal dihedral' (i.e. incidence) between fore and rear planes depends upon the conditions of balance in level flight, as we shall see in chapter 11. The stabiliser load is found from consideration of the location of the centre of gravity, the main aerodynamic forces and moments, and the effects of significant interference between the surfaces (such as that caused by upwash, downwash and turbulent wakes).

It is usual to give the rearplane a small negative angle of attack relative to the foreplane, so that the aeroplane will be in trim with zero pitching moment at one particular speed. It is customary with a small aircraft to provide some adjustment for a stabiliser through a range of, say ±3 deg. Adjustment in the air is preferred to adjustments which can only be made on the ground. Elevator trim tabs are used when there is no provision for stabiliser movement in flight.

Incidence of foreplane and rearplane surfaces tends to be as follows:

Conventional aeroplanes: wing, about +3 deg.
                              longitudinal dihedral, about +2.5 to +3 deg.
Tandem-wing: foreplane, about +2.5 to +3 deg.
                              longitudinal dihedral, about +2.5 deg.
                              (Note, longitudinal dihedral of *LDA–01*, +2.5 deg., while that of the *Flying Flea* (fig. 4.22) was +3 deg.)

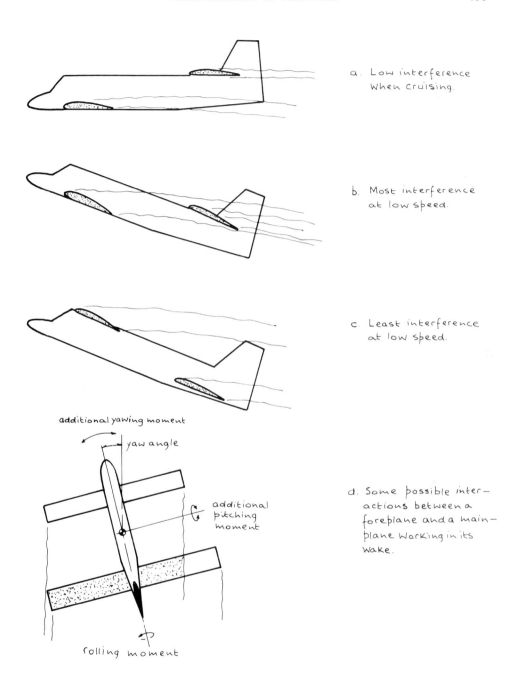

a. Low interference when cruising.

b. Most interference at low speed.

c. Least interference at low speed.

additional yawing moment

yaw angle

additional pitching moment

rolling moment

d. Some possible inter-actions between a foreplane and a main-plane working in its wake.

Fig. 4.16 Some things that can cause special trouble with pure tandem and canard surface arrangements. Although such factors affect a conventional tail, the interactions are often less complex.

Tail-first (examples):   *Vari-Eze*, canard, zero ± 1 deg
                              wing, zero ± 1 deg
                              (the planes must be within 0.5 deg incidence
                              of one another).
                      Long-EZ, canard, ± 0.3 deg
                              wing, ± 0.5 deg
                              (the planes must be within 0.3 deg incidence
                              of one another).

Biplanes

Biplanes dominated aviation into the 1930s, largely because of a series of catastrophic wing failures with early monoplanes. These happened because of an improper understanding of the complete role of the cabane bracing, consisting of a pylon structure above the centre section, from which bracing wires supported the weight of the wings on landing. The highly cambered wing sections of that period suffered powerful nose down pitching moments at high speed: in the language of the time, their centres of pressure moved a long way back. Wings began to fail downwards at high speed if the height of the cabane bracing had been reduced too far in an effort to cut drag and save weight, because the landing wires from the cabane pylon were taking tensile loads at high speed, keeping the wings in shape. Of course, the flatter the angle of the landing wires, the higher their tensile loading. In Britain, the War Office refused to have anything more to do with monoplanes and the biplane remained the mainstay of British military aviation for the next twenty years.

The biplane, on the other hand, was strong for several reasons. The reasons are still valid:

☐ They are compact, and their wingspans, which are shorter than those of comparable monoplanes, sustain smaller bending moments. Moreover, lift is shared between two planes instead of just one.

☐ Consequently, the wings of a biplane can be made 0.8 to 0.9 times the weight of a monoplane, with greater specific strength and stiffness (and the potential to make them lighter still (fig. 14.12)).

The modern metal monoplane, although superior in many areas, failed to oust the biplane completely. Figures given in table 4-1 show that one homebuilt aeroplane in four at the Experimental Aircraft Association Fly-In at Oshkosh in 1978 was a biplane.

TABLE 4–1 (ref 4.15)

Configuration	Percentage Present
Low wing	37
Biplane	25
High wing	19
Midwing	13
Parasol	5
Triplane (1), plus fractions left over above	1

Plate 4–11 Unique fillet and 'bite' at the trailing edge junction of the basically elegant *Heinkel He III* (1934) which reduced interference and change of downwash with angle of attack from the wing upon the tailplane. This one is ex-Spanish Air Force. (*Author*)

As long as one can live with lower lift/drag and therefore less range than a monoplane, biplanes can be superior to monoplanes for similar tasks because:

☐ They can carry more wing area for their size, can take off and land in shorter distances, and often have softer stall qualities.
☐ They can perform well into and out of short fields without needing elaborate and costly high lift devices, and can therefore lift more payload.
☐ They are more easily constructed for a lower price than a monoplane, all else remaining equal.

Some modern studies do not give such a pessimistic view of biplane lift/drag, suggesting that an unconventional layout, with proper choice of gap, stagger and negative decalage, can be aerodynamically more efficient than monoplanes (ref. 4.16). But their applications seem to be narrow and they may have unfavourable stall characteristics, because they differ considerably from conventional biplane arrangements.

Biplane theory is complicated by two factors. The most important is that mutual interference from the vortex system of each plane increases total downwash and induced drag, making it more than that of a monoplane with the same aspect ratio and wing area. Second, mutual interference from the curvature of the flow around each aerofoil section further increases downwash and induced drag, by an amount which depends upon the ratio of *gap/chord*.

Plate 4–12 *Westland Lysander* (1938) rebuilt from fragments, new materials, salvaged and refurbished parts, which now operates on a Permit to Fly. Wing is narrow at the root and in line with the pilot's eye, bestowing near-ideal field of view. The author, who is flying the *Lysander* here, found it to have remarkable low speed handling qualities and a wilful mind of its own. (*Flight International*)

Aspect ratio of a biplane is double that of a monoplane with the same span and total wing area:

$$\text{biplane aspect ratio, } A = \text{span}^2 / \tfrac{1}{2} \times \text{total wing area}$$
$$= 2\, b^2 / S \tag{4–24}$$

which should be compared with eq (2–4). But we cannot apply this value to a biplane in the same way as with a monoplane, because it would make it seem more efficient, when the reverse is the case. Mutual interference between the planes causes a biplane to be flown at a larger angle of attack so as to generate the same lift as a monoplane with the same section and area. The increase in angle of attack, $\Delta\alpha$, is proportional to the increase in angle of downwash, $\Delta\epsilon$, and we may write:

$$\text{biplane downwash, } (\epsilon + \Delta\epsilon) / \text{monoplane downwash, } \epsilon = (1 + \Delta\epsilon/\epsilon)$$
$$= (1 + \sigma) \approx 1.5 \tag{4–25}$$

If we now modify the equation for non-elliptic lift distribution by introducing the induced drag factor K or $K' = 1/e$, adapting it for comparison between the monoplane and biplane:

$$\text{monoplane downwash, } \epsilon = K'C_L/\pi A \approx 35\ C_L/A \text{ radians} \quad (4\text{--}26)$$
$$\text{biplane downwash, } (\epsilon + \Delta\epsilon) = K'C_L(1 + \sigma)/\pi A \approx 55\ C_L/A \text{ radians} \quad (4\text{--}27)$$

Biplane calculations can be simplified by replacing the wing arrangement by an *equivalent monoplane*, which has the same wing area and lift dependent drag. The concept was proposed by Max Michael Munk (1890–), a leading German aerodynamicist (who had been a student of Prandtl at Göttingen). Munk showed that in order to apply eq (4–8) to biplanes (and other multiplanes), the maximum span must be replaced by a monoplane wing of span kb having the same area and induced drag as the biplane. For a monoplane $k = 1$, but for a biplane k varies with the ratio of gap/span, the ratio of the spans, and the proportional area of the two wings.

If we use Prandtl's method of reducing any biplane arrangement to one that is orthogonal (equal span):

$$\text{mean span, } b = (\text{span of longer plane} + \text{span of shorter plane})/2 \quad (4\text{--}28)$$

then we may write the induced drag coefficients of the monoplane and biplane as:

$$\text{monoplane } C_{Di} = K'C_L^2(S/k^2b^2)/\pi \text{ from eq (4–9), and} \quad (4\text{--}29a)$$
$$\text{biplane } C_{Di} = K'C_L^2(S/2b^2)(1 + \sigma)/\pi \quad (4\text{--}29b)$$

To satisfy Munk's conditions, these are equal, and:

$$\text{Munk's span factor, } k = \sqrt{2/(1 + \sigma)} \quad (4\text{--}30)$$

For most practical biplanes $\sigma = 0.5$, with values varying between about 0.4 to 0.6.

There are various techniques for dealing with biplanes (refs. 4.3, 4.11, 4.17), but an easy geometrical way of solving the span of the equivalent monoplane is shown in fig. 4.17. This shows that the cylinders of air washed downwards by each wing of mean span b are reduced by the proximity of their overlapping cross-sections. Interference makes the total swept volume less than the sum of their swept volumes when separated. The equivalent monoplane has a span which sweeps out a volume equal to the remaining working volume (top and bottom lobes) of the biplane, *plus* an additional amount equal to that lost by interference. At first sight we might think that we have only to replace the shaded portion of the working mass in fig. 4.17b, approximately represented by the span $\times$ gap. In fact interference makes it necessary to add about $\sqrt{2}$ $\times$ gap $\times$ span (i.e. the mean span). When we draw the representative area as a ring around the circle circumscribing the mean span of the biplane, the overall diameter is that of the equivalent monoplane wingspan, within the range:

$$\text{gap/mean span} = 1/8 \text{ to } 1/4 \text{ (say, 0.1 to 0.25)} \quad (4\text{--}31)$$

Thus, if gap/mean span $= G/b$, it may be shown that:

$$\text{Munk's span factor, } k \approx \sqrt{[1.8(G/b) + 1]} \quad (4\text{--}32)$$

Fig. 4.18 shows the value of k for the range of gap/chord ratios in eq (4–31); it is pessimistic for biplanes with long wings. Table 4–2 shows how k is used.

Note that although we use gap/mean span when talking about interference effects, many other reference works employ the span of the longest wing for determining G/b. Generally the result is too small to be of much consequence now that biplanes are designed more for utility and sport than for aerodynamic efficiency. As a rough approximation, the loss of lift compared with a monoplane is about 3 to 9 per cent at large Reynolds numbers. The maximum lift of a biplane with gap equalling chord and no stagger is about 93 per cent that of a monoplane. Drag is 10 to 15 per cent more. This approaches a loss in total lift/drag ratio of 20 per cent. The lift slope, a, of a biplane is about 83 per cent of that of a monoplane with the same aspect ratio.

TABLE 4–2

Term	Finite monoplane span b	Orthogonal biplane span b	Equivalent monoplane span $= k \times$ biplane mean span, same total area
Aspect ratio A	b^2/S	$2b^2/S$ (i.e. double monoplane of same span and area)	$(kb)^2/S$ (i.e. $k^2 \times$ monoplane of biplane span and area)
Downwash α_i or ϵ	$K'C_L/\pi A$	$K'C_L(1+\sigma)/\pi A$	$K'C_L S/\pi(kb)^2$
Induced drag coefficient C_{Di}	$K'C_L^2/\pi A$	$K'C_L^2(1+\sigma)/\pi A$	$K^1 C_L^2 S/\pi(kb)^2$ (Munk's condition)

Munk's span factor k is taken from fig. 4.18(b), or by the approximation in eq (4–32), which relates it to the gap/span ratio of the biplane. In the equivalent monoplane column, where k^2 appears, we may introduce the term $(1.8(G/b) + 1)$

Location of equivalent monoplane wing

We need now to locate the equivalent monoplane wing relative to the pair of planes it is intended to replace. Figure 4.19 shows the method, using suffixes T and B for the top and bottom plane in each case. The mean chord of each plane is constructed as shown in fig. 2.5. When we have found the equivalent monoplane wing, it is necessary to assume that the aerodynamic centre is located about 2 per cent SMC further forward, at about 23 per cent $\bar{c}$, unlike the monoplane, which has the aerodynamic centre around 25 per cent. The reason for this is that the top plane generates more lift than the bottom.

The unmodified aerodynamic centre of the equivalent monoplane lies on a line joining the ac of the top and bottom planes. For simplicity, draw a line joining the quarter chord of each. The quarter chord of the equivalent monoplane will lie on the line. Now, to find the vertical position of the equivalent plane, distance Y above the bottom plane, take moments of the lift about the quarter chord of the bottom plane, using the gap, G:

$$\text{total lift} \times Y = (L_T + L_B)\, Y = L_T G$$

and, as lift can be expressed in proportion to $C_L S$, the lift coefficient and area respectively:

$$Y = (C_{LT} S_T/(C_{LT} S_T + C_{LB} S_B))G$$

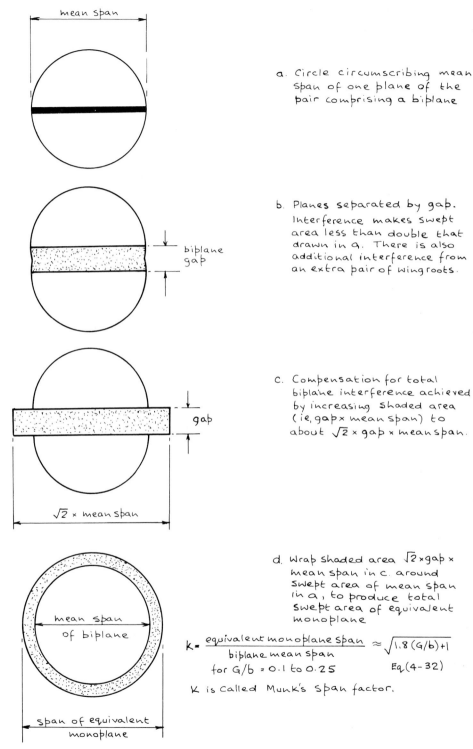

a. Circle circumscribing mean span of one plane of the pair comprising a biplane

b. Planes separated by gap. Interference makes swept area less than double that drawn in a. There is also additional interference from an extra pair of wingroots.

c. Compensation for total biplane interference achieved by increasing shaded area (ie, gap × mean span) to about $\sqrt{2}$ × gap × meanspan.

d. Wrap shaded area $\sqrt{2}$ × gap × mean span in c. around swept area of mean span in a, to produce total swept area of equivalent monoplane

$$K = \frac{\text{equivalent monoplane span}}{\text{biplane mean span}} \approx \sqrt{1.8(G/b)+1}$$

for G/b = 0.1 to 0.25   Eq (4-32)

K is called Munk's span factor.

Fig. 4.17   Approximate construction of equivalent wing span of a monoplane having the aerodynamic characteristics of a biplane of given mean span.

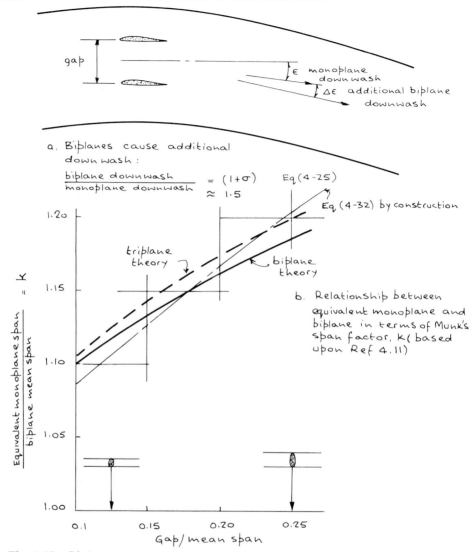

Fig. 4.18   Biplane (and triplane) characteristics.

$$= [pS_T/(pS_T + S_B)] \, G \tag{4–33}$$

where $p = C_{LT}/C_{LB} = 1$ with zero or negative stagger to 1.35 with positive stagger.

When both top and bottom planes are of equal size the lift of the top is about $\frac{1}{3}$ more than that of the bottom, so that:

$$\text{orthogonal biplane } Y = 4/7 \, G \tag{4–33a}$$

and an orthogonal triplane can be shown to be:

$$y = 7/12 \text{ total } G \tag{4–33b}$$

Similarly, for the standard mean chord $\bar{c}$ of the equivalent plane, area $S_T + S_B$:

$$\bar{c} \, (S_T + S_B) = \bar{c}_T \, S_T + \bar{c}_B \, S_B$$

i.e.

$$\bar{c} = (\bar{c}_T S_T + \bar{c}_B S_B)/(S_T + S_B) \tag{4–34}$$

While for the pitching moment coefficient of the equivalent plane, C_{Mac}:

$$C_{Mac}\,\bar{c}S = C_{Mac_T}\bar{c}_T S_T + C_{Mac_B}\bar{c}_B S_B$$

so that: (4–35)

$$C_{Mac} = (C_{Mac_T}\bar{c}_T S_T + C_{Mac_B}\bar{c}_B S_B)/\bar{c}S$$

Because the aerodynamic centre of the biplane lies about 2 per cent SMC further forward than a monoplane, it follows that a near-orthogonal biplane cellule must be mounted 2 per cent $\bar{c}$ further aft than a pure monoplane, to bring the centre of gravity of the aeroplane into the correct geometric alignment with the aerodynamic centre of the whole.

Wings are often staggered to improve the pilot's view. This has no effect upon the lift dependent drag of the whole, in theory anyway. The lift slope of each plane is modified slightly, as shown in fig. 4.20b and c (in which positive (top wing leading) stagger is employed).

Proportions of the most efficient biplane are given in fig. 4.20a (ref. 4.11), which is based upon the work of Munk. The diagram shows how to determine the best value of

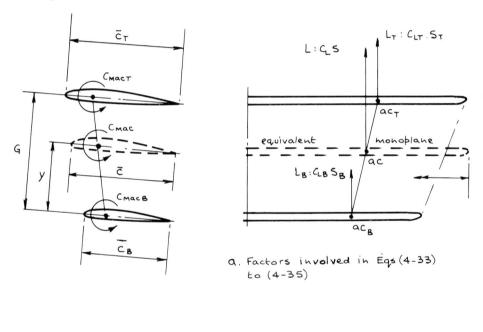

a. Factors involved in Eqs (4-33) to (4-35)

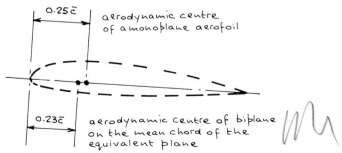

Fig. 4.19   Locating the equivalent monoplane.

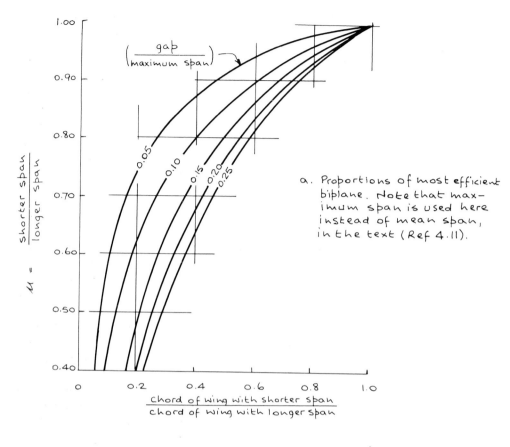

a. Proportions of most efficient
biplane. Note that max-
imum span is used here
instead of mean span,
in the text (Ref 4.11).

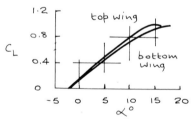

b. The top and bottom planes do
not generate equal lift.
Here each wing is identical to
the other, and there is no
stagger.

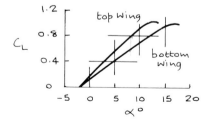

c. Stagger is often used to improve
the pilot's view, and it is positive
when the top wing is ahead of
the bottom. Here the effect
of 30° positive stagger is shown.
Theory shows that lift induced
drag is independent of stagger.

Fig. 4.20   Biplane geometry and its effects.

any one variable, $\bar{c}_2/\bar{c}_1$, G/b_1, or b_2/b_1 (where suffix 1 applies to the chord or span of the longer plane, and suffix 2 to the shorter), when the other two are assumed or known.

There is no place for triplanes, except as replicas of early aeroplanes – or perhaps for competition aerobatics (where low wing loading and plenty of drag might perhaps be combined with high power to produce an agile aeroplane, slow enough to keep within the box-like airspace limits). They can, nevertheless, be treated in a similar way to biplanes, and the curve for finding the span of the equivalent monoplane is shown in fig. 4.18b. The triplane has to be treated as two biplane cellules, so as to derive an equivalent plane between each pair. These equivalent planes are then used in turn to find the equivalent monoplane of the whole. Minimum drag is achieved when the lifts of the top and bottom planes are equal.

Rigging of biplanes

There is a conflict between theory, experiment and practice about the differing amount of incidence needed between the wings of biplanes. Induced drag theory suggests that the use of a small amount of negative declage (bottom plane at a larger angle of incidence than top) is needed for minimum induced drag. This is confirmed by ref. 4.16, but the use of negative decalage in practice is rare. The author discovered one example during a cursory search of records, the *Nieuport Scout* used in World War 1, which appears to have had about –2 deg between planes. The *Scout* had a large top plane and a small, narrow, bottom plane making it more of a *sesquiplane*, but this might not be significant.

Experiments, coupled with full-scale experience, show that a decalage angle of +1 deg for the top plane increases the minimum lift/drag ratio of the whole aircraft by +1 per cent (ref. 4.17). If decalage is increased further the effect is harmful to L/D. In many cases decalage appears to be 0 deg, with no difference between rigging with either forward or backward stagger.

A general summary shows the following values for decalage:

☐ Early biplanes (thin, undercambered wing sections):

average incidence of both planes,	+2 deg to +5 deg (extreme),
decalage between planes,	0 deg to +1 deg
	(with exceptions like the *Nieuport Scout*, with –2 deg),
longitudinal dihedral between wings and tail about +2 deg to +3 deg.	

☐ Triplane (e.g. *Sopwith Triplane* (1916)):

incidence of each plane,	+2 deg
decalage,	0 deg
longitudinal dihedral,	+½ deg.

☐ Later (post World War 1) biplanes with more advanced wing sections:

average incidence of both planes,	+2 deg to +3 deg
decalage,	0 deg to +1 deg
longitudinal dihedral,	about + 2 deg.

Comparing tandem with biplane wings

The arrangement of more or less equally sized wings in tandem has few applications, although there are now some exceptions: two are shown in plate 4.10. *Quickie* in fig. 6.9 is an example.

Biplanes and tandem planes are related by angle of stagger, θ, as shown in fig. 4.21a, in which a line joining the leading edges of the top and bottom planes is rotated forwards through 180 deg until the top plane is at the bottom. Munk's span factor, k, appears to vary with stagger from its value given in fig. 4.18b, to about 0.85 (minimum) in tandem, with the leading edges of equal planes 1.0 to 1.5 chords apart. This is sketched approximately in fig. 4.21a, while 4.21b is the tandem value of k for increasing distance apart of the planes (based upon ref. 4.11). Stagger is usually measured in chords.

Interference between the planes results in a moderate reduction in lift-dependent drag of the foreplane, and a marked increase for the rear. The consequence is an overall increase in drag for the whole.

An example of the result of interference between close-set tandem planes that was of historic proportion and is of importance to any designer and builder, was that of Henri Mignet's *HM 14, Pou-du-Ciel (Flying Flea*, in the carefree English translation), of 1933 (ref. 4.18). In its original form shown in fig. 4.22 it caused a number of fatal accidents from irrecoverable dives, and was ultimately banned in Britain and France. Later variants had the design faults corrected. After test flying one of these, the author believes that the configuration has much to offer anyone wishing to fly cheaply, for fun, with one of the simplest control systems that it may be possible to conceive (although it can be tricky when braking after landing for a conventionally trained pilot – as the author discovered).

Four factors appear to have contributed to the *HM 14* accidents, and they are worth recounting:

☐ The wings had a section invented by Mignet, with a sharp leading edge. Control in pitch was achieved by changing the angle of incidence of the foreplane by a direct linkage with the stick. Maximum incidence was limited to only about 4.8 deg on a specimen tested in the 24 ft (7.3 m) wind tunnel at the Royal Aircraft Establishment, Farnborough (ref. 4.19). It is possible that the pitch control lacked authority, and that the lack would have been worsened by the tendency of a sharp leading edge to force premature separation and loss of lift at moderate angles of attack.

☐ The foreplane trailing edge overlapped the leading edge of the rearplane. With the foreplane at its maximum incidence, a venturi effect might have been induced in the gap between the planes, increasing the lift of the rearplane, so that the nose-down moment of the rearplane about the centre of gravity could have become larger than the foreplane could counter.

☐ Longitudinal stability was dependent upon lift coefficient, being most stable at large angle of attack and high C_L, and least stable at low (due to the neutral point varying considerably with angle of attack).

☐ Inadequate control of the centre of gravity. The Farnborough tests showed the aeroplane to be unstable in normal flight with the **CG** further aft than 0.4 times the foreplane chord. In a dive steeper than –15 degrees, recovery could not be achieved.

There is also some evidence from later variants that the control power of the foreplane is affected by propeller diameter. Propeller tips have been sketched in fig. 4.22. A tip

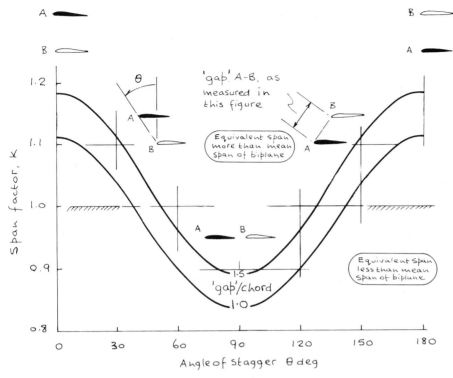

a. Estimated variation in Munk's span factor, K, with angle of stagger for a pair of biplane wings with 'gap'/chord 1.0 to 1.5 and aspect ratio 6.

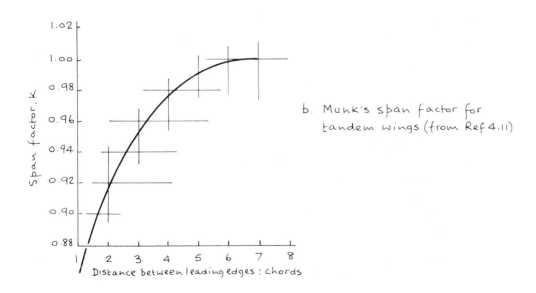

b. Munk's span factor for tandem wings (from Ref 4.11)

Fig. 4.21   Relationship between biplane and tandem wings.

that is not as high as the foreplane can cause a reversal of circulation beneath the centre section when power is applied, making it harder to lift the nose. A propeller tip should be about 4 in (10 cm) higher than the foreplane to maintain the authority of the control in pitch. Although *Flying Flea* variants can fly with quite low power engines, the small propellers used with such engines on gyrocopters, for example, should be avoided at all costs.

Among the cures applied to later variants of the *HM 14* were:

☐ The wing section was replaced by a tried design with a rounded leading edge.
☐ The distance between the foreplane and rearplane was increased, so that the overlap disappeared, being replaced by a gap.
☐ The rearmost position of the centre of gravity was limited to 0.25 times the total distance between the leading edge of the foreplane and the trailing edge of the rearplane.

Mignet's wing arrangement was close to that of a biplane with considerable stagger and a small gap. Or both wings could be taken as a single low aspect ratio wing, incorporating a slot, in which case aspect ratios varied between 3.2 and 3.43, depending upon the span of the foreplane. Zimmerman showed in 1932 that wings of very low aspect ratio have effective spans about 5 per cent longer than the actual span because of the closeness of the tip vortices, which dominate the aerodynamic picture. This caused him to advocate shapes like we saw earlier in the chapter. It is possible that the unusual, but effective, flying characteristics of the *Flying Flea* owe something to the phenomenon.

If the gap and stagger are increased in their proportions to wing span and chord, then another possible formula can be evolved for light aeroplanes. This is the configuration explored by *Arsenal Delanne* in the years from 1936 to 1939. Of eight tandem winged designs, two were built and flown. The foreplane was slightly larger than the rearplane, and they were located about two foreplane chords apart. The gap was about one foreplane chord. The advantages claimed were that such an arrangement provided a continuous slot effect. There is also some evidence that the *Arsenal Delanne 10C-2* tandem-wing two-seat fighter with retractable gear had a maximum level speed ratio, V_C/V_{so} around 7.5, whereas conventional aircraft with piston engines and tails achieve about 3 to 3.5.

Westland Aircraft Ltd test flew a Delanne-type *Lysander* variant, designated the *P12*, in 1941. The layout is shown in fig. 4.23. The company found that its behaviour, stability and control were an improvement on the standard *Lysander* (plate 4.12), and the lift-slope was 29 per cent better. Using the figures given by Westlands (ref. 4.20) and Warner (ref. 4.17) enables table 4–3 to be drawn.

The *P12* had fixed gear and it appeared to have a maximum speed ratio, V_C/V_{so}, about 5.17, compared with 7.6 for the *10C-2* given above. Certain other information obtained from the test flights showed that although the aeroplane was better longitudinally than the standard *Lysander*, directional control was degraded seriously at low speed, and when its tail turret was turned. Directional stability was reduced markedly when the centre of gravity moved aft. With the **CG** at 64.5 per cent chord the aeroplane was longitudinally and directionally uncomfortable. Further aft than that position the aircraft would spin. With the **CG** on the forward position at 45 per cent SMC take-off, general handling and stability were reported to be excellent, but full up elevator was needed to land. The design was not developed, although the *Westland* test

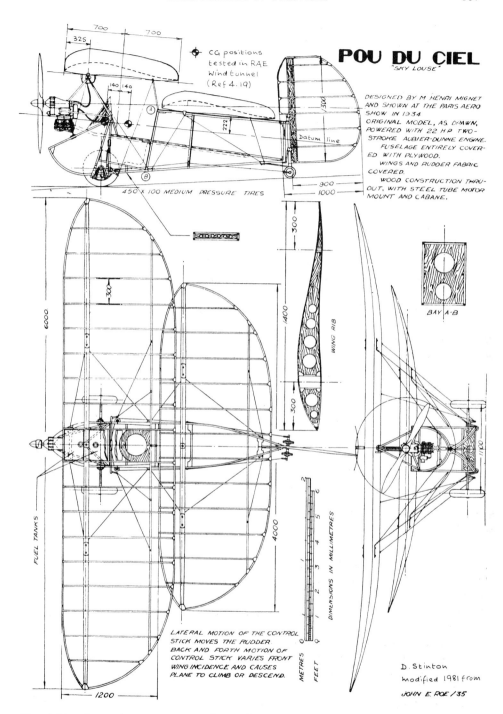

POU DU CIEL
"SKY LOUSE"

CG positions tested in RAE Wind tunnel (Ref 4.19)

DESIGNED BY M HENRI MIGNET AND SHOWN AT THE PARIS AERO SHOW IN 1934. ORIGINAL MODEL, AS DRAWN, POWERED WITH 22 H.P. TWO-STROKE AUBIER-DUNNE ENGINE.
   FUSELAGE ENTIRELY COVER-ED WITH PLYWOOD.
   WINGS AND RUDDER FABRIC COVERED.
   WOOD CONSTRUCTION THRU-OUT, WITH STEEL TUBE MOTOR MOUNT AND CABANE.

450 x 100 MEDIUM PRESSURE TIRES

Datum line

WING RIB

BAY A-B

FUEL TANKS

DIMENSIONS IN MILLIMETRES

METRES
FEET

LATERAL MOTION OF THE CONTROL STICK MOVES THE RUDDER. BACK AND FORTH MOTION OF CONTROL STICK VARIES FRONT WING INCIDENCE AND CAUSES PLANE TO CLIMB OR DESCEND.

D. Stinton
modified 1981 from
JOHN E. POE / 35

Fig. 4.22   General arrangement of Henri Mignet (1893–1965). *HM14 Pou du Ciel (Sky Louse* or *Flying Flea)*. Drawing based upon information given in refs. 4.18, 4.19 and 4.22.

pilot, Harald Penrose, proposed a light aeroplane with Delanne-type configuration around 1947.

TABLE 4–3

Configuration	Lift slope	Source
Infinite monoplane	$a_o = 2\pi/\text{radian} = 0.1/\text{degree}$	eq (4–18)
Finite monoplane	$a_A = 2\pi A/(A + 2)/\text{radian}$	eq (4–19a)
Biplane, $G/\bar{c} = 1$	$a_A \approx 0.83 \times \text{monoplane}$	(ref 4.17)
	$= 1.65\pi A/(A + 2)$	eq (4–36)
	for the same aspect ratio	
Westland Lysander monoplane	$a_A = 0.075$ ($A = 9.6$, estimated)	(ref 4.20)
Westland P12 monoplane (Delanne-type)	$a_A = 0.097$ ($A = 9.6$, estimated)	(ref 4.20)

Junctions, fillets and fairings

Junctions between surfaces are always sources of premature flow separation, aerodynamic buffet and drag. Mid-wing arrangements, and wings which meet relatively slab-sided bodies at right angles are the least likely to give trouble. With high and low wings, especially those which then meet curved fuselage skins, there is a natural tendency for wing and body surfaces to form an acute angle. Acute angles slow down flows, causing static pressures to rise and air to break away in small regions of high energy vortices left behind in the wake.

Losses with high wings are less than those which are set low on bodies with well curved cross-sections. The reason is that the increase in static pressure underneath the root of a high wing helps to generate and maintain lift. With a low wing, a rise in static pressure at the root of the top surface is anti-lift.

Wing fillets (and tail fillets) are designed to fill the volume between surfaces where they meet at an acute angle. A plot of cross-sectional area of such a trapped 'streamtube' shows a rapid contraction aft of the leading edge, to the point of maximum wing thickness, followed by a rapid expansion. Quite apart from adverse frictional effects, the air cannot cope with too rapid deceleration past the crest, so it separates. A fillet smooths and reduces the rate of change of cross-sectional area of the 'streamtube' between the leading and trailing edge of the wing, as shown in fig. 4.24.

Fillets give character to an aeroplane. A carelessly profiled wing root fillet can spoil the authenticity of a replica, quite apart from perhaps spoiling the flying qualities.

A particularly interesting fillet was the 'bite' at the trailing edge of the wing on the elegant and highly streamlined *Heinkel He 111* (1935), like that of the *He 70* (1932) before it. The marked 'bite' is shown in plate 4.14. It reduced the wing root chord, and gave a pronounced inverted-gull wing aspect to the trailing edge. The basic shape of both designs appears to have been so streamlined that the tailplanes lay almost in line with the crests of the wing root sections, where they were vulnerable to buffet. The bite was a geometric device which enabled the trailing edge of the wing to be swept

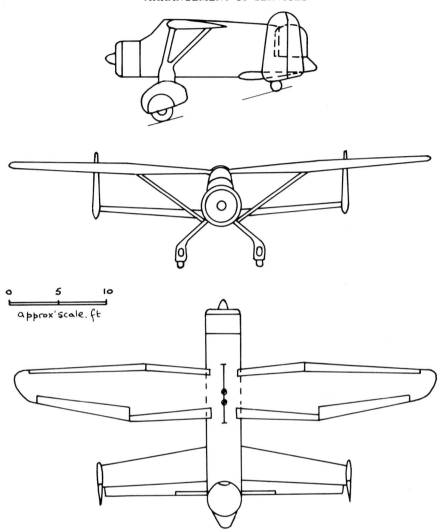

approx' scale, ft

Fig. 4.23   *Westland Aircraft Ltd.* P12, 1941 (ref. 4.20).

Weight	7167 lb (3251 Kg)
Centre of gravity	45 to 64.5 percent SMC
Span	50 ft (15.24 m)
Length	26.38 ft (8.04 m)
Mainplane area	260 ft² (24.15 m²)
Tailplane area	132.5 ft² (12.31 m²)
Elevators total area	32 ft² (2.97 m²)
Elevator trimmer area	2.82 ft² (0.26 m²)
Fins, total area	60.84 ft² (5.65 m²)
Rudders, area aft of hinge	17.36 ft² (1.61 m²)
Rudder trimmer area	1.98 ft² (0.18 m²)

upwards, to meet the curved fuselage skin almost at right angles, smoothing the wake.

The bite would also have had a favourable effect upon the reduction in change of downwash with change in angle of attack, $d\epsilon/d\alpha$, which is profoundly important in longitudinal stability calculations. The reduction in chord is substantially the same as we saw in fig. 4.13c, and can result in a 10 per cent reduction in $d\epsilon/d\alpha$ which, as we shall see in chapter 11, increases the effectiveness of the tailplane. If overdone, though, such a reduction of wing root chord can increase the induced drag, which spoils performance.

Shortening of the wing root chord on the *Lysander* (1936) as shown in plate 4.12 (see also the *Westland P 12*) can be a useful way of shedding wetted area where lift has been lost, provided that structural strength can be maintained. This type of wing planform is invariably associated with external bracing. Cutting away the wing leading edge at the root gave the *Lysander* (which was designed originally for army co-operation) the best all-round view for the pilot of any propeller engined aeroplane that the author has flown. The slats and flaps which were fitted to enable the *Lysander* to fly very slowly (V_C/V_{so} approximately 4) also gave it some of the most spectacularly useful – and wilful– flight characteristics.

In this chapter many general effects of different and distant arrangements of aerodynamic surfaces are seen to be related. There really is nothing new under the sun – as we have seen by going back to a number of older sources, while talking too about several quite old aeroplanes. It is always fruitful to look backwards – especially now that we have to find energy-saving ways of flying – there is always the chance that a fresh insight might be gained.

We have looked too at birds. As a lecturer at The College of Aeronautics, Cranfield, said to the author a few days before these words were written: 'Birds have been telling us how to do it for thousands of years, if only we had the wit to see'.

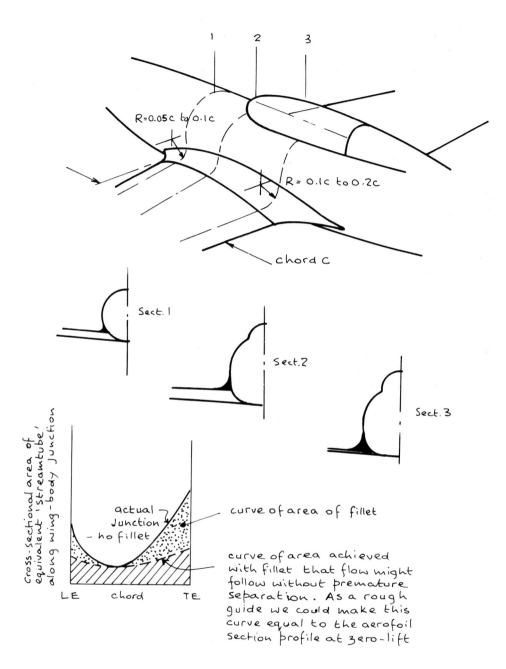

Fig. 4.24   Fillets smooth over and isolate areas between surfaces which, meeting at acute angles, would trap and slow the air, causing turbulence and separation.

References

4.1 Küchemann, D. (1978) *The Aerodynamic Design of Aircraft*. Oxford, New York, Toronto, Sydney, Paris, Frankfurt: Pergamon Press.

4.2 Bairstow, L. (1946) *Applied Aerodynamics*. London, New York, Toronto: Longmans Green & Co.

4.3 Hoerner, S. F. and Horst, H. V. (1975) *Fluid-Dynamic Lift*. Brick Town, New Jersey: Mrs Lisalotte Hoerner.

4.4 Judge, A. W. (1917) *The Properties of Aerofoils and Aerodynamic Bodies*. London and New York: Whittacker & Co.

4.5 Glauert, H. (1948) *The Elements of Aerofoil and Airscrew Theory*. Cambridge University Press.

4.6 *The Aviation Consumer* (1978) **VIII** no. 14. Belvoir Publications, 1111 East Putnam Avenue, Riverside, Connecticut 06878.

4.7 Blick, Prof. E. F. (1971) 'Bird Aerodynamics'. *Shell Aviation News* no 402.

4.8 Hoerner, S. F. (1965) *Fluid-Dynamic Drag*. Brick Town, New Jersey: Hoerner, S. F.

4.9 Spillman, J. J. (1978) 'The Use of Wing Tip Sails to Reduce Vortex Drag'. *The Aeronautical Journal, The Royal Aeronautical Society*.

4.10 Shaw, H. (1919) *A Text-Book of Aeronautics*. London: Charles Griffin and Company Limited.

4.11 Diehl, W. S. (1937) *Engineering Aerodynamics*. New York: The Ronald Press Company.

4.12 Marske, J. (1970) *Experiment in Flying Wing Sailplanes*. Indiana: Jim Marske, 130 Crestwood Drive, Michigan City.

4.13 Corning, G. (1953) *Supersonic and Subsonic Airplane Design*. Michigan: Edwards Brothers Inc., Ann Arbor.

4.14 Wolkovitch, J. (1979) 'Subsonic VSTOL Aircraft Configurations with Tandem Wings'. *Journal of Aircraft* **16** no 9, *American Institute of Aeronautics and Astronautics*.

4.15 Cox, J. (1978) 'Oshkosh 78 . . . A Year of Trends'. *Sport Aviation, Experimental Aircraft Association International, Inc, Hales Corners, Wisconsin*.

4.16 Olson, E. C. and Selberg, B. P. (1976) 'Experimental Determination of Improved Aerodynamic Characteristics using Biplane Wing Configurations'. *Journal of Aircraft*, **13**, no 4, April 1976, *American Institute of Aeronautics and Astronautics*.

4.17 Warner, E. P. (1936) *Airplane Design, Performance*. 2nd edn. New York and London: McGraw-Hill Book Company, Inc.

4.18 Mignet, H. (*c.*1934) *The Flying Flea*. Translated by The Air League of the British Empire. London: Sampson Low, Marston & Co Ltd.

4.19 Hartshorn, A. S. (1936) report no BA 1333, 'Tests of a *Pou-du-Ciel* in the 24 ft Tunnel'. *The Royal Aircraft Establishment, Farnborough.*

4.20 *Westland Aircraft Ltd* (Jan. 1941) report no 109, '*Westland P12*, Full Scale Results'.

4.21 Barnwell, F. S. and Sayers, W. H. (1916) *Aeroplane Design and a Simple Explanation of Inherent Stability* London: McBride, Nast & Co. (*Note*: Barnwell was the designer of the Bristol F2B Fighter (1916–17).)

4.22 Underwood, J. W. (1976). Henri Mignet and the Pou-du-Ciel *Air Trails*. Volume, no 1.

CHAPTER 5

Drag, Flaps and Wakes

'A scientific theory is a policy rather than a creed.'
Attributed to the British physicist, Sir Joseph John Thomson (1856–1940).

In the last chapter we looked in particular at induced drag, caused by surfaces in the act of lifting. Here we must look at ways of tackling lift/drag ratio, flaps, wakes and the non lift-dependent drag terms which are grouped collectively under the general heading of parasite drag. We shall adopt the view of the performance engineer, described where drag was defined in chapter 2.

Fig. 5.1 shows a convenient breakdown of total drag. Wave drag, which is caused by compressibility effects, has been set aside with broken lines, because it does not appear with most aeroplanes dealt with here. Under certain circumstances wave drag at zero lift, D_{fw}, could be treated as a parasite term.

Choosing an aerofoil section (wing profile drag, D_o)

There are many aerofoil sections from which to choose. The series published by the National Aeronautics and Space Administration includes three useful families: the (old designation) NACA four- and five-digit series for slower aircraft, and the six-series for fast (ref. 3.6):

☐ *Four-digit series*. The numbering system is based upon section geometry. The first digit represents the camber (maximum ordinate of the mean line above the chord line) as a per cent of the chord. The second digit indicates the distance from the leading edge to the location of maximum camber in tenths of chord. The last two digits show the section thickness in per cent of chord. Thus, *NACA 4415* has 4 per cent camber at $0.4 \times$ chord from the leading edge, and is 15 per cent thick.

☐ *Five-digit series*. The thickness distributions of the five-digit series is the same as the four-digit. The numbering system includes an indication of theoretical aerodynamic characteristics. The first digit represents the amount of camber in terms of the relative magnitude of the design lift coefficient: the design lift coefficient in tenths is $3/2 \times$ the first digit. The second and third digits indicate the distance from the leading edge to the point of maximum camber: the distance in per cent of chord is $\frac{1}{2} \times$ the number represented by the pair. The last two digits show the section thickness in per cent of chord. Thus, *NACA 23012* section has a design lift coefficient of $2/10$

$\times (3/2)$, i.e. 0.3; maximum camber is at $30/100 \times (1/2)$, which is 15 per cent; and the thickness ratio is 12 per cent.

☐ *Six-series* (usually, but not always, designated by a six-digit number). This was designed to achieve low drag, high critical Mach number and high maximum lift. The first digit is always 6, showing the series. The second digit denotes the chordwise position of minimum pressure, in tenths of chord behind the leading edge, for the basic symmetrical profile at zero lift. The third digit, which follows a comma, gives the range of lift coefficient in tenths above and below the design lift coefficient in which favourable, low drag, pressure gradients exist on both surfaces. The fourth digit, which follows a dash, gives the design lift coefficient in tenths. As before, the last two digits indicate the thickness of the section in per cent of chord. Thus, *NACA 65, 3–218* is for high speed and has minimum pressure $5/10$ chord behind the leading edge for the basic symmetrical section at zero lift. The 3 shows that the favourable lift coefficient is $\pm 3/10$ above and below the design lift coefficient, $2/10$. The thickness is 18 per cent.

A five-digit aerofoil in the six-series has the revised profile which results in a laminar low-drag 'bucket', and the coding is as follows for:

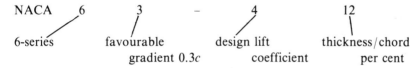

An A in place of the dash shows that a section is substantially straight on both surfaces from about $0.8c$ to the trailing edge. A section derived from an earlier profile with a different thickness ratio, but having minimum pressure at the same chordwise station, has the low drag range written as a subscript:

$$NACA\ 64_2\text{–}215$$

low drag range $\pm 2/10$ above and below $C_l = 0.2$

While removal of the cusp near the trailing edge of this section, by straightening aft of $0.8c$, would result in the redesignation:

$$NACA\ 64_2A215$$

the greater the extent of favourable pressure gradient aft of the leading edge, the more adverse the gradient over the rear of the section, and the lower the maximum lift coefficient. The earlier *NACA* four- and five-digit families have favourable gradients limited to about $0.15c$. Outside the drag 'bucket' of the 6-series section drag tends to increase faster than with an older section.

To achieve laminar conditions, maximum distributed roughness is about 0.002 in (0.05 mm), and about 0.01 in (0.25 mm) for isolated roughness, like rivet heads. Surface waviness must be held to ± 0.007 in (0.18 mm) over a 1 in (25.4 mm) length, or ± 0.02 in (0.5 mm) over a 2 in (51 mm) wavelength to avoid premature transition. The lower the section drag being aimed for, the closer must be the attention to maintaining both profile and surface finish.

Where a wing or tail is in the wash from a propeller, premature transition from

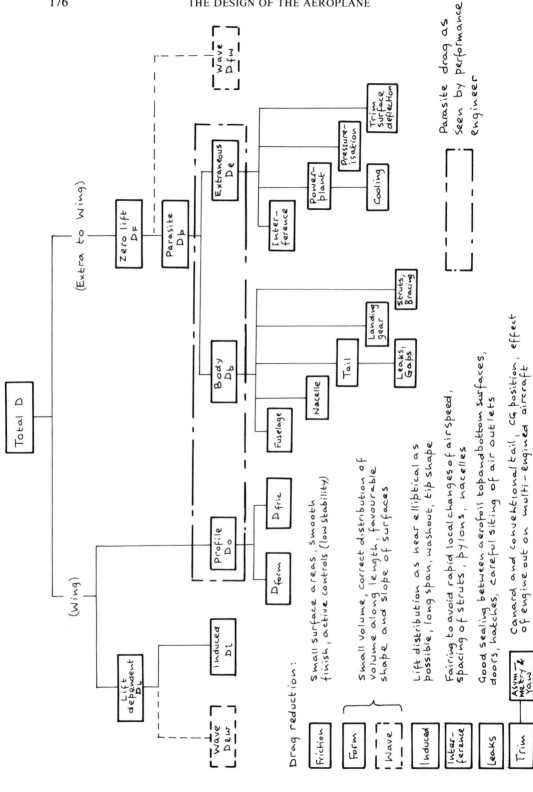

Total D

(Extra to Wing)

(Wing)

Zero lift D_F

Parasite D_p

Wave D_{fw}

Extraneous D_e

Inter-ference

Power-plant

Pressure-isation

Cooling

Trim Surface deflection

Body D_b

Fuselage

Nacelle

Tail

Landing gear

Leaks, Gaps

Struts, Bracing

Profile D_o

D_{form}

D_{fric}

Lift dependent D_L

Wave D_{LW}

Induced D_i

Parasite drag as seen by performance engineer

Drag reduction:

Friction — Small surface areas, smooth finish, active controls (low stability)

Form — Small volume, correct distribution of volume along length, favourable shape and slope of surfaces

Wave — Lift distribution as near elliptical as possible, long span, washout, tip shape

Induced — Fairing to avoid rapid local changes of airspeed, spacing of struts, pylons, nacelles

Inter-ference — Good sealing between aerofoil top and bottom surfaces, doors, hatches, careful siting of air outlets

Leaks

Trim — Canard and conventional tail, CG position, effect of engine out on multi-engined aircraft

Asymmetry & Yaw

laminar to turbulent flow is certain. The maximum extent of a laminar boundary layer will not exceed $0.1c$ (10 per cent of the local chord) and may be less in practice. It could be a waste of time and effort giving a laminar wing to an aeroplane designed to live out of doors in a field, because deposited dirt and squashed insects (coupled with propwash) would destroy laminar flow immediately.

Thin aerofoil sections do not cause much form drag, their profile drag is almost entirely due to friction: i.e. near enough double the frictional drag of a single surface. Finish is important and table 5-1 gives some idea of the relative drag of differently prepared surfaces at low Reynolds numbers, with turbulence:

TABLE 5-1

Relative drag of surfaces

Surface at cruise $C_L = 0.2$	Drag of surface/drag of same area of polished metal
Bare polished metal	1.0
Lacquered wood	1.2
Highly polished wood	1.06
Metal with carborundum walkway	2.0
Commercial finish (filler + lacquer + wax)	0.9
Filled and polished glass reinforced plastic	0.8

When looking for a satisfactory section, look carefully at what the aeroplane is expected to do. A racer needs low profile drag at the design lift coefficient. On the other hand an aeroplane designed for fast climbing needs high lift coefficient at low-ish speeds and higher profile drag may have to be accepted. The lift/drag ratio at the appropriate Reynolds number gives a useful choice.

A number of factors must be taken into account when selecting a section:

☐ *Design lift coefficient*: for low drag.
☐ *Structural considerations*: the depth of a section determines the depth of wing spar needed to take the bending loads; and the enclosed cross-sectional area is a measure of its ability to resist torque from the pitching moment. Spar weight is inversely proportional to *(depth of beam)*^{2}. Therefore, the deeper the spar and the thicker a section, the lighter the wing structure; and the more room for fuel and landing gear.
☐ *Stall qualities*: stall speeds and stall qualities lie at the heart of airworthy flying qualities. Pay attention to the shape of the lift-angle of attack curve at the point of the stall. The sharper the peak, the more violent the stall. Most aeroplanes are better when provided with docile stall characteristics. An exception might be an aeroplane designed for crisp international competition aerobatics.
☐ *Low pitching moment coefficient*: to keep stabiliser size small.
☐ *Low profile drag and high lift/drag;* for economy in the cruise, and the ability to accelerate out of trouble at low speed.
☐ *Ease of manufacture*: low drag profiles are all very well, as long as it does not cost the earth to make them, and then attempt to maintain them over a cost-effective

working life. Look for a section that has good characteristics with 'standard roughness'.
Laminar flow: nice to have, but don't be fooled into thinking that low drag laminar sections must *always* be the best. Look around.

Lift/drag ratio of plain wings

Data given in ref. 3.6, and similar sources show lift, drag and other aerodynamic information in the form of coefficients, corrected for aerofoils with infinite aspect ratios. Such results are strictly two dimensional. We must recalculate for real surfaces with tips, for use in a three-dimensional world.

When the two-dimensional angle of attack, lift and drag coefficients, α_0, c_l and c_d respectively, and variations with α_0 are given, we need to find α and C_{Do} for a finite wing with aspect ratio A, using the same section, at the same lift coefficient, $c_l = C_L$. Note that we use capital suffices for the wing of finite aspect ratio.
When wing lift distribution is elliptical, the angle of attack:

$$\alpha = \alpha_0 + \epsilon = \alpha_0 + c_l/\pi A \quad \text{from eqs (4–5) and (4–4b)}$$

But, when lift distribution is non-elliptic:

$$\alpha = \alpha_0 + K c_l/\pi A = \alpha_0 + K^1 c_l / \pi A \text{ (with interference)} \qquad (5\text{–}1)$$

and, induced drag coefficient,

$$C_{Di} = K c_l^2/ \pi A = K^1 c_l^2 /\pi A \qquad \text{from eq (4–9b)}$$

This enables the total drag coefficient to be written:

$$C_D = C_{Dp} + C_{Di} \qquad (5\text{–}2)$$

in which C_{Dp} is the parasite drag coefficient.

Now, if we have two wings with aspect ratios A_1 and A_2, using the same section (and with no other interference effects) their angles of attack at the same c_l are, from eq (5–1):

$$\alpha_1 = \alpha_0 + K_1 c_l/ \pi A_1$$
$$\alpha_2 = \alpha_0 + K_2 c_l/ \pi A_2$$

So that,

$$\alpha_2 = \alpha_1 + (c_l/ \pi)(K_2/A_2 - K_1/A_1) \qquad (5\text{–}3)$$

$$C_{D_1} = C_{D0} + K_1 c_l^2/ \pi A_1$$
$$C_{D_2} = C_{D0} + K_2 c_l^2/ \pi A_2$$

giving,

$$C_{D_2} = C_{D_1} + (c_l^2/ \pi)(K_2/A_2 - K_1/A_1) \qquad (5\text{–}4)$$

These may be simplified by assuming elliptic distributions, so that

$$K_1 = K_2 = 1$$

To derive three-dimensional characteristics from two-dimensional data, let $A_1 = \infty$ (so that $1/A_1 = 0$), $\alpha_1 = \alpha_0$, and $C_{D_1} = C_{D0} = c_d$. Fig. 5.2 shows such a set of two-dimensional date from ref. 3.6, for *NACA 63_1–412*, one of the laminar family. However, we shall use the standard roughness data, which does away with the drag bucket around $c_l = 0.4$. Further, let $A_2 = 7$, so that the above equations become:

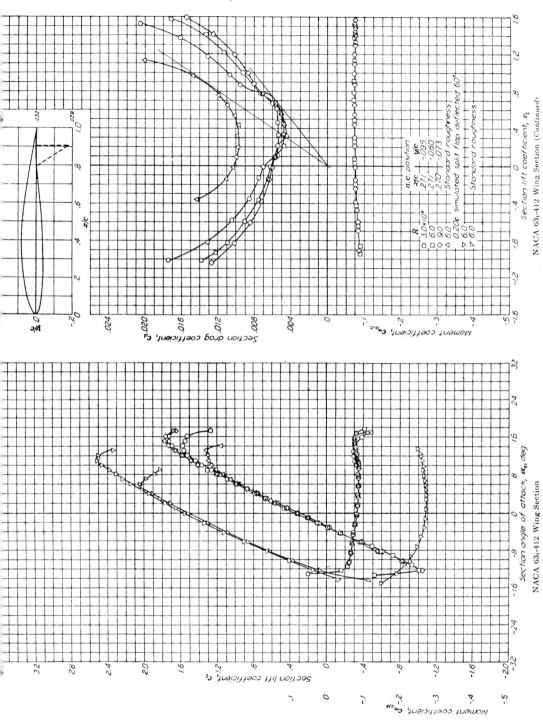

Fig. 5.2   *NACA 63₁–412 (ref. 3.6 with permission of Dover Publications, Inc., New York).*

$$\alpha = \alpha_0 + c_l/7\pi \qquad\qquad (5\text{--}3a)$$
$$C_D = c_{d_0} + c_l^2/7\pi \qquad\qquad (5\text{--}4a)$$

Table 5–2 shows the way in which such data is handled so as to correct from the two-dimensional to three-dimensional form. The figures are those for Reynolds number 6.0 $\times$ 10⁶ and are plotted in fig. 5.3. Note the dramatic effect of the lower aspect ratio upon lift/drag ratio, and the lift coefficient at which it occurs. Both are considerably reduced.

Surface roughness causes a marked loss of lift/drag, and so does propwash. When designing a sailplane for aerotowing, be prepared for the lift/drag to be halved by the effect of tug wake across the glider surfaces. This has an important effect upon the size of engine for the tug, which needs enough power for its task. It is no good engining a tug to cope with a sailplane generating lift/drag of 40 in free flight, when drag is doubled and L/D halved under tow.

A quick way of redrawing the lift curve for a wing of finite aspect ratio is to measure the slope a_0, for the particular two-dimensional section, somewhere around the middle of the straight line portion of the working range. The slope is usually slightly less than the theoretical 2π/radian (0.11/degree) of eq (4–18). As maximum lift depends upon Reynolds number, we can plot $C_{l\ max}$ (*see* fig. 5.2) as shown in fig. 5.4. A fairly straight line can be drawn through the points. Mark $C_{l\ max}$ with standard roughness, and draw a line through it, parallel with that through the laminar values. Pick off C_{lmax} for the required Reynolds number.

A modification can be made to the lift slope for wing taper, by the introduction of a planform factor, f_w (which is quite close to 1.0), as given by refs. 3.4 and 5.1, and shown in fig. 5.5.

$$\text{actual lift slope, } a = a_0 f_w A/(A + 2) \qquad\qquad (5\text{--}5)$$

which is derived from eq (4–19). Or we may multiply the value of theoretical a_A, shown in Figure 4.6(c), by f_w to give:

$$a = a_A f_w \qquad\qquad (5\text{--}6)$$

The angle of zero lift is unchanged by change of aspect ratio and lift slope, so that we may now plot a revised $C_L - \alpha$ curve for the wing, using an interpolated maximum lift coefficient, picked from fig. 5.4. The new line passes through the angle of zero lift for the basic section, and takes the form constructed in fig. 5.6. From these results we see that a reduction of aspect ratio:

☐ Reduces the lift slope, without changing the angle of attack for zero lift.
☐ Increases the stalling angle, but reduces the maximum lift coefficient.
☐ Increases drag throughout the whole range of angles of attack for any lift coefficient.
☐ Reduces the lift/drag ratio at any angle of attack.
☐ Reduces maximum lift/drag ratio and the corresponding angle of attack at which it occurs.
☐ With a full scale aeroplane, parasite drag of the remainder further reduces maximum lift/drag.

TABLE 5-2

Reduction of data for NACA 63_1-412, standard roughness at Reynolds number 6×10^6, aspect ratios $A = \infty$ and $A = 7$

α_0	-6	-3	0	3	6	9	12	14
$C_L = c_l$	-0.35	0.04	0.35	0.7	0.97	1.22	1.3	1.15
$C_{D_0} = c_d$	0.014	0.010	0.0098	0.0114	0.015	≈ 0.026	(extrapolated too far)	
C_L/C_{D_0}	-25	4	35.7	61.4	64.6	≈ 47	?	?
$C_L{}^2$	0.1225	0.0016	0.1225	0.49	0.94	1.64	1.69	1.32
$C_L/\pi A$	-0.016	0.0018	0.016	0.032	0.044	0.058	0.059	0.052
$C_L{}^2/\pi A$	0.0055	0.000072	0.0056	0.022	0.0427	0.0744	0.077	0.060
ϵ (degrees) $= (C_L/\pi A) \times 57.3$	-0.92	0.103	0.92	1.834	2.52	3.32	3.38	3.0
$\alpha = \alpha_0 + \epsilon$	-6.92	-2.89	0.92	4.83	8.52	12.32	?	?
$C_D = C_{D_0} + C_L{}^2/\pi A$	0.0195	0.0101	0.0154	0.0334	0.0577	≈ 0.1024	?	?
C_L/C_D	17.95	3.96	22.72	20.95	16.81	12.5	?	?

Although aspect ratio modifies the lift and drag characteristics of a two-dimensional wing section it does not have any appreciable effect upon the aerodynamic centre or the basic pitching moment of a real straight wing. Swept wings suffer great varia

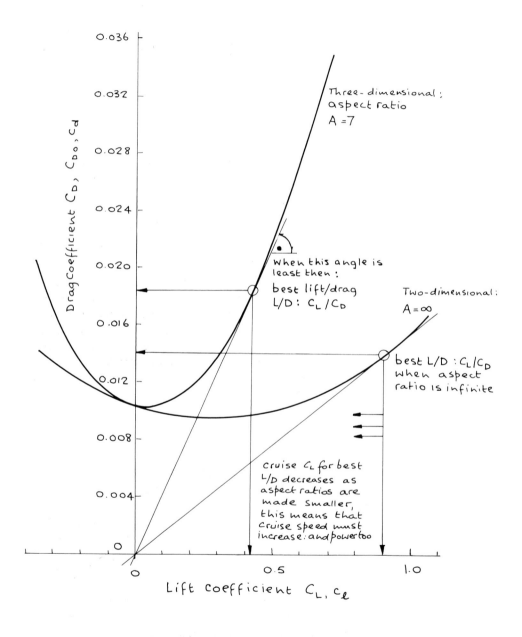

Fig. 5.3 Polar diagram of drag coefficient against lift coefficient for wings of aspect ratio $A = \infty$ and $A = 7$. Tangents drawn through the origin determine the best lift/drag ratios.

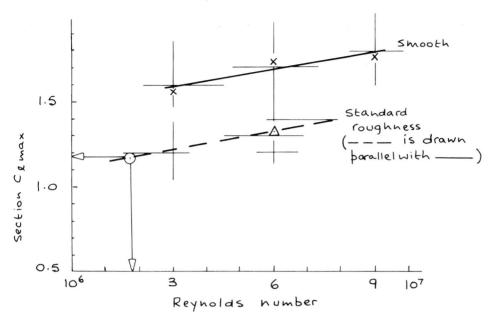

Fig. 5.4   Plot of section $c_{l\ max}$ with Reynolds number, making assumption that lift coefficient varies as a straight line. This method is applicable to the plain (unflapped) and flapped sections (e.g. *NACA 63₁–412* in fig. 5.2).

Fig. 5.3 is often drawn with the drag coefficient along the base. At shallow angles of attack profile drag is caused mainly by skin friction, which remains almost constant with angle of attack. But as angle of attack is increased, the separation point moves forwards and the wake thickens. Form drag, the pressure component, increases rapidly and dominates friction, swamping that component almost entirely by the time the stall is reached. Watching the wake of a wing in a wind tunnel makes it easy to see the way in which air becomes turbulently sluggish. It also makes it easy to appreciate the way in which drag is proportional to loss of momentum between the flow ahead of a body and the flow in its wake.

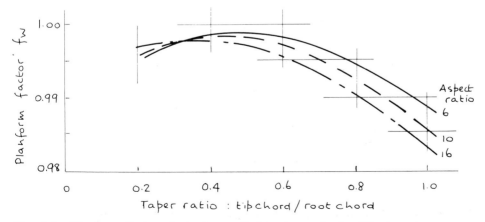

Fig. 5.5   Planform factor, f_w, to be applied to tapered wing lift slope in eq (5–5) (based upon ref. 5.1).

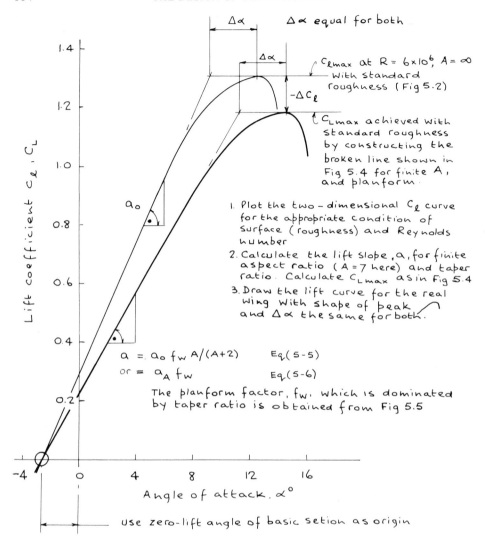

Fig. 5.6   Construction of lift curve for actual wing from two-dimensional data. The section used is *NACA 63₁–412* from fig. 5.2.

When a section has no drag bucket, drag coefficient can be approximated to a parabolic curve over a narrow working range of lift coefficients. This has the form:

$$\text{profile drag coefficient } C_{Do} \text{ (or } c_d) = c_{dx} + mc_l^2 \qquad (5\text{--}7)$$

which is a straight line as shown in fig. 5.7. The intercept, c_{dx}, is the point at which the line cuts the c_d ordinate. It has a value slightly less than the minimum drag coefficient of the section c_{dmin}. The slope of this line, m, is small when aspect ratio is infinite, being less than 0.01, but it is not negligible in its effect.

It is usually assumed that the slope of the C_{Do} line is directly proportional to $K/\pi A$, where K is the induced drag factor of the wing in plan; but closer examination shows that

$$\text{total drag coefficient } C_D = c_{dx} + mc_l^2 + Kc_l^2/\pi A$$
$$= c_{dx} + c_l^2\,(m + K/\pi A) \qquad (5\text{--}8)$$

which means that the effective induced drag factor is larger than K for planform alone.

We shall see later in the chapter that it is necessary to make fairly careful estimates of the induced drag factor, and the slope of $\Delta C_D / \Delta C_L{}^2 = m$.

In fig. 5.7, $m = 0.0075$. Recasting part of the second term in eq (5–8):

$$(m + K/\pi A) = K'/\pi A$$

so that,

$$K' = K + m\,\pi A \qquad\qquad\qquad (5\text{–}9)$$

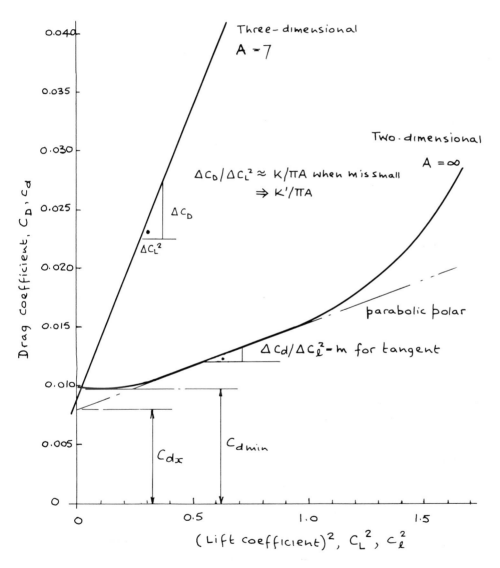

Fig. 5.7   Matching wing section characteristics to parabolic polars (converted to straight line form) so as to find induced drag factor $K = 1/e \rightarrow K'$

where K' is the effective induced drag factor of the wing when section profile drag characteristics have been taken into account. Thus, assuming $K = 1.2$ and $A = 7$:

$$K' = 1.2 + 0.0075 \times \pi \times 7$$

i.e.

$$K' = 1.36 \text{ an increase of nearly 14 per cent} \qquad (5\text{--}10)$$

This is one reason why drag estimates based upon theoretical values of planform efficiency, in terms of Oswald's factor e, tend to err on the low side. Section characteristics are important, and attention must be paid to the shape of the profile drag curve when selecting a wing section. Furthermore, as we have seen earlier, interference also contributes to K'. Glider values of K, assumed to be 1.05 or 1.06 for planform in the design stage, have grown to $K' = 1.3$ or 1.5 or more when the real aircraft has been bolted together. This makes a considerable difference to the aerodynamic optimum aspect ratio, which can be determined from the ratio K/A, shown in fig. 4.10a. The larger the value of K', the lower the aspect ratio for which K'/A is a minimum. This means that an underestimate of K on the drawing board can cause an aircraft to carry around a longer wing than is good for it – and long wings are heavy. Furthermore, maximum lift/drag ratio is achieved at a lower speed which spoils the ability to glide as far as possible, while making glide performance more susceptible to vagaries of the wind. Thus, a quite small underestimate in one direction has several important penalties dependent upon it.

Wing characteristics with flaps

Table 3–2 showed some generalised flap and slat characteristics, the performance of which depends upon the basic geometry of the surfaces to which they are attached, the amount of surface occupied by the device, and the amount of flap deflection. Analysis is complicated. Fortunately for us lighter and smaller aircraft tend to employ only mechanically simple plain, split and slotted (NACA) flaps. A few have slats. Thicker sections benefit most from trailing edge flaps, especially split flaps. Thinner sections, and those with sharper leading edges, perform better with leading edge flaps or slats to prevent leading edge separation and the thin aerofoil stall. Here, we concentrate only upon trailing edge flaps. Slats can be simple and useful, but their mechanical characteristics require care in the choice of speed at which they must open and close, so as to avoid spoiling climb performance. This can make them less of an asset off-design than they might seem to be at first.

Flap deflection usually produces a nose-down (negative) pitching moment of varying magnitude. This is associated with a change in the basic pitching moment of the wing at zero lift, M_o, C_{Mo} (see fig. 3.7). Generally, flaps do not alter the position of the aerodynamic centre of a wing and do not, therefore, alter the basic stability of an aeroplane. However, they do alter the trimming angles of tail surfaces and, therefore, the longitudinal dihedral between wing and tail. Because they usually occupy only part of the trailing edge of a wing their overall effectiveness is less than that implied by the data in table 3–2, which refers to sections of wings (or infinite wings with full span flaps). There are small order losses of flap effectiveness in the vicinity of junctions, which we may conveniently ignore.

Fig. 5.8 shows generalised lift characteristics of plain, split and simple slotted flaps. Selection of flap down in flight increases lift by an increment, ΔL, expressed here in terms of an increment in life coefficient, ΔC_L. The increment depends on the type of flap, the amount of flap chord/total chord, flap deflection, and the length of span that

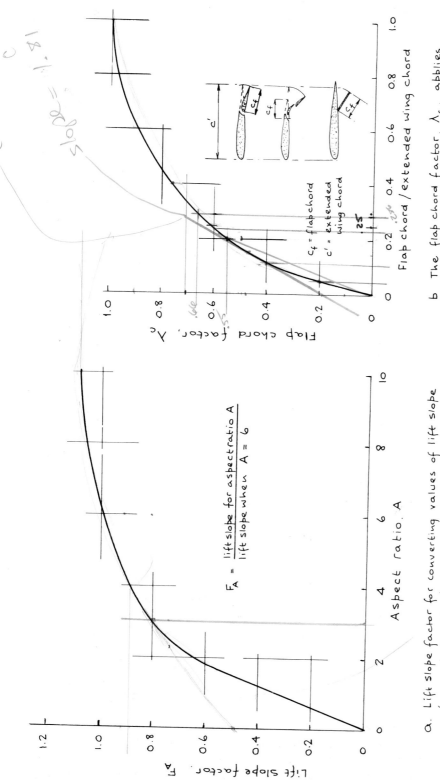

b   The flap chord factor, λ_c, applies to flaps of all kinds.

c_f = flap chord
c' = extended wing chord

Flap chord / extended wing chord

Flap chord factor, λ_c

a   Lift slope factor for converting values of lift slope from aspect ratio 6 to some other value between 0 and 10.

$$F_A = \frac{\text{lift slope for aspect ratio } A}{\text{lift slope when } A = 6}$$

Aspect ratio, A

Lift slope factor, F_A

Fig. 5.8   The effect of plain, split and slotted flaps on wing lift. The increment of wing lift coefficient due to flap is :

$$\Delta C_L = \lambda_c \, \lambda_\beta \, \lambda_b \quad (\text{eq } 5\text{-}11)$$

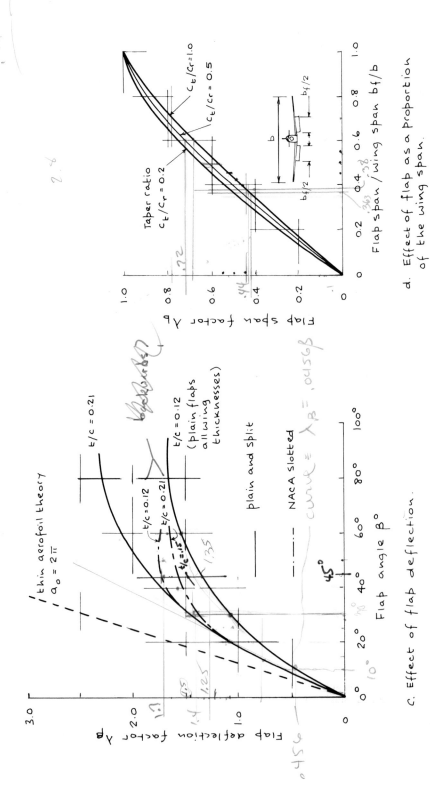

c. Effect of flap deflection.

d. Effect of flap as a proportion of the wing span.

Fig. 5.8 continued.

is flapped. Our method is approximate and based upon the work of Young (ref. 5.2) who is also drawn upon by ESDU in preparing flap data in Appendix A. We employ three factors, λ_c, λ_β and λ_b as follows:

$$\text{flap lift increment, } \Delta C_L = \lambda_c \lambda_\beta \lambda_b \qquad (5\text{–}11)$$

The first factor λ_c shown in Fig. 5.8b we have called the flap chord factor, which accounts for the change in lift coefficient caused by effective lengthening (or shortening) of the local wing chord by the presence of flaps. The second factor, λ_β (shown in c) is for flap deflections up to about 90 deg. The third, λ_b (shown in d) is the factor accounting for the amount of the wing span occupied by the total length of the flaps.

When basic data has been produced for a test aerofoil of aspect ratio 6 a crude correction can be made by means of fig. 5.8a. Thus, if a flap increment from tests when $A = 6$ is $(\Delta C_L)_6$, then:

$$(\Delta C_L)_A \approx F_A (\Delta C_L)_6 \qquad (5\text{–}11a)$$

for the case when aspect ratio A is other 6. The factor F_A has been derived from fig. 4.6c.

Selection of flap increases the profile drag of a wing by an increment ΔC_{Do}. This can be calculated in exactly the same way as before, using a different set of factors, as shown in fig. 5.9, which is also based upon ref. 5.2:

$$\text{profile drag increment, } \Delta C_{Do} = \delta_c \delta_\beta \delta_s \qquad (5\text{–}12)$$

The factor, δ_c, is a function of (flap chord/(wing+flap chord)). The next, δ_β is the factor for flap deflection. While δ_s is a factor dependent upon area of (flapped part of wing/total wing area).

Induced drag is increased by ΔC_{Di}, which may be calculated by means of the lift coefficient increment, ΔC_L, inserted in eq (5–13):

$$\text{induced drag increment, } \Delta C_{Di} = (C_L^2/\pi A)[1 + K'(\Delta C_L/C_L)^2] \qquad (5\text{–}13)$$

the terms having their previous meanings. The induced drag factor of the planform, K' (or K) is substantially unaltered by flap, even when there is a local increase in wing chord with flap deflection.

The increase in nose-down pitching moment with flap deflection is shown approximately in table 5–3:

TABLE 5–3

(ref. 5.2)

Type of flap	$\Delta C_{Mac}/\Delta C_L$
Plain and split (wing t/c 0.21 to 0.12)	−0.25 to −0.3
Slotted (single and double NACA)	−0.34

Flap deflection changes the angle of zero lift of a three dimensional wing by an amount:

$$\Delta \alpha_o = -F_f \Delta C_L \qquad (5\text{–}14)$$

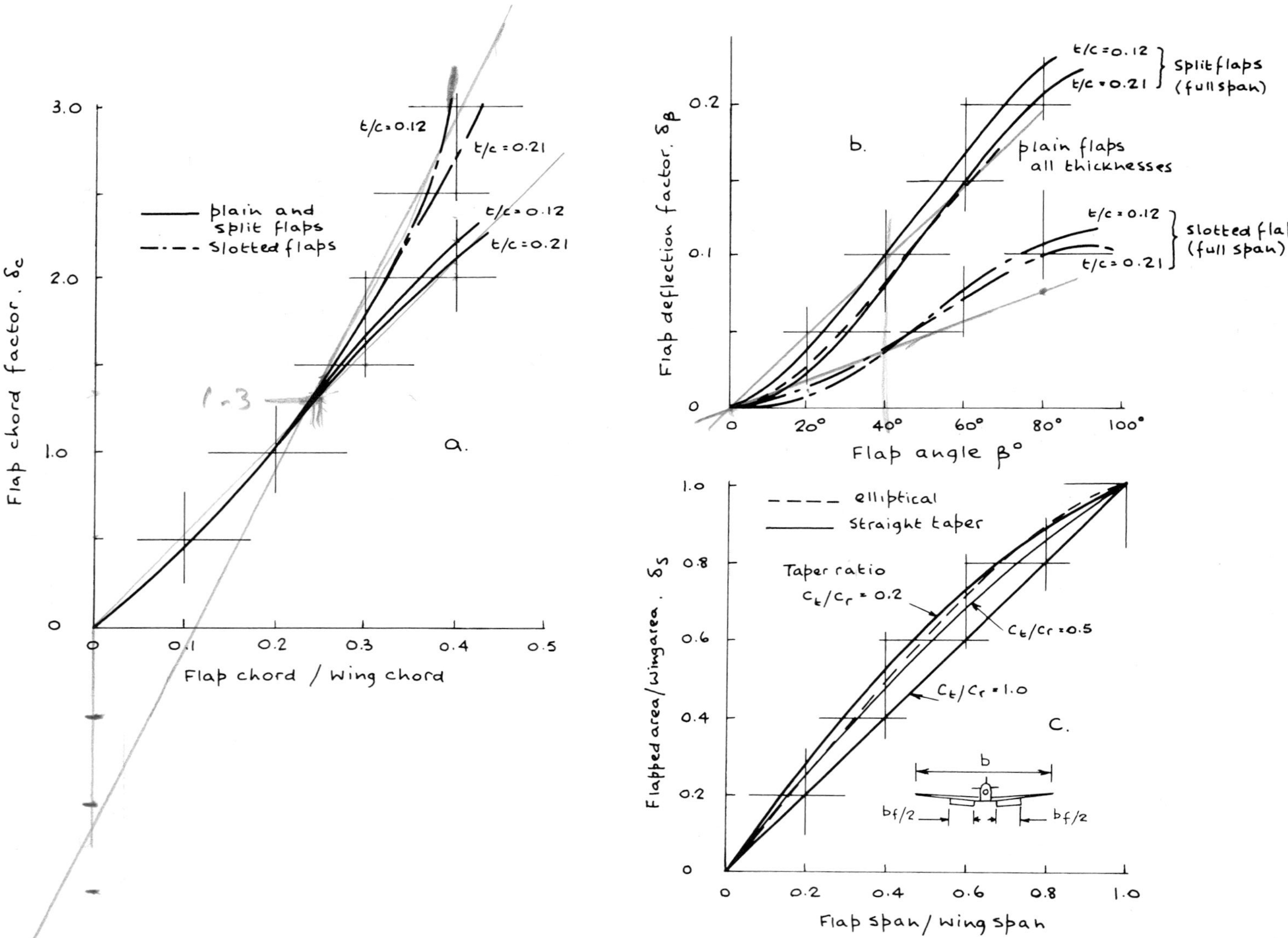

Fig. 5.9   The effect of plain, split and slotted flaps upon wing profile drag coefficient:

$$\triangle C_{Do} = \delta_c\,\delta_\beta\,\delta_s \quad \text{eq (5–12)}$$

Ref. 3.4 provides information upon which fig. 5.10 is based. Taper effects have been ignored in the figure for simplicity. The more tapered the wing, the larger the value of F_f. In the normal range of taper ratios, F_f increases in magnitude by one half of one unit, using part span flaps. (e.g. an untapered wing with $F_f = 5$ would suffer an increase in F_f to 5.5 with tip chord/root chord, $c_t/c_r = 0.2$).
Examination of figs 5.8b and 5.9b, and table 5–3, shows that:

☐ Split flaps are more effective than plain for increasing the lift of thicker sections, and they generate more drag when deflected 45 deg or more.
☐ Slotted flaps generate the most lift at shallow flap angles, but they can be equalled by some combinations of split flap and thick wing section at flap angles greater than about 30 deg. Slotted flaps do not generate as much drag as split and plain flaps.
☐ Slotted flaps decrease lift/drag ratio less than split and plain flaps. Plain flaps

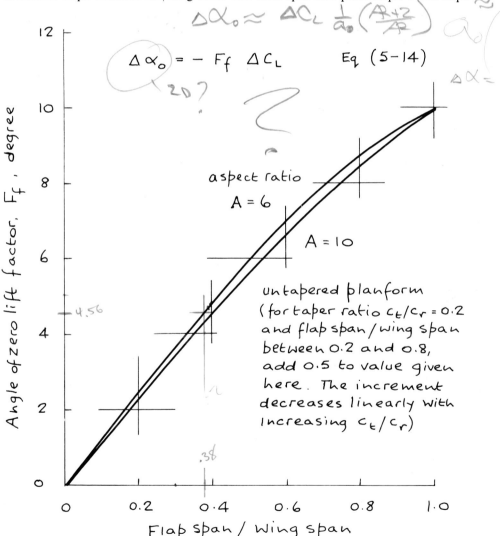

Fig. 5.10 Angle of zero lift factor, flaps down inboard (based upon data in ref. 3.4).

decrease lift/drag ratio most, steepening the glide angle more than the other two.
☐ Slotted flaps generate the most powerful nose-down pitching moments, and they
   therefore require larger, more authoritative elevator surfaces to raise the nose than
   are needed with plain and slotted flaps. Also, the centre of gravity cannot be located
   quite so far forward as with less powerful flaps.

We saw in fig. 5.6 how to draw the three-dimensional wing lift curve, knowing the two-
dimensional values given in data sheets. The flapped wing curve can be constructed in
much the same way, after calculating ΔC_L in eq (5–11), and the change in angle of zero
lift, $\Delta\alpha_o$, in eq (5–14). We must also make two assumptions:

☐ The lift curve for the flapped wing will be parallel to that of the plain wing without
   flaps.
☐ The shape of the curve of the finite wing with flaps, as it peaks towards the stall, is the
   same as that drawn for the two-dimensional wing with split flaps, given in the data
   sheets (e.g. fig. 5.2). The new maximum lift coefficient with flap is given by:

$$\text{flapped } C_{Lmax} = C_{Lmax}(\text{from fig. 5.4}) + \Delta C_L(\text{eq (5–11)}) \qquad (5–15)$$

The same value of ΔC_L is used in eq (5–14), to calculate the change in the angle of zero
lift – which can only be done after deciding how much of the wingspan is to be occupied
by flap (often less than one half).

The lift curve is constructed as shown in fig. 5.11, starting at the new origin: $\alpha_o +
\Delta\alpha_o$. The lift line is drawn parallel to that of the plain three-dimensional wing, to
intercept a line drawn through C_{Lmax} with flap. The top of the new curve is drawn using
the outline of the top of the two-dimensional lift curve with flap.

Knowing the maximum lift coefficient with flap, we may calculate the stall speed,
knowing the wing area; or we may calculate the wing area for a given stalling speed
needed to achieve a defined landing distance, using the formula:

$$S = W/C_{Lmax} q \qquad (5–16)$$

on substituting weight, W, for lift, L, in eq (2–3a). The true airspeed on landing, V, is
tied up in the dynamic pressure term, $q = \frac{1}{2}\rho V^2$.

Fig. 5.11 shows that the angle of attack for C_{Lmax} with flap is less than that of the
unflapped wing. The stall occurs at a shallower angle, and the pilot's view over the nose
is improved.

Ground effect

When an aeroplane flies close to the ground it comes into *ground-effect* at heights less
than half the wingspan. Ground effect is the family name for a number of things caused
when downwash is reduced by the proximity of its surface. As the aeroplane sinks
lower in the flare, the downwash angle, ϵ in eq (4–4), approaches 0 deg (which can only
be achieved with the wing on the ground). As the downwash angle at the wing may be
around 4 deg, the average reduction is one half of this, say 2 deg in practice. Thus, the
angle of attack on landing may be reduced by about 2 deg.

Take-off and landing flap

The above effects reduce the landing attitude, which allows the designer to use a
shorter, lighter landing gear. But the loss of downwash means that the induced drag is
also reduced. The lift/drag ratio improves, the aeroplane floats, lengthening the
theoretical landing distance. Low winged aeroplanes are more prone to floating at low

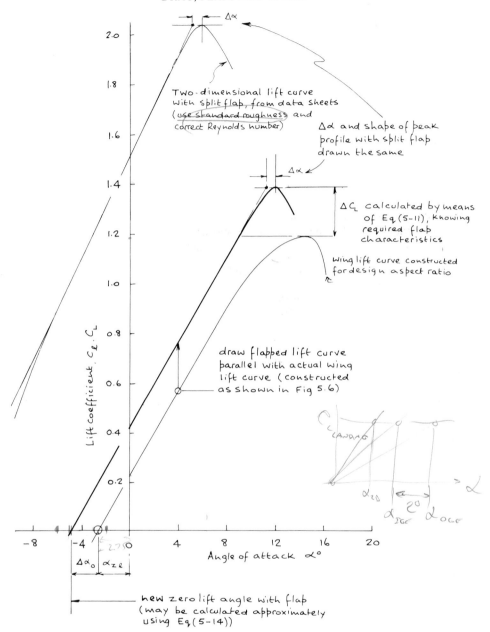

Fig. 5.11 Construction of lift curve for flapped wing, knowing profile of two-dimensional flapped wing curve, lift slope of actual wing and required flap characteristics.

speed than high winged, which can be made to sit down on the ground more positively. For this reason it is wise to arrange for flap to go down to something like 40 deg, increasing form drag so as to kill the float.

☐ The design of the landing gear should be shaped around an angle on touchdown corresponding with 0.9 × stalling angle with flap.

☐ The use of flap on take-off causes many arguments. Slotted flaps generate more lift at shallow angles of deflection than either split or plain. They also generate less drag. On a thick wing a split flap generates less drag than a plain flap at smaller flap angles, but the reverse is true on thinner wing sections. Plain flaps are the least efficient generators of additional lift. Thus, slotted flaps can be useful on take-off because they reduce the load on the landing gear earlier in the run, and their lower drag does not spoil the acceleration too much. Split and plain flaps lift the aircraft earlier, but the additional drag may spoil the acceleration so much that the take-off run is not reduced on a hard surface. On grass or soft soil the reduction in rolling friction by using even plain flaps for take-off, might make the difference between being able to take off, and not getting airborne at all. Under such conditions it often helps to put down a touch of flap.

Wake effects

All aircraft leave behind them a wake with characteristics which cannot be ignored. The thickness and reduction in dynamic pressure in the wake affect the control and stability of the aircraft because of its influence upon the tail surfaces. A tail working within a wake is less efficient, and has to be bigger, than one outside it. In this respect a T-tail has certain aerodynamic advantages over a low-set tail – but it has marked structural disadvantages, as we shall see later.

The position, dimensions and extent of the wake are functions of the circulation strength of the various parts of the horseshoe vortex system, formed by the bound vortex and two trailing tip vortices. They are also dependent upon the distance downstream of the point in question from the bound vortex of the wing, and upon the profile drag coefficient, C_{Do} which is a measure of the energy lost through air being dragged along by the aircraft. Taken together we can visualise a condition of pressure recovery at any point behind an aeroplane – measurable in terms of the ratio of local dynamic pressure to that of the free-stream (which is away from any disturbing effects of the engine(s) and airframe). Thus, a T-tail which is clear of most wake effects might be expected to have an efficiency of 90 per cent, because the dynamic pressure recovery would be about 9/10 of the free-stream value. But a stabiliser set at the back of a fat fuselage might only have an efficiency of 20 or 30 per cent. Generally, tail efficiency is around 0.6 to 0.7 (60 to 70 per cent). These figures mean that the *effective* tail area could be anything from 0.9 to as little as 0.2 to 0.3 times the *geometric* area, depending upon tail efficiency. This means that a tail stabiliser working at the back of a fuselage should be larger in area than one working outside the wake.

Propwash is another factor. The accelerated airflow behind a propeller is destabilising, as we shall see later in chapter 11, so that a stabiliser working in propwash must be larger than one which is clear of it. On the other hand, propwash increases the effectiveness of the elevator, because of the increased dynamic pressure. This means that, for a given area of tailplane-plus-elevator the proportion of the total occupied by the elevator can be less than it would be if the tail was out of the propeller wash. A consequence of this is that the pilot has more elevator control power ON than with power OFF.

The wake resembles a lumpy sheet of vortices following the wing, with local thickening and distortion in the way of the fuselage, nacelles and undercarriage. Its position relative to the plane of the wing depends upon the intensity of the vortex system, measured in terms of the lift coefficient, C_L, which is directly proportional to vortex strength Γ, as shown in eqs (4–10) and (4–13a).

Fig. 4.1b showed that the trailing vortices move inwards behind the wing during readjustment of the air after being displaced radially by the passing volume of the aircraft. Circulation around the bound and trailing vortices causes both of the trailing vortices to be washed downwards through an amount d, at a distance l behind the wing, as measured along the line of flight. Reason concludes that the wake starts at the trailing edge of the wing. Lifting line theory assumes that it starts at the bound vortex, located more or less at the $1/4$ chord of the wing. Either way the difference between each view is small, while the sheet of shed vortices curves downwards, with the concave surface upwards – its radius of curvature increasing downstream as the sheet flattens out when seen in elevation. The wake can be assumed to be nearly flat in a spanwise direction, across the middle third of the wing.

Wake displacement, d, is usually measured in terms of wing semispan (s or $b/2$) as d/b. This is a function of distance l downstream, so that we may also use the measure l/b along the line of flight to define the position of the wake in chords behind the wing. As we also need C_L to complete the picture, it may be introduced as follows:

$$\text{wake displacement factor, } d/sC_L = l/s$$

or,

$$2d/bC_L = 2l/b \qquad (5\text{–}17)$$

Wake factor curves are given by different sources, those of the Royal Aeronautical Society in the ESDU data sheets (Appendix A, Item 05.01.01) as ratios of the semispan, s. Hoerner, on the other hand uses wingspan b for his ratios (ref. 4.3), but this does not alter the shape of the curves, only the numbers for the ratios (by a factor of 2 on each side).

We assume that as wings, canards and tails are usually located between 2 and 4 chords apart, the following equations may be used for determining wake characteristics. Further, because we work in multiples of wing chord, we shall transform eq (5–17) into $d/\bar{c}$ and $l/\bar{c}$, by means of eq (2–4), where $\bar{c}$ is the SMC of the wing, such that s can be written $(A/2)\bar{c}$.

Fig. 5.12 shows the dimensions and pressure profiles of the wake shed by a wing operating at $C_L = 1.0$, over the middle third of the span. The wing has a taper ratio of $\lambda = 1/2$, and the vortices drift downwards at $1/4$ the final downwash velocity (ref. 4.3). There is no completely reliable theoretical solution which enables us to draw the wake accurately for design purposes. Wind tunnel tests are needed to check calculations and assumptions. However, the ESDU data sheet already mentioned (Appendix A) is a most useful guide.

The mean line of the wake leaves the zero lift line of the section tangentially. For the wing of taper ratio $1/2$, displacement of the wake below the $1/4$ chord point of the wing, as measured normal to the flight path is given in terms of wingspan:

$$\text{displacement ratio } d/b \text{ (for } \lambda = 1/2) = -(C_L/3\sqrt{A})\,l/b - 0.12/A \qquad (5\text{–}18)$$

or,

$$d/\bar{c} = -(C_L/3\sqrt{A})\,l/\bar{c} - 0.12 \qquad (5\text{–}19)$$

The path of the wake shed from a parallel chord wing is slightly less steep, because the circulation over the middle third of the wing is less intense. Therefore:

$$\text{displacement ratio, } d/b \text{ (for } \lambda = 1) = -(C_L/4\sqrt{A})\,l/b - 0.12A \qquad (5\text{–}20)$$

or,

$$d/\bar{c} = -(C_L/4\sqrt{A})\,l/\bar{c} - 0.12 \qquad (5\text{–}21)$$

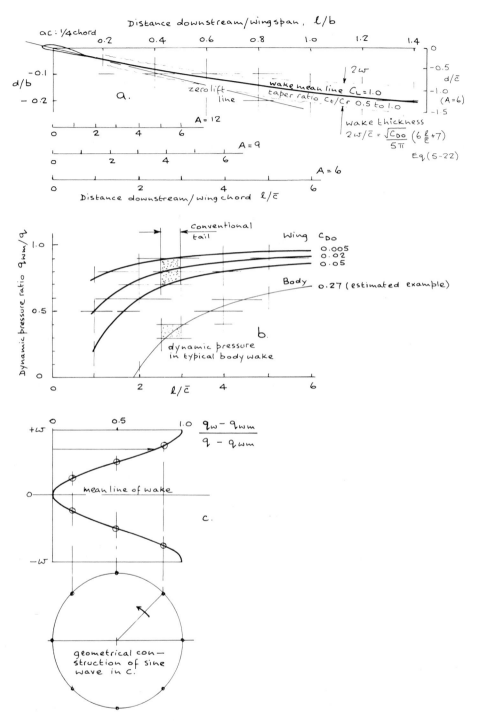

Fig. 5.12   Characteristics of wake behind a wing of a given aspect ratio and drag coefficient. (a) Average wake over middle ⅓ span *b*. (b) Dynamic pressure ratio on meanline q_{wm} relative to free stream, q. (c) Dynamic pressure distribution through depth of wake.

Fig. 5.12b shows the thickness of the wake, and the distribution of dynamic pressure along the length of its mean line, from the top of the wake to the bottom. The dynamic pressure within the wake is given in terms of q_{wm}/q, so that we have a direct indication of pressure recovery at any point.

If wake thickness is $2w$ and the profile drag coefficient of the wing is C_{Do}, then:

$$\text{wake thickness ratio, } 2w/\bar{c} = [\sqrt{(C_{Do})}/5\pi](6(l/\bar{c})+7) \qquad (5\text{--}22)$$
$$\text{dynamic pressure ratio, } q_{wm}/q = 1 - (3.6\sqrt{C_{Do}})/(l/\bar{c}) \qquad (5\text{--}23)$$

Dynamic pressure distribution through the wake over a distance $2w$ can be constructed as shown in fig. 5.12c, which is a portion of a sine wave.

The efficiency of a stabiliser is given in terms of the pressure recovery ratio, in effect the dynamic pressure at the tail to that available to the wing:

$$\text{stabiliser efficiency, } \eta_s = q_{ws}/q \qquad (5\text{--}24)$$

where q_{ws} is the dynamic pressure at the leading edge of the tail. η_s has values around 0.6 to 0.7 for a normal tail (and 0.9 for a T-tail, as we mentioned earlier). Ahead of the wing $q_{ws}/q \rightarrow 1.0$ and $\eta_s \rightarrow 100$ per cent. *power off!*

Although fig. 5.12 and the associated equations apply to wing wake, bodies also behave like aerofoil surfaces. Plate 5.1 shows Philip Meeson's *Marlboro Pitts Special* in knife-flight, during which the fuselage and propeller provide all of the lift. The angle of attack of the fuselage is about 25 deg, at which it is acting like a low aspect ratio aerofoil (see fig. 4.7), but the drag is so high that the aeroplane is decelerating quite rapidly. Substituting body length for wing chord, $\bar{c}$, in eqs (5–22) and (5–23), the wake thickness at the tail is about $1/3 \times$ length of the fuselage, and the pressure recovery is less than 0.4. It is not surprising that the drag is high, and we should also expect the starboard tailplane and elevator (upwards in the photograph) to be doing less than one half their normal work.

One of the many accidents which happened to the advanced family of *Gee Bee* racers in the early 1930s is said to have been caused by blanketing of one side of the tail of the *R–2* on landing (ref. 5.3). *Gee Bees* had exceptionally fat fuselages, to fair their large radial engines and to achieve low drag (see optimum thickness ratio v Reynolds number, in fig. 3.4). The aircraft appears to have had no flaps. The fuselage thickness ratio (in plan view) was about 0.29, and the aeroplane was short-coupled, making it quick-reacting to rudder. The pilot, Mae Haizlip, apparently sideslipped to kill airspeed when just above the ground and the aeroplane cartwheeled following the start of a snap (flick) roll to the left, which is said to have been assisted by half of the tail (and a large part of one wing?) being blanketed. All propeller-driven aeroplanes pitch nose-up or down, depending upon the direction of sideslip and propeller rotation (see P-factor in chapter 7); with a large right-handed propeller this could have been a contributory factor in causing the left wing drop.

Downwash

The angle of downwash does not change at the same rate as a change in angle of attack, and we need to be able to calculate the ratio $d\epsilon/dC_L$, or $d\epsilon/d\alpha$. Later, in chapter 11, we shall see that $(1 - d\epsilon/d\alpha)$ is of fundamental importance in longitudinal stability calculations. The rate of change of downwash angle with wing angle of attack is around $\frac{1}{2}$ at the tail. As an approximation, knowing that the angle of downwash at the wing is:

$$\epsilon \text{ deg} = 57.3 \ C_L/\pi A = 18.24 \ C_L/A \qquad \text{from eq (4–4b)}$$

Plate 5-1 An 'energetic hooligan of an aeroplane': the *Pitts S-1S Special* in knife flight with body angle of attack around 25 deg. (*Philip Meeson, UK*)

while at the tail ϵ is nearly double this value (actually, it is not double until the distance downstream is infinity). This enables us to write:

$$\mathrm{d}\epsilon/\mathrm{d}\alpha \text{ at the tail is approximately} = 2(\mathrm{d}\epsilon/\mathrm{d}C_L)(\mathrm{d}C_L/\mathrm{d}\alpha) \approx 2\mathrm{d}\epsilon/\mathrm{d}\alpha$$

and, as $dC_L/d\alpha = a$, the lift slope of the wing, per deg.:

$$d\epsilon/d\alpha \approx 2(18.24/A)a = 36.5\, a/A \tag{5-25}$$

In practice the average value of $d\epsilon/d\alpha$ at the tail is:

$$d\epsilon/d\alpha = 35\, a/A \text{ for a monoplane} \qquad \text{eq (4-26)}$$
$$= 55\, a/A \text{ for a biplane} \qquad \text{eq (4-27)}$$

Alternatively, if we look back to eq (5–5), in which $a = a_o f_w A/(A + 2)$, while knowing that $a_o \approx 0.11/\mathrm{deg}$, we may substitute in eq (5–25):

$$d\epsilon/d\alpha = 36.5 \times 0.11 \,[f_w A/(A + 2)]/A$$
$$\approx 4f_w/(A + 2) \tag{5-25a}$$

A more detailed expression may be derived from ref. 3.5, in which

$$d\epsilon/d\alpha = 20(a\lambda^{0.3}/A^{0.725})(3\bar{c}/l)^{0.25} \tag{5-26}$$

in which a is the actual lift slope of the wing, λ is the taper ratio (use $\frac{2}{3}$ when the wing is elliptical), A is aspect ratio, $\bar{c}$ is the wing SMC and l is the distance of the point in question downstream of the $\frac{1}{4}$ chord of the wing. Here, we shall use l_s in place of l as the distance between wing and tail $\frac{1}{4}$ chords, when making calculations of longitudinal stability.

If the tail is mounted more than $\pm0.5\bar{c}$ vertically from the centre line of the wake, use a constant of 18 instead of 20 in eq (5–26) (ref. 3.5).

Again, the ESDU data sheets in appendix A are an excellent source of guidance in

Plate 5–2 *Gee Bee R–2* racer (1932) with a barrel-like fuselage and a relatively small-span tailplane. (*TC Warren via Charles A Mendenhall, USA*)

these matters – but be careful. Here, taper ratio, λ, is defined as tip chord/root chord, so that it is conventionally less than 1.

For most aeroplanes the lift slope of the wing is about 0.085/deg for aspect ratios between 6 and 9; and the planform factor $f_w \approx 1.0$. This means that the average rate of change of downwash angle at the tail with wing angle of attack is between $\frac{1}{3}$ and $\frac{1}{2}$ and as an aircraft pitches nose up the tail comes down twice to three times as fast as the wake can get out of the way. Thus, at low speeds (and the large angles of attack achieved when manoeuvring) the tail may be increasingly affected by the wake. Of course, a fat 'draggy' fuselage with poor wing-fuselage junctions increases the profile drag coefficient C_{Do}, making the tail (stabiliser) efficiency factor, η_s, much less than it need be.

The important parameter is the height of the tailplane, $\pm h$, above or below the mean line of the wake. This can be treated in exactly the same way as the wake displacement ratio, by expressing it in terms of wingspan or chord:

$$\pm h/s = \pm 2h/A\bar{c} \qquad (5\text{-}27a)$$

or,
$$\pm h/b = \pm h/A\bar{c} \qquad (5\text{-}27b)$$

Fig. 5.13 shows fairly average values of $d\epsilon/d\alpha$ for different ratios of $h/s = 2h/b$ for a parallel chord wing of aspect ratio 6. To adjust for other aspect ratios multiply $d\epsilon/d\alpha$ by a factor $6/A$. To adjust for other taper ratios multiply by a factor which varies linearly from 1.0 when taper ratio $\lambda = c_t/c_r = 1$, to 1.7 when $\lambda = 0$. Thus, for taper ratio 0.5 the value of $d\epsilon/d\alpha$ measured from fig. 5.13b should be multiplied by 1.35 (i.e. 1.7/2).

Figs. 5.13c and d show an approximate solution for upwash ahead of a wing at a foreplane which is in effect a 'mirror image' of the tailplane reflected about the normal axis through the aerodynamic centre of the wing. The object is to calculate upwash from knowledge of the downwash at a tailplane (every source examined by the author has given tailplane data, and nothing for foreplanes). Thus having calculated $d\epsilon/d\alpha$ for the tail (let us call it $d\epsilon_t/d\alpha$) we may write for the foreplane rate of change of upwash angle with wing angle of attack:

$$d\epsilon_f/d\alpha = (\epsilon_f/\epsilon_t)(d\epsilon_t/d\alpha) \qquad (5\text{-}28)$$

Knowing that $d\epsilon_t/d\alpha$ is identical to the term $d\epsilon/d\alpha$ we may use values calculated by eqs (5-25), (5-25a) or (5-26) – or use the carpet in fig. 5.13b, with appropriate adjustments for aspect ratio and taper ratio of the wing. The ϵ_f/ϵ_t term in fig. 5.13(d) has been calculated for wing aspect ratio = 6. For other aspect ratios the values must be multiplied by a factor $6/A$. Decreasing wing taper ratio, which increases the wing chord inboard, causes the same increase in ϵ_f/ϵ_t as we have seen above, i.e., it must be multiplied by a factor which increases linearly from 1.0 when $\lambda = 1$, to 1.7 when $\lambda = 0$.

In the absence of wind tunnel results intuitive assumptions must be made about the effects of bumps and distortions of the downwash in the wake, caused by fuselage and nacelles. We saw earlier in chapter 4 how a bite, or shortening of the wing chord near the root can reduce $d\epsilon/d\alpha$ by around 20 per cent. Clearly, the actual reduction depends upon the amount by which the wing chord and, hence, strength of circulation at the root is reduced. If a reduction in taper ratio to 0 causes the length of the root chord to be doubled (for a given wing area), and this is accompanied by a 70 per cent increase in $d\epsilon/d\alpha$ seen above, a reduction of 20 per cent in $d\epsilon/d\alpha$ corresponds with a reduction in

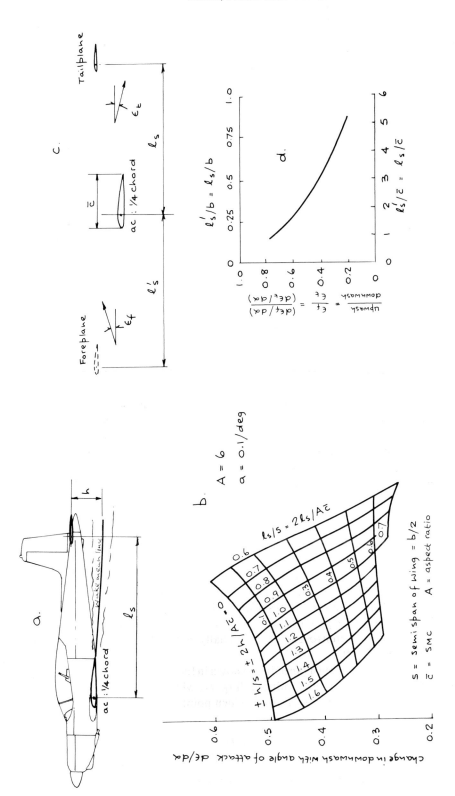

Fig. 5.13 a and b   A plot of typical, average rate of change of downwash angle with angle of attack, for a tailplane and parallel chord wing (*see also* Appendix A item 80020). *See* text for ways of handling other aspect and taper ratios. c and d enable upwash ahead of the wing to be calculated for a foreplane mirror image of a tailplane, knowing downwash at the tail.

wing root chord of about 0.25 to 0.3.

Similar reasoning can be applied to body effects. The lift of a fuselage is roughly proportional to the length, area and aspect ratio of that part of the body lying ahead of the wing (*see* chapter 11 and fig. 11.14). This data may then be used to estimate a lift slope for the fuselage, from fig. 4.6c. Downward displacement of the body wake compared with that of the wing wake will then be in the ratio of *lift slope of the body/lift slope of the wing*, resulting in a large local reduction in $d\epsilon/d\alpha$. Sometimes $d\epsilon/d\alpha$ may even change sign. It seems reasonable with such coarse guesswork to substitute body C_{Dp} for wing profile drag coefficient, C_{Do}, replacing $l_s/\bar{c}$ by the ratio $l_s/body\ length$. Much depends upon the shape and area distribution of a body, and it is probable that marked distortions and changes in $d\epsilon/d\alpha$, with serious loss of pressure recovery at the tail may occur over portions of tailspan equal to the width of the fuselage and any nacelles.

The next step is to look at ways of calculating parasite drag of various parts of an aeroplane, not only to enable us to estimate performance and power required, but to calculate parasite drag coefficient C_{Dp}, which is used above.

Estimating parasite drag (subsonic speeds)

Looking back to eq (5–9) and fig. 5.7, the profile drag coefficient is nearly constant, while the induced drag coefficient is a variable with (lift coefficient)². Extending the idea to the whole aeroplane, the total drag coefficient:

$$C_D = C_{Dp} + K'C_L^2/\pi A \qquad K' = \frac{1}{e} \qquad (5\text{--}29)$$

where C_{Dp} is the parasite drag coefficient, including the profile drag of the wing. Part of C_{Dp} varies with lift coefficient, as we saw in eq (5–8) for the wing. But this can be swept up into the induced part of the total drag equation, by the induced drag factor, K', fig. 5.14(b).

Parasite drag is estimated by adding together individual drags of different bits of the aeroplane in contact with the air. The sum is then factored by an amount varying from about 1.1 for a sailplane to even 1.4 to 1.7 for piston-engined aeroplanes, to account for interference, junctions, aerials, de-icer boots, and all of the paraphernalia of avionic 'bolt-on goodies' offered by manufacturers. The bulk of such drag is caused by bodies, struts, wires, landing gear, powerplant and cooling, in addition to interference and the rest mentioned above. However, we must also include leakage drag: caused by local flows between flap, wing, tail and control surfaces. There is also drag caused by leakage and location of outlets for the pressurisation system. Finally, there is trim drag caused by deflection of the various control surfaces, especially that caused in engine-out flight with a multi-engined aircaft.

Total drag can be drawn against (speed)² as shown in fig. 5.15, as the sum of parasite drag, D_p, which varies with V^2, and induced drag, D_i, which varies with $1/V^2$. Total drag is a minimum where both curves cross, which point marks maximum lift/drag ratio, $(L/D)_{max}$.

Thus, $D_{min} = 2\ D_p = 2\ D_i$

i.e. $C_{Dmin} = 2\ C_{Dp} = 2\ K'C_L^2/\pi A \qquad (5\text{--}30)$

The condition for maximum lift/drag ratio is marked in fig. 5.14b. The parasite drag

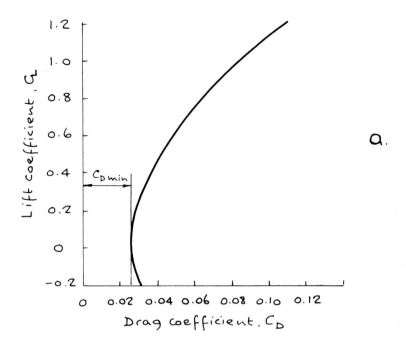

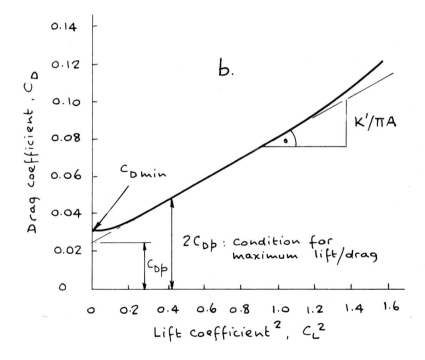

Fig. 5.14a Typical drag polar for whole aeroplane. b Treatment of total drag by parabolic approximation (i.e., use of $C_L{}^2$).

coefficient can be calculated in terms of equivalent parasite frontal areas, or wetted area of airframe, in the following ways.

Parasite (equivalent) area

Parasite drag of the aeroplane is made up of form drag components due to shape, and frictional components due to surface area and condition, in precisely the same way as shown for the wing in eq (2–7), so that we may write:

$$\text{parasite drag, } D_p = D_{form} + D_{fric}, \text{ of the whole} \tag{5–31}$$
$$= (C_{Dform} + C_{Dfric})qS = C_{Do}qS \tag{5–31a}$$

Although it is convenient to express an aerodynamic force in terms of a *coefficient* $\times$ *dynamic pressure* $\times$ *wing area*, this is not entirely satisfactory when dealing with drag from different sources. Instead we resort to another form of drag equation:

$$D_p = C_{D\pi} A_\pi q \tag{5–32}$$

Here, $C_{D\pi}$ is a coefficient based upon a more relevant area, A_π, which may be frontal or cross sectional area, in the case of form drag, and wetted area for drag caused by friction. If we rearrange this equation:

$$D_p/q = C_{D\pi} A_\pi = C_{Dp}S \tag{5–33}$$

it has dimensions of area, ft² or m², and we call the right hand side of the equation *parasite drag area*. There are three different ways of handling drag area, the first two by equating drag to that of surfaces normal to the flow, the third by means of wetted area.

Flat plate area. Here parasite drag is equated to the area of a flat plate, normal to the airflow, with air leaking around its edges, suction behind it and a turbulent wake. Such a plate has a drag coefficient of 1.28 times the force/unit area, q, of the free stream. If the flat plate has an area A_p:

$$\text{flat plate drag area, } C_{D\pi} A_\pi = D_p/q = 1.28 \, A_p \tag{5–34}$$

Equivalent parasite area. In this case a simpler expression is obtained by taking a hypothetical area of surface normal to the flow, which suffers no increase of drag due to leakage around its edges. The force on it is due to dynamic pressure alone, so that:

$$\text{equivalent parasite area} = D_p/q = f \tag{5–35}$$
because
$$C_{D\pi} = D_p/qf = 1.$$

Wetted area. When a shape is fine and well streamlined, parasite drag is caused mainly by skin friction acting upon wetted area, A_w. Fig. 5.16 shows the approximate ratios of wetted area to wing area for different arrangements of aircraft. In this case:

$$\text{drag area} = C_{D\pi} A_\pi = D_p/q = C_{Dfric}A_w \tag{5–36}$$

In each case the drag area is the same, so that:

$$D_p/q = C_{D\pi}A_\pi = 1.28 \, A_p = f = C_{Dfric}A_w = C_{Dp}S \tag{5–37}$$

This last equation enables us to work out the effect of different parts of an aircraft upon total drag, by calculating the drag area of any part, $C_{D\pi} A_\pi$, and adding all together:

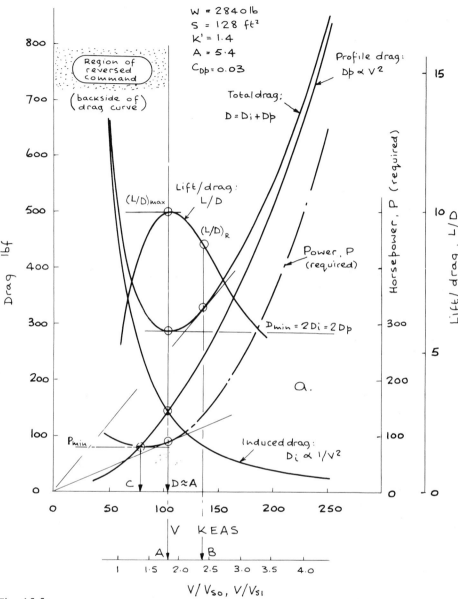

Fig. 15.5a

A = Speed for minimum total drag and, hence, best lift/drag.

   = $(L/D)_{max}$: best endurance speed for a jet aeroplane, and speed for best glide.

B = Best range speed, corresponding with $(L/D)_R$ and maximum speed/drag, V/D.

   ≈ 0.94 (L/D) max for a jet (here $(L/D)_R ≈ 0.9 (L/D)_{max}$ for piston propeller).

   ≈ 1.32 Vimd, the EAS for minimum drag.

C = Speed for minimum power: best piston-propeller endurance.

   = Vimp ≈ 0.76 Vimd, eq (6–27).

D = Best range speed for piston-propeller, corresponding with maximum speed/
   power, (V/P). As fuel consumption of a piston engine is roughly proportional to
   power, best range occurs at (max speed/unit fuel consumed). This speed is close to
   that for $(L/D)_{max}$ at point A.

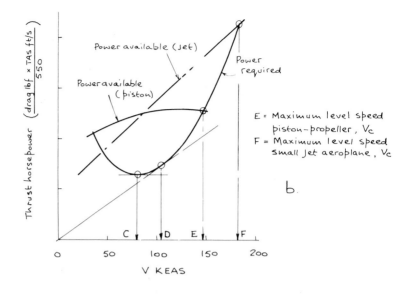

Power available (Jet)

Power available (piston)

Power required

E = Maximum level speed
piston-propeller, V_c
F = Maximum level speed
small Jet aeroplane, V_c

b.

Thrust horsepower ($\frac{drag\ lbf \times TAS\ ft/s}{550}$)

V KEAS

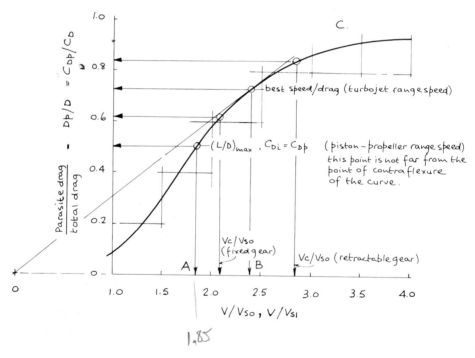

$Dp/D = C_{DP}/C_D$

Parasite drag / total drag

best speed/drag (turbojet range speed)

$(L/D)_{max}$, $C_{Di} = C_{Dp}$ (piston-propeller range speed)
this point is not far from the
point of contraflexure
of the curve.

V_c/V_{so} (fixed gear)

V_c/V_{so} (retractable gear)

V/V_{so}, V/V_{si}

1.85

Fig. 5.15b and c   Variation of drag, lift/drag and power with airspeed at constant lift
and weight. c may be for either speed ratio. The stall speeds clean and with flap are
close together with light aeroplanes.

$$\text{basic parasite area,} \quad f_b = f_1 + f_2 + f_3 + \ldots + f_n \tag{5-38}$$

Table 5–4 shows the main parts of aircraft contributing to total drag, together with drag coefficient, $C_{D\pi}$, and the area, A_π, upon which it is based. The values are fairly crude and conservative, because Reynolds number has been neglected. Frontal area, A_c, has been used for bodies contributing mainly form drag. Wetted area, A_w, is used for surfaces which generate mainly frictional drag. This is quoted alongside planform area, S and S_s or S_f, for wing, stabiliser, fin and rudder respectively.

Calculation of wetted area can be eased somewhat by the method shown in table 5–5, which shows the basic shapes into which bodies can be broken and approximated. These are a box or prism, a paraboloid, and a cone. Two factors are introduced: a form factor in elevation, m, which gives the ratio of the area of the actual shape in elevation to the area of a box, having the same length, L, and depth (or diameter), D. The latter is calculated as the square root of the maximum area of cross section, i.e., frontal area:

$$D = \sqrt{A_c} \tag{5-39}$$

The second is a section form factor, p, which gives the ratio of the circumference of the maximum cross section to the circumference of a circle. The method relies upon the relationship:

$$\text{wetted area,} \quad A_w = \pi \times \text{average area in elevation}$$
$$= \pi(LD)mp \tag{5-40}$$

Thus, in the case of a circular cylinder of length L and diameter D, form factors m and p both equal 1 and the wetted area is πLD.

Table 5–6 shows estimates of wetted area for several body shapes, and one typical aerofoil surface. The latter relies upon the formula:

$$\text{wetted area (top plus bottom),} \quad A_w = (2 + t/3c) \, S_{net} \tag{5-41}$$

where t/c is the thickness ratio of the root section, and S_{net} the planform area outside the line of the body.

When basic parasite area, f_b, has been calculated in the manner of eq (5–38), its sum should be factored by an appropriate value of n for the type of landing gear fitted. Values of n are listed at the bottom of table 5–4. About 5 per cent should then be added for interference, and another 5 per cent for aerials, pitot mast and protuberances on small aeroplanes. Engine cooling can cause drag through inefficient flows and badly fitting baffles, increasing basic parasite area by up to 30 per cent. A further drag increment is often associated with unfavourable cowl lines behind the propeller disc. Extensions to propeller shafts can help to sweeten cowl lines. Control gaps and leaks, badly fitting doors, fairings and panels can add another 5 per cent. Trim drag adds another indeterminate and variable increment – at most, say, another 5 per cent, depending upon centre of gravity, and asymmetry.
All of these increments are accounted for by modifying eq (5–38):

$$\text{total equivalent parasite area,} \quad f = C_{Dp}S$$
$$= f_b(n + 0.05 + 0.05 + 0.3 + 0.05) \tag{5-38a}$$

Thus, an inefficient propeller installation, coupled with a fixed, unfaired undercarriage might add as much as 95 per cent to parasite drag, and half as much to total drag at the speed for best lift/drag ratio. The least amount of interference might be about 5 per cent on parasite drag, say 3 per cent on the total.

When an aeroplane is very clean and highly streamlined, parasite drag may be attributed to skin friction drag, form drag being neglected. For this we need to work out wetted area, as shown in Fig. 5.16.

Fig. 5.17 shows equivalent parasite area as a function of skin friction drag coefficient, C_{Dfric}, and wetted area, A_w. A number of aircraft results have been marked. These show that piston-propeller aeroplanes have more parasite area than jets, and this is because of the turbulent effects of propwash. For a clean jet aeroplane, tunnel tests show average C_{Dfric} to be 0.003 to 0.0033; for a clean pusher 0.004 to 0.005; for a large propeller driven aeroplane with four engines, friction coefficient increases about 33 per cent, to approximately 0.004 to 0.0044 (ref. 4.13), because at higher Reynolds numbers applying to larger aeroplanes, C_{Dfric} is lower, being roughly 0.003 for wings, 0.0024 for fuselages, 0.006 for nacelles, and 0.0025 for tail surfaces, with 5 per cent for interference. Smaller aircraft working at lower Reynolds numbers may have values of ⅔ as much again. The reason for this can be deduced from fig. 3.9b, which shows the way in which C_{Dfric} rises with decreasing Reynolds number.

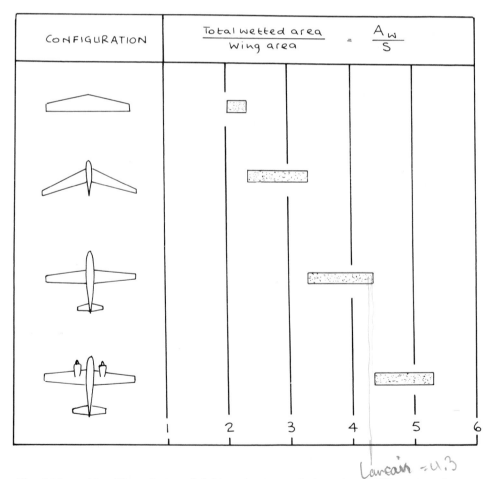

Fig. 5.16a and b   Wetted area of airframe in terms of wing area of different configurations. b shows a number of estimates.

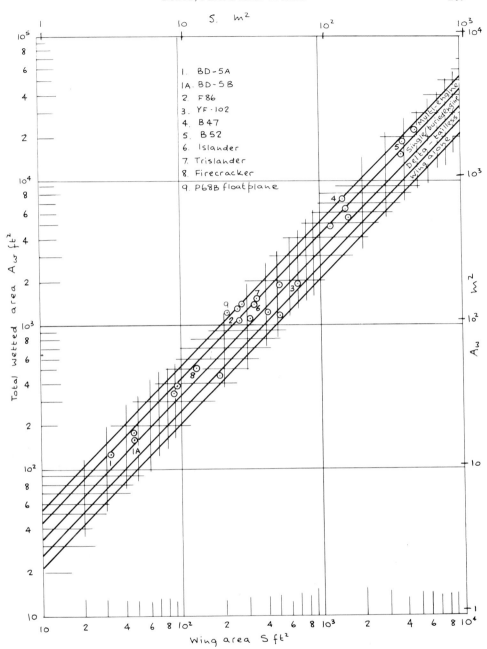

Fig. 5.16b.

Calculating the lift/drag ratio

Fig. 5.15 shows the importance of various points on the total drag and power curves, and the part played in theory by lift/drag ratio in range, endurance and condition for

TABLE 5.4 Drag estimation

Part	Description	$C_{D\pi}$	Area A_π upon which $C_{D\pi}$ is based
	Wing, t/c 0.1 to 0.2	Cantilever 0.005 to 0.009 braced 0.006 to 0.011	S, planform
		0.0025 to 0.005	A_w, wetted
	Stabiliser, t/c 0.08 to 0.12	cantilever wing values braced times 1.3	S_s, S_f, planform A_w, wetted
	Streamlined bodies (fineness ≈ 6/1) no excrecences	▨ 0.055 ◍ 0.045	A_c, frontal
		0.1 to 0.2	A_c, frontal
		0.07 to 0.12	A_c, frontal
	Tadpole, A_w reduced over length ℓ, so as to keep $f = C_{Dfric} A_w$ constant from nose to tail		A_w, wetted
	Nacelles, propeller	above wing 0.2 below wing 0.06	A_c, frontal
	Jet	0.05 to 0.07	A_c, frontal
	Wing tanks. Stores	0.2 to 0.25	A_c, frontal
		0.06	A_c, frontal
	Control, 50 percent span deflected 30°	0.02 to 0.03	S, planform
	Struts	0.12 to 0.2	A_c, frontal
	Bracing	0.22	A_c, frontal
	Hull	0.11 to 0.15	A_c, frontal
	Float	0.15 to 0.2	A_c, frontal
	Parachute	1.33	A_c, inflated diameter

	Arrangement		Factor η	
	Fixed tailgear,	unfaired	1.3	Multiply the sum
		faired	1.2	of the above drag
	Fixed nosegear	unfaired	1.35	areas by the
		faired	1.25	landing gear
	Retracting into	fuselage	1.08	factors shown
		nacelles	1.03	for each type
		wings	1.0	of arrangement

best glide. The values with which we are most concerned are $(L/D)_{max}$ for piston-engined aeroplanes, wing aspect ratio and the corresponding range speed. For a jet aeroplane, the equivalent range lift/drag ratio is $(L/D)_R$. The condition for minimum total drag and $(L/D)_{max}$ is:

$$C_D = 2K'C_L^2/\pi A = 2C_{Dp} \tag{5-30}$$
$$\text{giving: } C_L = \sqrt{[C_{Dp}\pi(A/K')]} \tag{5-42}$$
$$\text{and: } V = 1.06\sqrt{(W/\rho S)}\ \sqrt[4]{(K'/C_{Dp}A)}\ \text{KTAS} \tag{5-43}$$

in FPSR units, V being the true airspeed in ft/s. When we need equivalent airspeed in knots:

$$V_i = 12.9\sqrt{W/S}\ \sqrt[4]{(K'/C_{Dp}A)}\ \text{KEAS} \tag{5-44}$$

the remainder being in FPSR units.

It follows from the combination of eqs (5–30) and (5–42) that:

$$(L/D)_{max} = \tfrac{1}{2}C_L/C_{Dp} = \tfrac{1}{2}\sqrt{(\pi A/K'C_{Dp})}$$
$$\approx 8/9\sqrt{(A/K'C_{Dp})}\ \text{(piston and probably turboprop)} \tag{5-45a}$$

The lift/drag ratio for range of a jet aeroplane is about 0.94 of this:

$$(L/D)_R \approx 5/6\sqrt{(A/K'C_{Dp})}\ \text{(jet)} \tag{5-45b}$$

Transposing the equations in (5–45) for design aspect ratio needed to produce a given lift/drag ratio:

TABLE 5.5

Calculation of wetted area

Basic Shape	Form factor in elevation m	Form factor of section p	Wetted area (tangential to flow) $A_w = \pi m p L D$
Elevation:			See Eq (5-40):
rectangle, L, D, flow	1.0	—	$\pi p L D$
ogive, D, flow	$2/3 = 0.66\cdot$	—	$2/3\,\pi p L D$
triangle, D, flow	$1/2 = 0.5$	—	$\tfrac{1}{2}\pi p L D$
Section:			
circle, D	—	1.0	—
square, D	—	$4/\pi = 1.275$	—

$$A \approx (4/\pi) \, [K'C_{Dp}(L/D)^2_{max}] \text{ (piston and probably turboprop)} \quad (5\text{--}46a)$$

and:
$$A \approx (9/2\pi) \, [K'C_{Dp}(L/D)^2_R] \text{ (jet)} \quad (5\text{--}46b)$$

Of course, the success of any estimate depends upon the choice of values used in the calculations. Generally, most tend to err on the optimistic side. Parasite drag coefficient is very sensitive in this respect, and so is the induced drag factor. Our values are intended to be pessimistic.

TABLE 5.6

Wetted areas of components

Component	Approximate wetted area A_w
	See also Fig 14.14 for body estimates $A_w \approx 2.4 \text{ to } 2.5 \; DL$ $D = \sqrt{A_c} \qquad$ Eq. (5-39) $D/L = 0.15 \text{ to } 0.2 \quad$ Eq. (9-2)
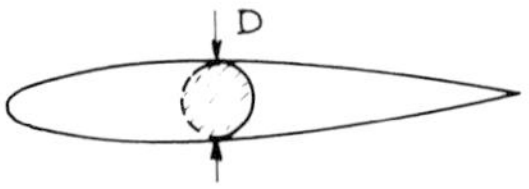	$A_w \approx 2 \, DL$
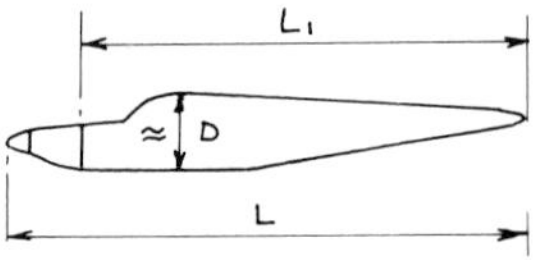	Conical tail: $A_w \approx 2.3 \, DL \quad$ overall $\approx 2.4 \, DL_1 \quad$ aft of firewall
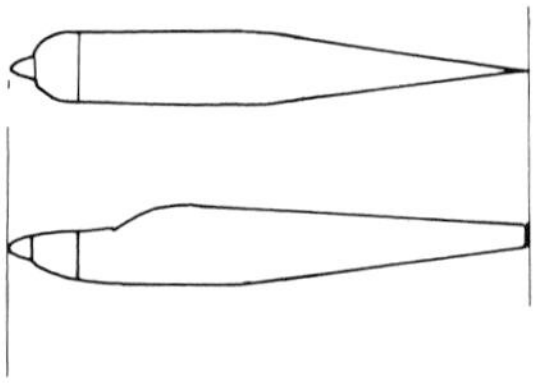	Chisel tail: $A_w \approx 2.7 \, DL \quad$ overall $\approx 2.85 \, DL_1 \quad$ aft of firewall
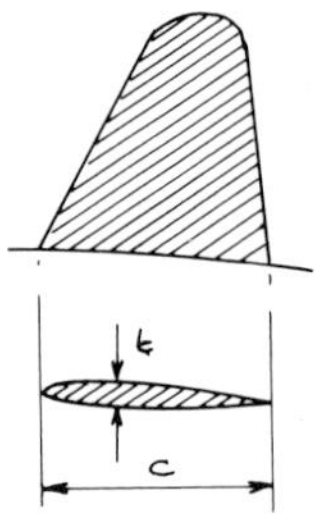	$S_{net} = \text{planform area outside body}$ $t/c = \text{thickness ratio of section}$ $A_w = (2 + (t/c)/3) \, S_{net}$ $= \text{Eq. (5-41)}$ For example, a tail surface with $t/c = 12$ percent would have a wetted area $2.04 \, S_{net}$

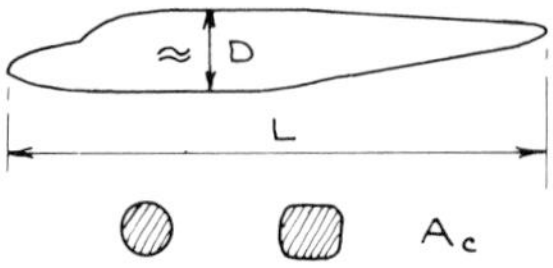

$$C_{Do} = C_{dfric} * \frac{A_{wet}}{S_w}$$

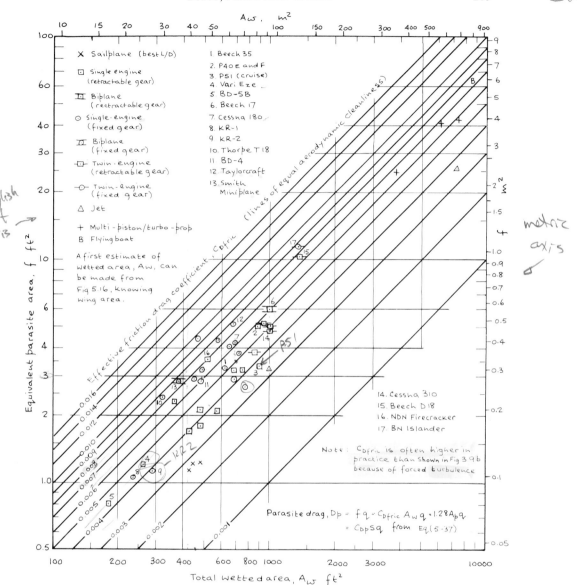

Fig. 5.17   Estimates of parasite drag and equivalent parasite area, *f*, as a function of skin friction drag coefficient and wetted area. (Some points are based upon ref. 5.4).

Table 5–7 summarises average parasite drag coefficients for different groups of aeroplanes, some of which are based upon ref. 5.5.

Knowing from eq (5–37) that:

$$C_{Dp}S = C_{Dfric}A_w$$

eqs (5–44) to (5–46) may have substituted $K'C_{Dp} = K'C_{Dfric}(A_w/S)$, giving the form:

$$(L/D)_{max} = 8/9\sqrt{[A/K'C_{Dfric}(A_w/S)]}$$

$$= 8/9\sqrt{(b^2/A_wK'C_{Dfric})} \qquad (5-47)$$

from which we see that b^2/A_w (span^2/wetted area), is a relative of aspect ratio. In general terms of aspect ratio too:

$$A \approx (4/\pi)[K'C_{Dfric}(A_w/S)(L/D)^2_{max}] \qquad (5\text{-}48)$$

Expressions for jet $(L/D)_R$ have exactly the same form, only the constants differ, so that we insert $9(L/D)^2_R/2\pi$ in place of $4(L/D)^2_{max}/\pi$.

Fig. 5.18 shows curves of $(L/D)_{max}$ plotted against aspect ratio, A, which apply to both eq (5-44) and (5-47). As $C_D = 2C_{Dp} = 2C_{Dfric}(A_w/S)$ (derived from eq (5-30)):

$$K'C_D/2 = K'C_{Dp} = K'C_{Dfric}(A_w/S) \qquad (5\text{-}49)$$

which represents terms in the denominators of eqs (5-44) and (5-47) and, therefore, the values of the different curves. If lift distribution is elliptical, $K = 1$, and the curves in fig. 5.18 are numerically equal to the parasite drag coefficient, C_{Dp}. Fig. 5.19 shows $(L/D)_{max}$ differently, in terms of span, friction and wetted area.

For example, a light aeroplane in table 5-7, with $C_{Dp} = 0.03$, induced drag factor, $K' = 1.4$, and $A_w/S = 4$, say, from fig. 5.16, would have:

$$C_{Dfric} = C_{Dp}/(A_w/S)$$
$$= 0.03/4 = 0.0075 \qquad (5\text{-}50)$$

so that, $K'C_{Dp} = K'C_{Dfric}(A_w/S) = K'C_D/2 = 1.4 \times 0.03 = 0.042$, i.e. factored drag coefficient $K'C_D = 0.084$. If the aspect ratio $A = 7$, then from eq (5-45a) or fig. 5.18, $(L/D)_{max} = 11.47$.

TABLE 5-7

Typical values of C_{Dp} and K'

Aircraft	Parasite drag coefficient C_{Dp}	Induced drag factor $K' = 1/e$
Subsonic jet	0.014 to 0.02	1.25 (increasing with wing sweep: e.g. 1.27 at 35 degrees)
Twin turboprop transport	0.02 to 0.03	1.2–1.3
Twin piston transport	0.025 to 0.04	1.35–1.45
Single engine trainer/tourer		
retractable gear	0.02 to 0.03	1.3–1.5
fixed gear	0.025 to 0.04	1.3–1.5
Homebuilt	0.02 to 0.04	1.3–1.5
Aerial work		
glider tug/agricultural (no spray gear)	0.06	1.35–1.5
agricultural (spray gear fitted)	0.07 to 0.08	1.35–1.5

The results of this analysis give some idea of the need for high quality surface finish, and the benefits that might accrue in theory (even though hard to achieve in practice), from boundary layer control. Cost is against active boundary layer control for light

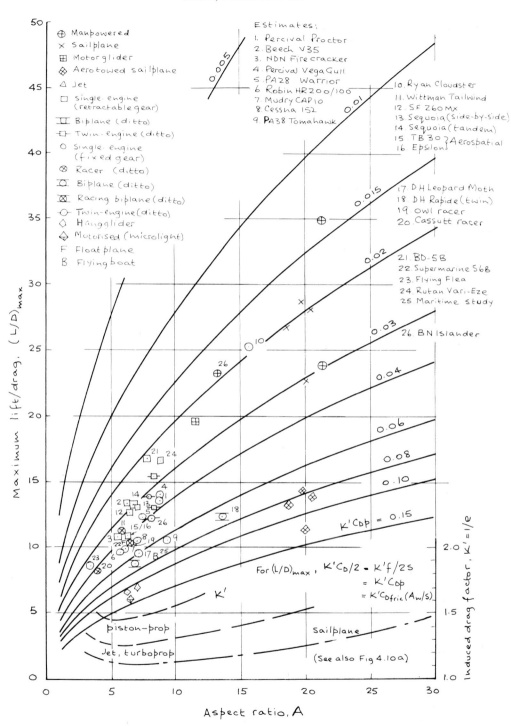

Fig. 5.18   Estimates of maximum lift/drag ratio from published data.

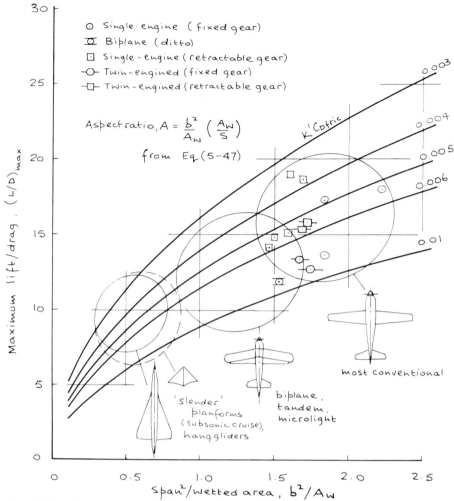

Fig. 5.19 Subsonic (subcritical) cruise relationship between span, wetted area, induced drag factor and frictional drag coefficient (b, A_w, K', C_{Dfric}). Note that (b^2/A_w) is a relative of aspect ratio $A = b^2/S$ (figure based upon Ref. 5.6).

aircraft, as well as for most others. Yet, parasite drag might be reduced by 4/5 using distributed suction, while careful finish alone can halve C_{Dfric}, increasing maximum lift/drag between 50 and 100 per cent, improving cruise performance and top speed, or reducing fuel consumption. Taking such benefits further, less powerful and quieter engines might be used, although power needed for active boundary layer control prevents much fuel and noise reduction in that direction.

Drag Counts

The term *drag count* is a commonly used measure of comparative drag, such as 'fairing the wing roots reduced total drag by 53 counts'. One drag count is defined as a change in total C_D, based upon wing area, S, of 0.0001. Thus, a reduction of total drag coefficient by this amount could be, e.g.

$$0.04 - (53 \times 0.0001) = 0.0347$$

References

5.1 Pazmany, L. (1963) *Light Airplane Design*. San Diego, CaliforniaL L. Pazmany.

5.2 Ministry of Supply. R & M No 2622 (1953) *The Aerodynamic Characteristics of Flaps*. London: Ministry of Supply, Her Majesty's Stationery Office.

5.3 Mendenhall, C. A. (1979) *A Legacy of Speed. The Gee Bee Racers*, Speciality Press Publishers and Wholesalers Inc, North Branch, Minnesota 55056.

5.4 Gregorek, G. M. and Hoffmann, M. J. (1978) *Observations on the Predictions of the Performance of Homebuilt Aircraft*. Ohio: Ohio State University, 2300 West Case Road, Columbus, Ohio 43220.

5.5 Torenbeek, E. (1976) *Synthesis of Subsonic Airplane Design*. Delft: Delft University Press.

5.6 Stinton, D. (1966) (1980) *The Anatomy of the Aeroplane*, London: G. T. Foulis & Co Ltd. St. Albans: Granada Publishing Ltd.

SECTION 3

PERFORMANCE

CHAPTER 6

Power for Flight

'An aeroplane, she is like a woman: for the best you must seduce here, not rape her.'
Polish Flight Commander flying instructor, Royal Air Force (1954)

'When landing this pilot flew his aircraft straight into the ground without apparently making any
attempt to hold off. Questioned later, he said: "I got slightly mixed up between the throttle and
the stick – holding off with the throttle and opening up with the stick".'
Tee Emm (*Training Memoranda*, Royal Air Force) **4** no 9 December 1944.

The first seventy years of powered flight were marked by the pursuit of high speed for
its own sake. Designers sought to increase productivity (eq (1–4)) more by increases of
block speed than weight. Increasing speed required the provision of high power. An
important consequence of this was that the engine industry became a leader industry
and a country which led the way in aircraft design had a firm engine industry in
support. A country lacking an engine industry tends to have the effectiveness of its
airframe industry reduced, because choice becomes limited and it can no longer
command its own destiny.

It is no longer socially acceptable to increase gross productivity in isolation – except
in very special circumstances, like defence. Fossil fuel reserves are progressively more
costly to extract. Also, there is no reason why people who are not interested in flying
should be assailed with noise and upset. The most important single factor today is the
reduction of fuel consumption, followed closely by the need to reduce noise. But if the
second is not heeded first in Britain, then very quickly there will be such a reduction in
available airfields, with social pressures preventing more being built, that general
aviation will cease to grow, and may be forced into retreat. This will be a negative way
of consuming less fuel.

Rate of fuel consumption rises proportionally with power output of a piston engine,
and with thrust generated by a turbojet. Noise is produced by the conversion of energy
into thrust by the propulsion system. Generally, the addition of a fan or a propeller to a
turbojet makes it more economical. But a propeller is a major source of noise.

Thus, if everything else remains unchanged with a given aircraft, an attempt to make
it carry more payload, by increasing the gross weight, merely causes the wings to place
a heavier footprint on the air, by increasing the wing loading. More drag is generated.
Higher power is needed to maintain cruising speed. More fuel is burned – and the
aeroplane cannot fly as far as it did when carrying less payload.

Conversely, an attempt to increase productivity merely by flying faster than the optimum for the combination of airframe and engine has the same thirsty, noisy consequences as the attempt to increase weight.

All propulsion systems perform the same basic function of transforming heat energy from fuels into propulsive thrust. For economy and efficiency we should have neither too much nor too little engine. The object is to provide just enough power to satisfy the operational requirements, with a small surplus included to give the pilot a reasonable margin for error. It is a major task of the airworthiness authorities to determine, and maintain, reasonable margins in all areas, so that manufacturers and operators have common yardsticks of safety.

Too much engine is too heavy and thirsty, reducing payload, fuel carried, and available range. Not enough engine reduces surplus thrust-minus-drag for a given weight, leaving smaller margins for manoeuvre and the performance needed to get out of trouble. Too little engine also limits payload and range due to inability to lift sufficient fuel off the ground.

Performance equations

The three flight conditions from which deductions may be drawn are: gliding, flying straight and level, and climbing. These are shown from top to bottom in fig. 6.1, while variation of rate of climb and descent with true airspeed, TAS is shown in fig. 6.2. We also assume that thrust and drag are in line.

In the case of the glide, when thrust $F = 0$, a descent gradient with an angle less than 10 deg., say, can be expressed in terms of lift, L, and drag, D, in the general form:

$$\sin \gamma = (F - D)/W \qquad\qquad (6\text{–}1)$$
$$= 1/(L/D) \text{ approximately} \qquad\qquad (6\text{–}2)$$

because lift and weight, W, are exchangeable when γ is small. This is applicable to sailplanes and gliders with no engines, or with engines switched off. It follows that the minimum descent gradient corresponds with $(L/D)_{max}$.

Eq (6–1) applies to the power-on cases too. As thrust is increased to the point at which it is equal and opposite to drag, $(F - D) = 0$, $\sin \gamma = 0$, and the aircraft just maintains steady level flight. If thrust is then increased further, $(F - D)$ becomes positive and the aircraft climbs.

The *'one-in-sixty rule'* can be useful when dealing with small angles. It assumes that an angle of 1 deg has a gradient of $1/60$ (actually $1/57.3$), so that as long as the angle is less than about 10 deg, its sine, tangent and measure in radians are roughly equal to the angle in degrees/60. Thus, an agricultural aeroplane, limited to a minimum climb gradient of 4.5 per cent on take-off under any ambient conditions, has a minimum permissible angle of climb of $(4.5/100) \times 60 = 2.7$ deg. Most climb and descent paths are inclined at 3 deg or so: the gradient being around $3/60 = 1/20$, or 5 per cent. This is the same as about 300 ft/nm (50 m/km).

We saw in fig. 5.18(a) that most light aeroplanes have maximum lift/drag ratios around 12 to 18, power-on. Gliding, with engines throttled back and propellers windmilling in the airflow, such aircraft suffer some loss of $(L/D)_{max}$ to around 10 to 12 on average. Their glide angles are steepened to 5 deg to 7 deg with throttle closed – although a braced biplane with fixed gear and a fixed pitch propeller may be nearer 8 deg or even more. This can have a marked effect upon the pilot's chance of making a successful forced landing in the event of engine failure, because (glide angle in degrees

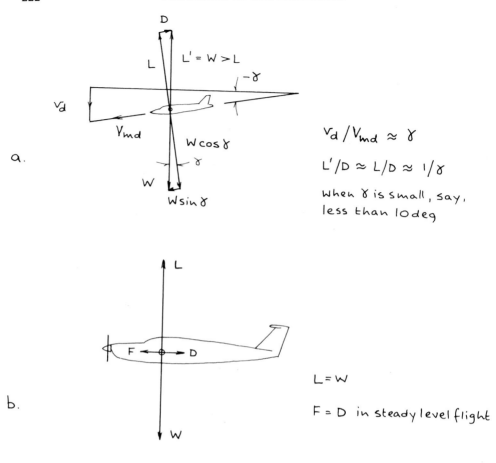

$v_d / V_{md} \approx \gamma$

$L'/D \approx L/D \approx 1/\gamma$

when γ is small, say, less than 10 deg

$L = W$

$F = D$ in steady level flight

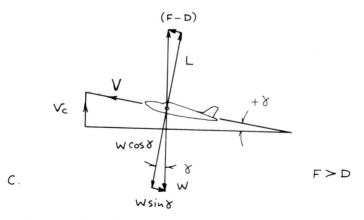

$F > D$

Fig. 6.1   Simplified force and speed diagrams in unaccelerated flight. (a) glide (thrust $F = 0$) (b) straight and level (c) climb.

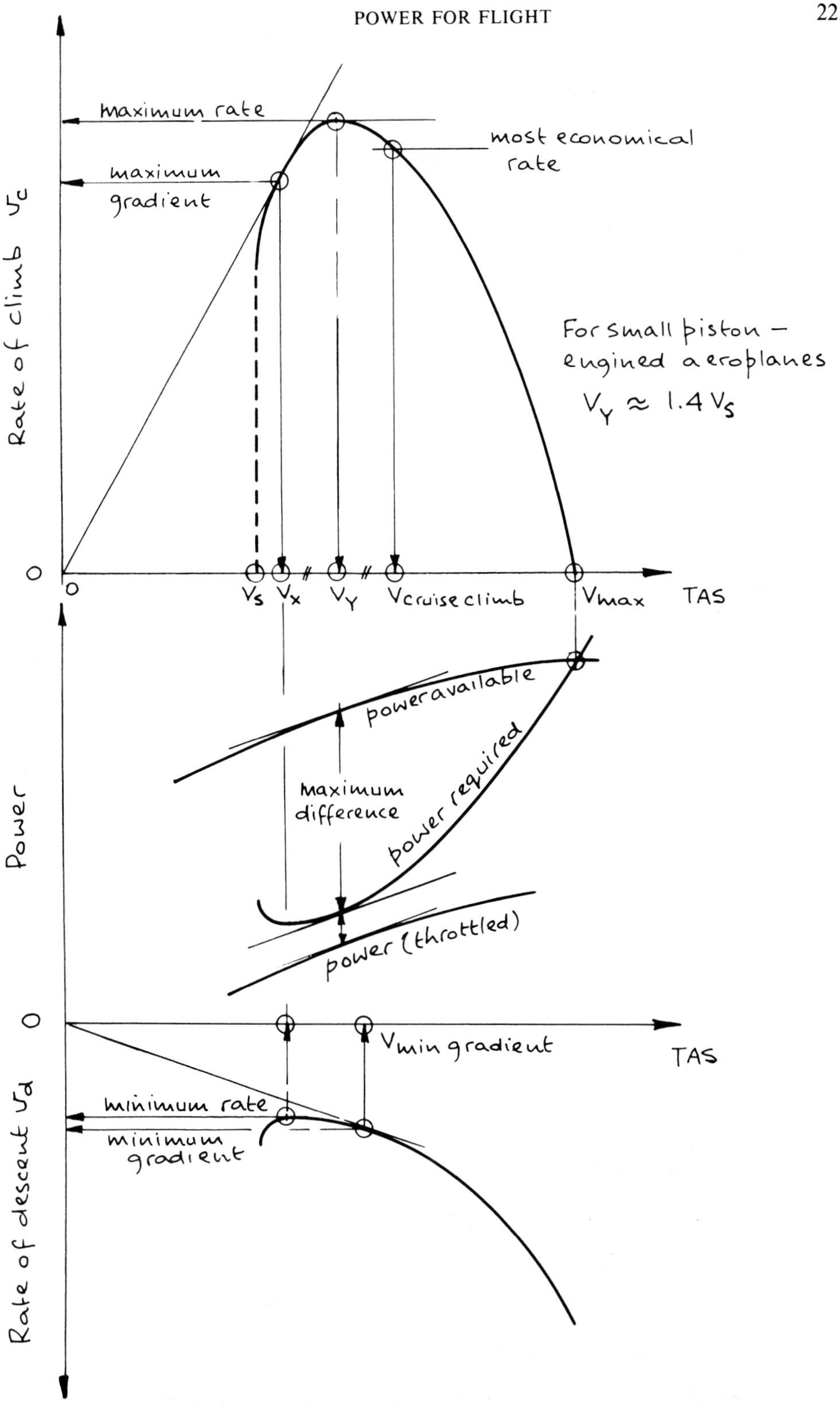

Fig. 6.2   Climb and descent. These sketches are diagrammatic only.

$\times$ 100) is roughly the height lost per nautical mile. In the case of the hypothetical, 'draggy' biplane the pilot could expect to cover at most about 1 nm in a straight line and still air, from 800 ft (244 m). A recorded rate of descent of a *Robin DR400* monoplane with propeller windmilling was 580 ft/min (2.95 m/s), suggesting an L/D around 10.5 at the glide speed, power off.

Fig. 6.3 emphasises the difference between rate of descent and angle of descent in their effects upon distance flown. Eq (2–54) showed that

rate of climb, v_c, or descent, v_d = gradient $\times$ true airspeed

when angles are shallow. The maximum angle of climb or the minimum angle of glide is achieved when drag is minimum, at $(L/D)_{max}$, but maximum rate of climb or minimum rate of descent are achieved at the angle of attack and the true airspeed for minimum power to fly level. For most light aeroplanes with aspect ratios around 7, we may resort to the rule of thumb:

□ For maximum rate of climb and minimum rate of descent, fly at 75 per cent of the speed for $(L/D)_{max}$ which is the speed required for minimum angle, or gradient of descent.

During the climb a component of thrust adds to the lift, although the actual lift of the wing is *less* than that required for straight and level flight. For maximum *rate* of climb we require the maximum difference between *power* available and power required. For maximum climb *gradient* we need the greatest difference between *thrust* available and thrust required to balance drag in level flight at the same speed.

These conditions are shown in fig. 6.4. In each case the maximum separation between the thrust or power available, and the thrust or power required curves, is a maximum when parallel tangents graze each curve at the same speed.

The best glide ratio, which is the longest distance flown for one unit of lost height, is inversely proportional to the angle of glide and to drag. For example one particular but typical four seat light aeroplane had a measured rate of descent of 280 ft/min (1.4 m/s) with the propeller windmilling, and 530 ft/min (2.7 m/s) with the engine stopped, at the same glide EAS for minumum drag with the engine throttled back) V_{md}. We measure glide ratio by

$$\text{glide ratio} = 1/\gamma \approx V_d/V_{md} \approx L/D \qquad (6\text{--}3)$$

and angle of glide, γ, can be derived in a number of ways from:

$$\gamma = \text{drag/lift} = (C_{Di} + C_{Dp})/C_L$$
$$= C_{Di} + C_{Dfric} A_w/S)/C_L \text{ radians} \qquad (6\text{--}3a)$$

The minimum value occurs when $C_{Di} = C_{Dp}$, so that

$$\gamma_{min} = (C_{Dp} + C_{Dfric} Aw/S)/C_L \text{ radians} \qquad (6\text{--}3b)$$

at the speed for $(L/D)_{max}$. We can also express minimum angle of glide in equations derived from eqs (5–44) and (5–47), i.e.

$$\gamma_{min} \approx (9/8) \sqrt{(K'C_{Dp}/A)} \text{ radians} \qquad (6\text{--}4)$$
$$= 1.125 \sqrt{(K'C_{Dp}S/b)} \text{ radians} \qquad (6\text{--}5)$$
$$= 1.125 \sqrt{(K'C_{Dfric}A_w/b)} \text{ radians} \qquad (6\text{--}6)$$

In chapter 2 (under Energy and other mechanical concepts) we saw how propeller efficiency, which is usually around 70 to 80 per cent, causes thrust horse-power available to be less than the brake horsepower produced by the engine:

$$\text{THP} = \eta \text{ BHP} \qquad\qquad \text{see eq (2--33)}$$

If we now write P for brake horsepower, BHP, and F for thrust produced, we may construct fig. 6.5 knowing:

$$\text{THP} = FV/550 = \eta P = P_t \qquad (6\text{--}7)$$

using FPSR units. We may also convert BHP into lbf/s

$$P_e = 550 \ P \ (7.456 \times 10^2 P \text{ watt}) \qquad (6\text{--}8)$$

Now, look again at figure 6.1, to see how power requirements may be stated:

☐ In unaccelerated level flight, when thrust F equals drag D, power required is

$$DV.$$

☐ When accelerating level at a constant rate, the net thrust force:

$$F - D = (W/g)a \qquad\qquad \text{from eq (2--12)}$$

in which the mass of the aeroplane is W/g and acceleration a.

☐ When climbing the weight of the aircraft is being lifted bodily at a rate equal to the rate of climb, v_c, such that the extra power required is:

$$W \ v_c$$

Adding all of these terms together, we can equate them to eq (6–8):

$$\eta Pe = FV = 550\eta P$$
$$= DV + Wv_c + (W/g)a \qquad (6\text{--}9)$$

This is called the *general performance equation*.

Power requirement and engine size

One of the hardest tasks for a designer can be settling which engine he should use. Sometimes he is given no choice, the engine being specified for him by an insistent operator, or fixed by availability, or some other circumstance beyond his control. Then he has to tailor and trim his design so as to get the most performance from the combination.

Too much power bestows lively performance and the ability to fly out of trouble, but

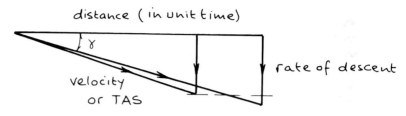

a. The fastest rate of descent occurs at the higher
   TAS, as shown, but the descent gradient is
   shallower, so that the aircraft flies further.

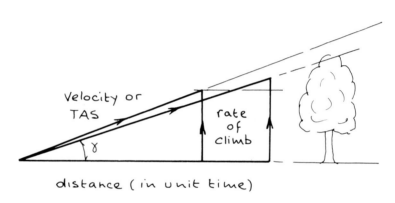

b. Similarly, while we may have a higher rate of
   climb at a higher TAS, as shown, the aircraft
   may have a better climb gradient at the lower
   airspeed: and it is climb gradient (angle γ)
   which gives obstacle clearance.

Fig. 6.3   Geometric difference between rates and gradients (angles) of descent and climb.

it can make a machine into a handful for the pilot, and uneconomical with fuel. Insufficient engine can be downright dangerous.

   A number of factors determine minimum power requirements:

☐ *Airfield.* The shorter the take-off distance, the higher the altitude and the hotter the climate, the bigger the engine needed to provide enough power, or thrust. Conventionally, power and thrust loading, W/P and W/F, can be used as indicators

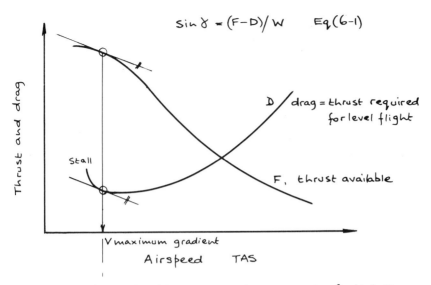

$$\sin \gamma = (F-D)/W \qquad Eq(6\text{-}1)$$

a. The true airspeed at which the maximum angle of climb, γ, is achieved is slow and often too close to the stall to be of much operational use.

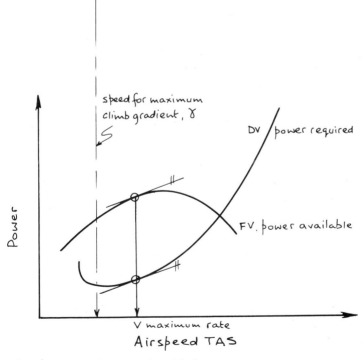

b. The true airspeed at which maximum rate of climb occurs is higher than that for maximum gradient, being around 1.4 times stall speed for a light aeroplane.

Fig. 6.4   Maximum angle of climb and maximum rate of climb.

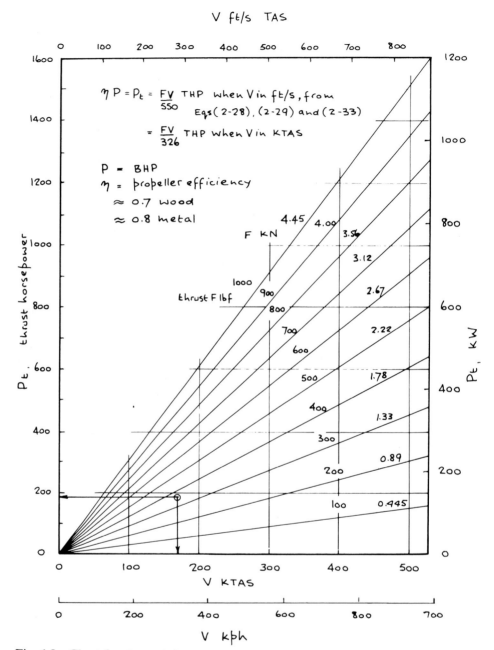

Fig. 6.5   Chart for determining thrust horsepower, and *vice versa*.

of design merit. Their reciprocals are useful at the project stage for determining the rated engine output needed to fly a given weight of aircraft.

Additionally, wing loading, W/S, and lift coefficient, C_L, at take-off safety speed, V_2 EAS, determine the ability of an aircraft to lift itself into the air, and to land, in the required distances.

☐ *Range in still air.* The distance that an aeroplane is able to fly with the fuel carried, which includes reserves, depends upon the specific fuel consumption of the engine, the weight of fuel carried, and upon the lift/drag ratio of the aircraft. Specific fuel consumption tends to be fixed by engine type and state-of-the-art, so that for a given weight of fuel, the lower the thrust and power requirements of the engine, the longer the range. But this must be coupled with clean design and small wetted area. This tends to imply the need for rudimentary variable geometry in the form of flaps, slats and other mechanisms needed to achieve high lift at low speed, so as to achieve field performance. The trend is towards higher wing loadings, faster cruising speeds, and denser airframes. The result is that aircraft are fitted with bigger and bigger engines, with power loadings like those shown in fig. 6.6.

The higher the altitude at which an aircraft is required to cruise, the bigger the engine provided by the designer, because high altitude means reduced air pressure and density, with reduced air swallowed for combustion. A normally aspirated piston engine swallows 13 lb (6 kg) air to burn 1 lb (0.5 kg) fuel at best power air/fuel ratio (the amount of oxygen contained is about 2.6 lb (1.2 kg)) i.e., 20 per cent by weight.

The rate at which energy is released by combustion determines the indicated horsepower, IHP (eq (2–30)), which varies as the mass of the air-fuel charge handled by the engine in the same interval of time. Therefore, the power produced depends upon the density of the air at any altitude and temperature. It follows that the engine must grow larger if it is to capture enough air to provide 2.6 lb oxygen for each pound of fuel burned. A piston engine grows by the incorporation of a supercharger for flight at high altitudes. A jet engine grows in diameter to increase its air-swallowing ability.

Fig. 6.8 shows the shape of the power and thrust curves with increasing altitude for given engines.

Minimum power to fly level (out of ground effect)

In fig. 6.1a and eq (6–2), if the angle of glide is such that the aircraft sinks at a minimum rate of descent, v_d, then its rate of change of potential energy is also a minimum. This is also the amount of power needed to prevent sink and to cause the machine to fly level:

$$\text{power to fly level at TAS, } V = \eta P_e = W v_d \tag{6–10}$$

where W is the weight. Generally, because the rate of descent is relatively shallow – usually less than 10 deg:

$$v_d/V = \gamma/57.3 \approx \gamma/60 = 1/(L/D)$$
$$\text{and, } v_d = V/(L/D) \tag{6–11}$$
$$\text{Hence, } \eta P_e = WV/(L/D)$$
$$= WV \sin \gamma \tag{6–12}$$
$$= DV \text{ (when } L \approx W) \qquad \text{from eq (6–9)}$$

But this is numerically the same as the power required to maintain airspeed, so that the requirement splits into two parts:

$$\eta \, P_e = \text{power to fly level} + \text{power to maintain airspeed}$$
$$= DV + DV = 2DV \tag{6–13}$$

This conclusion is the same as that made by Charles Renard (1847–1905), one of the leaders in early French aeronautics, who analysed the minimum power required for

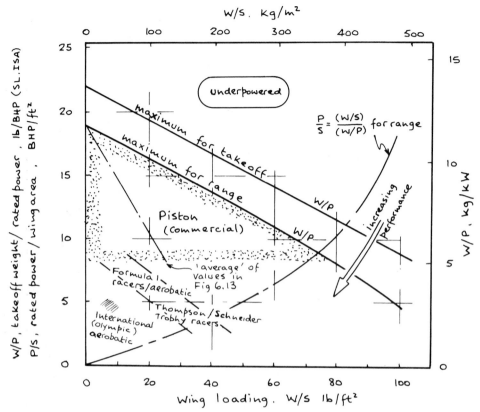

Fig. 6.6 Practical (and very generalised) state-of-the-art wing and power loading limitations. Wing loadings less than 20 lb/ft² (97.6 kg/m²) apply in the main to single engined light aeroplanes. Some of these curves are developed later in the chapter.

flight. His method tied together engine power, propeller efficiency, aircraft weight, wing area, and air density. Using the same terms as before, in straight and level flight:

$$\text{weight, } W = L = C_L \tfrac{1}{2}\rho V^2 S \qquad \text{from eq (2–3a)}$$
$$V = \sqrt{[(2/C_L)(W/S)(1/\rho)]} \qquad (6\text{–}14)$$

while minimum drag occurs when:

$$C_D = 2K'C_L^2/\pi A \qquad (5\text{–}30)$$

When gliding for range, flying level with minimum power, or cruise climbing, the lift/drag ratio is not far removed from $(L/D)_{max}$, i.e.:

$$(L/D)_{max} = \pi A/2K'C_L \qquad (6\text{–}15)$$

Combining eqs (6–13) and (6–14), and dividing throughout by W, we have an expression for power loading:

$$\eta P_e/W = (2/(L/D))\sqrt{[(2/C_L)(W/S)(1/\rho)]}$$
$$= 4K'(C_L/\pi A)\sqrt{[(2/C_L)(W/S)(1/\rho)]}$$
$$= 1.8K'(\sqrt{C_L}/A)\sqrt{[(W/S)(1/\rho)]} \qquad (6\text{–}16)$$

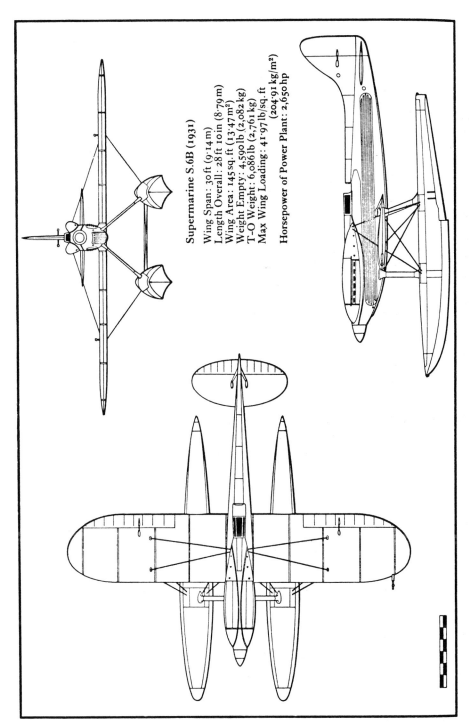

Supermarine S.6B (1931)

Wing Span: 30 ft (9·14 m)
Length Overall: 28 ft 10 in (8·79 m)
Wing Area: 145 sq. ft (13·47 m²)
Weight Empty: 4,590 lb (2,082 kg)
T-O Weight: 6,086 lb (2,761 kg)
Max Wing Loading: 41·97 lb/sq. ft
                              (204·91 kg/m²)
Horsepower of Power Plant: 2,650 hp

Fig. 6.7a The *Supermarine S6B* (ref. 6.1) which was outright winner of the Schneider Trophy and was hard to handle on take-off through torque, had a power loading of 2.3 lb/BHP (1.4 kg/kW. Of the 948 ft² (88.06 m²) wetted area, 470 ft² (43.66 m²) was radiator (and oil cooler) surface area. The designer, R. J. Mitchell (1895–1937) called the aeroplane a flying radiator. Mass balances on ailerons and rudder show there had been flutter problems.

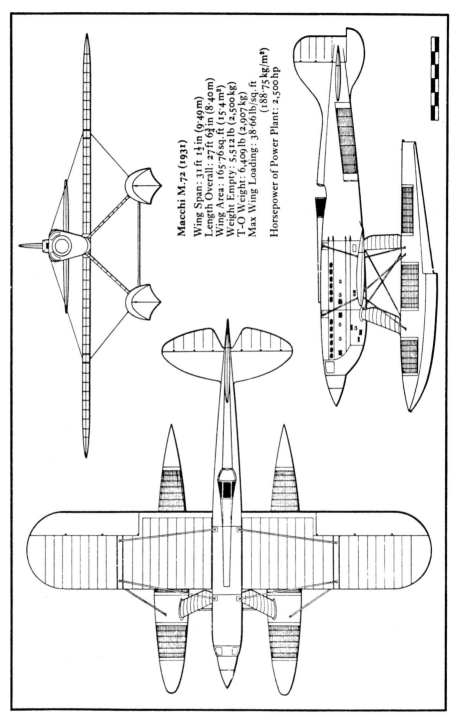

Macchi M.72 (1931)

Wing Span: 31 ft 1¼ in (9·49 m)
Length Overall: 27 ft 6¼ in (8·40 m)
Wing Area: 165·76 sq ft (15·4 m²)
Weight Empty: 5,512 lb (2,500 kg)
T-O Weight: 6,409 lb (2,907 kg)
Max Wing Loading: 38·66 lb/sq.ft
                          (188·75 kg/m²)
Horsepower of Power Plant: 2,500 hp

Fig. 6.7b   The Italian *Macchi M72* (ref. 6.1) had twin engines driving counter-rotating propellers to eliminate torque effects and a power loading of 2.56 lb/BHP (1.56 kg/kW).

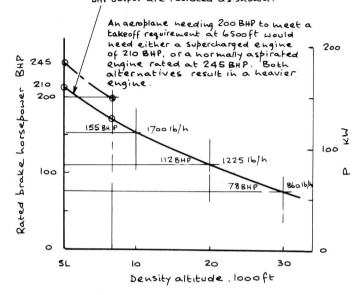

30,000 ft³ air swallowed per hour weighs 2,300 lb at sealevel.
As altitude is gained the engine still swallows 30,000 ft³
at the same rpm, but weight of air and corresponding
BHP output are reduced as shown.

An aeroplane needing 200 BHP to meet a
takeoff requirement at 6500 ft would
need either a supercharged engine
of 210 BHP, or a normally aspirated
engine rated at 245 BHP. Both
alternatives result in a heavier
engine.

a. Change of power with altitude for a normally aspirated
piston engine.

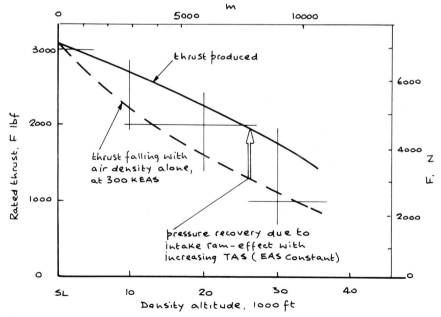

b. Change of thrust with altitude for a typical, relatively
small, gas-turbine engine.

Fig. 6.8   Engine output with altitude, showing typical variation of power and thrust
available.

The term $1.8K'\sqrt{C_L}$ is a constant for most practical purposes, because best lift/drag occurs around $C_L = 0.4$, give or take a bit, while $K' \approx 1.3$. With an aspect ratio of 6, the term outside the $\sqrt{}$ has a value around 0.25. For a motor glider with $A = 12$ to 15, the 'constant' is nearer 0.11. The average is about 0.18 in FPSR units (0.5 in SI) within the practical range of powered aspect ratios and induced drag factors. According to R. Henry (1891), a contemporary of Renard, the value of the constant was 0.18 (ref 2.1). Thus:

$$\eta P_e / W = k\sqrt{(W/S\rho)} \qquad (6\text{-}17)$$

with the constant k about $\frac{1}{4}$ for a conventional aeroplane, and $1/10$ for a motor glider, when working in FPSR units. Eq (6–16) shows too that, for a given wing loading and lift coefficient (which is an indication of angle of attack and, hence, attitude to the air) the term

$\eta P_e / W$ varies as $1/b^2$ (the reciprocal of (wingspan)^2)

Therefore, the longer the wingspan, b, the better the cruise and climb performance and also, from eq (6–17), which has $\sqrt{(1/S\rho)}$ on the right, the higher we may fly.

Plate 6–1 Long span for low induced drag and power for flight. Long wings also improve performance at high altitude (Top) John Monnet's *Moni*, aerobatic, fun motor glider (*Monnet Experimental Aircraft Inc, USA*) (Middle) *Ryson ST–100 Cloudster* (*Warren D. Shipp, USA*) (Bottom) *Lockheed TR–1/U–2* which flies at high altitude, where the never exceed and stall speeds ultimately coincide. (*Lockheed Aircraft Corporation, USA*)

Plate 6–1 (middle).

Plate 6–1 (bottom).

Plate 6–2 Amphibious *RFB–X114 Aerofoilboat*, which applies principles of Dr-Ing AM Lippisch, achieving lift/drag ratios around 30 in ground effect and 9 in free flight away from the surface. (*Rhein–Flugzeugbau GmbH, Federal Republic of Germany*)

Figure 7.23b shows an aircraft, the *RFB X114* designed to fly efficiently in ground effect, where lift/drag (through reduction of induced drag) is about 30. In free flight where induced drag is present, lift/drag ratio falls to around 9.

Fig. 6.9 shows another approach in the form of the Rutan designed, tandem-winged *Quickie* (ref. 6.2). Tandem planes can generate minimum induced drag, provided that the sum of their lift distributions is elliptical. The Quickie has two almost equal planes, each with an aspect ratio around 9, and an engine of 18 BHP (13.43 kW). The wing and power loadings are 9.05 lb/ft^2 (44.16 kg/m^2) and 26.67 lb/BHP (16.21 kg/kW) respectively.

If we are short of cash and cannot afford large and expensive engines, the best way to fly for fun is to use a wing with a low span loading, coupled with low wing loading.

The ratio P_e/W is the reciprocal of the power loading at one true airspeed. We may use a similar line of argument for a jet aeroplane under the same set of conditions, this time using $(F - D)V/W$ in place of P_e/W:

$$(F/W) - 1/(L/D)V = k\sqrt{[(W/S)(1/\rho)]} \tag{6–18}$$

where F/W is the reciprocal of the thrust loading, and L/D the lift/drag ratio at TAS V. The constant, k, is assumed to have the same values as in eq (6–17).

From these last equations we may deduce:

□ For a given aerodynamic efficiency, L/D, the lower the wing loading the lower the power and thrust requirements.

□ With propulsive and aerodynamic characteristics fixed by shape and power-plant, the higher we wish to fly the lower must be the wing loading.

☐ For a given wing loading, the higher the aerodynamic efficiency of the wing (really the whole aircraft, not just the wing alone) the lower are the thrust, power and fuel requirements. Also, the aircraft is probably quieter.

Thrust and power requirements affect the choice of powerplant, and the number of engines to be used. This means that we have to pay particular attention to the right hand side of eqs (6–17) and (6–18), with more than a passing look at eq (6–16), which tells us that the constant of proportionality, $k = 1.8K'\sqrt{C_L/A}$, wraps up three very fundamental aerodynamic terms.

Flight in ground effect

As an aeroplane approaches the ground its wing downwash is reduced by proximity, and this is accompanied by a decrease in the induced drag. The tailplane and a canard are similarly affected. The variables altered by the ground effect are downwash angle, ϵ, elevator effectiveness, wing angle of attack, lift slope and effective aspect ratio.

The change in wing and tail lift slope can be calculated from fig. 6.10, in which $b/2$ is the semispan of the aerofoil, sometimes denoted s, and d_g is the height of the aerodynamic centre of the wing or tail from the ground.

Ground effect increases lift slope from a to a_g, and aspect ratio from A to A_g. A bit of juggling with eq (4–19a) shows that:

$$\text{lift slope ratio, } a_g/a = a' = [A_g/(A_g + 2)][(A + 2)/A]$$
$$\text{i.e. } A_g = 2Aa'/[2 + A(1 - a')] \tag{6–19}$$

This means, for example, that a wing of aspect ratio 7, one semispan above the ground, has the effective aspect ratio increased by about 10 per cent, and induced drag (eq (4–9)) reduced reduced by a similar amount. Maximum lift/drag ratio is increased by about one half A_g/A.

$$\text{As, } C_L/\alpha = a \text{ and } C_L/\alpha_g = a_g$$
$$\Delta\alpha = (C_L/a)[(1/a') - 1] \tag{6–20}$$

which means that the angle of attack for landing is decreased, and the aircraft floats along with a flattened glide, stretching the landing distance.

Low-winged aircraft are more sensitive to ground effect than high-winged. A trickle of throttle is often enough to keep a very light aeroplane floating along almost indefinitely.

Provided a pilot does not take foolish risks, he can fly further at low altitude over water in a piston engined aeroplane than is possible out of ground effect. A similar reduction in downwash is achieved in formation flying, the leader in a formation *Vee* having less induced drag than if his wingmen were not there. This is the reason why migrating geese and swans fly in *Vee* formations, changing their leader fairly regularly, so that each bird has a rest.

Power to climb and manoeuvre

Power in excess of the minimum to fly level at a given TAS bestows the ability to climb and/or manoeuvre at the same speed: in short, the pilot is able to get the aircraft out of

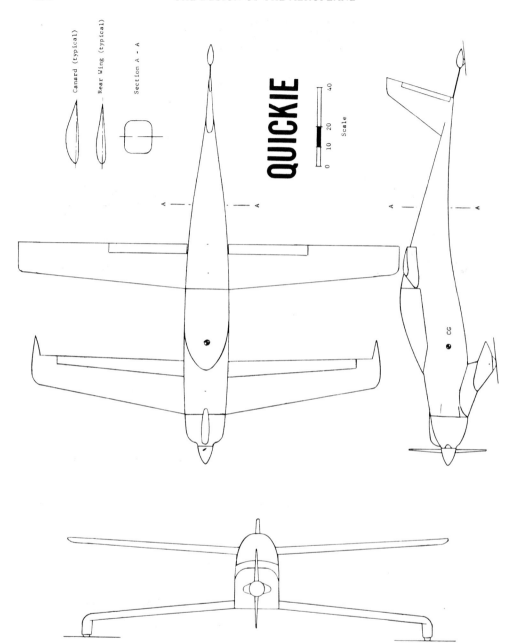

Fig. 6.9 *Quickie* (refs. 6.2 and 6.10) a concept which has forced fashion into another direction – and we do not yet know for how long.

QUICKIE LEADING DATA

Span 16ft (4·85m) **Length** 17ft 4in (5·3m) **Empty weight** 240lb (109kg) **Gross weight** 480lb (273kg) **Fuel capacity** 5·8gal **Baggage capacity** 20lb (9·1kg) **Take-off distance** 580ft (177m) **Landing distance** 490ft (149m) **Stall** 53 m.p.h. (85km/hr) **Cruise** 121 m.p.h. (195km/hr) **Range** 570 miles (920km)

HOW QUICKIE COMPARES

Aircraft	H.p.	75% cruise (m.p.h.)	M.p.g. 75% power (US gal)	Range (miles) @ 75% power	Empty weight (lb)	Gross weight (lb)	Useful load (lb)	Stall (m.p.h.)	Climb rate (ft/min)
Cessna 150	100	123	21·6	435	1,046	1,600	554	48	670
Bellanca Citabria	115	116	14·5	522	1,097	1,650	553	45	725
Piper Tomahawk	112	125	17·3	555	1,064	1,570	606	53	700
De Havilland DH.60 Moth	60	80	17·3	345	770	1,350	580	41	430
Sorrell Guppy	18	65	33	170	330	—	—	33	350
Quickie	18	121	81	570	240	480	240	53	425
Piper J-3	65	75	19	220	690	1,340	650	41	350
Whing Ding II	14	40	35	20	123	310	187	26	—
Volksplane	40	75	30	240	440	750	310	46	400
Pober Pixie	60	85	24	290	543	900	357	30	500
Birdman TL-1	14	50	25	100	130	350	220	20	300
Rand KR-1	40	150	48	420	355	600	245	45	600
Aerosport Quail	40	115	23	230	534	792	258	48	850
Teenie Two	40	110	40	400	310	590	280	50	800
Pazmany PL-4	50	98	28	340	578	850	272	48	650

trouble. When there is little power in hand, so that angles of climb are small, we may deduce from fig. 6.1c:

$$v_c/V \approx \gamma = \gamma \text{ deg}/57.3 = (F - D)/W \qquad (6\text{-}21)$$

which can be transposed into a power form on multiplying through by V, and by $L \approx W$, so that:

$$W \gamma \text{ deg}/57.3 \approx L \gamma \text{ deg}/57.3 = FV - DV$$

The term $FV = P_{e(climb)}$, while $DV = P_{e(level)}$, which we have dealt with already – it appeared as the *power to maintain airspeed*, in eq (6–13). Thus, transposing:

$$P_{e(climb)} = P_{e(level)} [1 + (L/D)\gamma \text{ deg}/57.3] \qquad (6\text{-}22)$$

Also, as lift/drag ratio varies with wing span, b, i.e. (L/D) varies as $\sqrt{A}$ varies as $\sqrt{b^2}$ varies as b then,

$$P_{e(climb)} = P_{e(level)} + f(b) \qquad (6\text{-}22a)$$

where (f) is a function which depends upon the terms in eqs (5–45a) and (5–45b).

Fig. 6.11 shows the forces in a level turn, for which the normal lift component is increased by an increment, ΔL. The larger the angle of bank, the more 'g' that must be pulled to keep the turn level. The increment can only come from increased angle of attack, which increases induced drag, and the power required to maintain speed.

The centripetal acceleration (towards the centre) is shown in fig. 6.11a, in which V is the true airspeed, R the radius of turn and ω the angular velocity in radians/sec:

$$\text{centripetal acceleration} = V^2/R \qquad (6\text{--}23)$$

The centripetal force required is the product of the mass of the aeroplane, W/g, and the centripetal acceleration:

$$\text{centripetal force} = (W/g)V^2/R \qquad (6\text{--}24)$$

Fig. 6.11c shows the lift units in terms of weight, nW, needed to sustain a turn with a constant angle of bank. The *applied* acceleration is $(n-1)$ units, and the diagram shows that $(n-1)=1$ when the angle of bank is 60 deg. Measurements can be made of *stick force per g* at different airspeeds in 60 deg banked turns. This is a measure of the stick-free stability (chapters 2 and 11).

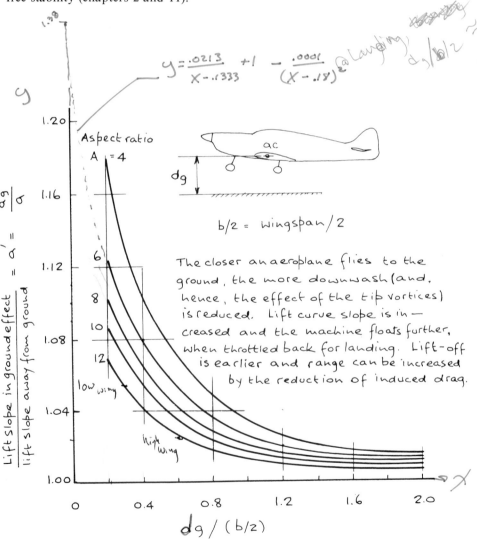

Fig. 6.10   Ground effect upon slope of the lift curve (*see* eq (6–19)).

Table 6–1 shows the effect upon lift, angle of attack and stall speed of a steady turn at different angles of bank.

TABLE 6–1

Lift and stall speed in a steady turn

Angle of bank ϕ deg	Effective weight nW	Percentage increase in lift and angle of attack	Percentage increase in stall speed: $\sqrt{n}$
0	W	0	0
30	$1.15W$	15	7
45	$1.41W$	41	19
60	$2.0\ W$	100	41
90	∞W	∞	∞

Note: The table is theoretical, because at a given speed the stalling angle of attack will be reached, limiting the angle of bank. Furthermore, induced drag increases, and there may not be enough power to maintain speed, so that even the stalling angle of attack might not be reached in certain cases.

Best endurance and range speeds

In fig. 5.15 we saw that the speed for minimum required power, V_{imp}, gives a *piston-engined* aeroplane its *longest endurance*. The speed for *best speed/drag ratio*, V_{imd}, gives a *jet* aeroplane its *longest range*.
We saw in eq (6–9) that in straight and level flight: $\eta P_e = DV$, i.e.

$$Pe \text{ varies as } C_D \tfrac{1}{2}\rho S V^2 \times V$$
$$\text{varies as } C_D V^3 \tag{6–25}$$

While from eq (6–14): V varies as $1/\sqrt{C_L} = C_L^{-1/2}$, so that by substitution for V^3 above:

$$P_e \text{ varies as } C_D/C_L^{3/2} \tag{6–26}$$

This has a minimum value at Point C in fig. 5.15, when $C^{3/2}/C_D$ is a maximum.
It may be shown that TAS and EAS for minimum power, V_{mp} and V_{imp}, are related to the corresponding speeds for minimum drag, V_{ma} and V_{imd}, by:

$$V_{mp}/V_{md} = 0.76 = V_{imp}/V_{imd} \tag{6–27}$$

Similarly, the maximum speed/drag ratio, V/D, occurs when:

$$V/D \text{ which varies as } C_L^{1/2}/C_D \tag{6–28}$$

is a maximum, and this occurs when $C_L^{1/2}/C_D$ is a maximum. The conditions are:

$$V_{max(v/d)}/V_{md} = 1.32 = V_{imax(v/d)}/V_{imd} \tag{6–29}$$

which is Point B in Figure 5.15. The ratio is almost the same for best speed/power ratio (i.e. speed for minimum drag, V_{imd}) of a piston-engined machine:

$$V_{max}(v/p)/V_{mp} \approx 1.3 \approx V_{imax}(v/p)/V_{imp} \tag{6–30}$$

which is Point D in fig. 5.15.

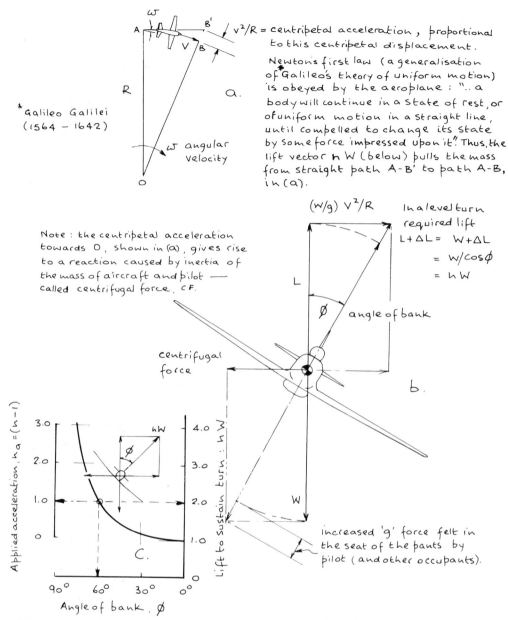

v^2/R = centripetal acceleration, proportional to this centripetal displacement.

Newton's first law (a generalisation of Galileo's theory of uniform motion) is obeyed by the aeroplane: "..a body will continue in a state of rest, or of uniform motion in a straight line, until compelled to change its state by some force impressed upon it". Thus, the lift vector nW (below) pulls the mass from straight path A-B' to path A-B, in (a).

*Galileo Galilei (1564 – 1642)

ω angular velocity

Note: the centripetal acceleration towards O, shown in (a), gives rise to a reaction caused by inertia of the mass of aircraft and pilot — called centrifugal force, CF.

$(W/g)\,V^2/R$

In a level turn required lift
$$L + \Delta L = W + \Delta L$$
$$= W/\cos\phi$$
$$= nW$$

ϕ angle of bank

centrifugal force

b.

increased 'g' force felt in the seat of the pants by pilot (and other occupants).

Fig. 6.11   Force diagrams in a steady (balanced) level turn.

An old fashioned rule of thumb for achieving 'good' performance from a very basic, simple kind of aeroplane (fixer gear, split flaps (if any), coupled with low wing loading) is to ensure that:

wing loading $\times$ power loading, that is W^2/SP

satisfies $90 < W^2/SP < 135$ (6–31)

small experimental go up to ~ 190 $\frac{W}{S}$ $\frac{W}{SP}$

$\frac{W^2}{SP}$

working in FPSR units. This rearranges into:

$$(W/S)/90 > P/W > (W/S)/135 \qquad (6-32)$$

The formula is certainly empirical and the origin and sources are unknown to the author. The numbers 90 and 135 are not 'pure', because they have dimensions based upon the units used. Nevertheless, in the author's experience, the formula appears to be reliable between wing loadings of 5 and 10 lb/ft² (24 and 49 kg/m²), For example, the single-seat *Pitts S-1S* which has been described by a test pilot-tutor as an 'energetic hooligan of an aeroplane', with an engine of 180 hp or more, has a value of W^2/SP around 75. Quick feet are needed to fly it accurately, and to take off and land safely. Yet the *Pitts S-2A*, which is a two-seater, marginally heavier and slightly larger, has W^2/SP nearer 90. This aeroplane, which is shown in single-seat configuration in fig. 6.12, has a little more inertia in pitch, roll and yaw, making it easier to control. Some aeroplanes can be so quick reacting when control is applied, that the pilot is left behind mentally. *Pitts Specials* roll at a rate of about 360 deg./sec with full aileron applied.

Plate 6-3 Author's *S37* designed for *Phoenix Aircraft Ltd* (UK) and built as *'Duet'* by Group Captain A. S. Knowles, has a *wingloading × powerloading* around 96 lb²/BHPft² (See eq (6-31)) (*John Hall*)

Fig. 6.13 shows a number of state-of-the-art combinations of wing and power loadings for a selection of typical light aeroplanes, many of which were plotted in fig. 5.18a. Most lie between two parallel lines represented by the following, worked in FPSR units:

$$W/P = 22 - 0.4 \ W/S \qquad\qquad (6-33)$$
$$\text{and, } W/P = 16 - 0.4 \ W/S \qquad\qquad (6-34)$$

The lower line marks the practical limit of liveliness that might be coupled with reasonable fuel-economy. The upper line is marked either by low drag (e.g. motor gliders), or not quite as much power as would be wished for most purposes. Fig. 6.13b shows a term BHP/S, the rated power per unit wing area, which can be a useful indication of potential merit for high performance aeroplanes.

When choosing the powerplant to produce a given power loading corresponding with an estimated wing loading, the following points should be considered:

☐ For a design to endure, it must have built-in stretchability for the inevitable increase in weight that is likely to follow in service. Therefore, there must be enough power avilable from the engine, without having to incur higher costs through re-engining the airframe to cope with increasing weight.

☐ An aeroplane should have the ability to go almost anywhere in the world. It should, therefore, have enough power in hand to satisfy field requirements at higher altitudes and temperatures than one might have in mind when first sketching a pretty shape.

We shall look at field performance towards the end of this chapter. Meanwhile, it is better to aim for combinations of wing and power loading in the lower half of the corridor, below the broken average line, when making first estimates during the project stage.

Fig. 6.14a and b show state-of-the-art values of power loading to achieve given rates of climb at sea level, ISA. Single-engined aeroplanes are shown in a, with fixed and retractable gears. Twin-engined aeroplanes are shown in b. In each figure the hatched line is the practical boundary, setting the upper limit beyond which estimates are too optimistic. The mean line for single-engined aeroplanes corresponds with the mean line for twins, with only one engine operating. Therefore to design a twin-engined aeroplane, select a power loading to achieve a desired rate of climb with one engine failed, then double it.

Thus, we may summarise for power loading at sea level, ISA:

☐ Single-engined, and twin-engined aeroplanes with one operating:

$$P/W = [(5.25/10^5)v_c + 0.03]BHP/lb \qquad\qquad (6-35)$$
$$= [(2.8/10^4)v_c + 0.05]kg/kW$$

☐ Twin-engined aeroplanes, both operating:

$$P/W = [(5.25/10^5) \ v_c + 0.015]BHP/lb$$
$$= [(3.46/10^4) \ v_c + 0.03]kW/kg \qquad\qquad (6-36)$$

in which v_c is in ft/min and (m/s) respectively.

Note carefully the minimum rates of climb (refs 1.1 and 2.4) in each case. All aeroplanes suffer from deteriorating rates of climb as they grow older. It is bad to have one's aeroplane slip too easily below the minimum as it becomes worn.

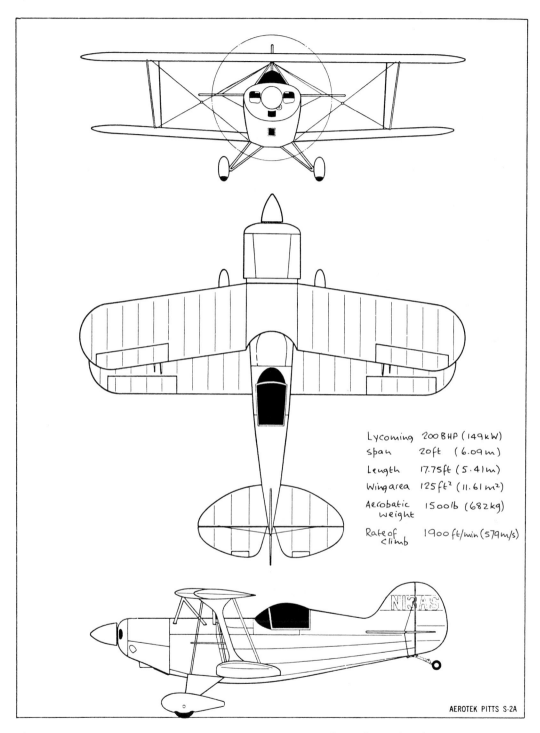

Lycoming   200 BHP (149 kW)
Span   20 ft   (6.09 m)
Length   17.75 ft (5.41 m)
Wing area   125 ft² (11.61 m²)
Aerobatic   1500 lb (682 kg)
weight
Rate of   1900 ft/min (579 m/s)
Climb

AEROTEK PITTS S-2A

Fig. 6.12 *Pitts S–2A* two seater in single-seat configuration (drawing from Underwood, John W., *Acrobats in the Sky*, Heritage Press, Box 167, Glendale, California 91209. Author's figures added).

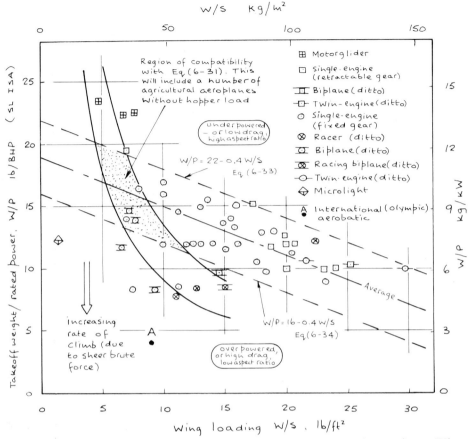

Fig. 6.13a and b   Typical combinations of loadings needed in project design a. Wing and power loading. b. Average power per unit (gross) wing area.

When all other aspects of aircraft configuration and geometry are fixed, rate of climb varies inversely with weight, for a given power. This is useful when working out flight test results, in which the rate of climb is know for one weight when the aircraft has been flown at another. As long as the difference between the weights is not large, and the aeroplane has been flown at the correct lift/drag ratio:

rate of climb at lighter weight/rate of climb at heavier weight
= heavier weight/lighter weight   (6–37)

Power and thrust loading, W/P and W/F, are useful indications of merit for comparing different aeroplanes. Their reciprocals, P/W and F/W, when multiplied by weight, tell how much power, or thrust, is needed to achieve a given rate of climb. But, the approach made here is crude, in the sense that we have not dealt with other important factors, like lift/drag ratio, which affect induced drag. Aeroplanes with long wings climb better and achieve higher service ceilings than those with short, for given power and wing loadings (see fig. 6.14c and d). Supercharging of various kinds maintains sea level power to higher altitudes, inhibiting the decrease in rate of climb with altitude experienced by aeroplanes powered with normally aspirated engines.

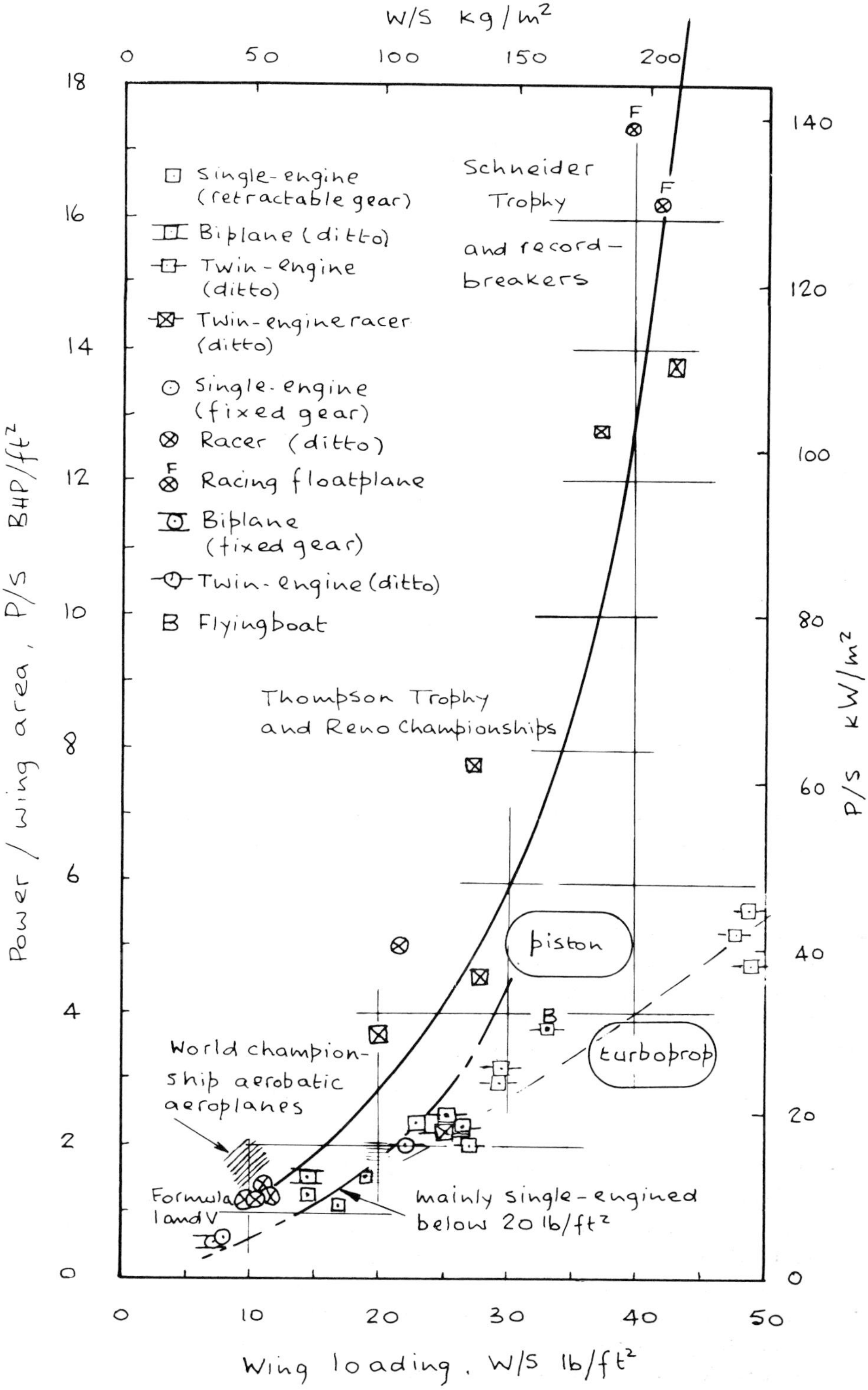
W/S kg/m²
0
50
100
150
200
18
16
14
12
10
8
6
4
2
0
140
120
100
80
60
40
20
0
Single-engine (retractable gear)
Biplane (ditto)
Twin-engine (ditto)
Twin-engine racer (ditto)
Single-engine (fixed gear)
Racer (ditto)
Racing floatplane
Biplane (fixed gear)
Twin-engine (ditto)
B Flyingboat
Schneider Trophy and record-breakers
F
Thompson Trophy and Reno Championships
piston
turboprop
B
World championship aerobatic aeroplanes
Formula I and V
mainly single-engined below 20 lb/ft²
Power / wing area, P/S BHP/ft²
P/S kW/m²
0
10
20
30
40
50
Wing loading, W/S lb/ft²

Fig. 6.13b.

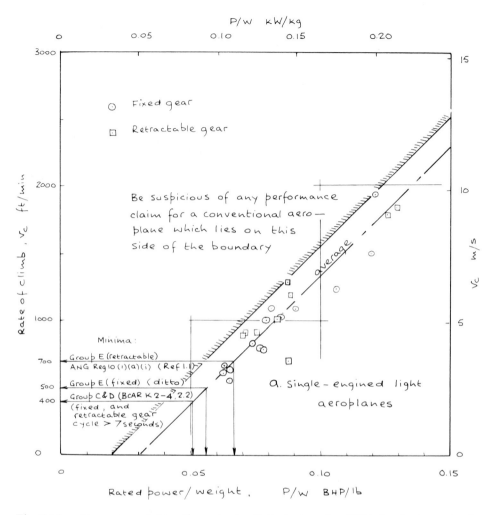

Fig. 6.14a   Power to weight ratio and rate of climb at sea level ISA for single-engined aeroplanes. Figures obtained from Aircraft Flight Manuals.

Looking again at eq (6–14), which expressed true airspeed in terms of characteristics of the aircraft, and the air, we see that the larger the lift coefficient, C_L, and the lower the wing loading, W/S, the slower the aircraft will fly. The slower the take-off and landing, the shorter, or the hotter and higher the field from which the machine can operate.

Low wing loading means more wing area. Although most aeroplanes need more wing as they grow heavier in service, more wing than is absolutely necessary is counter-productive. Even so, a modest increase in wing area rarely hurts a design in the early stages.

The limiting factor on wing area is high speed (EAS) flight, for which small wings with reduced wetted area are better than large wings, for a given altitude. Wing area for high speed is less than the optimum for field performance. Therefore, we shall look next at size of wing and power for high speed flight.

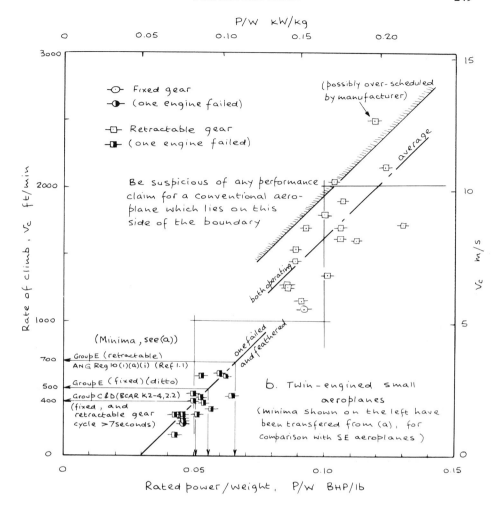

Fig. 6.14b Power to weight ratio and rate of climb at sea level ISA for twin-engined aeroplanes. Figures with full power, and one engine failed, obtained from Aircraft Flight Manuals.

High speed: Everling number

High speed demands high power and the amount a designer is able to provide depends upon a number of factors, which include:

☐ Powerplant availability: a rule of sound design is 'engine first, airframe second'.
☐ Strength of materials for the airframe and engine mounting. When fitting a more powerful engine in an airframe, one must always check the strength of the structure. To check the position of the centre of gravity alone is not enough. Nevertheless, this precaution has been ignored sometimes, with disastrous consequences.
☐ Effectiveness of control surfaces at low speeds on take-off and when over-shooting from a baulked approach, for coping with propeller torque, precession (*see* fig. 7.22) and propwash effects.

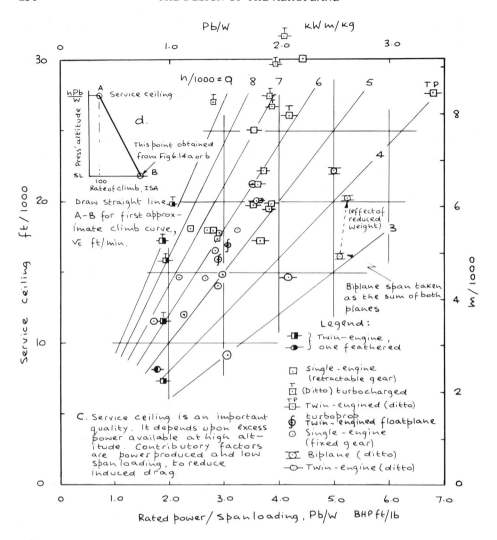

Fig. 6.14c and d   Service ceiling (at which rate of climb = 100 ft/min (0.5 m/s)). The data is calculated from manufacturer's sources. The way of using an estimate of service ceiling to construct an approximate climb curve with altitude, using sea level rates estimated from fig. 6.14 a and b, is shown inset in (d). Use the legend to 'eyeball' $n/1000$ for the configuration being considered.

☐ Constraints imposed by noise and other environmental rules.
☐ Cost.

As long as each factor can be accommodated, there is a universal tendency to fit the most powerful engine(s) that can be found. In the past that tendency has been forced by the pursuit of speed for its own sake, the conviction that: 'la vitesse est l'aristocratie du mouvement' (ref. 6.3).

Power needed to fly fast must be considered from two points of view:

☐ That needed to overcome the lowest attainable drag, unconstrained by take-off and landing requirements. As we saw earlier, this led to the World Speed record breaking

Schneider Trophy seaplanes, which had more room on water than was available on any airfield of the time.

☐ That needed to fly as fast as possible with a wing optimised for operation from a given airfield.

The second results in a larger, heavier, more complicated wing and flap arrangement than the first.

Table 6–2 gives some idea of the ratio of maximum to minimum speed of a number of different groups of light aeroplanes. The sample is not exhaustive, and it was chosen to give an idea of the magnitude of such ratios, with some room left for improvement:

Design cruising speed/stall speed, landing configuration = V_C/V_{SO}

Design diving speed/stall speed, landing configuration = V_D/V_{SO}

TABLE 6–2

Configuration	Design cruise V_C/V_{SO}	Design dive V_D/V_{SO}
Single-engine tourer-trainer, flapless, fixed gear	2.1	3.0
Single-engine tourer-trainer, flapped, retractable gear	3.2	4.5
Formula racer, flapless, fixed gear	5.2	7.3
Twin, five-seat, flapped, fixed gear	2.7	3.8
Twin, five-seat, flapped, retractable gear	2.85	3.95

Note: the last two sets of figures show that a well-designed fixed landing gear need not exact much of a drag penalty. The saving in weight and mechanical complexity might be worth more in some roles than the gains in speed (and rate of climb) achieved by retraction.

Stall speed, V_{SO}, is also the minimum flying speed in the landing configuration, if a proper stall does not occur. Speeds V_C and V_D are derived as follows:

Minimum design cruising speed:

$$\text{non-aerobatic } V_c = 38\sqrt{(W/S)} \text{ MEAS (ref. 2.4)} \tag{6–38}$$
$$= 33\sqrt{(W/S)} \text{ KEAS (ref. 6.4)} \tag{6–39}$$
$$\text{aerobatic } V_c = 42\sqrt{(W/S)} \text{ MEAS (ref. 2.4)} \tag{6–40}$$
$$= 36\sqrt{(W/S)} \text{ KEAS (ref. 6.4)} \tag{6–41}$$

where wing loading W/S is in lb/ft².

Minimum design diving speed:

$$\text{non-aerobatic } V_D = 1.4 \ V_C \text{ or } V_C + 40 \text{ KEAS}$$
$$\text{whichever is greater (ref. 2.4)} \tag{6–42}$$
$$= 1.4 \ V_C, \text{ normal category (ref. 6.4)} \tag{6–43}$$
$$= 1.5 \ V_C, \text{ utility category (ref. 6.4)} \tag{6–44}$$
$$\text{aerobatic } V_D = 1.6 \ V_C \text{ (ref. 2.4)} \tag{6–45}$$
$$= 1.55 \ V_C \text{ (ref. 6.4)} \tag{6–46}$$

The speed ratios in table 6–2 are indications of design merit, especially V_C/V_{SO}, because V_C is usually near enough the maximum level speed at full throttle – for our purposes anyway.

From eq (6–9), for straight and level flight at constant speed:

$$\eta\, Pe = DV$$

and, $$\eta P = DV/550 = FV/550 \text{ BHP}$$ (6–47)

while, from eq (2–3b), $$DV/550 = C_D \tfrac{1}{2}\rho S V^3/550 = \eta P$$ (6–48)

so that, transposing eq (6–48) for wing area:

$$S = (1100/\rho)(\eta/C_D)(P/V^3)$$ (6–49)

P is the rated power of the engine in BHP, with the remaining terms in FPSR units. This equation is converted further into forms which use KEAS and MEAS by multiplying through by 0.5921^3 for knots, and 0.6818^3 for miles per hour. Further, we can replace ambient density of the air, ρ, by relative density, σ, converting into equivalent airspeed using eq (2–53):

$$V = V_i/\sqrt{\sigma} = V_i/\sqrt{(\rho/\rho_o)}$$

which enables us to transpose eq (6–49) for power loading

$$W/P = 96000\ (\eta/C_D)(W/S)(\sqrt{=}/V_i^3)$$ (6–50)

when V_i is in KEAS; and:

$$W/P = 147000\ (\eta/C_D)(W/S)(\sqrt{\sigma}/V_i^3)$$ (6–51)

when V_i is in MEAS.

Plate 6–4 *Partenavia P68R*, a clean twin which did not show a significant improvement in productivity over the fixed (well faired) landing gear *P68B* (*Partenavia, Italy*)

Both equations confirm eq (6–26), if we substitute V_i varies as $1/\sqrt{C_L}$, which enables us to say also:

$$W/P \text{ varies as } C_L^{3/2}/C_D \qquad (6\text{–}52)$$

The term η/C_D in the above equations is the ratio of propeller efficiency to drag coefficient. Being the ratio of two non-dimensional numbers, it is non-dimensional too. The ratio is most useful in the project stage and was given the name *Everling number* after its discoverer. One tends to come across it in the period between the World Wars, but the author has so far been unable to find out anything about its origin, or the originator. Juggling eq (6–50) we obtain:

$$\text{Everling number } (\eta/C_D) = V_c^3 \,(96000\sqrt{\sigma}) \,(W_0/P)/(W_0/S) \qquad (6\text{–}53)$$

$$\text{while } (C_D/\eta) = 1/\text{Everling number} = 96000(\sqrt{\sigma}/V_c^3)(P/S) \qquad (6\text{–}53a)$$

when V_c is in KEAS. The term P/S, BHP/ft^2 may be thought of as a 'propwash factor' for want of a better name, because it is a measure of the power diffused per unit of wing

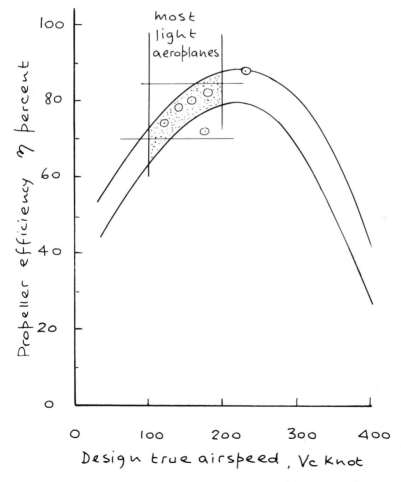

Fig. 6.15   Practical band of propeller efficiency (*see* chapter 7).

TABLE 6–3
Estimation of Everling Number
(ref. 6.6)

Aircraft	All-up weight W_o lb	Stall speed Vso KEAS	Wing loading W_o/S lb/ft²	Power loading W_o/P lb/bhp	Span loading W_o/b lb/ft	Aspect ratio $A = b^2/S$	Useful load AUW $\frac{W_u/W_o}{\%}$	Fuel load AUW $\frac{W_f/W_o}{\%}$	Max level speed ratio Vc/Vso	Everling number η/C_D
Beech V35B	3400	51	18.8	11.9	102	6.2	39	8	3.6	40
NDN–1 Firecracker	2840	57	22.2	10.9	109	5.4	32	22	3.1	28
Percival Vega Gull	2750	45	14.9	13.5	70	8.5	41	10	3.3	30
PA 28–161 Warrior	2325	50	13.5	14.5	66	7.2	42	13	2.5	23
Robin HR 200/100	1720	50	12.8	17.2	63	5.6	34	11	2.3	22
Mudry CAP 10	1675	44	14.3	9.3	63	6.0	29	14	3.3	22
Cessna 152	1670	42	10.6	16.7	51	6.8	34	9	2.6	20
PA 38 Tomahawk	1670	47	13.4	14.9	49	9.3	36	12	2.3	15
Ryson Cloudster	1650	37	7.8	16.5	29	15.6	27	12	3.5	48
Wittman W–8 Tailwind	1300 (Util)	48	14.4	13.0	58	5.6	46	12	3.0	28
SF 260 MX	2430 (Util)	57	22.4	9.3	87	6.4	37	16	3.6	37
Sequoia 300 (side by side)*	2800 (Util)	60	21.5	9.3	93	6.9	39	17	3.3	34
Sequoia 301 (tandem)*	2800 (Util)	60	22.4	9.9	96	6.8	39	17	3.4	38
Aerospatiale TB 30*	2645	62	27	9.1	109	6.1	?	?	3.1	24

$$\text{Everling number } (\eta/C_D) = \frac{\text{Max level speed}^3}{96000 \sqrt{\text{relative density}}} \times \frac{\text{(power loading)}}{\text{(wing loading)}} = \frac{Vc^3}{96000\sqrt{\sigma}} \times \frac{(W_o/P)}{(W_o/S)} \quad \text{from eq (6–53)}$$

$\eta = $ Propeller efficiency
$C_D = $ Total drag coefficient
$\approx C_{DO}$ at high speed

$\sigma = $ relative density
$Vc = $ max. level speed KEAS at altitude relevant to σ

*Project studies
Note: Data used in this table have been reproduced from published sources

w/s / p/w

Plate 6–5 Three efficient aeroplanes in terms of estimated Everling number ($\eta\,/\,C_D$, eq (6–53)) (Top) *Beech V35B*, a modern production aircraft with a value of 40 (*G. R. Wrixon, the Royal Aeronautical Society*) (Middle) Jean Batten's *Percival Gull* (1935), similar to the higherpowered *Vega Gull*, which had a value of 30, nearly one half century ago. (*Shuttleworth Collection*)

Plate 6–5 (Bottom) A slippery fast shoebox from Steve Wittman's
thoroughbred racing stable: the amateur-built *W-8 Tailwind*, with
a value of 28. (*AJE Perkins and Flight International*)

area and, hence, per unit total wetted area of airframe. Numerically it is equal to *wing loading/power loading*.

Eq (6–53a) can be used for calculating total and parasite drag coefficients, as long as reasonable estimates of propeller efficiency are available. It is also necessary to know accurately the speed and altitude so as to calculate $\sqrt{\sigma}/V_C^3$. (Rated power/wing area), P/S, is constant for any given aeroplane and can usually be obtained from published sources, like manufacturer's specifications or performance data prepared for potential customers. An excellent source is the annual *Jane's All the World's Aircraft* (ref. 6.5), obtainable from any good bookshop or library. Figure 6.15a shows broad values of propeller efficiency giving reasonable results in practice. Crude estimates for standard service propellers are $\eta = 0.7$ for wood and 0.8 for metal.

Table 6–2 showed design cruising speed ratio V_C/V_{SO}, while from fig. 5.15c we can find the corresponding ratio of (parasite drag/total drag), C_{Dp}/C_D varies from about 0.6 (for a single-engined aeroplane with fixed gear) to nearly 0.9 (for a twin with retractable gear). Thus within the limitations of the method:

$$\text{total drag coefficient, } C_D = k\eta(\sqrt{\sigma}/V_C^3)(P/S) \qquad (6\text{–}54)$$
$$\text{and parasite drag coefficient, } C_{Dp} \approx 0.65 C_D \text{ (fixed gear)} \qquad (6\text{–}55a)$$
$$\approx 0.85 C_D \text{ (retractable gear)} \qquad (6\text{–}55b)$$

The constant k in eq (6–54) is 96 000 when V_C is in KEAS, and 147 000 when given in MEAS.

Table 6–3 shows a range of Everling numbers for several different aircraft in the tourer-trainer category. From such figures and eq (6–53a):

$$C_D = \eta\,/\,\text{Everling number} \qquad (6\text{–}56)$$
$$\text{while, } C_{Dp} \approx 0.6\eta\,/\,\text{Everling number (fixed gear)} \qquad (6\text{–}56a)$$
$$\approx 0.85\eta\,/\,\text{Everling number (retractable gear)} \qquad (6\text{–}56b)$$

If we now know whether the propeller is made out of wood, or metal, we may reasonably insert $\eta = 0.7$ or 0.8 respectively in whichever equation is appropriate.

Table 6–4a has been added to show Everling numbers for different categories of aeroplane, for use when estimating achievable speeds during the project stage. It is prudent to pick Everling numbers on the low side of the range, because most drag estimates tend to be unrealistically low initially.

TABLE 6–4a

General Everling Numbers

Group	Everling number, η/C_D
Powered hang glider	5 to 9
Self launching motor glider	29 to 31
Biplane, flapless, fixed gear	8 to 14
Monoplane, flapless, fixed gear	15 to 22
Monoplane, flapped, retractable gear	25 to 40
Formula 1 racer, flapless, fixed gear	60 to 70
Twin-engined, 5-seat monoplane, fixed gear	27 to 29
Twin-engined, 5-seat monoplane, retractable gear	28 to 35
Twin-engined amphibian, 6–7 seat	about 20

Table 6–4b shows a range of improvements in Everling number by a reduction in drag coefficient, C_D for R. J. Mitchell's Supermarine Spitfire, assuming Everling number varies as $1/C_D$.

Field performance

Practical aircraft are designed to operate from fields having defined take-off and landing distances (fig. 6.16). Take-off distance depends primarily upon thrust loading, W/F, or power loading, W/P, closely followed by wing loading, W/S, and lift coefficient generated by the wing-plus-flap system, C_{Lto}.

Shortness of take-off depends upon how quickly lift greater than weight can be generated. The two forces to be overcome are due to the inertia of the aeroplane, $a(W/g)$, in which a is the acceleration and W/g is the mass of the aircraft; and $\mu\,(W-L)$ where μ is the coefficient of rolling friction. The ground run on take-off, s_1, is derived from the general equation:

$$F - D - \mu(W - L) = (W/g)\,a \qquad (6\text{–}57)$$
$$\text{giving, } s_1 = (W/2g)\quad V^2/[F - D - \mu(W - L)] \qquad (6\text{–}58)$$

in which thrust, drag and lift are usually calculated at a root mean speed (V_{RMS}) during the run ($V_{RMS} = 0.707 \, V_{LO}$, the lift-off speed) and the assumption is also made that thrust increases linearly with (speed)^2.

TABLE 6–4b

Improvement in Everling number and maximum level speed, based
upon Supermarine Spitfire
(ref. 6.11)

Improved item	Everling (% increase)	Factor	Speed (% increase)
Retractable tailwheel	2.8	1.028	1.38
Propeller root fairing	2.2	1.022	1.1
Undercarriage door	1.66	1.017	0.83
Whip aerial	0.3	1.003	0.14
Plain ailerons	3.3	1.033	1.67
Curved windscreen	3.3	1.033	1.67
Multi-ejector exhausts	2.2	1.022	1.1
Improved finish and wax polish	5.0	1.05	2.5
Clipped wing tips	0.5	1.005	0.28
Rear view hood and removal of external mirror	0.5	1.005	0.28

Braking coefficients of friction vary, but a reasonable standard value for a dry surface is 0.2. Deceleration distance on the ground is given by the following equation, assuming speed on touchdown is 1.15 V_{SO}:

$$S_G = 1.88 \, V^2_{SO}/-a \, \text{ft} \qquad\qquad (6\text{--}59)$$

where V_{SO} is in KTAS. The deceleration, $-a$, is a function of surface condition, brake and wheel size. Ref. 4.13 gives some values. Conventional brakes produce a deceleration of about $-6 \, \text{ft}/\text{s}^2$ (1.8 m/s^2). Reversible pitch propellers can increase this to $-10 \, \text{ft}/\text{s}^2$ (-3.0 m/s^2). A jet aeroplane with a drag or braking chute can achieve about $-8 \, \text{ft}/\text{s}^2$ (2.4 m/s^2). Jet engines tend to have thrust reverser efficiency less than 50 per cent and produce decelerations equivalent to about $-16 \, (F/W) \, \text{ft}/\text{s}^2$ where F/W is the ratio of thrust to weight on landing. This deceleration is added to the value for conventional brakes.

In much the same way, the coefficient of *rolling* friction is affected by surface condition and wheels: tyre size, tread pattern, and surface on which the wheel run, and wheel arrangement. For example, tandem wheels meet less resistance than wheels side by side, when running through slush and standing water, because the leading wheel clears a path for the follower; also reducing the chance of aquaplaning by the rear wheels. Thus, wheel arrangement affects directly the nose-down pitching moment about the centre of gravity caused by resistance, which must be overcome by the elevator. The effect is generally insignificant except on a soft or slushy surface. Table 6–5 shows values of rolling friction based in part upon refs 6.7 and 6.9.

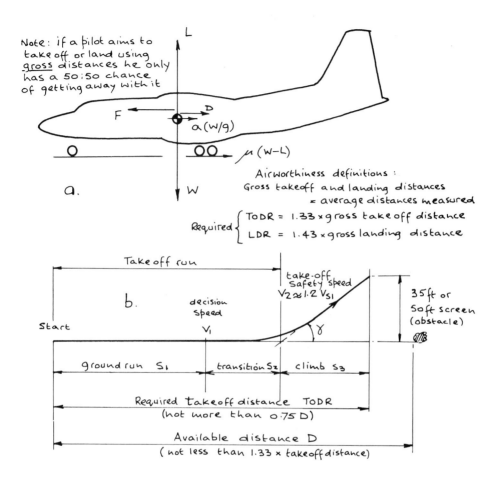

Note: if a pilot aims to take off or land using <u>gross</u> distances he only has a 50:50 chance of getting away with it

Airworthiness definitions :
Gross takeoff and landing distances
= average distances measured

Required { TODR = 1.33 × gross take off distance
           LDR = 1.43 × gross landing distance

Take off run

take-off safety speed $V_2 \approx 1.2 V_{S1}$

b.

decision speed

Start

V_1

35 ft or 50 ft screen (obstacle)

γ

ground run S_1 transition S_2 climb S_3

Required takeoff distance TODR
(not more than 0.75 D)

Available distance D
(not less than 1.33 × takeoff distance)

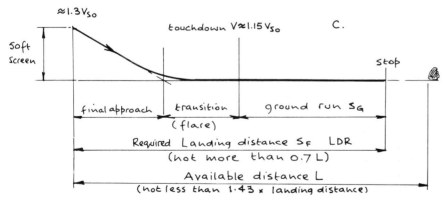

$\approx 1.3 V_{S0}$

touchdown $V \approx 1.15 V_{S0}$ C.

50 ft Screen

stop

final approach   transition
                  (flare)   ground run S_G

Required Landing distance S_F LDR
(not more than 0.7 L)

Available distance L
(not less than 1.43 × landing distance)

Fig. 6.16   Take-off and landing (a) General system of forces (b) Take-off distance (c) Landing distance.

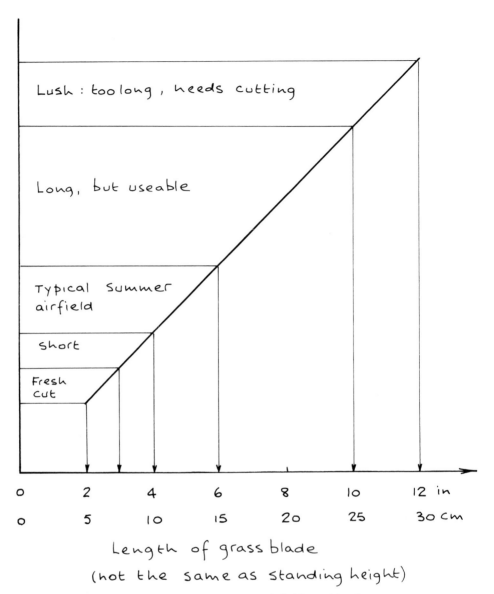

Fig. 6.17 Results of measuring grass on an airfield used by light aeroplanes.

Fig. 6.17 shows results of measuring grass on an English aerodrome used by light aeroplanes, which correspond reasonably well with the Australian figures. When rolling μ is applied to a light twin-engined aeroplane, the percentage increase in factored take-off distance is as shown in the right-hand column of the table.

Soil condition is defined in table 6–6, using the California Bearing Ratio, CBR. The table also shows the effect of the soil upon take-off and landing distance.

Factors are applied to take-off landing distances to provide a margin for numerous transient variables like pilot technique and actual conditions, and these are included.

If soil is soft, then take-off distances are increased. Fig. 6.18 shows the amount of

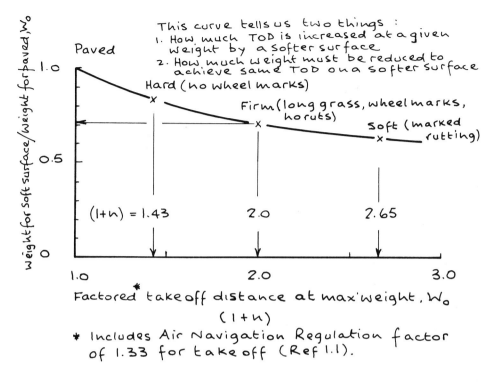

This curve tells us two things:
1. How much TOD is increased at a given weight by a softer surface
2. How much weight must be reduced to achieve same TOD on a softer surface

Paved

1.0

Hard (no wheel marks)

Firm (long grass, wheel marks, no ruts)

Soft (marked rutting)

0.5

$(1+n) = 1.43$ 2.0   2.65

0

weight for soft surface/weight for paved, W_0

1.0   2.0   3.0

Factored* take off distance at max weight, W_0
$(1+n)$

* Includes Air Navigation Regulation factor of 1.33 for take off (Ref 1.1).

Fig. 6.18   Take-off weight for operation from a softer surface to achieve same take off distance as from a hard paved surface.

TABLE 6–5

Surface	Rolling coefficient of friction, μ	Increase in factored take-off distance, per cent
Hard, paved (concrete, asphalt, wood)	0.02	0
Hard turf	0.04	+5
Short dry grass	0.05	+8
Short wet or long dry grass	0.08 to 0.10	+12 to +16
Long wet grass	0.13	+22
Soft ground	0.10 to 0.30	+16 to +55

take-off weight that must be reduced so as to become airborne in the same distance as would be achieved from a hard paved surface. The assumption is that:

take-off distance (TOD) varies as wing loading × power loading

i.e. $$s = k\, W^2/SP \qquad (6\text{–}60a)$$

which is also a function of (W/SF) for a jet, where W/F is the thrust loading as in a formula for jet take-off distance, derived from ref. 4.13:

TOD is a function of: $(W/S)(W/F)(1/C_{Lto})(1/\sigma)(420/g)[1/(1 - D/F]$ (6–60b) shown in fig. 6.19. Thus, take-off weight can be calculated:

$$\text{reduced take-off weight,} \quad W = W_o / \sqrt{(1 + n)} \qquad (6\text{-}61)$$

where n is the factored take-off distance using a hard paved surface.

TABLE 6-6

Soil condition	California bearing ratio, CBR per cent	Percentage increase in factored TOD	Percentage increase in factored landing distance (dry)	(wet)
Hard (no wheel marks)	50	+10	+10	+100
Firm (wheel impressions, no rutting)	12	+50*	+10	+50
Soft (marked wheel rutting)	5	+100	+10	+10

* Long grass on hard sub-surface
Distances include Air Navigation Regulation factors of 1.33 for take-off and 1.43 for landing (ref. 1.1)

If you have to take off from a limited field without scheduled performance to hand (e.g. after a forced landing, or for the first flight of an unknown prototype), the following rule of thumb should help (see also ref. 6.12):

☐ *Work out a lift-off speed in the take off configuration. If you cannot estimate this, then add 10 per cent to the calculated stall speed, V_{si} and treat the result, $1.1 V_{so}$ as the minimum unstick speed (take-off safety speed $V_2 \approx 1.2 V_{so}$).*
Note: if the weight has changed while the aeroplane is on the ground (unloading, refuelling):

$$\text{new stall } V_{si} = \text{old } V_{si} \times \sqrt{\frac{\text{new weight}}{\text{old weight}}} \qquad (6\text{-}61a)$$

☐ *Pace out the distance available – leaving room to accelerate enough when airborne to climb out over or to sidestep an obstacle.*
☐ *Make a clear mark at half the distance available to the point at which you must unstick.*
☐ *Check airspeed on the takeoff run to ensure that you have achieved at least $1/\sqrt{2}$, i.e., 71 per cent of the required speed by the time the half-way mark is reached. This is your decision speed, V_1*
☐ *If you have not reached your V_1 by the half-way point:*
STOP

On landing, the worst conditions are ice, and when the ground is hard and very wet, with standing water (e.g. the first heavy rain after a dry spell). Standing water and wet slush lift tyres off the ground hydrodynamically, causing aquaplaning. Low pressure tyres aquaplane earlier than high pressure tyres of the same size and tread condition, as shown by the empirical FPSR formula:

aquaplaning speed, $V_a = 9\sqrt{(\text{tyre pressure/slush density})}$
$$= 9\sqrt{(p/d)} \text{ knots} \qquad (6\text{--}62)$$

where pressure is in lb/in² and slush density is close to 1.0 (water).

The terms in eq (6–60b) give an indication of the complexity of the calculations needed for field performance. Although the formula applies to a jet, it can be manipulated for propeller-driven aircraft by converting for equivalent power:

$$\text{thrust, } F = \eta P \sqrt{\sigma}/V_{RMS} \qquad (6\text{--}63)$$

in which P is, of course, the rated horsepower of the engine. V_{RMS} is the mean speed on take-off (i.e. 0.707 V_{LO} referred to immediately after eq (6–58)), which is quite close to about 0.6 V_{SI}, the stall speed in the take-off configuration.

The amount of flap which might be needed for take-off cannot be calculated with certainty, and flight tests are needed. For example, flaps which double lift at low speed also quadruple aerodynamic drag, and this must be added to the effect of rolling friction. However, although the aerodynamic drag is increased by flap, the weight on the wheels decreases with increasing airspeed as lift bears more of the load, and the rolling friction term $\mu(W - L)$ in eq (6–57) is reduced. The lift coefficient on the ground in this phase is usually low, so that the drag coefficient of the aeroplane is approximately that due to parasite drag alone, C_{Dp}. Drag due to flap extension is not large until the aeroplane is rotated nose up at V_R.

Propeller-engined aeroplane take-off and landing distances are shown in figs 6.20 and 6.21, together with boundaries intended to squash a designer's optimism. The values apply to dry paved surfaces with zero gradient and zero wind. These distances must then be factored for different surface conditions, as shown in the preceding tables. The same average line can be extended to satisfy both single and twin-engined aeroplanes, so that if the rated power/lb take-off weight is P/W, then:

Take-off distance, $TOD = (W/P)(V_2{}^2/1000)$ ft $\qquad (6\text{--}64)$
and average design $P/W \approx V_{SI}{}^2/(23\ TOD + 4860)$ BHP/lb at SL ISA $\quad(6\text{--}64a)$

in which TOD is the gross take-off distance required from a hard paved surface, and V_{SI} is the stall speed in the take-off configuration. Take-off safety speed is assumed to be $V_2 = 1.2\ V_{SI}$ KEAS.

The equation can be modified for a higher altitude, or hotter ambient conditions by working out a new density altitude and then dividing through by the appropriate $\sqrt{\sigma}$. It can also be modified to cater for take-off from grass and soft surfaces by inserting the reduced weight W calculated from eq (6–61), in the ratio P/W.

The graphs in fig. 6.21 can be treated in a similar way, by assuming the approach speed to be:

$$V_{app} \approx 1.3\ V_{SO} = k(W/S) \qquad (6\text{--}65)$$

where k is some constant and W/S the wing loading. This reminds us that if everything else is equal in eq (2–3a), and if during a shallow approach lift is practically equal to weight, then the stall speed and the approach speed in the landing configuration are directly proportional to the wing loading. Therefore, we can size the wing needed for landing in a defined field length.

The two graphs shown in fig. 6.21 have the same slope. The lines have been extended to the left-hand side so as to measure their intercepts. Clearly, to have a value of $WV_{app}{}^2 = 0$ is impossible. By extending the lines the equations can be written in terms of

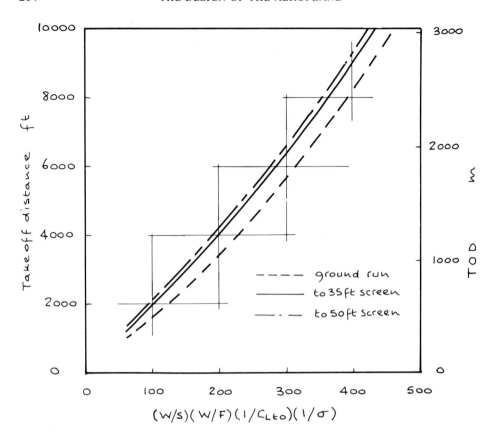

Fig. 6.19 Jet take-off distance, with aircraft characteristics, for hard paved surfaces (derived from formula in ref. 4.13).

approach speed, V_{app}, or stall speed in the landing configuration, V_{so}, when $V_{app} \approx 1.3 V_{so}$:

☐Single-engined aeroplanes (FPSR units)

$$\text{Average landing distance, } s_F = (20/10^6)WV_{app}^2 + 900 \text{ ft} \qquad (6\text{--}66)$$
$$\approx (33.8/10^6)WV_{so}^2 + 900 \text{ ft} \qquad (6\text{--}66a)$$

☐Twin-engined aeroplanes (FPSR units):

$$\text{Average landing distance, } s_F = (20/10^6)WV_{app}^2 + 1\,100 \text{ ft} \qquad (6\text{--}67)$$
$$\approx (33.8/10^6)WV_{so}^2 + 1\,100 \text{ ft} \qquad (6\text{--}67a)$$

The right-hand side of both equations can be juggled from eq (6–14) by substituting for stall speed in the landing configuration, i.e.

$$V_{so} = 1.414\sqrt{[(W/S)(1/C_{Lmax})(1/\rho)]} \qquad (6\text{--}68)$$

where C_{Lmax} is the maximum lift coefficient with flaps down. A further step introduces several aircraft parameters involving wing geometry:

$$WV_{app}^2 = 1.69WV_{so}^2 = 2.39(W/S)^2(b^2/A)(1/C_{Lmax})(1/\rho) \qquad (6\text{--}69)$$

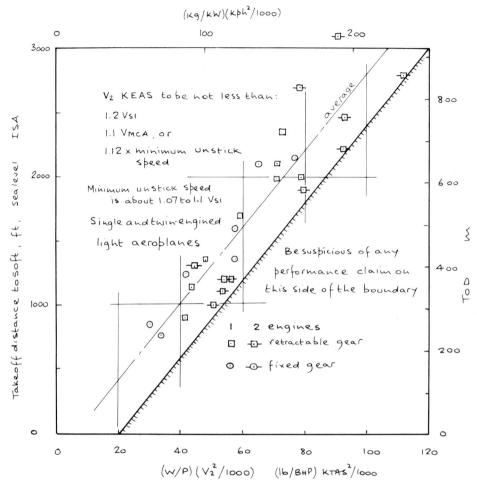

Fig. 6.20   Single and twin propeller-engined gross take-off distance to 50 ft (15 m) screen from hard paved surface. For grass an increment should be added from table 6–5, while for soil condition increments from table 6–6 should be used instead (Figures obtained from Aircraft Flight Manuals.)

(which is derived from the preceding equation by multiplying by (b^2S/b^2S)). Corning (ref. 4.13) introduces a formula for landing distance:

$$s_F = s_{50} + s_G \qquad\qquad (6\text{--}70)$$

in which s_{50} is the distance travelled from the 50 ft (15 m) screen (which distance presumably includes an increment for the flare). S_G is rolling distance on the ground. A factor of $1/0.6$ is then introduced as a factor of safety employed by the US Civil Air Regulations so that, in FPSR units:

$$S_F = (L/D)[(8.0 \, W/S)(1/\sigma \, C_{Lmax})] + 83.3) + 925(W/S[1/(-a\sigma C_{Lmax})] \quad (6\text{--}71)$$

Fig. 6.22 relates V_{SO}, the minimum level speed (which is almost the same as the stalling speed in the landing configuration), with factored landing distance from the 50 ft (15 m) screen. The Loughborough curve includes a factor of 1.5 on V_{SO}, together

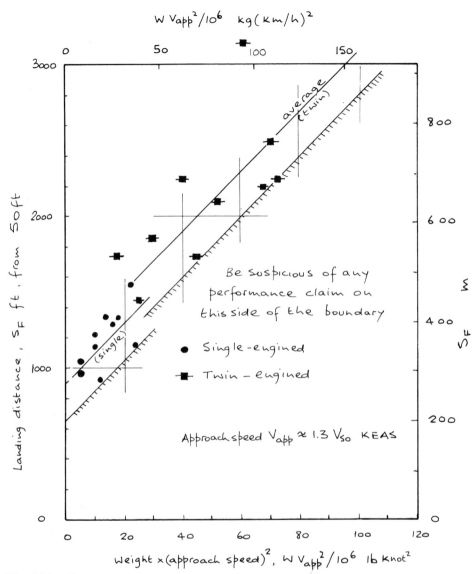

Fig. 6.21   Single and twin propellor-engined aeroplane landing distances from 50 ft (15 m) screen. Data from Aircraft Flight Manuals. Effects of different surfaces are given in tables 6–5 and 6–6.

with a further mandatory factor of 1.1 on landing distance from an obstacle clearance height of 50 ft (i.e., the screen (15 m)). The Loughborough curve is calculated from the *Special Terms of Approval of The Popular Flying Association* (ref. 6.8),which govern the design of light amateur-built aeroplanes in Britain. These require stall speeds of not more than 60 MEAS for aircraft with approved engines, or 50 MEAS with unapproved engines, and result in factored landing distances around 1 500 ft to 2 000 ft (457 m to 610 m). The Loughborough curve is published in ref. 11.1.

Minimum (level) flying speed can be derived from eq (6–68) in terms of lift

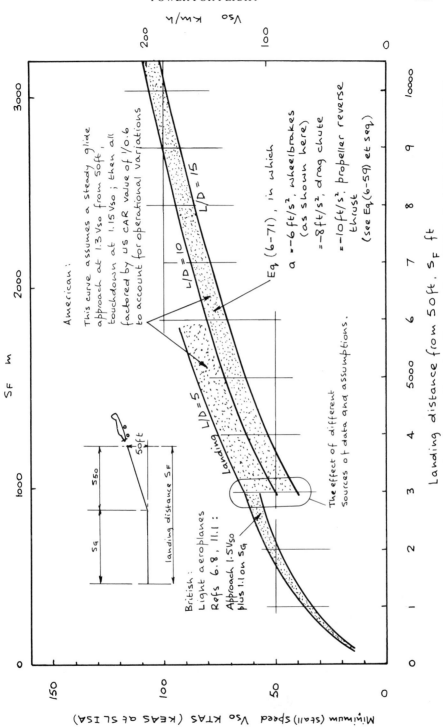

Fig. 6.22 Minimum flying (stall) speed to achieve factored landing distances from 50 ft (refs. 4.13, 6.8 and 11.1). To convert to EAS multiply by $\sqrt{\sigma}$, where σ = relative density at landing altitude.

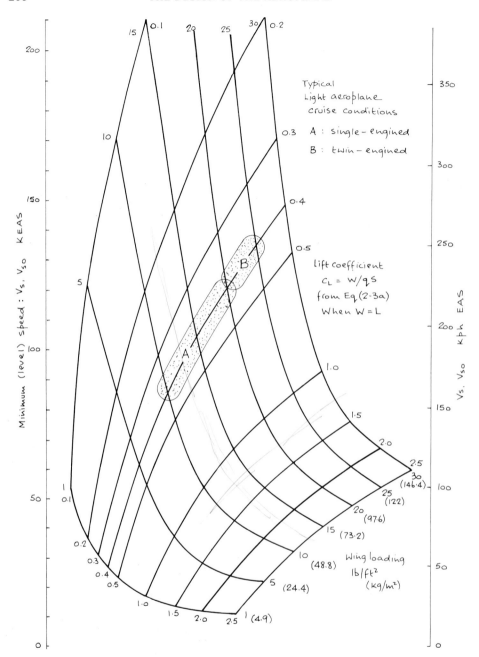

Fig. 6.23   Minimum level speed in terms of lift coefficient and wing loading, from eq (6–68).

coefficient and wing loading, as shown in fig. 6.23. This same carpet may also be used to find cruise, take-off and landing combinations of wing loading and lift coefficient. Three conclusions can now be drawn for field performance:

☐ Low wing loading results in low stall speed, so that plenty of wing area is needed to

Plate 6–6 (Top) Reference table 6–4b: hybrid *Supermarine Spitfire 1* airframe with a *Rolls-Royce Merlin 35*, flown by Tony Bianchi. The aeroplane is registered as G-AIST. (*Alain Ernoult via Tony Bianchi*) (Bottom) Later and perhaps the most beautiful of all *Spitfires, Rolls-Royce Griffon* engined MK XIV owned and flown by Spencer Flack as G-FIRE (*Spencer Flack and MC Searle*)

get into and out of small fields. The same applies to fields that are hot and high with reduced density altitudes. There is a direct trade-off between W/S and ambient density ρ, for a given V_{SO}, which may be seen from eq (6–68).

☐ Low span loading, W/b, reduces induced drag, which improves rate of climb. Therefore, if we want an aeroplane to climb fast, make the wingspan as long as possible (for a given structure weight).

☐ For high speed profile and parasite drag must be reduced, which means that fast aeroplanes need small frontal, wetted and wing areas. But small wing area spoils field performance, forcing one to provide flaps and other forms of variable geometry.

Having made this last point, it should be noted that many amateur-built light aeroplane designers do not bother to equip their aircraft with flaps. The trim changes which occur and the added mechanical complexity and weight are thought to outweigh any advantage in reducing a landing speed of 50 to 60 knots by around 5 knots. It is argued that the kinetic energy at such relatively low speeds can be dissipated more cost effectively by a combination of tail-down attitude after touchdown and wheelbrakes.

Now that we have some idea of the airframe factors which influence achieved performance, we shall look next at powerplant characteristics.

References

6.1 Mondey, D. (1975) *The Schneider Trophy*. London: Robert Hale.

6.2 Quickie Aircraft Corporation *Quickie*. Post Office Box 786, Mojave, Ca 93501.

6.3 Foxworth, T. G. (1975) *The Speed Seekers*. London: Macdonald and Jane's Publishers Ltd.

6.4 *Federal Aviation Regulations, Part 23*. Federal Aviation Administration Superintendent of Documents, US Government Printing Office.

6.5 Macdonald and Jane's Publishers Ltd (annually) *Jane's All the World's Aircraft*. London.

6.6 *Light Aeroplane Design Competition Guidelines* (1978–79). The Royal Aeronautical Society.

6.7 Air Navigation Order, Section 101.22, (1967) Australian Department of Civil Aviation.

6.8 *Special Terms of Approval granted to the Popular Flying Association, under Approval* Reference DAI/1172/48. (1973) Civil Aviation Authority (Airworthiness Division).

6.9 Smetana F.O., Summery D. C., Johnson W. D., NASA CR–2272. *Point and Path Performance of Light Aircraft* (June 1973). North Carolina State University for Langley Research Centre.

6.10 Barnett, C. (Apr. 1979) Quickie – lightweight extraordinary. *Flight International*.

6.11 Smith, J. (Dec. 1946) *The Development of the Spitfire and Seafire*. Royal Aeronautical Society, 706th Lecture.

6.12 Lerche, H-W (1980) *Luftwaffe Test Pilot*. London: Jane's Publishing Company Limited.

CHAPTER 7

Reciprocating Engines

'The whole problem is confined within these limits, *viz* – To make a surface support a given weight by the application of power to the resistance of the air.'
Sir George Cayley (1809)
(from *The Aeroplane, An Historical Survey of its Origins and Development*, C. H. Gibbs-Smith, Her Majesty's Stationery Office).

Matching an engine to an airframe involves a search for the best compromise between overall lift/drag ratio, airframe weight, cruise altitude, engine size and weight, and overall propulsive efficiency, η_p, which is the product of the 'internal' thermal process, η_i, and the efficiency of the mechanical process, η_m (eq (2–31)), such that:

propulsive efficiency, $\eta_p = \eta_m \eta_i$
= rate at which useful propulsive work is done/rate at which energy is
applied to the system $\qquad$ (7–1)
= brake thermal efficiency $\times$ propeller efficiency $\qquad$ (7–1a)

We saw in chapter 2 that energy and work have the same dimensions of force $\times$ distance through which it is applied. The introduction of a *rate* transforms the statement of efficiency into one of power input and output (eq (2–20)): thermochemical into mechanical.

Fig. 7.1 compares propulsive efficiency for a supercharged reciprocating engine, a turbojet, and a turbopropeller engine at speeds less than M 1.0. This shows that there is little or nothing to be gained from the pure turbojet at low airspeeds. Propellers, or fans, must be added. Nevertheless, there is profit for us in considering basic turbojet principles, and this is done in the next chapter.

Fig. 7.2 shows the way in which cruise efficiency, expressed in terms of the product:

$$\text{cruise efficiency} = \text{M}(L/D) \qquad (7–2)$$

jumps with each new breakthrough in aeronautical research and development. This measure of cruise efficiency can also be stated in terms of true airspeed and thrust specific fuel consumption, μ', (eq (2–36b)) in the ratio:

$$(V/\mu')(L/D) = k\eta_p \qquad (7–3)$$

which tends to have more or less set values for particular aerodynamic shapes, propulsion systems and altitudes of operation. For a typical subsonic jet aeroplane cruising at M 0.8, the constant $k \approx 40000$ in FPSR units when the lift/drag ratio is

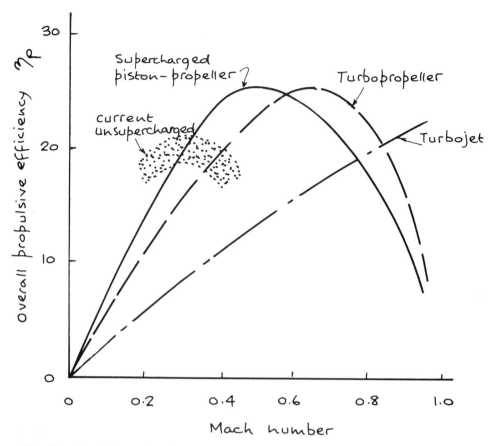

Fig. 7.1 Typical trends of overall efficiency of propulsion systems below M 1.0. The overall propulsive efficiency of a piston engine is the product of brake thermal efficiency and mechanical propeller efficiency. Thus the figures from table 2–1 would show a peak propulsive efficiency around 20 per cent, assuming a propeller efficiency of 80 per cent in eq (7–1a).

about 10. This shows how speed increases overall productivity, defined in eq (1–4), and the present superiority of the jet engine at high speeds.

There are five possible powerplants for light aeroplanes:

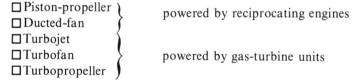

□ Piston-propeller
□ Ducted-fan } powered by reciprocating engines
□ Turbojet
□ Turbofan } powered by gas-turbine units
□ Turbopropeller

The last three are thirstier to run in the smaller sizes than the first two, and about five to eight times costlier to install than a piston engine of equivalent power.

Piston-propeller engines push a working mass of air rearwards by rotation of a propeller. Turbojets produce thrust by heating and expelling rearwards a mass of air and exhaust products. Turbofan and turbopropeller engines generate thrust predominantly by a 'cold flow' working mass: the fan within a duct, the propeller in

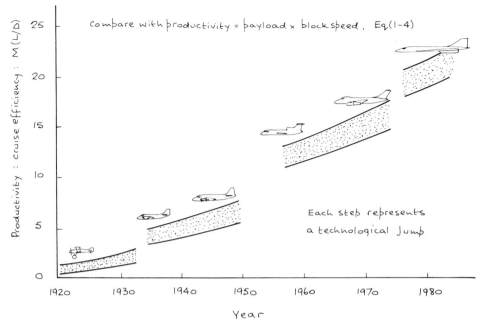

Fig. 7.2 Advances in aerodynamic cruise efficiency with each new breakthrough in research and development. The yardstick is (Mach number M) times (cruise lift/drag ratio).

free air. Both types of unit generate some additional jet thrust, as we saw in eqs (2–32a and b). Ducted-fans are essentially small diameter propellers, with more blades, working within cowled ducts.

Piston-propeller engines

The piston engine is the workhorse of light aviation. For many, the era of the big piston-propeller aeroplane, which gave way to the jet after World War 2, represented the quintessence of aircraft design. Then, a design could still be encompassed by one single mind. Today, with the exception of the sort of aeroplanes with which this book is concerned, big jets involve massive design teams, and it is impossible for the chief designer to be more than a general – with a subordinate staff making detailed decisions.

Piston engines are either air or liquid cooled. Most modern engines are air cooled, although a growing number of automotive conversions feature liquid cooling, as in plate 7.2 The commonest engines are fourstroke, employing the Otto cycle (Dr Nickolas Otto, 1876, but separately attributed to Beau de Rochas, fourteen years earlier):

induction – compression – power – exhaust

In such engines the crankshaft revolves twice for each complete cycle of four strokes, fig. 7.3. Two strokes are made outwards from the crankshaft, and two inwards, towards it. The power stroke occurs every other revolution, while the piston coasts through the unproductive revolution, forcing out the burnt gases from the working half-cycle.

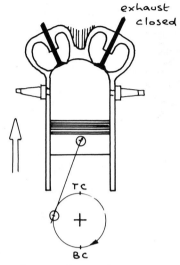

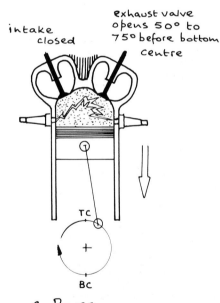

Fig. 7.3 Four-stroke Otto-cycle.
(Note: in US and British nomenclature:
    intake valve = inlet valve
    top centre TC = top dead centre TDC
    bottom centre BC = bottom dead centre BDC)

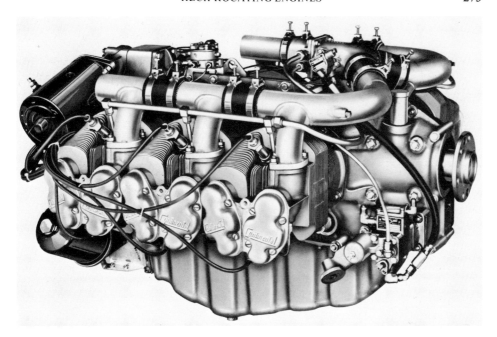

Plate 7–1 Typical modern air-cooled engines (Top) *Continental IO-360-D* (210 BHP) (*Teledyne Continental Motors*) (Bottom) *König* three-cylinder radial two-stroke (26 to 30 BHP at 4000 to 4500 rpm) for minimum aircraft (*König Motorenbau KG Berlin*)

Piston engines are classified as follows:

☐ *Unsupercharged, driving fixed-pitch propellers*. Their controls consist of a throttle lever (in effect an air control lever) and usually a mixture control. For any given throttle setting power, which is proportional to the mass of gas flowing through the cylinders and, hence, air density and swept volume, varies with rpm. In turn rpm vary with attitude of the propeller to the airflow, with airspeed, and with altitude – all of which affect mass airflow per minute (the last two through changing air pressure and, hence, intake manifold pressure). The mixture control is for regulating the fuel/air ratio as air density falls with increasing height.

☐ *Unsupercharged, driving constant-speed propellers*. An rpm control lever is added, which enables the pilot to select one particular engine speed. A constant-speed governor then automatically adjusts the propeller blade pitch angle over the constant speed range, to prevent the rpm varying. Mixture control is often automatic. At constant engine speed and TAS variations in power only occur with changes in altitude and, hence, indicated mean effective pressure, IMEP (eq (2–30)), which is dependent upon the manifold (or boost) pressure. With all normally aspirated (unsupercharged) engines, manifold pressure is always less than atmospheric. If rpm are increased at a given throttle setting, manifold pressure drops initially, because cylinder volume swept/minute increases, causing a greater suction downstream of the manifold, which is located between the air intake and the engine. At any given throttle and rpm setting, manifold pressure falls as altitude is gained. Progressive opening of the throttle maintains the original manifold pressure, but only up to the full throttle height (FTH) for that pressure.

☐ *Supercharged, driving constant-speed propellers*. Here, a mechanical device called a supercharger is added, which boosts manifold pressure – up to 20 lbf/in² (138.24 kN/m²) or more above atmospheric in some of the bigger engines. These are discussed later.

The way in which pressure within the cylinder varies throughout a fourstroke cycle is shown in fig. 7.4a. Summing the pressures during the whole cycle enables an average indicated mean effective pressure to be worked out, which is assumed to act during the working stroke. The areas under the respective parts of the curve represent power: those in A and C being power developed: the others in B and D being power expended (B in compressing the charge, D expelling the exhaust). Thus:

$$\text{indicated horsepower, IHP} = areas\ (A + C) - (B + D) \qquad (7\text{-}4)$$

Note that the spark is drawn occurring before *top dead centre*, TDC, as shown in a typical engine timing diagram, fig. 7.5. This is so that combustion will be complete by the start of the power stroke.

Charge burning time is about 0.0025 seconds (shorter in high-compression engines, in which the mixture has sustained adiabatic heating to a higher temperature). With an engine turning at 2500 rpm, the spark would have to occur about 37.5 deg before top dead centre. Rich mixtures burn fastest, lean mixtures slowest, so that spark timing can be advanced effectively or retarded by mixture strength. An incorrect mixture setting causes power loss. A single-engine *Beechcraft C23* with a faulty, over-rich carburetter lost 285 ft/min rate of climb at gross weight, only just clearing a hedge during an uphill take-off. That even reduced the rate below the 400 ft/min Group C and D minimum in fig. 6.14a.

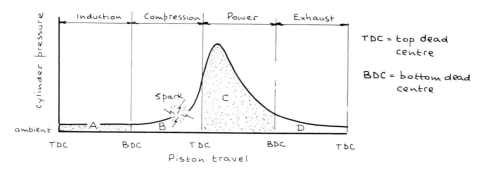

a. Cylinder pressure during four-stroke cycle. A and C develop power, B and D lose it; but exhaust losses can be much reduced by careful manifold and pipe design and tuning.

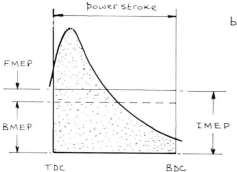

b. Loss of Indicated mean effective pressure, IMEP to friction mean effective pressure, FMEP (which collectively includes other mechanical losses). The remainder is brake mean effective pressure, BMEP.

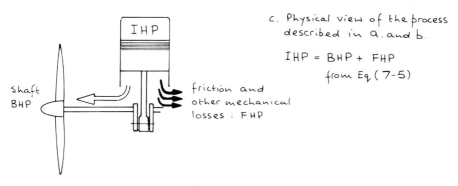

c. Physical view of the process described in a. and b.

IHP = BHP + FHP

from Eq (7-5)

Fig. 7.4   Four-stroke pressures and powers.

Indicated horsepower produced depends upon the charge weight of mixture burned in a given time, and that depends in turn upon the compression ratio of the engine. Indicated mean effective pressure, acting upon the area of each piston generates the indicated horsepower, IHP, part of which, the brake horsepower, BHP, is available for

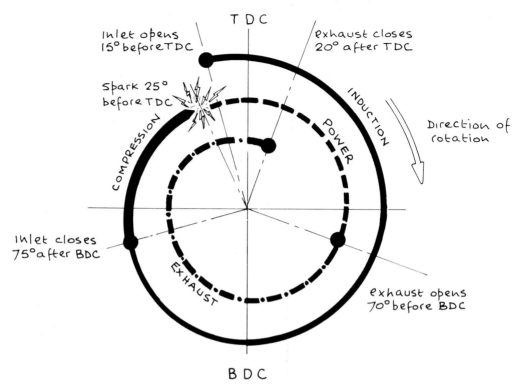

Fig. 7.5   Typical four-stroke timing diagram. (An error of 5 deg in spark timing made a difference in rate of climb, caused by a reduction in power, of 128 ft/min (0.65 m/s) in a gross 700 ft/min (3.56 m/s) for one brand new light aeroplane flown by the author.)

turning the propeller. This is the power left over after friction, power used to drive pumps, generators, cooling, and other mechanical losses have taken their toll. Such losses are swept up collectively as friction horsepower, FHP, produced by friction mean effective pressure, FMEP, acting on the piston areas.

Examination of eq (2–30) shows how indicated horsepower is a function of IMEP, capacity (i.e., piston area × stroke × number of cylinders) and engine speed, n rpm, such that:

$$IHP = plan/33\,000 \text{ hp} \qquad \text{from eq (2–30)}$$

Brake horsepower, so called because it is measured by a prony brake, a dynamometer, or a torquemeter, can then be written as:

$$BHP = IHP - FHP \qquad (7–5)$$
$$= \eta_m \, IHP \qquad \text{from eq (2–31)}$$

BHP can also be expressed in terms of torque, T, applied by the crankshaft, where:

$$\text{Work done per revolution} = 2\pi \times torque \qquad (7–6)$$
$$\text{so that, } BHP = 2\pi n T/33\,000 \text{ hp} \qquad (7–7)$$

Because the four-stroke engine has one working stroke every other revolution then, in FPSR units:

$$IMEP = (792\,000/c)(IHP/n) \qquad (7–8)$$

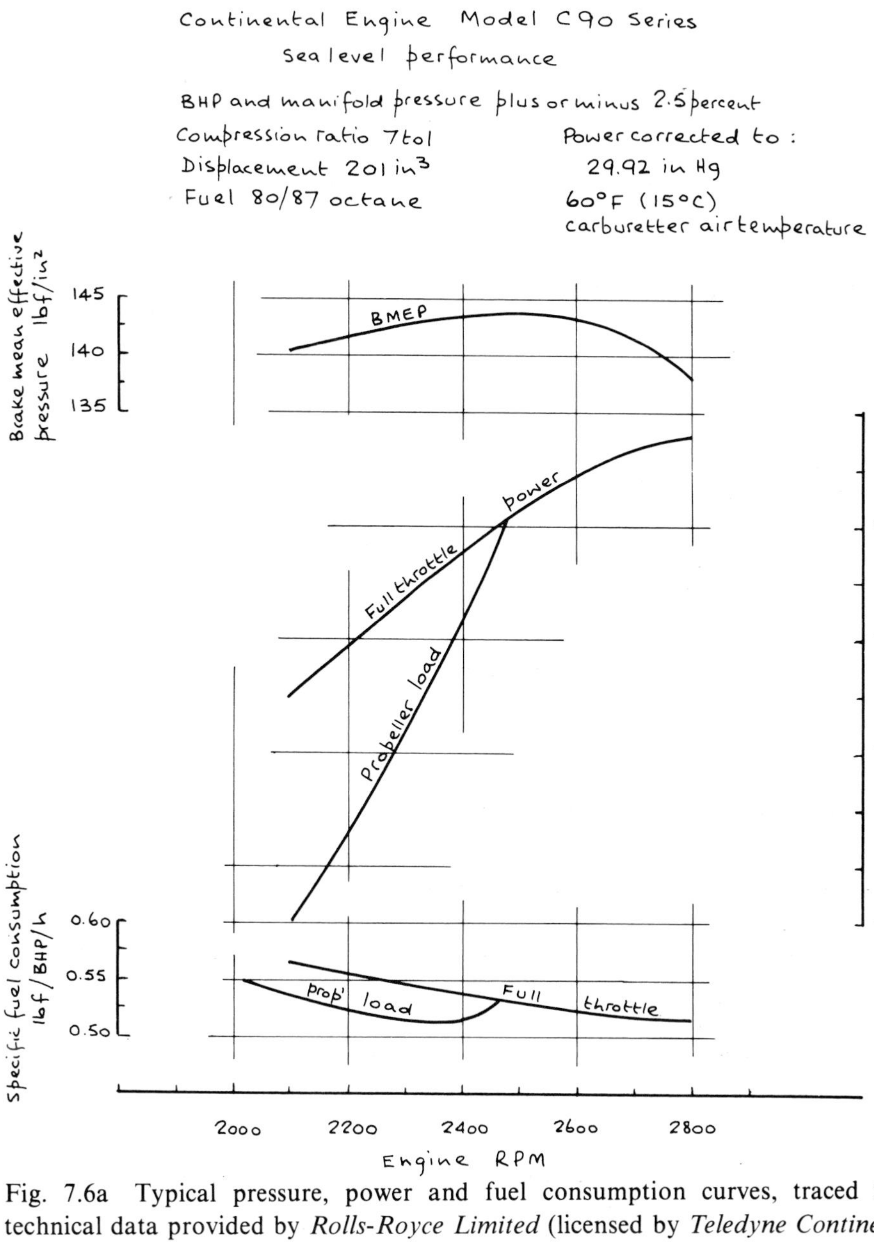

Continental Engine Model C90 Series

Sea level performance

BHP and manifold pressure plus or minus 2.5 percent

Compression ratio 7to1   Power corrected to :
Displacement 201 in³   29.92 in Hg
Fuel 80/87 octane   60°F (15°C)
                                   carburetter air temperature

Fig. 7.6a Typical pressure, power and fuel consumption curves, traced from technical data provided by *Rolls-Royce Limited* (licensed by *Teledyne Continental Motors* USA).

where c is the capacity, in³. In the same way:

$$\text{BMEP} = (792000/c)(\text{BHP}/n) \qquad (7-9)$$

Clearly, engine speed plays an important part in the magnitude of power lost to 'friction'. The higher the rpm the greater the loss, in a non-linear way, because the engine runs hotter, tolerances are used up, lubrication becomes less efficient. Fig. 7.6 shows BMEP and BHP curves against rpm for the *Continental C90*, which has a sea level rated power of 90 hp (67.14 kW). These curves, which are typical, show the way in

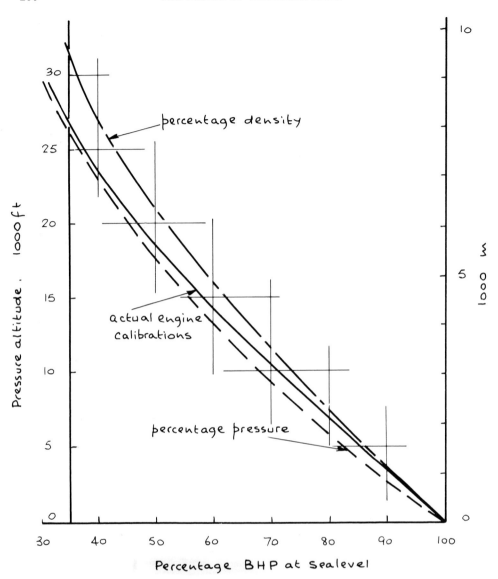

Fig. 7.6b   Percentage variation in power with altitude of a normally aspirated piston engine (based upon ref. 7.2).

which output varies with speed. The power curves are given for FULL THROTTLE and PROP′ LOAD: the first is power output measured on a testbed by means of a dynamometer, or brake. The second is while swinging a propeller.

Fig. 7.7 shows a number of engine results. The lines have been drawn according to the four-stroke formulae in eqs (7–8) and (7–9), while certain engines are two-strokes, i.e. there is a power stroke during each revolution, instead of every other. Nevertheless, the results give a clear indication of the way in which a given volume of mixture can be made more effective by working the engine at the highest cylinder pressure possible. A fast running engine is not a satisfactory way of achieving high power, because wear and tear is increased, friction losses are greater, and the engine is noisier (so is the

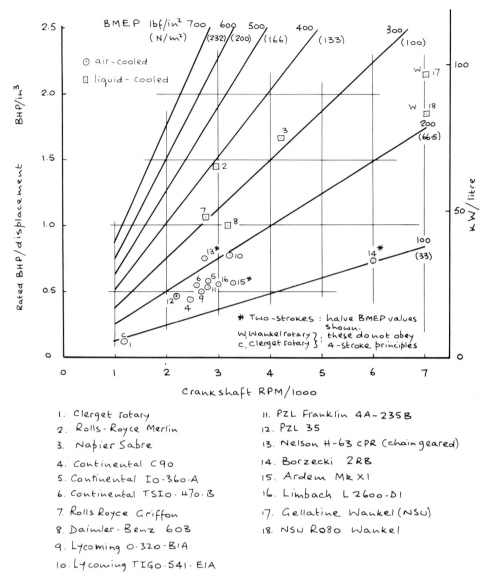

Fig. 7.7   Four-stroke engine performance. Some engines, like rotaries and two-strokes, do not fit without fiddling them, but that does not belie the overall message in the diagram.

propeller). In fact there is an old operational rule of thumb which applies as much to design as engine handling:

□ *'For efficiency, use high boost and low rpm'.*

Fig. 7.8 shows engine weight/horsepower as a function of specific weight (eq (2–40)). This shows how weight falls with increased working pressure within the cylinders, but cooling becomes more of a problem because high pressure engines are also hot engines.

The specific weight of a piston engine, given in eq (2–40) can be compared with that of a jet engine, given in eq (2–41):

Specific weight (jet)/true airspeed in ft/s × 550 is comparable with
specific weight (piston)   (7-10)

Propeller load

A power curve with propeller load was shown in fig. 7.6a. The load is caused by air resisting rotation in the same way as a wing generates drag. In fact the equation has the same form as eq (2-3b). Fig. 7.9 shows the way in which the drag of each blade acts at the centre of pressure, distance r from the shaft centre line. Torque is the sum of blade drag × radius, such that:

$$\text{Torque, } T = N(C_D\, q\, S)r \qquad (7-11)$$

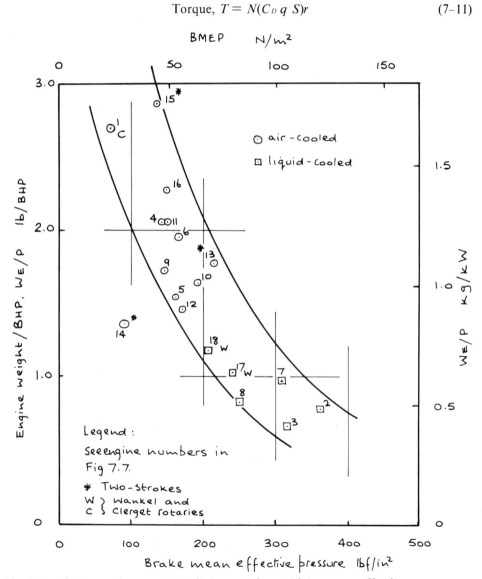

Fig. 7.8 Lighter engines can be built by working at higher mean effective pressures, but they cost more (see Fig. 7.7 for legend).

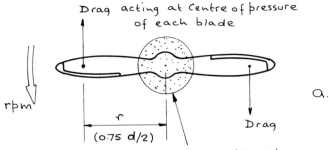

Drag acting at centre of pressure
of each blade

a.

rpm

r
(0.75 d/2)

Inner ¼ of propeller diameter, d,
does almost no useful work
(therefore, fair it with the largest
practicable spinner — most spinners
are far too small).

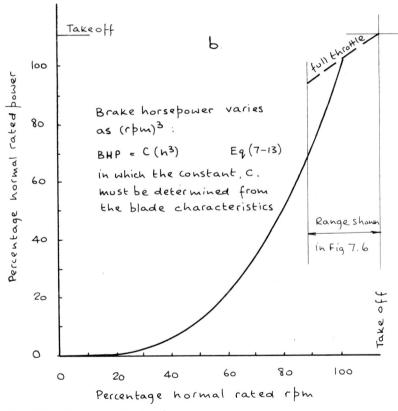

b.

Takeoff

full throttle

Brake horsepower varies
as (rpm)³ :

$BHP = C(n^3)$ Eq (7-13)

in which the constant, C,
must be determined from
the blade characteristics

Range shown
in Fig 7.6

Take off

Percentage normal rated power

Percentage normal rated rpm

Fig. 7.9   The propeller load curve.

where S is the area of each blade, and N their number. As long as a blade tip avoids compressibility effects (travelling less than about M 0.6) then blade drag coefficient is roughly constant. The term q involves V^2, where:

$$V^2 = (2\pi r \, n/60)^2 \qquad (7-12)$$

where n is the number of revolutions per minute. Thus torque varies as (rpm)². When an aeroplane is carrying out a static ground run, doubling engine rpm from 1 200 to 2 400 rpm increases propeller torque by 4.

It may be shown that power absorbed in swinging the propeller is:

$$BHP = (2\pi nT)/33\,000) = (nT)/5252 = C(n^3) \qquad (7\text{--}13)$$

from the combination of eqs (7–11) and (7–12). C is a constant. This means that power must be increased by 8 to double rpm, and by 27 to treble it. Thus, if ground static rpm should be 2 270, say, but only 2 250 rpm are achieved on the engine runup before a test flight, maximum rpm will be down by about 1 per cent and power by $(1 - 0.99^3)$, say 3 per cent.

Fuel–air ratio

Quite small changes in power can make relatively large changes in rate of climb. Sensitivity can be appreciated from eq (6–22) by substituting, say, lift/drag ratio $= 15$ and angle of climb, $\gamma = 2$ deg, so that the term $(L/D)\gamma/57.3 = 0.52$. An angle of climb of 2 deg has a gradient around 3.5 per cent, yet just over half as much power again is needed as to fly level at the same speed. This means that one third of the total power is being used for the climb. A three per cent loss in power, caused by a reduction in engine rpm, like we have just seen above, could therefore reduce the rate of climb by $0.03/0.52$ = near enough 6 per cent.

The mixture of fuel and air burned in the cylinders has constant volume, but density of the air (and so the mass of oxygen to support combustion) contained decreases with any gain in altitude. Fig. 7.10 (based upon ref. 7.1) shows the combustible range of fuel and air mixture, between the extremes of too lean and too rich. Very small changes in fuel/air ratio have a marked effect upon power produced. The curve suggests that a mixture 12 per cent rich causes a reduction of 4 per cent in power produced. In the example just given, a 4 per cent reduction in power could result in $0.04/0.52 =$ about 8 per cent reduction in rate of climb. This could be caused by the pilot failing to lean the mixture during the climb.

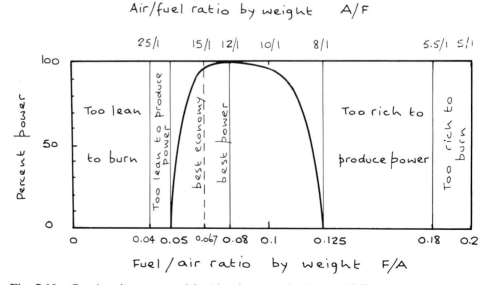

Fig. 7.10   Combustion range of fuel in air (see refs. 7.1 and 7.2).

Fig. 7.11 shows fuel–air ratio against power (ref. 7.2). Notice richening needed at high power, the addition of extra fuel being to cool the mixture, to prevent pre-ignition.

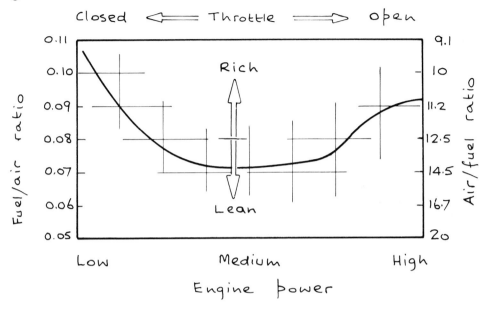

Fig. 7.11   Fuel-air ratio requirements of piston engines (ref. 7.2).

Proper mixture strength gives maximum Specific Air-Range, SAR, economic use of fuel and increased engine life. The most useful and direct instrument for this purpose is the Exhaust Gas Temperature gauge, EGT. A sensing probe is usually located in the exhaust of the leanest-running (therefore hottest) cylinder – it is almost impossible to distribute equal mixture strength to all cylinders, without a separate injector for each. When the mixture is stoichiometrically correct, the fuel–air ratio is 0.067 to 0.08 (between about 15 and 12 parts of air to one of fuel).

Fig. 7.12 (ref 7.3) has been added to show that for a given power setting a critical ratio within this range causes highest exhaust gas temperatures, so that combustion is complete, even though power is reduced slightly. *Cessna* is believed to have defined 'normal lean' mixture as that causing a loss of 2 mph (3.2 km/h) when leaned from that for best power. The normal lean mixture corresponds with highest EGT. The power curve in the lower part of the figure corresponds with that shown in reverse, in fig. 7.10.

Effect of humidity

Humid air is wet air. When we talk of saturated air we mean that it contains as much evaporated water (not free water) as it can hold. At ambient temperatures below freezing air is relatively dry because water turns to ice. Above freezing point the capacity of air to hold water is doubled with every 10°C (180°F) rise in temperature.

At a given pressure dry air is denser than saturated air. When relative humidity is 100 per cent (eq 2–38)), every 1 lb saturated air at standard temperature and pressure contains 0.023 lb (0.01 kg) water vapour. As the weight of water vapour is only 5/8 that of an equal volume of dry air, this means that water vapour displaces 8/5 × 0.023 =

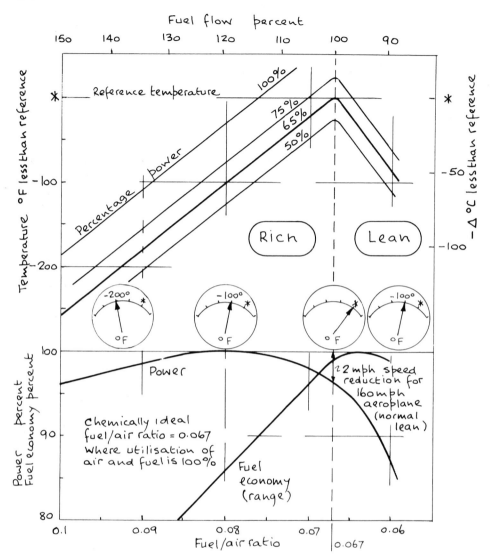

Fig. 7.12   Vital engine parameters in relation to fuel/air ratio (based upon *Alcor Aviation Ltd* data in ref. 7.3).

0.037 lb dry air (0.017 kg), leaving 0.963 lb (0.44 kg) containing oxygen to mix with the fuel. The effect upon the engine is:

☐ A reduction in the mass of combustion-supporting oxygen entering the cylinders, within a given volume of (air + water vapour) swallowed.

☐ A consequent richening of the mixture, reducing power as shown in figs 7.10 and 7.11.

☐ To slow the rate of combustion, partially drowning the process, with exactly the same effect as retarding the ignition.

All told there is an overall loss of power which can amount to 20 per cent in conditions of high humidity and temperature, found in the tropics. Even at 27° C (80° F), relative humidity of 90 per cent can reduce power by 6.5 per cent (ref. 7.4). In humid air expect an average power loss of 10 per cent, say. *Beechcraft* call for a reduction in rate of climb of 70 ft/min (0.36 m/s) in high humidity for the *C23 Sundowner 180* (as stated in the *Pilots Operating Manual* dated January 30, 1976).

Supercharging

An engine relying upon the combination of ambient pressure and its own suction to breathe air is said to be *naturally*, or *normally*, *aspirated*, and develops maximum power at sea level. At higher altitudes power is lost as the supply of oxygen falls. One of the most widely used formulae, certainly since 1934, is the following based on one attributed to Gagg and Ferrar of *Wright Aeronautical Corporation* (ref. 7.5). It expressed power at altitude, BHP_h, where the density of the air is ρ, in terms of sea level BHP_o, and ρ_o:

$$BHP_h = BHP_o[(\rho/\rho_o) - (1 - \rho/\rho_o)/7.55] \qquad (7-14)$$

The equation shows that power falls with altitude along a line lying between that for relative density, and the one for relative pressure. It lies closer to the relative pressure line than to density. Experimental results produce slightly higher values than the formula.

Power loss can be restored by supercharging but this is limited by the degree of overpressure that the engine structure is able to withstand, and by adiabatic heating of the air–fuel mixture which causes premature detonation. Supercharging once meant mechanical aspiration by means of a blower, connected directly to the engine through a gear-train. Today it has a wider use and applies to any kind of mechanical pressurisation of the mixture. Supercharging is expensive but, if the cost can be borne, it brings the following benefits:

☐ Field and climb performance are improved, especially at higher altitudes.
☐ It becomes possible to fly above weather that would upset operations in aircraft with normally aspirated engines, confined to lower altitudes.
☐ Range and cruising airspeed are increased (even though some extra fuel is burned getting up there).
☐ Adiabatic heating in the induction manifold delays or prevents icing.
☐ With supercharger OUT the aeroplane can usually be flown efficiently at low altitude, without spoiling the fuel consumption of the basic engine.

The modern turbosupercharger (contracted to turbocharger) consists of a free-running shaft, at one end of which is fixed a turbine, at the other a compressor. The turbine is acted upon by the hot exhaust from the engine. The compressor runs in a separate duct, boosting the manifold pressure to the cylinders, as shown in fig. 7.13. The first appearance of the exhaust-driven turbocharger was on a *Liberty* engine of 1918, which resulted in an altitude record of 33 000 ft (10 058 m) in 1920. But the first production turbochargers in regular use are said to have been used on the *Boeing* B17 of 1939.

When the turbocharger is not in use, the exhaust flow is dumped to atmosphere through a wastegate. Closure of the wastegate ducts gases through the turbine stage, boosting the mixture pressure by means of the impeller.

A further advantage of turbocharging is that the impeller provides cabin pressurisation if required, recycling energy that would otherwise run to waste.

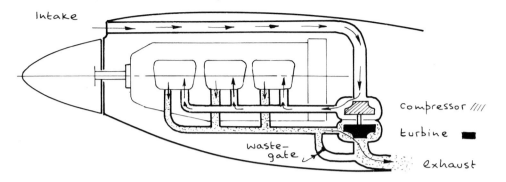

With the waste-gate closed, exhaust gases drive the turbine and the compressor — which turbo-charges air from the intake to the induction system. If the waste-gate is opened, exhaust gases by-pass the turbine and there is no supercharging.

Fig. 7.13   The turbo-supercharger.

The commonest forms of turbocharging light aeroplane engines are shown in fig. 7.14:

☐ *Ground boosting* of the normal sea level pressure of 14.7 lbf/in^2 (704 N/m^2, 1013.2 mb) to much higher values. A turbocharge ratio of 2:1 adds another 14.7 lbf/in^2, but raises the charge temperature considerably by adiabatic heating. A temperature rise of 6° C (11° F) reduces the knock limit of the fuel by 3 per cent. The result is that most flat-four and six engines used for light aircraft cannot be boosted beyond 500 hp (373 kW). A bigger and older breed of piston engine, like the *Rolls Royce Merlin,* using 100 octane fuel (see chapter 2, Engines and powerplants), was eventually boosted by 285 per cent, to 2050 hp and 25 lbf/in^2 (1535 kW and 1197 n/m^2) using a geared supercharger.

High boost involves the use of expensive inconel exhaust valves and vanes for the turbocharger unit, and special materials for other parts. Strengthened crankshafts are also needed.

☐ *Altitude boosting, or normalising* is achieved by means of a turbocharger that maintains approximately sea level power to altitudes around 16000 to 22000 ft (4900 to 6700 m). With such a system the wastegate is open on take-off, but it is then automatically closed progressively during the climb, until it is fully shut at the critical altitude, or Full Throttle Height, FTH. Above the critical altitude the turbocharger can no longer deliver sea level pressure, and power falls.

☐ *Ground and altitude boosting* is a combination of both of the above forms. Although sea level pressure is maintained to quite high altitudes, it is not correct to assume that sea level power is also maintained. As the aircraft climbs, the turbocharger runs faster and hotter, and gas temperatures of 650°C to 900°C (1200° F to 1650° F), and rotational speeds of 71000 to 125000 rpm are commonplace, so that adiabatic heating reduces air density in the induction manifold. Power output is reduced, even though manifold pressure remains constant.

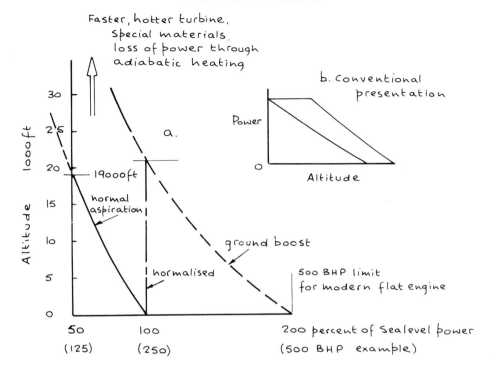

Faster, hotter turbine.
Special materials.
loss of power through
adiabatic heating

b. Conventional
presentation

Power

O

Altitude

a.

30

25

20 — 19000ft

normal
aspiration

15

10 ground boost

5 normalised

O

50 (125)   100 (250)   200 percent of Sealevel power

500 BHP limit
for modern flat engine

(500 BHP example)

Altitude 1000ft

Some points on turbocharger handling:

1. High altitude = high turbocharger rpm and cylinder head temperature

2. Cylinder head temperature, CHT, at least 30°F (20°C) higher at high altitude.

3. High CHT increases risk of detonation and damage to engine

4. Turbocharged engines need at least 100 octane fuel.

5. Open throttle slowly to avoid surge and over-boost.

6. Observe power-change sequence   (rich mixture = cooler CHT)
   Increasing power: enrich → increase rpm → open throttle
                                                    to increase
                                                    boost pressure
   Decreasing power: reduce throttle → reduce rpm → adjust mixture

7. Takeoff: consult Owner's Manual, Flight Manual or other approved manual for minimum oil temperature to prevent over-boosting.

8. Climb: unless specified in the appropriate manual use full rich mixture to improve cooling, so as to avoid detonation.

9. Cruising: observe CHT limits, turbine inlet, TIT, and exhaust gas temperature, EGT, limits

10. AVOID THERMAL SHOCK.

Fig. 7.14   Points about superchargers.

Some higher powered engines are supercharged as part of their design, others have kits than can be fitted later to the basic engine. While such kits have been successful, to be legal (and because most of the kits are American) a Supplementary Type Certificate is required from the FAA to cover installation. Engine manufacturers have a long-standing policy that anything which modifies an engine *after* it has left the factory cancels the warranty in the event of malfunction. The only kits which might be fitted without causing strength problems are for altitude boost, because sea level pressures and powers are not increased.

It is unwise to attempt to modify any old engine by installing a supercharger.

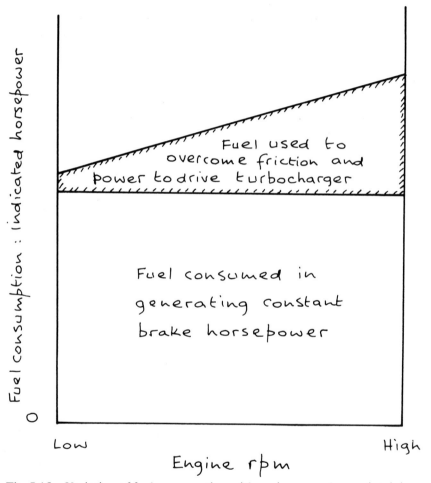

Fig. 7.15   Variation of fuel consumption with engine rpm when maintaining constant shaft brake horsepower. For economy use high boost pressure and low rpm (within engine limitations).

Fuel consumption

The specific fuel consumption of a piston engine was given in eq (2–37a), and in the lower portion of fig. 7.6a, as 0.5 lb/h/BHP (85μg/J). For most practical purposes we may draw a scale of fuel consumption proportional to indicated horsepower. If an engine is run faster than normal rpm, friction losses are increased, and to maintain BHP the throttle must be opened so as to increase the indicated horsepower, maintaining the balance in eq (7–5). Opening the throttle increases the fuel consumption, as shown in fig. 7.15, spoiling the specific fuel consumption. Thus, as we have already noted elsewhere, for best fuel economy an engine should be run with the highest mean effective pressure and the lowest rpm possible.

Two-stroke engines

Two-stroke engines are attractive as light and easily obtainable power units, being used for driving chain-saws, outboard motorboats, motorcycles, lawnmowers and snowmobiles. The problem is to make such units run as efficiently as a four-stroke over the same wide range of operating conditions – some of which are crippling. Fig. 7.16 shows a simple two-stroke engine with single ignition and no moving valves. Equations similar to eq (7–8) and (7–9) can be applied, except that the constant, 792 000, is halved to 396 000, because a two-stroke fires every revolution, while a four-stroke fires every other. Two-strokes are also called three-port engines, because they have inlet, transfer and exhaust ports – even though many may have twin exhausts and two or more transfer ports.

Unblown or unsupercharged two-stroke engines vary in specific weight from 0.8 lb/BHP to 2.0 lb/BHP (about 0.5 to 1.3 kg/kW). Specific fuel consumption varies from about 0.75 to 2.0 lb/h/BHP (128 to 340 μ g/J) as against the average 0.5 lb/h/BHP for a four-stroke cycle.

Rotational speeds of two-strokes are high, varying between 5 000 and 9 500 rpm, which makes them noisy.

Use of motor gasoline (Mogas)

There is much controversy about the use of motor gasoline in piston engines. Pressure has been exerted by light aeroplane owners upon CAA and FAA to approve the use of motor fuel. The reasons are fear of a shortage of normal gasoline (*Avgas*); its high price; the belief the *Avgas 100LL* has caused a lot of engine trouble and spark plug fouling due to lead; and the refusal of some oil companies to deliver small quantities required by many operators. CAA has now approved limited use of Mogas.

Mogas can only be approved with considerable testing. Gasoline is not a chemically unique fluid, unlike alcohol. It is a mixture of a large number of compounds, with a widely variable set of properties. Assurance is required about the consistency of behaviour of such fuel at altitude, where vapour locks might form in parts of the fuel delivery system. The vapour pressure of Mogas can vary from a level of 14 lbf/in² (670 N/m²) to the same value as Avgas (7 lbf/in² (335 N/M²) or less). Further, it is necessary to ensure proper engine operation under a number of adverse conditions, such as maximum manifold pressure, minimum rpm coincident with maximum cylinder temperature and maximum carburetter air intake temperature approved for use. Properly planned programmes are being run in the USA and the UK to produce the necessary evidence of the effects of Mogas on engine and aircraft fuel systems. Meanwhile many aircraft owners operate their aeroplanes on motor gasoline and risk the consequences. These include possible engine failure because of vapour locks in the fuel system, and inability of the engine to deliver full power on take-off, or when overshooting from a baulked landing.

piston rises, compressing
mixture in head, while
sucking fresh charge into
        crank-case

piston descends, compressing
mixture in crank-case

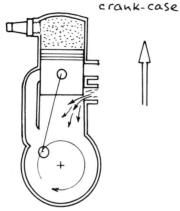

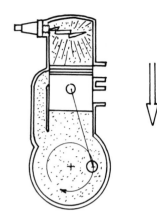

a. Induction — Compression.

b Power stroke

descending piston forces
fresh mixture into cylinder
through transfer port

all ports covered by
piston. Compression
stroke starts

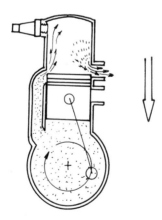

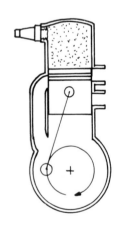

c. Exhaust — induction

d. Compression

Fig. 7.16   Two-stroke cycle.

The use of unapproved fuel in any aeroplane invalidates the manufacturer's guarantee, the insurance cover and the Certificate of Airworthiness.

Rotary combustion (Wankel) engines

A promising engine, though beset with practical development difficulties, is the small, relatively light, Wankel-type, shown in fig. 7.17a. The internal shape of the engine is a fat figure-of-eight trochoidal chamber, within which runs a triangular rotor, with seals at each corner. The engine as we now know it has been evolved by Felix Wankel, a German engineer, although the original idea dates back to a water pump, around 1588. Later, James Watt (*see* foot of table 2–5), unsuccessfully tried to apply the idea to a

mixture drawn through inlet port by rotor rolling around central gear in an eccentric orbit

path taken by tip of rotor,

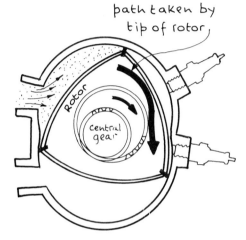

a. Induction

mixture compressed between seals (shown ▮ at each corner of rotor)

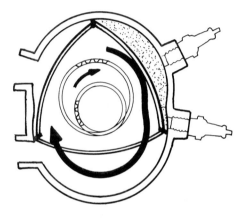

b. Compression

spark plugs ignite mixture, which expands, driving rotor onwards

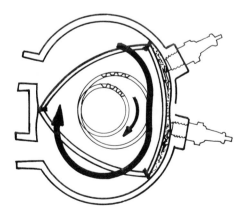

c. Power

burnt gases exhausted from expanding chamber

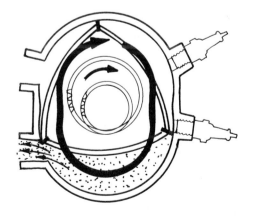

d. Exhaust

Fig. 7.17 Firing cycle of the *Wankel* rotary combusion engine. The cycle occurs three times in each revolution of the rotor.

steam engine. The principle was resurrected for internal combustion engines in 1908, with little success. Its present form is owed to work done by Wankel from 1954, culminating in the first effective model in 1957. The *Curtiss Wright Corporation* is currently running a programme, developing Wankel-type engines for light aircraft. In addition there is an advanced aircraft engine study being funded by NASA.

The weight of the Wankel, which employs twin chambers, is typically less than two-thirds that of a conventional six-cylinder engine of similar power. It is half the size, has forty per cent fewer parts, and is claimed to be half as costly to produce. It might be possible to reduce specific fuel consumption to around $\frac{2}{3}$ piston engine values, using a variety of fuels. Specific weights may be less than 1 lb/BHP (0.61 kg/kW). There have been vibration problems, caused by the rotor oscillating in its chamber (the reason for employing twin chambers) and problems caused by high temperatures and centrifugal forces (the same factor limited early rotary engines in World War 1). These cause excessive wear on the seals at the rotor tips.

In spite of early difficulties, the Wankel is the only known engine to meet US Federal pollution standards at reasonable cost. The engine is potentially quiet – in fact so quiet that *Curtis Wright* experimented with one in an aeroplane that could be heard 150 ft away (46 m). A factor which makes a notable contribution to overall quietness is the need to gear-down propellers, from engine speeds around 7000 rpm, so enabling propeller tips to operate at lower (less noisy) Mach numbers.

Summary of factors affecting piston engine output

A summary of various factors which affect engine power output is shown in fig. 7.18 (ref. 7.5). These split into:

☐ Ambient factors affecting the air mass and, therefore, the oxygen contained. They are of particular importance when we come to measuring performance.
☐ Mechanical losses within the engine.

Other sources of energy

A number of significant experiments are being carried out, especially by the Experimental Aircraft Association, in the United States, to find other sources of energy for light aircraft.

Shortages of gasoline in 1974 and 1979 caused people to look at alternative fuels, with emphasis upon renewable sources, like grain alcohol (ethanol). Light aircraft have been fuelled with straight alcohol, and with a mixture of gasoline and alcohol (gasohol). Ref. 7.6 outlines some of the results. These tend to show no significant difference in performance of an engine running on gasohol. An alcohol fuelled *Limbach SL1700EA* engine, fitted with a *Zenith 28 RX* carburetter, needed a slight increase in jet diameter (richening the mixture and increasing specific fuel consumption). It then had slower idling, and achieved the same ground static as when using gasoline. Temperatures, pressures and engine timing (30° before top dead centre) remained unchanged.

So far three solar powered aircraft have flown: *Solar One* (UK), *Solar Riser* (USA) and *Solar Challenger* (USA), with electrically-driven propellers, powered by arrays of solar (photovoltaic) cells mounted in the wings. Specific weight is high, but the principle has been shown to work. Such cells are byproducts of space research and technology, and they are expensive.

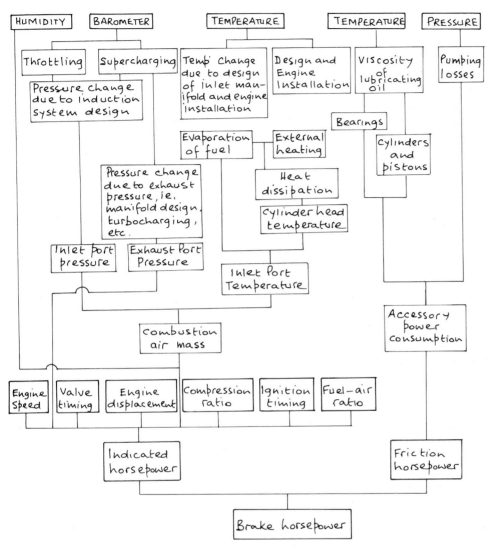

Fig. 7.18   Factors affecting engine power output (from ref. 7.5).

Space technology has brought about a range of semiconductors capable of transforming solar energy into power. Silicon is about 15 per cent efficient, gallium arsenide 11 per cent, and cadmium sulphide 8 per cent (ref. 7.7). Organic cells might be much more efficient, but they are some way off. Typical silicon cells are about 0.8 in square (2 cm $\times$ 2 cm), 0.4 to 0.5 in thick (10 to 12 mm), and weigh 0.62×10^{-3} lb (0.28 g). They are expensive: around \$75 to \$200 per watt generated, at 1974 prices.

Bright sunlight in the tropics has an energy equivalent to 0.124 BHP/ft² (1 kW/m²). A power unit with propeller having an efficiency of 80 per cent would be able to produce 0.015 BHP/ft² (0.12 kW/m²). This means that about 200 ft² (18.6 m²) of wing area covered with silicon cells would be needed to produce 3 BHP (2.24 kW), for a weight of 28 lb (12.7 kg) minus electric motor and propeller. The specific weight of such a bank of cells would be something like 9.33 lb/BHP (5.7 kg/kW).

Plate 7–2 Liquid-cooled automotive engine developments considered for *Blackburn B-48* replica in chapter 15, example 33. (Top) *Bonner Sapphire V6* (200 BHP), installed in a *De Havilland Chipmunk*. (*Aero-Bonner Company Ltd, Shoreham, UK*) (Bottom) *TE495–TC700* (700 BHP) (*Thunder Engines Inc, USA*)

Power produced varies linearly with incident sunlight. There is marked degradation with latitude and the amount of cloud. On a cloudless day in a temperate latitude, around 53 deg north, say, we might expect solar input and propulsive output around 75 per cent of the values given.

Propellers

A propeller consists of a number of wing-like aerofoils designed to convert torque into thrust, each one of which is subject to the same aerodynamic laws and influences as any other lifting surface. To generate thrust a propeller blade has to be rotated at an angle of attack to the local airflow. The local airflow is conveniently seen as a helix, caused in the main by the addition of two velocity vectors: one due to the forward motion of the aircraft, V, the other caused by rotation of each blade at n rpm. The picture is complicated by the addition of 'downwash' by the blades ahead. The helix angle of flow varies between blade root and tip, as shown in fig. 2.8a. If the angle is denoted ϕ, the radius of a particular blade section out from the axis of rotation, r, then with the propeller rotating at n rpm in flight at TAS V, the helix angle is given by:

$$tan \ \phi \ \text{deg} = (2\pi r \ n)/V = \pi[(nd)/V] \qquad (7\text{--}15)$$

in appropriate units. The term V/nd is called the advance ratio:

$$J = V/nd \qquad (7\text{--}16)$$

Each section of a blade from root to tip must be set at the most efficient angle of attack for the design condition. In high speed flight the TAS V might be calculated from minimum design cruising speed, V_C (*see* eqs (6–38) to (6–41)). On the other hand a climb propeller to give best rate or gradient of climb would be designed for the appropriate speed. When buying an aeroplane one should always ask if it is fitted with a climb or a cruise propeller, so as to avoid confusion when finding that it flies fast, but climbs badly, or *vice versa*.

It follows that, for constant pitch, blade section and angle must vary from root to tip, which accounts for the thickness/chord variations, and twist along the length of a blade. Because of the variable conditions, a blade is represented by a section located 0.75 of the distance out from axis to tip. The innermost 25 per cent is assumed to do no useful work at all. Fig. 2.8 summarises the salient features of a two-bladed propeller. The main propeller design problems are:

☐ Settling the maximum possible diameter within the constraints of undercarriage length, contact with the ground, and proximity of other airframe surfaces. While it is obvious that a propeller must not come into contact with parts of the aircraft while rotating, it is not a good thing to have blades running too close to structure located ahead of or behind them. The airflow is slowed down locally, pressure rises, and the blades suffer pulsations in load, mainly in bending, which affect fatigue-life, and causes vibration throughout the airframe.

☐ Choosing the design rotational speed. While most propellers are bolted to the main crankshaft, which rotates at engine speed, gearing may be necessary at times, to avoid high tip speeds.

☐ Deciding the blade area and, hence, the number of blades needed to absorb engine power and to generate adequate thrust.

To be able to settle such features we need to know:

Total drag of the aircraft (drag coefficient C_D) at the design speed.
Horsepower needed to fly at the design speed.
Tip speed of the propeller.
Total propeller blade area.
Rated pitch of the propeller.

Total drag of the aircraft is calculated by any of the methods discussed already in chapter 5.

The required horsepower at the design speed, whether it be for climb, cruise or high speed flight, is calculated from eqs (6–7) to (6–9).

Propeller tip speed should be as high as possible. Metal propellers, which have thinner sections than those of wood, are able to achieve higher tip speeds without running into compressibility effects. A tip speed of M 0.6 (660 ft/s) is about the limit for wooden profiles, while metal profiles with tip sections thinner than about 6 per cent might run up to M 0.8 (800 ft/s). Profiles suffer degradation through contact with stones, rain, hail and other foreign objects. Blade drag coefficients rise, and torque with them, so that maximum rpm cannot be attained, and propeller efficiency falls rapidly. Tip speed is calculated from:

$$V_t = \pi n d \qquad\qquad (7\text{–}17)$$

where n and d have the meanings in the preceding equations. Tip Mach number, M_t, is given by the ratio of tip speed to acoustic speed, a:

$$M_t = V_t/a \qquad\qquad (7\text{–}18)$$

Watch the units in these calculations.
The higher the rotational speed of a propeller:

☐ The smaller the required pitch angle, so that the lift generated by a blade lies more nearly along the line of flight, reducing the drag component opposing rotation.
☐ The smaller the blade area and/or the fewer the number of blades needed to generate the thrust (conversely, blades must be added to cope with high powered engines with propellers of limited diameters).
☐ The lighter the propeller and drive system.

Offsetting these advantages is the fact that high tip speed means more propeller noise.

The rated pitch of a propeller is the geometric distance that a blade would advance in one revolution were it free to slide on its flat undersurface (measured at a section 75 per cent of the distance out from its axis of rotation to tip), as shown in fig. 7.9a. The pitch angle, β, is usually about 4 deg to 5 deg more than the blade helix angle, ϕ, of a flat-bottomed section. The actual pitch angle depends in fact upon the aerofoil section used, and its angle of best lift/drag (as determined by construction in fig. 5.3).

Ref. 7.8 shows how propeller diameter may be calculated as follows in the first two equations:

☐ For a two-bladed wooden propeller:

$$d = 10000 \; \sqrt[4]{[P/(53.5 \; n^2 V)]} \qquad\qquad (7\text{–}19a)$$

For a four-bladed wooden propeller:

$$d = 10000\ ^4\sqrt{[P/(111\ n^2 V)]} \tag{7–19b}$$

Another formula which is useful in the range 300 to 600 BHP (223.8 to 447.6 kW) is based upon ref. 15.12:

$$d = 4.18\ \sqrt{P} \tag{7–20}$$

Other rough 'eye ball' equations can be found useful which are based upon 'convenient fit' values in fig. 7.19b:

☐ Mainly two bladed piston propeller, including two-strokes:

$$d = 22\ ^4\sqrt{P} \tag{7–20a}$$

[handwritten: P = 115 hp, d = 72"]

from around 10 BHP (7.5 kW) to 600 BHP (448 kW) when noise is not a factor.
☐ Three bladed piston and turbopropeller engines when noise is a consideration:

$$d = 18\ ^4\sqrt{P} \tag{7–20b}$$

This equation is more useful at higher powers for commuter-type operations.
☐Three bladed turbopropellers for agricultural use:

$$d = 20\ ^4\sqrt{P} \tag{7–20c}$$

where noise is less important on the whole, but cannot be ignored.

In each equation d is the diameter in inches and P the rated brake or shaft horsepower of the engine, n is the rotational speed of the propeller and V the true airspeed, MTAS, at sea level, ISA. Always check for critical tip speeds when a value of d has been determined.

It is often convenient to treat a propeller as an imaginary *actuator disc*, in which there is no specification of blade characteristics. Such a disc gives an impulse, a change of momentum, to the air passing through it – thrust being proportional to that change of momentum. This is the *Rankine-Froude* momentum theory of propulsion, after Rankine (see foot of table 2–5) and William Froude (*see* Froude number, F, in chapter 2). The effect upon the airflow is shown in fig. 7.19, with the characteristic *vena contracta* shape caused by speeding-up of the flow.
The area of the actuator disc is given by:

$$A_p = \pi/4\ (d^2) = 0.7854\ d^2 \tag{7–21}$$

and its thrust, F, is the product of the disc area and the pressure rise Δp imparted to the air:

$$\text{propeller thrust } F = A_p \Delta p \tag{7–22}$$

If we apply Bernoulli's law from an undisturbed point upstream of the disc to a point downstream, well behind it, using eq (2–5), such that:

$$p + \tfrac{1}{2}\rho V^2 = C, \text{ a constant} \tag{2–5 plus 2–9}$$

it may be shown that:

$$\Delta p = \rho 2v(V + v) \tag{7–23}$$

It is convenient to express the increment of increased velocity, v, in terms of the propeller *inflow factor*:

$$a' = v/V \tag{7–24}$$

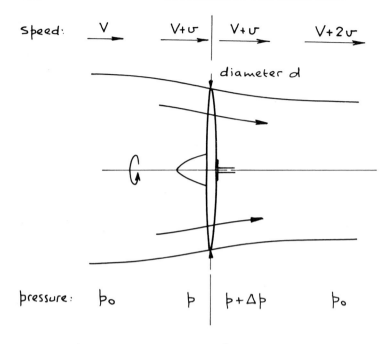

Speed: V   V+υ | V+υ   V+2υ

diameter d

pressure: p₀   p | p+Δp   p₀

The propeller gives an impulse to the air. The final
propwash velocity (V+2υ) is the sum of the true
airspeed, V, and twice the impulsive increment of
velocity, υ, given to the air in passing through the
propeller disc. The reason is that the air continues
to accelerate for a short distance downstream.
There are several physical analogies with downwash
imparted to air by a passing wing (see Figs 4.1 and 4.2b).

Fig. 7.19a   The propeller as an actuator-disc, forming a *vena-contracta* in the airflow.

from which eq (7–22) may be developed to give:

$$F = A_p^2 \rho V^2 a'(1 + a')$$ (7–25)

In straight and level flight thrust = drag, i.e.

$$F = C_D \tfrac{1}{2} \rho S V^2$$ (from eq (2–3b))

Substituting eq (7–25), we have:

$$C_D S / A_p = 4_a'(1 + a')$$ (7–26)

which expands into the quadratic form:

$$4a'^2 + 4a' - (C_D S / A_p) = 0$$

Using the standard solution for a quadratic we obtain:

$$a' = \tfrac{1}{2}[\sqrt{(1 + C_D S / A_p)} - 1]$$ (7–27)

i.e.

$$v = V/2[\sqrt{(1 + C_D S / A_p)} - 1]$$ (7–28)

$$v = \frac{V}{2}\left(\sqrt{1 + \frac{2T}{\rho V^2 A_p}} - 1\right)$$

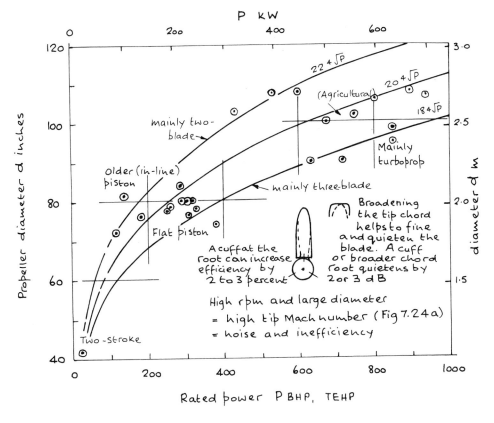

Fig. 7.19b State-of-the-art propeller diameter against rated power.

as $v = a'V$. This enables us to state the final propwash velocity, $V_p = (V + 2v)$ in the form:

$$\text{final propwash velocity, } V_p = V\sqrt{(1 + C_D S/A_p)} \qquad (7\text{–}29)$$

so that the factor for increased dynamic pressure is given approximately by:

$$K_p = q_p/q = 1 + F/qA_p \qquad (7\text{–}30)$$

which may be used to estimate the increase in dynamic pressure at the tail when bathed in propwash and, hence, the increase of efficiency, η_s (eq (5–24)). Fig. 7.19b shows state-of-the-art propeller diameters against rated power, so giving scale to the calculations.

Propeller efficiency

The efficiency of the propeller was sketched broadly in fig. 6.15. A number of factors cause the band to be wide. One is the number of propeller blades (each sheds a system of trailing vortices which upsets the others). Another is whether the blades are made of wood, or metal (there is a wider scatter among 'identical' wooden propellers). A third is proximity of parts of the airframe changing the static pressure behind the disc, and compressibility effects at blade tips. The ideal Froude efficiency, $\overline{\eta}$, which is never realised in practice, is given by:

$$\overline{\eta} = FV/F(V + v) \qquad (7\text{--}31a)$$

but, as $v/V = a'$, we may cancel the thrust terms and write:

$$\overline{\eta} = 1/1 + a' \qquad (7\text{--}31b)$$

In the case of a real propeller, subject to all of the above losses at some time or another, we may write:

$$\text{actual propeller efficiency, } \eta = \eta_{max} f_J f_\eta \qquad (7\text{--}32)$$

In this expression we use three terms to take into account a multiplicity of adverse effects, as shown in fig. 7.20. η_{max} is the theoretical maximum efficiency for blades made of wood, or metal. The factor f_J accounts for the propeller operating off–design. It may be rotating at the wrong speed, n rpm; or a change of attitude may have altered the true airspeed, V; or the blades may have been 'cropped' as a result of damage, so that the diameter, d, has been changed. The final factor, f_η, is a propulsive efficiency factor (ref. 7.10) which takes care of blockage of propwash by parts of the airframe, tip and any other losses.

Another rough approximation for propeller efficiency, which introduces certain airframe factors, assumes that ideal Froude efficiency is reduced by something like 20 per cent on average, so that:

$$\eta \approx 0.8\overline{\eta} = 0.8/(1 + a) \qquad (7\text{--}33)$$

Substituting for a' by using eq (7–27):

$$\text{propeller efficiency, } \eta \text{ is roughly } 1.6/[1 + \sqrt{(1 + C_D S/A_p)}] \qquad (7\text{--}34a)$$

It should be noted that the term $C_D S$ is a member of the equivalent drag area family, related to others in eq (5–37). Thus, for an aeroplane cruising at maximum lift/drag ratio, where total drag is double the parasite drag, i.e. $C_D = 2C_{Dp}$, shown in eq (5–30), and knowing that total equivalent parasite area, $f = C_{Dp}S$, from eq (5–38a):

$$\eta \text{ is roughly } 1.6/[1 + \sqrt{(1 + 2f/A_p)}] \qquad (7\text{--}34b)$$

Finally, ref. 7.11 gives an equation for propeller efficiency which has the form:

$$\eta = 0.85/(1 + F/qd^2) \qquad (7\text{--}35)$$

in which thrust in cruise, F, is equal and opposite to the total drag. Under such conditions lift is equal to weight and the aeroplane is cruising at maximum lift/drag, so that we can replace propeller thrust, F by $W/(L/D)_{max}$. Thus, knowing the propeller diameter, d:

$$\eta = 0.85/(1 + W/(L/D)_{max}qd^2) \qquad (7\text{--}36)$$

in FPSR units, where q is the dynamic pressure at the cruising speed for $(L/D)_{max}$ (see eq (5–43)).

Constant speed and feathering propellers

Fixed pitch propellers suffer losses when run off-design, as we saw in fig. 7.20b. A

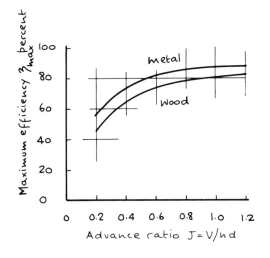

a. Maximum efficiency of two-bladed propellers. Four-bladed produce about 95 percent of these values. Assume the efficiency of three-bladed to fall in between two and four-bladed.

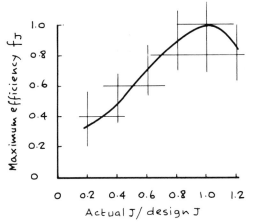

b. General variation of efficiency with change of advance ratio

$$J = V/nd \quad (Eq (7-16))$$

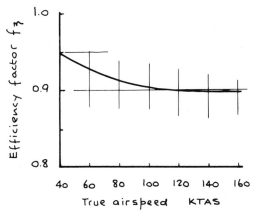

c. Variation of propulsive efficiency factor, f_η, with true airspeed, for the Britten–Norman BN-2, Islander. This curve can probably be applied generally, without much error.

Fig. 7.20   Propeller efficiency, $\eta = \eta_{max} f_J f \eta$ (eq (7–32)), based upon refs. 4.17, 7.8, 7.9 and 7.10.

propeller with variable pitch can be run at high efficiency ($f_J = 1$ in eq (7–32)) over a wide range of conditions, defined by V/nd.

Most modern variable pitch propellers incorporate a Constant Speed Unit, CSU, which enables pitch to be changed automatically, so as to maintain constant rpm, regardless of airspeed. In the case of propellers made by *Hartzell* in the USA, for example, counterweights are attached to the clamps holding the blades into the hub spider. To control blade pitch, an arrangement of a hydraulic piston and cylinder is mounted on the front of the hub spider, connected to the blade clamps by means of linkages, fig. 7.21. The piston is moved forward by internal oil pressure, supplied by a governor, pulling the blades into fine pitch by means of each linkage. If the engine speed drops below the rpm for which the CSU governor is set, then oil is forced into the cylinder head, sliding it forwards, decreasing the blade pitch (and torque), so that rpm increase.

If rpm rise above the governed speed, oil is allowed to flow out of the cylinder. Increased centrifugal force, acting on each blade counterweight, causes it to attempt to move into the plane of rotation of the propeller. This makes the counterweights move the blades to coarser pitch, which draws the piston rearwards. Torque is increased by coarsened pitch and the engine slows down, until the governed speed is reached, at which point oil pressures and centrifugal forces are in balance. Adjustable coarse and fine pitch stops enable the blades to be set for the best operating range of rpm.

Feathering propellers are broadly similar to variable pitch propellers, except that a feathering spring, within the hub, assists the blade counterweights to increase pitch. Feathering is accomplished by releasing the governor oil pressure, allowing the feathering spring and counterweights to move the blades. A safety feature of such systems is that if oil pressure drops to zero (signifying failure within the engine) the propeller can be caused to feather automatically, saving the engine from further damage.

Propeller 'P' effects

A rotating propeller causes several complicated effects, especially when it is pitched or yawed and is no longer more or less normal to the relative airflow. Together they add up to *P factor*, or *P effect*.

Taking the effects in order and looking at fig. 11.9, we have:

☐ *Asymmetric blade effect*, when the plane of a propeller is not at right angles to the flight path so that the blades in one half of the disc have an added component of flow because they are advancing into wind. Those on the other side are retreating and have a reduced flow over them. The result is an uneven lift, i.e. thrust: that generated on the advancing side being higher than on the side where the blades are retreating. This produces a pitching or yawing couple.

☐ *Rigidity*, in that the direction of the propeller axis tries to remain fixed in space, and this gives rise to:

☐ *Precession*, in that if a couple is applied to tilt the plane of rotation, the resulting motion is precessed 90 deg onwards, in the direction of rotation. For example, an aeroplane with a right handed propeller (rotating clockwise as seen by the pilot sitting behind it) will, when pitched nose-up, be made to yaw to the right, and *vice versa*.

☐ *Pitching moment* is introduced when a propeller, which is invariably mounted forward or aft of the centre of gravity, is tilted up or down, causing a component of thrust to act in the pitching plane. This affects longitudinal stability and aggravates the above effects.

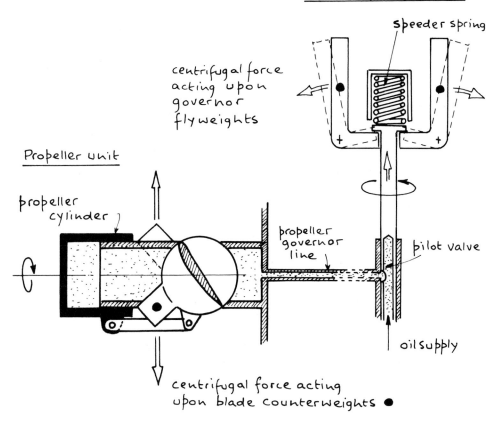

Constant Speed governor

speeder spring

centrifugal force
acting upon
governor
flyweights

Propeller unit

propeller
cylinder

propeller
governor
line

pilot valve

oil supply

centrifugal force acting
upon blade counterweights ●

The constant speed propeller, shown diagramatically,
depends upon a balance between governor speed
(a function of propeller speed) and oil supplied under
pressure by means of the pilot valve to the
propeller cylinder. Movement of the propeller-
cylinder operates a simple linkage to increase
or decrease the pitch of the blades. When the
engine is exactly at the rpm set by the governor
the centrifugal reaction of the flyweights balances
the force of the speeder spring, positioning the pilot
valve so that oil is neither supplied to nor drained
from the propeller. With this condition blade
angle does not change. Thus, the rpm
setting depends upon the amount of compression
in the speeder spring.

Fig. 7.21 *Hartzell*-type constant-speed propeller.

Plate 7–3 Solar-powered aircraft have a power output and, thus, performance directly proportional to the area of solar cells (Top) *Solar One* by Frederick Ernest To and David Williams, flown by Derek Piggott at Lasham, England, on 19th December 1978 (*Dennis Fowler, London Express News*) (Bottom) Wholly successful *Solar Challenger* by the team of Dr Paul MacCready, flown from France to England by Stephen Plácek, 7th July 1981. Note the dark areas covered by 16000 or more solar cells (spin-off from the Space Programme) occupying 245ft² wing and tail surface area, developing 2.676 kW. Only one half of this power is needed for level flight, as long as the cells are nearly perpendicular to reasonably intense sunlight. (*The Times, London*)

Propwash moves as a helix, spiralling backwards around the aeroplane like a corkscrew rotating in the same direction of motion as the propeller. The wash strikes body, wing and tail surfaces at an angle and has an especially powerful effect upon yaw by changing the angle of attack of the fin and rudder (which must be deflected to make the aeroplane fly straight). A right-hand propeller (rotating to the right, i.e. clockwise when seen from behind) causes propwash to come from the left, inducing a fin sideforce to the right, which yaws the nose to the left, so that the pilot has to apply right rudder, and *vice versa*.

☐ *Torque* is the opposite reaction to the engine turning the propeller: the propeller tries to stand still while the aeroplane is caused to rotate in the opposite direction around the shaft. Thus, a right hand propeller would cause the aeroplane to roll to the left. The pilot has to apply some right aileron (left down) to counteract the effect. There is induced drag, from the downwards deflected left aileron (aileron drag) which yaws the nose to the left – adding to the effect of propwash – requiring rudder to correct. Propeller-driven aeroplanes with powerful engines can get into trouble if full power is applied too quickly at airspeeds which are too slow for rudder and ailerons to 'bite'. *Torque-rolls* caused many accidents, especially when opening up to go around again after a wave-off from an aircraft carrier. Aeroplanes like the *Supermarine Seafire 47*, with a 2350 BHP *Rolls Royce Griffon* engine needed counter-rotating propellers (contra-props) to deal with the problem. The *Macchi M72* (fig. 6.7b) was another example of an aeroplane with such propellers. The *Spitfire 1* from which the *Seafire* grew, started life with a two-bladed fixed pitch propeller and a *Rolls Royce Merlin* engine of 1050 BHP. The *Merlin* propeller was right-hand (clockwise rotating), while the *Griffon* propeller rotated left-hand. The *Merlin* engine pilot had to push with his right foot, the *Griffon* pilot with his left. This caused some accidents and incidents when pilots were converting between these *Spitfire* variants.

Gyroscopic properties of propellers have been known for a long time, and have caused numerous accidents. One of the commonest, due to precession, is ground looping of tail-dragging aeroplanes when the tail is lifted too soon and too high on take-off. This is shown in fig. 7.22. Precession shows itself in side-slips, causing aeroplanes to pitch nose-up and down, depending upon direction of yaw and the direction and speed of propeller rotation. But it can be turned to advantage in advanced aerobatics, in manoeuvres like the *lomçovàk* (ref. 7.12), which is achieved by initial use of the flying controls, to set up conditions during which the gyroscopic properties of the propeller take over.

In fact, gyroscopic effects are always present in some degree, because the behaviour of an aeroplane in flight is the outcome of a tussle between dynamics and aerodynamics. At high airspeeds, aerodynamics win. At low airspeeds the propeller is in a better position to win – the art is to keep control of the situation at all times.

The magnitude of the gyroscopic couple must be known for stressing the engine mounting and other parts of the powerplant group. For a two-bladed propeller it is given by (ref. 7.13):

$$Q = 2\,I\Omega_1\Omega_2 \qquad\qquad (7\text{--}37)$$

in which I is the polar moment of inertia (eq (2–24)), Ω_1 radians/s is the rate of

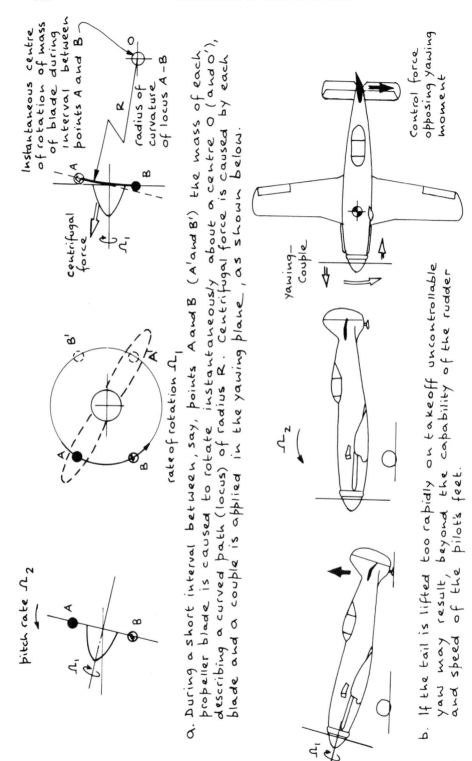

a. During a short interval between, say, points A and B (A' and B') the mass of each propeller blade is caused to rotate instantaneously about a centre O (and O'), describing a curved path (locus) of radius R. Centrifugal force is caused by each blade and a couple is applied in the yawing plane, as shown below.

b. If the tail is lifted too rapidly on takeoff uncontrollable yaw may result, beyond the capability of the rudder and speed of the pilot's feet.

Fig. 7.22   The propeller as a precessing gyroscope.

a. Free-propeller

b. Ducted fan (showing separate high and low-speed lip profiles

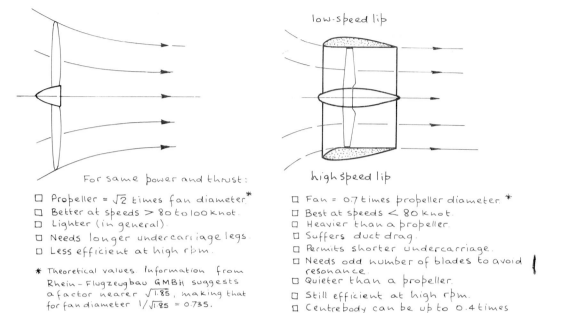

low-speed lip

high speed lip

For same power and thrust:

☐ Propeller = √2 times fan diameter.*
☐ Better at speeds > 80 to 100 knot.
☐ Lighter (in general).
☐ Needs longer undercarriage legs.
☐ Less efficient at high rpm.

* Theoretical values. Information from Rhein-Flugzeugbau GMBH suggests a factor nearer √1.85, making that for fan diameter 1/√1.85 = 0.735.

(see also Fig 7.23b).

☐ Fan = 0.7 times propeller diameter.*
☐ Best at speeds < 80 knot.
☐ Heavier than a propeller.
☐ Suffers duct drag.
☐ Permits shorter undercarriage.
☐ Needs odd number of blades to avoid resonance.
☐ Quieter than a propeller.
☐ Still efficient at high rpm.
☐ Centrebody can be up to 0.4 times fan diameter.
☐ Duct chord 1/5 to 2 times fan diameter.
☐ Close tolerances needed between fan tip and duct.

Fig. 7.23a   Comparison between propeller and ducted-fan.

propeller rotation, and Ω_2 radians/s is the rate of pitch or yaw. The polar moment of inertia is taken about the centreline of the propeller shaft.

Fans (ducted) propulsors

A ducted fan, or ducted propulsor, is basically a propeller running inside a circular shroud – except that it has perhaps 5, 7 or even 9 blades. Its usefulness depends upon the design speed of an aircraft, because it is not precisely equivalent to a free propeller, in that it is a better thrust-producer at low airspeeds, but it is not as efficient at higher speeds.

Advantages of the ducted fan are:

☐ The duct reduces the inflow effect of the propwash, making the flow downstream parallel with the walls of the duct. The result is that, for a given horsepower, the fan produces the same static thrust as a free-propeller $\sqrt{2}$ times larger in diameter, *see* fig. 7.23; although from *Rhein-Flugzeugbau GmbH* suggests that a more practical value is $\sqrt{1.85}$.

☐ The fan is protected by the duct – and people are protected from the fan.

☐ It is quieter than a propeller (especially in the plane of rotation) because the fan is only about 0.7 to 0.73 times the diameter of an equivalent propeller and it can be run at

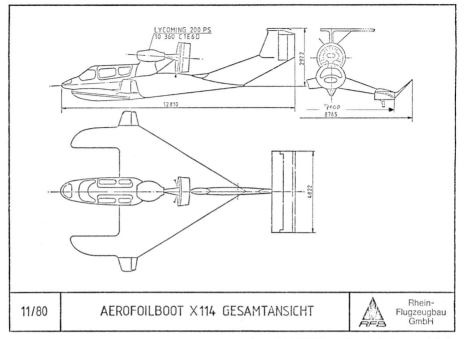

Fig. 7.23b   The *X114 Aerofoil boat* by *RFB* has a 200 BHP engine, 2400 rpm, driving a fan of 55 in (1.4 m) diameter. See also plate 6–2.

higher rpm without exceeding the critical Mach number of the tips. For a given critical tip speed, fan and propeller are related by:

$$\text{diameter of fan/propeller diameter} = \text{rpm of propeller/rpm of fan} \qquad (7\text{–}38)$$
$$= 1/\sqrt{2} \text{ theory} \qquad (7\text{–}38a)$$
$$= 1/\sqrt{1.85} \text{ Rhein Flugzeugbau} \qquad (7\text{–}38b)$$

☐ Running tolerances between blade tip and duct must be finely controlled to thousandths of an inch, if quite large losses are to be avoided. Some experimental fans use an ablating surface in the duct, so that the tips wear their own close-fitting track.

☐ Ducts must be strong enough to contain bursting fans. This, and the shape of the duct, makes a fan unit heavier than the equivalent propeller.

☐ To avoid resonance to which fans are susceptible, odd numbers of blades are required.

Duct drag may be calculated in isolation, being the drag coefficient of the duct section, and the projected area when opened out flat. Thus:

$$\text{projected area of duct, } S_d = 2\pi r_d c_d \qquad (7\text{–}39)$$

where r_d and c_d are the duct radius and chord. Area S_d is then used in the standard drag equation, with a tolerance added for interference and drag of supporting struts, or stators. A standard roughness drag coefficient of $C_D = 0.01$ might be used, with a factor of 1.5 to account for interference:

$$\text{duct drag, } D_d \approx 0.015 \, q/S_d \qquad (7\text{–}40)$$

The projected area of the duct in plan and elevation is $2r_d \, c_d$. This can have a

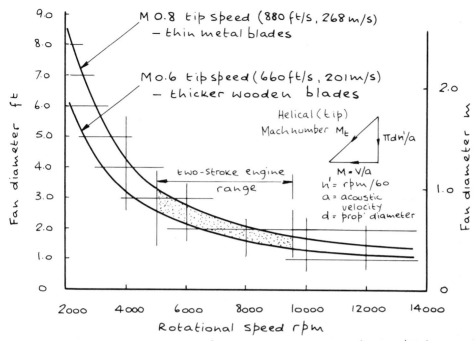

a. Fan diameter and rpm to avoid compressibility and loss of efficiency.

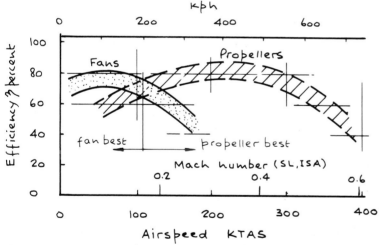

b. The fan is a low-speed device, suffering a loss of gross thrust because of increasing duct-drag. But, a propeller for the same job would have to be 50 percent larger in diameter.

Fig. 7.24 Fan characteristics.

considerable effect upon stability, because there is evidence of ducts behaving like tubular ring-wings when pitched and yawed, or like biplane aerofoils of very low aspect ratio.

Noise

Noise is sound that annoys. Very intense sounds can cause physical damage. It has become one of the commonest, socially unacceptable forms of pollution, and a political issue in communities surrounding airports. No modern designer can afford to ignore noise requirements.

A pure sound is caused by a fluctuating pressure pulse detected by the ear, or by an instrument, and it has two measurable properties:

☐ Magnitude of the fluctuation.
☐ Frequency of pressure fluctuation.

These are shown in fig. 7.25a. Pure sound is hard to achieve, because other frequencies intrude to adulterate the simple note, as shown in b. The average pressure during the cycle, which has a basically sinusoidal form, is called the Root Mean Square value, RMS. This is calculated by cutting the cycle into vertical strips as shown, squaring the value measured at the mid-point of each strip, averaging the resulting sum of the squares, and then finding the square root of their average. This gives:

$$\text{RMS or effective pressure} = 0.707 \times \text{maximum pressure} \qquad (7\text{--}41)$$

The faintest sound detectable by the human ear is roughly 20μ N/m^2, or about 2×10^{-10} times standard atmospheric pressure. This is the reference unit of sound pressure. Sounds are made up of pressure pulses of different frequencies and magnitudes. A sound of a given pressure and low enough frequency may be tolerated without discomfort, while the same pressure at a somewhat higher frequency may cause pain.

The level of sound intensity is measured in decibels, dB (which is one tenth of one bel), relative to the reference sound pressure level given above. The associated pressure levels are measured in terms of RMS values, so that:

$$\text{sound pressure level} = 10 \log_{10}(p/p_{ref})^2 \text{dB} \qquad (7\text{--}42)$$
$$= 20 \log_{10}(p/p_{ref}) \text{ dB} \qquad (7\text{--}43)$$

p_{ref} being the pressure of the sound usually 20 uN/m^2. It may be shown that if we double the ratio, p/p_{ref}, then:

$$20 \log_{10}(2/1) = 20 \times 0.301 = 6 \text{ dB}$$

while multiplying the ratio by $4 = 20 \times 0.602 = 12$ dB. Subjectively, an increase of 10 dB would be judged to make a sound twice as loud to the ear (ref. 7.14).

$$\text{sound frequency, } f = \text{speed of sound/time for one pressure cycle, } \tau \quad (7\text{--}44)$$

Various measures have been introduced. The commonest used for quantifying community disturbance is the dB(A), which is used for traffic, trains, industry, light aircraft – in fact everything except heavy aircraft. Sound is filtered by 'weighing' which is dependent only upon frequency measured in cycles/s, or hertz (Hz) (*see* foot of table 2–5). The weighting is independent of pressure, and is an attempt to simulate the effect of sound upon the human ear, i.e. a small receiver within a large box of bone and tissue. The method gives full weighting to frequencies around 1 000 Hz, and low weighting to low frequencies.

A more precise development of the dB(A), which attempts to measure the subjective effects of loudness and annoyance, in terms of level of perception, is the *Perceived*

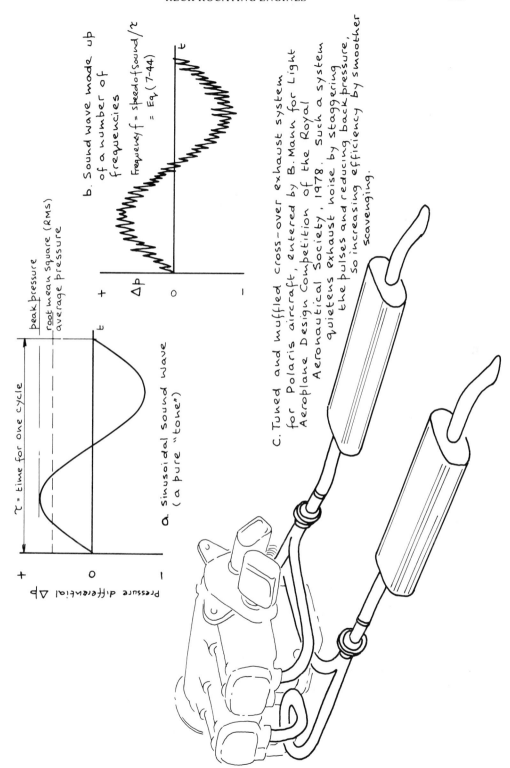

a. Sinusoidal Sound Wave ("a pure tone")

τ = time for one cycle

peak pressure
root mean Square (RMS)
average pressure

Pressure differential Δp

b. Sound wave made up of a number of frequencies

Frequency f = speed of sound/τ
= Eq (7-44)

c. Tuned and muffled cross-over exhaust system for Polaris aircraft, entered by B. Mann for Light Aeroplane Design Competition of the Royal Aeronautical Society, 1978. Such a system quietens exhaust noise by staggering the pulses and reducing back pressure, so increasing efficiency by smoother scavenging.

Fig. 7.25   Sound wave characteristics, and a design for a quietened exhaust.

Noise deciBel, PNdB, in which weighting changes with sound pressure level. This is used for monitoring noise of heavy aircraft.

Yet another measure is the *Effective Perceived Noise deciBel*, EPNdB, which is a modification of the PNdB to cater for 'spikes' in the spectrum of frequencies. This measure, which also takes into account the duration of the noise of a single aircraft flying over the measuring point, is used for noise certification work.

Piston engined aeroplanes have four main sources of noise:

☐ Engine exhaust;
☐ Engine intake;
☐ Propeller tip;
☐ Propeller blade loading.

Engine exhaust emits a broad spectrum of sound, mainly caused by combustion and turbulence. The lowest frequencies come from the firing rate. Gas pressure at the discharge end of the exhaust stack pulsates as each mass of exhaust products discharged from a cylinder meets the resistance of ambient air. The way to smooth pulsation is to discharge the exhaust into a muffling chamber, large enough to diffuse the energy somewhat before it reaches free air. Baffling inside the muffler helps to stagger the inlet and outlet pulses.

Exhaust pulses can be staggered and the exhaust quietened by careful design to reduce backpressure, which is resistance to outflow of the gases. The lower the backpressure the higher the engine efficiency. Engine cylinders fire in a set sequence, e.g. 1–3–2–4 for a four-cylinder horizontally-opposed engine. If two cylinders, like 1–3 and 2–4, fire in quick succession into the same pipe, backpressure is high because pulses occur close together. Highest efficiency is achieved by manifolding the exhaust from pairs of cylinders, so that pulses are evenly spaced. With a four-cylinder engine this is brought about by arranging cylinders 1 and 2 to share one stack, while 3 and 4 share another. But each cylinder in a pair is on the opposite side of the engine to the other, so that cross-over pipes are needed. Careful design of exhaust pipes with smooth curves and no sharp corners (especially at welded seams and joints) can increase engine efficiency by up to 7 per cent – with reduced noise.

Length of exhaust pipe also affects engine efficiency and muffling of the noise. The length of pipe can be critical, like an organ pipe. If the pipe is long enough then standing pressure waves are set up, exhaust backpressure is minimised and power ouput peaks.

A four-cylinder engine running at 2700 rpm needs about 270 in³ (4.42 litre) for good attenuation (ref. 7.15). A cylindrical chamber, about 6 in diameter × 10 in length (15.25 cm × 25.4 cm) provides sufficient volume for such an engine. The muffler should be located as close to the engine exhaust ports as possible. A length of exhaust pipe downstream of the muffler improves its efficiency. As a general rule, the further the muffler is downstream of the engine, the longer should be the tailpipe from the muffler.

Automotive practice is a good source of exhaust design. Engine intake noise is caused by turbulence, more often than not. Again, attenuation is the key to silencing. A large diffuser volume is needed downstream of the intake, located close to the carburetter. The inlet duct should be about 2/3 × diameter of the exhaust pipe, and at least 10 in (25.4 cm) in length. The flow should be as smooth and turbulence free as possible. The diffuser volume should be at least half the volume of the exhaust muffler (ref. 7.15).

Propeller blade noise is caused by tip vortices and compressibility. Fig. 7.26 applies to propellers and fans, and shows that critical noise levels have already been passed. Gearing is needed to reduce rpm. Blade chord has then to be increased so as to maintain thrust. If propellers are made slower and larger in diameter, they become heavier and more expensive. Ground-clearance becomes critical and, in the case of twins, engines must be located further outboard on the wing. This worsens engine-out handling, or bigger, heavier, costlier fin and rudder surfaces are needed to cope with the effects of engine failure.

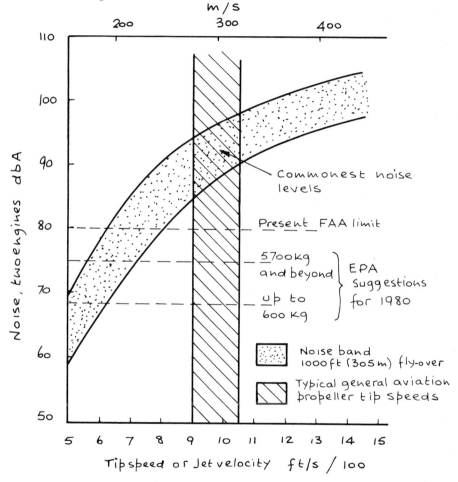

a. This diagram, based upon Ref 7.16, shows how noise generated by two propeller engines, passing overhead at 1000 ft (305 m) changes with tip speed. The curve also applies to jet engine efflux velocity. Commonest noise levels are higher than the present Federal Aviation Administration limit; and much higher than limits being suggested by the American Environmental Protection Agency (EPA) for 1980, with far more optimism than hope.

Fig. 7.26a and b Two aspects of the noise problem.

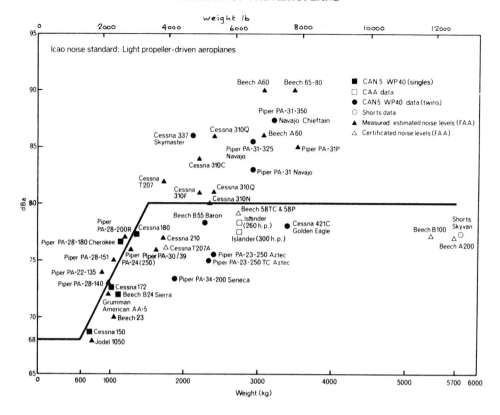

b. Proposed International Civil Aviation Organisation noise standards and a selection of general aviation aeroplanes, based upon information prepared jointly by the Civil Aviation Authority and the Department of Trade, and presented in Ref 7.17. Measurements assume maximum continuous power at 1000ft (305m), with a correction for a function of take off / climb performance. WP40 refers to working paper 40 of CAN5 (of the ICAO Committee of Aircraft Noise).

Fig. 7.26b.

If Federal Aviation Administration noise requirements are made tighter by the 1980s, problems will become much worse. Limiting noise to the 68 to 75 dBA range shown in fig. 7.26a would involve tip speeds of 500 ft/s (M 0.45), with rotational speeds of 1 200 rpm. Propeller diameters would have to increase from about 80 in to 96 in or so (2.03 m to 2.44 m) to produce enough thrust.

One experimental modification has been to bend over the tip of each propeller blade, so as to form a flat end-plate blocking flow on the underside. Diameter has been reduced, and the propeller is said to be less noisy.

Blade loading causes noise which is dependent upon thrust, diameter, and number of blades (i.e. the *solidity* of the propeller, measured in terms of the ratio of the sum of the blade chords at $0.7 \times$ tip radius, to the length of the circumference of the circle swept out by that radius). A propeller is most efficient when all parts from root to tip work at the same high lift coefficient. Therefore, high aspect ratio blades are more efficient than those with low aspect ratios, for the same reason as wings are so. Tractor propellers are quieter than pushers, which are affected by turbulent wakes. The lower the blade loading the lower the blade drag. Low aspect ratio blades tend to stir the air too much while pushing it backwards. The limits upon blade aspect ratio are:

☐ Blade stall;
☐ Blade strength.

Quiet propellers are generally less efficient than noisy ones of the same design. If a propeller is noisy, in spite of low tip speeds, it could pay to increase the number of blades, which is far better than broadening blade chord. However, there are advantages to be gained by broadening blade chords at the root. The inner quarter of a propeller blade is almost 'dead' (fig. 7.9a) and can be filled with spinner, as long as this has no detrimental effect upon cooling intake area. The combination of a large spinner with cuffs at the blade roots, to maintain chord almost to the spinner line, is quieter and more efficient than the usual practice of combining small diameter spinners with nearly cylindrical blade roots.

Although liquid-cooled engines are heavier than air-cooled, they tend to be quieter (the larger mass absorbs more energy). Furthermore, because radiators can be located away from the engine it is easier to design more efficient combinations of propeller and spinner than is possible when the engine air intake is just downstream of the blade root.

Ducted propulsors are claimed to have noise levels about 1/6 those of propeller units of the same power. This is due to the lower tip speeds of fans, and the shrouding effect of the duct itself. Comparable reductions are claimed for other forms of noise-shrouding, using other parts of the airframe, like wing roots and tails. Fig. 7.27 shows

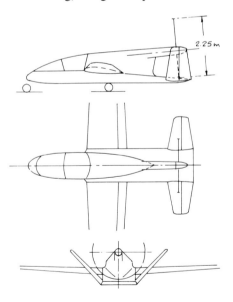

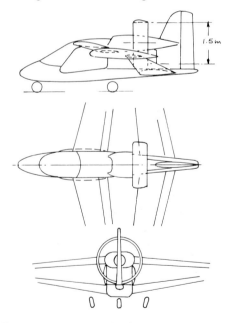

a. Light aeroplane from Ref 7.18 with propeller shrouded by V-tail surfaces and beaver-tail rear fuselage.

b. Warren-winged project with ducted propulsor producing the same thrust as in a. This arrangement of the author's looked inefficient: too little lift, too much wetted area and interference wayward static and manoeuvre margin not enough speed and agility.

Fig. 7.27   Configurations shaped to reduce propeller and fan noise.

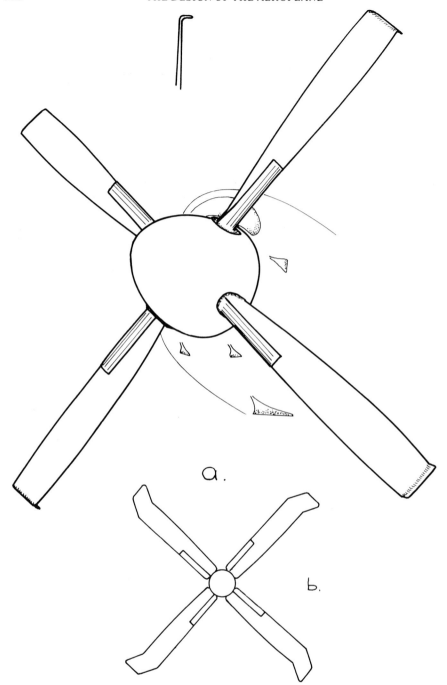

Fig. 7.28 a and b.

Q-tips shown in (a) are shaped to form small end-plates. In theory they enable the blades to operate with higher span loadings, and such propellers are said to be quieter because they can be run with reduced tip speeds.

Swept-back tips in (b) increase the critical Mach number which, by reducing stress upon and energy imparted to the air, is said to quieten the propeller.

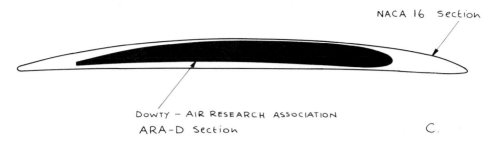

Fig. 7.28c   The *ARA-D* section improves upon performance of *NACA 16*, used for many propellers, by carrying higher loadings at higher lift/drag ratios. The chord is narrower and the leading edge more rounded, reducing vulnerability to damage by stones. Weight is lighter and, because of the higher blade loading noise levels are said to be reduced. (*Dowty Rotol Limited*).

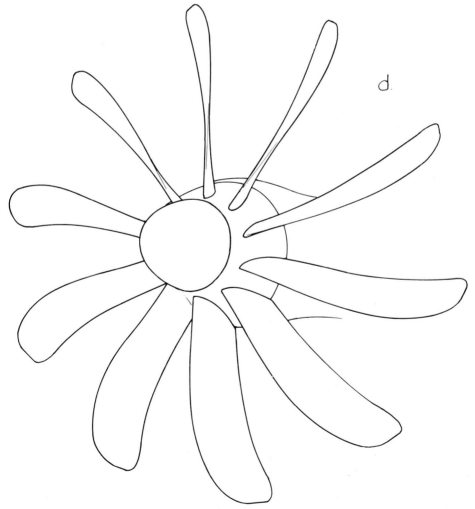

Figure 7.28d   *NASA Lewis* advanced turboprop.

two light aeroplane projects from a French source (ref. 7.18) which were designed for quietness – one uses the rear fuselage and tail surfaces, the other a ducted fan. Fig. 7.28 shows some propeller developments.

In spite of claims for the quietness of ducted fans, there is some evidence that a free propeller fitted to a full-scale model in a wind-tunnel may be quieter than a shrouded propeller, under certain circumstances (ref. 7.19). Results showed the propeller to generate 97 dB(A) as against 102 dB(A) from the shrouded unit, for the same thrust.

One should beware of results and claims of this kind, regardless of which unit is being supported by them. Comparability depends upon design features and the stations around the aircraft at which measurements are made. It may be that shrouded propellers and ducted fans emit narrow lobes of intense noise in certain directions, the duct acting rather like a megaphone, or loud-hailer, so that the noise energy is directed. Certainly, the noise pattern of a shrouded or ducted unit is very different from that of a free propeller.

British and American noise requirements are to be found in refs. 7.20 and 7.21.

References

7.1 Pratt & Whitney Aircraft (May 1976) *The Aircraft Engine and its Operation.* United Aircraft Corporation, East Hartford, Conn.

7.2 (Jan. 1949) *Aircraft Powerplant Handbook.* CAA Technical Manual No 107, Experimental Aircraft Association, EAA, Hales Corners, Wisconsin.

7.3 Nelson, J. L. (1974) *Modern Lightplane Engines.* Modern Aircraft Series, Sports Car Press, New York.

7.4 Federal Aviation Administration (Nov. 1970) 'Wet Air'. *Aviation News.*

7.5 Lycoming Avco Corporation (Aug. 1960) Report no. 2268, **1**, *Horsepower Correction Factors and Operating Techniques for Engine Development and Calibration.*

7.6 Experimental Aircraft Association (Oct. 1979) 'A Year of Energy and Ultralights'. *Sport Aviation.*

7.7 Irving, F. G. and Morgan, D. (1974) *The Feasibility of an Aircraft Propelled by Solar Engergy*, AIAA Paper no. 74–1042. American Institute of Aeronautics and Astronautics.

7.8 Booth, H. (1921) *Aeroplane Performance Calculations.* The Directly Useful Technical Series, London: Chapman & Hall Ltd.

7.9 The Royal Aeronautical Society (1934) *Handbook of Aeronautics*, **1**, London.

7.10 Wilson, R. (Nov. 1979) 2A/AERO/1, *Propulsive Efficiency Factor: Islander, Pilatus Britten-Norman.*

7.11 Hovey, R. W. (Oct. 1972) *Simplified Propellers for Low Speed Homebuilt Aircraft.* 2nd edn., PO Box 1074, Saugus, Cal 91350: the Author.

7.12 Williams, N. (1975) *'Aerobatics'.* Airlife Publications, England.

7.13 Civil Aviation Authority. *BCAR, Section K 3–4.*

7.14 Burns, W. (1973) *Noise and Man.* London: John Murray.

7.15 Welch, W. A. (June 1971) 'Airplanes Needn't be Noisy'. *Sport Aviation.* Experimental Aircraft Association.

7.16 The Technical Editor (July 1977) 'Dowty ducted propulsor flies'. *Flight International.*

7.17 Barnett, C. (May 1978) 'What's all the noise about? *Flight International*, 27 May 1978.

7.18 D'après Aerokurier, Traduction, Pagnon, A. 'Propulsion et Bruit'. *Les Cahiers du RSA, no. 97–98,* Réseau du Sport de l'Air.

7.19 Rathgeber, R. K. and Sipes, D. E. March 29–April 1, 1977/770444. *The Influence of Design Parameters on Light Propeller Aircraft Noise.* Business Aircraft Meeting. Society of Automotive Engineers Inc, 400 Commonwealth Drive, Warrendale, Pa 15096.

7.20 Civil Aviation Authority BCAR Section N, Noise.

7.21 Federal Aviation Administration FAR Part 36, Noise Standards.

CHAPTER 8

Turbine Engines – and a Range Equation

'If an engine fails, lower the nose to maintain speed . . . It is better to hit the far hedge at five knots than to stall into the near hedge at fifty five knots.'
Old instructor's adage.

Few light aeroplanes are propelled by gas turbine engines. Nevertheless, small turbojet engines are available, and turbopropeller units are appearing in increasing numbers, especially for agricultural and aerial work aeroplanes.

Turbojets

The principal parts of a turbojet are shown in fig. 8.1. The optimum installation houses the engine within a low drag cowling, accessible for servicing, with the shortest, straightest intake and exhaust ducting possible. Ducts introduce frictional losses, while curvature which changes the direction of the airflow suffers a reaction to the changing momentum, called momentum drag.

Momentum is the product of mass × velocity (eq (2–26)) and this may be changed at different rates: the greater the rate of change of momentum, the greater the force involved. In the case of a jet engine, air is swallowed, heated and ejected at high speed. The shorter the time in which the change of momentum has to occur, the more heat energy that is required. Hence, the greater the thrust the higher the fuel consumption. For our purposes we shall assume for a moment that specific fuel consumption (eq (2–36)) remains constant with true airspeed and engine rpm. In fact it does not, but changes in sfc are of second order compared with changes in other factors affecting the range equation.

If a stationary jet engine imparts a velocity V_J to a mass of air, W_a/g every second, then using Newton's fluxional notation (placing a dot over a term to show rate), i.e. $dm_a/dt = \dot{m}_a (= \dot{W}_a/g)$

$$F = (p - p_o)A + (\dot{W}_a/g)V_J = (p - p_o)A + \dot{m}_a V_J \qquad (8-1)$$

as shown in fig. 8.1b (ref. 8.1). But when the engine is moving through air at TAS V (while jet velocity V_J is measured relative to the engine) the total rate of change of momentum and thrust becomes:

$$F = (p - p_o)A + \dot{m}_d(V_J - V) \qquad (8-2)$$

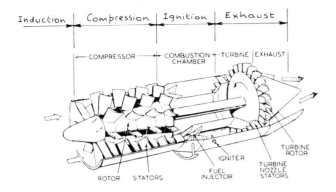

a. Principal parts of a turbojet engine, showing that its cycle is comparable with that of a four-stroke piston engine.

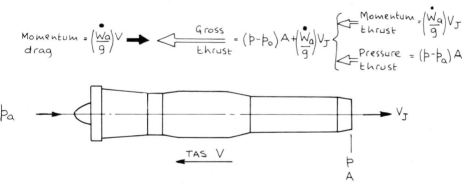

All pressures are total pressures except p, which is the static pressure at the propelling nozzle :

$\left(\dfrac{\dot{W_a}}{g}\right)$ = mass flow of air through engine lb/s
    where g = gravitational constant, 32.2 ft/s^2

V_J = jet velocity at propelling nozzle . ft/s

p = static pressure at nozzle . lbf/in^2

p_a = atmospheric pressure, lbf/in^2

A = nozzle area, in^2

V = true airspeed . ft/s

b. The balance of forces and expression for thrust and momentum drag (FPSR units), Ref 8.1.

Fig. 8.1   The turbojet engine.

The term $\dot{m}_a V$ is called *ram drag* by the propulsion engineer, and *intake momentum drag* by the aircraft engineer. Either way it represents a propulsion loss caused by scooping up the air and carrying it along with the aircraft. The process of adding heat to accelerate the air back again to atmospheric conditions is a way of overcoming the

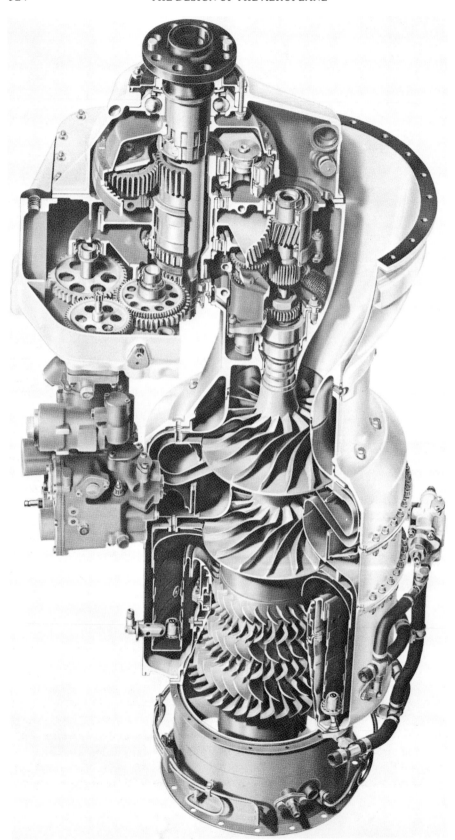

Fig. 8.1c A typical turbopropeller engine (by permission of the Garrett Corporation, USA).

loss of efficiency involved. Positive thrust is only possible if the jet velocity is greater than that of flight.

The expression of thrust in eq (8–2) suggests that if jet velocity remained constant and somehow independent of airspeed, then by the $(V_J - V)$ term, thrust would be reduced. Although this does happen it is partially offset because a pressure recovery takes place within the engine called *ram-ratio-effect* or, usually, just *ram-effect*. This increases the air-swallowing ability of the engine and with it the jet velocity. The result is a partial thrust recovery with airspeed, as shown in fig. 8.2a.

We saw in eq (2–37b) crude figures for the specific fuel consumption of a jet engine. The quantity varies somewhat as shown in fig. 8.2b, because of ram-effect increasing the mass of air flowing through the engine, and the amount of fuel needed to burn it.

Altitude affects thrust and fuel consumption as shown in fig. 8.3. Thrust falls with air density, but the combination of ram-effect and falling ambient temperature brings about a pressure recovery. This is shown in a, together with the near-flat curve of specific fuel consumption with altitude, in fig. 8.3b.

Turbopropellers

Turboprops are hybrid, filling the gap between the relatively low-speed piston-propeller unit and the higher speed jet. There have been few turboprop engines for light aircraft, although they have much to offer now in the agricultural and aerial work fields (fig. 8.4 shows one example). Such engines produce both propeller and jet thrust, so that the total power is referred to as Thrust Equivalent Horse Power. A formula was given in chapter 2 for the take-off case:

$$\text{TEHP} = \text{SHP} + \text{jet thrust}/2.6 \qquad \text{eq (2–32b)}$$

Eq (2–42) shows how the constant 2.6 is obtained. The expression is more complicated in flight, because the jet engine part of the cycle produces thrust more or less as shown in figs 8.2 and 8.3, while propeller efficiency imposes changes that we have seen already in the last chapter.

Some idea of relative effectiveness of different powerplants over a range of airspeeds can be gained by comparing them in terms of a criterion proposed by L. Laming in 1949, and used by Maurice Roy in the *Fourth Louis Blériot* Lecture in 1951 (ref. 8.2):

$$\text{criterion of propulsive effectiveness} = \text{net thrust}/\text{propulsive weight} \qquad (8–3)$$

where: propulsive weight, W_{PF} = powerplant weight, W_p
         + weight of fuel, W_{Fuel}
         + weight of oil, W_{Oil}
         + weight of fuel and oil system, W_{FO} (8–4)

The last three terms can be lumped together by assuming that the amount of oil needed by the engine is a fraction of, and directly proportional to the much larger weight of fuel. Similarly, the system weight is roughly 6 per cent to 9 per cent of the weight of fuel carried. Thus, propulsive weight can be dealt with in two parts: one directly proportional to the weight of the engine and its installation; the other a function of the weight of fuel carried.

The first term, which is powerplant weight, W_p, is dependent upon engine weight and an installation factor, F_p, shown later in the book (table 14.5). If the specific weight of

100 300 500 700 900 kph
static thrust percent
thrust with ram-effect
thrust without ram effect
True airspeed KTAS
a. Thrust recovery with true airspeed.
Mach number SL ISA
specific fuel consumption lb/h/lbf
Author's estimate of Garrett TFE 731-3 turbofan at 10,000 ft
mg/N sfc
True airspeed KTAS
b. Specific fuel consumption increases with airspeed and, hence, with mass flow (Ẇa/g in Fig 8.1b) — but the actual shape of this curve depends upon the engine control system.

Fig. 8.2 The effect of speed upon turbojet thrust and specific fuel consumption (refs. 8.1 and 8.5).

Altitude km
Static thrust percent
thrust recovery with ram effect of increasing TAS at constant 300 KEAS
thrust falling with air density at 300 KTAS
Tropopause
Density altitude 1000 ft
a. The effect of altitude upon thrust
Specific fuel consumption lb/h/lbf
mg/N sfc
Density altitude 1000 ft
b. The effect of altitude upon specific fuel consumption

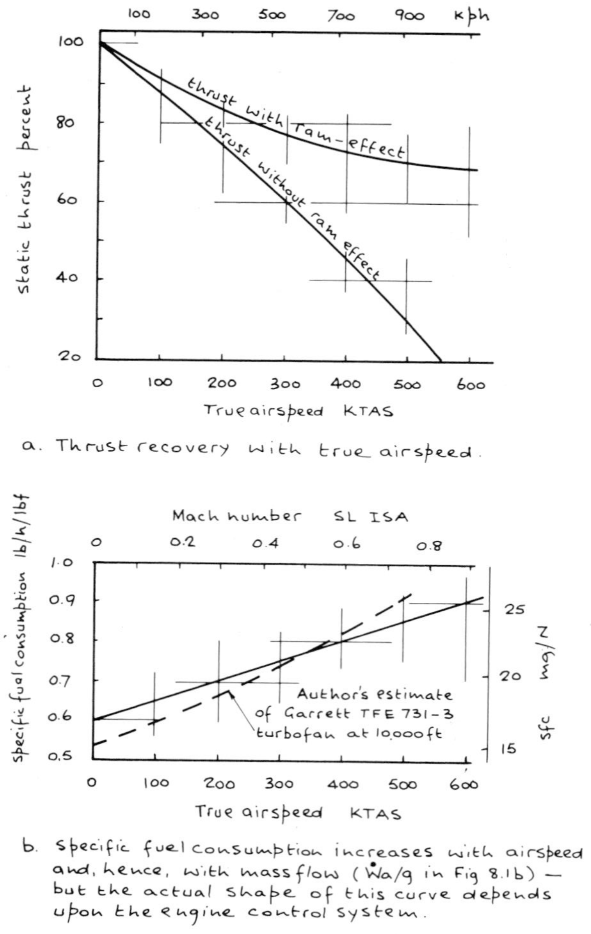

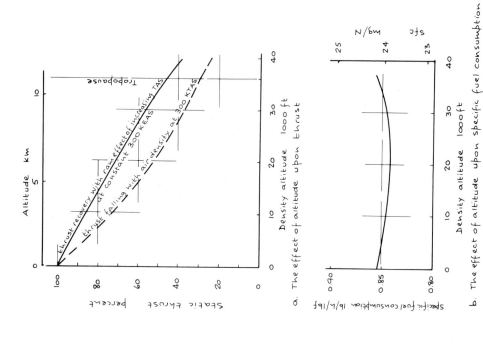

Fig. 8.3 The effect of density altitude upon turbojet performance (ref. 8.1).

Plate 8–1 Turbopropeller engines are lighter and smaller than equivalent piston engines. They cost more, but fuel is cheaper. This *Ayres Turbo Thrush* ag-aeroplane is powered by a *Pratt & Whitney PT6A–34*, 750 SHP *Agro-Turbine* drawing air from a box called a *plenum chamber*, located behind the engine. (*Ayres Corporation, USA*)

a piston or turboprop engine is $\overline{w}$, while that of a jet is $\overline{p}$, each being related to power output, P, and thrust F, respectively, we have power plant weight in each case:

$$W_p = F_p \overline{w} P \text{ (piston or turboprop)} \tag{8–5}$$
$$= F_p \overline{p} F = F_p \overline{p} D \text{ (turbojet or turbofan, cruising)} \tag{8–6}$$

Drag D has been introduced into the last equation because we are most interested in the cruise case.

Assuming that the aeroplane is cruising for range, R nm at a speed V KTAS, the time taken is R/V, and the weight of fuel consumed is:

$$W_{Fuel} = c' PR/V \text{ (piston or turboprop)} \tag{8–7}$$
$$= \mu' DR/V \text{ (turbojet or turbofan)} \tag{8–8}$$

Specific fuel consumptions c' and μ' are as defined in eqs. (2–36a and b), with a fraction of 6 to 9 per cent added for system weight. Therefore, if we call the criterion of effectiveness, E:

$$E \text{ varies as } 326 \, \eta/(F_p \overline{w} P + c'R) \text{ (piston or turboprop)} \tag{8–9}$$
$$\text{and as } V/(F_p \overline{p} \, V + \mu'R) \text{ (turbojet or turbofan)} \tag{8–10}$$

The last two equations, when plotted, give two different kinds of curve, as shown in fig. 8.5. Turboprop and piston engines have similarly shaped curves, which show them to become less effective with increased cruising speeds. The turboprop, although thirstier than the piston, has a lighter specific weight for the same power, and a lower propulsive weight. Beyond point A turboprops are more effective than piston-prop engines. The

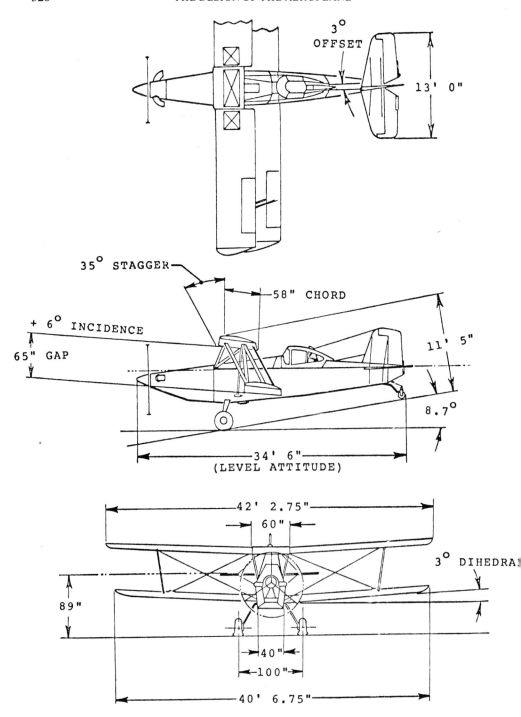

Fig. 8.4   *Schweizer Aircraft Corporation* Turbo Ag–Cat D (8500 lb (3864 kg)) with 680 SHP (507 kW) *Pratt and Whitney PT6* turboprop engine. (drawing from Aircraft Flight Manual).

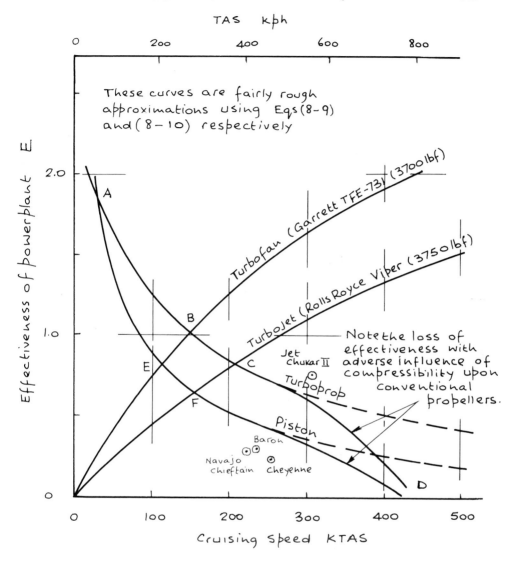

Fig. 8.5 Typical curves showing comparative effectiveness of different subsonic powerplants, using method given in ref. 8.2. Four rough estimates of actual aircraft installations are shown.

Values given in the figure, and the intersections, vary from engine to engine, so that the curves are very general.

Turboprop engines have the disadvantages of being from four to around eight times more expensive than their piston equivalents. But fuel costs are lower, and kerosene is easier to obtain than gasoline, making turboprops cheaper to run.

If propeller efficiency remained constant with increasing airspeed, the piston and turboprop curves would fall asymptotically as shown by the broken lines in the figure. But propeller efficiency eventually drops to zero, so that the curves are caused to bend downwards to zero at some point D. By modifying and improving propeller design efficiency can be maintained to slightly higher speeds, but it always falls to zero in the end.

Turbojets (and turbofan, or bypass engines, which are rather like ducted propulsors, driven by turbojets) are less effective than propeller-engines at low speeds: below points B, C, E and F in the figure. But, as cruising speeds increase, jet engines rapidly come into their own as the most effective means of propulsion.

Turbofans

Turbojets make a lot of noise when accelerating comparatively small masses of air to high jet velocities: noise level varies as the eighth power jet velocity. Noise can be reduced by accelerating larger masses of air more slowly: double the mass of air and it needs $1/\sqrt{2}$ (about 0.7) times the original acceleration to produce the same thrust. The noise level drops to 0.7^8, i.e., about one sixteenth of the original value.

The higher the disc loading of a compressor, the louder the noise, because of the high energy input to the air. Disc loading, like helicopter rotor loading is related to propeller blade loading, which we saw as a cause of noise in the last chapter. Here:

$$\text{disc loading} = \text{thrust}/\text{compressor (or fan) disc area} \qquad (8\text{--}11)$$

Turbojets have high disc loadings, around 1 500 to 2 000 lbf/ft² (72 330 to 96 440 N/m²). Fans, on the other hand, are more lightly loaded and quieter. Coupling a fan to a turbojet engine makes the whole unit more efficient (*see* the comparison in fig. 8.6). They are quieter and operate efficiently at lower air speeds than turbojets, because of the mixing of a large mass of external 'cold' flow by-passing the hot flow through the core of the engine:

$$\text{by-pass ratio} = \text{total mass of air swallowed by (engine + fan)}/\text{mass passing}$$
$$\text{through engine core alone} \qquad (8\text{--}12)$$

The fan engine in fig. 8.6 has a by-pass ratio of 2.8 to 1, which means that $(2.8-1)/2.8$ or about 2/3 of the thrust-producing flow passes through the 'cold' fan.

Technical detail	Garrett TFE 731-3	Rolls Royce Viper
Thrust at SL lbf	3700 (16.8 kN)	3750 (16.7 kN)
Weight lb	736 (334 kg)	790 (356 kg)
Specific weight lb/lbf	0.199 (0.05 kN/kg)	0.21 (0.053 kN/kg)
width in	34.2 (86.9 cm)	-
height in	39.7 (100.8 cm)	-
diameter in	-	24.55 (62.5 cm)
length in	49.73 (126.3 cm)	64.6 (164.1 cm)
Specific fuel consumption lb/h/lbf	0.818 (20.8 mg/Ns)	0.94 (25.2 mg/Ns)
by-pass ratio	2.8	-
gear ratio	0.555	-

Fig. 8.6 Comparison between turbofan and turbojet engines of similar thrust. Garrett information ref. 8.3.

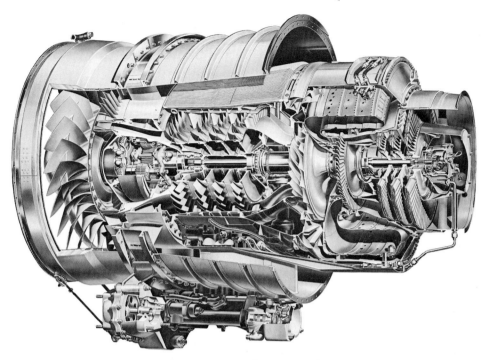

Garrett TFE 731   fan engine
(by permission of the Garrett Corporation)

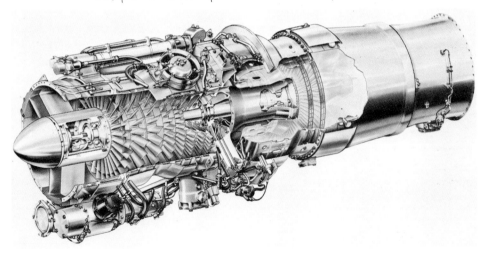

Rolls-Royce Viper single shaft turbojet
(by permission of Rolls Royce Ltd)

Fig. 8.6 (continued)

Breguet range equation (Louis Breguet, pioneer French aircraft designer (1880–1955))

The distance that payload can be carried is a basic operational requirement for any aeroplane designed for a commercial market. Disposable load is the sum of payload plus fuel and, to a certain extent, payload can be exchanged for additional fuel, so that range R might be increased, from A to B in fig. 8.7a. Point D is one of the hardest for a designer to fix, because it determines fuel volume and weight, arrangement of tanks, structure weight in certain areas, and ultimate stretchability of the basic design. In short, it has a profound influence upon cost-effectiveness and utility.

As fuel is consumed the aircraft becomes lighter and flies at a shallower angle of attack, reducing drag. If the pilot maintains a constant cruise EAS he can throttle back and use less fuel, or he can cruise climb a jet aeroplane, gaining true airspeed at constant EAS. Either way, range is increased. This is shown in fig. 8.7b, which introduces Specific Air Range (SAR), $\bar{R}$, measured as distance flown per unit weight of fuel consumed, in this case nm/lb.

Now, let us juggle one or two of the terms that we have come across already so as to derive a useful expression called the *Breguet range equation*. We start with:

range = (miles per hour/lb per hour) × (total fuel lb – fuel for other flying lb)

i.e. $R = (V/\mathring{f})\Delta W_{Fuel}$ (8–13)

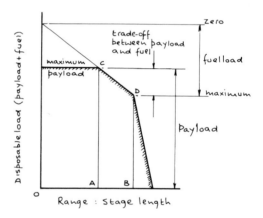

a. Disposable load and range (stage-length)

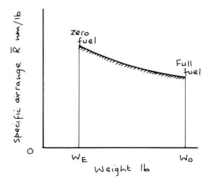

b. Fuel quantity and range

Fig. 8.7   Fuel and range.

and   endurance = weight of fuel consumed / fuel consumption   (8–14)

Fuel consumption rate, $\dot{f}$, written in terms of power specific fuel consumption, c', and thrust specific fuel consumption, μ', becomes:

$$\dot{f} = P_t c'/\eta \text{ (piston and turbopropeller engines)} \qquad (8\text{–}15)$$
$$= F\mu' \qquad \text{(turbojet)} \qquad (8\text{–}16)$$

where P_t and η are the thrust horsepower needed for cruising and propeller efficiency, respectively, and F is thrust lbf, which equals drag, D, in straight and level flight. Thus, using eq (6–7) and writing cruising speed as V KTAS:

$$\text{Thrust horsepower, } P_t = \eta P$$
$$= FV/326 = DV/326 \qquad (8\text{–}17)$$

which enables us to derive the *Breguet range equation* as follows:

☐ *Piston and turboprop aeroplanes*:

From eq (8–13), $R = (V/\dot{f})\Delta W_{Fuel}$

Knowing too that drag may be written in terms of aircraft weight and lift/drag ratio:

$$D = W/(L/D) \qquad (8\text{–}18)$$

using eq (6–7) *et seq*:

$$R = 326 \, (\eta/c')(L/D)(\Delta W_{Fuel}/W) \text{ nm} \qquad (8\text{–}19)$$

Maximum range is achieved when ΔW_{Fuel} is equal to the usable fuel on board, and L/D is maximum, given in eq (5–45a). The fuel ratio:

$$\Delta W_{Fuel}/W_O = (W_O - W_E)/W_O \qquad (8\text{–}20)$$

[handwritten: $We = Wo - \Delta W_{fuel}$]

in terms of gross and zero fuel weights. For the benefit of readers who prefer a more precise mathematical solution:

$$(W_O - W_E)/W_O = \int_{W_E}^{W_O} dW/W = \log_e (W_O/W_E)$$
$$= 2.3 \log (W_O/W_E) \qquad (8\text{–}21)$$
$$\text{so that: } R = 326 \, (\eta/c')(L/D)_{max} \log_e (W_O/W_E) \qquad (8\text{–}22a)$$
$$= 750 \, (\eta/c')(L/D)_{max} \log (W_O/W_O) \qquad (8\text{–}22b)$$

☐ *Turbojet and turbofan aeroplanes*
Again, from eqs. (8–13) and (8–18):

$$R = (V/\dot{f})\Delta W_{Fuel}$$
$$= (V/\mu')(L/D)_R \log_e (W_O/W_E) \qquad (8\text{–}23a)$$
$$= 2.3 \, (V/\mu')(L/D)_R \log (W_O/W_E) \qquad (8\text{–}23b)$$

Note that in both sets of equations we may conveniently substitute:

$$W_O/W_E = W_O/(W_O - W_{Fuel}) \qquad (8\text{–}24)$$

and that the units chosen are: R nm, V KTAS, c' lb/h/hp, μ' lb/h/lbf, while $D = F$ lbf. $(L/D)_R$ is obtained from eq (5–45b).

As a first approximation, range may be calculated from fig. 8.8. This and the foregoing show that the range of an aeroplane depends upon three parameters: one relating to the efficiency of the engine installation, in terms of η/c' or V/μ' (also M/μ');

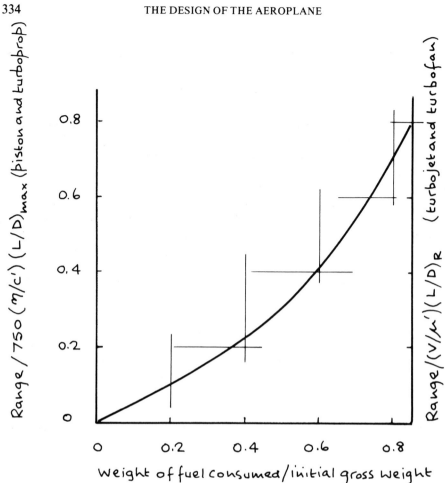

Fig. 8.8   Solution of the *Breguet range* equation for propeller and turbojet aeroplanes, working in Rnm, c' lb/h/BHP, μ' lb/h/lbf and V KTAS.

L/D, which measures aerodynamic efficiency; and $\log_e(W_O/W_O - W_{Fuel})$, a measure of structural efficiency.

With certain exceptions the maximum range of a jet aeroplane increases markedly with height, being commonly twice as great at 30 000 ft (9 144 m) as at sea level. The opposite is true with normally aspirated piston-propeller aeroplanes, which cruise furthest at low altitudes. Turboprop machines cruise most efficiently somewhere between the two.

Why use of $(L/D)_{max}$ is optimistic

Although theory shows that propeller-driven aeroplanes fly furthest at the speed for best lift/drag ratio, in practice they are operated at higher speeds and a lower L/D. There are two main reasons:

☐ Aerodynamically, the wing section of an aeroplane (especially a light aeroplane) is chosen for high C_{Lmax} and good stall qualities, closely followed by a low drag design lift coefficient, and not to optimise some overall lift/drag ratio (which is an amalgam of wing, body, interference and other effects).

☐ The speed for best range L/D is usually too slow for efficient operation of the engine, which might have been sized for the airfield case (e.g., short, hot, high), or for a fast climb to altitude.

Look back to fig. 5.2 *et seq*, and we see that the *NACA 63₁–412* wing section used as an example has a design (low drag) $C_L = 0.4$. Yet, if a tangent is drawn through the origin of the polar so as to graze the curve at the C_L for best section L/D (*see* fig. 5.3) we find that this occurs at a lift coefficient about double the design value, i.e. 0.8 (which is the lift coefficient for best C_L/C_D of all low-speed sections). This implies that, for the section to operate at the angle of attack for best L/D, the aeroplane must cruise at a much lower speed than the one at which the section generates least drag.

One reason why an aeroplane would not be flown at such a slow speed is the airworthiness requirement to fly at a design cruising speed not less than $V_C = 33\sqrt{W/S}$ KEAS (eq (6–39)). Were the aeroplane to be flown at the speed for $(L/D)_{max}$, which would be much slower than V_C, it might be too close to the minimum flying speed (or stall speed, V_S) for comfort, especially in turbulence.

In the examples given in fig. 5.15c, the speed for $(L/D)_{max}$ occurs around 1.85 V_{SO}, while the design cruising speed, V_C, is nearer 3.0 to 3.5 V_{SO}. This means that the achievable L/D at the higher speed is less than $(L/D)_{max}$, and the range is correspondingly less than that calculated by means of the Breguet equation using $(L/D)_{max}$. The loss of range would be quite dramatic, were it not for the effect of the improving engine specific fuel consumption, which decreases with increasing speed. Thus, for a given fuel load, the rapidly falling L/D, when multiplied by the rising $1/c'$ (the reciprocal of the specific fuel consumption) results in a loss of range which is nowhere near as great as that caused by L/D alone.

The Breguet range equation is accurate when the representative lift/drag ratio and specific fuel consumption are used for the product $(1/c')(L/D)$.

References

8.1 Rolls Royce (1971) Ltd (July 1969) *The Jet Engine*. Publication Ref TSD 1302 3rd Ed.

8.2 Roy, M. (May 1951) The Fourth Louis Bleriot Lecture, 'Power versus Weight in Aviation'. *The Journal of the Royal Aeronautical Society*, London.

8.3 Fulton, K. (May 1977) 'TFE-731 Inherits General-Aviation Fan Market'. *Flight International*.

8.4 Gunston, W. T. Editor (1962) *Flight Handbook*. 6th edn. London: Iliffe Books Ltd.

8.5 Garrett Corporation *Garrett TFE 731-3 Tubofan Pilots Brief*. AiResearch Manufacturing Company, 402 South 36th Street, PO Box 5217, Phoenix, Arizona 85010.

SECTION 4

OPERATIONAL CHARACTERISTICS

CHAPTER 9

Fuselages, Hulls and Floats

'Too much detail too soon leads to poor design.'
David·Rendel, past Head of Mechanical Engineering Department, The Royal Aircraft Establishment, Farnborough; and the Civil Aviation Division, New Zealand Ministry of Transport.

'The avoidance of strict accuracy is a general sign of good breeding.'
Socrates (*circa* 470–399 BC)

In this chapter we begin to draw together operational threads which help us to answer a number of pertinent questions in design procedure:

☐ What operational constraints (like geography and terrain) affect the layout and internal environment needed by passengers and freight?
☐ Shall the aeroplane be a landplane, seaplane, or amphibian?
☐ Where shall we put the undercarriage and what will be the wheel arrangement?
☐ How shall payload be carried (e.g. in a conventional fuselage or hull, which spreads the load along the length of the machine, affecting longitudinal and directional stability and control; or across the span, affecting lateral stability and control in the main)?
☐ How shall payload be loaded and unloaded?
☐ What constraints apply to body shape (given Reynolds number and Mach number, how sharp or blunt can it be)?
☐ How shall powerplants be installed, and do their requirements affect body arrangement and shape?
☐ How will the answers affect the layout of stabilising and control surfaces, their shapes and sizes?

The answers are not always obvious. For many aircraft the designers failed to get them right.

Design method from operational requirements

The first consideration in design is what the aeroplane is intended to do. After payload (number of passengers, weight of baggage), range, field length, speed and altitude have been specified and agreed, the designer needs criteria to help him shape the best aeroplane for the job. Measurement of 'best' is hard and various formulae and rules of thumb have been invented over the years – an example is given in eq (6–31) and fig. 6.13, while others might be deduced from chapter 6. In commercial terms 'best' comes down to *profitability*, low Direct Operating Cost, DOC. Where light aeroplanes are concerned low DOCs may be interpreted in terms of lightness, simplicity (which implies maintainability and repairability), low fuel consumption, choice of materials, and 'stretchability' (growth potential).

Selection of criteria depends upon the specification. Care must be taken when writing it to ensure that not only does it ask enough, but that it does not demand too much. It is too easy in these committee-minded times to wreck otherwise good specifications by letting too many people have a say. That is especially true of the military. The author, at a mature age and in a team of equally mature colleagues was once involved in writing a simple paper, which was then forced to run to fifteen drafts. Part of its subject was technical 'sophistication', a precise old word meaning: to spoil simplicity or purity or naturalness (Oxford English Dictionary, OED), now wrongly used to mean complex and advanced. At the end of fifteen drafts the paper was sophisticated (OED) and unintelligible. It is very easy to do the same with specifications. That is why the two quotations at the head of the chapter are thought to be apposite.

The first step in writing a specification is to have a clear idea in mind of what the aircraft is to do: select the aim and stick to it. For the rest, set down a number of headings – as many as you like – and then prune and collate them when you have written everything relevant under each. For example, we might draft a specification along the following lines when setting out to design a light training aeroplane:

Specification

1. *Purpose and Role*
   To design an *ab initio* training aeroplane for use in flying clubs, and for glider towing, with the following characteristics.

2. *Payload*
   (a) Minimum of two occupants, weighing 200 lb (91 kg) each.
   (b) Provision for 25 lb (11 kg) personal baggage, each;
        15 lb (7 kg) navigational equipment (manuals, charts, plus weight of holdall).

3. *Performance*
   (a) To operate from an unprepared grass strip in 2000 ft (610 m) to and from a screen height of 50 ft (15 m) at an elevation of 2000 ft (610 m), ISA + 15°C.
   (b) Range to be at least 540 nm (1000 km), with 45 minutes reserve, with the specified payload.

4. *Handling*
   (a) The controls are to be well harmonised.
   (*Note: see* chapter 2 under Handling Terms and chapter 12).
   (b) Stall characteristics shall be docile, with natural warning.
   (c) The aircraft shall be aerobatic. Manoeuvres shall be at least those specified in BCAR Section K2-12.
   (d) Unlimited spinning is required, both erect and inverted. Spin entry may be achieved with up to full power, but the throttle shall be closed for the recovery, which shall be achieved in not more than one additional turn.

The remaining side headings are a matter of choice. The following are suggested, without elaboration:

5. *Equipment*
   (a) Harness and intercommunication
   (b) Avionics
   (c) Cockpit and instrument layout
   (d) Stowage space

6. *Structural Design*
   (a) Simplicity
   (b) Fatigue and safe life
   (c) Protection of occupants in an accident
   (d) Stretchability (ability to improve cost-effectiveness through increased load-carrying ability and performance)
   (e) Choice of materials
   (f) Maintenance and Repair

7. *Engine Installation and other Systems*
   (a) Powerplant
       (i) Induction system
       (ii) Cooling
       (iii) Silencing
       (iv) Maintenance and Repair
   (b) Systems
       (i) Fuel and Oil
       (ii) Electric
       (iii) Hydraulic
       (iv) Pneumatic
       (v) Ventilation, heating, air conditioning
       (vi) Flying controls
       (vii) Maintenance and Repair

8. *Production and Costing*
   (a) Engineering
   (b) Manufacture
   (c) Maintenance
   (d) Costing
       (i) Non-recurring costs
       (ii) Recurring costs

9. *Marketing and Product Support*

The specification is the yardstick against which the resulting aircraft is measured. It must always take account of the state-of-the-art of aeronautical technology and practice. Advanced aircraft, for which long lead-times are necessary, need almost incredible acts of foresight on the part of manufacturers to cope with the large changes in technology flowing from research and development.

Because specifications are practical documents, one finds that the lines first drawn by a designer are greatly altered by what is achievable in practice (fig. 9.1). The real aeroplane grows heavier than was first estimated. We should always look carefully at similar machines to see in what ways our own can be improved – and also to see where

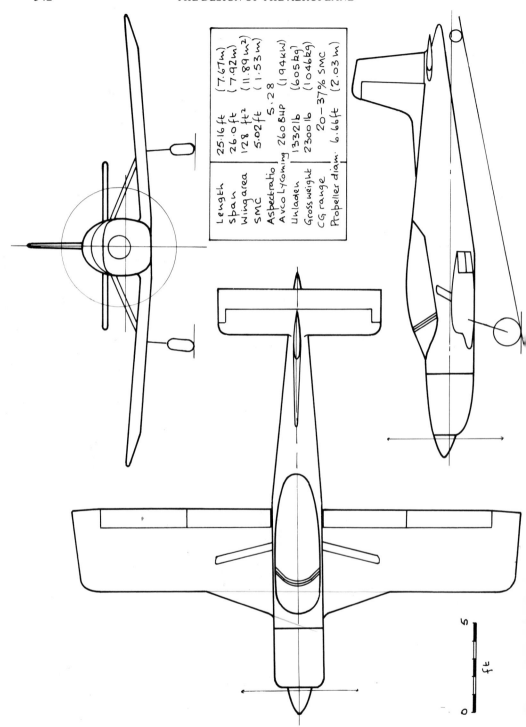

Length	25·16 ft	(7.67 m)
Span	26·0 ft	(7.92 m)
Wing area	128 ft²	(11.89 m²)
SMC	5·02 ft	(1.53 m)
Aspect ratio	5.28	
Avco Lycoming	260 BHP	(194 kW)
Unladen	1332 lb	(605 kg)
Gross weight	2300 lb	(1046 kg)
CG range	20–37% SMC	
Propeller diam.	6.66 ft	(2.03 m)

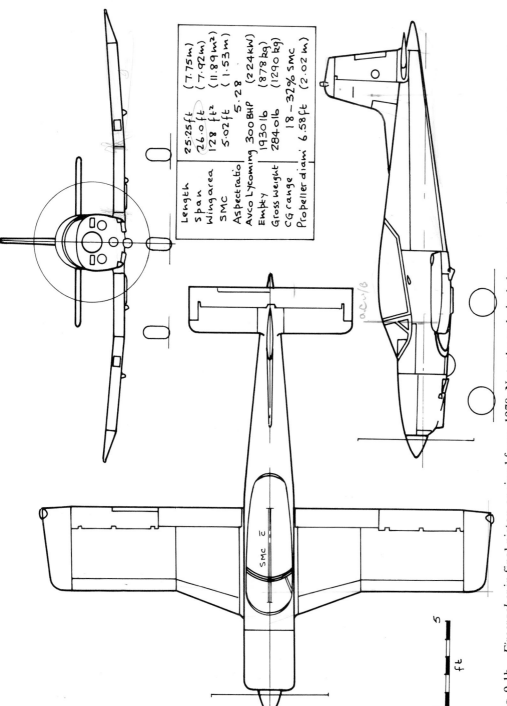

Length	25.25 ft	(7.75 m)
Span	26.0 ft	(7.92 m)
Wing area	128 ft²	(11.89 m²)
SMC	5.02 ft	(1.53 m)
Aspect ratio	5.28	
Avco Lycoming	300 BHP	(224 kW)
Empty	1930 lb	(878 kg)
Gross weight	2840 lb	(1290 kg)
CG range	18 – 32% SMC	
Propeller diam	6.58 ft	(2.02 m)

Fig. 9.1b *Firecracker* in final piston-engined form, 1978. Note the technical changes, especially in growth of weight and power. The growth in weight is attributable in part to the adoption of heavier nosewheel gear, a larger engine and a cantilever wing in place of one externally braced. (Data obtained from *NDN Aircraft Limited*.)

we are perhaps being too optimistic. The aeroplanes in table 6–3 were the result of such an exercise carried out in connection with the above specification (ref. 6.6).

Generally, the smaller the tolerances by which a design might be allowed to fall short of what is required, and the greater their number, the more expensive will be the eventual aeroplane. The tolerances are set by the customer (usually the operator), typical examples being:

☐ Range within ±3 per cent at best range speed.
☐ Maximum speed within ±3 per cent.
☐ Equipped airframe and structure weights within ±2 or 3 per cent.
☐ Take-off and landing distances within ±5 to 7 per cent.
☐ Noise levels no more than 2 or 3 dB(A) above that specified (which should be a like amount below the legally required limit).

The tolerances usually include upper and lower limits, even though one of them represents a bonus for the operator. If the bonus is too large, however, one should suspect that some other quality in the design has suffered.

Sometimes a specification is written around a completely new technological concept, as a private venture and there have been many famous examples, both military and civil. Apart from the private venture (which often contains many unknowns) the formal specification gives the designer his first ideas of how big and how heavy the aeroplane will be. Therefore, we shall look at some aspects of interpreting specifications, to see what tends to fix the form an aircraft will take.

What shall we draw first?

It is impossible to calculate an exact solution at the first attempt. Quite apart from lack of data, much of the designer's personality intrudes artistically. This is no bad thing, because it contains any special genius, or insight, that might be present. The most successful designers are those with the best feel for real problems, and the wit to know when to stop paper studies running too far into the realms of fantasy. One should never be more accurate than is necessary. It is a waste of time calculating to third and fourth decimal places data that can only be measured to the first decimal place.

In spite of arguments to the contrary, which advocate drafting the planform first (because everything depends upon the arrangement of the flying surfaces), more people sketch the side view before any other. It is the side view and fuselage that we are most aware of on the ground, because it embodies most of the practical and aesthetic lines which attract or repel us at first sight. The fuselage is the streamlined shape fairing the payload-carrying volume, incorporating features which facilitate loading and unloading; and the beam which enables economically-sized tail surfaces to exert their moments.

Another good reason for drawing the fuselage first is that it has to fit the human body, the size and proportions of which dominate cockpit and cabin shape, door sills, steps and seat arrangements, windscreen and window shapes, sizes and angles.

Cockpit and cabin

Fig. 9.2 shows the shape of a standard airman, based upon values given in *AvP 970* (ref. 9.1). Joints are marked with small circles, and the centres of gravity of each part of the body with small quartered circles. The weight of the standard man, clothed, is shown in

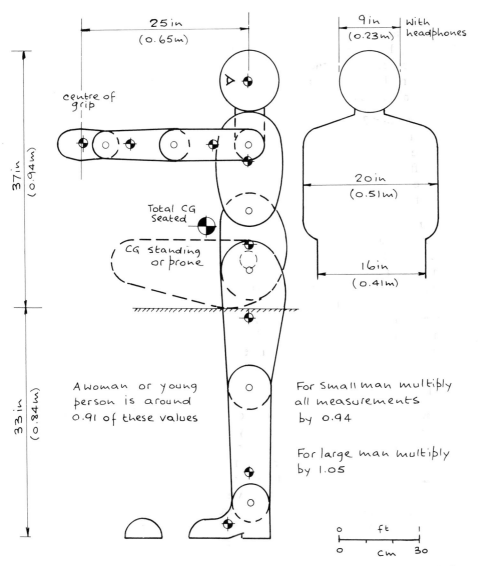

Fig. 9.2 Geometrical construction of standard man (without parachute) from straight lines and circles. Partial centres of gravity shown as small quartered circles, joints as plain circles (based upon ref. 9.1).

table 9–1. The profile can be cut out of cardboard and pinned at the joints, for use in cockpit layouts.

Allow at least 5 in (13 cm) for the cushion, and 2 in (5 cm) for the padded seat back. The generalised cockpit dimensions in fig. 9.3 are based upon the seat datum with cushions compressed. Parachutes are a different matter, and there are many variants. A bucket seat, or seat back, is needed for parachute stowage, dimensions depending upon size and shape of individual packs. Table 9–2 shows two common parachute packs, one seat-type, the other back-type, for use in gliders.

Cockpit height must be sufficient, because there is nothing so wearing on nerves,

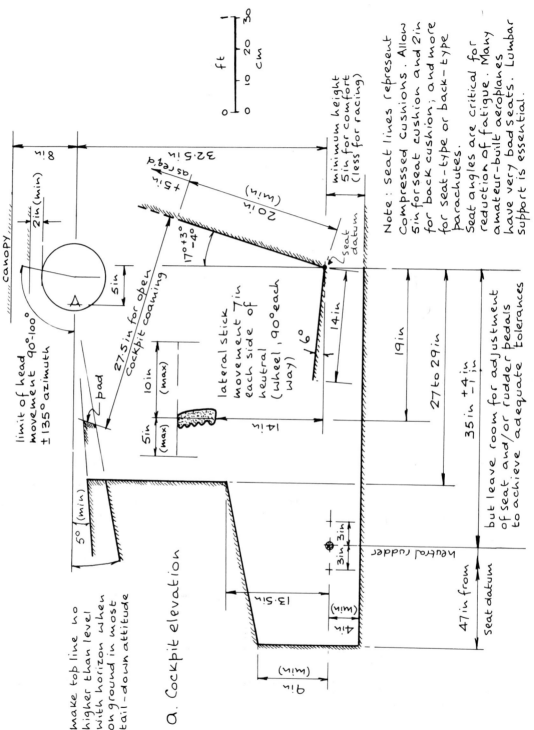

a. Cockpit elevation

Fig. 9.3a Cockpit elevation

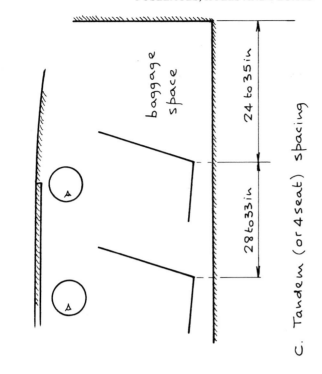

C. Tandem (or 4 seat) spacing

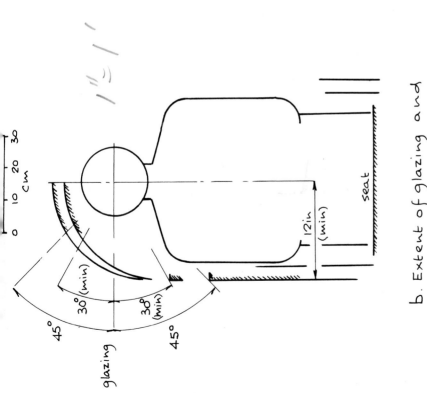

b. Extent of glazing and cockpit sills to enable the pilot to look out sideways in 30° and 45° banked turns it is essential to be able to look inwards during any turn, with an unobstructed view in the plane of a manoeuvre.

Fig. 9.3b and c Cockpit and cabin dimensions.

tissue and temper as cramped seats and headroom. Modern sailplanes have markedly reclining seats so as to reduce frontal area to a minimum, but the workload is low. The higher the workoad on the pilot and crew, the more convenient ergonomically and comfortable should be the cockpit, with ample legroom, elbow room, headroom and scope for adjustment.

Space should be left under each seat for lifejackets. Pockets should be to hand for maps, charts and sick-bags. There must be room for baggage: the longer the range and the greater the number of occupants, the more space that is needed for comfort and convenience. In a tourer it is worth thinking about baggage space large enough to take a temporary child-seat. The larger the baggage space the more thought that must be given to loading and unloading, and to the shape and sizes of doors and hatches. If baggage is to be stowed in the fuselage nose in particular, take care to provide for lashing-down points. The author has come across several executive aircraft with enough space for bags, but no provision for lashing them securely, so that when decelerating, or in turbulence, they could move forward to foul the weather radar or landing lamp, and shift the centre of gravity.

Cuts-out for doors and hatches affect fuselage frame-spacing, and the amount of structure left to provide stiffness and strength. Weight of baggage is an important consideration: 44 lb (20 kg) per passenger, allowed by airlines (economy class) could be cripplingly heavy for many four-seat light tourers.

TABLE 9–1

Characteristics of the standard man
(based on ref. 9.1)

Part of (clothed) body	Per cent Weight	lb	kg
Head and neck	8.3	15	7
Upper trunk	27.2	49	22
Lower trunk	15.5	28	13
Thighs	22.2	40	18
Legs and feet	16.7	30	13.5
Upper arms	5.6	10	4.5
Forearms and hands	4.5	8	4
Total	100	180	82

(For a small man multiply by 0.86; for a large man multiply by 1.14; for a woman or young person multiply by, say, 0.55.)

Adjustments have to be made to balance payload against fuel and number of passengers, so as to arrive at the optimum aircraft for the job. But light aeroplanes are used for air taxi work, as third-level transports, and the following airline baggage allowances must be taken into account when designing a light aeroplane with such work in mind.

For many years the standard man weighed 170 lb (77 kg), but people are growing bigger. The western Caucasian male is heavier and bulkier than his pre-World War 2 counterpart. Racial variations in human size and shape can make a considerable difference to weight and balance calculations, and to fuselage proportions. The average weight today is nearer 180 lb (82 kg) clothed, with deviations of $\pm$ 14 per cent. Measurements also vary $\pm$5 per cent.

TABLE 9–2
Generalised Parachutes

Parachute type	Dimensions
 Weight 25 lb (11.36 kg)	Seat pack length 13 in (33 cm) width 15.5 in (39.4 cm) depth 8 in (20.3 cm) (including 2 in (5.1 cm) cushion) back pad 27 in × 0.5 in thick (68.6 cm × 1.3 cm)
 Weight 18 lb (8.2 kg)	Back pack length 23 in (58.4 cm) width 14.5 in (36.8 cm) depth 6 in (15.2 cm) (including back pad) This type is often used in gliders

TABLE 9–3

Airline class	Baggage allowance
First	30 kg (66 lb)
Economy	20 kg (44 lb)
	Both of the above include 5 kg (11 lb) hand luggage

Note: the 5 kg hand luggage is limited in size to the sum of length + breadth + width = 45 in (1.15 m).

The bulkier and the more sedentary the pilot or passenger, the greater the attention that must be paid to legroom, space for wriggling and moving about. This should include twisting and turning around in one's seat to attend to a distressed child sitting behind.

The *UK Air Navigation Order 1976, Scale A of Schedule 5* (found in ref. 1.1) requires all aeroplanes (helicopters and gyroplanes) to be fitted with either safety harness or a seat-belt and diagonal shoulder strap for the pilot's seat, and for any seat alongside. The Experimental Aircraft Association in the USA requires its members to sign the following pledge when they join (ref. 9.2):

'I, _____ hereby promise to install and wear shoulder harness and safety belts in my custom built aircraft to protect myself, passenger and the good name of the Association. Air Force and Navy tests have proved that a 20G harness will eliminate 90% of aircraft accident injuries.'

Fig. 9.4 shows recommended British practice (ref. 9.3) based upon the standard of the FAA.

Never cramp a cockpit. Irritation and general discomfort cause overpowering subjective stimuli, frayed tempers and errors of judgement. Although airsickness may have physical causes, there is an informed school of thought which holds that it is more often a symptom of wishing to escape from intolerable surroundings. A cramped cockpit can often cause nausea. The same applies to cabin design.

☐ As a rough rule: if an aeroplane flies at speeds for which a wing section of a given thickness ratio provides satisfactory lift/drag characteristics, then the fuselage thickness ratio (1/fineness ratio) may be:

$$\text{fuselage diameter/length} = \text{wing thickness ratio} \, ^{+\,5}_{-\,0} \text{ per cent (max)} \quad (9\text{--}1)$$

When fuselage width and depth differ, they may be averaged as follows, or as shown in table 5–6:

average diameter of fuselage $D = \sqrt{area\ of\ maximum\ cross\ section,\ A_c}$

i.e. $= 0.15$ to $0.2 \times$ length $\quad (9\text{--}2)$

for most subsonic aeroplanes.

Overall dimensions can be estimated by assuming a thickness of wall-plus-lining as shown in table 9–4.

TABLE 9–4

Number of seats	Approximate thickness (wall + lining) per side	
	in	cm
1	1.0 to 2.0	(2.5 to 5.0)
2	1.0 to 2.0	(2.5 to 5.0)
4	2.0	(5.0)
4 to 10	2.5 to 3.5	(6.0 to 9.0)
10 to 30	3.5 to 4	(9.0 to 10.0)

The minimum width of fuselage for a single seat (or tandem) aeroplane is 24 in (0.61 m). A side-by-side arrangement for large occupants must be at least 40 in internally (1.02 m), while 43 in (1.1 m) is common. The widest and most comfortable cockpit measured by the author was 47 in (1.2 m) internally. The narrowest and least comfortable was 38 in (0.97 m), with a mere head-hitting distance from seat to roof (wing spar) of 34 in (0.87 m) (i.e. 3 in (7.6 cm) less than for a standard man).

If an aeroplane has a cabin with an aisle between the seats, aisle width should not be less than 6 in (say 15 cm). Fig. 9.5 shows how fuselage height and width affect body length, while Fig. 9.5c is a typical cabin cross-section.

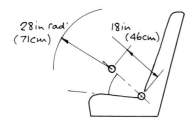

a. Radius of travel of head of occupant, allowing for stretch of seat belt and tall occupant. Within the arc all surfaces should be smooth and either flat, or of large radius.

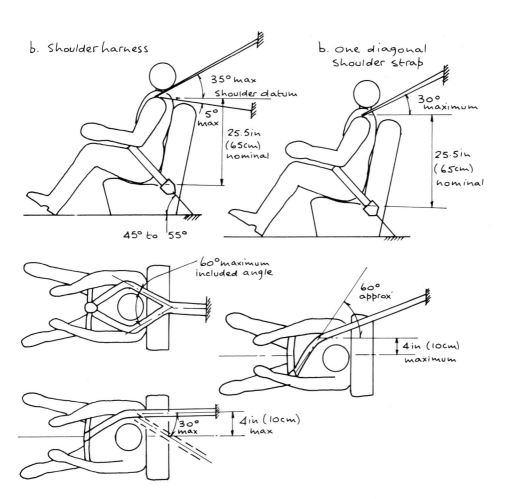

Note: Anchorage of shoulder harness or diagonal straps affects structural layout and arrangement of other seats. The anchor points into the structure must be able to take a load of 9.0g, plus an appropriate safety factor.

Fig. 9.4   Safety belts and harness (ref. 9.3).

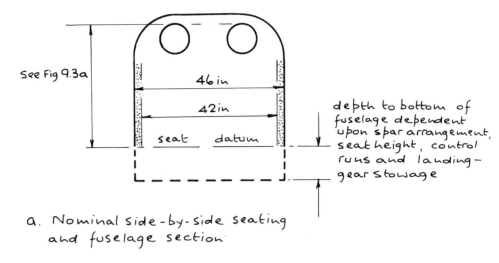

See Fig 9.3a

46 in

42in

seat   datum

depth to bottom of
fuselage dependent
upon spar arrangement,
seat height, control
runs and landing-
gear stowage

a. Nominal side-by-side seating
and fuselage section

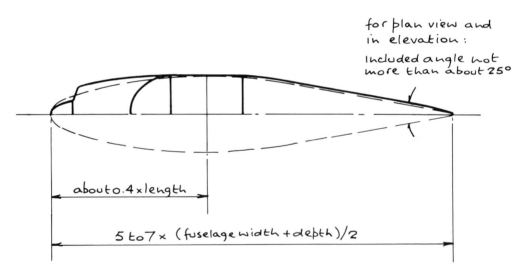

for plan view and
in elevation:

Included angle not
more than about 25°

about 0.4 × length

5 to 7 × (fuselage width + depth)/2

b. General planform of fuselage should have lines
comparable with an aerofoil section. The same
should be true for the side view, but this is much
harder to achieve because of other considerations.
The slope of surfaces towards the tail should not
be too steep for the air to negotiate, so causing
premature separation in normal flight.
A Reynolds number and, hence, fuselage thickness
ratio can be worked out using Fig 3.4.

Fig. 9.5a, b and c   Fuselage proportions and inboard profile.

Surrounding cockpit structure should be strong enough to resist penetrating the enclosed volume shown below. The floor and supporting structure should be able to resist deformation which, in turn, distorts the seats, causing injury.

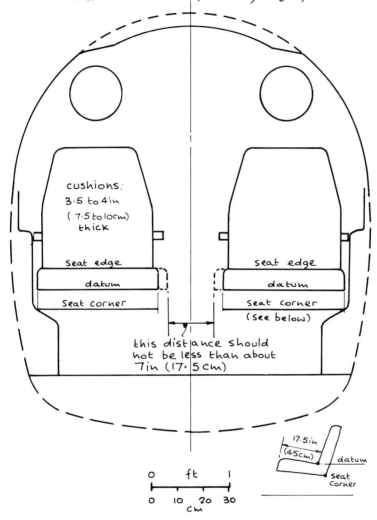

cushions:
3.5 to 4 in
(7.5 to 10 cm)
thick

Seat edge

datum

Seat corner

Seat edge

datum

Seat corner
(See below)

this distance should not be less than about 7 in (17.5 cm)

17.5 in
(45 cm)
datum
Seat Corner

0   ft   1
0   10   20   30
        cm

c. Generalised inboard profile of cabin or cockpit section of light business-executive aeroplane.

Fig. 9.5c.

Choosing wing position

The view from an aircraft must be the best possible, and this is affected by:

□ wing position;
□ extent of cockpit glazing.

High-winged aircraft tend to have better fields of view from just above the horizon, downwards, than low-winged, for which the reverse is true. They make better touring aeroplanes for this reason, because passengers can see more below them. But high-winged aeroplanes can be lethal when manoeuvring, because it is usually hard to see in the direction of turn.

Low-winged aeroplanes provide a better arrangement when agility is required, because they tend to have good fields of view in the direction of turn and manoeuvre. The wings blanket downward view more than a little in straight and level flight. They generate more favourable ground effect on take-off and landing (fig. 6.10), but low-winged machines tend to float further than high-winged, while flaps and ailerons, being closer to the ground, are more easily damaged. However, low wing structure is a useful anchorage and stowage for landing gear, which can be made shorter and lighter. Deeper spars can often be used, by incorporating them into seat structure, without increasing the depth of fuselage needed for a high-winged aeroplane with a wing of the same thickness. But, fairing between wing root and body can be more critical aerodynamically than with a high wing, because the upper surface generates about $\frac{2}{3}$ of the lift and some is lost by imperfect fillets; while imperfections beneath the root of a high wing increase static pressure and increase lift.

High wings tend to be strutted, because they are often thinner, so as to leave enough headroom. This can make them more 'draggy' than low-winged arrangements. But a high wing provides more lateral stability through dihedral effect, as shown in fig. 9.6.

The extent of cockpit glazing should be determined by the pilot's needs. An agile aeroplane which regularly exceeds angles of bank of 60 deg needs wider fields of view than a stately transport machine, which rarely exceeds 30 deg. A pilot, strapped into the seat, sees in azimuth about 135 deg to right and left from dead ahead. In the vertical plane, and as long as there is no restrictive headrest, a supple pilot without arthritis can look upwards from the horizon through 90 deg to 100 deg. These angles should be unrestricted and glazed appropriately, as far as possible. In any case the angular extent of glazing either side of the pilot(s) should not be less than the anticipated angles of bank – plus a degree or two more, as long as the structure can withstand the cuts-out. This means that:

□ Aerobatic, training and crop-spraying aeroplanes should have windows which enable a pilot to see at least 60 deg upwards and 45 deg downwards, either side.
□ Transport and other cruising aircraft, which may need adequate cabin structure to cope with pressurisation, can perhaps be built with less extensive glazing in the vertical plane. Even so, it should not be less than about 40 deg up and down.

In the author's opinion, collision is such an in-flight hazard that it is foolish to provide narrow vizor-like windscreens and windows in light aircraft. Some manufacturers still do so.

When designing the cockpit and cabin, think about crashworthiness. A tough and resilient structure is needed to take the weight of the aircraft when on its back. Too little attention seems to be paid to designing doors which can be opened obviously and

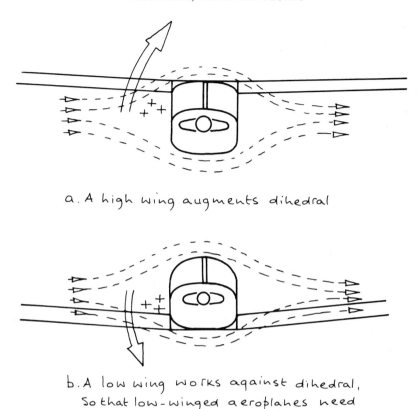

a. A high wing augments dihedral

b. A low wing works against dihedral,
   so that low-winged aeroplanes need
   more dihedral than those with high.

Fig. 9.6   Effect of wing position upon dihedral during a sideslip.

easily from the outside by rescuers in an accident. Emergency access, indications of the positioning and operation of latches and handles, tends to be overlooked. Always think about 'sod's law' in flying: if something is going to go wrong, it will do so in the worst way possible, usually in the shortest time. When a designer has completed his elegant cockpit layout he should then ask himself: 'could an old lady, who does not read the language, release the occupants from the outside in a survivable accident – possibly with a fuel-fire inhibiting clear thought?'

The slope of a windscreen should not be more acute than 30 deg to the line of sight: 40 to 50 deg is common, 35 deg is just acceptable for lower quality materials. Too shallow an angle causes distortion by refraction and unwanted internal reflections, especially at night. A rectangular windscreen panel is useful for judging attitude by reference outside the cockpit.

Bubble or teardrop canopies are popular with designers of sporting and training aeroplanes. Although as a rough guide a length/diameter of 2.5 to 3 causes least drag, straight and level, the slope of the downstream portions of the canopy can cause trouble with changing angles of attack and yaw. Premature separation may be forced by large changes of attitude, often buffeting tail surfaces in the wake. Therefore, look at the slope of the rear surfaces when angles of attack and yaw are around 15 deg and if necessary make the profile finer. At subsonic speeds the shape of the rearward facing surfaces is more important than the slope of those which face forwards. At transonic and supersonic speeds the slope of a forward facing surface is more critical than the reverse.

Always bear in mind the need to provide some form of clear vision in the event of flight in heavy rain, or icing, or when you have splattered a bird across your windscreen. A direct-vision, DV, window should be placed where the pilot can see comfortably enough to make an emergency landing. Such a window should be large enough to enable a clothed arm to reach through it, far enough to wipe the windscreen. The thick, heated, plate-glass de-icer panels often fitted on the outside of modern light aeroplane windscreens are no substitute for a good DV window. They can trap water between glass and screen, reducing vision in moderate rain.

Hulls and floats

The shape of a seaplane hull, or floats, is a compromise to meet the following requirements:

☐ Buoyancy and static stability.
☐ Low water-drag, and the provision of hydrodynamic lift at low speeds to reduce wetted surface area as much as possible.
☐ Spray must be suppressed from reaching propellers, intakes and other vulnerable parts.
☐ Dynamic stability on the water.
☐ Manoeuvrability and control while taxying.
☐ Adequate performance and versatility.

Buoyancy and static stability are provided by the volume of the hull and floats: the weight of water displaced being equal to the weight of the aircraft: the righting moment by the arrangement of the centre of gravity and the metacentre (fig. 2.18).

A buoyant flat plate immersed in water has static lift when at rest, but it generates hydrodynamic lift as well when moving forward at a positive angle of attack. We speak of the displacement regime where lift is predominantly hydrostatic; and of the planing regime in which hydrodynamic lift provides most of the support.

Fig. 9.7 shows parts of a seaplane hull and the way in which it is shaped so as to reduce drag from its different sources. As a floating body moves through water, waves are produced which resemble shockwaves in air – in fact the phenomena are similar. If we look over the bow of a boat moving in smooth water we see a number of low waves radiating away from the hull, like those sketched in fig. 9.8a. As speed is increased the waves grow steeper and they are reduced in number, i.e., there is an increase in both amplitude and wave length. Although the bow wave remains fixed, the remaining waves are spread out towards the stern. Fig. 9.8b shows the condition where the second wave has moved far enough aft to just begin pushing on the stern, in the manner of a wave pushing a surfboard. At this point, where the wave length is equal to the waterline length, we would notice a flattening of the slope of the resistance curve. But if speed is increased further a marked change occurs: the second wave trails behind the stern, the hull pitches nose-up as it tries to climb its own bow-wave, and resistance increases disproportionately. In this condition wave drag is a maximum.

Water drag is made up of frictional, normal pressure and wave-making components. The total resistance, R is shown in fig. 9.9 as a ratio of drag/weight, R/W, against unstick speed ratio, V/V_{us}. Two other curves have been added: the thrust/weight, F/W,

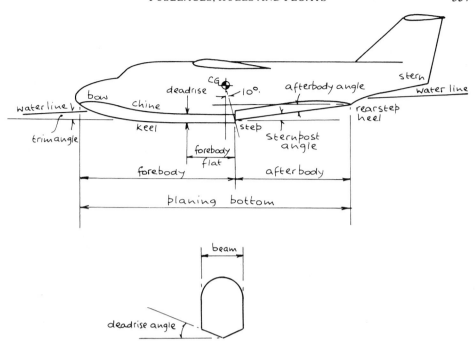

Fig. 9.7 Parts of a seaplane hull (and float).

Plate 9-1 Waves formed by a ship. The basic structure of the formation may be compared with the shock waves in plate 3-4 (Top) (*National Maritime Institute, UK*)

and trim-angle. All seaplanes have had marginal performance in the vicinity of the 'hump', where $(F/W - R/W)$ is least.

Wave-making is a cause of highest resistance. Motion of the hull thrusts molecules of water aside, and downwards, piling the water into crests alternating with troughs. Thus, two sets of forces are most noticeable at first: those caused by inertia, and those due to gravity. Viscous forces are also present, caused by the viscosity of water (look back to eq (3–11) *et seq*), but these are small enough to be ignored initially. If we consider only:

factors affecting inertia forces/factors affecting gravitational forces

in much the same way as we treated Reynolds number in eq (2–11), we have a dimensionless number called the Froude number, F, where:

F varies as (density of water $\times$ (speed through water)^2)/(density of water $\times$ gravitational constant $\times$ waterline length of hull)

In this equation we may cancel the density terms, ρ, so that:

$$F = \sqrt{(\rho V^2/\rho g L)} = \sqrt{\lambda/2\pi L} = V^2/gL \qquad \text{eq (2–67)}$$

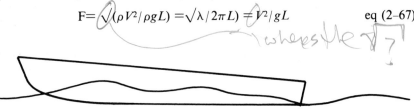

a. Wave-making at low speed.

b. Critical condition in which second wave is pushing forward on the stern.

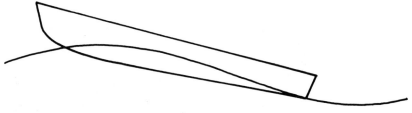

c. Higher speed, at the 'hump' where drag is a maximum, with the hull climbing its own bow wave.

Fig. 9.8   Wave development.

As speed is increased wave-making drag increases and rises steeply beyond the critical condition shown in fig. 9.8b (where the second wave is just leaving the stern). Beyond this speed the hull is climbing a hill, shown in c. To go faster a hull must accelerate past the 'hump speed', lift out of the water and plane. Planing generally occurs by the time:

$$V = 1.7\sqrt{(\text{waterline length in feet})} \text{ knot} \qquad (9\text{-}3)$$

$V = 1.6\sqrt{L} \text{ knots}$

with an average value of the constant around 1.6.

The change in attitude, represented by the trim-angle, is caused by the increased normal pressure on the forward facing hull surfaces and suction on the rearward facing surfaces. Conditions are similar to those affecting a convex aerofoil surface in supersonic flight. The normal pressure and suction forces cause a nose-up couple that must be countered by elevator deflection to hold the aircraft at the optimum trim-angle for planing.

Suction acting on the afterbody tends to hold the stern down and causes porpoising. It is necessary to break down the suction by ventilation: introducing a layer of air between the afterbody and the water, and this is done by making a step about half-way along the planing bottom, slightly aft of the aircraft CG. The main step may be located by the intercept of a line some 10 deg aft of the vertical through the centre of gravity, as shown in fig. 9.7.

Unfortunately, steps cause high aerodynamic drag, and various shapes have been tried in an effort to reduce it. The earlist simple transverse step increased the drag of the basic streamlined hull by about 48 per cent. An elliptical step, as seen in planform, has a drag increment around 15 per cent, with a minimum close to 12 per cent.

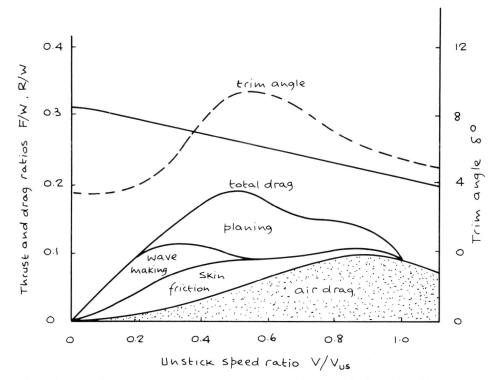

Fig. 9.9 Combined resistance, with thrust and trim-angle during take-off.

Alternatives are *hydrofoils* and *hydroskis*, examples of which are sketched in fig. 9.10. *Skis* work at larger trim-angles than *foils*, and they do not *cavitate* (the flow vapourises at the foil surface causing loss of lift). They have a further advantage in that they can be retracted quite easily to form the bottom surfaces of the hull. Their disadvantage is that they do not permit much freeboard in choppy water. *Foils*, on the other hand, are small water-wings which are completely immersed and generate lift/drag ratios in water around 30:1. They generate intense suction and are susceptible

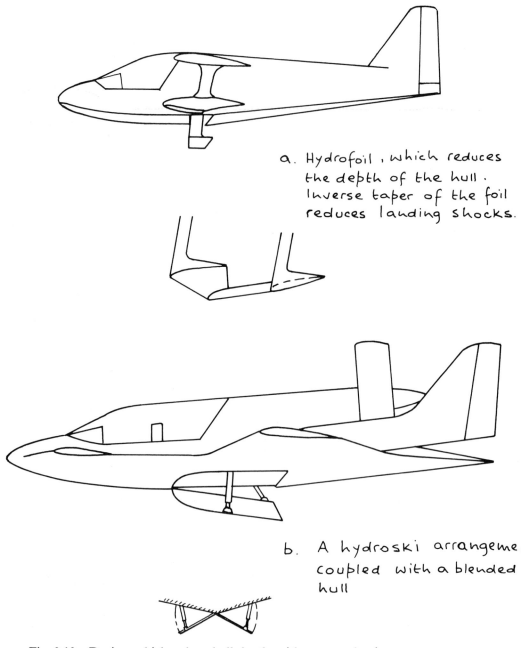

a. Hydrofoil, which reduces the depth of the hull. Inverse taper of the foil reduces landing shocks.

b. A hydroski arrangeme coupled with a blended hull

Fig. 9.10   Devices which reduce hull depth, with spray reduction.

to cavitation over their upper surfaces causing reduced lift/drag, and instability. They can be designed to lift the hull bodily, creating much needed freeboard, and for this reason they present certain attractions. Although both enable cleaner hulls to be designed, their mechanisms and structures introduce weight penalties.

Spray

Planing surfaces are vee-shaped to absorb the shocks of high speed motion. Spray is caused by the peak pressure developed in the area where the planing bottom enters the water and occurs in two forms. The first, ribbon or velocity spray, is flung sideways in a flat trajectory from the line of forward contact of the planing bottom with the surface of the water. Being light it causes few problems, apart from misting windscreens. The second kind, called blister spray, is heavy and far more damaging. Blister spray is thrown upwards and rearwards by the chine in a heavy cone. The height to which it rises determines the heights of wings, engines and tail-surfaces.

Spray is suppressed by hollowing the forebody from keel to chine, by increasing forebody fineness (length/beam) by attaching strips called spray dams to the forebody chine, and by building an inverted gutter just inside the chine, as shown in fig. 9.11. The spray dam and more elaborate gutter must lie along the airflow. For this reason they cannot run too far aft along the chine, which has marked curvature. The dam protrudes at right angles to the spray path and derives its effectiveness from mixing air with the spray as it is deflected back to the water. The aerated mass penetrates the free water surface with high velocity and little or no reflection.

Dynamic stability on water

There are three kinds of dynamic longitudinal instability which affect a planing hull:

- ☐ *Porpoising* is a cyclic oscillation in pitch and rise, and if allowed to persist it may become divergent and result in the destruction of the aeroplane.
- ☐ *Skipping* is like a flat stone bouncing across the surface of the water.
- ☐ *Pattering* is a short period oscillation in pitch, without rise.

Porpoising at large trim angles is caused by the afterbody dipping into the water. This is prevented by maintaining large afterbody keel and sternpost angles. Porpoising at high speeds results in skipping, the aeroplane being thrown clear of the water before stalling back again. Another cause of porpoising is location of the step centroid too far in front of or behind the centre of gravity.

Skipping is caused by the step being too shallow, so that there is insufficient ventilation of the planing-bottom. Tests indicate that the depth of the step should be about 4 per cent to 8 per cent of the beam for (afterbody length/beam) ratios between 2.5 and 4 (with straight line variation between the corresponding points). For a light seaplane (forebody length/beam) ratio should be about 3.

At shallow angles of trim porpoising is reduced by a flattened portion of the forebody, called the forebody-flat. This extends 1.5 beam widths forward of the step and, being flat, sustains more or less constant pressure over the whole of its surface. Curvature would cause variation of the longitudinal pressure distribution with trim and alter the metacentric height with any disturbance in pitch, so that resulting motion would be aggravated. Later hulls with refined slender lines do not have a marked forebody-flat. Instead the deadrise-angle is increased forward of the step, which makes the vee at the keel more acute. Increasing the deadrise-angle in this way is called

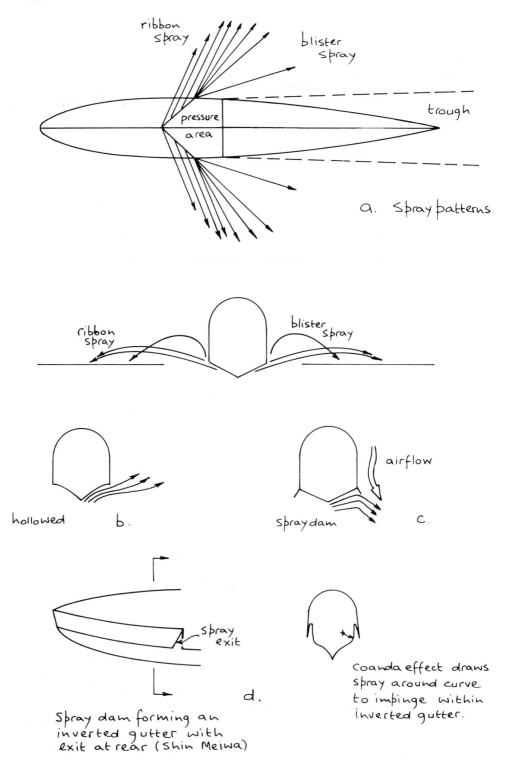

Fig. 9.11   Spray formation and devices for its suppression.

forebody-warp. An increase in deadrise-angle decreases the tendency to porpoise, but causes the forebody keel to run deeper in the water, which decreases directional stability.

Forebody deadrise-angle should not be less than 15 deg for the smallest aircraft, increasing to 25 deg at the step of larger machines. Deadrise reduces landing impact (fig. 9.12) (after ref. 9.4)), but it can cause ground clearance problems with amphibians. Forebody-warp permits the deadrise-angle to be increased to about 40 deg towards the bow, enabling the aircraft to operate among waves of greater height from trough to crest.

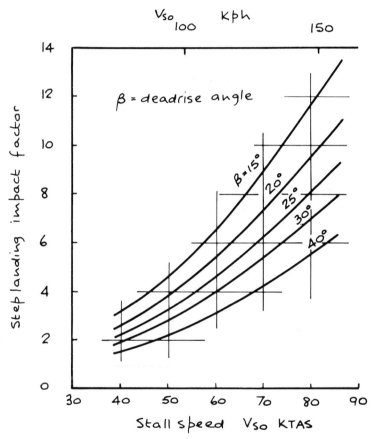

Fig. 9.12   Variation in step landing impact with stall speed and deadrise angle for a 4000 lb (1818 kg) seaplane (after ref. 9.4).

Most light seaplanes weighing less than 4000 lb (say, upn to 2000 kg) can cope with waves around 1.5 ft (0.45 m), although much depends upon actual hull design. Fig. 9.13 shows an approximate range of wave heights plotted against gross weight (displacement) for conventional hulls. This emphasises one reason why light seaplanes are fairly unpopular novelties in Britain, for example, which lacks large enough lakes and expanses of inland water to make them cost-effective. The sea-state around Northern Europe and the British Isles, even close inshore, is rarely smooth enough for safe operation of small seaplanes. There is little work for larger ones, which suffer greater logistic support problems than helicopters.

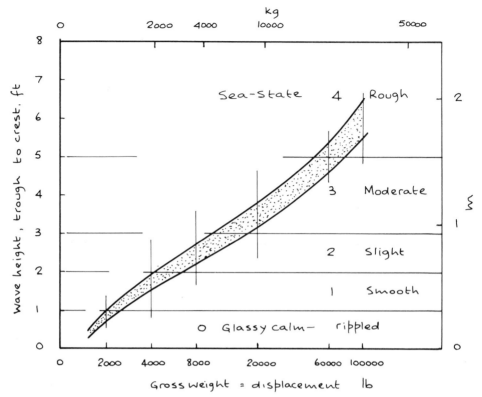

Fig. 9.13　Limiting wave heights for hulls of different displacements, with description of sea-state (after ref. 9.5). Typical wave heights in sheltered waters of Britain and Northwestern Europe are around 1.5 ft, making most light seaplane operations fairly impractical.

Figs 9.14a and b show land and seaplane versions of the *Partenavia P68* with geometry which illustrates a number of points covered above. Note the ventral fin added to the fuselage of the seaplane to improve directional stability in flight, by compensating for the increased side area forward of the centre of gravity.

Directional control

Although long forebodies with plenty of warp suppress spray, they decrease directional stability and make the hull prone to ground (water) looping, because the centre-of-lateral-area is moved forward of the centre of gravity. Such instability may be cured by a skeg, a small fin, protruding into the water from the afterbody keel, but its effectiveness depends upon the range of trim angles at which it runs in solid water.

Water-rudders or water-flaps are needed for directional control, and all seaplanes have increased fin area at least to cope with the destabilising effect of the growth of keel area forwards. If the sides of the hull bulge outwards too much above the chines, spray striking the curved surfaces causes yaw if it touches one side before the other. This feature affects the design of fin and rudder surfaces. Jet seaplanes need special consideration in the design of water-rudders and water-flaps, because they lack beneficial effects of propwash to help with manoeuvre and control.

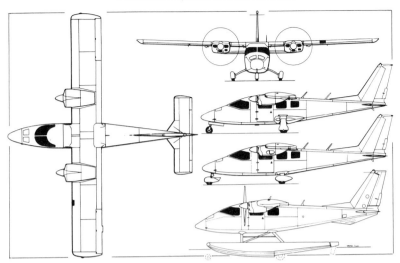

Fig. 9.14 *Partenavia P68B* with additional sideviews of floatplane/amphibian version and *P68R* with retractable gear. *See* table 9–5 for gain and loss account.

TABLE 9–5
Comparison between P68 variants shown in fig. 9.14.

Item	P68B (fixed gear)	Percentage change from basic P68B		
		P68R (retractable gear)	P68B (floatplane)	P68B (amphibian)
Gross weight	4321 lb (1960 kg)	0	+20	+20
Empty weight	2800 lb (1270 kg)	+2.5	+31	+41
Useful load	1521 lb (690 kg)	−4.6	0	−19
Maximum speed	174 KTAS (322 kph)	+5	−15	−15
Best rate of climb	1600 ft/min (8.13 m/s)	+4	−31	−31
Single engine rate of climb	318 ft/min (1.62 m/s)	+16	−28	−28
Service ceiling	20000 ft (6096 m)	+10	−20	−20
Maximum fuel range 45 min reserve	1100 nm (2038 km)	+4.5	−38	−38
Estimated drag	100 %	−9.5	+38	+38
Estimated productivity	100 %	0	−15	−31
Data compiled from Partenavia, Jane's All the World's Aircraft and author's estimates				

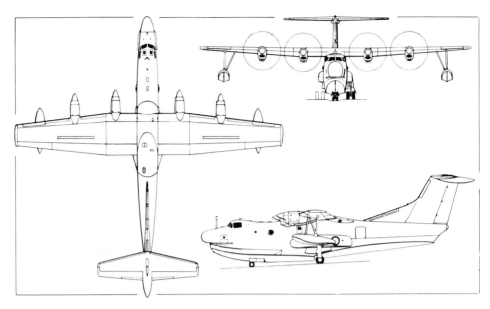

Fig. 9.15   *Shin Meiwa US-1* search and rescue amphibian, showing how hard it is to make amphibious aeroplanes aerodynamically clean as well as operationally efficient. (*Pilot Press Limited*)

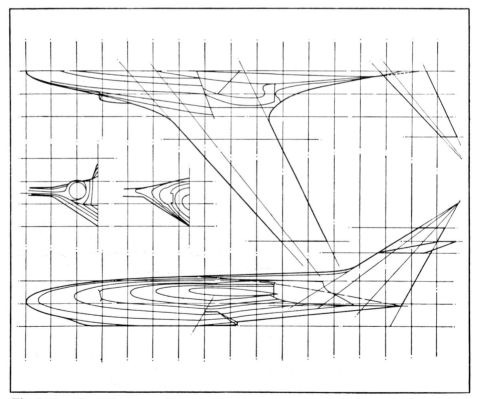

Fig. 9.16   Lines of a transonic blended-hull seaplane used in the *Skate Project*, USA, about 1950 (ref. 9.6).

Plate 9–2 Amphibian seaplanes have relatively heavy empty weights. Japanese *Shin Meiwa US–1*, Search and Rescue aircraft (which has more than one pilot) shows tip vortices from the propellers (*Shinn Meiwa Industry Co Ltd,* Japan)

Blended hulls

Existing hull and float-forms suffer penalties in weight and performance, in that speed and rate of climb are reduced. Loss of speed is around 10 per cent at the cruise. Flying boats can be made more efficient than floatplanes (which tend to be modified landplanes with landing-gear replaced by floats). Even so, with their chines and additional wing-tip floats (or stabilising sponsons grown laterally from the hull) it is hard to refine their aerodynamic shapes to the point at which they are equal in every way to landplanes. Furthermore, it is hard to make a seaplane as flexible as a landplane without the addition of landing gear, making it amphibious. Then weight penalties become higher still, as shown in table 14–10 (ref. 5.6).

Some indication of the problem and the resulting 'bittiness' of the amphibian can be gleaned from the drawings of two *Shin Meiwa* designs, based upon the *PX–S* maritime reconnaissance flying boat, as shown in fig. 9.15. Attempts to clean up small amphibians by retracting their wheels can cause weight problems when cutting holes in planing bottoms. Nevertheless it can be done, although some designers have resorted to merely swinging the wheels upwards, out of the water, while leaving them in the wind underneath the wing.

In the 1940s the American *Convair* company modified a jet bomber, called the *XB-46*, for operation from water. The modification involved the addition of a large wing-hull fillet, which faired into the bow and stern, giving the hull an aerofoil section when viewed from the side. The increased volume of the new type of hull, brought about by the fillets, eliminated the need for separate engine nacelles, because there was room enough to bury the engines within the hull. Buoyancy was provided by fillet-volume, while spray was controlled by spray-dams. The inherent lateral stability of the new hull form (fig. 9.16 (ref. 9.6)) eliminated separate floats (fig. 2.18).

The blended-hull lines shown here allow a large payload-volume/surface area of airframe, with room for retracting the undercarriage without too much trouble. The higher structure weight, including the landing gear, is compensated to a certain extent by a saving in wing-tip floats and their supporting structure.

References

9.1 AvP970 **2**, Book 2, App 8 (1955) *Design Requirements for Aircraft for the Royal Air Force and Royal Navy*. Ministry of Aviation.

9.2 Experimental Aircraft Association Membership Application, EAA, PO Box 229, Hales Corners, Wisconsin 53130.

9.3 BCAR Section K 4–4 *Seats, Safety Belts and Harnesses*. Civil Aviation Authority.

9.4 Thurston, D. B. (1978) *Design for Flying*. New York, London: McGraw-Hill Book Company.

9.5 BCAR G 4–10, Appendix. Civil Aviation Authority.

9.6 Stout, E. G. (1951) 'A Review of High-Speed Hydrodynamic Development'. *Proceedings of the Third Anglo-American Aeronautical Conference*. Brighton: The Royal Aeronautical Society.

CHAPTER 10

Choice of Landing Gear

'Between the limits of absolute theory and absolute practice lies horse-sense.'
From an anecdote about Herbert Eugene Chaplin (1896–1979) Chief Designer (Aircraft) Fairey
Aviation recounted by Harold Best-Devereux, Consulting Engineer.

'A good landing is one you can walk away from.'
Anon (early).

The undercarriage, or landing gear, serves a triple purpose in providing a stable
support for an aircraft at rest on the ground, forming a suitable shock-absorbing
device, and acting as a rolling chassis for taxying and during manhandling. It is dead-
weight in flight and much art is needed to fair it, or to retract it in such a way as to cause
least interference with the external aerodynamics and the internal load-carrying
volume. Also, it represents a considerable cost item in the total maintenance bill.

A complex retraction mechanism is heavy and there is much skill needed in making
retractable gear light and simple, yet strong enough to absorb the repeated shocks of
moderately heavy landings. Superimposed upon the design case of coping with high
rate of descent is the drag load caused by rotational inertia of the wheel about the axle
during the time of quite violent spin-up on touchdown. More drag loads are caused by
braking, while additional sideloads come from lateral skidding and crosswinds.

Where light aeroplanes are concerned it is possible to design very clean gear with
wheel fairings, which cause few aerodynamic penalties, and which are light and cheap,
by utilising flat spring steel legs. Such relatively simple but durable units are even
employed on a number of heavy agricultural aeroplanes, which, with some of them
operating at weights of 8 500 lb (3,864 kg) are hardly light.

The number of wheels and tyre sizes are determined by the requirement that an
aeroplane should be able to operate at maximum take-off weight from both rigid and
flexible bearing surfaces, having specified load-bearing properties. The size of tyre and
its pressure determine the 'footprint' area in contact with the ground. The load applied
by the wheel is thus felt as a pressure, a stress over the area of the footprint. Multiple
small-wheel units can be made lighter and folded away more easily than single big
wheels, but bogey-trains, more complicated axle-units and retraction mechanisms tend
to cancel any theoretical benefits. Further, multiple small-wheel units may become
clogged with mud and there are distinct benefits for ag-aeroplanes relying on quite big,
relatively soft, tyres with only one wheel per leg. One tends to find that ground-support
vehicles get into difficulties before the aircraft, which gives pilots a good indication of
when to give up.

Choice of gear layout depends upon a number of factors, and the author believes that one should not automatically assume that a nose-gear (tricycle unit) is necessarily best. While they make for reasonably easy ground handling, pilots trained on the current range of aircraft fitted with them tend to have slow feet, and they are less well co-ordinated than pilots trained on tail-draggers. This is no idle prejudice. The *Tiger Club* in Britain operates a wide range of tail-dragging aeroplanes, and the greatest single problem for its check-pilots is sharpening up the footwork of new members, who have to demonstrate their ability to fly the *Tiger Moth* before being accepted as flying members. The *Tiger*, which likes to fly sideways and is far from responsive, shows up the deficiency within seconds.

Each type of gear has certain advantages and disadvantages, and choice depends upon practical considerations.

Tailwheel gear

Tailwheel undercarriages have two main units forward of the centre of gravity and one behind which, in the simplest case, may be only a skid. At rest the aircraft sits tail-down at an angle of attack slightly less than the stalling angle of the wings with high-lift devices extended. This allows the aeroplane to be three-pointed onto the ground with power off. Among amateur-built aeroplanes there are more taildraggers than any other.

☐ *Advantages*. The advantages of taildraggers lie in their aerodynamic cleanliness (potential if not in fact), relative lightness, simplicity and cheapness. With care they can be made to generate less drag so that they contribute to increased lift/drag and higher performance than nose-wheel gear. The tail-down attitude enables pilots to cope better when flying into and out of small rough fields. On the ground they can be pushed around and manhandled into smaller spaces than similar machines with nosegear.

☐ *Disadvantages*. The disadvantages lie in handling on take-off and landing, loading, and view over the nose when taxying. Because the centre of gravity of the aeroplane lies behind the mainwheels, there is a powerful tendency for the tail to swing outwards in a turn, leading to a ground-loop (especially if the tailwheel is free swivelling). More powerful machines tend to be fitted with tailwheels which can be locked so as not to swivel, when the aircraft is running straight. Passengers and crew have to walk uphill when boarding, and *vice versa*. Engine starting can be harder in cold weather – the *Tiger Moth* is only one of a number of aeroplanes which start better if the tail is lifted when priming the engine, so that fuel runs freely along the manifold towards the front cylinders.

Although an aeroplane fitted with tailwheel gear is more demanding for students, lengthening time taken to solo for many, disconcerting others, it may be argued that there are more gains than losses in causing student pilots to learn how to cope. There is evidence in Britain (where training is mainly on nosegears) that the general standard of flying does not appear to be high enough consistently to produce pilots with the right skills and aptitudes for flying the more demanding older types of aeroplanes. For example, a study carried out at Old Warden aerodrome over several days during a recent season showed that a small but significant number of pilots, drawn from a sample with a wide spread of experience, did not achieve an acceptable standard on landing (ref. 10.1). What occurred at Old Warden occurs elsewhere too. Sloppier landing habits, failure to get the tail down on landing (regardless of whether an aeroplane is a tricycle or a tail-dragger), cause too many ballooning, wheelbarrowing and mishandling incidents. The result is that numbers of *Cherokee, Cessna 150* and *Grumman American AA–5* type aircraft end up with broken nosegears.

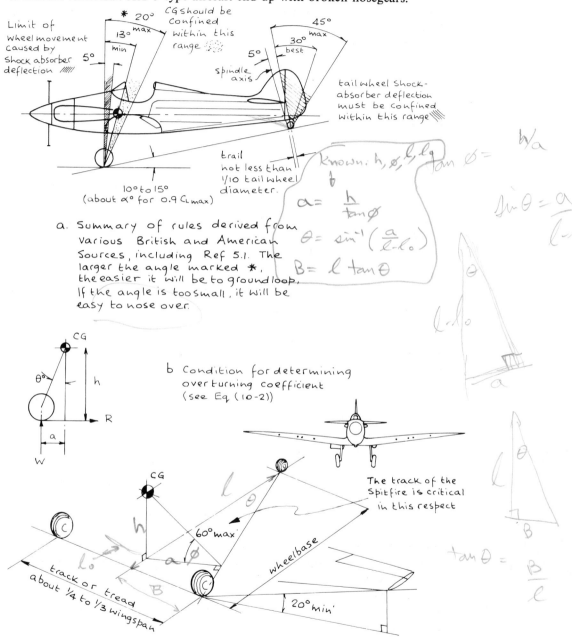

a. Summary of rules derived from various British and American sources, including Ref 5.1. The larger the angle marked *, the easier it will be to groundloop. If the angle is too small, it will be easy to nose over.

b Condition for determining overturning coefficient (see Eq (10-2))

The track of the Spitfire is critical in this respect

c. If the track is too narrow wing tips will be damaged by the aeroplane tipping sideways when groundlooping, or in a strong crosswind

Fig. 10.1 The tailwheel undercarriage.

Fig. 10.1 shows the general arrangement of a tailwheel undercarriage. The centre of gravity for the design gross weight should fall within 13 deg to 20 deg aft of vertical, tail-up, with the average about 17 deg. Wheel motion during shock absorber deflection should fall inside the area enclosed by the vertical and a line 5 deg aft of it. With shock absorber compressed and flat tyres there should be propeller tip ground clearance of not less than 1.5 in (say 4 cm). Under the same conditions the closest that flaps and elevators should be to the ground is about 2.5 in (6.5 cm).

The castor or spindle axis for the tailwheel should be inclined forward of the normal to the ground by 5 deg. The spindle axis should intercept the ground line not less than 1/10 tailwheel diameter ahead of the point of contact between the wheel and the ground. This is to ensure that there is enough trail to avoid shimmy (rapid oscillation about the spindle axis). Tailwheel shock absorber deflection should place the wheel within the angle formed by a line normal to the ground at the point of contact and a line inclined 45 deg aft. The optimum angle is 25 deg to 30 deg aft of the normal.

The track or tread of the mainwheels should be arranged as shown so that the aeroplane cannot roll over too easily. Both the *Messerschmitt Bf 109* and the *Supermarine Spitfire* were critical in this respect.

The gear is arranged in elevation so that the main wheels touch first with the point of contact with the ground subtending an angle α deg at the **CG**, when the wing is flying at an angle of attack corresponding with:

$$\alpha_{0.9} = \text{angle of attack for } 0.9\ C_{Lmax}, \text{ i.e. } 1.05\ V_{SO} \qquad (10\text{--}1)$$

which depends upon wing section, planform, incidence and flap, but rarely exceeds 15 deg for reasons shown in fig. 4.7. Some aeroplanes have such shallow ground angles that the tailwheel or skid touches first every time.

The aircraft should not be in danger of nosing over when brakes are applied. The critical condition is shown in fig. 10.1b in which, taking moments about the centre of gravity and expressing them as a ratio we obtain:

$$\text{overturning coefficient, } K = Rh/Wa = R/W \tan \theta \qquad (10\text{--}2)$$

in which R = braking force = μW, where W = weight of aircraft, μ = braking coefficient ≈ 0.25, a = deceleration and $K = 0.7$ to 0.8. Given these values:

$$\theta = \tan^{-1}(\mu/K)$$
$$= 17 \text{ deg to } 19 \text{ deg} \qquad (10\text{--}3)$$

The angle θ should be checked throughout the estimated CG range so as to avoid making it too large. It is advantageous to have enough elevator power to lift the tail early in the take-off run, and elevator size is affected by the magnitude of θ.

Nosewheel gear

Most commercial and training aeroplanes have nosegear, although these too have both advantages and disadvantages.

☐ *Advantages.* The more or less level attitude of nosewheel aircraft makes them easier to load and unload most of the time. The view over the nose can be excellent. They are less demanding and can be taxied faster, and straighter, without the need to swing the nose from side to side, so as to see ahead. Shallower angle of attack makes for a faster acceleration on take-off. It is usually harder to damage the tail with blown debris. There is less risk of nosing over when forced landing.

☐ *Disadvantages.* Because nosewheel units have to take greater loads than tailwheels or skids, they are heavier. They cause higher drag and overall lift/drag of the aircraft is reduced. Therefore, there is a greater need to retract nosewheel undercarriages. One or two designers have compromised by folding only the nosewheel leg away. Because they are easy and forgiving on the ground they are less demanding, and the standard of pilot handling can be inadequate when converting initially to tailwheel types. The position of the centre of gravity gives a static nosewheel reaction varying between 6 and 15 per cent gross weight. If there is too much load on the nosewheel:

☐ It is hard to rotate nose-up on take-off through insufficient elevator power.

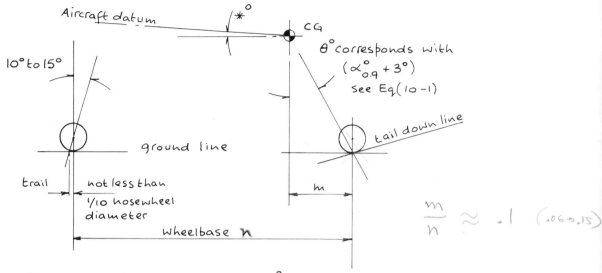

Aircraft datum

θ° corresponds with
$(\alpha_{0.9}^\circ + 3^\circ)$
see Eq(10-1)

tail down line

10° to 15°

ground line

trail

not less than
$1/10$ nosewheel
diameter

wheelbase n

m

$$\frac{m}{n} \approx .1 \quad (.06 \to .15)$$

a. Summary of rules. The angle $*^\circ$ should not be too large, otherwise the nose wheel will touch first in a tail-up landing, causing wheelbarrowing and loss of directional stability.

$a = n$
$b = n - m$

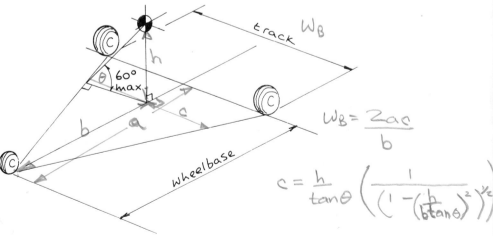

track W_B

60° max

wheelbase

$$W_B = \frac{2ac}{b}$$

$$c = \frac{h}{\tan\theta}\left(\frac{1}{\left(1 - \left(\frac{b}{h}\tan\theta\right)^2\right)^{1/2}}\right)$$

b. If the track is too narrow wing tips may be damaged (see Fig 10.1c)

Fig. 10.2   The nosewheel undercarriage.

$$W_B \approx \frac{2ah}{b\tan\theta}$$

☐ The marked reduction in mainwheel load reduces braking drag.

☐ The mainwheels lie well aft, which makes it hard to counterbalance by rudder (and differential braking) the couple caused by a crosswind acting on the fuselage ahead of the mainwheels.

☐ A tandem-winged aeroplane flown by the author in a strong crosswind had the mainwheels so far aft (to cater for a large usable **CG**-range) that $\frac{1}{3}$ right rudder and most of the right brake were needed to keep straight with a strong wind from the right, and *vice versa*. This meant that the nosewheel was deflected about $\frac{1}{3}$ right, with much tyre-scrubbing, brake-wear and heating of brake pads – as well as increased rolling resistance on take-off. If the nosewheel reaction is too light:

☐ There is a tendency for the aircraft to sit on its tail. This can be avoided by locating the mainwheels aft of the perpendicular dropped from the centre of gravity to the ground, tail-down, as shown in fig. 10.2a. The angle of attack $\alpha_{0.9}$ deg is given by eq (10–1), the angle θ deg is measured in a level attitude.

☐ It may be that the force exerted by the nosewheel in a turn will be too light for effective steering, especially in a crosswind.

☐ The increase in the ratio of (dynamic/static nosewheel load) makes shock-absorber performance critical.

Nosewheel load is deduced in terms of gross weight by taking moments about the mainwheels in fig. 10.2a:

$$W_n/W = m/n = 0.06 \text{ to } 0.15 \tag{10–4}$$

Bicycle gear

Bicycle arrangements of wheels, with the main load-carrying units on the centre-line, and outriggers beneath the wings, have appeared sporadically. Fig. 10.3 shows the three basic arrangements. Their merit lies in less weight and drag than full nose and tailwheel gears. The position of the wheels in fig. 10.3a allows little margin for variation of landing attitude, and speeds must be maintained within 2 to 3 knots. If the aeroplane is landed nose-high, the pitching moment of the centre of gravity about the rear wheels forces the nosewheel down with a high risk of bouncing and vice versa. For equal, optimum sized units front and rear wheels should be placed at a distance from the **CG** equal to the radius of gyration of the aircraft in pitch (*see* eq (2–25b)). But if bouncing is to be avoided, i.e. if the pilot is to be given a reasonable margin of freedom in landing speeds for different weights and cross-wind conditions, the mainwheels should lie as close to the **CG** as possible.

In the other cases we may resort to the conditions for determining the geometry in elevation of nosewheel and tailwheel undercarriages, applied as shown in fig. 10.3b and c. In general, if units are placed at a distance from the centre of gravity less than the radius of gyration in pitch, then the gear touching first suffers the greater load. If they are placed further away than the radius of gyration, then the unit touching last is most heavily loaded.

Bicycle gear as shown in fig. 10.3a has been used on large jet bombers (e.g. the *Boeing B–47*) designed to operate from well prepared airfields. Type b has found a number of military applications, especially with VTOL machines in recent years. Type c is commonly used for motor gliders.

Although bicycle gear has few vices – beyond vulnerability of lightweight outriggers – the author finds it tiresome. Slight changes of wind tilt light aeroplanes from side to

Front view applicable to a, b and c.
Minimum outrigger loads occur when they
are located at the radius of gyration
of the aircraft in roll.

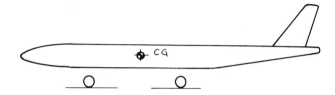

a.

If each maingear unit is located at the
radius of gyration of the aircraft in pitch,
critical loads front and rear will be
equal and a minimum.

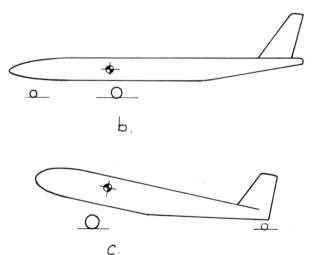

b.

c.

Fig. 10.3   Bicycle arrangements with outriggers.

side, moving the centre of rolling resistance in the direction of the downwind outrigger.
There is a tendency of the aircraft to yaw with roll, which brings into play
centrifugal effects, which cause the pilot to meander while rolling alternately from side
to side. Crosswind landings can be difficult, necessitating crosswind gear, as on the
Boeing B-52.

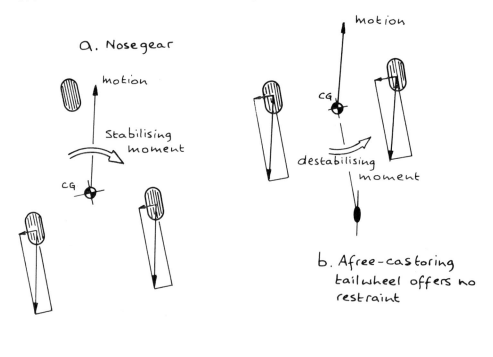

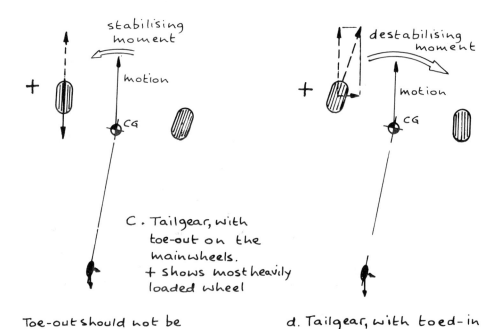

Fig. 10.4 Directional stability of landing gears. Nosegear a is more stable than tailgear b. Tailgear with toe-out c is less unstable than with toe-in d.

Directional stability – toed wheels

Directional stability of nosegear layouts is positive, in the sense that if the aircraft yaws slightly while taxying, the rolling and skidding resistance of the mainwheels, acting behind the centre of gravity, tends to straighten the aircraft out. This is shown in fig. 10.4a.

Tailwheel layouts are unstable. The bulk of the weight of the aircraft is taken by wheels ahead of the CG so that yaw or skid causes instability, tending to make matters worse. This is accentuated by a free-castoring tailwheel, which rides with the turn and offers no corrective restraint. The larger and heavier an aeroplane fitted with tailwheel gear, the more necessary is a tailwheel locking device, to be engaged as soon as the machine is running straight when lining up for take off, and again for landing. The longer the tail remains on the ground at such times, the more dangerous is any resulting swing caused by the propeller with full power selected, i.e., during a touch-and-go or going round again.

The situation can be improved somewhat by toeing-out the mainwheels of a taildragger very slightly – say, one or two degrees. The reason is shown in fig. 10.4c and d. Yaw or a turn throws the main weight on to the outside wheel which, because of toe-out, tends to run straight. Toe-in makes matters much worse. In fact a taildragger which is normally quite docile can become unexpectedly hard to handle on take-off and landing because something as simple as an eyeballed repair to damaged gear has caused slight toe-in that was not there before.

Skis

Skis vary from modified water-skis, suitably strengthened and with proper fittings, to highly streamlined glass reinforced plastic units, incorporating hydraulics. Regardless of design and cost all must have the proper area, fittings and rigging to suit the aeroplane.

Fig. 10.5 (based in part upon ref. 10.2) gives an indication of 'footprint pressure' of skis on snow, for a range of different gross weights. The inset shows the way in which skis are braced so as to parallel the flight path, attitude being maintained by cables at the back, tensioned by bungee-sprung cables to the toe of each at the front. A retainer wire also runs to the toe of each ski, to prevent it becoming inclined at 90 deg to the airflow, should a bungee unit break. The retainer wire and bungee should never be attached to the same fitting, in case it is the fitting which fails.

Skis mounted on nosegears can suffer rough usage, and it is advisable to double the strength of nosegear units and fittings. Skis fitted to tailwheels and skids tend to be broad and shovel-like, and they are often ridged underneath, or have rods welded into place to aid steering. The footprint pressure on the tailski should be less than that of the mains (by being made relatively larger for the weight it must support). Some aircraft keep a steerable tailwheel, running it through a slot in the ski, so as to facilitate steering, and to use it as a brake by pumping the rudder from side to side.

Shock absorption

When an aircraft hits the ground on touchdown, landing gear shock absorbers and tyres deflect and kinetic energy of descent is changed into a mixture of thermal and potential (including pressure) energy. The energy absorbed by the landing gear (shock

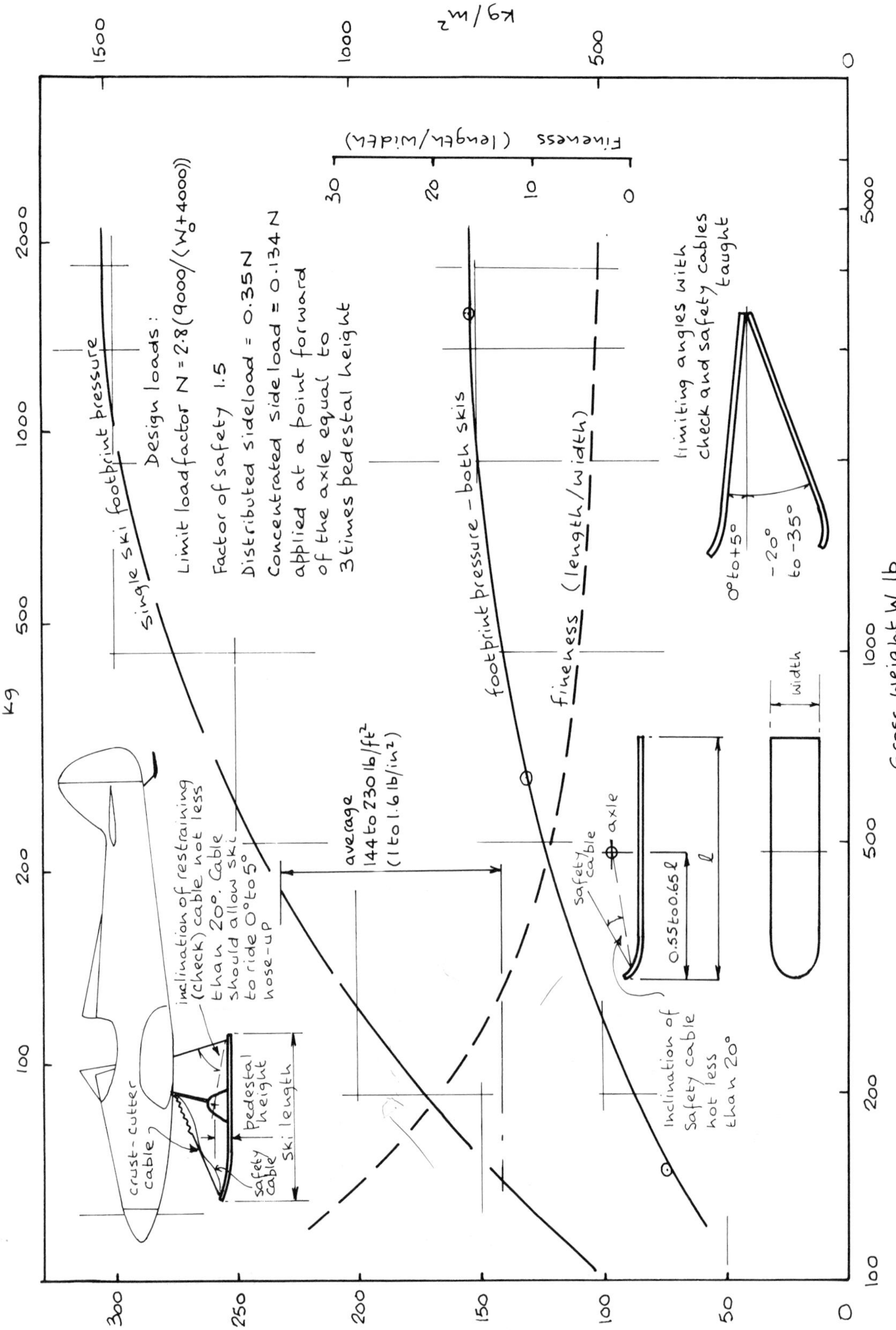
kg/m²
1500
1000
500
0
Fineness (length/width)
30
20
10
0
2000
1000
500
200
100
kg
Design loads:
Limit load factor N = 2·8(9000/(W₀+4000))
Factor of safety 1.5
Distributed sideload = 0.35N
Concentrated side load = 0.134N
applied at a point forward of the axle equal to 3 times pedestal height
single ski footprint pressure
footprint pressure – both skis
fineness (length/width)
limiting angles with check and safety cables taught
0° to +5°
-20° to -35°
average 144 to 230 lb/ft² (1 to 1.6 lb/in²)
inclination of restraining (check) cable not less than 20°. Cable should allow ski to ride 0° to 5° nose-up
crust-cutter cable
safety cable
pedestal height
ski length
safety cable
axle
0.55 to 0.65 ℓ
ℓ
width
Inclination of safety cable not less than 20°
300
250
200
150
100
50
0
Footprint pressure lb/ft²
100
200
500
1000
5000
Gross weight W₀ lb

Fig. 10.5 Ski design

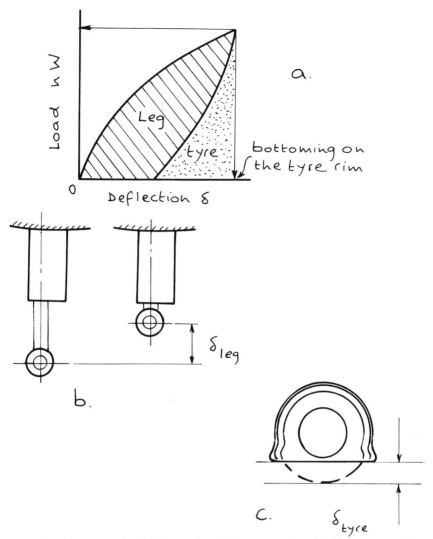

Fig. 10.6 Landing gear shock absorption. The energy absorbed is measured by the area under the curves in a.

absorbers plus tyres) is roughly as shown in fig. 10.6, being equal to the sum of the areas under the curves, and this equals the total kinetic energy (eq (2–16a)), where:

$$\text{Energy absorbed} = \eta n W \delta \qquad (10\text{–}5)$$

η = efficiency of process, nW = maximum vertical load, δ = total deflection of tyre + shock absorber.

A civil aeroplane is assumed to touch down with a vertical velocity not exceeding 10 ft/s (3.05 m/s) (refs. 10.3 and 4), and 12 ft/s (3.7 m/s) for most military aeroplanes. A good landing on a smooth, paved surface gives only 2 or 3 ft/s (0.6 to 0.9 m/s). The overall kinetic energy absorbed is given by:

$$KE = W v^2 / 2g \qquad (10\text{–}6)$$

which is equal to eq. (10–5). Here W = gross weight lb, v = maximum velocity of descent ft/s, and $g = 32.2$ ft/s². Thus:

$$KE = Wv^2/2g = \eta n W \delta \qquad (10\text{–}7)$$

i.e.
$$\eta \delta = v^2/2ng$$

The minimum value of n is 2, but 3 is used for most aircraft. These values when applied to a civil aeroplane touching down at 10 ft/s give: $= 6.2$ in

$$\eta \delta = 10^2/2 \times 3 \times 32.2 = 5.\cancel{X}\text{ in (13 cm)}$$

which represents the total travel resulting from deflection of tyre and shock absorber together, i.e.

$$\eta \delta = \eta_{tyre}\,\delta_{tyre} + \eta_{leg}\,\delta_{leg} \qquad (10\text{–}8)$$

so that, for a given tyre deflection, where:

$$\delta_{tyre} = \text{inflated radius} - \text{radius when flat} \qquad (10\text{–}9)$$
$$\delta_{leg} = (\eta \delta - \eta_{tyre}\,\delta_{tyre})/\eta_{leg} \qquad (10\text{–}10)$$

The efficiency of different types of shock absorbers is given in table 10–1:

TABLE 10–1

Shock absorber efficiency

Type of shock absorber	Efficiency η
Tyre	0.47
Cantilever spring	0.50
Compressed rubber rings	0.60
Oleo-pneumatic	0.75

(handwritten: $.47\,k\,x^2$; spring rate!)

Using the appropriate values in eq (10–10), we have:

$$\delta_{leg} = (5.\cancel{2}^{6.2} - 0.47\delta_{tyre})/\eta_{leg} \text{ in} \qquad (10\text{–}11)$$

in which the deflection of the tyre when flat, δ_{tyre}, is obtained from the tyre manufacturer's catalogues. Table 10–2 shows typical American light aeroplane tyre characteristics (ref. 5.1):

TABLE 10–2

Tyre characteristics

Static load lb	Tyre size	Ply rating	Tyre diam. in D	Flat radius in	Max deflection in
700	5.00–4	4	13.25	3.6	3.02
800	5.00–5	4	14.20	4.1	3.00
1100	6.00–6	4	17.50	4.5	4.25

Assuming that these tyre proportions are typical, deflection when flat is about 0.45 times the inflated radius. This enables us to make an educated guess at total shock absorber travel, during the paper project stage, knowing roughly the diameter of tyre of a similar aeroplane.

(handwritten: $\delta_{tyre\,max} \approx .45 \dfrac{D}{2}$)

References

10.1 Roscoe, A. H., Keating R. F. and Ellis, Flight Lieutenant G. A. (June 1979) Tech Memo FS264 *Landing Performance of Pilots in Single-Engine Light Aircraft.* Royal Aircraft Establishment, Bedford.

10.2 Husek, D. G. (Dec. 1980) 'Aircraft Skis'. *Sports Saviation.* Experimental Aircraft Association International Inc, Hales Corners, Wisconsin.

10.3 BCAR Section K3–5 *Grounds Loads.* Civil Aviation Authority.

10.4 FAR Part 23.473. Federal Aviation Administration.

Tire size	Ply	load rating #	Wt (tire+tube) #	Diameter inches	Wheel+brake wt #
				8"	3.75 #
2.8/2.5 x 4	4			10"	3.75 #
4.10/3.50 x 4	4				
5.00 -4	4/6	700/1200 #	3.8 #	13.25"	5.0 #
5.00 -5	4/6	800/1285 #	5.0 #	14.20" MAX	5.75 #
6.00 -6	4/6	1150/1750	7.6 #	17.50" MAX	7.75 #

CHAPTER 11

Longitudinal stability

'Keep the aeroplane in such an attitude that the air pressure is always directly in the pilot's face.'
H. Barber (1916)
(from *The Aeroplane: an Historical Survey*, Charles H. Gibbs-Smith, Her Majesty's Stationery Office, 1960).

'Inherent stability'...being a tendency of the machine to retain the same attitude to its flight path or to its *relative motion to the air*, it follows that the more stable is a machine in this sense the more does it tend to follow alterations in wind direction, and this quality in excess makes for discomfort in flying and danger in landing. Hence we want to ensure that our machine has a *slight* margin of stability and that ample controlling power is afforded to the pilot to enable him to quickly alter at will its attitude in any direction.
F. S. Barnwell, *Aeroplane Design* 1916 (ref. 4.21) (designer of *Bristol F.2B*)

Stability and control are complementary and in certain respects each represents a different philosophical approach to flight. The early pioneers of aviation in Europe tended to concentrate upon making inherently stable aeroplanes, control being employed to make them change direction. The Wright brothers in the USA took a different line and built an aeroplane, their *Flyer*, which was controllable, but which had no stability to speak of. For very short flights it is quite practicable to fly aeroplanes which are neutrally stable (like Gustave Limbach's *Gusty* in fig. 15.15, a machine that is neutrally stable about all axes, is highly aerobatic, and which does not care which way up it is flying). It is also possible to get used to flying an aeroplane which is marginally unstable – but it takes little to make marginal and unstable aeroplanes dangerous when the pilot's attention is divided, as when tired, or when distracted by passengers, or in an emergency.

We saw in chapter 2, fig. 2.12 that stability is possessed by an aeroplane if it responds to a disturbance in such a way as to oppose it and return to its original state. The condition is like that of a ball in a saucer, which always rolls back to the lowest point after being pushed to one side. Stability makes an aeroplane point into the relative wind – but too much stability can be tiring when the wind is chopped up into gusts.

Instability, to take the ball-in-the-saucer analogy further, is the condition when the saucer is inverted. The ball might be balanced momentarily, but a slight disturbance causes it to roll away down the slope. Neutral stability, on the other hand, is like placing the ball on a perfectly smooth and level surface, so that it stays wherever it is put.

Plate 11–1 Modest control circuit friction makes this aeroplane feel neutrally stable about all axes. *Limbach Gusty* (flown here by Gus Limbach) neither knows nor cares which way up it is. (*Howard Levy, USA*)

Control may be thought of as a disturbance of equilibrium by the pilot, which can then be maintained against the basic trim of the aeroplane. It is for this reason that control has been placed in the next chapter, letting longitudinal stability act as a prologue.

The formal study of stability and control has a certain elegance – but it is heavy-going in places, because of the many factors which enter the picture. Therefore, it will probably pay to read quickly through the chapter (and chapter 12 if you are game) before settling down to the detail later. The ideas are digestible enough, it is the multiplicity of complicated-looking terms which tends to be overwhelming at first.

Take a piece of paper and let it fall from the hand. As it falls it is flying, in a sense, because its descent is slowed by aerodynamic forces. But without control there is no real flight with direction and purpose – its motion is more random than directed (except by gravity). Whenever a pilot wishes to direct and manoeuvre an aeroplane it is necessary to alter the position of the control surfaces. Conventional surfaces are basically simple flaps, hinged portions of wing and tail trailing edges. Movement of the surfaces alters the local pressure distributions and the resultant aerodynamic forces. Reactions, in effect hinge-moments, are felt by the pilot as a feedback through the control system. The feedback may be direct (but reduced by the mechanical advantage of the system), or, if hinge-moments are too powerful it may be necessary to use power control jacks, with artificial forces transmitted back to the pilot by an artificial feel-system, e.g. *q-feel*, which is proportional to the dynamic pressure, q. Ideally, control forces should increase with airspeed, angle of attack, normal acceleration, and with increasing control deflection, so as to safeguard against the pilot breaking the aeroplane.

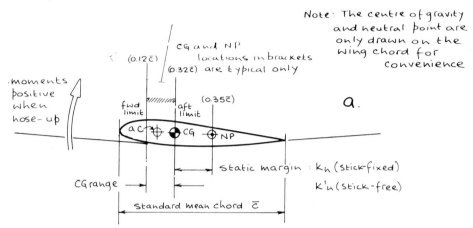

ac   The aerodynamic centre of the aircraft – minus – stabiliser, which is shifted forwards of the aerodynamic centre of the wing alone, by the presence of the fuselage (and any nacelles or floats). The shift due to the fuselage is approximately 4 to 5 percent SMC (see Fig 11.14).

NP   Neutral point: the aerodynamic centre of the complete aircraft with stabiliser fitted.

CG range   The centre of gravity of an aircraft has forward and aft limits set by diminishing ability to trim by means of control surface deflection (forward limit) and diminishing stability (aft limit). The CG range and limits are expressed more often than not in terms of percentage SMC. Assuming the ac of the aeroplane – minus – stabiliser to lie at $0.22\bar{c}$, forward and aft CG limits might be from 0.12 to $0.32\bar{c}$, ie 12 to 32 percent SMC respectively, with the neutral point at $0.35\bar{c}$. These positions depend upon the size of the stabilising surfaces, eg, tailplane plus elevator

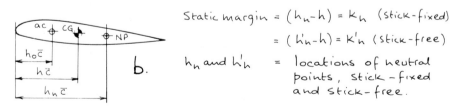

Static margin   The distance measured as a fraction of the SMC between the CG and the appropriate neutral point. In the absence of aeroelastic distortion and compressibility effects, the static margin = CG margin (which is what is really shown in this figure.

Fig. 11.1   Some terms used when analysing longitudinal stability.

Stability and control are analysed in three planes:

☐ pitch, longitudinally;
☐ yaw, directionally;
☐ roll, laterally.

The fundamental state is that of longitudinal balance and stability. Fig. 11.1 shows some of the special terms used in this chapter, and table 2–7 shows notation used in stability and control analysis.

Longitudinal balance (trim)

Although a state of balance is at the root of stability, we must be careful. Balance about the centre of gravity of an aeroplane is achieved when it is *in trim*. An aeroplane could be in trim in perfectly smooth air, like the undisturbed ball balanced on an upturned saucer. But, like the ball, the slightest disturbance (in the form of a gust, or transient control movement by the pilot) would cause it to be away. Therefore, the second requirement is for stability, so that when the aeroplane is disturbed in pitch, it must tend to return to the trimmed state of *zero pitching moment about the centre of gravity*.

It is possible to have unsatisfactory states of trim without stability, or stability without trim at a useful angle of attack, if we design the aeroplane incorrectly.

Consider the aerodynamic loadings which cause pitching moments about the **CG** – they might look rather like fig. 11.2a. When the aeroplane is in equilibrium about the **CG** the resultant moment of the pressure distributions is zero and we say that the moment about the centre of gravity $M_{CG} = 0$, i.e., the machine is *trimmed*.

Now, imagine a small disturbance like an upgust which increases the angle of attack and changes the aerodynamic loadings, as shown in fig. 11.2b. The loading increments have their own overall Centre of Pressure, **CP**, which may or may not coincide with the original **CP** (which coincided with the **CG** – the condition for trim). What concerns us is the change of pitching moment $\pm \Delta M_{CG}$ resulting from the additional loading increments – and, eventually, the rate of change of pitching moment with magnitude of the disturbance. For example, if the CP of the combined increments lies aft of the **CG** (as in fig. 11.2c) the aeroplane is stable, because the nose-down moment about the **CG** caused by an increase in angle of attack tends to push the nose down and to restore equilibrium. A pitching moment increment which tends to reduce the angle of attack is defined as negative, $-\Delta M_{CG}$. The adjacent figures in d and e show the cases of neutral stability and instability which occur when ΔM_{CG} is zero, and positive, respectively.

The centre of pressure of the incremental aerodynamic loadings – the point at which the lift increment, ΔL may be considered to act – is the aerodynamic centre of the aeroplane complete with stabiliser. It is given the special name of *neutral point*, **NP**.

The trouble with centres of pressure is that they tend to wander about and are very hard to pin down with certainty. For example, fig. 11.3 shows the typical **CP** movement of a flat-bottomed aerofoil section at different speeds in undisturbed flight. The position of the **CP** on the aerofoil chord is defined in terms of:

centre of pressure coefficient = (distance to **CP** from leading edge)/(chord) (11–1)

which is a means of locating the resultant crossforce in fig. 3.6b. It is possible for a centre of pressure to move to infinity at one particular angle of attack, and this makes it unusable. Therefore, it is better to avoid dealing with the **CP** quite as much as people

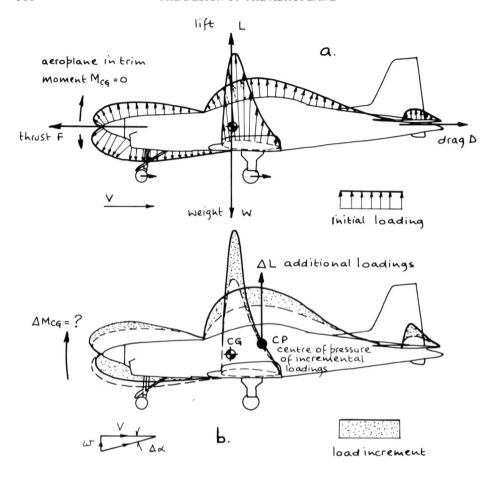

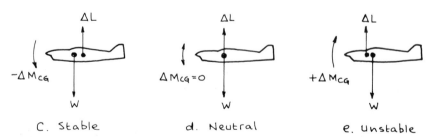

Fig. 11.2   Sketches (not to scale) of the origin of the stable and unstable moments about the **CG** when an aeroplane is disturbed in pitch by an upgust. Suctions only are shown in (a) and (b).

used to do in the early days of aviation. Even so, it is a useful concept especially when it comes to descriptive explanations of what appears to be happening to an aircraft at any moment.

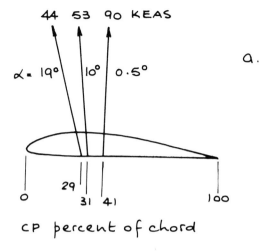

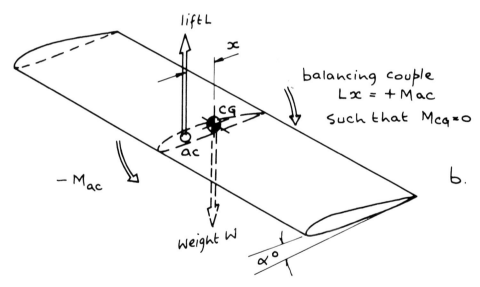

Fig. 11.3a Variation of centre of pressure with airspeed and angle of attack in level flight. b A simply trimmed tailless plank wing which is not statically stable, but which will fly as long as it is undisturbed.

Because of the fickleness of the centre of pressure, later aerofoil sections, like *NACA 23012*, were designed to have near-stationary **CP**s over their working ranges of angles of attack.

A plank-like aerofoil surface, like that shown in fig. 11.3b, can be made to fly in trim (as long as it is undisturbed in pitch) by arranging the aerodynamic centre and the centre of gravity in such a way as to make the nose-up couple of weight and lift just balance the nose-down aerodynamic pitching moment, $-M_{ac}$, so that about the centre of gravity $M_{CG} = 0$. But, to make such a surface stable so that it returns to its trimmed state after a disturbance we have to reflex the trailing edge, or resort to some other trick like those shown in fig. 4.11, each one of which incorporates decalage, or longitudinal dihedral.

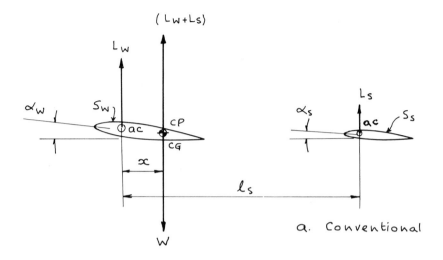

a. Conventional

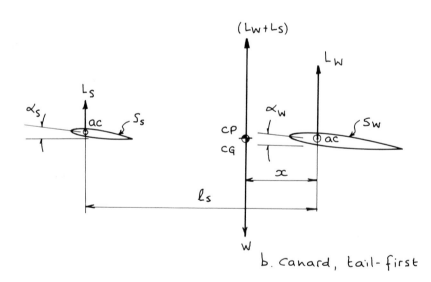

b. Canard, tail-first

The centres of pressure and gravity coincide when each system is in trim, so that the total lift and weight are equal and opposite in each case. The sections are assumed to be uncambered, for simplicity, since pitching moment about an aerodynamic centre, M_{ac}, is then zero.

Fig. 11.4 Basic arrangements of trimmed (initially undisturbed) tandem, uncambered aerofoil surfaces.

Longitudinal dihedral (decalage)

Although decalage is the correct term to use in this context, it is more usefully reserved to describe the differences in incidence between the separate planes of a biplane. Here, we shall use the term *longitudinal dihedral* to define the difference in rigging angle between surfaces, or parts of surfaces, the spacing of which is predominantly longitudinal.

The commonest way of providing such longitudinal dihedral is to introduce separate foreplane and tailplane surfaces as stabilisers of the mainplane. Of these, the tailplane is commonest and most popular, because a relatively small and light surface can be made to provide control and stability over a fairly wide range of centres of gravity, with economy of effort and a fairly modest penalty in weight.

Fig. 11.4 shows two arrangements of tandem planes. The first is a wing-plus-tail, the second a wing-plus-canard foreplane. The centres of gravity are assumed to be located at the centres of pressure in their initially undisturbed (and therefore trimmed) positions. Although the surfaces are distinguished by suffixes, S_w and S_s, etc. it would be just as easy to resort to S_1 and $S_2 \dots$, or S_f and S_r respectively, so as to be able to set up general equations for equilibrium. Finally, we shall see what happens to each arrangement with positive, zero and negative longitudinal dihedral, when each is disturbed by an upgust.

Assuming that the upgust is such that the angle of attack of each surface of a pair is instantaneously increased by 1 deg, we summarise the remaining conditions as follows:

☐ There are no downwash, wake or propwash effects to reduce the change in angle of attack at one surface and not the other. Both suffer the same change.
☐ The lift of each surface increases linearly with angle of attack – the angle being measured from the angle of zero lift.
☐ Each surface has the same lift slope, so that lift is directly proportional to the product:

$$\text{lift unit} = (\text{surface area}) \times (\text{angle of attack}) \qquad (11-2)$$

☐ Lift acts at the 1/4 chord point, which is assumed to be the aerodynamic centre of each surface, **ac**.
☐ We can neglect M_{ac}, the aerodynamic pitching moment about the *ac* of each surface, if we consider symmetric, uncambered aerofoils.

Neutral stability

For our first case let us imagine that in fig. 11.4a:

$$L_w = 5\,L$$
$$\text{and } \alpha_w = \alpha_s = 4 \text{ deg}$$

i.e. there is zero longitudinal dihedral between the planes. The wing lift will be $(5 \times 4) = 20$ units and that of the tail $(1 \times 4) = 4$ units, so that if we take moments about the aerodynamic centre of the wing:

$$4\,l_s = (20 + 4)x$$
$$\text{and the } \mathbf{CP} \text{ lies at } x = l_s/6 \qquad (11-3a)$$

and this is also the position for the **CG** when the aircraft is initially in trim.

Now, let an upgust increase the angle of attack of both planes by 1 deg. What happens to the **CP** of the combination? Taking moments about the wing **ac** as before:

$$5 \; l_s = (25 + 5)x$$
$$\text{i.e. } x = l_s/6 \qquad\qquad (11\text{--}3\text{b})$$

This shows that the **CP** has not moved and the condition corresponds with that shown in fig. 11.2d. In other words, the combination is neutrally stable, because there is no change in pitching moment about the centre of gravity, M_{CG}.

Trimmable and untrimmable arrangements

For the second case imagine that in fig. 11.4a the wing area and tail area remain unchanged, but:

$$\alpha_w = 4 \text{ deg and } \alpha_s = 2 \text{ deg}$$

i.e. the longitudinal dihedral $=+2$ deg. The wing lift is still 20 units, but the tail lift has decreased to $(1 \times 2) = 2$ units. Taking moments as before, the new centre of pressure of the combination lies at:

$$2 \; l_s = (20 + 2)x$$

so that, $\qquad\qquad\qquad x = l_s/11 \qquad\qquad (11\text{--}3\text{c})$

which if further forward than the position calculated in eqs (11–3a and b). Thus, the **CG** would have to be moved forward to coincide with the **CP** for initial trim, from $x = l_s/6$ to $l_s/11$.

Let the same upgust strike the new combination, so that the wing and tail lift increase as before. Taking moments about the wing *ac*:

$$3 \; l_s = (25 + 3)x$$
i.e. $\qquad\qquad\qquad x = (3/28) \; l_s \qquad\qquad \text{eq } (11\text{--}3\text{b})$

which shows that the **CP** has moved aft. As the **CG** is at $l_s/11$, there is now a nose-down (stable) pitching moment exerted by the total lift, tending to restore equilibrium. Therefore, longitudinal dihedral makes the aeroplane stable, restoring trim. It can be shown in exactly the same way that a downgust produces a stable response too.

Now look at fig. 11.4b where the canard stabiliser is in front of the wing. Let:

$$S_w = 6 \; S_s$$
$$\text{and } \alpha_w = 1 \text{ deg while } \alpha_s = 4 \text{ deg}$$

so that the longitudinal dihedral $= +3$ deg.

The **CP** of the canard combination is found by taking moments about the **ac** of the wing. Thus, wing lift is $(6 \times 1) = 6$ units, while that of the canard is $(1 \times 4) = 4$ units, so that:

$$4 \; l_s = (6 + 4)x$$
$$\text{i.e. } \quad x = (2/5) \; l_s \qquad\qquad (11\text{--}3\text{d})$$

forward of the wing.

If the canard combination is disturbed by the same gust as before, the CP moves to:

$$x = (5/17)l_s \qquad\qquad (11\text{--}3\text{e})$$

which is aft of $(2/5) \; l_s$, and so causes a nose-down (stable) pitching moment about the **CG**, which is of course located at $(2/5) \; l_s$ for initial trim.

We can go further with such exercises to show that negative longitudinal dihedral (obtained by setting the rearplane at a larger angle of attack than the foreplane) is destabilising, because the **CP** moves in an unstable direction.

Cautions and Rules of Thumb

So far we have made one or two assumptions which might tend to break down in practice. For example, the *CG* is fixed and, although it was not stated, there is the implication that the aerofoil surfaces are rigid at all times, regardless of loading. But all structures are elastic to a certain extent and they twist and bend in response to changes in loading. We already know that a gust will not produce exactly the same change in angle of attack at the tail as it does at the wing, because of wake effects described in chapter 5. Similarly, the wake of the foreplane can adversely affect the local angle of attack of the wing, reducing longitudinal stability to a certain extent. Thus, aero-elasticity, trailing vortices, and turbulence shed by junctions and excrescences all conspire to alter stability. For these reasons it is imprudent to make other than cautious guesses about many effects which might seem obvious at first sight.

We may state one or two rules of thumb about static longitudinal stability and trim:

☐ *Positive longitudinal dihedral is needed for trim at a positive lift coefficient.*
☐ *Longitudinal dihedral reduces the total lift of combined planes (and flying-wings with reflexed trailing edges). Therefore, the surface(s) must be flown at a larger angle of attack, which increases the induced drag and reduces the lift/drag ratio.*

All of this is not saying that tailless aircraft are wrong. Their advantages depend upon precisely defined operational requirements – even more so than conventional aeroplanes. The tailless aeroplane must not be thought of as an obvious solution to the problem of securing high overall efficiency, because they carry around with them more wetted area than is strictly necessary.

Finally, if we look back to where we made the assumption that lift units generated vary directly with angle of attack, then from eq (11–2) we may say that:

$$\text{wing (or stabiliser) loading} = \text{lift units}/\text{plan area} \qquad (11\text{–}4)$$

which is directly proportional to the angle of attack in each of the examples.

This gives the third rule of thumb:

☐ *An aerofoil surface (or part) lying ahead of the* **CG** *must carry a heavier loading than any part following behind.*

This rule ensures that the leading plane stalls first, pitching the aircraft nose-down, so as to regain speed. This is perhaps the most fundamental of all airworthiness requirements.

Moment equation – importance of stabiliser volume

In practice the centre of gravity does not remain conveniently fixed in flight. Fuel and oil are consumed, passengers wander about in larger aircraft, crew may move, and load arrangements can change (as when stores are dropped or off-loaded). Changes in configuration caused by raising and lowering flaps and gear move the overall centre of pressure. Alterations of power-settings change the velocity of propwashes and introduce pitch, roll and yaw effects. The result is that the pilot must retrim the aeroplane everytime the **CP** and **CG** cease to coincide. This is done by movement of the control surfaces, so as to bring the centre of gravity and the centre of pressure together again, reducing any out of balance moment about the CG to zero. Movement of the control surfaces introduces hinge moments, which are reacted and overcome by hands and feet as stick and rudder forces. These forces in turn must be removed for comfort by movement of the trimming controls.

Previously we made certain simplifying assumptions and then argued that they break down to a greater or lesser degree in practice. Downwash and wake effects cannot be ignored. Drag and thrust should really be taken into account, because they introduce moments about the CG more often than not. But because their effects are often small compared with that of the CP and CG ceasing to coincide, we shall continue to ignore them for the time being.

Consider now the simplest case shown in fig. 11.5a, in which the moments of the wing and tail (or foreplane and mainplane) lifts must be in equilibrium about the centre of gravity, acting as a fulcrum. The moment of the wing acting at a distance x from the CG must be balanced by the tail lift acting at a distance I. Normally, the distance x is so small relative to the tail arm, I_s, that we can go further and say that the moment about the CG:

$$M_{CG} = L_w \, x - L_s \, l = L_w \, x - L_s \, (l_s - x)$$
$$\approx L_w \, x - L_s \, l_s = 0 \text{ for trim} \qquad (11\text{--}5)$$

The equation shows three things:

☐ An equation for tail (stabiliser) lift can be written:

$$\text{tail lift, } L_s = Lw \, (x/l_s) \qquad (11\text{--}6a)$$

so that if the tail is three times as far from the CG as the wing, the tail lift will be one third of the wing lift.
☐ If the CG is forward of the aerodynamic centre of the wing a download is needed at the tail for balance.
☐ Moving the CG forwards, towards the ac of the wing, reduces the tail load required for trim.

The same moment equation can be written in aerodynamic terms, using lift and moment coefficients:

From,   eq (11–5)
$$M_{CG} \approx L_w \, x - L_s \, l_s$$
$$C_{MCG} \, q \, S_w \bar{c}_w \approx C_{Lw} \, q \, S_w \, x - C_{Ls} \, q_s \, S_s \, l_s$$
i.e. $$C_{MCG} \approx C_{Lw} \, (x/\bar{c}_w) - C_{Ls} \, (q_s/q) \, (S_s \, l_s/S_w \, \bar{c}_w)$$
$$= 0 \text{ for trim} \qquad (11\text{--}5a)$$

There is no longer any need to use the suffix w when referring to wing characteristics (like SMC and lift coefficient). For simplicity we shall write C_L for C_{Lw}, and $\bar{c}$ for $\bar{c}_w$ (the standard mean chord of the wing). But do remember that the total lift coefficient of the aircraft is made up of numerous contributions from wing, tail, fuselage, nacelles, flaps, landing gear, and anything else subject to an aerodynamic pressure distribution. This means that the suffixes should still be there in our minds when making analyses. Of the items remaining in eq (11–5a):

$$x/\bar{c}_w = x/\bar{c} = (h - h_o)\bar{c} \qquad (11\text{--}6b)$$

In the tail part of the equation there are two unique terms in addition to C_{Ls}:

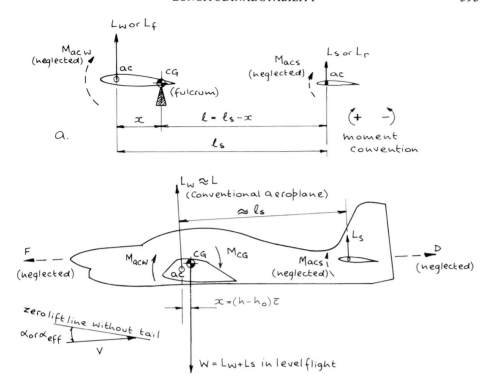

b. The centre of gravity is rather like a fulcrum, about which an aircraft pitches (rolls and yaws).

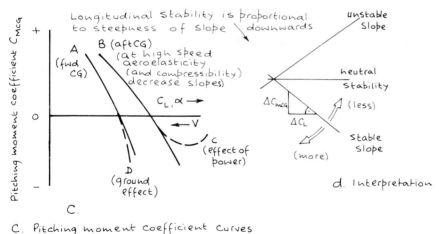

C. Pitching moment coefficient curves in different configurations

Fig. 11.5   Conditions for static longitudinal stability.

(q_s/q) which is the same as $(q_{ws}/q) = \eta_s$ in eq (5–24) and, tail (stabiliser) volume coefficient, $\overline{V_s} = (S_s/S)\,(l_s/\overline{c})$ (11–7)

The first is a measure of the reduction in tail effectiveness when working in or near the wake of the wing and body. The second is an important measure of the geometry of the aeroplane.

We are now able to recast eq (11–5a) in a general form which also incorporates the pitching moment coefficient of the wing about its aerodynamic centre, C_{Mac}, a term which we have so far ignored (and which is usually negative):

$$C_{MCG} = C_L (h - h_o) + C_{Mac} - \eta_s C_{Ls} \overline{V}_s = 0 \text{ for trim} \qquad (11\text{–}8)$$

This equation can be expanded into a rather unwieldly version, eq (11–8a), which is shown in fig. 11.6. Although it is clumsy-looking it enables various contributions to be pointed out, so giving a feel for what static stability is all about.

If we need to consider a tandem-winged aeroplane with two planes that are somewhere near equal in size, we would have to include the pitching moment of each. Instead of writing C_{Mac} for the wing alone we would write for the foreplane and rearplane respectively, $(C_{Macf} + C_{Macr})$. Apart from this refinement, the method would be the same. Similarly, a tail-first (canard) arrangement might be treated as an aeroplane with a small wing at the front, a large tail at the back (with a short moment arm and relatively large rearplane volume coefficient). The aerodynamic moment of the foreplane, C_{Macf}, would be small enough to be neglected, while for C_{Mac} we could write C_{Macr} if we so wished.

The larger the tail volume coefficient the larger the usable **CG** range, and the greater the length of fuselage that might be occupied by disposable load. Transport aeroplanes have larger tail volume coefficients than sporting and agricultural aircraft, so as to achieve greater flexibility in stowage of awkward loads. Sporting and agricultural machines need to be lively. Thinking of control and stability as opposite sides of one coin, the smaller tail volumes of the latter aircraft enable them to be flown with much reduced stick forces. Typical values of stabiliser volume coefficient are given in table 11–1.

Looking again at eq (11–8), even if tail volume and aerodynamic pitching moment coefficient remain constant there are still two other factors which affect the restoring moment: the position of the **CG** relative to the aerodynamic centre $(h - h_o)$; and the lift coefficient of the rearplane or stabiliser, C_{Ls}.

As far as the first is concerned, if we could pick up the centre of gravity and carry it bodily towards the tail, the tail moment arm would decrease and with it the restoring moment. A point would eventually be found, distance $h_n \overline{c}$ from the foreplane or wing leading edge, at which the nose-up moment caused by the surface ahead of the **CG** would be equal and opposite to the nose-down moment provided mainly by the surface behind it. The aeroplane would be neutrally stable, and that particular **CG** location is called the neutral point, **NP**, see fig. 11.1.

We would only know that the neutral point had been found if, when the aeroplane is disturbed in pitch (as measured by a small change in angle of attack, $\Delta\alpha$), the restoring moment about the **NP**:

$$\Delta C_{MCG} / \Delta\alpha = 0 \qquad (11\text{–}9a)$$

Within the working range of angles of attack, lift coefficient is directly proportional to α, so that we may also write more conveniently:

$$\Delta C_{MCG} / \Delta C_L = 0 \qquad (11\text{–}9b)$$

This is written dC_{MCG}/dC_L as the disturbance becomes infinitely small.

TABLE 11–1

Horz Stabiliser volume coefficient

Power, flap	Stabiliser volume coefficient V_s		
	Sport, competition (and agricultural aeroplanes*)	Transport	All-moving stabilator
Propeller-driven, simple flaps	0.3–0.65	0.5–0.8	0.35–0.55
Propeller-driven, high lift flaps	rare	0.85–1.2	0.5–0.65
Jet, simple flaps	0.2–0.55	0.4–0.65	0.2–0.4
Jet, high lift flaps	0.3–0.4	0.5–0.68	about 0.4
Sailplane	0.57–0.6 (0.64 based on total area of a vee tail)	—	0.53–0.59
Manpowered			about 0.2–0.25

Note: Canard designs are not commonplace enough for there to be much evidence, but the tail volume coefficient with an economically-sized foreplane appears to be about 0.8 to 0.85 times V_s with a tailplane.

*Too much stability makes agricultural aeroplanes exhausting to handle and pilots want stick forces to be light.

If the centre of gravity lies ahead of the neutral point, the aeroplane will be statically stable. If it moves aft of the **NP** the aeroplane will be statically unstable.

CG static (and manoeuvre) margins

When an aeroplane is rigid (strictly an unreal condition), stability can be measured in terms of fixed geometrical factors, like configuration and location of the centre of gravity. Aerodynamic properties, like wing and tail lift slopes are theoretically constant and do not change with speed or Mach number, or with loads applied to the skin and structure. Then we are able to assume that the neutral points are fixed, and distances measured between the **CG** and **NP** called **CG** *margins stick-fixed* and *free* (H_n H'_n respectively), are absolute measures of stability. In the real world they are not.

Real aeroplanes bend and twist. Their skins deform, and there is a constant aeroelastic interaction between what the pilot and other disturbances do to the apparent constants. For example, fuel is consumed and the **CG** moves. Aerodynamic pressures suck the skin out here and push it in there, altering profiles. **CG** margins cease to have strict relevance. Instead we measure stability in terms of *static margins, stick-fixed* and *free*, denoted K_n and K'_n.

In a similar way, when an aeroplane is manoeuvring, extra effects caused by rotation in pitch about the centre of gravity can increase the effective static margins, giving fresh

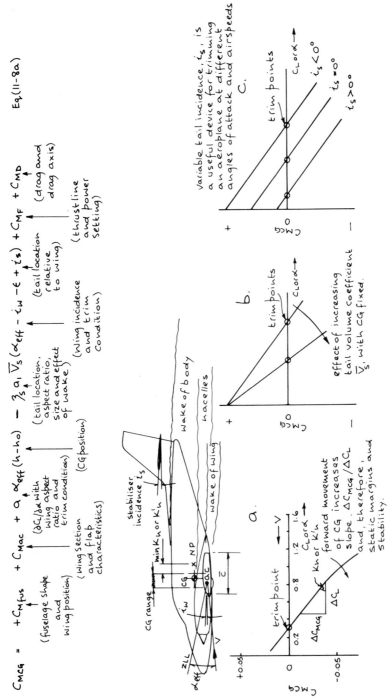

$$C_{MCG} = +C_{Mfus} + C_{Mac} + a\,\alpha_{eff}(h-h_o) - i_s\,a_1\,\bar{V}_s(\alpha_{eff} - i_w - \epsilon + i_s) + C_{MF} + C_{MD} \qquad \text{Eq(11-8a)}$$

Eq(11-8) can be written in the expanded form of Eq.(11-8a), shown above, to give a feel for the different contributions, some of which are shown here, others elsewhere in the chapter. In (a) the static margins stick fixed and free (K_n and K'_n) depend upon the slope of the C_{mcg} curve, and this is steepened by forward movement of the CG. (b) shows how stability is increased by increased tail volume coefficient $\bar{V}_s$ (which depends upon the size of the tail and the magnitude of its moment arm about the aerodynamic centre of the wing — and, hence, about the CG). (c) shows the effect of stabiliser incidence (its rigging angle). Note that the slope of the three curves does not change with incidence of the tail, only the intersection, and therefore the trim point.

Fig. 11.6 Various factors affecting longitudinal stability.

measures of stability, called *manoeuvre margins, stick-fixed* and *free,* H_m and H'_m. We shall discuss these in due course.

If we plot C_{MCG} against C_L for different **CG** locations, as shown in fig. 11.5c and 11.6, the downward (negative) slope of a line indicates the degree of static stability. The steeper the negative slope, the more stable the aeroplane.

Most of the aeroplanes in which we are interested do not suffer significant aeroelastic distortion, so that we shall take a short cut and use terms like static margin when discussing stability. Whereas in theory:

static margin, stick-fixed, $K_n = \psi_1\, H_n$, the stick-fixed **CG** margin

we shall simply assume

$$K_n = H_n = -dC_{MCG}/dC_L \qquad (11\text{--}10a)$$

and although, static margin, stick-free, $K'_n = \chi_1\, H'_n$, the stick-free **CG** margin

we shall assume,

$$K'_n = H'_n = -dC_{MCG}/dC_L \qquad (11\text{--}10b)$$

The difference between the stick-fixed and free cases depends upon the difference in rearplane, or stabiliser lift coefficient with the elevator free to trail. The symbols ψ_1, and χ_1, are factors of proportionality, which we assume to be unity in this book.

For those who wish to find out more about the theory, there are plenty of useful works on the subject, and these include refs. 3.4, 3.5 and 11.1 to 11.4 inclusive, together with relevant items from Appendix A.

Stick-free stability: effect of control deflection

If the pilot holds the stick firmly, so that the elevator cannot move, and if the centre of gravity is then moved steadily aft, the aeroplane will grow less and less stable (as well as going out of trim). Now, if the stick is released so that the elevator is able to take up its own position when the aircraft is disturbed in pitch, we say that it is free to float, or trail. The direction in which it trails depends upon the aerodynamic characteristics of the control surface. If the elevator trails down, against the relative wind, it increases the lift of the stabiliser, and the lift coefficient is increased by an increment $+\Delta C_{Ls}$. If, on the other hand, the surface trails up, with the wind it decreases the stabiliser lift coefficient by $-\Delta C_{Ls}$.

It follows that if we are able to move the **CG** of the aeroplane aft with the elevator free to trail, it will be possible to locate the **CG** further aft if the elevator trails downwards than if it floats upwards. In the former case the down-trailing elevator increases static stability to more than when the stick is fixed. In the latter, static stability is correspondingly reduced.

Another way of looking at this is to see elevator movement, either caused by the trail characteristics, or by the pilot's hand, shifting the centre of pressure of the whole aeroplane. When trimming the pilot is faced with an out of balance moment about the **CG**. The elevator is then moved so as to bring the **CG** and **CP** of the aircraft into line. The elevator is then 'fixed' by adjustment of a trim tab, or by a spring-loaded trim lever, to remove any out of balance control force, so that the stick can be released, if necessary, and the pilot's attention given to other tasks.

Many light aircraft and gliders can only be trimmed in pitch by the pilot exerting a force on the controls. Often trimming is achieved on the ground by bent plate tabs, or lengths of cord doped on one side or the other of the trailing edge of a control. These bias the control so that it trails to the correct angle for trim at, say, the cruising speed and power setting. The pilot is then committed to holding out of balance forces at other speeds and power settings.

Fig. 11.7 shows the origin of hinge moments, and what happens to an elevator when there is a change in local angle of attack, or when it is deflected. The hinge moments are the origin of the control forces. They also cause a freed surface to float to a new angle, at which the hinge moment is zero.

Hinge moments can be stated as follows:

hinge moment = effect of the camber of the main aerofoil
+ effect of aircraft incidence
+ effect of elevator movement
+ effect of tab movement

i.e. $H = H_o + H_\alpha + H_\eta + H_\beta$ (11–11a)

They are expressed in terms of their hinge moment coefficients, which are worked out in exactly the same way as pitching moment coefficients, except that we use elevator area and chord instead of wing area and chord:

i.e. $C_H = H/qS_\eta \bar{c}_\eta$
$= b_o + b_1\alpha_s + b_2\eta + b_3\beta$ (11–11b)

where: b_o = hinge moment coefficient caused by camber of surface ahead of control. This can usually be ignored, since most stabilisers are of symmetric section.

b_1 = $\delta C_H/\delta\alpha_s$, the rate of change of elevator hinge moment coefficient with change in stabiliser angle of attack alone.

α_s = angle of attack of stabiliser, measured from its line of zero lift (ZLL).

b_2 = $\delta C_H/\delta\eta$, the rate of change of elevator hinge moment coefficient with elevator deflection alone.

η = elevator deflection.

b_3 = $\delta C_H/\delta\beta$, rate of change of elevator hinge moment coefficient with tab deflection alone. This can usually be ignored.

β = tab deflection.

q = dynamic pressure, $\frac{1}{2}\rho V^2 = \frac{1}{2}\rho_o V_i^2$.

$\bar{c}_\eta$ = standard mean chord of elevator.

S_η = area of elevator, measured aft of the hinge line.

The sign convention is *that if the hinge moment results from or causes control movement which increases lift, then the moment is positive.* Thus, if b_1 is negative this means that the elevator trails with the relative flow, trailing edge up, which reduces lift. If b_2 is negative, the control will always generate a self-centring force which opposes the pilot's hand. When b_2 is positive the control is said to be *overbalanced*, because when it is deflected it tries to increase the angle of deflection, so that the pilot has to restrain the control to prevent it from moving further. Thus, b_2 is a measure of control heaviness. When overbalance occurs it can give the pilot an initial impression that the aeroplane is unstable – as the author found with the ailerons of a *Helio Courier* that had been misrigged.

If, for simplicity, we ignore the effects of H_0 and H_β in eq (11–11a) then we can express algebraically the lift of the stabiliser with elevator fixed or free to float. When fixed, a positive increase in stabiliser angle of attack, $\Delta\alpha_s$, increases the stabiliser lift

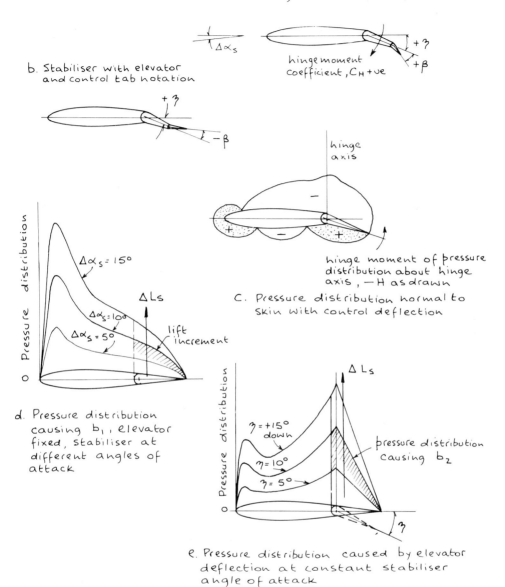

a. Sign convention

b. Stabiliser with elevator and control tab notation

hinge moment coefficient, C_H +ve

hinge axis

hinge moment of pressure distribution about hinge axis, $-H$ as drawn

c. Pressure distribution normal to skin with control deflection

Pressure distribution

$\Delta\alpha_s = 15°$

ΔL_s

$\Delta\alpha_s = 10°$

$\Delta\alpha_s = 5°$

lift increment

d. Pressure distribution causing b_1, elevator fixed, stabiliser at different angles of attack

Pressure distribution

ΔL_s

$\eta = +15°$ down

$\eta = 10°$

$\eta = 5°$

pressure distribution causing b_2

e. Pressure distribution caused by elevator deflection at constant stabiliser angle of attack

Fig. 11.7 Control surface deflection, pressure distributions, hinge moments (and their coefficients).

coefficient by an amount:

$$\Delta C_{Ls} = a_1 \Delta\alpha_s \qquad (11\text{--}12)$$

If the control tries to float and exerts a hinge moment H_α then, if the pilot releases the stick, the surface will float to a new angle at which H_α has decreased to zero. If the angle through which the control trails (the same as floats) is $\Delta\eta$, then:

$$b_1\Delta\alpha_s = -b_2\Delta\eta \qquad \text{from } 11-11b$$

i.e.

$$\Delta\eta = -(b_1/b_2)\,\Delta\alpha_s \qquad (11\text{--}13)$$

angle it floats for $C_H = 0$

Plate 11–2 *Fairchild Republic A–10* has marked wing under-camber, which results in a large negative (nose-down) pitching moment coefficient and – 7 deg tail incidence to trim with the wing producing no lift at Mach number 0.6. (*Fairchild Republic Company, USA*)

Thus, the change in stabiliser lift coefficient, stick-free, becomes:

$$\Delta C_{Ls} = a_1 \Delta \alpha_s + a_2 \Delta \eta$$
$$= a_1 \Delta \alpha_s (1 - a_2 b_1 / a_1 b_2) = \bar{a}_1 \Delta \alpha_s \qquad (11\text{–}14)$$

in which,   equivalent lift slope, $\bar{a}_1 = a_1 (1 - a_2 b_1 / a_1 b_2)$ (11–14a)

If the elevator floats upwards, so that $\Delta \eta$ is negative, then stabiliser lift is reduced. For this to occur b_1 must be negative. The lift slopes a_1 and a_2 are always positive. The term b_2 must be negative if the control is to feel right to the pilot – and, of course, $\Delta \alpha_s$ is positive, because we said so earlier. Inserting these conditions in eq (11–14a), we see that the effective lift slope of the stabiliser, $\bar{a}_1$, is less than a_1 with the stick fixed, when the elevator is free to move upwards. When b_1 is positive the elevator trails downwards and stabiliser lift is increased, through the stick-free $\bar{a}_1$ then being greater than a_1 stick-fixed.

Thus, the degree of static stability stick-free is increased when b_1 is positive, and decreased when it is negative. Elevator-fixed stability is considered to be the measure of basic static stability, just as with any free-flight model aeroplane. Freeing the elevator adds to or detracts from the basic stick-fixed stability.

Effects of drag, thrust and propwash

So far we have assumed that thrust and drag produce no pitching effects, and the moment equation has been expressed in terms of wing and stabiliser lift alone. In reality there are five forces affecting equilibrium: wing and stabiliser lift, thrust, drag and weight. We saw in fig. 6.1b only a simplified drawing of the balance of forces in straight and level flight, in which lift and weight were equal and opposite, and thrust and drag were equal and opposite. In reality they are not in line. Lift and weight are offset, thrust and drag too, more often than not.

Fig. 11.8 shows the forces acting in straight and level flight, in which the lift is again the sum of the wing lift plus that produced by the stabiliser. Stabiliser lift may be upwards, acting in the same direction as wing lift, or it may be downwards, depending upon the actual location of the centre of gravity, and the wing C_{MO}. A conventional aeroplane with the CG forward requires a download at the tail to hold up the nose. This acts against the wing lift, so that the wing has to be flown at a larger angle of attack than when the CG is aft. Consequently, such an aircraft stalls at a higher speed with the CG forward than it does with the CG aft.

Figs 11.8a and b show the arrangement of lift, weight, thrust and drag for most conventional aeroplanes. The drag resultant acts through the centre of drag of the aeroplane, and this can be found by taking moments of all the drag elements about some convenient datum, like the bottom of the lowest wheel in level flight. With the thrust line lower than the drag line the aeroplane pitches nose-down if the engine fails, so as to establish a glide. With the main lift resultant acting behind the weight there is no tendency to pitch nose-up into a stall.

The lower figure shows the arrangement when the thrust line is high. The aeroplane could just as easily have been a flying-boat with a pylon-mounted engine. This is an adverse arrangement, because opening the throttle pushes the nose down, while engine failure causes the nose to rise. Furthermore, the lift acting ahead of the weight causes a nose-up moment which is pro-stall. An arrangement of this kind results in a considerable download on the tail in straight and level flight, and this increases trim drag, reducing the lift/drag ratio. The situation can be improved by tilting the thrust line so as to produce a component which reduces the download. A forward-set propeller, when tilted upwards, forces a downwards component of propwash on to the tail. Engine failure then makes the propwash disappear, the tail rises and the aeroplane pitches nose-down so as to glide.

Most modern aeroplanes achieve relatively low tail loads by using wing sections with low moment coefficients. Aft-loaded sections, like the $GA(W)$-1, are at a disadvantage in this respect, because they have large moment coefficients and tail surfaces must be bigger. Similarly, high lift flaps with strong pitching moments have the same effect on tail surface required.

High performance sailplanes, which need the highest possible lift/drag ratios cannot afford trim drag. Their tail loads are reduced to zero, or as near as possible, by flying with the CG so far aft that the nose-up moment of lift and drag just balances $-M_{ac}$ (which is the condition seen in fig. 11.2).

The effect of thrust and drag upon the moment coefficients in eq (11–5a) is to add two increments:

$$\Delta C_{MF} \text{ due to thrust} = \pm (C_{FZF}/\bar{c}_f) \qquad (11\text{–}15)$$
$$\Delta C_{MD} \text{ due to drag} = \pm (C_{DZD}/\bar{c}_f) \qquad (11\text{–}16)$$

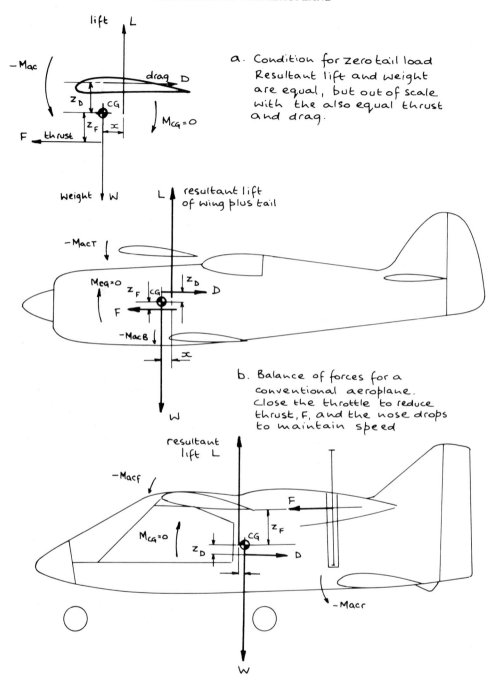

a. Condition for zero tail load. Resultant lift and weight are equal, but out of scale with the also equal thrust and drag.

b. Balance of forces for a conventional aeroplane. Close the throttle to reduce thrust, F, and the nose drops to maintain speed

c. Arrangement of forces with a high thrust line

Fig. 11.8 Balance of forces in trimmed straight and level flight.

in which $\bar{c}_f = \bar{c}$, when the wing is in front, and C_F is the thrust coefficient, which is numerically equal to the drag coefficient, C_D, in straight and level flight. The positive and negative signs are assigned according to the effect of each increment pitching the aeroplane nose-up or nose-down.

The condition for zero tail load in steady straight and level flight is shown in fig. 11.8c, in which the centre of gravity of the aeroplane is displaced a distance Δx from the aerodynamic centre of the aircraft, where $\Delta x = \Delta(h - h_0)\bar{c}$. It may be shown, by taking moments about the centre of gravity, that if we also introduce $(C_{Mac} + C_{Mfus})$ – which is C_{MO} and can be large and negative – then the displacement becomes:

$$\Delta(h - h_0) = \Delta x/\bar{c} = (C_{Mac} + C_{Mfus}) + (z_D + z_F)/\bar{c}(C_L/C_D) \qquad (11\text{--}17)$$

The ratio C_L/C_D is the cruise lift/drag ratio (including $(L/D)_R$, or $(L/D)_{max}$, depending upon whichever is preferred, calculated at the end of chapter 5). It follows from this equation that when $(C_{Mac} + C_{Mfus})$ is small, then the distance Δx is equal to the vertical distance between the thrust line and the drag line of action, divided by the lift/drag ratio of the aeroplane. The value of L/D is somewhere around 10 to 15 for most light aeroplanes, making the required offset around 7 to 10 per cent of the distance $(z_D + z_F)$.

A disturbance in pitch increases drag very slightly, but the effect is usually so transient that we can ignore it. It is not the same with a propeller, because three effects are introduced, as shown in fig. 11.9.

Propeller contributions

☐ Asymmetric blade effect (*see* chapter 7 fig. 11.9a, which causes yaw.)
☐ When the plane of rotation of the propeller is no longer normal to the airflow the thrust line is inclined at an angle of attack to the flow fig. 11.9b. If an aeroplane is pitched nose-up, for example, then thrust can be resolved into components normal and tangential to the flight path, the normal component acting in the lifting-plane. If the propeller is ahead of the **CG** the lifting component is destabilising; and stabilising when the propeller is behind it. *A tractor propeller is destabilising in both pitch and yaw.*
☐ Propwash (*see* chapter 7 and fig. 11.9c).
   A gust has a much smaller effect upon a tail bathed in propwash than upon one that is not, reducing the relative value of the restoring moment of the former. A pusher aeroplane stabilised by a foreplane is not affected in this way.

If follows that stabilisers immersed in propwashes, like those working in wakes, are less efficient than stabilisers working in relatively free air. Measurements of stabiliser efficiency between two variants of substantially the same transport aeroplane showed that a stabiliser on the rear fuselage, more or less in line with the wings and engines, had an efficiency around 80 per cent (eq (5–24)). But when the tailplane was raised to near the top of the fin its efficiency increased to 94 per cent. This was equivalent to a rearward movement of the neutral point of 7 to 8 per cent SMC.

Expressions for static, stick-fixed stability

To measure static stability with the elevator held (stick-fixed) by the pilot, we must modify eq (11–8) by considering what happens when a disturbance in pitch occurs. The disturbance is measured by $\Delta\alpha \rightarrow d\alpha$, expressed in terms of $\Delta C_L \rightarrow dC_L$, so that it is very small. Other changes occur too:

C_{MCG} grows by an increment $\Delta C_{MCG} \rightarrow dC_{MCG}$;
C_L grows by an increment $\Delta C_L \rightarrow dC_L$;
C_{Ls} grows correspondingly by $\Delta C_{Ls} \rightarrow dC_{Ls}$;

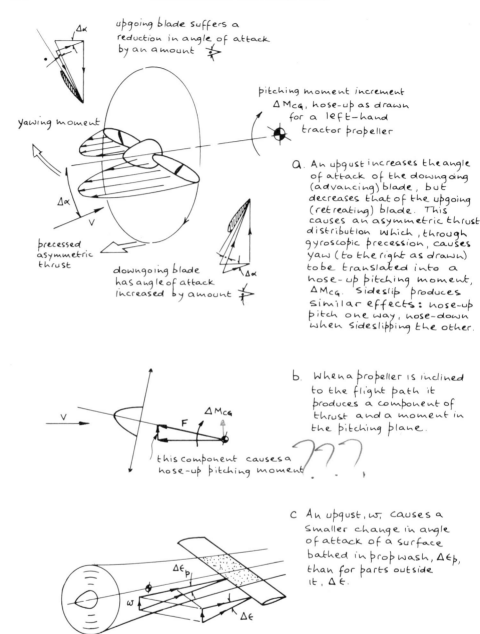

upgoing blade suffers a
reduction in angle of attack
by an amount $\frac{\dot{\gamma}}{?}$

pitching moment increment
ΔM_{CG}, nose-up as drawn
for a left-hand
tractor propeller

yawing moment

$\Delta \alpha$

V

precessed
asymmetric
thrust

downgoing blade
has angle of attack
increased by amount $\frac{\dot{\gamma}}{?}$

$\Delta \alpha$

a. An upgust increases the angle
of attack of the downgoing
(advancing) blade, but
decreases that of the upgoing
(retreating) blade. This
causes an asymmetric thrust
distribution which, through
gyroscopic precession, causes
yaw (to the right as drawn)
to be translated into a
nose-up pitching moment,
ΔM_{CG}. Sideslip produces
similar effects: nose-up
pitch one way, nose-down
when sideslipping the other.

V

ΔM_{CG}

F

this component causes a
nose-up pitching moment

b. When a propeller is inclined
to the flight path it
produces a component of
thrust and a moment in
the pitching plane.

???

c An upgust, w, causes a
smaller change in angle
of attack of a surface
bathed in prop wash, $\Delta \epsilon_p$,
than for parts outside
it, $\Delta \epsilon$.

$\Delta \epsilon_p$

ω

$\Delta \epsilon$

Fig. 11.9   Power is destabilising, most of all when a propeller is forward of the **CG**.

C_{Mac} cannot grow by any increments because, by definition, the pitching moment about the aerodynamic centre of a surface remains constant with changing angle of attack, i.e. $\Delta C_{Mac} = 0$.

Therefore, inserting these changes in eq (11–8) and dividing through by dC_L, as in eq (11–10a):

stab efficiency (reduced in prop wash)

static margin, $K_n = -dC_{MCG}/dC_L$

$$= -(h - h_o) + \eta_s\overline{V}_s(dC_{Ls}/dC_L) \text{ with tail} \qquad (11-18)$$

$$= -(h - h_o) + \eta_r\overline{V}_r(dC_{Lr}/dC_{Lf}) \text{ with tandem wings} \qquad (11-18a)$$

$$= -(h - h_o) - \eta_f\overline{V}_f(dC_{Lf}/dC_L) \text{ with canard stabiliser} \qquad (11-18b)$$

This is the physical distance between the neutral point, h_n, and the location of the centre of gravity, h, expressed as a fraction of the foreplane, or wing standard mean chord. When the **CG** is so far aft that it lies at the neutral point, $h = h_n$, and the static margin = 0, making static stability neutral.

To find the neutral point, we may write: $-(h_n - h_o) = -(h - h_o)$, and as eq (11–18) also equals 0, we can transpose to give:

neutral point, $h_n = h_o + \eta_s\overline{V}_s(dC_{Ls}/dC_L)$ with tail $\qquad (11-19)$

$$= h_o + \eta_s\overline{V}_r(dC_{Lr}/dC_{Lf}) \text{ with tandem wings} \qquad (11-19a)$$

$$= h_o - \eta_f\overline{V}_f(dC_{Lf}/dC_L) \text{ with canard stabiliser} \qquad (11-19b)$$

Thus, both neutral point and static margin can be expressed in terms of the physical geometry of the aircraft. The term h_o is the distance of the aerodynamic centre aft of the leading edge of the foreplane, or wing. The wake efficiency, η_s, affects the volume coefficient $\overline{V}_r$ or $\overline{V}_s$ of the rearplane, or tail. Although the characteristics of the wake change as an aeroplane pitches, the angle $d\alpha$ is so small that we assume η_s remains constant. When a foreplane surface is small compared with a rearplane (dC_{Lf}/dC_L) is about 1, and η_f, the efficiency of the foreplane, is around 100 per cent. The negative sign in eq (11–19b) is necessary because here the stabiliser is ahead of the wing.

All that we need now is to see what goes on inside the bracket, with the tail, or rearplane contribution, (dC_{Ls}/dC_L) or (dC_{Lr}/dC_{Lf}). To reduce some of the hieroglyphics and squiggles let us look only at the case of a tail. It is easy enough to replace the tail terms by dC_{Lr} and dC_{Lf} if we need them.

Tail contribution, dC_{Ls}/dC_L

The lift coefficient of the stabiliser consists of three parts:

☐ The lift increment caused by change in local angle of attack:

$$\Delta C_{Ls} = a_1\Delta\alpha_s \qquad\qquad \text{from eq (11–12)}$$

in which a_1 is the lift slope of the tail. This can be calculated in exactly the same way as shown in eqs (4–18) to (4–20), or from fig. 4.6c.
☐ The lift increment due to elevator deflection alone, η:

$$\Delta C_{Ls} = a_2\Delta\eta \qquad (11-20)$$

which appeared in eq (11–14), where a_2 is the lift slope of the tail with elevator deflection, $dC_{Ls}/d\eta$

☐ The lift increment due to trim tab deflection alone, β:

$$\Delta C_{Ls} = a_3\Delta\beta \qquad (11-21)$$

where $\qquad\qquad a_3 = dC_{Ls}/d\beta$

We shall ignore the last term, which tends to be small compared with the remainder, so that the total tail lift increment corresponds with that given by eq (11–14), when we saw what happened if the pilot released the stick.

The local angle of attack of the tail depends upon the angle of incidence at which it is rigged (the tail setting) and the angle of downwash from the wing. These must both be added to the angle of attack of the wing, such that:

$$\text{stabiliser angle of attack, } \alpha_s = \alpha_{eff} - \epsilon + \alpha_{si} \tag{11–22}$$

as shown in fig. 11.10. This equation includes eq (4–5). The tail setting angle is constant and cannot change with tail angle of attack, when the tailplane is bolted to the fuselage. Therefore, the only parts of eq (11–22) which change generate increments $\Delta\alpha_s$, $\Delta\alpha$ and $\Delta\epsilon$. If these increments are small enough we can write:

$$\alpha_s = \alpha_{eff}(1 - d\epsilon/d\alpha_{eff}) + \alpha_{si}$$

and as $d\alpha_s \approx d\alpha_{eff}$

$$d\alpha_s/d\alpha = (d\alpha_{eff}/d\alpha)(1 - d\epsilon/d\alpha) + d\alpha_{si}/d\alpha$$

in which $d\alpha_s/d\alpha_{eff} \approx 1$ and $d\alpha_{si}/d\alpha = 0$, so that

$$d\alpha_s/d\alpha = (1 - d\epsilon/d\alpha) \text{ when the change is small} \tag{11–23}$$

The term $d\epsilon/d\alpha$ appeared in eqs (5–25) and (5–26). Knowing from chapter 4 that the slope of the lift curve $a = dC_L/d\alpha$, we may substitute dC_L in the above equation so as to make it consistent with the expression for K_n, such that $dC_L = ad\alpha$. Similarly, $dC_{Ls} = a_1 d\alpha_s$, so that:

$$dC_{Ls}/dC_L = (a_1/a)(d\alpha_s/d\alpha)$$
$$= (a_1/a)(1 - d\epsilon/d\alpha) \tag{11–24}$$

a w/B

and with a foreplane, $dC_{Lf}/dC_{Lf} = (a_r/a_f)(1 - d\epsilon/d\alpha_f)$ (11–24a)

Thus, inserting these equations into eqs (11–18) and (11–19), we have

$$\text{static margin, stick-fixed, } K_n = (h_o - h) + \eta_s \overline{V}_s(a_1/a)(1 - d\epsilon/d\alpha) \tag{11–25}$$
$$\text{neutral point, stick-fixed, } h_n = h_o + \eta_s \overline{V}_s(a_1/a)(1 - d\epsilon/d\alpha) \tag{11–26}$$

The equations can be adapted for a tail-first, or a tandem-winged aeroplane, except that we then use $\overline{V}_r$, a_f, a_r and $d\alpha_f$ in place of $\overline{V}_s$, a_1, a and $d\alpha$. This means that we can apply the values given in table 11–1 to both. The difference between the conventional aeroplane and one with a wing at the back, is that the former has a small surface on a long arm behind the centre of gravity; while the latter has a large surface on a much shorter arm.

Expressions for static, stick-free stability

When the elevator is free to trail the lift coefficient of the tail is modified (and generally reduced) by the trail characteristics that we saw in eq (11–14a). This enables us to write:

$$\text{lift slope of tail with elevator trail, } \overline{a}_1 = a_1(1 - a_2b_1/a_1b_2) \text{ eq (11–14a)}$$

Hence:

$$\text{static margin, stick-free, } K'_n = (h_o - h) + \eta_s \overline{V}_s(\overline{a}_1/a)(1 - d\epsilon/d\alpha) \tag{11–27}$$
$$\text{neutral point, stick-free, } h'_n = h_o + \eta_s \overline{V}_s(\overline{a}_1/a)(1 - d\epsilon/d\alpha) \tag{11–28}$$

We now have some expressions with which to calculate stabiliser size. Before seeing how this is done we must look at longitudinal manoeuvrability.

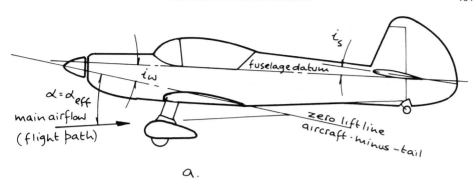

a.

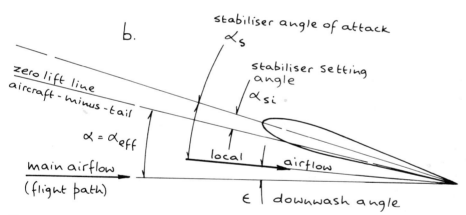

b.

Fig. 11.10   Factors affecting stabiliser angle of attack, α_s.

Longitudinal manoeuvrability

At first sight this title is confusing, and it will seem even more so when we read that it is all about longitudinal manoeuvrability stick-fixed and stick-free.

Don't worry, instead look at it this way. An aeroplane has a certain amount of static stability at any moment in flight, depending upon its geometry and upon the position of the centre of gravity (and upon whether the pilot is holding the stick firmly, or is flying 'hands off'). If a manoeuvre is then carried out, like pulling out of a dive, there is an additional change in angle of attack at the tail, caused by rotation of the aeroplane in space. That additional increment increases the contribution of lift from the tail, increasing the static stability. The result is that the static margins appear to grow larger, because the manoeuvre points move further aft. The new points are called the *manoeuvre points, stick-fixed* and *stick-free*, while the new static margins are called the *manoeuvre margins, stick-fixed* and *stick-free*.

Their usefulness lies in the clues they give to the 'feel' of an aircraft when the pilot moves the stick. This shows itself as the stick forces felt when manoeuvring. The two elements which arise are:

☐ Stick *movement* per applied g, measured by the stick-fixed manoeuvrability.
☐ Stick *force* per applied g, measured by the stick-free manoeuvrability.

The first is rarely measured in practice, but it is of some importance when understanding the theory. The second is more readily measured and is more real in a sense, because a pilot can feel the aircraft through his hands, and that feel is more often than not the stick force when the flight path and attitude are changed, without retrimming.

Imagine that an aeroplane is trimmed and that the pilot then pulls out of a dive, as shown in fig. 11.11, by pulling back on the stick and moving the elevator upwards, by an amount $\Delta\eta$. If speed remains constant, the result is a steady applied acceleration:

applied (centripetal) acceleration, $n_a g = (n - 1)$ g units, from fig. 6.11

$$= V^2/R \qquad \text{eq (6–23)}$$
$$= qV \qquad (11–29)$$

where q is the angular velocity. This is the result of elevator deflection rotating the aeroplane nose up, increasing the wing angle of attack by an amount $\Delta\alpha$, and the lift coefficient by ΔC_L. The relationships are, therefore:

$$\text{wing } C_L + \Delta C_L = (1 + n_a)C_L$$

i.e.
$$\Delta C_L = n_a C_L = a\Delta\alpha \qquad (11–30)$$

During the manoeuvre we assume that the aeroplane is more or less level, so that it is in equilibrium as shown in fig. 11.11a but, because of its curvilinear motion, it is pitching steadily nose up at the same rate q as it is flying around the instantaneous centre, O. The pitching motion in fig. 11.11b causes the tail to move downwards with velocity w where, from fig. 11.5c:

$$w = l_s q \qquad (11–31)$$

When dealing with a canard, or tandem-wing, the foreplane and rearplane sustain corresponding components of velocity, the foreplane in an upwards direction, where $-w_f = l_f q$: while the rearplane value is $w_r = l_r q$. These cause changes in angle of attack at each plane. In the case of a tail, the change in angle of attack is the origin of the *tail damping contribution*, $\Delta\alpha_{sw}$ (really, $a_1 \Delta\alpha_{sw}$), where:

$$\Delta\alpha_{sw} = w/V = l_s q/V \qquad (11–32)$$

and, as $q = n_a g/V$, on transposing eq (11–29):

$$\Delta\alpha_{sw} = (n_a g)(l_s/V^2) \qquad (11–33)$$

Knowing that $V^2 = 2W/C_L\rho S$, from eqs (2–3a) and (2–9):
tail damping contribution, $\Delta\alpha_{sw} = (C_L n_a)(g\rho S\ l_s/2W)$
$$= \Delta C_L/2\mu_1$$
$$= (a/2\mu_1)\Delta\alpha \qquad (11–34)$$

This is a far-reaching relationship, because μ_1 is called the *longitudinal relative aircraft density* which, in effect, expresses the 'density' of the aeroplane relative to the density of the surrounding air, i.e.:

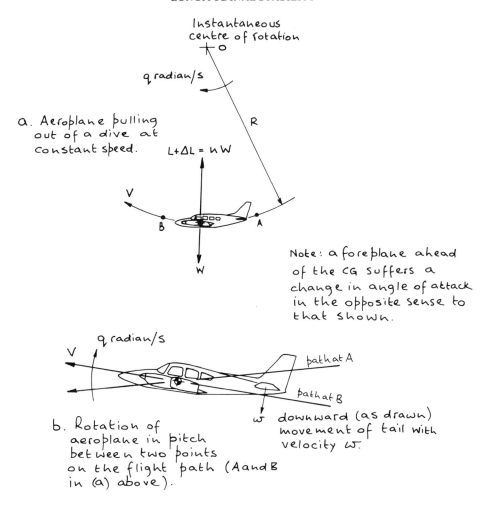

Instantaneous centre of rotation

q radian/s

R

a. Aeroplane pulling out of a dive at constant speed.

$L + \Delta L = nW$

V

B

A

W

Note: a foreplane ahead of the CG suffers a change in angle of attack in the opposite sense to that shown.

q radian/s

V

path at A

path at B

w downward (as drawn) movement of tail with velocity w.

b. Rotation of aeroplane in pitch between two points on the flight path (A and B in (a) above).

$\Delta \alpha_s$

Wind component caused by motion of tail

w

w relative wind

V_{TAS} at low altitude

V_{TAS} at high altitude

c. Change in angle of attack at tail caused by rotation rate in pitch, q, at low and high altitude

Fig. 11.11 Forces and motions while manoeuvring (in this case, when pulling out of a dive).

non dimensional

$$\text{longitudinal relative aircraft density, } \mu_1 = (W/g\rho(l_sS)) \qquad (11\text{--}35)$$

This last equation is composed of a mass term, W/g, divided by a 'volume' term which is the product of the wing area and tail moment arm about the **CG**, Sl_s, and by ambient air density, ρ. Relative aircraft density is non-dimensional and, as air density falls with increasing altitude, its value increases as $1/\rho$.

Plate 11-3 T-tails on General Aviation aircraft can be costly gimmicks. The author estimates that stabiliser volume of the *PA-28R-201 Cherokee Arrow III* (Top) is about five per cent more than that of the *PA-28RT-201 Cherokee Arrow IV* (Middle) making the T-tailed stabiliser lighter. But the tail cone aft of the wing rear spar and the fin are heavier, making the total weight of fuselage cone, fin, rudder, stabiliser and control runs about $1/3$ heavier on the IV than for the III. (Bottom) The *PA-44-180 Seminole* twin-engined derivative, with many common parts, but sweeter control harmonisation. (*Piper Aircraft Corporation*)

Plate 11.3 (Bottom).

It follows that for a given control deflection and equivalent airspeed, the change in angle of attack at the tail is reduced at high altitude, because true airspeed is faster. Therefore, tail damping is reduced and response of the aeroplane to control is more brisk than when flying at low altitudes. It is easier to over-control an aeroplane at high altitude, and when flying in a hot climate, than when flying lower down, and when the weather is cold.

Now consider what happens to stability, as expressed in terms of our static margins, when an aeroplane is disturbed in pitch while pulling out of a dive. The angle of attack of the tail is increased by two increments instead of one. The first is $\Delta\alpha_s$ due to a disturbance, $\Delta\alpha$, which is exactly the same as before. The second is the tail damping contribution, $\Delta\alpha_{sw}$, such that:

$$\text{total change in tail angle of attack} = \Delta\alpha_s + \Delta\alpha_{sw} \qquad (11\text{--}36)$$
$$\text{total change in tail lift coefficient} = a_1\Delta\alpha_s + a_1\Delta\alpha_{sw} \qquad (11\text{--}37)$$
$$\text{total change in } -\mathrm{d}C_{MCG}/\mathrm{d}C_L = \eta_s\overline{V}_s(\mathrm{d}C_{Ls}/\mathrm{d}C_L + \mathrm{d}C_{Lsw}/\mathrm{d}C_L) \qquad (11\text{--}38)$$

Expressions for manoeuvrability, stick-fixed

If we now take eq (11–38) and compare it with eq (11–18), we see that it has gained one additional term, which we shall call ΔK_n:

$$\text{increase in static margin, } \Delta K_n = \eta_s\overline{V}_s(\mathrm{d}C_{Lsw}/\mathrm{d}C_L)$$
$$\text{in which,} \qquad \mathrm{d}C_{Lsw} = a_1\mathrm{d}\alpha_{sw}$$
$$= a_1(a/2\mu_1)\mathrm{d}\alpha \qquad \text{from eq (11--34)}$$

as $\Delta\alpha \rightarrow \mathrm{d}\alpha$. Now write $\mathrm{d}C_L = a\,\mathrm{d}\alpha$ and the $\mathrm{d}\alpha$ terms cancel top and bottom, leaving:

$$\Delta K_n = \eta_s\overline{V}_s(a_1/a)(a/2\mu_1)$$
$$= \eta_s\overline{V}_s a_1/2\mu_1 \qquad (11\text{--}39)$$

This increment can be added to both the static margin and neutral point, stick-fixed, to give:

$$\text{manoeuvre margin, stick-fixed, } H_m = K_n + \eta_s \overline{V}_s a_1 / 2\mu_1 \qquad (11\text{--}40)$$

while,
$$\text{manoeuvre point, stick-fixed, } h_m = h_n + \eta_s \overline{V}_s a_1 / 2\mu_1$$
$$= \textbf{CG} \text{ position for zero stick-}$$
$$\text{movement per applied } g \qquad (11\text{--}41)$$

The magnitude of the increase in static stability when the aircraft is manoeuvring is about 0.01 of the standard mean chord of the wing for a lively aerobatic aeroplane, to 0.1 SMC for a large transport aircraft flying at low altitude. Generally, we shall assume that:

$$\Delta K_n = \eta_s \overline{V}_s a_1 / 2\mu_1 \approx 0.03 \, \overline{c} \qquad (11\text{--}39a)$$

for most light aircraft dealt with here.

Expressions for manoeuvrability, stick-free

When the elevator is free to trail the lift slope of the stabiliser, a_1, becomes $\overline{a}_1$, as we saw in eq (11–14a). Manoeuvrability affects precisely the same change in tail angle of attack as we saw in the stick-fixed case above, so that we may add to the static margin, stick-free, K'_n, an increment with the same basic form as eq (11–39a):

$$\Delta K'_n = \eta_s \overline{V}_s a_1 / 2\mu_1$$
$$= \eta_s \overline{V}_s a_1 \, (1 - a_2 b_1 / a_1 b_2) / 2\mu_1 \qquad (11\text{--}42)$$

Again, this increment can be added to the neutral point stick-free as well so that taking both together:

$$\text{manoeuvre margin, stick-free, } H'_m = K'_n + \eta_s \overline{V}_s \overline{a}_1 / 2\mu_1 \qquad (11\text{--}43)$$
$$\text{manoeuvre point, stick-free, } h'_m = h'_n + \eta_s \overline{V}_s \overline{a}_1 / 2\mu_1 \qquad (11\text{--}44)$$

The manoeuvre margin, stick-free, is larger than the static margin, stick-free. The relative positions of the neutral and manoeuvre points, stick-fixed and stick-free, play an important part in influencing the dynamic stability of the aeroplane.

Stick force per applied g

When an aeroplane is rigid, stick force per applied g depends upon the stick-free manoeuvre margin, and is independent of speed, unlike ailerons, which suffer from the (speed)^2 law. Stick force per g is critically dependent upon **CG** position, growing less as the centre of gravity moves aft, until it becomes zero at the stick-free manoeuvre point.

Stick force per g as such is not spelt out by BCARs, for example. Instead we find that ref. 11.6 specifies that the control force needed to apply a normal acceleration, which would impose Proof Load on the structure, shall not be less than:

☐ For a wheel, $(W/10)$N (where $W \ldots$ kg $\ldots$ is max weight), or 90N (20 lbf), whichever is greater, but need not exceed 225N (50 lbf).

☐ For a stick, $(W/14)$N (where $W \ldots$ kg $\ldots$ is max weight), or 70N (15 lbf), whichever is greater, but need not exceed 160N (35 lbf).

☐ There shall be no decrease in stick force with increasing applied g.

However, a general rule for piston engined fighters around 1945, which might very well be applied to aerobatic, training and agricultural aeroplanes, was that designers should aim for 3 lbf to 8 lbf/g. Under no circumstances should the value be allowed to drop below 3 lbf/g. It was also suggested that 100 lbf to reach breaking g of 4 (i.e. 1 + 3 applied) could be used for larger aircraft, giving stick force/g around 35 lbf. These figures will be found in ref. 12.1, when we come to deal with control surface design. Alternative values, taken from ref. 11.1, are given in table 11–2.

We shall not prove the equation, but it may be shown that if the stick force is P, the applied acceleration is n_a, the elevator gear ratio is m_e, the elevator area and chord are S_η and c_η respectively, and the wing loading is W/S, then, because b_2 is always negative and a positive stick force is a 'pull':

$$\text{stick force}/g, \quad P/n_a = -m_e S_\eta \ c_\eta \ (b_2/a_2 \bar{V}_s)(W/S) \ H'_m \qquad (11\text{–}45)$$

H'_m is given by eq (11–43).

Bobweight effect

If there is static underbalance or overbalance, or a bobweight in the elevator circuit, then the hinge moment can be represented by a factor K which is positive when tending to pull the elevator downwards (heavying the control). The stick force and stick force per g are then changed by:

$$\Delta P = -K \, m_e n_a$$

i.e.
$$\Delta P/n_a = -K \, m_e \qquad (11\text{–}46)$$

and it follows that the feel of an aeroplane can be altered by the addition of a bobweight without changing control surface and circuit geometry. In these last two equations the mechanical term, m_e, is defined as:

elevator gear ratio, $m_e = ($ elevator deflection in degrees/57.3$) \times$ movement of
$$\text{stick at handgrip in ft} \qquad (11\text{–}47)$$

TABLE 11–2

Stick force per applied g
(Ref. 11.1)

Class of aeroplane	SF/g, lbf
Docile, non-aerobatic	10–15
Trainer	5–12
Aerobatic ('hot ship')	2–7

Relationships between the static and manoeuvre margins

It is useful at this point to compare the various stability equations, to see how we can build up from the basic static margin, stick-fixed:

$$K_n = (h_o - h) + \eta_s \bar{V}_s(a_1/a)(1 - d\epsilon/d\alpha)$$
$$= \text{static margin, stick-fixed} \qquad \text{eq (11–25)}$$
$$K'_n = (h_o - h) + \eta_s \bar{V}_s(\bar{a}_1/a)(1 - d\epsilon/d\alpha)$$
$$= \text{static margin, stick-free} \qquad \text{eq (11–27)}$$
$$H_m = (h_o - h) + \eta_s \bar{V}_s(a_1/a)(1 - d\epsilon/d\alpha) + a_1/2\mu_1)$$
$$= K_n + \eta_s \bar{V}_s a_1/2\mu_1$$
$$= \text{manoeuvre margin, stick-fixed} \qquad \text{from eq (11–40)}$$

$$H'_m = (h_o - h) + \eta_s \overline{V}_s((a_1/a)(1 - d\epsilon/d\alpha) + \overline{a}_1/2\mu_1)$$
$$= K'_n + \eta_s \overline{V}_s \overline{a}_1/2\mu_1$$
$$= \text{manoeuvre margin, stick-free} \quad = h_m - h \qquad \text{eq (11–43)}$$

The $\overline{a}_1 = a_1(a_2 b_1/a_1 b_2)$ term is the effect of the pilot releasing the stick, so as to fly hands-off, letting the elevator float freely. For a_2/a_1 see eq (11–56) and fig. 11.15c.

Determination of stabiliser size

We are now in a position to use the above equations for calculating stabiliser volume. Too much tail is uneconomically heavy, and an excess of stability makes an aeroplane sluggish in response to control and tiring to fly. Not enough tail limits **CG** range, makes an aeroplane hard to trim, tiring to fly, and difficult when it comes to loading. One should always keep in mind the particular problems of an operator on, say, a hot and wet tropical airstrip, with a flat calculator battery, no proper load sheet, and an inaccurate set of bathroom scales, trying to keep the **CG** within the aft limit.

Table 11–3 and fig. 11.12 summarise the main points. Table 11–4 gives typical values for the ratios of surface area to wing and other dominating areas. Table 11–1 gave similar first estimates for tail volume coefficient.

TABLE 11–3

Summary of definitions and notation

Name	Stick condition	Symbol	Meaning	Used to determine
Neutral point	fixed	h_n	*CG* for neutral static stability	*CG* for zero stick travel to change speed
	free	h'_n	as above	*CG* for zero stick force to change speed
CG margin (theoretically rigid aeroplane)	fixed	H_n	$h_n - h$	Guide to permissible *CG* range
	free	H'_n	$h'_n - h$	ditto
Static margin (real, flexible aeroplane)	fixed	$K_n = H_n$ ψ_1	Measures stick-fixed static stability	Stick travel to change speed
	free	$K'_n = H'_n$ χ_1	Measures stick-free static stability	Stick force to change speed
Manoeuvre point	fixed	h_m	*CG* position for zero man-oeuvre margin	*CG* for zero stick travel per *g*
	free	h'_m	as above	*CG* for zero stick force per *g*
Manoeuvre margin	fixed	H_m	$h_m - h$	Stick travel per *g*
	free	H'_m	$h'_m - h$	Stick force per *g*

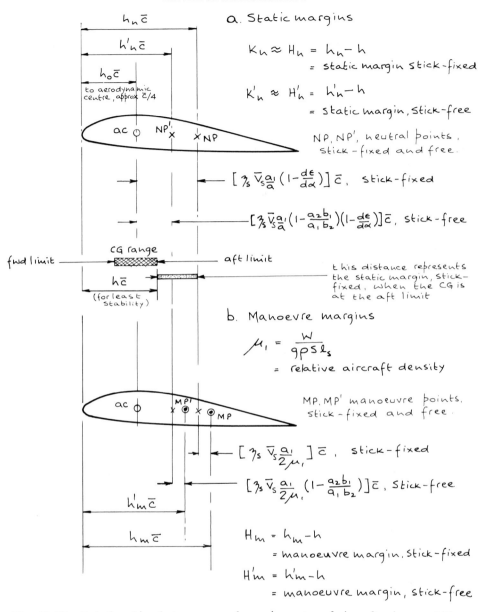

a. Static margins

$$K_n \approx H_n = h_n - h$$

= static margin stick-fixed

$$K'_n \approx H'_n = h'_n - h$$

= static margin, stick-free

NP, NP', neutral points, stick-fixed and free.

$$\left[\%_s \bar{V}_s \frac{a_1}{a} \left(1 - \frac{d\epsilon}{d\alpha} \right) \right] \bar{c}, \quad \text{stick-fixed}$$

$$\left[\%_s \bar{V}_s \frac{a_1}{a} \left(1 - \frac{a_2 b_1}{a_1 b_2} \right) \left(1 - \frac{d\epsilon}{d\alpha} \right) \right] \bar{c}, \quad \text{stick-free}$$

this distance represents the static margin, stick-fixed, when the CG is at the aft limit

b. Manoeuvre margins

$$\mu_1 = \frac{W}{g \rho S \ell_s}$$

= relative aircraft density

MP, MP' manoeuvre points, stick-fixed and free.

$$\left[\%_s \bar{V}_s \frac{a_1}{2\mu_1} \right] \bar{c}, \quad \text{stick-fixed}$$

$$\left[\%_s \bar{V}_s \frac{a_1}{2\mu_1} \left(1 - \frac{a_2 b_1}{a_1 b_2} \right) \right] \bar{c}, \quad \text{stick-free}$$

$$H_m = h_m - h$$

= manoeuvre margin, stick-fixed

$$H'_m = h'_m - h$$

= manoeuvre margin, stick-free

Fig. 11.12 Relationships between aerodynamic centre of aircraft-minus-stabiliser, the neutral points stick-fixed and free, and the manoeuvre points stick-fixed and free.

Fig. 11.13 shows the general arrangement and proportions of a conventional aeroplane with a tail, and a canard. Stabiliser arm, l_s is given in terms of mainplane SMC, $\bar{c}$. The area of the stabiliser is best estimated as a ratio of S_s / S. The aerodynamic centres of the surfaces correspond with $\bar{c}/4$ of each.

As a first and very crude approximation to the planview drawing of a single engined aeroplane, the wing 1/4 chord can be located about 0.3 of the fuselage length back from the nose. With a twin the distance is generally nearer $0.4 \times$ fuselage length. Both dimensions are flexible and, if adopted too firmly, can lead to gross errors.

The aspect ratio of a tail should be less than that of the wing. Because the forward plane must always stall first, it is prudent to give the foreplane a higher aspect ratio than the rearplane. A fair compromise is to make the aspect ratio of the foreplane 1.2 to 1.5 times that of the rearplane.

We may estimate the lift slope ratio of the two planes as follows, using eq (4–19), while inserting the value of each different aspect ratio as required:

$$a_A = 2\pi A/(A + 2)/\text{radian} \qquad \text{eq (4–19a)}$$

For a stabiliser of lift slope a_1, and a wing of lift slope a, the ratio of their aspect ratios is $A_s/A = R_A$, so that

$$\text{lift slope ratio, } (a_1/a) = (A + 2)/(A + 2/R_A) \qquad (11–48)$$

We start by picking a tail area/wing area ratio appropriate to the aeroplane being drawn, using table 11–4. A crude tail volume coefficient can then be calculated, based upon the proportions in fig. 11.13, and this should be checked against table 11–1.

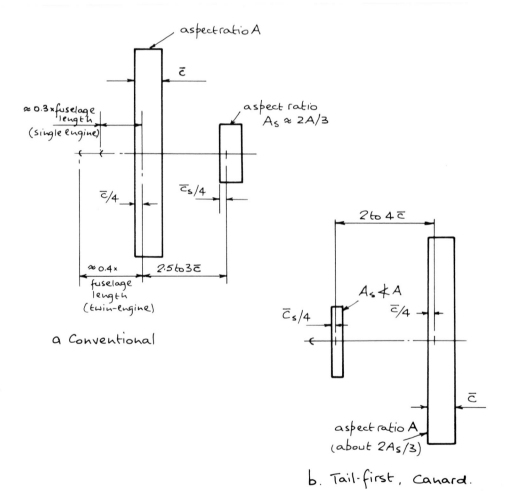

Fig. 11.13   Wing-plus-stabiliser arrangements and proportions.

total area (6 of 4)

TABLE 11–4

Stabiliser, fin and control surface areas

Surface area ratio	Stabiliser plus elevator	Fin plus rudder	Aileron
Total surface area / wing area	Conventional: older: 0.1 to 0.17 modern: 0.16 to 0.2 Canard: 0.15 to 0.25	0.03 to 0.06 0.075 to 0.085	0.08 to 0.1
Control-plus-tab area / total surface area	0.5 to 0.55	0.5 to 0.6	0.18 to 0.30
Balance area ahead of control hinge / control-plus-tab area	0.15 to 0.25	0.16 to 0.25	0.20 to 0.25
Control-tab area / control-plus-tab area aft of hinge	0.05 to 0.1	0.05 to 0.1	0.04 to 0.06
Aspect ratio	Conventional: 3.5 to 4.5 (say $2A/3$) Canard: 1.2 to $1.5A$ A = wing aspect ratio	1.0 to 1.8 Note: *see* fig. 13.11 for definition of vertical surface area	

Notes: Estimation of areas depends upon geometric factors like those shown in fig. 13.11. The principles can be applied to horizontal surfaces too, the areas of which should be calculated as net, i.e. counting only area outside body lines. Base aileron area upon grossest wing area (i.e. including areas marked a in fig. 2.2)

The **CG** ranges are roughly as follows. These reflect the tendency of modern designers to bring centres of gravity forwards, so as to reduce stall/spin misbehaviour:

$$\text{older aeroplanes: 0.25 to 0.35 SMC} \qquad (11\text{–}49a)$$
$$\text{modern aeroplanes: 0.16 to 0.28 SMC} \qquad (11\text{–}49b)$$

Checks using stability margins

We have just seen how the stability margins can be expressed in terms of the static margin, stick-fixed, which represents the basic static stability of the aeroplane. The various terms involved are as follows:

☐ h_o: the aerodynamic centre of the wing-plus-fuselage. In effect this is the 'neutral point' of the combination. The *ac* is caused to move forward of $\bar{c}/4$ by the addition of the fuselage, particularly by the length of nose ahead of the wing 1/4 chord, and the width of the fuselage, resulting in a shift of 4 to 5 per cent SMC (Appendix A, item 76015 shows a method of calculating the forward shift of the combined aerodynamic centre).

A crude estimate can be made as shown in fig. 11.14, in which the fuselage forward of the wing 1/4 chord is treated as a very low aspect ratio aerofoil surface of rectangular form. The method is more accurate if the nose 'aspect ratio' is calculated using *maximum body width²/area of nose in planform* (eq (11–50) in fig. 11.14). We assume an equivalent aerodynamic centre for the nose, 1/4 of its length back from its extremity, or from the front of the cowling (when the spinner area is smaller than, say, total $S_{nose}/10$). The lift slope of the equivalent aerofoil surface is estimated from fig. 4.6c, or by multiplying the nose 'aspect ratio' by $\pi/2$ (*see* eq (4–19b)). The lift slope of the wing is calculated in the normal fashion, using eq (4–19a). Finally, the forward (i.e. negative) displacement of the *ac*, h_o is calculated by taking moments about the wing aerodynamic centre:

forward shift of wing+body *ac*, $-\Delta h_o = -0.75(a_{nose}/a_A)/((a_{nose}/a_A)+(S/S_{nose}))$ (11–51)
in which, $(a_{nose}/a_A) = 0.25A_{nose} + 0.5(A_{nose}/A)$.   (11–52)

This latter equation is derived from the ratio of eq (4–19b)/eq (4–19a). The lift slopes of the nose and the wing are a_{nose} and a_A, while A_{nose} and A are the equivalent aspect ratio of the nose, and the wing aspect ratio respectively. For most light aeroplanes h_o moves forward to 0.19 to 0.22 $\bar{c}$, i.e. $-\Delta h_o = -0.02$ to -0.06.

☐ V_s: stabiliser volume, which is the factor most easily adjusted in the early stages.
☐ η_s: stabiliser efficiency, usually 0.8 to 0.9, but can be as low as 0.65.
☐ a and a_1: wing and stabiliser lift slopes, both of which are proportional to aspect ratio.
☐ $d\epsilon/d\alpha$: rate of change of wing downwash with angle of attack (*see* eqs (5–25) to (5–26)).
☐ h: centre of gravity position (which should be located well forward to reduce excessive tail area) but which may be altered in the early stages by moving the wing on the fuselage. Adjustment may also be accomplished by sweeping wings forwards or backwards to a certain extent, so as to bring everything into alignment. This is a favoured solution when compressibility effects are not involved.

Experience suggests that the tail should be large enough to give at least neutral static stability, stick-fixed ($K_n \not< 0$) when cruising with the **CG** at the aft limit. Aerobatic

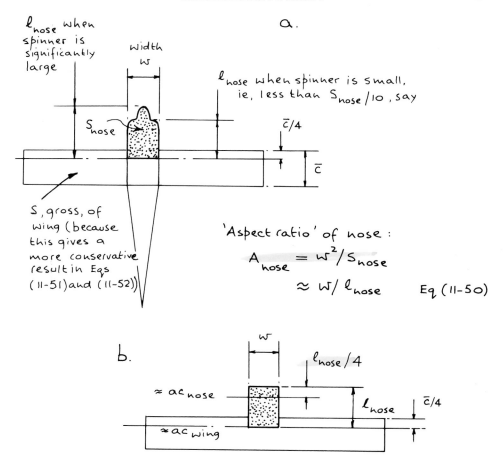

ℓ_{nose} when spinner is significantly large

width W

ℓ_{nose} when spinner is small, ie, less than $S_{nose}/10$, say

$\bar{c}/4$

S_{nose}

$\bar{c}$

S, gross, of wing (because this gives a more conservative result in Eqs (11-51) and (11-52))

a.

'Aspect ratio' of nose :

$$A_{nose} = w^2/S_{nose}$$

$$\approx w/\ell_{nose} \qquad Eq \ (11-50)$$

b.

w

$\ell_{nose}/4$

$\approx ac_{nose}$

ℓ_{nose}

$\bar{c}/4$

$\approx ac_{wing}$

This figure shows a way of approximating planform of the nose of an aeroplane, forward of the wing $\frac{1}{4}$ chord (aerodynamic centre, in fact) to a very low aspect ratio aerofoil surface, for calculation of the forward shift of the aerodynamic centre of the wing – plus – body. The method can be applied to nacelles, each one of which contributes to shifting the combined ac even further forward of that of the wing alone.

Fig. 11.14 Simplified treatment of body effect upon forward shift of aerodynamic centre of aircraft-minus-stabiliser.

aeroplanes can sustain a smaller negative stick-fixed static margin, as long as the stick-free static margin is positive. This means that in eq (11-27): $(\bar{a}_1/a) = -(a_2 b_1/a_1 b_2) < 0$, which can only be so if (b_1/b_2) is negative – because the lift slope terms are always positive.

The difficulty is that as aeroplanes progress through the various design stages, and later as they grow old, they become more and more tail heavy. Therefore, it is prudent

$b_1 \oplus$

$b_2 \ominus$

over balanced elevator

to start with a stick-fixed static margin of 0.02 to 0.04 SMC in the aft **CG** cruise. From there we can then build up the remaining margins using table 11–5.

TABLE 11–5

Practical values of static and manoeuvre margins

Margin	Stick-fixed	Stick-free
Static, K_n	0.02 to 0.04 (but could be 0 for a 'hot ship')	—
K'_n	—	$\triangleright K_n + 0.03$, but with most light aeroplanes $K'_n < K_n$.
Manoeuvre, H_m	$K_n + 0.03$ = 0.06 for most light aeroplanes	—
H'_m	—	$K_n + 0.02$ to $0.03 = 0.08$ to 0.25, i.e. a ratio around 1 to 3 between aft and forward **CG** limits

If we compare the values given in the table with eqs (11–25), (11–27), (11–40) and (11–43), while using eq (11–48) to calculate the lift slope ratio, a_1/a, it is a straightforward matter to transpose the required increments for tail volume coefficient, $\overline{V}_s$. However, we need to know something about control surface characteristics, and a brief introduction is given in chapter 12.

Trim

Assuming that K_n has the right value, the next step is to check that the aeroplane can be trimmed in two critical conditions:

☐ At the stall, with the wing working at C_{Lmax}, flap down, and the **CG** on the forward limit.
☐ At the low C_L and aft **CG** case.

Power and ground effects must be allowed for, using eq (7–30) and fig. 6.10.
    The checks amount to ensuring that the net moment about the **CG** is zero in each case, i.e.

$$C_{MCG} = C_L(h - h_o) + C_{Mac} - \eta_s\overline{V}_sC_{Ls} = 0 \qquad \text{from eq (11–8)}$$

Some of these terms need attention:

☐ C_{Mac}: C_{Mo}: the pitching moment coefficient at zero lift, which is mostly due to the wing-plus-fuselage. The wing contribution is obtained from sources like ref. 3.6. The fuselage contribution can be estimated using results for similar shapes (wind tunnel results are most useful). The nose produces the most powerful effects. Light aeroplane fuselages produce C_{Mo} values which vary between 0.03 and –0.03, based upon wing area. The width of the fuselage in terms of the wing span is important, the greater the ratio the more powerful the moment. Large broad canopies produce a nose-up pitching moment. In the absence of better data assume $C_{Mofus} = 0$ in the equation:

$$C_{Mo} = C_{Mac} + C_{Mofus} \qquad (11\text{-}53)$$

C_{Mo} from this equation should be used in eq (11–8) in place of C_{Mac}, whenever a reliable value of C_{Mofus} is available.

☐ C_{Ls}: the effect of an elevator is to change the effective angle of attack of the basic aerofoil section as shown in fig. 11.15. The increment is given by the following which uses fig. 11.15c (based upon ref. 3.4):

$$\Delta \alpha_s \eta = \Delta \eta (d\alpha_s / d\eta)$$

and, $\qquad\qquad \Delta C_{Ls} = a_2 \Delta \eta = a_1 \Delta \eta (d\alpha_s / d\eta) \qquad (11\text{-}54)$

from which we also see that:

$$a_2 = dC_{Ls}/d\eta = a_1(d\alpha_s/d\eta) \qquad (11\text{-}55)$$

i.e. $\qquad\qquad\qquad (a_2/a_1) = (d\alpha_s/d\eta) \qquad (11\text{-}56)$

Now, the lift coefficient of the stabiliser within the straight line working range is:

$$
\begin{aligned}
C_{Ls} &= a_1\alpha_s + a_2\eta & \text{from eq (11–14)} \\
&= a_1(\alpha_{eff} - \epsilon + \alpha_{si}) + a_2\eta & \text{following eq (11–22)} \\
&= a_1[\alpha_{eff}(1 - d\epsilon/d\alpha) + \alpha_{si}] + a_2\eta & \text{from eq (11–23)}
\end{aligned}
$$

and this must be inserted in eq (11–8) to give:

$$C_{MCG} = C_L(h - h_o) + (C_{Mac} + (C_{Mofus}) - \eta_s \bar{V}_s \left\{ a_1[\alpha_{eff}(1 - d\epsilon/d\alpha) + \alpha_{si}] + a_2\eta \right\} = 0 \qquad (11\text{-}57)$$

This must satisfy the critical cases.

Checking stabiliser size

We can make a rough check of stabiliser area by drawing the plan view of our aeroplane, including rectangles for propellers, on a piece of stiff card, as shown in fig. 11.16. Leave a margin around the anticipated stabiliser outline, so that card can be trimmed away with scissors. The area of the stabiliser within the anticipated outline is first estimated in terms of S_s/S, from table 11–4. Mark the ¼ chord points for each surface (the general proportions of the layout should correspond with fig. 11.13).

Cut out the shape of the aircraft and then balance it fore and aft on a knife blade. Trim away the spare area around the anticipated stabiliser outline until the lamina balances at a point P on the centre line, aft of the wing ¼ chord. The distance from the wing ¼ chord to P should be about 0.58 SMC with variations as follows:

$$\text{extreme: } 0.54 \text{ to } 0.75 \text{ SMC} \qquad (11\text{-}58)$$
$$\text{average: } 0.56 \text{ to } 0.6 \text{ SMC} \qquad (11\text{-}59)$$

The above values apply to an aeroplane with a tail at the back, and possibly a pure tandem arrangement, with both planes the same size. In the latter case we have to find the centre of gravity (centroid) of both planes, taking area moments about their ¼ chords. Point P is then measured aft of the centroid of both, as a fraction of the appropriate SMC of whichever plane is the larger of the two.

a. Deflection of the elevator by an amount $\pm\Delta\eta$ in effect changes stabiliser angle of attack by $\pm\Delta\alpha_{s\eta}$ (thin aerofoil theory)

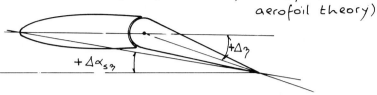

b.

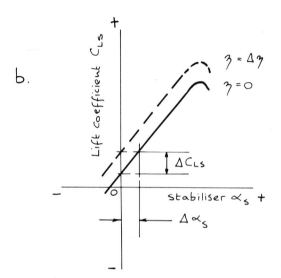

The incremental change in stabiliser lift coefficient with elevator deflection (downwards as drawn). The curve has the same shape, but in reverse, for upward deflection

c.

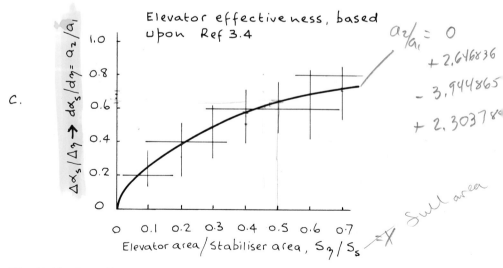

Elevator effectiveness, based upon Ref 3.4

$a_2/a_1 = 0$

$+ 2.646836$

$- 3.944865$

$+ 2.303780$

Fig. 11.15   The effect of elevator deflection upon lift of the whole stabiliser (tailplane, or foreplane-plus-elevator).

$(0,0)$ $(.2, .39)$
$(.4, .575)$
$(.7, .71)$

$\dfrac{S_e}{S_H}$

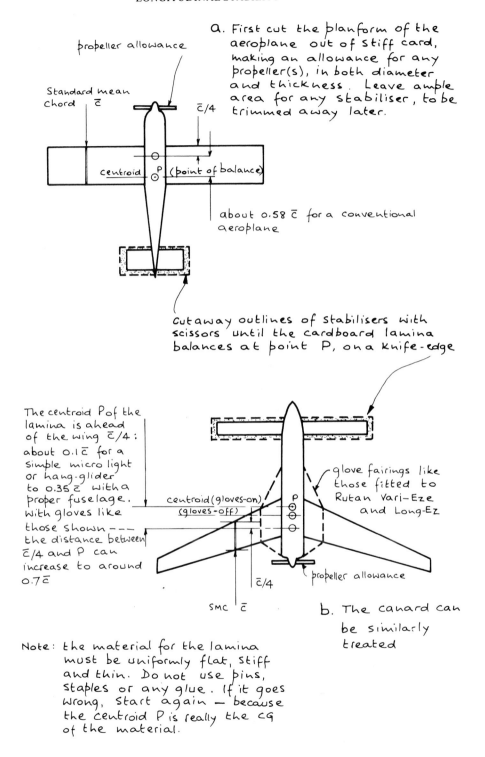

propeller allowance

Standard mean chord $\bar{c}$

$\bar{c}/4$

a. First cut the planform of the aeroplane out of stiff card, making an allowance for any propeller(s), in both diameter and thickness. Leave ample area for any stabiliser, to be trimmed away later.

centroid P (point of balance)

about 0.58 $\bar{c}$ for a conventional aeroplane

Cut away outlines of stabilisers with scissors until the cardboard lamina balances at point P, on a knife-edge

The centroid P of the lamina is ahead of the wing $\bar{c}/4$: about 0.1 $\bar{c}$ for a simple micro light or hang-glider to 0.35 $\bar{c}$ with a proper fuselage. With gloves like those shown - - - the distance between $\bar{c}/4$ and P can increase to around 0.7 $\bar{c}$

centroid (gloves-on) (gloves-off)

glove fairings like those fitted to Rutan Vari-Eze and Long-Ez

propeller allowance

$\bar{c}/4$

SMC $\bar{c}$

b. The canard can be similarly treated

Note: the material for the lamina must be uniformly flat, stiff and thin. Do not use pins, staples or any glue. If it goes wrong, start again — because the centroid P is really the CG of the material.

Fig. 11.16   A rough check of stabiliser area using planform of aeroplane cut out of card.

Very few modern types of aeroplanes with foreplanes have been built, so that we lack statistical evidence. However, similar experiments with laminae produce large variations. The shortest distance to the centroid of wing-plus-foreplane forward of the $\frac{1}{4}$ SMC of the wing, measured by the author, is about 0.1 SMC (for a tail-first powered hang-glider). Others of the *Rutan VariEze* type appear to have distances approaching 0.35 to 0.7 SMC forward of the $\frac{1}{4}$ SMC of the basic wing (the latter figure referring to the aeroplane with 'glove' wing root fairings).

Success of the method, which is only a crude guide, depends upon the use of a plain lamina. If pins, staples or glue are introduced, they will have a drastic effect upon the centroid.

Checking the neutral point

The crude check on stabiliser size can be developed along the lines of that suggested in ref. 11.5, which uses wing and stabiliser laminae to find the neutral point, stick-fixed, of the combination. We make an allowance for effectiveness of the stabiliser, and this needs guesswork. The neutral point stick-fixed was shown in eq (11–26) to contain an efficiency term, η_s, which depended upon dynamic pressure recovery at the tail, and the stabiliser/wing lift slope ratio, a_1/a. Combining both:

$$\text{factor of stabiliser effectiveness} = \eta_s(a_1/a) \qquad (11\text{–}60)$$

The values we might expect in practice for the two terms are 0.7 to 0.8 for η_s and a_1/a about 0.85 from eq (11–48), with the result that stabiliser effectiveness lies somewhere between about 0.6 and 0.7 for most conventionally-mounted tails.

The method given in the reference involves making stiff card templates of the *front half* of the wing and the stabiliser (using identical weight card for both). The front half of the tailplane must be reduced in size from the anticipated area, in proportion to the factor given above. As we are only considering the front half of the stabiliser, the area involved will be $S_s/2$, the size being:

$$\text{stabiliser template area} = \eta_s(a_1/a)S_s/2 \approx S_s/3 \qquad (11\text{–}61)$$

Mount both templates in their correct relation to each other on two stiff, light, balsa wood strips (for lateral stability). These should have length to spare, so that they can be trimmed when balancing the arrangement on a knife edge to find the neutral point. The strips should have equal lengths overhanging the fulcrum on either side.

The centre of gravity of the aeroplane must lie ahead of the neutral point.

In-flight measurement of static margins

It is possible to determine static margins by flight tests, during which the pilot measures elevator and trimmer deflections at different lift coefficients (calculated at different airspeeds) and positions of the centre of gravity. The main assumption is that the angle of the flight path is shallow enough for:

$$\text{crossforce coefficient, } C_R = \sqrt{(L^2 + D^2)}/qS \approx C_L \qquad (11\text{–}62)$$

Fig. 11.18 shows the curves that can be obtained by this technique.

Stick-fixed

The pilot trims the aeroplane initially at some particular airspeed, weight and **CG**

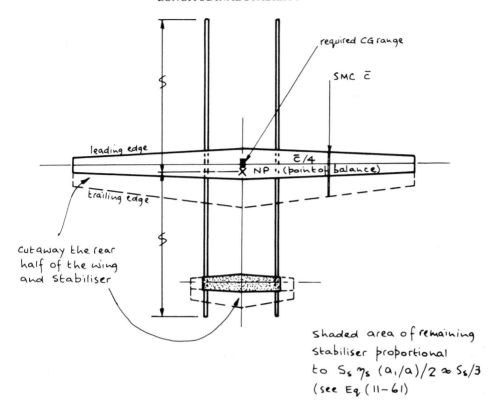

Shaded area of remaining
stabiliser proportional
to $S_s \eta_s (a_1/a)/2 \approx S_s/3$
(see Eq (11-61))

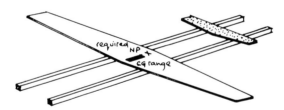

The effectiveness of this method of finding the neutral
point, stick-fixed, depends upon care in juggling the
lengths of the supporting sticks, and in not over-
estimating the size of the remaining area of the
stabiliser. Remember, the centre of gravity of the
aeroplane must lie ahead of the neutral point NP,
otherwise it will be longitudinally unstable.

Fig. 11.17   Estimation of neutral point, stick-fixed, by balancing front halves of wing and stabiliser laminae on light balsa wood strips (*see* ref. 11.5). The method works for canard surfaces, except that **NP** must then lie forward of the wing (rearplane) ¼ chord.

position. All three have to be known accurately – the airspeed being either the calibrated (equivalent) airspeed, or the true airspeed. We can start with indicated airspeed, but the instrument and pressure errors must be known so as to make the appropriate conversions. Speed is then changed by a small movement of the elevator

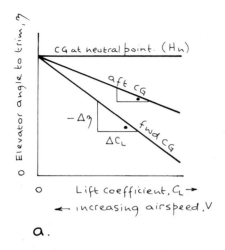

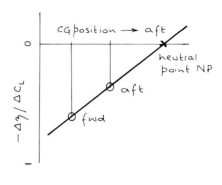

a.

b.

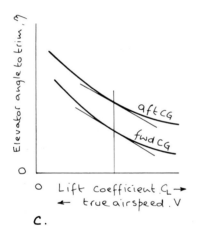

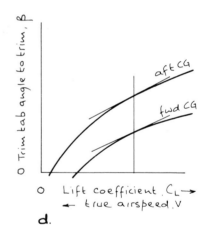

c.

d.

(a) Shows the ideal straight line relationship between elevator angle, or stick position, and lift coefficient. If the slope of each line is measured and plotted in (b) the neutral point can be found geometrically. However, realities intrude, like aeroelasticity, scale effects and compressibility, changing the straight line forms in (a) to shapes like (c). Such effects make themselves felt in measurements of trimmer deflection, β, with lift coefficient, C_L (and airspeed, V), as shown in (d). It is because of awkwardly shaped curves like these that we cannot accurately determine stick-free stability using CG margins.

Note that the method depends upon accurate calculation of lift coefficient, and this requires accurate knowledge of fuel consumption

Fig. 11.18   Trim curves used to measure stick-fixed and free static margins, K_n and K'_n.

alone (leaving the trimmer fixed), and an out of trim stick force is then needed to maintain the new speed. The lift coefficient must change with airspeed, and we shall change ΔC_L. Finally, to hold the new airspeed, stabiliser lift must have changed by an increment $a_2\Delta\eta$, which appeared in eq (11–20).

As the aeroplane is in trim at the new airspeed, $\Delta C_{MCG} = 0$, so that:

$$-\Delta C_{MCG} = -a_2\eta_s\overline{V}_s\Delta\eta \tag{11–63}$$

This enables the static margin to be calculated, knowing that:

$$\text{static margin, } K_n{:}H_n = -dC_{MCG}/dC_L \approx -\Delta C_{MCG}/\Delta C_L$$
$$\text{(no elasticity or compressibility)}$$
$$\approx -a_2\eta_s\overline{V}_s(\Delta\eta/\Delta C_L) \tag{11–64}$$

(be careful, don't confuse η_s with η here).

Thus, knowing that the lift coefficient $C_L = W/qS$, in which weight and wing area are fixed at any moment, while q is dependent upon airspeed[2], we may measure the elevator angle to trim, η, in terms of stick position and plot it as shown in fig. 11.18a. Stick position can be measured from the instrument panel by means of an expanding rule.

If the measurements are made at two different **CG** positions (e.g. at the forward and aft limits) a curve may be plotted like fig. 11.18b by measuring the slope of each different curve in (a). The intercept of the curve with the **CG** position axis gives the location of the neutral point, stick-fixed. The slope of the curve is a measure of $a_2\eta_s\overline{V}_s$, which may be written as $\overline{A}$, such that

$$K_n \approx \overline{A}(\Delta\eta/\Delta C_L) \tag{11–64a}$$

Stick-free

In a similar way we can find the stick-free static margin by measuring elevator trimmer deflection $\Delta\beta$ (in terms of trimmer control movement in the cockpit) at different airspeeds. Then the stick-free static margin is found from:

$$K'_n \approx -a_3\eta_s\overline{V}_s(1 - a_2b_3/a_3b_2)(\Delta\beta/\Delta C_L) \tag{11–65}$$

For normally proportioned and balanced controls a_2b_3/a_3b_2 is usually greater than 1.0. Consequently, for positive stability we expect $\Delta\beta/\Delta C_L$ to be positive. Measurement of trimmer position at different airspeeds (and lift coefficients) saves us the trouble of needing to insert actual values of:

$$a_3\eta_s\overline{V}_s(1 - a_2b_3/a_3b_2) \text{ which may be written as } \overline{B}, \text{ such that:}$$
$$K'_n \approx -\overline{B}(\Delta\beta/\Delta C_L) \tag{11–65a}$$

The procedure is exactly the same as in the case of elevator (stick) deflection. Trimmer position is plotted against lift coefficient at different airspeeds and **CG** positions. When there is no aeroelastic distortion, or compressibility effects, fairly straight lines are obtained. In practice the curves tend to resemble fig. 11.18d. Measurement of the slope of the curve for each **CG** position enables a curve like 11.18b to be drawn (except that it will be the other way up, because the trimmer is deflected downwards, in a positive direction, to trim up-elevator needed to increase C_L).

As long as a static margin is positive an aeroplane will be statically stable. When the margin is zero the **CG** coincides with the neutral point and the machine is neutrally stable. When the **CG** is aft of the **NP** the static margin is negative and the aeroplane is unstable.

Location of horizontal tail

The vertical location of the horizontal tail is affected by aerodynamic and structural considerations. Fuselage, wing and nacelle wakes reduce stabiliser efficiency, η_s, and such reduction is usually worse when manoeuvring at high lift. Propwash is destabilising. The best position for the tail is away from all such influences. Unfortunately, the ideal locations from the aerodynamic point of view, i.e. very high or very low, are bad structurally, or introduce ground clearance problems.

A general guide to location is shown in fig. 11.19 (ref. 11.7). Although the figure refers specifically to pitch-up, nevertheless the general principles apply, because pitch-up is exacerbated by the reduction in tail effectiveness caused by bad interference from other parts of the airframe.

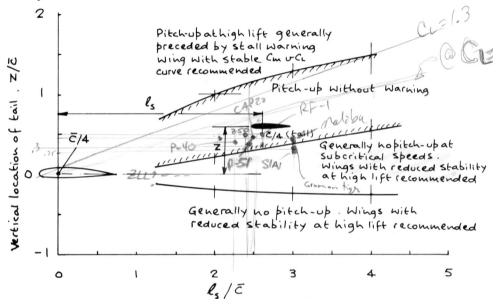

Fig. 11.19 Boundaries of horizontal tail locations, after ref. 11.7. The same observations apply in general when considering rearplane – foreplane arrangements; although the total effect of foreplane upon rearplane will depend upon relative size.

References

11.1 Maccabee, F., editor (Apr. 1968) TT6801, *Light Aircraft Design Handbook*. Loughborough University of Technology.

11.2 Irving, F. G. (1966) *An Introduction to the Longitudinal Static Stability of Low-Speed Aircraft*. Oxford: Pergamon Press.

11.3 Duncan, W. J. (1952) *The Principles of the Control and Stability of Aircraft*. Cambridge University Press.

11.4 Babister, A. W. (1961) *Aircraft Stability and Control*. Oxford: Pergamon Press.

11.5 Simons, M. (1978) *Model Aircraft Aerodynamics*. England: Model and Allied Publications, Argus Books Limited, Watford, Herts.

11.6 BCAR Section K2-8. Civil Aviation Authority.

11.7 Spreeman, K. P. (Aug. 1959) NASA TMX-26 *Design Guide for Pitch-up Evaluation and Investigation at High Subsonic Speeds of Possible Limitations due to Wing–Aspect Ratio Variations*. Washington: National Aeronautics and Space Administration.

CHAPTER 12

Control Surfaces

'... many take the line that control surface design is still far more of an art than a science.'
M. B. Morgan and H. H. B. M. Thomas (ref. 12.1).

'I'm all for keeping the art in life'
Professor L. F. Crabtree.

The handling quality of an aeroplane is dependent to a large degree upon the quality of its controls combined, of course, with response to stability, and its dynamic properties. Control surfaces (with one or two exceptions, like spoilers and stabilators) take the form of flap-like devices which change the camber. Some may be like plain flaps, some like slotted, but they all belong to the flap family. Movement of a control enables the pilot to alter the attitude of an aircraft in pitch, roll or yaw. Assessment of control qualities is one of the hardest tasks of a test pilot, and this involves art every bit as much as discipline.

Controls are either effective, or they are not. There are no degrees of effectiveness – although the efficiency of a surface may vary considerably with deflection, or airspeed (or both) by comparison with others. They must cause an aircraft to perform all required manoeuvres safely. Control forces must act progressively in a logical sense and be well within the physical capability of the pilot. Moreoever they should be easy and pleasant. An aeroplane with 'sweet', well harmonised controls is a pleasure to fly, and far less tiring then one that is not. Cut pilot fatigue and we are a good halfway on the road to safety.

Under Handling Terms in chapter 2 we saw a rule passed down from World War 2, that for sweet handling the aileron: elevator: rudder force needed to produce a given rate of response about each axis should be:

$$A:E:R = 1:2:4 \qquad \text{eq (2–43)}$$

An assessment of this kind is highly subjective and can lead to strong differences of opinion, but it can be useful on concentrating the pilot's mind.

Pilot effort

We are only concerned with manual control systems. Table 12.1 shows typical values of control forces that can be applied by the average pilot. The last column (ref. 12.1) is very important. The forces are the highest which a pilot cares to exert under normal circumstances, e.g., when taking off, landing, or raising and lowering flaps, and during exceptional manoeuvres (asymmetric engine failure, or baulked landing). Reaction times are taken from the same reference. It shows that the time taken for a pilot to react to a situation may exceed the subsequent time taken to apply the necessary control. This has a direct bearing on action following an engine cut.

The remainder of table 12–1 is culled from ref. 12.2.

Control circuit mechanics

Friction and backlash in control circuits are sources of trouble and must be avoided. Friction causes 'breakout forces' which a pilot must exert before a control can be moved. Ref. 12.1 recommends that friction of aileron, elevator and rudder should not be higher than 2, 4 and 6 lbf (9.1, 18.2 and 27.2 N) for the sort of aircraft with which we are concerned. The danger of such friction is that when the pilot has overcome it, the control moves suddenly, resulting in overcontrol and imprecision.

Backlash is lost motion caused by excessive tolerances, slack, wear and tear. Flutter can result, especially with spring and servo tab system.

Response effect

In the last chapter we were introduced to hinge moments, and saw what an important part they played in relation to the differences between stick-fixed and free longitudinal stability. Response effect (sometimes called b_1 effect) is the name given to the alteration in the control hinge moment during response of an aircraft to control movement. To refresh our memories:

$b_1 = \delta C_H / \delta \alpha_s$, the rate of change of elevator hinge moment coefficient with stabiliser angle of attack, with elevator and tab fixed.

$b_2 = \delta C_H / \delta \eta$, the rate of change of elevator hinge moment coefficient with elevator deflection, the angle of attack of the stabiliser and tab deflection remaining unchanged. The curve is only linear part of the way each sie of neutral, and usually non-linear over large deflections.

$b_3 = \delta C_H / \delta \beta$, the rate of change of elevator hinge moment with trimmer deflection, stabiliser angle of attack and elevator deflection remaining unchanged.

Imagine that we have an elevator which tends to float or trail with the wind when the stick is pulled back and the nose of the aeroplane rises (increasing the angles of attack of the wing and the stabiliser). The trail is caused by negative $\delta C_H / \delta \alpha_s$, i.e. $-b_1$. The hinge moment to hold the elevator in its deflected position will thus be reduced. Conversely, positive b_1 means that the elevator will tend to trail downwards (against the wind) and the hinge moment will be increased.

The ratio of pilot's effort with response effect to what it would be with no response, is termed the:

response factor, $K =$ effort with response/effort without response   (12–1)

If a change in elevator angle $\Delta \eta$ produces a change in stabiliser angle of attack $\Delta \alpha_s$, then change in hinge moment coefficient:

$$\Delta C_H = b_1 \Delta \alpha_s + b_2 \Delta \eta \tag{12–2}$$

TABLE 12-1

Pilot characteristics
(A combination of refs. 12.1 and 12.2)

Control	Maximum pilot effort		Minimum pilot effort	Greatest force pilot cares to exert for a short while
	$W = 12540$ lb (5700 kg)	$W \leqslant 5060$ lb (2300 kg)		
Aileron				
Stick lateral	72 lbf (325 N)	67 lbf (300 N)	40 lbf (180 N)	20 lbf (one hand)
Wheel lateral	72 lbf (325 N)	67 lbf (300 N)	40 lbf (180 N)	20 lbf (one hand)
Wheel up and down	80 lbf (360 N)	67 lbf (300 N)	50 lbf (225 N)	30 lbf (two hand)
Wheel torque	63 D lbf in (280 D Nm)	53 D lbf in (235 D Nm)	40 D lbf in (180 D Nm)	
Minimum reaction time stick ¼ second wheel ½ second				
Elevator				
Stick	180 lbf (805 N)	167 lbf (745 N)	100 lbf (445 N)	30 lbf (one hand)
Wheel	220 lbf (980 N)	200 lbf (890 N)	100 lbf (445 N)	30 lbf (one hand) 40 lbf (two hand)
Minimum reaction time not applicable				
Rudder				
On one side of rudder bar	237 lbf (1055 N)	200 lbf (890 N)	130 lbf (580 N)	60 lbf (push)
Simultaneously on each side of rudder bar	180 lbf (805 N)	180 lbf (805 N)	180 lbf (805 N)	
Minimum reaction time ½ second (push)				

Reaction time, any control: anything up to 3 seconds

W: Maximum design weight
D: Control wheel diameter, in (m)
Linear variation of force assumed for intermediate values of W

with response (omitting trimmer contribution); while without response:

$$\Delta C_H = b_2 \Delta \eta, \text{ when } \Delta \alpha_s = 0 \qquad (12\text{--}3)$$

If we now insert them in eq (12–1), we obtain:

$$K = (b_1 \Delta \alpha_s + b_2 \Delta \eta)/b_2 \Delta \eta$$
$$= 1 + (b_1 \Delta \alpha_s / b_2 \Delta \eta) \qquad (12\text{--}4)$$

and the pilot's effort, instead of being proportional to b_2 is proportional to Kb_2. Since $\Delta \alpha_s / \Delta \eta$ and b_2 are negative, K is less than unity when b_1 is negative. This means that negative b_1 lightens control forces. A positive b_1 makes the response factor greater than unity, and the stick force feels heavier.

Usually, response effects are more marked on elevator and rudder than on ailerons. The reason is that unit change of elevator or rudder angle produces larger angles of attack in pitch and yaw than unit aileron deflection produces in roll. The relative magnitude of the resulting motions may be around 5 to 1.

For a given control movement at any one speed, the hinge movement and consequently the pilot's effort is proportional to Kb_2 and stick force depends upon the square of the speed. Thus, for any one control, the force for a given displacement varies as the square of the equivalent airspeed, in the absence of distortion and compressibility effects. This means that control forces between V_{SO} and V_C, or V_D, vary in the ratio of V_C/V_{SO} and V_D/V_{SO} (table 6–2), with ranges of around 10:1 in the cruise case, to 50:1 for a formula racer at V_D. But the pilot needs small values of Kb_2 to help in the manual operation of the controls. To lighten them 'aerodynamic balance' is provided in many cases – although formula racers, being small and simple, tend not to have such refinements. They start with very light stick forces at low speed instead; some of them so far below any certification standard that they are fit only for Permits to Fly, or Experimental Cs of A.

Aerodynamic balancing

Aerodynamic balancing of control surfaces is a way of reducing hinge moments by geometry, and distribution of surface area about the hinge line, so that the resultant of control lift acts on a small moment arm from the hinge (fig. 12.1). It should be noted that such balancing alters both b_1 and b_2 simultaneously, but by differing amounts, so care is needed to avoid overbalance giving positive b_2.

$$\text{aerodynamic balance} = \text{area moment fwd of the hinge}/\text{area moment}$$
$$\text{aft of the hinge} \qquad (12\text{--}5)$$

Horn balance

A horn is the commonest balance, which reduces numerically b_2 but at the same time heavies the control, changing $-b_1$ numerically by making it positive. Two kinds of horn are shown in fig. 12.2. The first extends to the leading edge of the fixed surface, and is called *unshielded*. The second has some of the fixed surface ahead of it and is said to be *shielded*.

Effectiveness of a horn balance depends upon the moment of the area of horn ahead of the hinge, to the area moment of the flap surface behind it. Sometimes we see aircraft on which an unshielded horn has been too powerful, and it has been cropped back from the leading edge to something approaching the shape of a shielded horn, so that there is

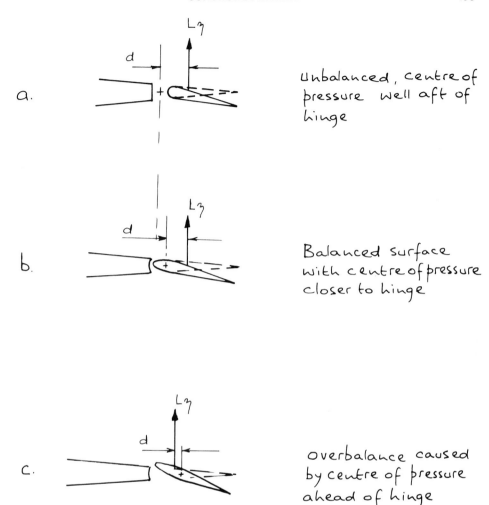

a. Unbalanced, centre of pressure well aft of hinge

b. Balanced surface with centre of pressure closer to hinge

c. Overbalance caused by centre of pressure ahead of hinge

Fig. 12.1   Control balance and overbalance, which affect the stick force felt by the pilot and the mathematical term b_2: a measure of the rate of change of hinge moment (felt by the pilot) and elevator deflection.

— like a Wilga

a step in the leading edge, from the fixed surface to the horn. Occasionally, we will also see the tip of the elevator on one side of the aeroplane has been cut off square, while the one on the other side remains curved. In this case too the total area moment of the horn surfaces has been too powerful when influenced by the asymmetric effects of propwash, power ON, and has been reduced by chopping off one of them.

Overhanging balance (or set-back hinge)

This is another way of increasing the area moment of surface ahead of the hinge, relative to that behind. In this case the hinge line is set back from the leading edge of the flap, allowing the control leading edge to emerge into the airstream when deflected.

If the control is unshrouded, blunting the leading edge lightens the control by causing a suction around the radius ahead of the hinge. Sharpening the leading edge heavies the control by reducing the suction ahead of the hinge when the surface is

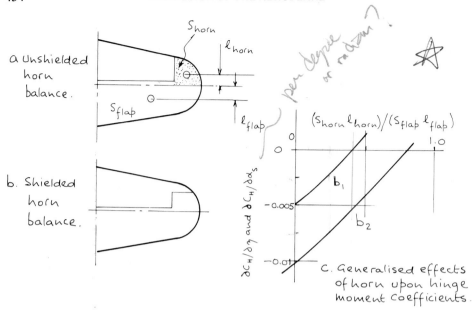

Fig. 12.2   The horn balance.

deflected, increasing the local static pressure. Thus, efficiency of overhang depends upon the secondary effect of altering pressure distributions on the leading edge extension.

Various leading edge profiles have been investigated, and it is not for us to consider them here. Suffice it to say that when the angle of attack of a surface is changed, the differential pressure between the upper and lower surface causes flow to leak through the gap ahead of the control leading edge, and this can have a powerful influence upon control characteristics. Fig. 12.3 shows the generalised effect of a simple rounded overhang.

If the control gap is sealed, the control is heavied by causing the centre of pressure to move aft, making b_1 and b_2 more negative, improving lift slope. Sealing also increases the lift slopes a_1 and a_2 and, therefore, the efficiency of the control.

Internally balanced (sealed) control

Fig. 12.4 shows a newer kind of aerodynamic balance, called an *internal* balance, which is usually sealed, but which may have no sealing. The overhang is contained within the profile of the control surface shrouds. Each side of the seal is vented to atmosphere at the shroud trailing edges.

With this type of control more balance is required for a given b_2 than on an unsealed blunt-nosed control, but less than on an unsealed control with sharp-edged overhang. Removal of the seal heavies the control by moving the centre of pressure aft. Control deflection alters the external pressures affecting the overhang, and accounts for the marked effect on b_2. The internal balance works well at high speed, but b_1 and b_2 are sensitive to changes of Mach number.

Frise balance (Leslie George Frise, British aircraft designer (1895–1979))

The Frise balance is a specialised type evolved for ailerons. It is characterised by an unsymmetrical nose profile, which protrudes below the wing contour when the aileron

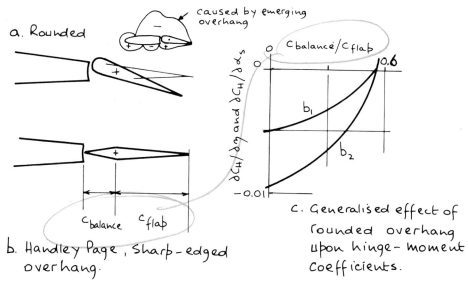

a. Rounded

caused by emerging
overhang

$C_{balance}/C_{flap}$

b_1

b_2

$\partial C_H/\partial \eta$ and $\partial C_H/\partial \alpha_s$

-0.01

$c$balance $c$flap

b. Handley Page, Sharp-edged
overhang.

c. Generalised effect of
rounded overhang
upon hinge-moment
coefficients.

Fig. 12.3   Overhanging balance (or set-back hinge).

is deflected upwards. Its main purpose is to minimise adverse yaw caused by aileron drag (*see* chapter 13). At small angles of deflection the upgoing aileron is overbalanced, and this helps to deflect the downgoing aileron on the other side. Fig. 12.5 shows the effect.

The net balance of a pair of Frise ailerons is a function of the neutral riggins position of the controls. Consequently, careful rigging is needed for good balance. Changes in rigging produce the following:

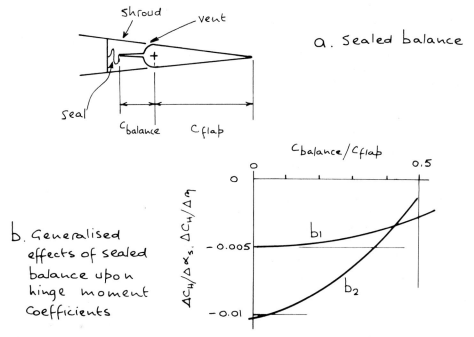

shroud   vent

a. Sealed balance

seal

$C_{balance}$ C_{flap}

$C_{balance}/C_{flap}$

0.5

b_1

b_2

$\Delta C_H/\Delta \alpha_s, \Delta C_H/\Delta \eta$

-0.005

-0.01

b. Generalised
effects of sealed
balance upon
hinge moment
Coefficients

Fig. 12.4   Sealed internal (*Westland–Irving*) balance.

☐ Rigged up from neutral: overbalance for small deflections.
☐ Rigged down from neutral: heavy forces for small deflections.

The advantages of Frise ailerons are a large balance effect with a small set-back hinge; and they are relatively easy to construct. Disadvantages are: sensitivity to rigging; tendency to flow separation from the nose of the upgoing aileron, causing buffet and loss of effectiveness; aileron upfloat at high speed can cause overbalance; and there is a tendency to overbalance caused by aeroelastic distortion, which can lead to snatching (see under Handling terms in chapter 2).

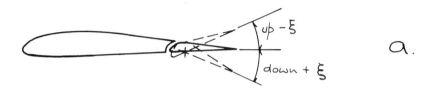

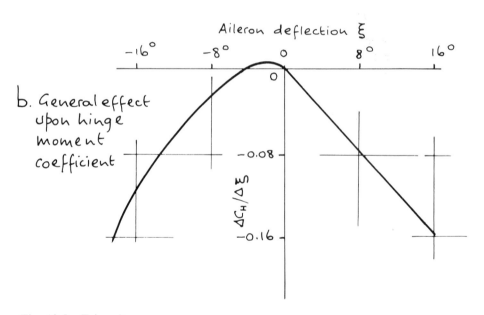

Fig. 12.5   Frise aileron.

Balance by contouring control surfaces

Conditions at the trailing edge of controls have large effects upon hinge moments, due to the influence of the trailing edge upon circulation. Sections with large trailing edge angles have hinge moments which are sensitive to conditions in the boundary layer (i.e. transition points, interference, separation, shock waves). As trailing edge angle is increased, the change of hinge moment with control deflection ceases to be a straight line. Trailing edge angles larger than 16 deg should be avoided.

Control surfaces tend to be flat in their runs to the trailing edge (fig. 12.6a). A bulged (convex) control gives lightness for small angles of deflection, and heaviness with

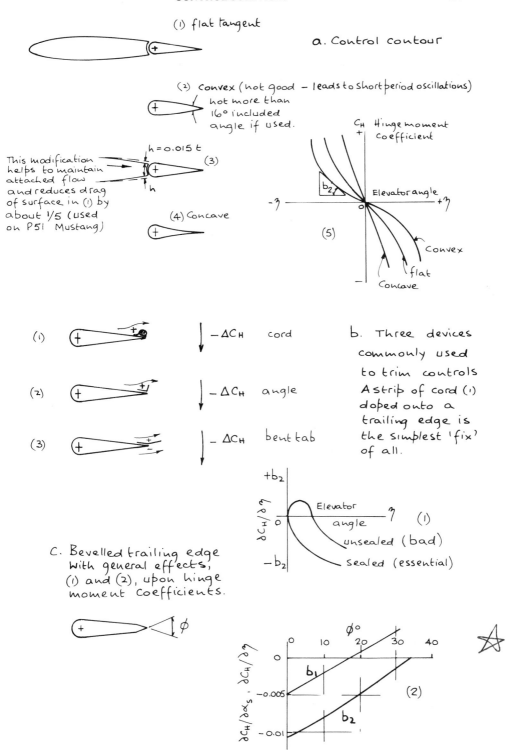

Fig. 12.6   Tricks for modifying control feel characteristics.

increasing deflection. Convex control surfaces are sensitive to changes in boundary layer thickness, which have little effect upon thin, or concave control surfaces. They are also susceptible to short-period oscillations. A concave surface heavies a control. Small trailing edge modifications produce large effects. Commonest and simplest is the old-fashioned addition of a length of cord (fig. 12.6b), or a short length of angle, or a strip of bent tab. If cord or angle is added to one side only at the trailing edge it 'pushes' the trailing edge in opposition (i.e. away from the cord or angle) increasing b_1 and b_2 negatively in the ratio:

$$b_1/b_2 = 0.7 \qquad\qquad (12–6)$$

Since it is the last 20 per cent or so of the chord of a control surface which has the greatest effect upon hinge moment, the shape of the trailing edge, and modifications to is, can be powerful and out of proportion to thei apparent size.

Short pieces of cord or angle added to the trailing edges on both sides are useful for heavying ailerons and rudders, and also prevent rudder snaking. Be careful with elevators though, because such modifications can have adverse effects upon stick-free stability.

A bevelled trailing edge has the effect of increasing the trailing edge angle. It is a powerful, tricky device, which lightens the control by making b_1 and b_2 less negative. When the *Spitfire* changed from fabric covered ailerons to sheet metal surfaces, riveted at the trailing edges, the effect was to exchange a rounded edge (which would not cut fabric) to one that was bevelled as far as the air was concerned. This changed control characteristics enough to affect repeatability of flight test results.

One must also be careful with bevelled trailing edges and friction in control circuits (a fault of *many* modern light aeroplanes, both commercial and amateur-built – due to over-simple and often crude hinges more often than not, constructional techniques, and materials employed). Friction can introduce the effect of a positive control force over a small angle of deflection (it is the origin of control break-out force) but, as the control moves the force lightens and there may even be overbalance as the pilot deflects the control still further.

Small dissimilarities between the bevel on one side and that on the other can cause marked asymmetry of balance. Controls with bevelled trailing edges must be sealed, otherwise there is a danger of overbalance with small deflections. An increase in the included angle of bevel, ϕ, lightens the control as shown in fig. 12.6c.

Control surface drag reduction

Control gaps cause drag and this can be reduced by contouring as shown in fig. 12.6a(3). The control may be bulged above the skin line of the basic section, or the thickness of the fixed surface ahead of the control may be reduced by the same amount. Either way, bulging the control by about 15 per cent of section thickness on each side causes a separating flow to re-attach, because the air is forced to accelerate over a hump. Drag is reduced by about 1/5 locally so that it is not much higher than that of the basic profile with no control surface and gap. Examples are to be found on the *North American P51–D* and *Westland Lysander*.

Tabs

All of the devices shown so far for balancing controls have the disadvantage that the

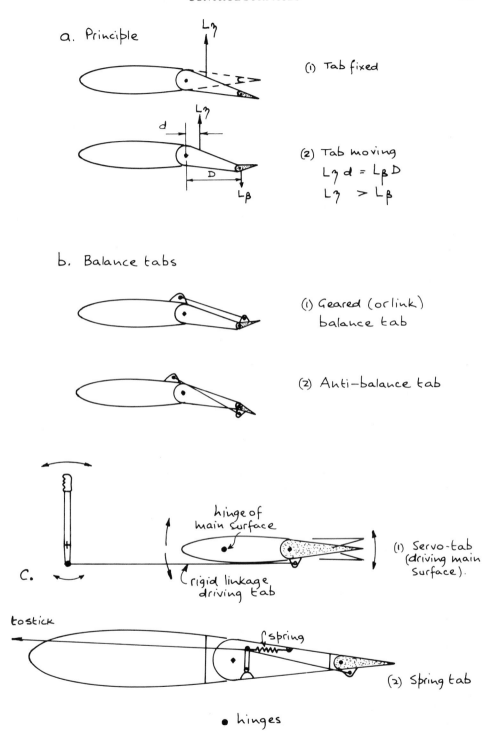

a. Principle

(1) Tab fixed

(2) Tab moving
$$L\eta\, d = L_\beta D$$
$$L\eta > L_\beta$$

b. Balance tabs

(1) Geared (or link) balance tab

(2) Anti-balance tab

hinge of main surface

rigid linkage driving tab

(1) Servo-tab (driving main surface).

to stick

spring

(2) Spring tab

• hinges

Fig. 12.7   Control tabs.

pilot's control forces vary as the square of the airspeed. For aircraft with a wide speed range, this means either putting up with high forces at high speed, or balancing the controls very closely. If the latter, the control will be light and sloppy at low speeds, with dangers of overbalance.

Trailing edge tabs can be used in various ways of defeat the (speed)^2 law. Basically, they are most commonly and easily used as variable trimming devices, operated by wheel or lever directly from the cockpit. They work as shown in fig. 12.7a, in which the hinge moment exerted by the tab when deflected just belances the hinge moment of the control:

$$L_\eta d = L_\beta D \qquad\qquad (12\text{–}7)$$

The terms L_η and L_β used here will be recognised as $a_2\Delta\eta$ and $a_3\Delta\beta$ which appeared in eqs (11–20) and (11–21).

Geared balance tabs

The geared balance tab is sometimes called a link tab, and this is geared to the control surface in such a way that it moves in a given ratio to the control surface movement. The ratio is usually expressed as $m_t = \Delta\beta / \Delta\eta$. The general effect is to change the value of b_2 without affecting b_1. When the tab moves in the opposite direction to the control surface it is called a balance (or lagging) tab, which lightens the hinge moments and stick forces. If the tab moves in the same direction as the surface, it is called an anti-balance (or leading) tab, which increases them. These tabs are shown in fig. 12.7b. An anti-balance tab is often used to increase an initially low stick-force per g.

Servo and spring tabs

A *servo control* is one in which the stick is connected directly to the tab, which is hinged to the control surface (fig. 12.7c). Operation of the tab by the pilot deflects the control surface. The extent of the deflection of the main control for a given tab angle depends upon the relative effectiveness of the tab and the main surface.

Such control systems are applied to larger aircraft, in which the stick forces in a normal control system may be excessive. Problems with servo tabs are:

☐ Effectiveness at low speed, to ensure accurate control during take-off and landing.
☐ Effectiveness at the stall.
☐ Avoiding tab damage caused by the main control hitting the stops when taxying and in flight.
☐ Prevention of flutter.

A *spring tab* is a variable servo tab, in that a spring is incorporated in the tab circuit. This enables the (speed)^2 law to be defeated, while giving a high degree of balance, without fear of overbalance. It consists of a tab geared to the stick force: the higher the force the greater the tab deflection and, consequently, its hinge moment contribution. The spring changes the tab gearing with airspeed. As drawn the linkage to the stick deflects the tab and the spring in proportion to the applied stick force. The net result is that the input force is less than it would be with a rigid crank and no tab. Spring tabs should be avoided in elevator circuits, but are suitable for ailerons.

Defeating aeroelastic effects

Structural members have torsional and flexural axes, along which they twist and bend respectively, as shown in fig. 12.8. Both axes tend to be close to one another, but their juxtaposition can be critical. To avoid complication, we shall talk in terms of one elastic axis. The amount of material comprising the structure is there to provide strength and stiffness. Small aircraft are usually both strong and stiff. But a larger aircraft, while being strong enough, tends to become floppy (unless a designer is

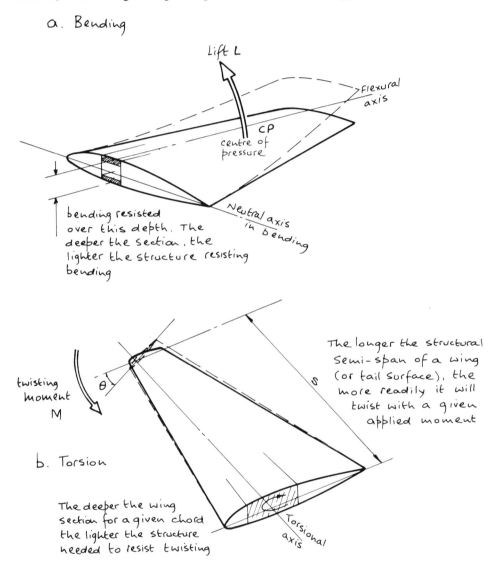

a. Bending

Lift L

Flexural axis

CP
centre of pressure

bending resisted over this depth. The deeper the section, the lighter the structure resisting bending

Neutral axis in bending

twisting moment M

θ

S

The longer the structural semi-span of a wing (or tail surface), the more readily it will twist with a given applied moment

b. Torsion

The deeper the wing section for a given chord the lighter the structure needed to resist twisting

Torsional axis

Note: If the flexural axis of a surface is ahead (upwind) of the CP (see(a)), the arrangement is anti-flutter; whereas a flexural axis behind the CP is pro-flutter, in that the combination does not provide flutter-resistance.

Fig. 12.8 The interaction between bending (flexure), torsion and structural properties.

prepared to add dead weight of material to stiffen it). Bending and torsion caused aerodynamically, together with accompanying side effects upon control and stability, fall under the heading of aeroelasticity. They can lead to flutter, fatigue and structural failure.

Aileron reversal (within the operating speed of the aircraft)

Lack of torsional rigidity in a wing can result in the aileron twisting the wing, instead of the wing remaining rigid, so that the aileron can do its job. For example, upward deflection of the aileron twists the wing leading edge up, increasing the angle of attack, and this in turn increases the wing lift instead of decreasing it as intended by the aileron. If the torsional axis of the wing is behind the centre of pressure, an increase of lift causes the **CP** to move forward, making matters worse.

There is a critical divergence speed at which lift builds up faster than the opposing torsional rection. Twist continues until the wing breaks off. Long before that happens, lift generated by the wing could have overcome the effect of the aileron, causing roll in the opposite direction. This is the state of aileron reversal.

Aileron reversal can be avoided by making the wing so stiff that the divergence speed is faster than 1.2 V_D at least. Or, the wing may be designed so that the torsional axis is ahead of the centre of pressure at all times.

Flutter

Flutter is a high frequency oscillation of the aerofoil surfaces caused by a struggle between the aerodynamic forces and the stiffness of the surface. It is dynamic, arising from a wing, tailplane or fin being relatively free in bending and torsion.

Inertia and trail characteristics of control surfaces can modify the overall aerodynamic state, so that the initial disturbance is increased, or the tendency to overshoot the original condition is increased. This can lead to cyclic fluttering of the structure which, if it does subside, can be catastrophic – or it may severely reduce airframe life.

High aspect ratio surfaces are more flutter prone than those with low aspect ratio.

There are three kinds of flutter:

☐ torsional-flexural flutter;
☐ torsional aileron flutter;
☐ flexural aileron flutter.

The first, *torsional-flexural flutter*, is shown in fig. 12.9a, in which there are three kinds of forces: aerodynamic L, acting through the aerodynamic centre; structural resistance, R, acting along the flexural axis; and inertia, $m_w a$ (due to the mass and acceleration of the displaced wing) acting through the **CG** of the wing. If the wing is given an upward impulse, due to a gust, say, and the centre of gravity of the wing as drawn is aft of the elastic axis, the wing pitches nose up, increasing the lift. Structural resistance builds up and slows the wing, reducing the acceleration, so that when the displacement reaches maximum amplitude, $m_w a$ is zero, and the lift returns to its undisturbed value. At this point, (3), structural resistance is a maximum and accelerates the wing back the opposite way. The inertia of the wing now acts upwards, pitching the section nose down, reducing the lift, causing the wing to bend downwards. As soon as it passes the undisturbed position (shown with a broken line), structural resistance builds up the other way, slowing the motion, until the wing reaches maximum amplitude downwards, (6). At this point the lift returns to its undisturbed value, $m_w a = 0$, and the wing begins to spring back again due to R. This starts the process all over again, and the wing is seen pitching nose up in (7).

Thus torsional-flexural flutter is akin to divergence and occurs at a critical speed determined by the rigidity of the wing. It can be prevented by mass balancing (one reason for hanging podded engines out in front of a swept wing) which, simply but rather inaccurately, is a way of bringing the **CG** of the wing forwards, so as to coincide

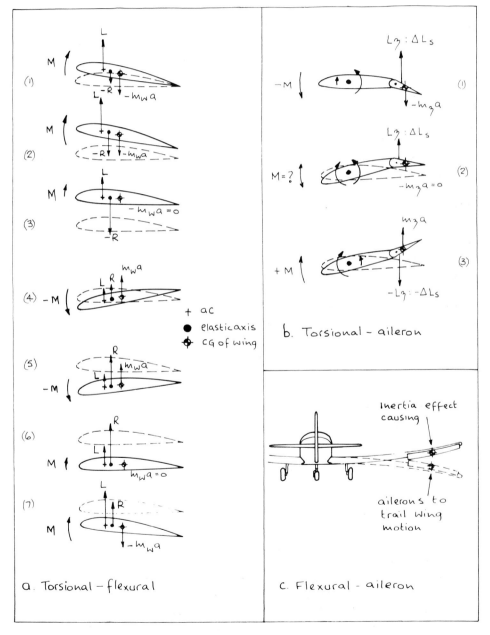

Fig. 12.9   Flutter and control surface profiles which affect flutter characteristics.

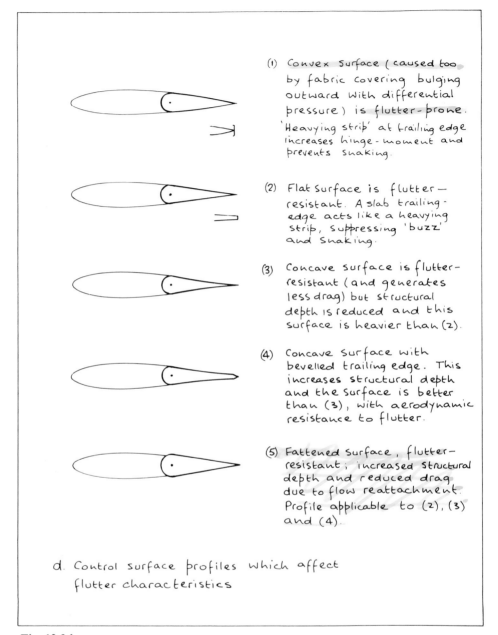

(1) Convex surface (caused too by fabric covering bulging outward with differential pressure) is flutter-prone. 'Heavying strip' at trailing edge increases hinge-moment and prevents snaking.

(2) Flat surface is flutter-resistant. A slab trailing-edge acts like a heavying strip, suppressing 'buzz' and snaking.

(3) Concave surface is flutter-resistant (and generates less drag) but structural depth is reduced and this surface is heavier than (2).

(4) Concave surface with bevelled trailing edge. This increases structural depth and the surface is better than (3), with aerodynamic resistance to flutter.

(5) Fattened surface, flutter-resistant; increased structural depth and reduced drag due to flow reattachment. Profile applicable to (2), (3) and (4).

d. Control surface profiles which affect flutter characteristics

Fig. 12.9d.

with the elastic axis. Alternatively, wing stiffness can be increased until the critical speed is higher than the maximum permissible speed of the aircraft (i.e. at least 1.25 V_D). As we saw earlier, this adds weight and reduces disposable load.

The second, *torsional aileron flutter*, is shown for the first half-cycle in fig. 12.9b. This time the three elements contributing to the motion are aileron lift L_η, aileron inertia, $m_\eta a$, and the hinge. This kind of flutter has a number of features in common with aileron reversal. Torsional aileron flutter can be prevented by mass balancing to bring the aileron **CG** on to, or slightly ahead of, the hinge – or by making the aileron control irreversible. Of the two methods, mass balancing is often the lightest solution.

The third, *flexural aileron flutter*, is shown in fig. 12.9c. It is generally similar to torsional aileron flutter, but is caused by the inertia of the aileron lagging behind the cyclic rise and fall of the wing as it flexes. This tends to increase the oscillations, because lift due to aileron deflection boosts wing bending. This type of flutter is prevented by mass balancing the aileron.

The position of the mass balance weight is important: the nearer the wing tip the greater the acceleration, so that for a given $m_\eta a$ the balance weight can be made smaller and less penalising. However, on many aircraft the balance weight may be distributed along the leading edge and within the profile of the ailerons, so that concentration of the mass at one point does not start torsional flutter of the ailerons themselves.

Although we have talked about flutter in terms of wing and aileron combinations, the same strictures and rules apply to rudders and elevators. Mass balancing of elevators and rudders is also needed if their inertia, and springiness of the fuselage in bending and torsion, is to be prevented from making them flutter too.

Mass balancing

Imagine a control surface hinged to a wing, tailplane, or fin, being accelerated in a direction perpendicular to its plane – and that it is in a vacuum (so that there are no aerodynamic forces to consider). If the **CG** of the control surface does not coincide with its hinge axis, inertia will cause it to deflect, and a hinge moment would be needed to hold the control fixed preventing what is happening in fig. 12.9c.

If, however, a counterbalancing mass were to be set ahead of the control we could reduce the hinge moment to zero. The condition for mass balance would be, then:

$$\Sigma x \Delta m = 0 \qquad (12\text{--}8)$$

for accelerations in the pitching and rolling planes. Here, x is measured from the hinge line, parallel with the surface, and the sum covers every element of mass, Δ_m, for the whole. If the control is deflected as shown in fig. 12.10, then it should also balance for accelerations along the flight path:

$$\Sigma z \Delta m = 0 \qquad (12\text{--}9)$$

where z is measured normal to the plane of the surface (i.e. more or less normal to the flight path in the case of ailerons and elevators (*see* table 2–7)). Both equations must be satisfied for complete static balance.

Precisely the same considerations apply to tabs.

For mass balancing of ailerons another condition is involved:

$$\Sigma x y \Delta m = 0 \text{ or is } -ve \qquad (12\text{--}10)$$

In addition to x having the same definition as in eq (12–8), y is the distance of the element of mass perpendicular to the axis of symmetry of the aeroplane. When ailerons have little or no forward aerodynamic balance, at least 10 per cent mass overbalance should be provided.

For biplanes, the weight of any inter-aileron member should properly be accounted for in eq (12–10), by halving the weight and treating each half as a separate isolated mass. Each half is then considered as being fixed to the upper and lower ailerons at the points of attachment of the inter-aileron member.

Similarly, where a T-tail stabilator or elevator is operated by a push rod linkage, the rod and its members which act about the control hinge should be counted.

The disposition of non-structural loads, like fuel, engines, baggage and other stores housed in (or carried under) wings should be placed well forward. If possible the *CG* of each, or of each assembly, should lie ahead of the flexural axis. Where this cannot be accomplished, the loads should be carried as close to the wing roots as possible.

Similar considerations apply to painting control surfaces. It is sound practice to avoid painting markings on ailerons, elevators and rudders, which adds extra weight aft of the control hinges, eventually destroying the equilibrium achieved by otherwise careful mass balancing.

Weights and springs to improve stick-free stability

Many light aircraft and gliders which do not fly fast do not have mass balanced controls. The situation is that shown in fig. 12.10a, with the **CG** of the control aft of the hinge. The weight of the control, W_η in the case of an elevator, imposes a hinge moment H_{mech} due to the mechanical arrangement of the system. This alters the hinge moment of the elevator, H_η, in eq (11–11a) to $(H_{mech} + H_\eta)$, such that:

$$H = H_o + H_{mech} + H_\alpha + H_\eta + H_\beta \qquad (12\text{–}11)$$

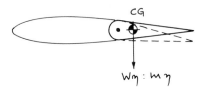

a. Unbalanced surface with centre of gravity aft of hinge (thus the weight of the surface acts as a bob-weight, which applies a moment proportional to normal acceleration. Bob-weights are used to increase static margins stick-free, increasing too stick-force per applied g).

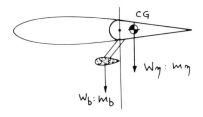

b. Mass balanced control.

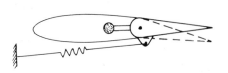

c. Mass balanced control with elevator down-spring. The latter is used to increase stick-free stability.

Fig. 12.10   Mass balancing and improvement of stick-free stability: the use of weight and spring.

in which we can ignore the effect of H_o. When H_{mech} acts in an elevator-down sense as shown, it increases the static margin, stick-free. The equation can be changed into the form of a hinge moment coefficient, dividing by $q_o S_\eta \bar{c}_\eta$, in which $q_o = W/SC_L$, so that:

$$C_{Hmech} = (H_{mech}/W\bar{c}_\eta)(S/S_\eta)C_L = \kappa \; C_L \tag{12-12}$$

and the hinge moment coefficient from eq (11-11b) becomes:

$$C_H = \kappa \; C_L + b_1\alpha_s + b_2\eta + b_3\beta \tag{12-13}$$

This additional term is carried through all subsequent equations making:

$$\eta = -(\kappa C_L + b_1\alpha_s + b_3\beta)/b_2 \tag{12-14}$$

It also changes eq (11-27) into:

$$K'_n + \Delta(K'_n)_\kappa = (h_o - h) + \eta_s \bar{V}_s(a_1/a)(1 - d\epsilon/d\alpha) - \kappa(a_2/b_2)) \tag{12-15}$$

such that:
$$\Delta(K'_n)\kappa = -\eta_s\bar{V}_s\kappa(a_2/b_2) \tag{12-15a}$$

and $\bar{a}_1$, we remember, $= a_1(1 - a_2 b_1/a_1b_2)$.

Similarly, the neutral point stick-free changes by the same amount, i.e., to $h'_n + \Delta(h'_n)_\kappa$ where:

$$\Delta(h'_n)\kappa = -\eta_s\bar{V}_{s\kappa} \; (a_2/b_2) \tag{12-15b}$$

The mechanical factor also changes the response factor equation, eq (12-4), to:

$$K + \Delta K = 1 + (b_1\Delta\alpha_s)/(\kappa C_L + b_2\Delta\eta)$$
$$= 1 + (b_1\Delta\alpha_s/b_2\Delta\eta)[1 + 1/(\kappa C_L - 1)]$$

in which:
$$\Delta K = (b_1\Delta\alpha_s/b_2\Delta\eta)[1/\kappa C_L - 1)] \tag{12-16}$$

Exactly the same effect can be produced with a mechanical spring, like that shown in fig. 12.10c where, in this case, the control is mass balanced. The magnitude of the mechanical moment, $H_{mech,}$ can be calculated for the spring rate and the deflection.

Since, in general, a_2 is positive and b_2 is negative, $-\kappa(a_2/b_2)$ has the same sign as κ. Hence, a positive value of H_{mech} (elevator down) increases the static margin stick-free, moving the neutral point aft by the amount $\Delta h'_n$ given in eq (12-15b). While a negative H_{mech} (elevator up) moves the neutral point forwards.

Although the effect of a given mechanical moment on the stick-free static margin is the same, regardless of whether it is produced by a bob-weight or a spring, the effect on the stick force per g is influenced by the way in which the moment is applied. Nevertheless, both methods represent a means of artificially increasing stick-free stability by adjusting control characteristics, without altering the overall aerodynamics and layout of the aeroplane.

Use of a stabilator to improve stick-free stability

The all-moving tail, or stabilator, is a useful device for altering the stick-free neutral point within very wide limits. It can also be used to alter the stick-force to change speed.

In fig. 12.11 we have a symmetrical section stabilator and geared tab replacing the conventional combination of tailplane, elevator and tab. Assuming the stabilator to be supported at its aerodynamic centre, the moment coefficient about the pivot is due to the tab alone, such that:

$$C_{Ms} = C_{Mac} = b_3\beta \tag{12-17}$$

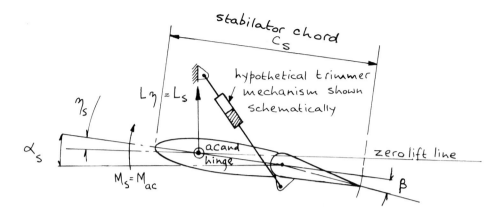

a. Stabilator hinged at the aerodynamic centre
of the surface. The hypothetical (as drawn)
trimmer would look too complicated to include
here. It exists to enable the pilot to set the
tab to an angle β_0, which is the datum
setting for trimming purposes.

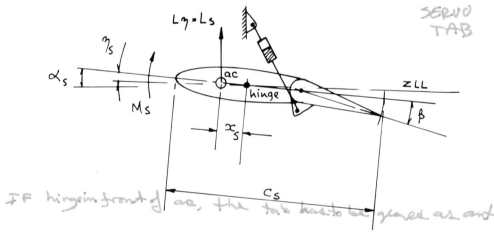

IF hinge in front of ac, the tab has to be geared as anti servo

b. Here we have the same stabilator with the
hinge arranged so that the surface pivots
about a point x_s behind the aerodynamic
centre. The larger this displacement, the
more stable the aeroplane with stick free,
ie, 'hands-off'. With the hinge forward of
the ac, stick-free stability is reduced.

if tab geared
properly

Fig. 12.11   The all-moving tail, or stabilator, which the French also call 'monobloc'.

If the tab gearing is defined by $m_t = \Delta\beta/\Delta\eta_s$, then we can say that the tab angle:

$$\beta = \beta_o + m_t\eta_s \qquad (12\text{--}18)$$

where β_o is the datum setting of the tab for trimming purposes, and m_t is a positive gear ratio. If the stick is released $C_{Mac} = 0$ and the angle of the stabilator becomes:

$$\eta_s = -\beta_o/m_t \qquad (12\text{--}19)$$

Under these conditions the stick-fixed and free neutral points coincide.

If we now mount the stabilator with the pivot aft of the aerodynamic centre by an amount x_s, the hinge moment increases to:

$$C_{Ms} = C_{Mac} + C_{Ls}(x_s/c_s) \qquad (12\text{--}20)$$

in which the lift coefficient of the stabilator, C_{Ls}, changes from the form:

$$C_{Ls} = a_1\alpha_s = a_1\eta_s \qquad \text{(e.g. see form of eq (11--12))}$$

to:
$$C_{Ls} = a_1\eta_s + a_3\beta \qquad (12\text{--}21)$$

In short, the stability is increased stick-free. Conversely, pivoting the stabilator ahead of its aerodynamic centre reduces stick-free stability. In the limiting case with the pivot aft of the **ac** it may be shown that the stick-free neutral point approaches the aerodynamic centre of the basic symmetrical stabilator.

It is not our purpose to examine refinements of this kind, but ref. 11.2 is a valuable source for those who wish to read further.

Thus, for a given tail volume, $\overline{V}_s$, and stabilator lift slope, a_1, variation of tab size and gear ratio, coupled with the position of the stabilator pivot, the stick-free neutral point can be varied almost at will, to lie anywhere between h_o and $(h_o + l_s/c_s)$. Throughout all of this the stick-fixed neutral point remains unchanged.

Control surface travel

The angles through which control surfaces are deflected should be neither too large, making them stall-prone through flow separation, nor too small – which makes them ineffective with not enough 'bite'.

Elevators often have equal travel, but some have more up than down. Typically:

$$\eta = \pm 25 \text{ deg}$$

but,
$$\rhd \pm 30 \text{ deg} \qquad (12\text{--}22)$$

Ailerons often have differential movement with more up than down, to reduce aileron drag:

$$\xi \text{ up} = 15 \text{ to } 20 \text{ deg}$$
$$\text{down} = 10 \text{ to } 15 \text{ deg} \qquad (12\text{--}23)$$

Rudders have lower aspect ratios, so as to cope with large angles of sideslip, and they have more angular movement than elevators and ailerons:

$$\zeta = \pm 30 \text{ deg} \qquad (12\text{--}24)$$

Crosswind handling

The combination of aileron and rudder authority, which depends in no small measure upon travel, affects handling in crosswinds. Rough practical estimates of crosswind speeds for which light aeroplanes should be designed to cope are given in table 12–2:

TABLE 12–2

Crosswind Limitation

Configuration	Crosswind minimum (as fraction of approach speed V_{app})
Nosewheel, low wing high wing Tailwheel, low wing biplane	$\approx \frac{1}{4}$ $\approx \frac{1}{6}$

Spoilers

We are mainly concerned with flap-like control surfaces, the deflection of which increases aerodynamic forces and moments. Spoilers are sometimes used as aileron-substitutes, for roll control, especially when torsional aero-elasticity is critical. Spoilers kill lift locally and increase drag, so that their effect can be favourable in roll and yaw, as well as torsion.

The disadvantage of spoilers is that they degrade lift, an important consideration at low speeds. Some types have caused negative control response for small deflections when used with flap down (ref. 12.3). As a broad generalisation, they are most effective roll controls at high speeds; and they make useful lift-dumpers to achieve maximum effect of wheel brakes on touchdown. Sailplanes and gliders employ spoilers to steepen angles of glide by direct increase in drag and reduction of lift/drag ratio.

Location of ailerons

An aileron should be located along the wing span in the region where the spanwise lift distribution is largest, i.e., about ⅔ to ¾ out from the plane of symmetry of the aeroplane. There they have the greatest effect for their size and weight. Putting this the other way, it results in the smallest, lightest and most economical aileron surfaces. But, as we have noted elsewhere, if a large part of the trailing edge is occupied by powerful flaps, then the ailerons may have to be run outboard, even as far as the wing tips (*see* fig. 15.9).

The same principle applies with biplanes. If the ailerons are not required on both sets of planes, then they should be located on the plane which bears the greatest aerodynamic load. Thus, with forward (positive) stagger, the top wing makes a greater contribution to the lift than the bottom wing, so that the ailerons might be more economically effective when mounted on the top wing. Much depends upon interference between the planes, and upon other mechanical and geometric considerations. Thus, because ailerons are mounted on the bottom wing only, it does not mean that the designer made a wrong decision.

By the same token, when a biplane has negative (back)stagger then, the bottom wing might carry the largest load and, on balance, the ailerons should be located on the bottom plane. Even so, there may be other constraints to consider and this too might not be a hard and fast rule.

References

12.1 Morgan, M. B. and Thomas, H. H. B. M. (Aug. 1945) 'Control Surface Design in Theory and Practice'. *Journal of the Royal Aeronautical Society*.

12.2 BCAR, Section K4–8. *Control System Loads and Design*. Civil Aviation Authority.

12.3 Wentz Jr. W. H. (May 1975) NASA CR–2538. *Effectiveness of Spoilers on the GA(W)–1 Airfoil with a High Performance Fowler Flap*. National Aeronautics and Space Administration, Washington.

CHAPTER 13

Lateral and Directional Stability and Spinning

'With the machine moving forwards, the air flying backwards, the propellers turning sideways, and nothing standing still, it seemed impossible to find a starting point from which to trace the various simultaneous reactions. Contemplation of it was confusing. After long arguments we often found ourselves in the ludicrous position of each having been converted to the other's side, with no more agreement than when the discussion began.'
The Wright Brothers, The Century Magazine (September 1908)
(from 'Simple bicycle-makers', Philip Jarrett, *Flight International*, 13 December 1973).

'Most aeroplanes start life with insufficient fin and rudder area.'
'Tommy' Campbell
while teaching design. *Blackburn Aircraft Ltd, Brough, E. Yorks 1945.*

We lump lateral and directional stability together because they are interdependent. For example, imagine an aeroplane flying straight and level, and the pilot applies a touch of aileron to the right. Moving the control to the right puts the left aileron down and the right up. Initially this increases the lift and drag of the left wing, while decreasing lift and drag of the right. This causes the machine to roll right and yaw left, so that the left wing slows down and the right wing speeds up in the plane of the wings. But as the aircraft begins to roll right, the lift vector is inclined to the right, and the aeroplane begins to sideslip in that direction. This causes the relative wind to come from the right, to affect the fuselage, fin and rudder surfaces (and all other side areas).

If the aeroplane has been properly designed, the centre of lateral area will lie behind the centre of gravity, so that there is a 'weathercock' effect, turning the nose of the machine into the relative wind, reducing the sideslip and angle of yaw. At the same time the dihedral effect of the wing, tail and other surfaces should come into play, in an attempt to roll the aircraft level again.

Note that the pilot has moved only one control, the aileron, but this action has generated a complex set of forces and moments. The response of the aeroplane has been dynamic, not static, as in the case of static longitudinal stability. In all of the motions we can detect two paramount effects: one in roll; the other in yaw. The complexity of behaviour in yaw and roll may be simplified by an elegant method of analysis.

Lateral derivatives

Table 2–7 shows the conventional notation used for analysing the problem. To do this

TABLE 13–1

Lateral Derivatives

Moment or force (Effect) \ Derivatives caused by (Cause)	Control displacement: Aileron ξ	Control displacement: Rudder ζ	Angular velocities: Roll rate p	Angular velocities: Yaw rate r	Sideslip velocity v	Weight* W
Rolling moment L	**$L\xi$**	$L\zeta$	L_p	L_r	L_v	0
Yawing moment N	$N\xi$	**$N\zeta$**	N_p	N_r	N_v	0
Side force Y	$Y\xi$ (negligible)	$Y\zeta$	Y_p (negligible)	Y_r	Y_v	$W \sin \phi$*

* Weight and its effect, due to angle of bank ϕ has been added for completeness, even though $W \sin \phi$ is not a derivative.

□ Primary effects of aileron and rudder controls.

we resort to force and moment coefficients, in the same way as for longitudinal stability, so that if L is the rolling moment about the OX axis, l is the rolling moment coefficient. Note the convention that motions about axes obey the right-hand corkscrew rule when looking in the $+X$, $+Y$ and $+Z$ directions from the origin, O. But, control surface deflections are positive when opposing the positive roll, pitch and yawing motions.

We can now break down the motions according to their causes, as shown in table 13–1. Along the top we list the cause, while down the side we have effect. These are called aerodynamic derivatives (more precisely lateral aero-dynamic derivatives).

To see how it works, look back to our description of a pilot moving aileron alone. The yaw which followed was caused by aileron drag, and this was followed by sideslip velocity (relative airflow from the right). Therefore, splitting yaw in precisely that way, by looking at an effect in terms of its cause, we have:

☐ *Rate of change of yawing moment per unit aileron deflection:*

$$\delta N/\delta \xi = N\xi, \text{ for the moment derivative}$$
$$= n_\xi, \text{ for its coefficient.}$$

☐ *Rate of change of yawing moment per unit sideslip velocity:*

$$\delta N/\delta v = N_v, \text{ for the moment derivative}$$
$$= n_v, \text{ for its coefficient.}$$

In order to convert the basic force and moment derivatives into non-dimensional coefficients, we must divide them by the factors shown in table 13–2. For example, $n_\xi = N_\xi/\rho V^2 S(b/2)$

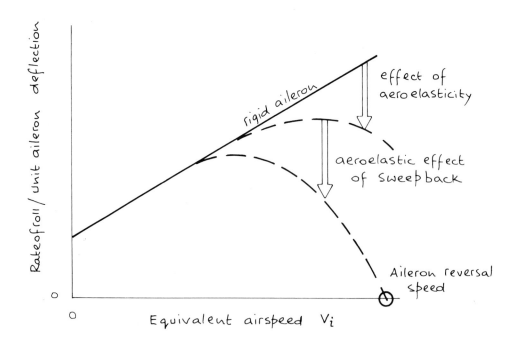

Fig. 13.1   Effect of aileron deflection on rate of roll.

TABLE 13–2

The dividing factor for converting the lateral derivatives in
Table 13–1 into non-dimensional coefficients

(handwritten: $\frac{8}{\partial \partial} S b$)

	Control Displacement $\rho V^2 S$	Angular Velocity $\frac{\rho V S b}{2}$	Sideslip $\rho V S$
Force			
Moment	$\rho V^2 S\left(\frac{b}{2}\right)$	$\rho V S\left(\frac{b}{2}\right)^2$	$\rho V S\left(\frac{b}{2}\right)$

(handwritten: $\frac{1}{2}\rho V^2$)

b = wing span   S = wing area
ρ = ambient density   V = TAS, in compatible units,
                                        e.g. ft/s

Example: the yawing moment due to rudder deflection,
$N_\zeta = \delta N/\delta\zeta$, and this is converted into a moment coefficient:

$$n_\zeta = (N_\zeta/\rho V^2 S)(2/b)$$

Although not a lateral derivative, the contribution of the weight of the aircraft to the lateral forces and moments is included in table 13–1.

Let us look at the derivatives in turn (ref. 11.4 is a comprehensive):

Rolling moment due to aileron, L_ξ by convention the angle of aileron deflection, ξ, is positive with the right aileron down. The convention breaks down with spoilers: raising the right spoiler causes the aeroplane to roll to the right.

Aileron power is especially important when taking off and landing in a crosswind. This determines aileron area. Performance at high speed determines the degree of balance. A mathematical way of plotting aileron performance is by showing the helix angle obtainable for a given displacement (usually per degree, sometimes per unit aileron deflection). The angle is given by: *(handwritten: $= S_a \times (r\,S) \times Cl_a / Cl_a$)*

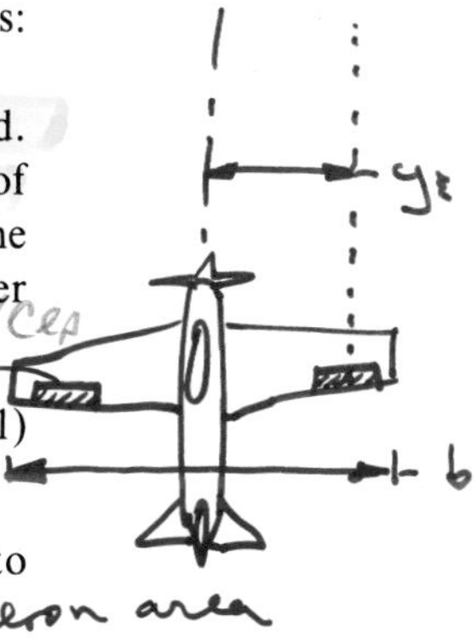

$$\text{aileron helix angle} = (pb/2V) \cdot \delta a \quad \frac{\xi_\xi}{2} \qquad (13\text{–}1)$$

where p is the rate of roll in deg/s, b is the wingspan, and V the TAS in ft/s.

Table 11–4 shows state-of-the-art values of control surface area. This enables us to introduce: *(handwritten: P9 417 values are high — total aileron area)*

$$\text{aileron volume coefficient, } V_\xi = [S_\xi y_\xi / Sb] \qquad (13\text{–}2)$$

where y_ξ is the distance of the centroid of one aileron outboard of the axis of symmetry. Values of V_ξ should not be less than 0.03 or higher than 0.044. Average values are 0.038 to 0.042.

Rolling moment due to rudder, L_ζ, is the subsidiary effect which is caused when the rudder sideforce produces a moment about the **CG** of the aircraft, fig. 13.2a. Although it is usually small enough to be neglected, it can be significant with a fin and rudder set high on top of the fuselage. In that case rudder to the left causes the aircraft to roll to the right. The value of L_ζ changes with altitude at a given true airspeed. At low altitudes an aircraft flies relatively tail-up, compared with high altitude, where the EAS is lower for a given TAS and the aeroplane, flying at a larger angle of attack, is relatively more tail-down. This means that L_ζ is most powerful at

(handwritten annotations in right margin:)
$\frac{S_\xi}{S} \approx .09$

$\frac{y_\xi}{b} \approx .41$

lancer 200
$V_\zeta = .0178$

Firecracker
$V_\zeta = .0284$

(handwritten at bottom:) Smyth Sidewinder $V_\zeta = .0234$

low altitude, when the rudder is higher above the **CG**, than at higher altitudes, where the tail rides lower.

☐ *Rolling moment due to rate of roll*, L_p, is the result of the increased angle of attack of the downgoing wing increasing the lift. This has a damping effect, which slows the rate of roll, fig. 13.2b. In rolling manoeuvres L_p usually dictates the final, steady roll rate. Its sign is –ve because it opposes the rolling motion.

$$\text{moment coefficient, } l_p = -0.2 \text{ to } -0.5 \tag{13–3}$$

☐ *Rolling moment due to rate of yaw*, L_r, is caused almost entirely by the wing during rotation of the aircraft in yaw. The outer wing travels faster than the inner, and generates more lift, fig. 13.2c. Positive yaw to the right causes positive roll to the right. The larger the angle of attack of the wing, the more powerful L_r becomes. The value of the moment coefficient:

$$l_r = \text{about } 0.25 C_L, \text{ i.e. } 0.02 \text{ to } 0.3 \tag{13–4}$$

for all aeroplanes.

☐ *Rolling moment due to sideslip*, L_v, is the important 'dihedral effect'. A straight wing with positive dihedral from root to tip, when sideslipping, experiences a geometric increase in the angle of attack of the upwind wing, fig. 13.2d. The upwind wing generates more lift than the downwind wing, so that the resulting roll is –ve (e.g., sideslip right, roll left). However, interference caused by the position of the wing on the fuselage, by locations of nacelles, undercarriage and flaps, and power, may be large enough to equal the contribution made by the wing alone.

Most straight-winged light aircraft have dihedral angles around:

$$\text{low wing: 5 deg to 7 deg (extreme)}$$
$$\text{high wing: } 2\tfrac{1}{2} \text{ deg (about } \tfrac{1}{2} \text{ low wing).} \tag{13–5}$$

When a wing is swept back there is an additional factor caused by the increase in relative airspeed over the upwind wing, fig. 13.2e. Forward sweep has the reverse effect. For this reason sweptback wings have less dihedral than straight. High performance jet aircraft, which operate at high altitude (and, thus, relatively larger angles of attack than at low altitude, because of the lower EAS for a given TAS) often have no dihedral, and even feature anhedral, to keep L_v within tolerable bounds. Too much dihedral <u>and</u> not enough weathercock stability causes an oscillatory motion called 'Dutch roll', during which the aircraft snakes along, while rolling from side to side.

$$\text{moment coefficient } l_v \text{ should be negative and not too large}$$
$$= -0.03 \text{ to } -0.2 \tag{13–6}$$

☐ *Yawing moment due to aileron*, N_ξ, is a secondary effect of aileron, caused by the increased drag of the downgoing control. Commonly called 'aileron drag', or 'adverse aileron yaw', the effect is unfavourable, because the aircraft is caused to yaw out of a turn. Frise-type ailerons, fig. 12.5, are designed to minimise aileron drag. Spoilers give a favourable N_ξ, because the wing with the spoiler out is on the inside of the turn and generates the most drag.

☐ *Yawing moment due to rudder*, N_ζ, is negative, because positive rudder deflection (left) causes negative yawing moment (nose moves to the left). If we regard the fin and rudder as an upright half tailplane and elevator, then an identical set of coefficients can be applied, such that as $a_2 = \mathrm{d}C_L/\mathrm{d}\eta$ in the case of the elevator, then

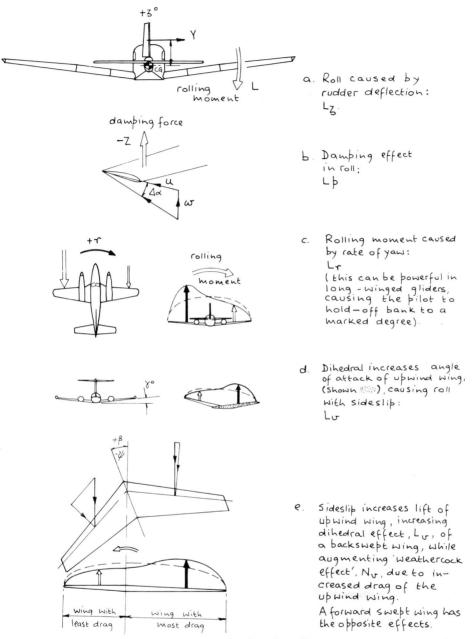

Fig. 13.2   Some less obvious lateral derivatives in roll.

the equivalent for the rudder may be written $(a_2)_\zeta = dC_L/d\zeta$. Now, as the yawing moment due to rudder deflection is N_ζ, it may be translated into its coefficient, n_ζ, on dividing through by $\rho V^2 S(b/2)$ in table 13–2, whence:

$$N_\zeta = -Y_\zeta l_f = \tfrac{1}{2}\rho V^2 S_f (a_2)_\zeta$$

and,
$$n_\zeta = -\tfrac{1}{2}(a_2)_\zeta (S_f/S)[l_f/(b/2)] = -\tfrac{1}{2}(a_2)_\zeta \overline{V}_\zeta \tag{13–7}$$

$$\overline{V}_\zeta = \left(\frac{S_f}{S}\right) \cdot \left(\frac{l_f}{b/2}\right)$$

The term $\overline{V}_\zeta$ is the 'fin-volume coefficient' based upon the semi-span, $s = b/2$, the area of fin-plus rudder, s_f, and distance l_f from the aerodynamic centre of the fin-plus-rudder to the **CG**. Some authorities prefer to state fin-volume coefficient in terms of the wingspan, b, such that:

$$n_\zeta = -\tfrac{1}{2}(a_2)_\zeta \, \overline{V}_\zeta \text{ (using } s = b/2)$$
$$= -(a_2)_\zeta \, \overline{V}_f \text{ (using } b)$$
$$= -0.02 \text{ to } -0.10 \tag{13--7a}$$

From this $\overline{V}_f = \tfrac{1}{2} \, \overline{V}_\zeta$

while, $\overline{V}_\zeta = 0.015$ to 0.06 (average 0.035) for most conventional aeroplanes.   (13--8)
The lift slope $(a_2)_\zeta \approx 3.5$ per radian (0.06 per deg) for many of the aeroplanes considered here.

☐ *Yawing moment due to rate of roll*, N_p, is shown in fig. 13.3a and is a development of the situation shown in fig. 13.2b. Both should be compared with fig. 11.3a, which showed the way in which the aerodynamic crossforce is apparently rotated forwards with increasing angle of attack, and backwards as angle of attack is reduced. The faster the rate of roll, p, the greater the induced angle of attack of the downgoing wing – so that an increasing forwards component of the crossforce pulls the wing forwards. The reverse happens to the upgoing wing. This effect is increased by increasing angle of attack. With a conventionally rounded wing leading edge positive roll causes negative yaw. If the leading edge is sharp, however, suction fails to develop and N_p is positive. The reason is that induced drag is increased on the downgoing wing and reduced on the upgoing, and this counteracts the yawing moment by acting in the opposite sense. The actual value of N_p depends, therefore, upon the outcome of a struggle between suction causing –ve yaw and induced drag increments opposing the suction by introducing components of +ve yaw.
Fin and stabiliser surfaces also make similar contributions to N_p. Typical values of the total

$$\text{moment coefficient, } n_p = +0.1 \text{ to } -0.1. \tag{13--9}$$

☐ *Yawing moment due to rate of yaw*, N_r, is commonly referred to as the 'yaw damping factor', which is always negative because it opposes yaw. The main contribution comes from the fin and rudder, which are given an additional angle of attack (like that shown in fig. 13.2b) by virtue of their swinging about the **CG** in an arc about the OZ axis. The lift generated by the increment gain in angle of attack provides the yawing moment which damps the motion.
Fuselage surfaces also contribute to yaw damping, sections with sharp corners being better than circular or oval sections. Table 13–3 shows relative damping ratios of different body cross sections at an angle of attack of 45 deg. This is an important consideration when designing an aeroplane to have safe spin characteristics.
There is a close relationship between the effect of yaw on the vertical tail surfaces, and sideslip:

$$N_r(tail) = -N_v(tail)$$
so that,
$$n_r(tail) = -n_v(tail) \tag{13--10}$$

To this must be added the body contribution, and a contribution from the wings (caused by the outer wing having greater drag than the inner wing, through travelling faster), so that:

$$\text{total moment coefficient, } n_r = n_r(tail) + n_r(body) + n_r(wing)$$
$$= -0.01 \text{ to } -0.3 \tag{13--11}$$

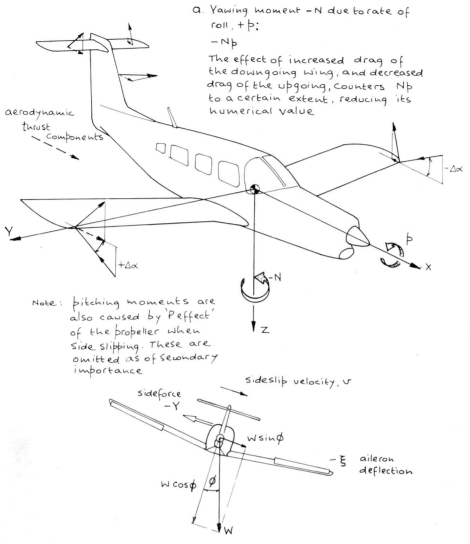

a. Yawing moment $-N$ due to rate of roll, $+p$:

$-Np$

The effect of increased drag of the downgoing wing, and decreased drag of the upgoing, counters Np to a certain extent, reducing its numerical value

aerodynamic thrust components

$-\Delta\alpha$

$+\Delta\alpha$

p

$-N$

Note: pitching moments are also caused by 'P effect' of the propeller when side slipping. These are omitted as of secondary importance

sideslip velocity, v

sideforce $-Y$

$W\sin\phi$

$-\xi$ aileron deflection

$W\cos\phi$ ϕ

W

b. Sideforce, Y, a lateral drag component, due to component of weight, $W\sin\phi$, acting in the plane of the wings, causing sideslip.

Fig. 13.3   Some lateral derivatives caused by roll and slip.

for many modern aircraft. Because of the wing contribution, yaw damping increases with angle of attack.

☐ *Yawing moment due to sideslip, N_v,* is a measure of 'weathercock stability', because it arises from the required tendency of the aircraft to point into the relative wind (N_v must be positive). Contributions from the wing, body, landing gear, tail, and any other components with side area affected by the wind, may be added in the same way as shown in eq (13–11).

The body tends to be destabilising, because its centre of lateral area lies ahead of the **CG**, more often than not. In addition there is a strong suction over the forebody and an increased static pressure aft of the wing when an aircraft is yawed. This is exacerbated by jet engine air intakes located well forward. The mass flow of air into the intake is caused to follow a curved path which introduces a sideforce and moment tending to increase the angle of yaw, making the aeroplane directionally

TABLE 13–3

Effectiveness of body cross-sections and fin and rudder disposition on damping in rotation (yaw), based upon ref. 13.1

	Body cross-section	Damping coefficient	Damping ratio at $\alpha = 45°$ $\epsilon/\epsilon_{\text{circular}}$
○	Circular	+0.6	1.0
□	Rectangular	+1.5	2.5
0	Elliptical	+2.1	3.5
⌂	Round top, flat bottom	+1.1	1.8
⌂	Round top, flat bottom + strakes	+1.7*	2.8
∪	Round bottom, flat top	+2.5	4.2
∪	Round bottom, flat top + strakes at tailplane roots	+3.5*	5.8
Fin {	Free	+1.5	Not comparable
	Under tailplane	+3.0	
	Above tailplane	–0.4	
Rudder {	Free	+1.5	Not comparable
	Under tailplane	+2.0	
	In tailplane wake	–0.25	

anti spin ↓

* Depends on width of strake. Values quoted refer to width 0.014 *l*, where *l* is distance from **CG** to the rudder post.

unstable at low speeds. An aeroplane with a propeller forward of the **CG** is destabilised directionally for the same reason as that shown for longitudinal stability in fig. 11.9b – a pusher propeller aft of the the **CG** is stabilising. These effects tend to make the body swing out of wind (in the same way as an aerofoil surface would pitch up if pivoted at a point aft of its centre of pressure). In general:

$$n_v(body) = 0 \text{ to } -0.6 \qquad (13\text{–}12)$$

Directional stability is usually provided by the fin and rudder together forming a total surface, rudder-fixed. Burt Rutan appears to have broken with this tradition with at least one version of his push-pull tail-first *Defiant*, which has the rudder surface mounted forward of the **CG** beneath the forebody. Fins are at the tips of the mainplane.

Fin surfaces are mounted aft of the **CG**, so that the lift force on the fin when sideslipping generates a moment about the **CG** which tends to reduce the slip. The tail contribution to n_v depends on the fin area and position and is given in terms of the vertical tail constants by:

$$n_v(tail) = \tfrac{1}{2}(a_1)\beta \overline{V}_\zeta = (a_1)\rho\beta \overline{V}_f = 0.02 \text{ to } 0.2 \qquad (13\text{–}13)$$

where $(a_1)_\beta = dC_L/d\beta$. The angle of attack of the fin, $\beta = \tan^{-1}(v/\overline{V})$. V_f and $\overline{V}_\zeta$ are

Plate 13-1 Design for spin recovery. (Top) British *NDN-1 Firecracker*, flown by Desmond Norman, can be a trainer or a cheap and cheerful ground attack aeroplane. It has some of the best spin recovery characteristics found by the author, even power ON, and this is mainly due to the layout of the tail, helped by the shortish wing. (*Peter J. Bish, via NDN Aircraft Ltd*). (Middle) after initial problems the *Scottish Aviation Bulldog* settled down with anti-spin leading edge strakes at the tailplane roots, and a ventral fin (*British Aerospace, Scottish Division*). (Bottom) French *Aerospatiale TB10 Tobago* with two ventral anti-spin strakes, aft of the wing trailing edge, suggest early troubles. (*James Gilbert via Air Touring Services Ltd, UK*)

recognised as the two forms of fin volume coefficient given in eq (13–7a). Lift slope is about 3.5 per radian, 0.06 per deg (depending upon fin aspect ratio, discussed at the end of this chapter). Estimates can be made from fig. 4.6c and data given in Appendix A for vertical tails.

$$\text{total moment coefficient } n_v = n_v(body) + n_v(tail)$$
$$= +0.02 \text{ to } +0.15 \qquad (13–14)$$

☐ *Sideforce due to rudder, Y_ζ,* is caused by rudder deflection producing a yawing moment about the centre of gravity. Thus, it also makes a contribution to the side forces on the aircraft, no matter how small compared with those due to sideslip, and the component of weight when banked. Positive rudder (left) causes a positive force (to the right), so that the coefficient y_ζ is positive. In terms of vertical tail constants:

$$y_\zeta = \tfrac{1}{2}(S_f/S)(a_2)_\zeta \qquad (13–15)$$

where S_f/S is as previously defined, and $(a_2)_\zeta$ is the same as in eq (13–7). It is worth mentioning that:

$$y_\zeta = \text{approximately } -n_\zeta = -(a_2)_\zeta \, V_f \qquad (13–16)$$

☐ *Sideforce due to rate of roll, Yp,* is usually insignificant, although a tall fin may produce some force, which is –ve because it resists the rate of roll.

$$\text{force coefficient } y_p \approx 0 \qquad (13–17)$$

☐ *Sideforce due to rate of yaw, Y_r,* is numerically small and often neglected. Keel surfaces aft of the **CG** make a positive contribution, while those ahead have a negative effect.

$$\text{force coefficient, } y_r \approx 0 \qquad (13–18)$$

☑ *Sideforce due to sideslip, Y_v,* is the lateral resistance of the aircraft to sideways motion. A sharp cornered fuselage generates more drag than one with a rounded section. Data in table 13–3 is relevant. The value of the coefficient:

$$\text{force coefficient, } y_v \approx -0.03 \text{ to } -0.5 \qquad (13–19)$$

☐ *Weight components.* Since all moments are measured about the centre of gravity, the weight of the aircraft has no effect upon rolling and yawing moments. But, when the aircraft is banked, the sideforce due to weight is of great significance, because it produces the lateral acceleration which gives the component of turn in the plane of the wings (fig. 13.3b), where:

$$\text{sideforce} = W \sin \phi \qquad (13–20)$$

There are no static cases in lateral and directional stability, unlike longitudinal stability. Even directional, or weathercock stability, N_v (the presence of which can be indicated by balancing a paper lamina) cannot be used for trimming in azimuth, in the way that the stabiliser can adjust and hold a desired wing angle of attack.

In general, all lateral and directional motions are dynamic. They cannot be predicted adequately without knowledge of the moments of inertia of the aircraft about each axis. But knowledge of the meaning of these lateral derivatives makes it possible to analyse any particular motion of an aircraft and to interpret its behaviour in terms of the physical design characteristics.

For example, let us look back again to the beginning of the chapter, to our description of the pilot applying a touch of aileron to the right and the subsequent motion of the aeroplane, and translate it into the language of derivatives, using table 2–7 as a guide:

... the pilot applies a touch of aileron to the right (right aileron up, $-\xi$) ... which puts the left aileron down ... Initially this increases the lift and drag of the left wing ($+Z_\xi$, $-X_\xi$), while decreasing lift and drag of the right. This causes the machine to roll right ($+L_\xi +p_\xi$) and yaw left ($-N_\xi -r_\xi$), so that the left wing slows down and the right wing speeds up in the plane of the wings. But as the aircraft begins to roll right (angle of bank ϕ), the lift vector is inclined to the right, and the aeroplane begins to sideslip in that direction (through the accelerating force, $W\sin\phi$). This causes the relative wind to come from the right (component, $-v$), to affect the fuselage, fin and rudder surfaces (and all other side areas) (causing a change in angle of attack $\beta = \tan^{-1}(v/u)$, although in this book we use V instead of u (in table 2–7), so that the right hand side becomes $\tan^{-1}(v/V)$).

If the aeroplane has been properly designed, the centre of lateral area will lie behind the centre of gravity, so that there is a 'weathercock effect' ($+N_v$) turning the nose of the machine into the relative wind, reducing the sideslip ($-v$). At the same time the dihedral effect of the wing ($-L_v$), tail and other surfaces should come into play in an attempt to roll the aircraft level again.

It will be appreciated that this translation into derivative form could have been more comprehensive. We could have mentioned L_p, L_r, N_p and the rest. Their omission in the interests of brevity only shows the power of the method.

Spiral instability

It is easy to forget that a spiral resulting from spiral instability can be very dangerous if a pilot is unable to regain control before structural limits are exceeded. The spiral dive was one of the earliest dangers encountered by aviators, and replicas of some of the oldest historic aeroplanes are as vulnerable to spiral instability today as were the originals upon which they are based.

Spiral instability is caused by an aeroplane possessing too much directional stability (N_v) and insufficient lateral stability ($-L_v$). If the machine is then upset by a gust which raises one wing, the aeroplane banks, the nose drops and a sideslip starts towards the lower wing. N_v yaws the nose into the relative wind and L_r, the rolling moment due to rate of yaw, increases the angle of bank, which increases the sideslip. If $-L_v$ due to dihedral is insufficient then the condition worsens, with the angle of bank increasing and the nose dropping further still. The pilot flying on instruments alone would be aware of increasing indicated airspeed and a rate of turn on a turn indicator. An attitude indicator like an artificial horizon would show an increasing angle of bank in a dive. The balance instrument (a slip-ball or bubble, or slip-needle) might give no indication, showing almost zero sideslip if directional stability is powerful.

The cure is to build dihedral into the wing and/or to sweep the wings backwards. Pendulous stability helps, as when the CG is located well below the wing.

Dutch roll

An excess of lateral stability, when $-L_v$ is much more powerful than N_v, causes an aeroplane to wallow along, rolling from side to side and snaking directionally. We may argue the way in which it comes about in exactly the same way as we pictured spiral instability above. In this case when sideslip starts dihedral effect raises the wing on the lower side, perhaps with little or no yaw accompanying the motion.

Slight dutch roll is commonly encountered with high performance swept-wing aeroplanes, especially at high altitude in clear air turbulence. Usually, it is not uncomfortable, showing as little more than rotary motion of one's drink when sitting near the tail in a jet airliner.

Spinning

Almost since man first flew, spinning has caused many fatal accidents. In the early days this was due to pilots not knowing how to take recovery action. There is some doubt about who first discovered the control movements needed to effect recovery. Some say that it was Lieutenant Wilfrid Parke in 1912, at Larkhill Aerodrome on Salisbury Plain. Certainly, the spin was called 'Parke's dive' for a long time. Others attribute it to Harry G. Hawker in a *Sopwith* aeroplane. However, the results were not known generally until the accurate flight test work of Major Frank W. Gooden at the Royal Aircraft Establishment, Farnborough, in the 1920s – which is not the same as saying that pilots were not spinning and recovering earlier. The work of Major Gooden was part of the research which resulted in a consistently applicable theory, whereas before that things were rather hit or miss. For example, a book entitled *Practical Flying* by Flight-Commander W. G. McMinnies RN (Temple Press, 1918) after describing a 'tailspin' – also called a spinning nose dive or corkscrew spiral – says: 'He can get out of the spin, if he has sufficient height, by placing the controls – rudder and stick – central, whereupon the machine will take on a nose dive, when the engine can be restarted and the flight continued in the ordinary manner … It is generally found that a pupil will get into a spinning nose dive through making a faulty spiral on certain types of machine on which the area of the stabilising tail fin is too small'. Later, there was more to it than that.

Spinning is included in this chapter because it represents the special case of an aeroplane making what is technically termed a 'departure' simultaneously in yaw, roll and pitch. The author sees it as equivalent to an aeroplane bolting with its pilot, like a horse, running out of control. The machine may do so inadvertently by mishandling, or by asymmetry in the stall; or it may be caused to spin by deliberate control actions of the pilot. A large number of stall-spin accidents occur among aerobatic homebuilt aeroplanes.

The following distinction must be made:

☐ *Spin.* A self-sustaining (autorotational) spiral motion of an aeroplane about a vertical axis, during which the mean angle of attack of the wings is beyond the stall. A spin follows departures in roll, yaw and pitch from the condition of balanced flight. The developed spin is achieved when there is general (sometimes oscillatory) equilibrium between the predominantly pro-spin moment due to the wings and the generally anti-spin moments due to other parts of the aircraft.

☐ *Incipient spin.* The region between spin entry and a developed spin, in which the outcome of the struggle between growing and changing pro-spin and anti-spin moments has not been resolved.

It is operation of the wings beyond the stall and low airspeed which differentiates the spin from a spiral dive, during which the aeroplane is not stalled. Also, the spin axis is closer to the centre of gravity of the aeroplane than the axis of a spiral dive. During a spin the airspeed is more or less steady, a turn indicator needle points in the direction of yaw, and the balance indicator usually shows a sideslip away from the axis of rotation. A spiral dive, on the other hand, is marked by increasing airspeed and, usually, no slip or skid. Furthermore, the pilot is generally aware of a rapid increase in the rate of rotation in yaw, as an aeroplane enters into an actual spin. It is as if the aeroplane suddenly 'bites'. Typical rates of yaw for many conventional light aeroplanes are about 120 deg per second, i.e. 3 seconds per turn when the spin has stabilised.

Rotation in a spin may be in either direction, the motion being imparted by aerodynamic moments. These may be caused initially by the pilot deflecting the controls in a pro-spin direction. But a spin can result more dangerously from asymmetry in the stall, during which one wing drops before the other and so becomes more stalled than the other. Both causes lead to autorotation, which is an essential element of any spin.

Spins are either erect or inverted. The erect spin may often start with a barrel roll-like motion, or even a flick (snap) roll, more or less along the original flight path of the aeroplane. Gradually the nose drops and the motion becomes oscillatory, in a downward direction. As the spin develops the oscillatory motions usually decay and the rate of rotation increases. Spins in one direction may be different from spins in the other. A *Zlin 5 Ol* flown by the author took 1 sec/turn spinning to the right and around 2 sec/turn to the left, depending upon the effects of propeller rotation. The erect spin can be identified if the roll (seen visually) and the yaw (indicated by the turn needle) are in the same direction. In an inverted spin the roll and yaw are in opposite directions.

The characteristics of a developed spin differ between types of aeroplanes and, often, between individual examples of a type. The spins are affected to a great degree by the amount of control deflection of each surface used to initiate and maintain the motion. In aeroplanes in which fuel constitutes an appreciable proportion of the total weight, the fore-and-aft and lateral distribution of the remaining fuel load can be a major influence upon spin characteristics, through its effect upon the moments of inertia (fig. 13.14 a to c).

Straight winged aeroplanes are less likely to enter inverted spins than those with swept wings, because one of the natural requirements is that the control column should be forward of neutral when an aeroplane is inverted at low speed. This is not true for swept winged machines, some of which may spin inverted with the control column held hard back (i.e., in the position for an erect spin). The most common abused manoeuvres which can lead to inverted spins are a loop or a half roll off the top, when the airspeed is too low.

In some swept winged aeroplanes the inverted spin is accompanied by pronounced negative g loads. When an inverted spin is flat the amount of roll is small compared with yaw, which is marked. When an inverted spin is steep the yawing motion may be masked by the high rate of roll. It is essential always to check the turn needle to confirm the spin direction. Sometimes negative g in an inverted spin is slight enough for it to be masked by the rate of roll.

To achieve satisfactory recovery from a spin, be it intentional or (more dangerously) accidental three phases must be handled by the pilot.

☐ The type of spin must be identified from roll and yaw: a turn indicator or, better still,

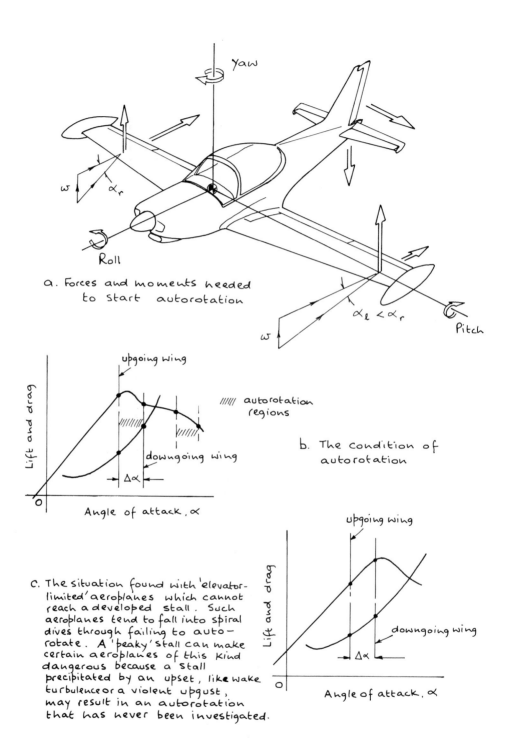

a. Forces and moments needed
   to start autorotation

b. The condition of
   autorotation

c. The situation found with 'elevator-
   limited' aeroplanes which cannot
   reach a developed stall. Such
   aeroplanes tend to fall into spiral
   dives through failing to auto-
   rotate. A 'peaky' stall can make
   certain aeroplanes of this kind
   dangerous because a stall
   precipitated by an upset, like wake
   turbulence or a violent upgust,
   may result in an autorotation
   that has never been investigated.

Fig. 13.4   Spin conditions.

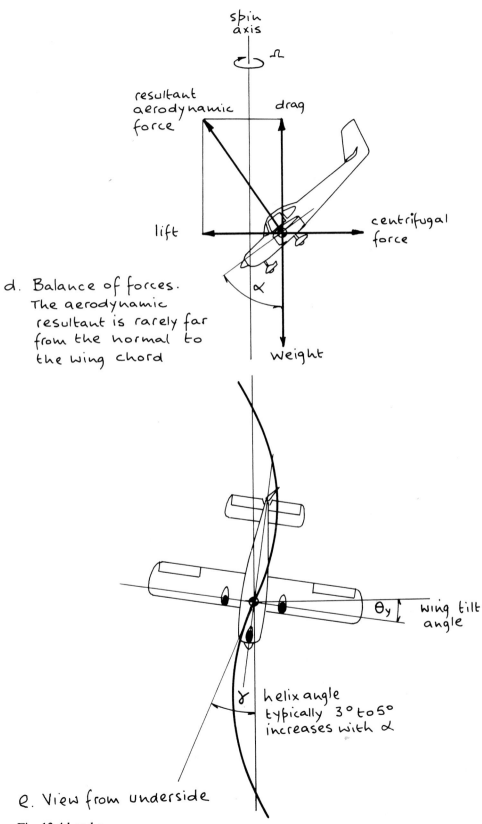

d. Balance of forces.
The aerodynamic
resultant is rarely far
from the normal to
the wing chord

e. View from underside

Fig. 13.4d and e.

a combined turn and slip indicator is the pilot's best friend for this.

☐ The correct recovery action detailed in the *Aircraft Flight Manual*, or other relevant manual, must be applied until the spin stops.

☐ The controls must be centralised and normal flight regained.

It is essential that the first phase is appreciated and followed every time. The author believes that, as a turn and slip indicator is so essential, it is downright foolish to fly an aeroplane without one fitted.

Basically, there are two kinds of erect spin, with variations in between. The first is steeply nose-down, with the mean angle of attack of the wings around 30 deg (so that the nose is about 60 deg to 70 deg below the horizon). There is outward sideslip and the spiral motion of the centre of gravity has a marked radius of gyration about the spin axis. At the other extreme is the 'flat' spin, with the nose around 30 deg (sometimes less) below the horizon. The mean angle of attack may be 60 deg to even 80 deg. The rate of rotation is about double that of the steep spin, with a much smaller radius of gyration about the spin axis. Outwards sideslip is still present. A steep spin usually precedes a flat spin, and recovery is much easier from the former.

The forces and moments needed to start autorotation are shown in fig. 13.4, starting with the stick back (elevators up) to stall the aeroplane, and full rudder applied by the pilot in the desired direction of the spin. The rudder causes side-slip to the left as shown, so that the downwind (right) wing stalls before the left. The result is a combination of roll and yaw to the right, with nose-down pitch.

All aeroplanes spin differently, some will not even begin to spin initially. Only when an aircraft is very light, with aerodynamic effects more powerful than those due to rotational inertia (e.g. like a powered hang glider) is it possible for a full spin to develop in about one turn.

Certain modern light aeroplanes are elevator limited, so that they cannot stall, achieving instead a minimum flying speed with the stick fully back. The situation is shown in fig. 13.4c, so that the downgoing wing, although generating more drag than the upgoing wing as the pilot attempts to provoke a spin, nevertheless produces more lift. The tendency then is to roll out of the entry, so that a spin does not develop. However, because an aeroplane will not enter a spin as a result of deliberate (or even accidental) control movements, this does not indicate that a spin might never develop. There is some evidence to suggest that aeroplanes that are reluctant to enter a spin can be bad if something untoward (like the wake of a heavy aeroplane) forces a spin. Then there may not be enough control authority to effect recovery.

Depending too upon the shape of the lift and drag curves, and the angles of attack of the wings, some aeroplanes can only be made to spiral dive. The danger is that if pro-spin controls are held too long in a spiral, the speed may build up so fast that structural limits are exceeded before the pilot can recover.

Although the autorotational property of a wing, when a large part of it is at an angle of attack beyond the stall, is the primary cause of a spin, this does not necessarily mean that a spin will occur. There are damping moments provided by the fuselage, as we saw in table 13–3, and the anti-spin moment from the fin which together counter the propelling moments from the wings. The result is that for a given combination of control settings there is one equilibrium rate of rotation at each angle of attack. A spin can only follow from autorotation if the equilibrium of pitching moments, and inertial rotary moments (caused by the aeroplane behaving like a set of dumb-bell masses gyrating about a common centre) can be sustained. If equilibrium of the pitching

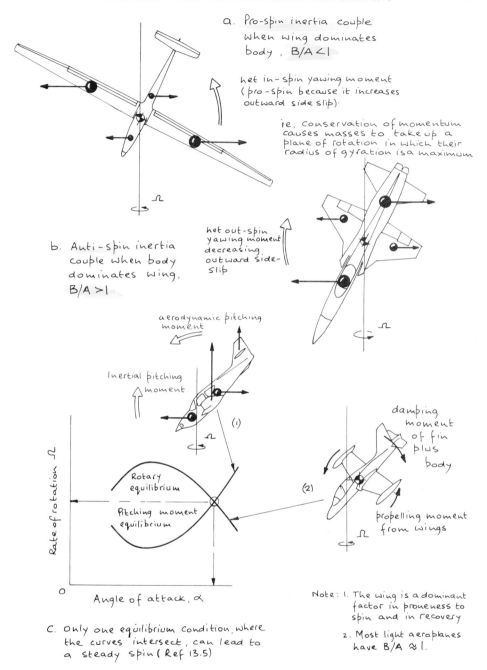

a. Pro-spin inertia couple
when wing dominates
body, B/A < 1

het in-spin yawing moment
(pro-spin because it increases
outward side slip).

ie, conservation of momentum
causes masses to take up a
plane of rotation in which their
radius of gyration is a maximum

b. Anti-spin inertia
couple when body
dominates wing,
B/A > 1

het out-spin
yawing moment
decreasing.
outward side-
slip

aerodynamic pitching
moment

Inertial pitching
moment

(1)

damping
moment
of fin
plus
body

Rate of rotation Ω

Rotary
equilibrium

Pitching moment
equilibrium

(2)

propelling moment
from wings

O

Angle of attack, α

Note: 1. The wing is a dominant
factor in proneness to
spin and in recovery

2. Most light aeroplanes
have B/A ≈ 1.

c. Only one equilibrium condition, where
the curves intersect, can lead to
a steady spin (Ref 13.5)

Fig. 13.5 Interaction between inertia and aerodynamic effects in a spin.

moments and the inertial rotary moments cannot be obtained simultaneously, then
either an oscillatory spin results, or the aeroplane recovers itself. Fig. 13.5 summarises
this in general.

The failure of aeroplanes to have satisfactory spin recovery characteristics can be
attributed to one or more of the following:

☐ *A heavy wing*, in the sense that a large mass is spread predominantly along the Y-axis, giving rise to the moment of inertia, A (table 2–7). Under-wing stores, wing-mounted engines, fuel spread along the wings, and tip tanks, all help to make A large, increasing the tendency to predominance over the moment of inertia, B, of the masses spread out fore and aft along the X-axis (fuselage). Aeroplanes with mass spread out mainly along the fuselage ($B/A > 1$) tend to recover from spins more easily than when the wing is heavy ($B/A < 1$), fig. 13.5a.

☐ *An inefficient body section*, i.e., one producing low body damping. This is a reason for the various strakes which appear on fuselages, especially near the tail, designed to generate favourable (anti-spin) vortices.

☐ *Deficiency in side area*, which again produces low damping.

☐ *Shielding of the rudder* by the tailplane, fig. 13.6.

The use of power in a spin can have a seriously inhibiting effect upon recovery. As we saw in chapter 11, propwash is destabilising, and it reduces the effective angles of attack of the fin and fuselage strakes, and the effective angles of deflection of the rudder and elevator surfaces.

Spin recovery

Because stall-spin misbehaviour continues to be a major cause of accidents, and because there is so much (sometimes confused) argument and debate about recovery techniques, it is valuable to look at a number of historical precedents, spanning the period 1918 to the present. All aeroplanes can be made to spin if they are seriously enough abused. Those which are claimed to be spin-proof usually have been designed in ways which limit their ability to be abused badly enough – for example, the *Aircoupe F–1A* with the ' simplomatic' controls from which the rudder pedals were eliminated, so that the pilot could not yaw the aeroplane as a prelude to autorotation.

Most conventional aeroplanes with a single engine in the nose can be caused to recover from spins using what the British call *Standard* and the American call *Basic Spin-Recovery Procedure*. This differs from the recovery technique given in *Practical Flying* of 1918, which was quoted as 'placing the controls – rudder and stick – central'. Later, two distinct control movements were advocated as follows:

☐ *NACA Technical Note No 555 Procedure (1936)* (ref. 13.2)
  '(1)   Briskly move the rudder to a position full against the spin.
  (2)   After the lapse of appreciable time, say after at least one-half additional turn has been made, briskly move the elevator to approximately the full down position.
  (3)   Hold these positions of the controls until recovery is effected.'

There are a number of reasons why the rudder movement should precede the elevator movement. The effect of the reversed rudder is to check the rate of rotation and cause the nose of the airplane to go down. The blanketing (shielding, *see* fig. 13.6c) of the rudder by the elevator is generally less, and hence the effectiveness of the rudder greater, when the elevator is up. While the rate of rotation is being checked by the rudder, the elevator becomes increasingly effective in assisting recovery. An opposite sequence of operation, that is, one in which the elevator movement precedes the rudder movement, is decidedly objectionable because the usual effect of putting the stick forward while the rudder is held with the spin is an increase in the rate of rotation.

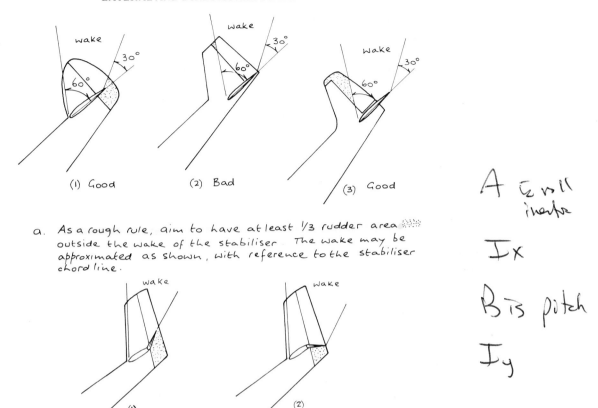

(1) Good   (2) Bad   (3) Good

a. As a rough rule, aim to have at least 1/3 rudder area
    outside the wake of the stabiliser. The wake may be
    approximated as shown, with reference to the stabiliser
    chord line.

b. Effect of elevator deflection on shielding of the rudder.
    This shows why, with most aeroplanes, it is wise to
    attempt spin recovery by applying corrective rudder, before
    applying nose down elevator.

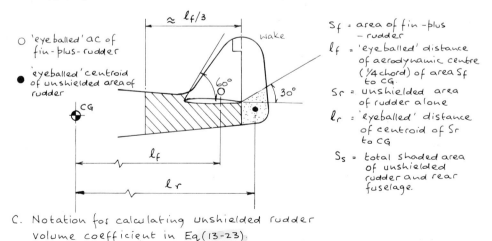

O 'eyeballed' ac of
   fin-plus-rudder

• 'eyeballed' centroid
  of unshielded area of
  rudder

S_f = area of fin-plus
      - rudder

l_f = 'eyeballed' distance
      of aerodynamic centre
      (1/4 chord) of area S_f
      to CG

S_r = unshielded area
      of rudder alone

l_r = 'eyeballed' distance
      of centroid of S_r
      to CG

S_s = total shaded area
      of unshielded
      rudder and rear
      fuselage.

C. Notation for calculating unshielded rudder
    volume coefficient in Eq (13-23).

Fig. 13.6   The influence of a stabiliser upon rudder shielding and volume needed for
spin recovery.

A ε roll
   inertia

I_X

B is pitch

I_y

Slow and cautious movement of the controls during recovery is to be avoided. In certain cases it has been found that, with a slow and cautious reversal of the rudder and elevator, spinning will continue indefinitely; whereas brisk operation of these controls would have effected recovery.'

In 1943 the British Air Ministry issued a *Cadet's Handbook of Elementary Flying Training* which advised as follows:

AP 1979A Procedure (1943) (ref. 13.3)

(1) '... *apply full opposite rudder* ... with your full strength ...'

(2) '... when you see that the rotation has practically stopped, press the stick forward (the amount of forward pressure on the stick varies with different types of aircraft – for most training types it will not be great) ...'

(3) '... and finally ease off the rudder ...'

'It is no use pressing the stick forward while the aircraft is in full rotation; the elevators will not then have the effect you are seeking, although they may *steepen* the spin, which is sometimes desirable ... They will in fact delay, or even prevent the rudder from stopping the rotation. This is because they will shield the rudder to some extent from the airflow, and thus reduce its effectiveness.'

The advice continues for *emergency action*:

'If ... the aircraft does not cease rotating within 1 000 feet of your applying full opposite rudder, the following methods should be tried. They should not be resorted to otherwise.

1. *Throughout, always keep full opposite rudder applied.*

2. Press the stick right back and keep it there to remove or reduce the shielding effect of the elevators.

or

3. Rock the stick sharply, full forward and full backward, pausing for about a second at each extreme position. The aim is to achieve a rocking motion in the aircraft so that it may swing into a position favourable to recovery. This rocking may be intensified by opening the throttle as the stick is pressed forward and closing it as the stick is pressed backward.'

Later, from the author's copy of the Royal Air Force AP129 *Manual of Flying, Volume 2*:

☐ *Royal Air Force Procedure (1955)*

'The standard spin recovery action is to apply full opposite rudder, holding the control column hard back and the ailerons neutral (control column central) then, after a short pause, moving the control column progressively forward until the spin stops, *keeping the ailerons neutral*. These actions are taken to stop the yawing motion and unstall the wings. On many aircraft there may be a momentary increase in the rate of rotation after recovery action has been taken. The moment rotation stops, the rudder and control column should be centralised; the rudder to prevent another spin in the direction of application, and the control column to prevent too steep a dive during recovery. As airspeed increases, the aircraft should be eased into level flight and power applied, care being taken to avoid a *g* stall.'

The recommended emergency action again included:

'(a) Full anti-spin rudder must be held on continuously, whatever other action is taken; but *see* sub-para (c)(i).

(b) Ensure that normal recovery action is properly taken and held long enough to take effect ...

(c) Try to change the stable character of the spin by:
(i) Applying full pro-spin control for one or two turns and then repeating the normal recovery action.
(ii) Opening and closing the throttles, or using full power on the engine on the "inside" of the spin.
(iii) Induced fore-and-aft rocking by use of elevators. On single engined propeller-driven aircraft the throttle should be closed when the control column is moved back and opened when it is moved forward; the slipstream then increases the unstalling effort of the elevators.
(d) *Use of Aileron.* Ailerons should be used as recommended in *Pilot's Notes.*
(e) If the *g* increases markedly, re-examination of the situation may show that the aircraft is in a tight spiral and not a spin. Recovery action should be appropriate to a spiral and not a spin ...'

We see that recovery procedures became more comprehensive as time brought better research and experience, and aeroplanes grew more advanced. There was always the continuing need to teach a universal spin recovery procedure that could be applied to all conventional aeroplanes, because this increased flight safety through standardisation. Under stress pilots almost invariably regress to earlier and more long-learned techniques and patterns of behaviour – and this is especially true when flying to the limit, which is the case when spinning inadvertently.

The developing procedures show awareness of the separate importance of the rudder and elevator, and then of their inter-relationship (risk of shielding by the elevator). There was early recognition of the influence of rotational inertia, and the recommendation to try rocking the aeroplane if it would not recover normally – and to introduce the effects of propwash. Next came specific reference to the ailerons which, when other than central, could introduce aerodynamic asymmetry and proneness to (further) autorotation. Finally, there was the growing appreciation of the need to give the controls *time* to take effect. In fact, ref. 13.2 noted:

'It is not uncommon for a bad-spinning airplane to make at least 5 turns before the recovery control begins to give any satisfactory results ... In the event, then, of a vicious spin, a rule of great importance is to hold the controls applied for recovery for at least 5 turns before attempting any other measure to promote recovery.'

As a light aeroplane may lose, typically, 250 ft to 350 ft per turn (76 to 110 m), plenty of height above ground level is needed for spin tests. In the event of having to bale out of a spinning aeroplane, it can take 1 500 ft (460 m) for the pilot to fall clear. Therefore, tests should not be carried out on an unknown or doubtful aeroplane below 10 000 ft above ground level (AGL) (3 000 m); and a decision height to leave the aeroplane should be set so that one can be clear of the machine by 1 000 ft AGL (300 m). A minimum decision height is about 3 000 ft AGL (900 m).

Thus, taking the main elements together:

□ *Standard (or basic) spin recovery procedure*
(1) Check the direction of turn (yaw).
(2) Check throttle *closed.*
(3) Check ailerons *central.*
(4) Apply full *opposite* rudder to the indicated direction of turn (this works whether the aeroplane is spinning erect or inverted).
(5) *pause* (one-half additional turn at least, takes about 1 second).

(6) Move the control column firmly and progressively *forward* (against any increasing stick force and buffet), *if necessary to the front stop* and hold it there until rotation ceases.
(7) When rotation ceases *centralise* the rudder control and ease out of the ensuing dive.

With an increasing number of modern light aeroplanes (6) is redundant. Instead the stick is either held back (elevator fully up) or it is eased forward to the elevator-central position. We can see from the procedural precedents and their explanatory passages given above, why such advice in these cases is not contradictory. It may be that the design of the tail is more prone to blanketing of the rudder by the elevator – or the aeroplane may be more of a spiral-diver than a spinner. If the stick is pushed forwards regardless the aircraft might bunt quite smartly (i.e. start an outside loop), and lose more height during the ensuing dive than it would have done if the stick had not been moved forward so far. Also, much depends upon the shielding of the lower portion of the rudder when the elevator is moved downwards, thus forcing downwards the bottom edge of the wake in fig. 13.6b(2). Pushing the stick forwards has been known to flatten a spin. However, these are comments made in passing. No two aeroplanes of a type ever spin exactly alike; and no two types spin alike. One must never speculate too much on paper about spinning and spin recovery. This is something the test pilot has to find out the hard way. Even tests with models in the spinning tunnel, as well as in radio controlled flight, cannot be correlated exactly with full scale behaviour, if only because of Reynolds number effects. The rule is always to be guided by the manufacturer's advice scheduled in the Aircraft Flight Manual, or related documents – or to find out the hard way during flight tests.

Inverted spin recovery

The normal recovery from an inverted spin is

(1) Check the direction of turn (yaw).
(2) Check throttle *closed.*
(3) Check ailerons *central* (this is essential throughout).
(4) Apply full *opposite* rudder to the indicated direction of direction of turn.
(5) Move the control column progressively *backwards* until the spin stops.

Note that the pause which is present in standard of basic recovery procedure has been omitted; this is because the rudder is generally un-blanketed (unless the aeroplane has a T-tail) and movement of the elevator introduces no adverse effect (*see* fig. 13.6).

A particular danger in recovery from an inverted spin is that a pilot's g threshold may be seriously reduced if negative g has been present.

In some swept-winged aeroplanes the correct recovery action is to oppose yaw with rudder and then, with ailerons central, to move the control column fully forward. Even this may not be wholly effective and it may then be necessary to add full aileron deflection in the direction of roll introducing aileron drag which assists the rudder.

Often, when anti-spin rudder is applied the spin will stop, but the aeroplane will pitch nose down like a pendulum and enter an erect spin, in the opposite direction. This must be watched and the appropriate recovery action applied.

Spin recovery criteria

There are a number of different spin recovery criteria in use wherever aeroplanes are

designed. We shall note only two. The first formulae below were given by Latimer
Needham (ref. 13.6) before World War 2:

Rudder power to prevent an incipient spin is given by the following equation, which
has been modified very slightly so as to use our nomenclature. The result is more
conservative than that given in the reference:

$$10^3 \, C'(S_f/S)(l_f/b) \nless 5 \tag{13-21}$$

where, S_f, S, l_f and b have the meanings in eqs (13-7) and (13-7a) while the
coefficient $C' = 0.35$ for a fixed fin
$\qquad = 0.3$ for an all-moving rudder.
Thus, substituting fin volume coefficient, $\overline{V}_f$, from eq (13-7a) the criterion in eq
(13-21) becomes:

$$\overline{V}_f \nless 0.005/C' \tag{13-22}$$

Rudder volume to recover from a spin is given by a rough formula based upon the
same reference, which has again been modified to suit our nomenclature, while
giving a conservative result compared with the original:

$$(S_s/S)(l_s/\overline{c}) \nless 0.065 \tag{13-23}$$

Here, S_s is the shaded area in fig. 13.6c.

To these may be added the following recommendations:

☐ Use a wing section with docile stall characteristics. It might also be necessary to
introduce washout towards the tips and, in the case of tapered wings, to avoid sweepback of the leading edge, which can precipitate a tip stall on one wing before the
other. Differential (Frise) ailerons can be beneficial.

☐ The tailplane and elevator should be set as high as possible (without incurring
structural penalties), so as to leave plenty of rudder area underneath. Mount the
tailplane and elevator with the bulk of the total area either well forward of the fin
post, or well aft. Slight tailplane dihedral can be beneficial.

☐ A drooped (notched or saw tooth) leading edge extension of about 0.03 SMC to the
outboard half of the wings, or leading edge slats, can benefit anti-spin
characteristics. A drooped outboard leading edge extension should *not* be faired
into the wing leading edge inboard. The inboard end of the extension should form a
sharp-edged step. Its purpose is to suck a component of flow towards the tips, so that
a favourable chordwise vortex is shed by the sharp inboard end of the extension.

A second source of criteria is given in ref. 13.1, in which it is assumed (incompletely)
that for equilibrium, the pro-spin moment caused by the wings must equal the anti-spin
moments from other parts of the aeroplane. The situation can be stated in terms of the
following equation, representing the case of a borderline aeroplane, which just fails to
be able to recover from a spin.

The moments in the equation are about the *wind axes*, which are chosen because the
centrifugal forces on all parts of the aircraft act radially from the axis of the spin. It
follows that there can be no centrifugal couple about the wind axis, and equilibrium in
the spin can be analysed in terms of aerodynamic properties of the configuration of the
aircraft. Thus, for equilibrium in the spin the pro-spin moment due to the wings must
equal the anti-spin moments due to the other parts of the aeroplane:

| anti-spin moment coefficient due to body | + | anti-spin moment coefficient due to unshielded rudder volume when rudder deflected against the spin | + | pro-spin rolling moment coefficient due to wing | = 0 |

i.e. $\bar{l}_{pb} + \bar{l}_\zeta + \bar{l}_{pw} = 0$, for an aircraft which just fails to recover $\qquad$ (13–24)

If the above equation does not equal zero, there is a residual unbalanced rolling moment coefficient about the wind axis (*see* eq (13–31)). When positive it is anti-spin, and the aeroplane should recover. But if the residual moment is negative, recovery will probably be impossible. The first two terms are positive, while the wing term is negative. Thus, to be better than borderline:

$$\bar{l}_{pb} + \bar{l}_\zeta \text{ must not be less than } \bar{l}_{pw}$$

and it follows that recovery will hang upon the effectiveness of the unshielded rudder, given by the magnitude of $\bar{l}_\zeta$.

The relative merit of each part of the equation depends upon the ratio of the pitching moment of inertia, B, to the rolling moment of inertia, A, expressed as B/A (which appeared in fig. 13.5a and b). This follows from the rolling and yawing inertia couples, with moments of inertia A and C, which influence the angle of the wings and thus sideslip in a spin. The three moments of inertia, A, B and C are linked by the ratio of the yawing and rolling inertia couples, which can be expressed in the form:

$$(A - B)/(C - B), \text{ where } A + B \geqslant C \qquad \text{(table 2–7)}$$

so that,
$$(A - B)/(C - B) \approx (A - B)/A = (B/A) \qquad (13–25)$$

Therefore, eqs (13–24) and (13–25) are the two most important parameters affecting the probability of an aeroplane recovering from a spin. Plotting the first against the second enables fig. 13.7 to be drawn, with boundaries between *pass, borderline* and *fail* marked by empirical test results. This shows that as the pitching moment of inertia, B, increases, $(1 - B/A)$ decreases, and the required anti-spin rolling moment needed for recovery is correspondingly reduced. Therefore, the more powerful the flywheel contribution of the wing in a spin, the harder it is to effect recovery. But the more powerful the flywheel contribution of the body, the easier recovery becomes.

In the following analysis of each effect in eq (13–24), the assumption is that the aircraft is spinning in a 45° nose-down attitude. This is a reasonable average for most aeroplanes, and the rate of rotation about the spin axis is then a minimum. As such, it represents the case for the least body (plus fin and rudder damping) and, therefore, the greatest input from the unshielded rudder to overcome the wing.

□ *Anti-spin moment coefficient due to the body, $\bar{l}_{pb}$:*

$$\bar{l}_{pb} = (\lambda/Sb^2) \, \Sigma\,_{l_1}^{l_2} \, \epsilon h x^2 \, \Delta x \qquad (13–26)$$

in which the damping coefficient, ϵ, is obtained from table 13–3, while the terms h, x and Δx are defined in fig. 13.8. The rotational term:

$$\lambda = \Omega b/2 \, v_d \qquad (13–27)$$

where Ω is the rate of rotation about the spin axis in radians/s, b the wingspan in ft,

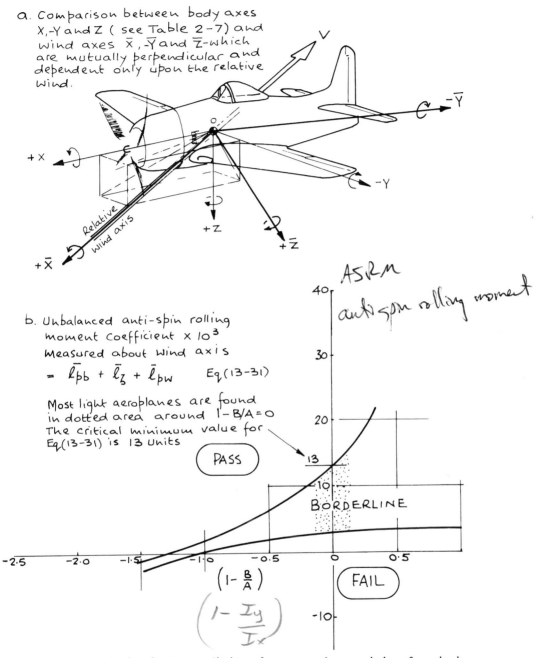

a. Comparison between body axes
X,-Y and Z (see Table 2-7) and
wind axes $\bar{X}$, $\bar{Y}$ and $\bar{Z}$-which
are mutually perpendicular and
dependent only upon the relative
wind.

b. Unbalanced anti-spin rolling
moment coefficient × 10^3
measured about wind axis

$= \bar{\ell}_{pb} + \bar{\ell}_{z} + \bar{\ell}_{pw}$ Eq (13-31)

Most light aeroplanes are found
in dotted area around 1−B/A=0
The critical minimum value for
Eq (13-31) is 13 units

PASS

ASRM
anti spin rolling moment

BORDERLINE

FAIL

$\left(1- \dfrac{B}{A}\right)$

$\left(1- \dfrac{I_y}{I_x}\right)$

Fig. 13.7 The criterion for the prediction of recovery characteristics of a spinning aeroplane (*after* ref. 13.1).

$\lambda = .55$

$\Omega \simeq 2 \text{ rad/s}$

and v_d the true rate of descent in ft/s. Many light aeroplanes take about 2 to 4 seconds per revolution with the nose down something like 60 deg, while losing some 200 to 300 ft/turn. These correspond with rates of rotation around 2 radians/s (rising to 4 or more radians/s in a flat spin), and 80 ft/s (24.38 m/s) average rate of

$V_d \simeq 100 \text{ ft/s}$

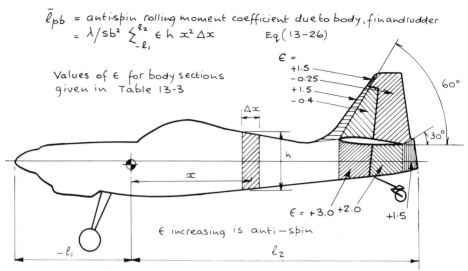

$\bar{\ell}_{pb}$ = anti-spin rolling moment coefficient due to body, fin and rudder

$$= \lambda/sb^2 \sum_{-\ell_1}^{\ell_2} \epsilon h\, x^2 \Delta x \qquad \text{Eq (13-26)}$$

Values of ϵ for body sections given in Table 13-3

ϵ increasing is anti-spin

Fig. 13.8 Body, fin and rudder damping coefficients.

descent. Ref. 3.1 also gives the following equation for λ:

$$\lambda = \sqrt{[1.3/(b_1 \times \text{aspect ratio})]} \qquad (13\text{--}28)$$

where, $b_1 = (C - A)/\rho S(b/2)^3$ (13–29)

A = rolling moment of inertia, slug ft^2, I_{xx}
C = yawing moment of inertia, slug ft^2, I_{zz}
   $\leqslant A + B$, where B is the pitching moment of inertia, slug ft^2,
S = wing area, ft^2,
ρ = air density, slug/ft^3.

The aspect ratio of the wing is, of course, equal to (span^2/area). The success of the method depends upon the estimation of the damping coefficient, ϵ. Only rarely can a simple estimate be made for the whole fuselage, although it may be possible more often with amateur-built aircraft of a simple type, like those with rectangular-sectioned bodies. Usually, because of changing sections and tail locations, it has to be calculated section by section.

☐ *Anti-spin moment coefficient due to full opposite rudder,* $\bar{l}_c$:

$$\bar{l}_c = S_r l_r/Sb \qquad (13\text{--}30)$$

in which S_r is the shaded area of the rudder alone, and l_r the distance of its centroid from the **CG** (the centroid can usually be 'eyeballed'). These are shown in fig. 13.6b.

☐ *Wing rolling moment coefficient,* $\bar{l}_{pw}$, can be estimated from fig. 13.9, in which values have been plotted against the rotational term, λ, in eq (13–27). The curves are based on the assumption that the wing rolling moment is a linear function of section thickness/chord ratio.

The estimates enable the unbalanced (anti-spin) rolling moment coefficient to be calculated from:

ASRM   anti-spin rolling moment coefficient $= \bar{l}_{pb} + \bar{l}_c + \bar{l}_{pw}$ (13–31)

and the result plotted against $(1 - B/A)$ in fig. 13.7. Most modern light aeroplanes have values of B/A around 1, so that their results are close to $(1 - B/A) = 0$. They require the above sum to come to at least 13 units if they are to have a reasonable chance of recovery.

An example of the method is shown in table 13–4, calculated for spins at 45 deg, for a good and a bad aeroplane. The initial total is for $(\bar{l}_{pb} + \bar{l}_{pw})$, before the pilot moves the rudder, so as to introduce $\bar{l}_\zeta$. The final sum is with full opposite rudder applied.

TABLE 13–4

Moments Due to Rotation about the Spin Axis

Contribution	Good aircraft	Bad aircraft
Wing, $\bar{l}_{pw}$	–6 units	–21 units
Body, $\bar{l}_{pb}$ and fin, $\bar{l}_{pf}$ i.e. $(\bar{l}_{pb} + \bar{l}_{pf})$	+34 units	+7 units
Total without $\bar{l}_\zeta$	+28 units	–14 units
Full opposite rudder, $\bar{l}_\zeta$	+17 units	+5 units
Final total	+45 units	–9 units

These results show that the condition for equilibrium rate of rotation (eq 13–24) is not achieved when spinning 45 deg nose down. The good aeroplane is still strongly positive in its total without $\bar{l}_\zeta$, showing that equilibrium might be achieved at a shallower angle of attack (steeper nose-down attitude). But when the rudder is deflected fully against the spin, the final total is dramatically more positive, showing that recovery should be easy. In the case of the bad aeroplane the initial total, being negative, is pro-spin. It also indicates that the equilibrium condition will be reached at a larger angle of attack, i.e. in a flatter spin. Even when the rudder is deflected against the spin, the sum remains negative, showing that recovery will be unlikely.

In general, the key to autorotation lies in the amount of outward sideslip that can be given to the wing. Equilibrium through a balance of moments about the axis of a spin can take place over a wide range of angles of attack, by adjustment of the sideslip.

Recovery is achieved by movements of the controls which reduce the outward sideslip. This may be done, for example, by applying opposite rudder so as to point the nose out of the spin (everything else remaining unchanged). Or, depending upon the inertia ratio, B/A, and the consequent behaviour of the aeroplane as a rotating flywheel, the pilot may first have to adjust the attitude of the machine by using elevator and aileron before rudder, so as to tilt the flywheel in a favourable direction. Gyroscopic precession then causes out-spin yaw, which reduces outwards sideslip, so as to bring about recovery. These are things the test pilot must try.

Effect of aileron

So far we have talked of spin recovery with ailerons *central*, but it is also important to appreciate that the use of aileron may make all of the difference between a quick recovery or no recovery. However, use of powerful ailerons while stopping a spin may then suddenly cause a spin in the reverse direction. Generally, use of aileron to aid recovery depends upon inertia distribution – and this may alter in flight if wing fuel is carried, for example.

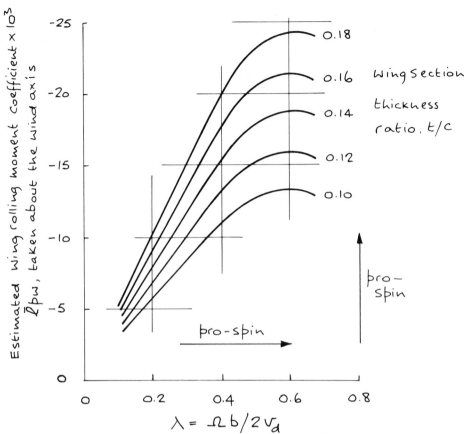

Fig. 13.9 Estimation of wing rolling moment coefficient, $\bar{l}pw$, about the wind axis in a spin (ref. 13.1), assuming that the wing rolling moments are functions of thickness/chord ratio.

☐ use of aileron must be related to direction of roll and not yaw

If an aeroplane has most of its weight concentrated into a long fuselage and has relatively lighter wings and a short span. ($B/A > 1$), then aileron applied in the direction of roll tends to assist recovery. The longer the fuselage and the greater the weight concentrated in nose and tail, the larger the numerical value of B/A, the greater the beneficial effect of aileron in the direction of roll during recovery.

If an aeroplane has long and relatively heavy wings, so that $B/A < 1$, then aileron applied against the direction of roll is most beneficial. Thus, if an aeroplane can be fitted with wing tip tanks, which alter the value of B/A, the effect of aileron upon spin recovery must be thoroughly investigated with tanks ON, both full and empty, and tanks OFF.

Checking fin size

In chapter 11 we saw experimental ways of checking stabiliser size, and finding the stick-fixed neutral point, using laminae. Given the limitations of the method, we can do the same here, so as to roughly gauge the area of the fin and rudder together.

The method relies upon the provision of enough keel surface aft of the **CG** to compensate for destabilising effects of fuselage, landing gear, propellers, stores carried externally, and wings. Dihedral of wings, when projected in elevation, causes them to act like small keel surfaces. We therefore treat the elevation of an aeroplane in exactly the same way as the plan view was used for checking stabiliser size.

Each portion of the side view of an aeroplane should be dealt with as follows:

☐ Body-draw the side view.
☐ External stores and nacelles – these are dealt with in the same way as the body. Where their shapes are hidden behind or within the outline of the aircraft when seen from the side, they must be added above or below the fuselage in the correct fore and aft location, so that each has its contribution accounted for.
☐ Propeller(s) – draw a rectangle equal to the diameter and thickness of each (in effect, construct a rectangular outline in elevation around each propeller). If the aircraft is multi-engined, add the equivalent area of each propeller above and below the body outline, at the appropriate station.
☐ Wing dihedral – increase the rise between tip and root as seen in elevation, by half as much again. The new projected area of the wing seen end-on must be added either to the top or the bottom of the side view of the body in the correct position. In the case of a biplane, an allowance must be made for both planes, together with the additional areas of struts.
☐ Undercarriage – each wheel plus leg is represented by a rectangle of side equal to the diameter of the wheel, and length equal to the distance from the wing or body to the bottom of the wheel. An allowance must be made for spats or other fairings (and the same with floats).
☐ Fin – leave an area slightly larger than expected around the outline of the fin plus rudder, so as to be able to trim some of it away with scissors when it comes to achieving the required balance.

The outline of the aircraft may be unrecognisable when these things have been done (fig. 13.10), but that does not matter as long as the relative sizes and distributions of areas are accurate. On no account use paste or glue, or staples, to attach bits and pieces to the lamina, because the centroid is really its centre of gravity. Even a small touch of paste can make a large difference to the result.

The centroid of the resulting lamina should lie at a point P, which is generally found between 10 and 18 per cent of the total length of the fuselage aft of the anticipated *CG* (the $\frac{1}{4}$ SMC of a conventional aeroplane). More accurately:

$$\text{conventional aeroplanes (single and twin):} \quad 0.175 \, l \text{ aft of } CG \quad (13\text{–}32)$$
$$\text{canard aeroplanes:} \qquad\qquad 0.135 \, l \text{ aft of } CG \quad (13\text{–}33)$$

The tail-first arrangement has a smaller margin because of the problems of balance caused by the relatively larger fin surfaces. Older conventional aeroplanes tend to have margins nearer 10 to 15 per cent of the fuselage length aft of the **CG**, i.e. at 0.11 to 0.15l, giving them less weathercock stability and making them easier to spin than most modern machines. Some early trail-dragging aeroplanes with wire-spoked wheels became spin-prone when the spokes were faired with fabric discs.

Some notes on vertical tail surfaces

Calculation of the area of the fin-plus-rudder and its effectiveness as a stabiliser is

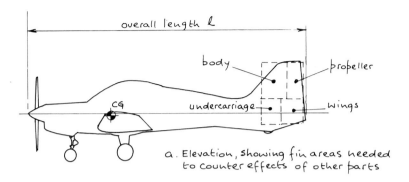

overall length ℓ

body

propeller

CG

undercarriage

wings

a. Elevation, showing fin areas needed to counter effects of other parts

b. Conversion of elevation into lamina, with equivalent keel areas added for wing dihedral, gear and propeller(s)

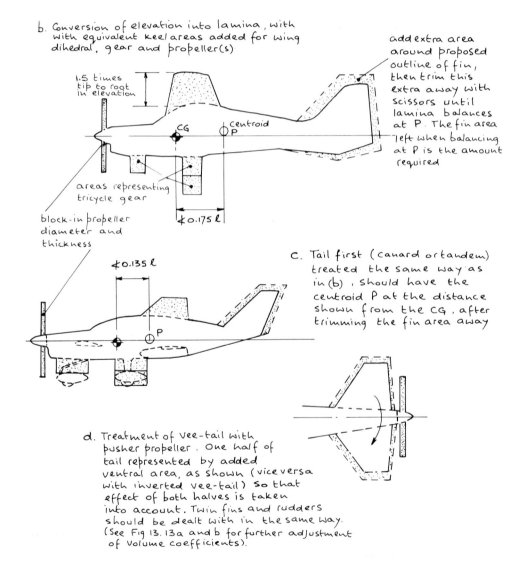

1.5 times tip to root in elevation

CG

Centroid
P

add extra area around proposed outline of fin, then trim this extra away with scissors until lamina balances at P. The fin area left when balancing at P is the amount required

areas representing tricycle gear

block-in propeller diameter and thickness

$\leftarrow 0.175\,\ell$

$\leftarrow 0.135\,\ell$

P

c. Tail first (canard or tandem) treated the same way as in (b), should have the centroid P at the distance shown from the CG, after trimming the fin area away

d. Treatment of Vee-tail with pusher propeller. One half of tail represented by added ventral area, as shown (vice versa with inverted vee-tail) so that effect of both halves is taken into account. Twin fins and rudders should be dealt with in the same way. (See Fig 13.13a and b for further adjustment of volume coefficients).

Fig. 13.10 Checking minimum fin size using a paper lamina.

fraught with difficulty. A project designer who lectured to the author as a student used to say that no matter what one did, an aeroplane always ended up without enough fin and rudder area for some flight conditions.

The difficulty arises because of a number of factors. The boundary layer of the fuselage is thick by the time it reaches the tail, its depth varying with angle of attack. The fuselage wake is turbulent, relatively sluggish, and takes up a path dependent upon the downwash from the wing. Fin effectiveness depends, therefore, upon the location of the wing on the fuselage: low wings result in more efficient fins than high wings. High-winged aeroplanes often have larger vertical surface areas than those with low (plate 13.3). A nose-mounted propeller causes additional turbulence, while propwash in general (being helical) introduces asymmetry in the flow at the tail. The same asymmetry also introduces lateral and directional interactions between stability and control. Finally, as the aeroplane pitches, the fin and rudder move up and down relative to the wake, altering the efficiency of the tail, expressed by η_s, in eq (5–24).

Various methods have been used for calculating areas and lift slopes. Some are shown in fig. 13.11, based upon refs. 3.5, 5.5, 13.7, and Appendix A, C01.01.01, C01.01.02 and C01.01.05. A determining factor is the vertical location of the stabiliser and the way in which the rudder is arranged. This tends to fix the effective 'span' of the surface, b_f (others use b_v).

Thus, if S_f is the effective area of the fin-plus-rudder:

$$\text{aspect ratio of vertical surfaces, } A_f = f_{Af}\,(b^2_f / S_f) \qquad (13–34)$$

This equation is based upon ref. 5.5 and results in values which are smaller than an equation given in ref. 3.5 (which introduces a constant, 1.55), upon which the following is based:

$$A_f = 1.55\,f_{Af}\,(b^2_f / S_f) \qquad (13–34a)$$

We have introduced a factor, f_{Af}, to account for the effect of vertical location of the stabiliser, in fig. 13.12.

As a first shot we may estimate the lift slope of the vertical surface, $(a_1)_B$, using fig. 4.6c. We can, if we wish, then factor the value so obtained by $\eta_s = q_{ws}/q$ in eq (5–24). It is really a matter of detailed choice.

The Royal Aeronautical Society (ESDU Data, Appendix A) uses a different method and introduces a body contribution, as shown in fig. 13.11f. The same source also has a data sheet which shows how a T-tail increases fin aspect ratio and lift slope (Appendix A, C01.01.05).

Veetails

See fig. 13.13 and caption.

Moments of inertia

Moments of inertia A, B and C which appeared in table 2–7 and in the section on spinning are defined as:

$$\text{moment of inertia about OX, } A = \Sigma^{M}_{o}(y^2 + z^2)\,\Delta m \qquad (13–36)$$
$$\text{moment of inertia about OY, } B = \Sigma^{M}_{o}(z^2 + x^2)\Delta m \qquad (13–37)$$
$$\text{moment of inertia about OZ, } C = \Sigma^{M}_{o}(x^2 + y^2)\Delta m \qquad (13–38)$$

where x, y and z are the co-ordinates of any element of mass of aeroplane, Δm. Fig. 13.14a, b and c shows representative values of A, B and C.

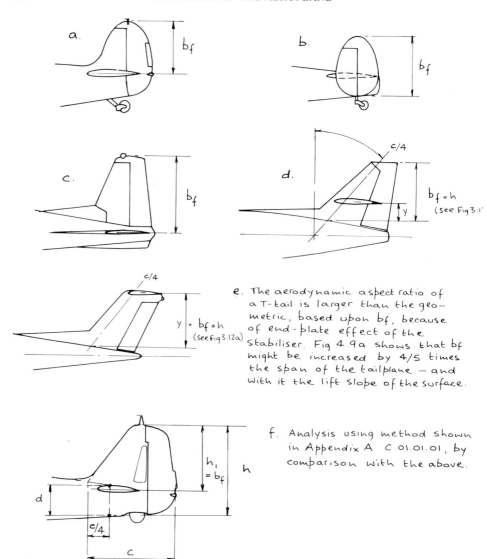

Fig. 13.11   Definition of vertical surface area and its 'span'. The determining factor is vertical location of the stabiliser (a to e after refs. 3.5, 5.5 and 13.4) (f based upon Appendix A, C.01.01.01). The principles are also applicable to horizontal surfaces.

Steiner's parallel axis theorem

It is sometimes necessary to calculate a moment of inertia about one axis (e.g. $O'–Z'$ or $O'–X'$ in fig. 15.7, as when determining the centre of gravity) and then convert it to a moment of inertia about a parallel axis somewhere else. For example, we may calculate moments of inertia in fig. 15.7 by introducing columns for $W_w x^2_w$, or $W_{Tail} x^2_{Tail}$ and dividing throughout by the gravitational constant, $g = 32.2$ ft/s^2 (9.8 m/s^2) so as to convert the weight terms into masses. In fig. 13.15 let $\bar{x}$ and $\bar{z}$ be the distances of the **CG** of an aeroplane from the **CG** datum axes O–Z and O–X respectively. The parallel axis

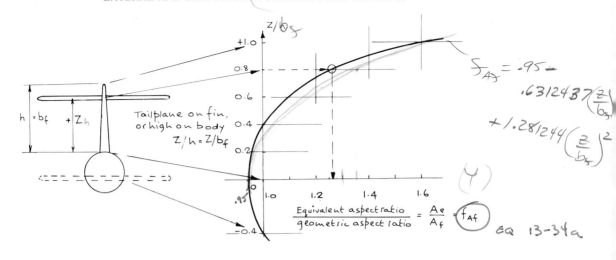

$$f_{A_f} = .95 - $$
$$.631243 7 \left(\frac{z}{b_f}\right)$$
$$+ 1.281244 \left(\frac{z}{b_f}\right)^2$$

$$\frac{\text{Equivalent aspect ratio}}{\text{geometric aspect ratio}} = \frac{A_e}{A_f} = f_{Af}$$

EQ 13-34a

a. Effect of tailplane (tending towards an endplate for the fin) upon equivalent aspect ratio of fin as location is varied. This figure is related to Fig 13.11 d and e. See Fig 4.6c for lift slope of fin-plus-rudder with geometric aspect ratio, A_f; and Appendix A, C.01.01.05 for more comprehensive treatment.

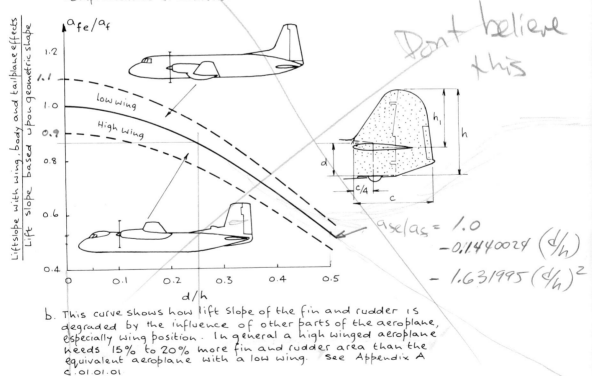

Don't believe this

$$a_{se}/a_s = 1.0$$
$$-0.144002 4 \left(d/h\right)$$
$$- 1.631995 \left(d/h\right)^2$$

b. This curve shows how lift slope of the fin and rudder is degraded by the influence of other parts of the aeroplane, especially wing position. In general a high winged aeroplane needs 15% to 20% more fin and rudder area than the equivalent aeroplane with a low wing. See Appendix A C.01.01.01

Fig. 13.12   Factors affecting fin characteristics.

a.

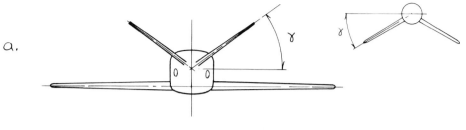

$$\frac{\text{Volume coefficient of vee-tail}}{\text{Volume coefficient of stabiliser}} = \frac{\overline{V_U}}{\overline{V_s}} = 1 + (\tan\gamma)/2 \qquad \text{Eq (13-35a)}$$

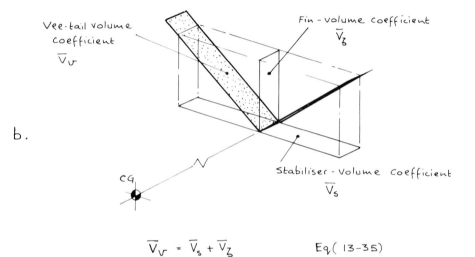

$$\overline{V_U} = \overline{V_s} + \overline{V_z} \qquad \text{Eq(13-35)}$$

Fig. 13.13   Vee-tails need more total volume than a conventional arrangement, and eq (13–35) shows the minimum. This means that such tails are not necessarily the answer for efficiency. An upright vee increases lateral stability while an inverted vee decreases it. A more complicated control system is inevitable, employing a mixer box for rudder and elevator functions. Volume coefficients are as defined in eqs (11–7), (13–7) and (13–8).

theorem tells us that:

$$\text{moment of inertia about O'-Z', } I_{o'z'} = \Sigma_o^M x^2 \Delta m + M(\bar{x})^2 \qquad (13\text{--}39)$$

in which x is the distance of an element of mass, Δm from the CG of the aeroplane and $\Sigma_o^M x^2 \Delta m$ is one of the terms needed when calculating moment of inertia B in eq (13–37):
Similarly, $I_{o'x'} = \Sigma_o^M z^2 \Delta m + M(\bar{z})^2$ (13–40)

Thus, as $M = W/g =$ mass of the aeroplane, then pitching moment of inertia B about the centre of gravity is given by:

$$B = \Sigma_o^M (z^2 + x^2)\Delta m$$
$$= I_{o'z'} + I_{o'x'} - M((\bar{x})^2 + (\bar{z})^2) \qquad (13\text{--}41)$$

Rolling and yawing moments of inertia A and C can be calculated in a similar way, except that if the axis O'–X' lies in the plane of symmetry, then the **CG** (which is usually close to the centreline of the aeroplane) will have a moment arm y ≈ O.

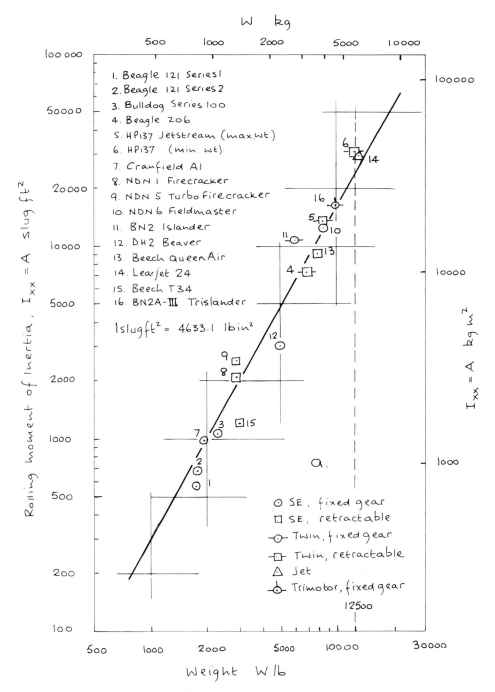

Fig. 13.14a   Variation of rolling moment of inertia $I_{xx} = A$ with weight of aeroplane.

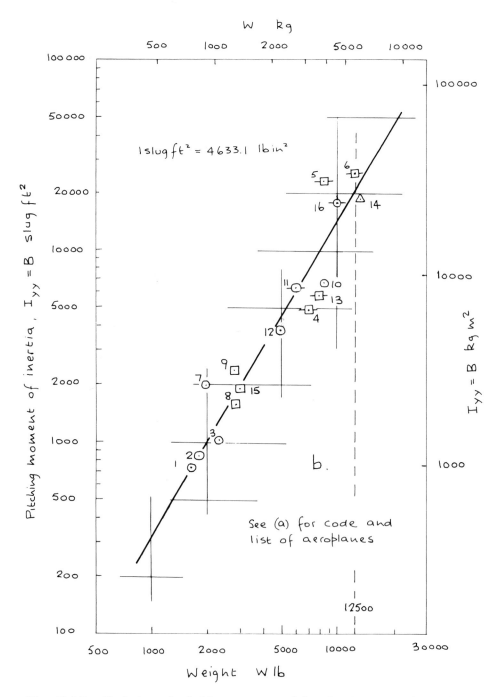

Fig. 13.14b   Variation of pitching moment of inertia, $I_{yy} = B$, with weight of aeroplane.

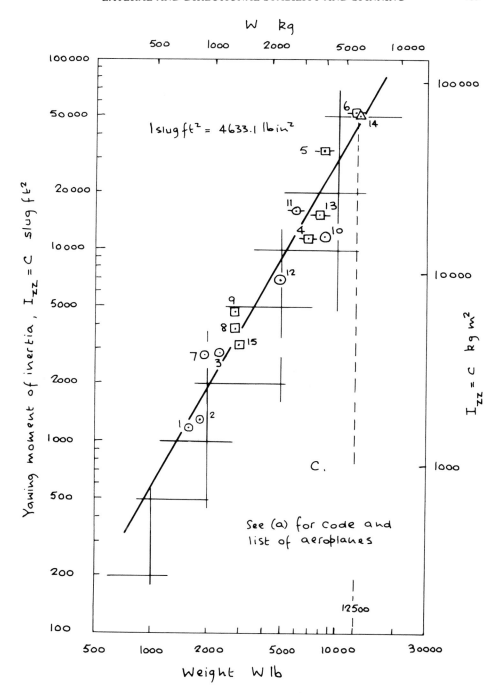

Fig. 13.14c Variation of yawing moment of inertia, $I_{zz} = C \leqslant A + B$, with weight of aeroplane.

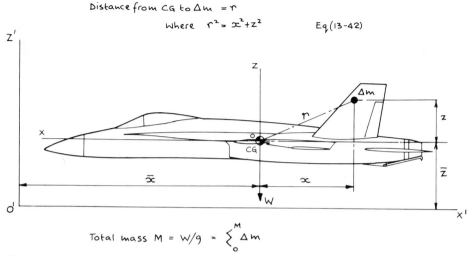

Distance from CG to Δm $= r$

where $r^2 = x^2 + z^2$ Eq (13-42)

Total mass $M = W/g = \sum_{0}^{M} \Delta m$

Fig. 13.15   System used to find moments of inertia about axes through aircraft centre of gravity, $O–X$, $O–Z$, knowing distances $\bar{x}$ and $\bar{z}$ of the **CG** from displaced axes $O'–X'$ and $O'–Z'$.

References

13.1 Kerr, T. H. (Aug. 1953) Tech Note Aero 2251, *A Criterion for the Prediction of the Recovery Characteristics of Spinning Aircraft*. Royal Aircraft Establishment, Farnborough.
   (*Note,* the method can also be found in AvP970 (Aug. 1959), *Design Requirements for Aircraft for the Royal Air Force and Royal Navy*, **1**, Book 1, Leaflet 208/2, published by the then Ministry of Aviation. This latter document might still be classified Restricted, although the subject matter of the leaflet is not.)
13.2 McAvoy, W. H. (Jan. 1936) Technical Note No 555, *Piloting Technique for Recovery from Spins*. National Advisory Committee for Aeronautics.
13.3 Air Publication 1979A. (Apr. 1943) Air Ministry. *Cadets' Handbook of Elementary Flying Training*. 1st Edition, His Majesty's Stationery Office.
13.4 Air Publication 129 (1955) *Royal Air Force Manual of Flying*, **2**. Aircraft Operation, Air Ministry and Ministry of Supply.
13.5 Burns, B. R. A. (Mar. 1972) 'Anatomy of Spinning, An Aerodynamicist's Comments'. *Flight International*.
13.6 Latimer Needham, C. H. (1939) 'Aircraft Design'. *Aerostructures*, **2** New York: Chemical Publishing Company Inc, Brooklyn.
13.7 Roskam, J. (1977) *Methods for Estimating Stability and Control Derivatives for Subsonic Aircraft*, 3rd edn. Ottawa, Kansas: Roskam Aviation and Engineering Corporation, Route 4, Ottawa, Kansas 66067.

CHAPTER 14

How Big and How Heavy?

'Crinkle, crinkle, little spar,
strained beyond the yield-point, far.
Up above the world so high,
bits and pieces in the sky.'
Quoted by A. J. Coombe, Technical Director, *NDN Aircraft Limited.*

The specification gives the designer his first idea of how big and heavy an aircraft must be, if it is to satisfy the requirements. Its proportions tend to be determined by role, and the design point selected either for most efficient cruising, or best manoeuvrability in the flight envelope.

Cruising aeroplanes designed to transport awkward loads have long wing spans and relatively large stabilisers, with plenty of tail volume to cope with flexibility in loading. Agile, highly manoeuvrable aeroplanes, like racers, aerobatic machines and agricultural aircraft, have smaller tail volumes and lower aspect ratios. The main reason for the former is that they have smaller **CG** ranges and tighter natural stability margins. The reason for the latter is the weight penalty caused by manoeuvres, and the modest range requirement.

Weight is estimated by controlled guesswork. The process is critical, and we shall use this chapter to look at the factors which affect the weight of the different components.

Looking back to eqs (1–1) to (1–2a) we see that the weight of an aeroplane is made up as follows:

gross weight $\quad\quad\quad$ = standard empty weight + usable fuel + payload
$\quad\quad\quad\quad\quad\quad\quad\quad\quad$ + crew + ballast $\quad\quad\quad\quad\quad\quad\quad\quad$ eq (1–1)
standard empty weight = (powerplant weight + structure weight + weight of
$\quad\quad\quad\quad\quad\quad\quad\quad\quad$ controls + weight of equipment and services)
$\quad\quad\quad\quad\quad\quad\quad\quad\quad$ + (weight of unusable fuel, full operating fluids
$\quad\quad\quad\quad\quad\quad\quad\quad\quad$ and full oil) $\quad\quad\quad\quad\quad\quad\quad\quad\quad\quad\quad$ (14–1)

The weight of controls is not always treated separately. It depends upon how complicated and heavy they are, and upon the technical necessity of making such a split.

In this chapter we concentrate mainly upon:
☐ powerplant weight;
☐ structure weight;
☐ weight of equipment and services;
☐ weight of controls.

Of these the most difficult is the design of the structure so as to achieve minimum weight and adequate strength. Much of the art of aircraft design lies in the creation of economical aircraft structures. The weight of those items comprising 'structure' is made up as follows:

$$\text{structure weight} = \text{weights of wing(s)} + \text{fuselage} + \text{engine nacelles} + \text{tail unit} + \text{landing gear} \qquad \text{eq (2--65)}$$

Structural design affects the achievable flight envelope, stability and control, the operational role and the development potential of an aeroplane. To understand how such effects come about we must know something of the principles involved.

Structural forms and applications

In its purest form a structure is a system of individual members arranged in frames. The simplest structures used in aeronautics are readily recognised as frames, but more advanced varieties lose their simplicity as members are made to do more than one job. This may be seen by comparison between figs. 14.1 and 2. Analogies can be drawn between the human body, with a soft external skin which fairs and protects the load-bearing skeleton (which holds everything in shape) and the body of the crab or the lobster, both of which have shells which serve a dual purpose. Although such structures appear to differ at first sight, the separate load-bearing skeleton and the load-bearing shell share features which obey similar principles.

Quite apart from fundamental tensile, compressive and shear-stressed members (fig. 2.17), parts behave as beams, struts, ties and thin-walled tubes. Although larger aeroplanes rely heavily upon thin-walled shell forms, light aeroplanes exhibit greater variety. Table 14–1 gives an idea of the percentage of structural arrangements among aircraft displayed at Oshkosh, Wisconsin in 1978 (ref. 4.15). The figures are not necessarily absolute. For examples, low-winged aeroplanes tend to have better shapes and lift/drag ratios than those with struts and wires. As the aircraft appearing at the EAA Fly-in come from all over the USA, it would be reasonable to expect a large number to be clean monoplanes, simply because they can get there more easily, with their better cruise lift/drag ratios.

TABLE 14–1

Percentage of structural arrangements seen among amateur-built
aircraft in the USA
(Based upon ref 4.15)

Construction	Structural form	Percentage present
Tube and fabric	Triangulated truss	48
All metal	Mainly thin-walled tube	29
All wood	Mixed	14
Composite	Development of thin-walled tube, with foam stabilised skin – but there are arguments about what constitutes 'composite' construction	8

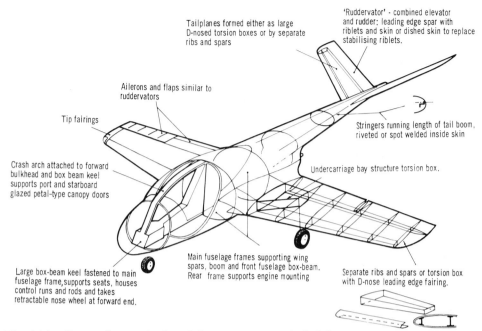

Tailplanes formed either as large
D-nosed torsion boxes or by separate
ribs and spars

'Ruddervator' - combined elevator
and rudder: leading edge spar with
riblets and skin or dished skin to replace
stabilising riblets.

Ailerons and flaps similar to
ruddervators

Tip fairings

Stringers running length of tail boom,
riveted or spot welded inside skin

Crash arch attached to forward
bulkhead and box beam keel
supports port and starboard
glazed petal-type canopy doors

Undercarriage bay structure torsion box.

Large box-beam keel fastened to main
fuselage frame, supports seats, houses
control runs and rods and takes
retractable nose wheel at forward end.

Main fuselage frames supporting wing
spars, boom and front fuselage box-beam.
Rear frame supports engine mounting

Separate ribs and spars or torsion box
with D-nose leading edge fairing.

Fig. 14.1 Parts of a particular airframe structure (ref. 5.6).

In a year or two we may see a large growth in aeroplane designs utilising man-made materials. Already many sailplanes and gliders are composite. These could well overtake one or two of the others. Such materials have technical and aesthetic potential. Their lightness allows advantage to be taken of low-powered lightweight engines now available in the commercial and domestic fields for chainsaws and snowmobiles. The main danger to supplies is that many materials are by-products of the oil industry.

Aerostructures are never 'perfect', in the sense of having only just enough members to keep them stable and in equilibrium under any system of forces. When a structure has too few members it is said to be deficient. If it has too many, it is redundant. Paradoxically, aerostructures feature a great many redundancies in the endless pursuit of safety and lightness. This introduces difficulties when calculating stresses in individual members.

The basic triangulated truss and the thin-walled tube are used in one form or another in almost every aircraft. The truss is the easiest and cheapest to repair, but it is not as fail-safe as the thin-walled tube. Even so, a classic example is that of the *Hawker Hurricane* and *Supermarine Spitfire*, which together formed the main fighter strength of the Royal Air Force in 1940. The *Hurricane* served in greater numbers than the *Spitfire* (33 Squadrons, as against 19 *Spitfire* Squadrons). It had a tough pin-jointed tubular frame fuselage covered with a soft skin of stringers and fabric, and metal wings (fig. 14.3 (ref. 13.6)). Light damage was easily repaired at Station level, and overall serviceability was high, at 63 per cent. The *Spitfire* had a load-bearing stressed skin which was more vulnerable to light damage. Repairs often had to be made away from Stations, at Maintenance Units and factories, and its serviceability was only about 37 per cent. Although the *Spitfire* had a better performance than the *Hurricane*, the superior front-line strength of the latter enabled it to shoot down three aircraft to every

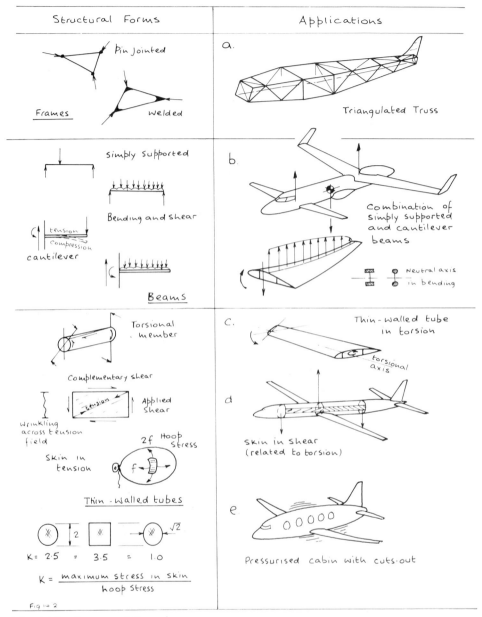

Fig. 14.2   Structural forms.

two of the *Spitfire*, in spite of the *Spitfire* being the better gun-platform. Nevertheless, the *Spitfire* is sentimentally regarded as the main British fighter of the Battle of Britain.

Both *Spitfire* and *Hurricane* weighed about 6 600 lb (3 000 kg) in their 1940 versions. That was only marginally heavier than the limiting weight of a light aeroplane today (6 000 lb, 2 730 kg).

Composite structures are likely to satisfy many, if not most, of the needs of the light aeroplane designer in the future. They are not the absolute answer at present, because it is impossible to prove their integrity under all required conditions.

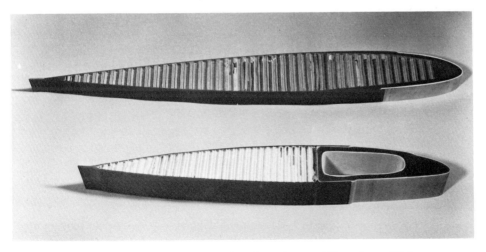

Plate 14–1 (Top) Composite foam/epoxy/fibreglass *Viking Dragonfly*, designed by Bob Walters and Al Nelson, is powered with a 1600 cc *Volkswagen* engine and won the 'outstanding new design' award at Oshkosh 1980. (*Viking Aircraft, USA*) (Bottom) Composite structure by *Ciba-Geigy*, makers of *Fibrelam* and *Aeroweb*. (*Ciba-Geigy Plastics and Additives Company, UK*)

Skins are made of glass-reinforced plastic (GRP) and plastic sheet sandwiching foam plastic and honeycomb filling. Thin metal skins have been successfully stabilised by bonding foam plastic sheet inside. A test specimen made by the author had 0.25 in (6 mm) polyvinylchloride (PVC) foam sheet bonded to 30 SWG (0.0124 in, 0.3 mm) sheet aluminium. Alone, the aluminium was structurally useless. Stiffened by the foam (which must not be allowed to crumple in compression) it became as resistant as 18 SWG sheet aluminium (0.048 in, 1.22 mm), with a weight equivalent to 22 SWG material (0.028 in, 0.7 mm).

Proof of structural integrity and adequate bonding between stressed skin and stabilising material (like comparatively inelastic foam, which collapses when bent) is a source of worry. Good quality control is essential. Reserve and safety factors must be adequate. Certification authorities which have the legally imposed task of proving that they have done a responsible job after there has been an accident, need reassurance that composite materials can withstand wear, tear, fatigue and weathering in the same way as conventional materials, before an accident occurs. Doubtless, reasonable proof of integrity will be forthcoming one day, but techniques are not quite reliable enough at present. In the case of the author's experiments with the foam-stabilised aluminium, properties seemed excellent until the material was dented – whereupon the foam collapsed and stiffness was not much better than that of a sheet of paper.

So far, composite materials have their widest applications among amateur-built aircraft, which operate on Permits to Fly in the UK and Experimental Cs of A in the USA (neither of which carries the burden of airworthiness needed for public transport operations).

Although it is no part of this book to dig into the principles of structural design, which is a separate subject in its own right, a number of useful references are included at the end of this chapter (refs. 5.1, 11.1, and 14.1 to 14.8 inclusive).

Second moments of area (moments of inertia)

We saw in chapter 2 (eq (2–24) *et seq*, and fig. 2.7) and in chapter 13 that a moment of inertia is a measure of the kinetic energy of rotation of a mass about a particular axis. We may imagine material to be cut into sections, and each section with its own finite mass (which is dependent upon its thickness) then has its moments of inertia which depend upon the shape of the section, and upon the density of the material.

When designing structures it is necessary to find the 'moments of inertia' of cross sections of members. Here a cross section has no mass, so that we must deal with the second moments of area instead. Mathematically, the way of finding a second moment of area is exactly the same as that given in eqs (2–23) and (2–24), except that in place of the mass terms m and M we use areas ΔA and A:

$$\text{second moment of area of section} = \Sigma_0^A \Delta A r^2 \qquad (14\text{–}2)$$

Thus, a second moment of area is the moment of inertia of a section, the mass of which is unity. In structural design we loosely talk about moments of inertia when we are really referring to second moments of area.

The importance of moments of area in structural design is that they are measures of the ability of certain cross sections of material to resist bending and torsion – the larger the value for a section, the lighter it can be built. If we have a spar which must not exceed a given weight, say, but we can play around with the shape of its cross section, then the shape with the largest moment of area (inertia) will be the one with the lowest

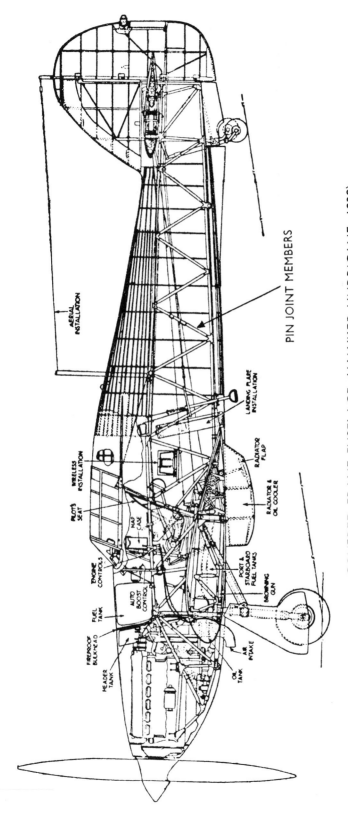

COVERED FRAME FUSELAGE (HAWKER HURRICANE, 1939)

Fig. 14.3 This construction helped to keep more *Hurricanes* than *Spitfires* in combat in 1940, making this aeroplane the more effective fighter in terms of shooting down enemy aircraft in the *Battle of Britain* (reproduced from ref. 13.6).

stress level. The smaller the second moment of area of a section, the heavier the structure.

It may be shown that if M is the bending moment of a system of loads applied to a section, I is the relevant 'moment of inertia', E is Young's Modulus of Elasticity:

$$E = \text{stress}/\text{strain} \qquad (14\text{--}3)$$

R is the radius of curvature of the neutral axis, and f is the compressive or tensile stress at some distance y from the neutral axis, then:

$$M/I = f/y = E/R \qquad (14\text{--}4)$$

From this we see that for a given bending moment:

  intensity of stress varies as $1/$moment of inertia (i.e. second moment of area)

all else remaining equal. The structural designer must therefore explore the use of cross sections which combine the largest second moments or area with the least material.

Similarly, we can consider a member in torsion, in which case we measure the polar moment of inertia (polar second moment of area) as if it were a flywheel rotating about the torsional axis (fig. 14.2c). In this case let T be the applied torque at the section, J the polar 'moment of inertia', q the shear stress at some radius r from the torsional axis, C the Modulus of Rigidity of the material, θ the angle of twist, and L the length along which the twist is applied (e.g. the length of the semispan of a wing), then:

$$T/J = q/r = C\theta/L \qquad (14\text{--}5)$$

From this we see again that, for a given torsion:

  intensity of shear stress varies as $1/$polar 'moment of inertia'

Therefore, the farther out from the torsional axis that material can be arranged, the lighter will be the shear-carrying structure.

Generally, light aeroplane structures are not too critical, so that designers can choose freely among commercially-produced materials. Thus, although an I-section beam is theoretically superior in bending to one of O-section, for the same overall depth (because of its larger moment of inertia about its neutral axis), the tubular spar is better in torsion and does not need additional structure in that respect. It is simple – and its volume can sometimes be filled with fuel. Jim Bede, who designed the *AA–1 Yankee*, the *BD–4* and *BD–5*, is understood to have chosen the tubular wing spar form for such reasons.

First estimate of weight

Accurate estimates of weight must be made early in the design process. These must be checked, rechecked and updated at frequent intervals. The process splits into:

☐the preliminary estimate, of which there may be several;
☐the second (continuously updated) estimate.

If the preliminary estimate is optimistically light, the final weight will be heavier than originally thought. The result will be a sluggish, underpowered, nondescript performer with inferior handling qualities. If the initial estimate is pessimistic, the aeroplane will be designed from the start with oversized wings and tail, and it will be too heavy in other directions. Again, flying qualities will suffer, and there will be increased manufacturing and operating costs.

The effectiveness of a design can be judged by the ratio:

$$\text{useful (disposable) load} / \text{gross weight} = \tfrac{1}{3} \text{ to } \tfrac{1}{2} \qquad (14-6)$$

for modern light aeroplanes. Fig. 14.4 has been averaged from a number of sources (ref. 11.1, 14.9 to 14.14 inclusive). Manufacturers' data from *Beech, Cessna, Gulfstream American* and *Piper* were obtained from company specifications, which are often updated annually.

Several observations can be made from fig. 14.4:

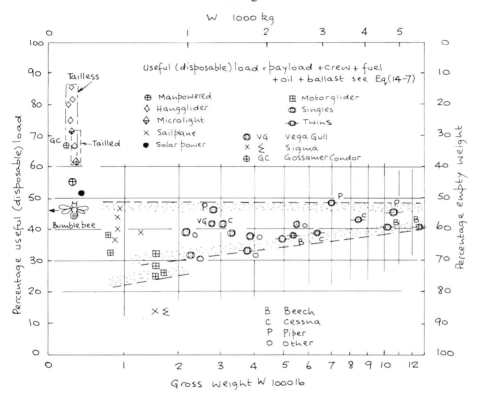

Fig. 14.4   Typical useful loads and empty weights (some averaged, some estimated, some single examples).

☐ The addition of a tail increases structure weight and reduces the percentage load that can be carried (compare the hang gliders).

☐ Manpowered aircraft have lighter useful loads than hang gliders, although the canard *Gossamer Condor* (ref. 14.9), which won the *Kremer prize* in 1977 just managed to achieve the useful load of microlights.

☐ Many of the glass sailplanes, and some modern twin-engined aeroplanes, have comparable percentage useful loads around the value calculated for the highly efficient, longranging aerial-work insect, the bumblebee (46 per cent).

☐ Motor gliders and single engined aeroplanes tend to have the lowest percentage useful loads.

☐ The British experimental *Sigma* (Σ) sailplane had the lowest percentage useful load, but one of the highest glide ratios (ref. 14.12).

The starting point for the first estimate is eq (1–1), in which:

$$\text{useful load} = \text{usable fuel} + \text{oil} + \text{payload} + \text{crew} + \text{ballast} \qquad (14\text{--}7)$$

Sometimes the weight of oil is included in this total, instead of counting it in the standard empty weight, as in eq (14–1). However, the weight of oil is such a small fraction that often it can be ignored without too much error. Weight of ballast ought to be zero, but sometimes it has to be included if the centre of gravity has come out in the wrong place, or when an aircraft is being tested at design gross weight.

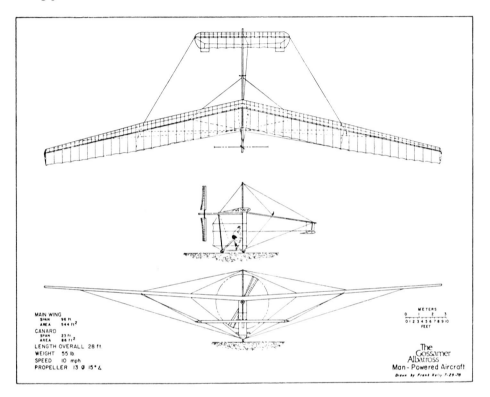

MAIN WING
SPAN   96 ft
AREA   544 ft²
CANARD
SPAN   23 ft
AREA   86 ft²
LENGTH OVERALL 28 ft
WEIGHT   55 lb
SPEED   10 mph
PROPELLER 13 0 15° ∠

METERS
0   1   2   3
0 1 2 3 4 5 6 7 8 9 10
FEET

The
Gossamer
Albatross
Man - Powered Aircraft
Drawn by Frank Kelly, 7-29-78

Fig. 14.5 *Gossamer Albatross* which flew the channel in 1979 has a similar configuration to its predecessor, *Gossamer Condor*, which won the *Kremer Prize* for man-powered flight in August 1977. (*Hang Gliding*, May 1979)

Many modern sailplanes are designed to carry water ballast as an aid to fast cruising to an area of lift. This may weigh between 12 and 15 per cent of the gross weight.

The amount of fuel carried by most light aeroplanes is modest, around 15 per cent for most piston-propeller aeroplanes, with singles carrying 2 to 3 per cent less than twins. Turboprop aircraft carry about double the fuel because of their thirstier engines, but their powerplants are lighter, and they fly faster. The result is that useful loads are about 2 per cent of gross weight heavier than for piston-propeller machines. Agricultural aeroplanes are permitted to carry overloads around by allowing smaller structural reserve strength, so increasing the actual payload by about half to almost as much again.

Table 14–2 gives some idea of the relative proportions of the different items of weight dealt with so far. Knowing the payload to be carried (e.g. number of occupants plus baggage), and then adding the percentage fuel load, we arrive at a notional useful load for a projected design. The gross weight is then calculated as the reciprocal of the

TABLE 14–2

Generalised weight breaksdown

Aircraft	Percentage of gross weight			
	Payload (occupants plus bags/ freight)	Fuel load (includes oil)	Useful load	Standard empty weight
A Manpowered:				
(1) conventional	55	—	55	45
(2) canard	66	—	66	34
B Hang glider:				
(1) conventional	70	—	70	30
(2) tailless	80	—	80	20
(3) powered	64	1	65	35
C Sailplane	40	—	40 (excluding ballast)	60
D Motorglider	28	4	32	68
E Single-piston trainer/tourer/ business	30	10	40	60
F Single-piston agricultural	40	10	50	50

(Note: such aeroplanes are usually permitted to be overloaded by about 1.5 to 1.75 times design weight in the USA, and 1.25 to 1.5 times design weight in the UK)

G Twin-piston tourer/ business-executive/ light-transport	23	15	38	62
H Turboprop-twin business-executive/ light transport	10 (min)	30 (max)	40	60

(Note: the turboprop, being a jet, is thirstier than the piston counterpart, but it is faster and gets there in a shorter time so that, with relatively lightweight engines, useful load is improved)

---

percentage useful load obtained from the table, times the actual weight of payload plus fuel, i.e.:

project gross weight, W_o = (weight of payload + fuel)/useful load ratio   (14–8)

where useful load ratio = percentage useful load/100.

The standard empty weight has numerous components, shown in eq (14–1) and developed in tables 14–3 and 14–4. The breakdown selected should be the one which the

TABLE 14–3

Weight component groups

Item	Typical components
Powerplant	Dry engine, propeller, spinner, gearing or belt drive (if any), engine mounting, exhaust system, coolers, oil-system, fuel-system on engine-side of firewall, alternators, accumulator (which may be treated alternatively as part of the electrical system), cowling.
Structure	Wing, ailerons, tabs, flaps, slats, struts, bracing. Body (fuselage, hull). Nacelles (but these might also be summed under powerplant, or wing). Canopy, canopy mechanism. Stabilator, tailplane, elevator, tabs (i.e., total horizontal empennage). Fin, rudder, tabs (i.e. total vertical empennage). Landing gear, floats, struts, bracing.
Controls	Flying control: stick, wheel, pedals, bar, rods, bellcranks, pulleys, brackets, hinges. Engine controls on cockpit-side of firewall.
Equipment and services	Basic cockpit instrumentation (ref. 14.15). Seats, furnishing. Electrical system. Hydraulic system. Pneumatic system. Fuel system. Avionic (nav'-comm') system. Paint. Antennae, de-icing gear. Miscellaneous airframe equipment.

designer believes to be most useful for his particular purposes. For example, a fuel system which is integral with 'wet' wings (wing structure forming the actual tanks), or engine nacelles which form tanks out of their own structures, might be treated most easily under the general heading of structure weight. On the other hand, an aeroplane with separate tanks, located within but not part of the structure, might warrant a completely separate heading under 'fuel and oil supply'.

Powerplant weight

The powerplant is a heavy item and its weight, if miscalculated, can throw everything else awry. Theoretically, powerplant weight depends upon the amount of power required, in the form of rated power, or sea level static thrust. In practice, the weight depends upon whichever engine is available, more often than not. Fig. 14.6 shows a number of mainly average points taken from manufacturer's sources for propeller-driven aeroplanes. Being averages they do not reveal the scatter. Care must be taken with very light aircraft, which suffer large variations in powerplant weight below 1 000 lb (455 kg) gross. This is caused by the chunky, commercial stock engines, with comparatively large nuts, bolts, studs, alternators and spark plugs. There is little choice or chance of neat engine-airframe matching.

TABLE 14–4

Aircraft weight breakdown

Item	Weight
Engine (dry)	
Propeller	
Engine mounting	
Engine systems (forward of firewall)	
Total powerplant	_____
Wing	
Fuselage (or hull)	
Tail unit (empennage)	
Landing gear	
Total structure	_____
Fuel tanks and structure	
Fuel system	
Oil tanks and structure	
Oil system	
Residual fuel and oil	
Total fuel and oil supply	_____
Flying control system	
Hydraulic system	
Pneumatic system	
Electrical system	
Total systems	_____
Avionics and instruments	
Furnishing	
Air conditioning	
Safety equipment	
Total fixed equipment	_____
Removable equipment	
Paint	_____
Empty weight	_____
Operating equipment	
Unusable fuel	
Operating fluids	
Oil	
Crew and its baggage (if required)	_____
Standard empty weight	_____
Passengers and baggage	
Freight	
Fuel	
Provisions (consumables)	_____
Disposable (useful) load	_____
Gross, all-up, take-off weight	_____

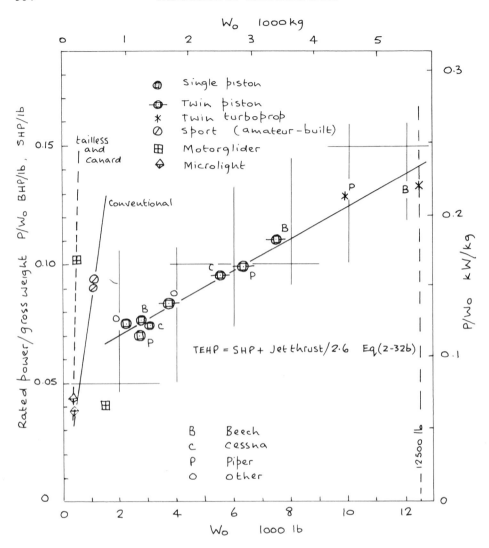

Fig. 14.6   Power/gross weight ratios of propeller-driven aeroplanes up to 12 500 lb (5 700 kg).

Very light (microlight) aeroplanes (with the exception of manpowered aircraft and motor-gliders) tend to be overpowered in terms of power/weight ratio, P/W_o. Canard and tailless machines are cases in point. They have relatively light and efficient structures in the ranges shown in fig. 14.6, but the available powerplants spoil the picture. They are commercial units, almost without exception, with weights fixed by other considerations (like the ability to be knocked around in the field, and in the back of a pick-up truck). The result is that rated power/gross weight is so dominated by the relative weight of the engine to the light airframe, that both the canard and the tailless aeroplane appear to need more power per unit gross weight than aeroplanes with tails. The simple truth is that their structures, being light and efficient, cannot be matched with equally efficient low-powered engines.

Motorgliders are hybrids. We should expect them to be different. Manpowered

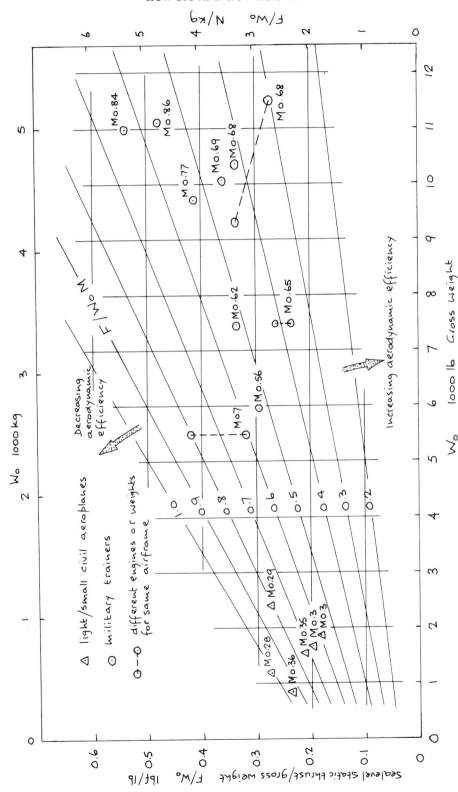

Fig. 14.7 Thrust/weight ratios of light/small civil jets and military trainers, for constant aerodynamic efficiency, as indicated by F/W_0M.

aircraft have only been plotted in fig. 14.6 for consistency.

The result of a plot like that shown in the figure implies the existence of two quite separate worlds in light aviation, distinguished by two differently applied technological cultures. A dichotomy of this kind is of service to the major industry which, certainly in the USA, watches amateur research and development, gaining insights, knowledge and fresh ideas at low cost to itself. Innovation of the ideas of amateurs within the industry then produces feedback and spin-off later, which can be used in turn by the amateur.

Powerplant weight (which includes the many items covered in tables 14–3 and 14–4) may be factored from the dry engine weight, or basic engine weight, by means of the installation factors in table 14–5 (from ref. 14.16). If the engine weight is W_E and the powerplant weight, W_P, the powerplant weight ratio W_P/W_O may be calculated in terms of gross weight, W_O, rated power, P, and installation factor, F_P, from the following formula:

$$\text{propeller-powerplant weight ratio, } W_P/W_O = F_P\,(W_E/P)(P/W_O) \quad (14\text{–}9)$$

Rated power/gross weight, P/W_O, is selected from fig. 14.6 for the kind of aeroplane, engine and gross weight the designer has in mind. The specific weight of the engine, W_E/P, is picked from fig. 14.8.

The weight of a jet powerplant is treated in the same way, except that the formula becomes:

$$\text{jet powerplant } W_P/W_O = F_P\,(W_E/F)(F/W_O) \quad (14\text{–}10)$$

The values are again found from table 14–5 and figs. 14.7 and 14.9.

Unfortunately, the factors applying to small jet engines are based upon scanty information. Light jet aircraft are fuel-gulping novelties, although the price of avgas is causing designers to turn more and more towards light turboprop and jet propulsion, because kerosene is cheaper. Some of the results upon which fig. 14.7 is based are twenty-five years old. With scatter like that shown, the only reasonable curves that might be drawn through the points are those for aerodynamic efficiency, expressed in the form:

$$(V/\mu')(L/D)_R, \text{ or } (M/\mu')(L/D)_R$$

the first of which appeared in eq (8–23a), while a general version of the second appeared in eq (7–2) and fig. 7.2.

These expressions enable us to make two simplifying assumptions. First, that specific fuel consumption varies little for the sort of engines available, so that it remains more or less constant. Second, that aerodynamic shape, construction and standard of finish enable them to be lumped into one comparable group. Thus, because in level flight *lift = weight* and *thrust = drag*, we may use the reciprocal of $M(L/D)_R$ as a measure of 'inefficiency', while replacing L by W_O and D by F, such that:

$$M(W_O/F) \text{ varies as } M(L/D)_R \quad (14\text{–}11)$$

and, $F/W_O M$ grows as an aeroplane becomes less efficient.

The lines drawn in fig. 14.7 are 'eyeballed' averages for the empirical results quoted It would be wrong to attempt to use the same lines for big jets, supersonic strike aeroplanes, or aircraft in other groups – although the method still applies.

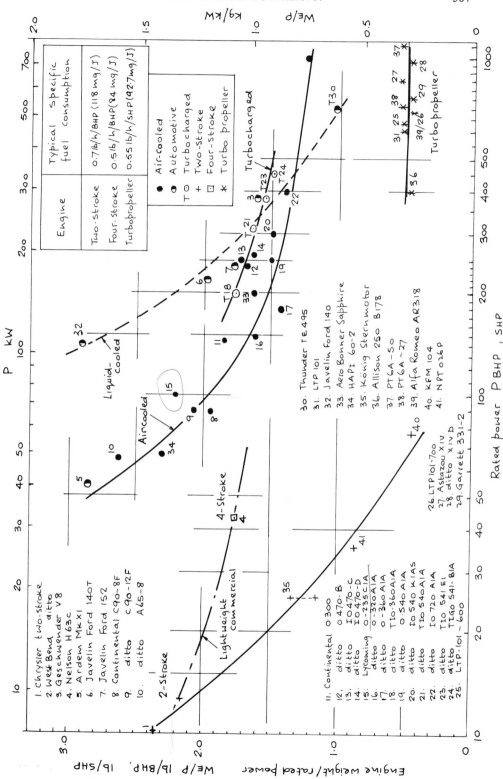

Fig. 14.8 Specific equipped weights of piston and turbopropeller engines (data from various published sources and author's estimates).

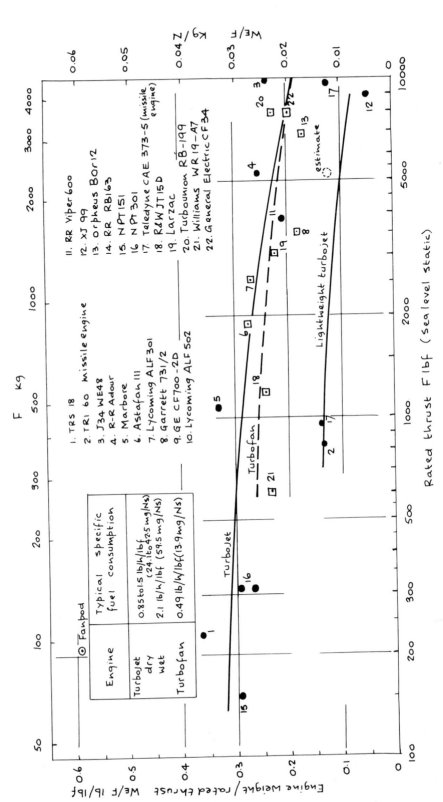

Fig. 14.9 Turbojet and turbofan engine specific (equipped) weights (data from various published sources and author's estimates).

TABLE 14–5 (from ref. 14.16)

Engine installation weight

Engine	Installation factor, F_P
Piston, single, air-cooled	1.3
twin, air-cooled	1.4
large multi, air-cooled	1.6
liquid-cooled	1.9
Turbopropeller	1.7

All of the above include the weight of the propeller:
propeller weight, $W_{prop} = 0.2515\ P^{1.04}$ (ref. 15.12)
(The liquid-cooled factor includes the weight of the cooling system:
radiator, pipes, etc. We assumed that the weight of such items makes the
unit 45 per cent heavier than an equivalent air-cooled engine)

Ducted fan (plus bracing and stators)	1.03 times F_P for engine
Turbojet, within wings	1.25
within fuselage	1.2
in wing pod	1.05 to 1.2
	(depending upon silencers and thrust reversers, which may increase factor to 1.3)
in fuselage pods	1.3

[handwritten margin notes: metal 35# for 115 hp; 11# for wood]

The lightest jet aeroplanes in the figure are the least efficient. There are few engines
from which to choose. Thrust/weight ratios are determined by what can be achieved
with the only 'hardware' available. Because of the square-cube law the surface area per
unit volume of such aeroplanes (proportional to length²/length³) is high. Therefore,
the drag generated/unit weight, and the corresponding thrust required/unit weight is
higher than for larger aeroplanes.

Wing group weight

The weight of the wing group is usually the second heaviest item, so that
miscalculations can again be critical. The group includes spars, booms, shear webs,
ailerons, flaps, struts, wires and all attachments. Variations in wing group weights can
be large, depending upon:

☐ Design gross weight, W_O.
☐ Wing area, S, which is determined most of all by the stall speed, unless the aeroplane
   is optimised for cruising, or is a racer, in which case wing and wetted area depend
   upon the need for low drag.
☐ Aspect ratio, A, and span, b.
☐ Design diving speed, V_D.
☐ Design manoeuvring load factor, n, multiplied in turn by the ultimate factor of
   safety, 1.5 (but which may sometimes be as high as 2 for special applications), which
   together produce the ultimate load factor, N.
☐ Wing chord, c, and section thickness ratio, τ, which taken together define both the

depth of spar opposing bending, and the circumference of skin taking torsional shear.

☐ Taper ratio, λ, which is the tip chord/root chord, and which determines geometrically the moment arm of the resultant lift load, acting at a distance from the plane of symmetry, which applies a bending moment to the wing.

☐ Type of structure: cantilever, braced, monoplane, biplane, 'rag and tube', wood, metal, man-made fibre.

☐ Magnitude and location of relieving loads in the wing, in the form of engines, pods, overload and other fuel tanks, landing gear, underwing stores, spray gear, etc.

The commonest way of calculating the weight of the wing group is to split the structure into parts which resist bending, and those which resist shear (like ribs, which are designed to transmit air loads into the main structure). Comprehensive formulae are usually complicated. Among the simplest, which also give reasonably average values for the sorts of light aircraft with which we are mainly concerned, is the following derived from Sechler and Dunn (ref. 14.8), by means of some recent test results (ref. 14.16). We express the weight of the wing group as a ratio of the gross weight:

$$\text{wing group weight ratio, } W_w/W_o = a_w F_w N(2.5b + 120)/10^4 \qquad (14\text{--}12)$$

in which the terms have just been defined, with the exception of the weight factor, a_w given in table 14-6, and a structural factor, F_w, given in fig. 14.12.

TABLE 14–6

Ultimate load and weight factors

Ultimate load factor, N	Weight factor, a_w
5	1.00
6	0.88
7	0.78
8	0.71
9	0.65
10	0.61
11	0.56
12	0.53

The ultimate load factor is obtained from table 14-7 (from ref. 14.17), the relevant value being multiplied by 1.5 for a conventional structure. The factor should be 4.0 for one that is composite in this present learning period.

Table 14-7 is quite close to that given in ref. 14.17, except that the old British semi-aerobatic category is being dropped in favour of the FAA utility category (ref. 14.18). However, although the load factors given in the table tend to produce the severest cases, aircraft with low wing loadings suffer more from gusts than those with higher wing loadings. The reason may be seen by considering the change in angle of attack at a wing caused by a vertical gust, $\pm U_i$ (expressed in the same units as equivalent airspeed, V_i):

$$\text{lift increment caused by gust, } \Delta L = \pm q a_A (U_i/V_i)S$$
$$= \pm \rho_o a_A U_i V_i S \qquad (14\text{--}13)$$

Here a_A and S are the lift slope and wing area respectively. The incremental change in wing loading is obtained by dividing this equation by S. The incremental change in load factor, $\pm\Delta_n$, is then obtained on dividing through by the wing loading of the aeroplane before meeting the gust. Thus, the total gust load factor is given by:

$$n = 1 \pm \Delta_n = 1 \pm \rho_o a_A U_i V_i / w \qquad (14\text{-}14)$$

in which w is the undisturbed wing loading.

The above expression shows that the lower the wing loading of an aeroplane, the larger is the effect of a given gust. The basic gust envelope for design purposes is shown in fig. 14.10b, and the increments are calculated by working U and V, or U_i and V_i in the same units. In the figure we have deliberately mixed up the units, the gusts being given in ft/s, while speed is in knots (KTAS or KEAS). Gust response and load increase rapidly when the wing loading is less than 10 lb/ft² (48.8 kg/m²), so that an aerobatic aeroplane which tends to have a low wing loading also needs to have gust cases investigated in detail. Racing aeroplanes with relatively high wing loadings are designed more by manoeuvring criteria.

Another useful formula (ref. 14.19) derived from work of Ivan H. Driggs, past Director of the Research Division of the Bureau of Aeronautics Department of the United States Navy, can be transposed as follows, using the same notation as before, and working in FPSR units:

$$W_w / W_o = F_w S \sqrt{(N/1000\,\bar{c}\,W_o)} \qquad (14\text{-}15a)$$
$$= F_w \sqrt{[(N/1000)(b/w)]} \qquad (14\text{-}15b)$$

in which b is the wing span. When the span loading W_o/b has been determined by rate of climb requirements and we wish to juggle with a number of other parameters, like wing loading and aspect ratio, w and A, the formula becomes:

$$W_w / W_o = \sqrt{[(N/1000)(W_o/b)A]/w} \qquad (14\text{-}15c)$$

So far the equations have not included the effect of taper ratio, λ, thickness ratio, τ, or applied to anything other than a cantilever metal monoplane wing. However, a number of approximate adjustments can be made for variations in taper, thickness ratio, wing loading and ultimate load factor, as shown in fig. 14.11 (based on a method given by Howe in ref. 14.16). If we take the wing group weight ratio for a given set of operational conditions as unity (or 100 per cent), then the figure shows how W_w/W_o changes as each term varies separately. A diagram of this kind can be drawn for any wing.

The method given by Howe is based upon the following relationships:

Wing weight varies as (wing loading w)$^{0.27}$;

(wing area S)$^{0.9}$;
(taper ratio $C_i/C_r = \lambda$), in the form $((1 + 2\lambda)/(3 + 3\lambda))^{0.27}$;
(aspect ratio A)$^{0.45}$;
(thickness ratio $t/c = \tau$)$^{-0.45}$;
(ultimate load factor N)$^{0.27}$;
(wing span b)$^{0.9}$;
$1/$(cosine ¼ chord sweep angle Λ)$^{0.9}$ $\qquad (14\text{-}16)$

Very crudely these can be expressed for a quick assessment:

$$\sqrt{(\sqrt{w})},\ ((1 + 2\lambda)/(3 + 3\lambda)),\ \sqrt{A},\ 1/\sqrt{\tau},\ \sqrt{(\sqrt{N})},\ b,\ 1/\cos\Lambda \quad (14\text{-}16a)$$

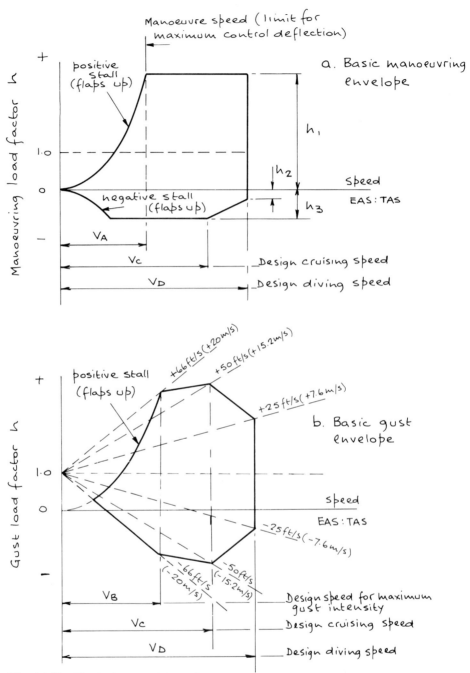

Fig. 14.10   Typical normal load factor versus speed (called *V–n*) diagrams.

Thus, we may approach the problem by considering each factor in turn, while shaping our wing to suit operational requirements;

☐ Wing area for stall speed, and to give a high enough wing loading for cruising and avoidance of damage by gusts.

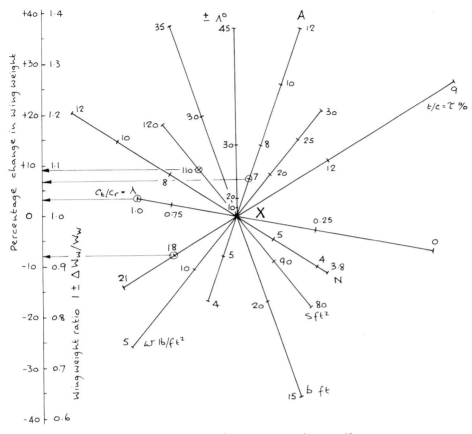

Datum wing at intersection of lines, X:

Wing loading ω = 15 lb/ft² (0.734 kg/m²)

area S = 100 ft² (9.29 m²)

thickness ratio t/c = τ = 15 percent

taper ratio c_t/c_r = λ = 0.5

aspect ratio b²/S = A = 6

Ultimate load factor = N = 1.5n = 6

Wing span b = 24.6 ft (7.5 m)

Sweep at ¼ chord Λ = 0°

Thus, if we wish to change the datum wing, the percentage changes in wing weight might be, for example:

S = 110 ft² = +9%

τ = 18% = −8%

A = 7 = +7%

c_t/c_r = 1 = +3%

Fig. 14.11 Effect of changes in wing geometry upon weight of wing of a light aeroplane.

☐ Span loading for low lift-dependent drag and, therefore, good climb and cruise performance.

☐ Taper for reduction of structure weight, and reduced aerodynamic damping in roll.

☐ Section for lift/drag, the thickness being determined by the need for stowage volume

TABLE 14–7

Load factor
(based upon ref. 14.17)

Speed	Load factor	Aeroplane type		
		Non-aerobatic	'Utility'	Aerobatic
V_A, V_C, V_D	n_1	$2.1 + 24\,000/(W_0 + 1\,000)$ or $+ 3.8$ whichever is the lesser. W_0 is in lb.	$+4.4$	$+6.0$
V_D	n_2	0.0	-1.0	-1.0
V_C	n_3	$-0.4\,n_1$	-1.8	-3.0

and the lowest possible structure weight. Choice of thickness ratio needs considerable care, especially for high speed. Wing sweep is in many ways a geometric trick played upon the air to reduce compressibility effects by making a wing of a given depth aerodynamically thinner. However, with most light aeroplanes which operate at lowish Reynolds numbers, there is not much difference in maximum lift coefficients and minimum drag coefficients between 12 and 21 per cent thick sections in any one aerofoil family, so that choice of thickness is less critical at low speeds.

Fig. 14.12 extends the possibility of calculation beyond the cantilever monoplane to the braced monoplane, and biplane, using data provided by Wood (refs. 14.13 and 14.14). The values given are factors F_w by which cantilever wing weight ratios may be multiplied to obtain braced monoplane and biplane weight ratios. The weight of the tail unit is included for treatment in due course, and this is shown as a factor, F_T.

When calculating weight it pays to use more than one formula, so as to be able to reject any results that look wild.

Fuselage structure weight

The weight of the fuselage is another large item. Estimates are complicated by many factors. These include: the number of load cases involved and design diving speed, V_D; doors, hatches and cuts-out (all of which require surrounding structure); cockpit and cabin arrangement, and the extent of glazing; whether or not the fuselage is pressurised; flooring and the load it must carry; landing gear arrangement. There is then the weight of structure needed to take the wing and tail attachments.

Fig. 14.13 shows the way in which the surface area of fuselage is related to the weight of the aeroplane, A_{wf}/W_0, which is an example of the square-cube law. Fig. 14.14 shows the way in which the 'form factor' of the fuselage affects the surface area/gross weight of aeroplane. The term form factor is used for the ratio of surface area of fuselage to the product of fuselage length and diameter, A_{wf}/DL. The equivalent diameter of the fuselage is found by taking the square root of the area of the maximum cross section. A way of dealing with body surface area was shown in chapter 5: eqs. (5–39) and (5–40), and tables 5–5 and 5–6.

Table 14–8 shows the approximate weight of fuselage/surface area, W_F/A_{wf}, for

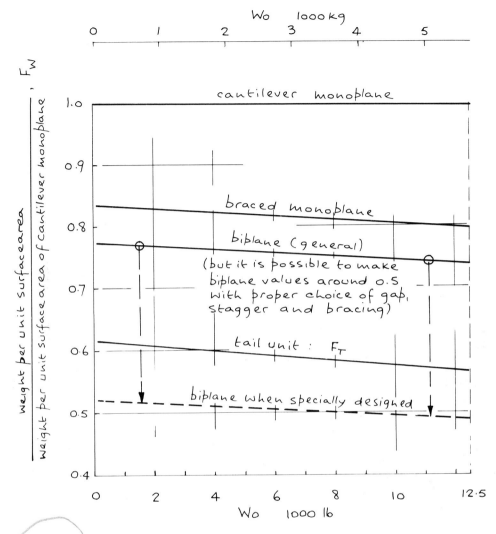

Fig. 14.12 Relative surface weight per unit area of wings and tails (based upon refs. 14.13 and 14.14).

various groups of light aeroplanes. The values include weights of skin, structure, glazing, flooring, attachments and fittings. Table 14-9 shows how other details of fuselage design, like landing gear, change the fuselage structure weight. These are given in the form of a design factor, F_F, rather like the installation factor F_P, used when calculating powerplant weight. Thus, when these terms are multiplied together:

$$\text{fuselage weight ratio, } W_F/W_O = F_F(W_F/A_{wf})(A_{wf}/W_O) \qquad (14\text{--}17)$$

Eq (14–17) appears to give reasonable 'ballpark' results for aeroplanes weighing less than 10000 lb (4536 kg), but it looks optimistic at heavier weights. Alternative formulae for heavier aeroplanes given by Howe can be manipulated into the form

$$\text{short range transport, } W_F/W_O = 0.0125 \ W_O^{0.18} \qquad (14\text{--}17a)$$
$$\text{long range transport, } W_F/W_O = 0.0013 \ W_O^{0.32} \qquad (14\text{--}17b)$$

TABLE 14–8

Ratio of fuselage weight/surface area

Aircraft group	Metal fuselage weight per unit surface area, W_F/A_{wf} lb/ft² (kg/m²)	
Single engine	1.27	(6.2)
Twin engine	1.24	(6.05)
Jet trainer	2.2	(10.7)
Jet executive	2.45	(11.9)
Weight of glazing (windscreen, canopy, windows)	1.5 to 2.0	(7.3 to 9.7)

TABLE 14–9

Fuselage weight factor
(mainly based upon ref. 5.5)

Type of fuselage	design factor, F_F
Pressurised	1.08
Rear-mounted engines	1.04
Landing gear:	
in wings	1.0
in fuselage	1.07
fixed, with no bay structure	0.96
Freighter	1.1
Wood, or tube and fabric structure	about 1.8 × weight of metal fuselage (this factor is about 2.0 for an aeroplane weighing 1 000 lb (455 kg), decreasing through 1.6 at 2 500 lb (1 140 kg) (the square-cube law again))
Flying boat hull	about 1.25 × above values (*see* fig. 14.16)

The allowance for engines mounted on the rear fuselage requires the same factors as those given above.

Seaplane hulls and floats

Hulls and floats are heavier than fuselages of equivalent surface area, because they must be strong enough to take severe water loads. Their weights increase as (water speed)². The weight of a hull, which includes the planing surfaces, keel and chines, is lighter than the weight of fuselage-plus-weight of landing gear. The square-cube law

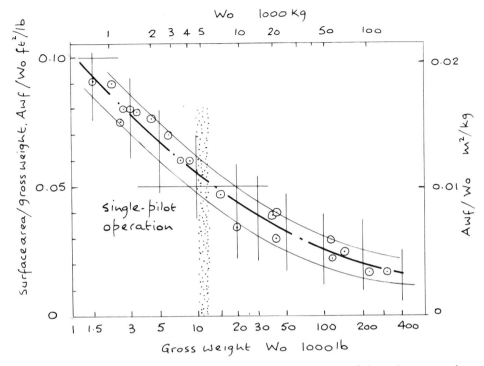

Fig. 14.13 Variation in fuselage surface area ratio with gross weight (a demonstration of the effect of the square-cube law, which shows that although weight increases roughly with length³, surface area only increases with length²).

affects the ratio of surface area/gross weight in a similar way to that shown in fig. 14.13, i.e., the larger and heavier the aeroplane, the lower the weight of hull and float structure per unit gross weight.

Seaplanes are not as common as landplanes and there is not the same quantity of data available for analysis. Nevertheless, work done by the author in 1965 to compare a military flying boat and amphibian, all with the same basic airframe, performance, and gross weight, produced the values shown in table 14–10 (from ref. 5.6).

TABLE 14–10

Structure weight/gross weight

Aircraft	Percentage structure weight	Gross weight ratio
Basic landplane	28	1.0
Flying boat variant	33	1.2
Amphibian variant	38	1.35

Data published by Thurston (ref. 9.4) suggests that the hull of a flying boat is about ¼ heavier again than the fuselage of an equivalent landplane up to 3000 lb (1370 kg), and this is confirmed by Wood in the larger sizes, up to 30000 lb (13700 kg) (ref. 14.13 and 14.14). The weight of seaplane floats/gross weight of aircraft is given in fig. 14.15, which was drawn from data given in refs. 13.6, 14.13 and 14.14 and some data published by *Edo-Aire* of New York in 1976. The weight of supporting struts and structure has not been included. The total weight of two floats and their attachment gear can be around 3 times the weight of a single float.

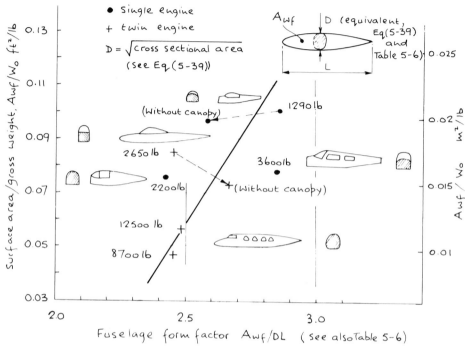

Fig. 14.14   Variation in fuselage surface area ratio with gross weight plotted against form factor A_{wf}/DL (*see* table 5–6).

The minimum volume of a single float must be enough to support the maximum design weight of a seaplane when the whole float is only just submerged in fresh water (which is less dense and therefore less supportive than sea water). Displacement in fresh water is 62 lb/ft³ (993 kg/m³), so that the volume (ft³) of a single float is the gross weight (lb) of the aeroplane/62. Most floats have a length/maximum diameter (roughly the depth from deck to keel), calculated as in eq (5–39), around 7.5 to 8. The weight per unit surface area of float varies between about 2 lb ft² (10 kg/m²) at $Wo =$ 1000 lb (454 kg) around 3 lb/ft² (15 kg/m²) at 7000 lb (3175 kg). Surface area is calculated in the same way as for a fuselage (table 5–6).

Fig. 14.17 shows a way of calculating the volume of a float, or any other awkwardly shaped body, by plotting a curve of area of cross-section at any station from bow to stern. The volume is the area under the curve, and this can be calculated by dividing the area into strips. The total area is then the sum of the areas of the strips.

Other approximations can be made by saying that the area under the curve of areas is equal to the mean height of the curve times the length of the float. If the curve is roughly sinusoidal as drawn, then the mean height is less than if the curve is semi-circular, and we have:

displacement is approximately $0.36\ (A_c)_{max}L$, when sinusoidal   (14–18a)

$\qquad\qquad\qquad 0.39\ (A_c)_{max}L$, when semi-circular   (14–18b)

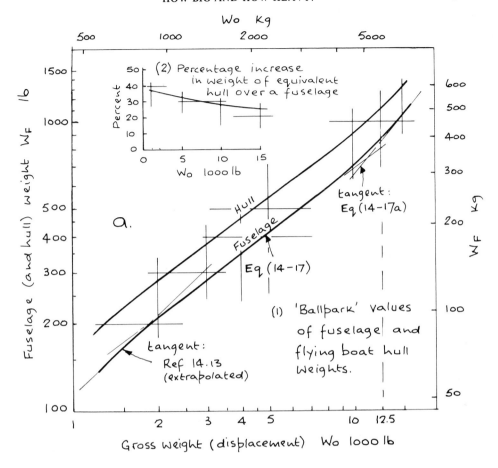

Fig. 14.15 a and b   Fuselage, hull and float weights.

The weight of a seaplane is not simply that of a similar landplane, plus a bit for the additional weight of the hull, or floats-plus struts (except in the case of a landplane fitted with floats). If performance is to be comparable, as in the projects shown in table 14–10, then bigger engines are needed to cope with the additional drag, and this means heavier powerplant, fuel and fuel system weights. In short, there is a 'domino, or 'snowball effect', in which the disturbance of one element ultimately disturbs the remainder.

Exactly the same effect can be seen in all weight calculations. Any simple change or improvement in one area snowballs to affect other areas. This is one good reason for not attempting to make one design do everything – which tends to be a costly and sometimes fatal flaw in many military projects.

Nacelle weight

The weights of engine nacelles, wing and fuselage pylons have not been swept up into the installation factor, F_p, in table 14–5. Instead they are treated as structure weight. However, the weight of a nacelle depends upon the size of the engine, for which reason we often find weight formulae based upon power and thrust. Other factors which affect the weight of nacelles are the position of the engines: either within wings and fuselages,

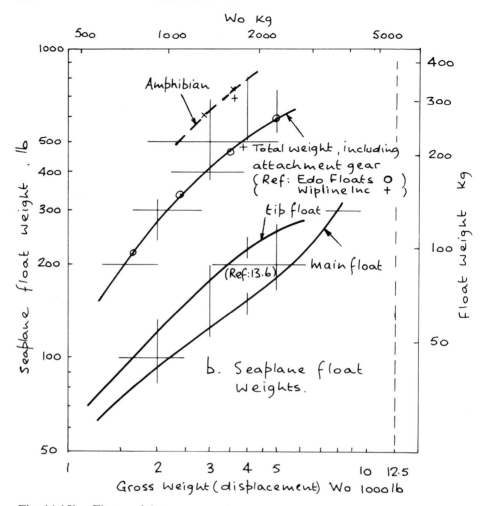

Fig. 14.15b   Float weight.

or supported outside them on pylons. When an engine is buried within a structure it is often more sensible to treat the weight of its mounting as structure weight, rather than as powerplant weight. Thus, some juggling may be necessary. This does not matter as long as we are consistent.

Table 14–11 summarises some of the weight ratios of nacelles and pylons. When an engine mounting is counted as structure weight, its weight must be subtracted from the powerplant weight, i.e. about 0.01 to 0.015 W_O must be taken away from the powerplant weight ratio.

Stabiliser and tail unit

We include under this heading the weight of the tailplane, or a canard foreplane, together with elevators, fin, rudder, and tabs of various kinds. Typically, the total weight of the stabilising, control and trimming surfaces is 2 to 4 per cent of the gross weight. Further the weight of these items can be treated as a fraction of the wing weight, because it is affected by similar factors.

TABLE 14–11
Nacelle Weight Estimation

Nacelle Arrangement	W_{Nac}/W_0	Other Estimates
Simple fairing	0.015 to 0.02	2 to 3 lb/ft² (10 to 15 kg/m²) based upon surface area
Fuel tank forming fairing	—	When nacelle forms alloy fuel tank skin, weight (lb) is roughly equal (numerically) to capacity in Imperial gallons/2 (but see also Table 14–13).
Nacelle + engine mounting	0.03 (0.01 to 0.015 for engine mounting)	4 lb/ft² (19.5 kg/m²) based upon surface area
Wing pylon	0.01 to 0.015 per engine	About 0.2 × powerplant weight.
Fuselage pylon	0.005 to 0.01 per engine	About one half the value given above.

Estimations of the weight of the whole tail unit and its parts can be made from fig. 14.12 and table 11–4. The first shows the tail unit weight as a ratio of the weight/unit area of the tail to the weight/unit area of a cantilever monoplane wing. To be more precise, the weight/unit area of the wing outside the lines of the fuselage, i.e., the net area. However, the method is sufficiently accurate if we work in gross area.

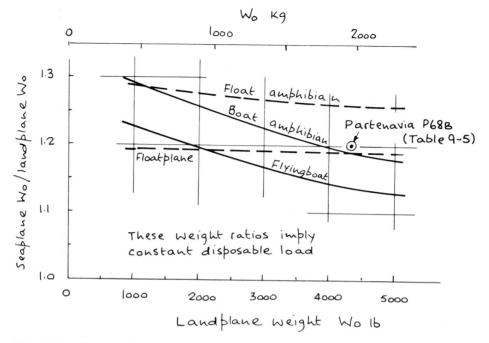

Fig. 14.16   Gross weight ratios of light seaplane arrangements with landplanes for the same task. When floats are fitted to a landplane it is often necessary to reduce disposable load so as to keep close to the original design gross weight.

Foreplanes are generally 0.15 to 0.25 of the gross area of the mainplane, unless the aeroplane has a pure tandem winged arrangement. This means that foreplanes are heavier than tailplanes.

In the case of a T-tail, three main effects occur:

☐ The area of the horizontal tail can be reduced somewhat, because it is working out of the worst wake effects, and it can therefore be made lighter.
☐ The vertical tail must be larger and stronger and therefore heavier, to support the high tail, with its inertia loads and vulnerability to 'round the clock' gust loads.
☐ The rear fuselage must be stronger to resist the heavier loading imposed by the high tail, it is therefore heavier.

Table 14–12 summarises in ratio form an example of the changes which took place between the *Piper PA–28R–201*, which had a fuselage-mounted horizontal tail, and the *PA–28RT–201*, which had a T-tail. The twin-engined *PA–44–180* has been included, because it belongs essentially to the same family, with some common units. The figures given for the *PA–28* variants show that the empennage weight alone was increased by a total of 38 per cent by using a T-tail. With the weight of empennage and tail cone added together, the weight of the new 'back-end' was nearly 32 per cent heavier.

TABLE 14-12

The effect upon weight and area of changing from a fuselage-mounted tail to a T-tail (the number is F_T, by which tail component weights might be multiplied in eqs (14-19) and (14-20)

Aircraft	Empty wt ratio	Tailcone wt ratio	Stabilator ratios		Vertical tail ratios	
			Area	wt	Area	wt
Stabilator on fuselage						
PA-28R-201 *Arrow III* (single-engine)	1.00 (1638 lb, 745 kg)	1.00 (45.3 lb, 20.6 kg)	1.00 (31.6 ft², 2.93 m²)	1.00 (44.7 lb, 20.3 kg)	1.00 (11.6 ft², 1.08 m²)	1.00 (16.46 lb, 7.5 kg)
T-tail						
PA-28RT-201 *Arrow IV* (single-engine)	1.02	1.23	0.84	0.90	1.52	2.68
PA-44-180 *Seminole* (twin-engine)	1.44	1.23	0.77	0.94	1.88	2.98

Note: the T-tail increased tail surface weight to 1.38 × that of *PA-28R-201*; and weight of new 'back-end' (aft of wing) including tail-cone to 1.32 × that of aircraft with stabilator on fuselage.

Thus, there are gains in using a T-tail, and there are losses. If losses outweigh gains there is no point in pursuing a change. It is perhaps significant that the T-tailed *PA–28* appears to have been abandoned as this is written.

To calculate tail weight we may take any appropriate wing weight formula for W_W/W_O from eqs (14–12) to (14–15c) and factor it as follows:

$$\text{tail weight ratio,} \quad W_T/W_O = (F_T/F_W)(S_T/S)(W_W/W_O) \qquad (14\text{–}19)$$

The values of F_T and F_W are shown in fig. 14.12. The ratio (S_T/S) is rather crude and represents the sum of the horizontal and vertical tail areas/wing area, such that we obtain from table 11–4:

$$S_T/S = (S_s + S_f)/S \qquad (14\text{–}20)$$

This assumes that the weight/area of the horizontal tail is almost the same as that of the vertical tail. The assumption is not far out, for if we calculate the weight/unit area of the stabilator and the vertical tail of the *PA–28R–201* in table 14–12, we see that:

$$44.7/31.6 = 1.414 \text{ lb/ft}^2 \text{ (6.9 kg/m}^2)$$

while, $\qquad\qquad\qquad\qquad\qquad\qquad\qquad\qquad\qquad\qquad\qquad$ (14–21)

$$16.46/11.6 = 1.418 \text{ lb/ft}^2 \text{ (6.92 kg/m}^2)$$

The assumptions begin to fall down when we resort to a T-tail, and we have to multiply each component by a relevant factor F_T which, in the absence of more comprehensive data, may be taken from table 14–12 and applied as required to the different weight and area terms.

Undercarriage

The weight of the landing gear is about 4 to 6 per cent of the gross weight of an aeroplane. Much depends upon its layout and the role of the machine. Military aircraft have the heaviest landing gears, while large civil aircraft have the lightest, in terms of weight ratio.

The following values have been given by Pazmany (ref. 5.1) and Howe (ref. 14.16):

☐Light aeroplanes, less than 10 000 lb (4 545 kg)
$\quad W_U/W_O = 0.055$ (nosewheel type) (ref. 5.1)
$\qquad\quad = 0.045$ (tailwheel type) (ref. 5.1)
$\qquad\quad = 0.048$ (ref. 14.16) $\qquad\qquad\qquad\qquad\qquad\qquad\qquad$ (14–22a)

☐ Transport aeroplanes
$\quad W_U/W_O = 0.038$ to 0.04 $\qquad\qquad\qquad\qquad\qquad\qquad\qquad\qquad$ (14–22b)

☐ Fighter and bomber aeroplanes (added for comparison)
$\quad W_U/W_O = 0.07$ to 0.08 $\qquad\qquad\qquad\qquad\qquad\qquad\qquad\qquad$ (14–22c)
$\qquad\quad = 0.09$ for naval aircraft $\qquad\qquad\qquad\qquad\qquad\qquad\qquad$ (14–22d)

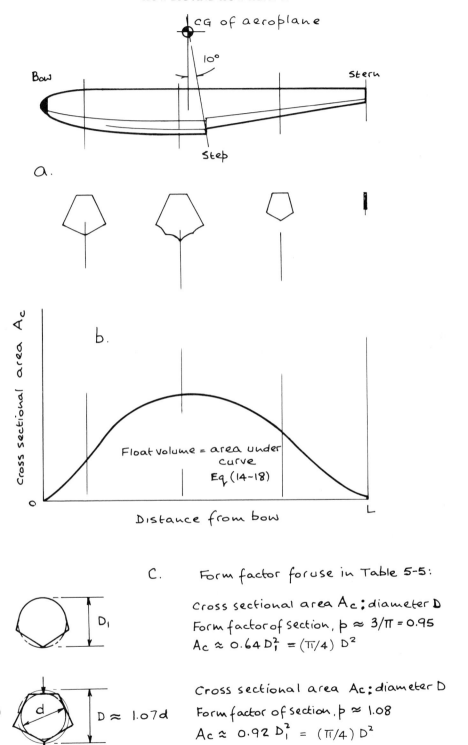

a.

b.

Float volume = area under curve
Eq (14-18)

c. Form factor for use in Table 5-5:

(1) Cross sectional area A_c: diameter D
Form factor of section, $p \approx 3/\pi = 0.95$
$A_c \approx 0.64 D_1^2 = (\pi/4) D^2$

(2) $D \approx 1.07d$
Cross sectional area A_c: diameter D
Form factor of section, $p \approx 1.08$
$A_c \approx 0.92 D_1^2 = (\pi/4) D^2$

Fig. 14.17   Float volume and surface area (use the method of tables 5–5 and 5–6).

Weights of landing gear units are, in terms of total gear weight, W_u

Nosegear unit
nosegear = about 0.3 W_u
maingear = about 2 × 0.35 W_u = 0.7 W_u (14–23)
Tailwheel gear
maingear = about 0.8 W_u
  tailgear = about 0.2 W_u (14–24a)
or, when such aircraft have tailskids:
maingear = about 0.9 W_u
  tailskid = about 0.1 W_u (14–24b)

Layout and design can cause marked variations in undercarriage weight. A retractable gear is roughly 1/20 to 1/15 heavier than fixed. A nosewheel arrangement is between 1/5 and 1/4 heavier than one with a tailwheel for the same aeroplane. Finally, because there is more of it sticking out in the wind, nosewheel units generate more drag, reducing lift/drag ratio more than for a tailwheel undercarriage.

Fuel and oil supply

The fuel and oil supply may be as simple as a plastic bottle and a pipe, gravity feeding a petrol and oil mixture to a two-stroke engine. It may, on the other hand, be as complicated as a multiple cell arrangement of tanks, with individual pumps, cocks, pipes and cross-feed cocks. Whichever system is used, it can usually be split into tank weight on one side, the cocks, pumps and pipes on the other.

For ordinary systems the weight ratio of cocks, pumps and pipes of a piston engined aircraft is:

$$W_{FP}/W_O = 0.05 \ P/W_O \qquad (14\text{–}25)$$

in which the ratio of power/weight, P/W_O, is obtained from fig. 14.6.

Weights of fuel tanks and supports are based upon capacities. Care must be taken when analysing American and British data, because:

1 US gal = 6 lb (2.7 kg) aviation gasoline,
1 Imp gal = 7.2 lb (3.28 kg) ditto = 1.2 US gal
  = 7.7 to 8.0 lb (3.5 to 3.63 kg) kerosene
  = 9 lb (4.09 kg) oil
  = 10 lb (4.54 kg) water (14–26)

It is impossible to make a general estimate of fuel system weight which is applicable to a wide range of aircraft, because of the variation in quantity carried between different makes and types. However, analysis shows that the weight ratio of fuel designed into most single and twin engined light aeroplanes:

design fuel load, W_{Fuel}/W_O = 0.13, single engined (14–27)
  = 0.16, twin engined (14–28)

If we divide through both equations by the weight of fuel/Imp gal, they convert into the number of gallons carried per unit of gross weight, G/W_o. These average:

$$\text{Imp gal carried, } G/W_o = 0.018 \text{ Imp gal/lb } (0.18 \text{ litre/kg}), \text{ single engined} \quad (14\text{--}29)$$
$$= 0.022 \text{ Imp gal/lb } (0.22 \text{ litre/kg}), \text{ twin engined} \quad (14\text{--}30)$$

Table 14–13 shows fuel tank weights based upon capacity G Imp gal, in the form of tank weight alone, and as a weight ratio, W_{Tank}/W_o.

TABLE 14–13

Type of fuel tank	Tank weight W_{Tank} lb (ref. 14.16)	Tank weight ratio W_{Tank}/W_o
Rigid metal	$10 + 0.69G$	$10/W_o + 0.69\ G/W_o$
Rigid fibreglass or GRP	$7 + 0.4\ G$	$7/W_o + 0.4\ G/W_o$
(actual 8.3 Imp gal tank):	$8 + 1.0\ G$	$8/W/o + 1.0\ G/W_o$
Crashproof	$7 + 0.38\ G$	$7/W_o + 0.38\ G/W_o$
Flexible (bag)	$10 + 0.12\ G$	$10/W_o + 0.12\ G/W_o$
Drop (external overload)	$1.0\ G$	$1.0\ G/W_o$

[handwritten annotation: $0.48 \times G$ u.s. gallons]

where G is the total capacity in Imp gal

Note: in the case of the measured weight of a GRP tank of 8.3 Imp gal (10 US gal) capacity, the tank is small. Wall weight varies roughly as (length)², while volume varies as (length)³. Therefore we would expect weight due to capacity, G, to fall below $1.0\ G$ in largest sizes. This is a way of saying that the tabulated formula ($7 + 0.4\ G$) is not necessarily wrong.

The total weight of the fuel system is the sum of the tank weight, W_{Tank}, plus the remaining items already mentioned, W_{FP}, given in eq (14–25), such that:

$$\text{fuel system weight ratio, } W_{FS}/W_o = (W_{Tank}/W_o) + (W_{FP}/W_o) \quad (14\text{--}31)$$

Fuel system weights for military aeroplanes tend to be about $\frac{1}{7}$ (say, 15 per cent) heavier than civil, for the same gross weight.

Weights of systems

Under this heading we include flying controls, hydraulic, pneumatic, electric and de-icing systems. Generally:

$$\text{total system weight ratio, } W_{Sys}/W_o = 0.06 \text{ to } 0.12 \quad (14\text{--}32)$$

The lower value is the minimum for flying controls and electrics together. Military aeroplanes can have system weights heavier than $0.12\ W_o$.

Flying control system

The total weight of the flying controls is roughly proportional to the weight of the wings. If W_{FC} is the weight of the system, then for a high-winged machine:

$$\text{control weight ratio of manual system, } W_{FC} = 0.0075(b^2/W_o)$$
$$+ 0.3(b/W_o) \quad (14\text{--}33)$$

in which W_o/b is the span loading. The weight ratio for a low-winged aeroplane is about $\frac{4}{5}$ this value.

When dual controls are fitted, the weight ratio is increased in eq (14–33) by a factor of 1.47 for a high-winged aeroplane, and by $1.47 \times \frac{4}{5} = 1.2$ for one that is low-winged.

Powered flying controls are heavier than manual, the comparable equation for solo controls with a high wing being:

$$\text{powered control weight ratio, } W_{PFC}/W_o = 0.01(b^2/W_o) + 0.4(b/W_o) \qquad (14\text{–}34)$$

The same factors can be applied for low-winged aircraft, and for dual controls as were used for eq. (14–33), i.e. 1.47 and 1.2 respectively.

Hydraulic and pneumatic systems

Such systems are usually taken together, because they provide the bulk of the power sources for actuating mechanisms. Generally, if W_{HP} is the system weight, then:

$$\text{hydraulic and pneumatic weight ratio, } W_{HP}/W_o = 0.03 \qquad (14\text{–}35)$$

Electrical system

Electrics involve wide variations in weight, because of the equipment and services fitted for different customers. A good working average is:

$$\text{electrical weight ratio, } W_{ES}/W_o = 0.03 \qquad (14\text{–}36)$$

De-icing system

De-icing is usually an optional extra. Some systems use heated elements, others use liquids, while among the commonest are pneumatic boots. Differences between them are small enough to be ignored, because the overall contribution to gross weight tends to be small:

$$\text{de-icing weight ratio, } W_{DI}/W_o = 0.006 \qquad (14\text{–}37)$$

Weight of fixed equipment

Under this heading fall furnishing, navigational and communications equipment, safety equipment, air conditioning and instruments. Furnishing, for example, is determined by the job the aeroplane is designed to do, and the number of occupants to be accommodated. The weight of air conditioning equipment depends upon similar considerations. The nav/comm equipment carried can account for anything between $\frac{1}{4}$ and, say, $\frac{3}{5}$ of the fixed equipment weight. The total weight, W_{FE}, is obtained from:

$$\text{fixed equipment weight ratio, } W_{FE}/W_o = 0.06 \text{ to } 0.1 \qquad (14\text{–}38a)$$

For a light aeroplane, flight and engine instrument weight is given by:

$$\text{flight and engine instrument weight ratio, } W_{FEI}/W_o = 0.015 \qquad (14\text{–}38b)$$

While the minimum nav/comm weight for a light aeroplane engaged upon public transport operations is around:

$$\text{nav/comm weight ratio, } W_{NC}/W_o = 0.03 \qquad (14\text{–}39)$$

Weight of miscellaneous items

Under this heading are seats, paint, removable equipment (like covers, picketing gear, and items like oars and anchors for a seaplane), so that:

$$\text{miscellaneous weight ratio, } W_{Misc}/W_O \qquad (14\text{-}40)$$

is the sum of the following:

☐ Seats

There are considerable variations in weights of seats. In a very simple single-seat light aeroplane this may be no more than a sheet of plywood with a horsehair cushion, totalling 5 lb/occupant (2.3 kg). More complex seats vary from 17 lb/person (8 kg), to 25 lb or 30 lb (11 to 14 kg) including harness.

☐ Paint and finish

The weight of this item is a function of surface are, which is in turn a multiple of the wing area, such that:

$$\text{paint weight ratio, } W_{PF}/W_O = 0.1/\text{wing loading} = 0.1\, S/W_O \qquad (14\text{-}41)$$

☐ Removable equipment

This is usually light and W_{RE}/W_O is probably indeterminate, much depends upon the requirements of the operator.

The weight sum

The total weight of the aeroplane is the sum of the parts dealt with in this chapter. We have worked in weight ratios, such that:

$$(W_P/W_O) + (W_W/W_O) + \ldots + (W_{FE}/W_O) + (W_{Misc}/W_O)$$
$$+ (\text{disposable load}/W_O) = 1.0 \qquad (14\text{-}42)$$

and this should be compared with eqs (1–1) and (1–2a). All told there are more than 15 items, so that an error of one half of one per cent of gross weight in each can add up to about one half of the fuel load carried. Much care is needed if an aeroplane is not to be crippled by carelessness. The estimates given here should only be taken at their face value, and it pays to modify and update them as often as worthwhile data appear. One such example of limited updating was introduced into table 14–13, after measuring the actual weight of a GRP fuel tank of known capacity.

References

14.1 *File No 3, Design,* **1**. Experimental Aircraft Association. Hales Corners, Wisconsin.

14.2 *File No 3, Design,* **2**. Experimental Aircraft Association.

14.3 Hoffman, R. J. *'Engineering for the Amateur Aircraft Builder'.* Experimental Aircraft Association.

14.4 Contractor Report NASA CR-1285 (Mar. 1969) *Potential Structural Materials and Design Concepts for Light Aircraft.* San Diego Aircraft Engineering, Inc. National Aeronautics and Space Administration, Washington, DC.

14.5 Peery, D. J. (1950) *Aircraft Structures.* New York: McGraw Hill Book Co Inc.

14.6 The Royal Aeronautical Society (1952) Handbook of Aeronautics no. 1, *Structural Principles and Data*. 4th edn. London: Sir Isaac Pitman & Sons, Ltd.

14.7 The Royal Aeronautical Society 1954 Handbook of Aeronautics no. 2, *Component Design*. 4th edn. London: Sir Isaac Pitman & Sons, Ltd.

14.8 Sechler, E. E. and Dunn, L. G. (1963) *Airplane Structural Analysis and Design*. New York: Dover Publications Inc.

14.9 Hirst, M. (Oct. 1977) 'America's Man-Powered Prizewinner'. *Flight International*.

14.10 Sherwin, K. (1971) *Man-Powered Flight*. Hemel Hempstead: Model & Allied Publications Ltd, 13/35 Bridge Street, Hemel Hempstead, Herts.

14.11 Organisation Scientifique et Technique Internationale du Vol à Voile (Jan. *1963) The World's Sailplanes*, **II**, Ist edn. OSTIV.

14.12 Coates, A. (1978) *Jane's World Sailplanes and Motor Gliders*. London: Macdonald and Jane's.

14.13 Wood, K. D. (1934) *Airplane Design*. New York: College of Engineering, Cornell University.

14.14 Wood, K. D. (1963) *'Aerospace Vehicle Design'*, **1**, *Aircraft Design*. Colorado: Johnson Publishing Company, Boulder.

14.15 Air Navigation Order, Schedule 5. (1976) Civil Aviation Authority.

14.16 Howe, Prof. D. Cranfield Institute of Technology, College of Aeronautics, Cranfield, Bedfordshire.

14.17 *British Civil Airworthiness Requirements*, Section K3-2. Civil Aviation Authority.

14.18 Federal Aviation Administration. Federal Aviation Regulations Part 23, Appendix A, Table 1, Limit flight load factors, FAA, Washington, DC 20591.

14.19 Jenkinson, L. (Apr. 1970) TTI, Light Aircraft Design Example, Loughborough University of Technology.

SECTION 5

PROJECT EXAMPLES

CHAPTER 15

Layout

'If you want to build a replica you have to get the engine right ... the aeroplane must be to scale, or else it is nothing.'
Vivian Bellamy, replica builder extraordinary.

'Strive for design simplicity: you never have to fix anything you leave out.'
Saying attributed to Bill Lear (1903–1978) of *Gates Learjet Corporation.*

To make a practical drawing of an aeroplane involves certain steps. It is impossible to calculate an exact solution at the first attempt and by now the reason why should be obvious. The design of each component is inextricably related to the design of every other, as well as to the aeroplane as one whole, so that no single item can be fixed with sufficient finality in isolation at such an early stage. Much of the art of aircraft design depends upon judging when to stop. All is compromise. As we read in an earlier quotation (chapter 9) one should never be more accurate than is necessary at any stage.

Ideally, the design of an aeroplane is dictated by the specification, but it can often be dictated by the predilections and prejudices of the customer. Each feature and design characteristic depends in turn upon numerous other factors. The order in which they are taken varies between designers and their particular ordering of priorities. Each designer has his own methods, so that even the starting point of an aeroplane doodled on a pad will be different each time, being prompted more often than not by the design feature which is uppermost in the mind.

The method outlined here might not suit everyone, but it fits the book and provides a fair starting point from which the reader might progress. The stages stem from questions a designer needs to ask himself, and they are written instead as side headings, with arguments underneath.

What payload, to where?

This is the most fundamental question and corollary. We need to know how many people, or how much freight. A separate decision is how much baggage is to be allowed for each occupant. Air conditioning and pressurisation requirements depend upon where the aircraft is likely to fly (fig. 1.3). It pays to look at the market and attempt either to fill a gap, or to innovate in a way that promises to beat the competition.

Books like *Jane's All the World's Aircraft*, or *Jane's World Sailplanes and Motor Gliders* (both of which are updated periodically) are eminently useful sources of data.

This can be augmented by information from a number of good international aviation journals. Other valuable data for amateur-built and similar light aircraft can be found in publications of the Experimental Aircraft Association, and in books like ref. 15.1.

Preliminary design estimates should be based upon characteristics of actual aeroplanes. Performance estimates need aerodynamic data. Start by making a careful choice of the number of passengers and crew, their baggage and any freight. In table 9–1 it was suggested that the average weight of Western man is about 180 lb (82 kg) fully clothed, with variations ±14 per cent. Baggage was given in table 9–3.

First estimate of gross weight

For most of the aeroplanes with which we are concerned, gross weight is given by:

$$\text{gross weight, } W_O = \text{roughly } 4 \times \text{payload, } W_{Pay} \qquad (15\text{–}1)$$

although the factor varies. Very light aeroplanes may have gross weights nearer 2.5 times payload. Aircraft designed for longer ranges, which must therefore carry large quantities of fuel, may have gross weights nearer 6 to 8 times payload.

Example 1

An aeroplane is to carry two adults of 200 lb (91 kg) each, and two children of 70 lb (32 kg), each with a total of 175 lb (80 kg) baggage. What is the gross weight of the aeroplane likely to be?

$$W_O = 4((2 \times 200) + (2 \times 70) + 175)$$
$$= 2860 \text{ lb } (1\,300 \text{ kg})$$

First estimate of wing area

Knowing from eq (2–3a) that lift $L = C_L qS$, and replacing lift by weight, W_O in level flight:

$$\text{wing area, } S = W_O/C_L q = 295 \ W_O/(C_{Lmax} V_s^2) \text{ ft}^2 \qquad (15\text{–}2)$$

when working in FPSR units, and V_s is the stall speed or minimum flying speed, KEAS.

The maximum lift coefficient, $C_{Lmax} = 1.4$ to 1.5 for a wing without flaps. With half span split and plain flaps, C_{Lmax} is about 1.8. Single slotted flaps reach 1.9 or a little more (*see* fig. 5.8 and eq (5–11)). Although flaps generate lift they are as useful for increasing drag (unless an aeroplane is specially designed for short take-off and landing), and to adjust flight attitude nose-down on the approach, improving the view. Where light aeroplanes are concerned the use of flaps to reduce stalling speed is often a secondary consideration.

Field performance depends upon wing loading, as we saw from eq. (6–65) and fig. 6.21. Knowing field size, fig. 6.22 enables us to determine V_s (in the landing configuration this is denoted V_{so}) in eq (15–2).

Example 2

What wing area is needed to land in a field of factored landing distance 2 100 ft (640 m), assuming half span plain flaps and a weight of 2860 lb (1 300 kg) at sea level ISA?

The stall speed KTAS is shown in fig. 6.22. At sea level ISA the relative air density and, hence, $\sqrt{\sigma} = 1.0$, so that we should expect $V_S = V_{so} = 52$ KTAS $= 52$ KEAS. Inserting the values in eq (15–2):

$$\text{wing area, } S = 295 \times 2860/(1.8 \times 52^2)$$
$$= 173 \text{ ft}^2 \ (16.1 \text{ m}^2)$$

The use of a single slotted flap instead of a plain or a split flap would reduce the wing area in the ratio of their maximum lift coefficients, 1.8/1.9, to 164 ft². Although this would represent a saving in wing structure weight, based upon area, the mechanism of a slotted flap would be slightly heavier than for a plain or split, so that we would have to balance gain against loss when the time came.

The wing loading with 173 ft² would be:

$$\text{wing loading, } W_O/S = 2860/173 = 16.5 \text{ lb/ft}^2 \ (80.8 \text{ kg/m}^2)$$

These figures may be cross-checked from the carpet in fig. 6.23.

First drag estimate

Much depends upon the configuration of the aeroplane. Fig. 5.16 shows wetted area of airframe in terms of wing area for different kinds of aeroplanes, while fig. 5.17 enables us to estimate parasite drag, knowing equivalent parasite area, f ft². Fig. 5.15d enables us to estimate total drag coefficient, C_D, knowing the parasite drag coefficient, C_{Dp}.

Example 3

We will continue with the machine in example 2, letting it be a single piston-engined light aeroplane with retractable gear. If wing area $S = 173$ ft², what will be the drag at $(L/D)_{max}$?

From Fig. 5.16, a single engined aeroplane has wetted area about 4 times wing area:

i.e.   total wetted area, $A_w \approx 700$ ft² (65 m²)

Choosing $C_{Dfric} = 0.005$ on average from fig. 5.17:

equivalent parasite area, $f = 3.5$ ft² (0.325 m²)

From fig. 5.15c the speed for maximum range occurs at $(L/D)_{max}$ i.e. at $1.85\, V_{so}$ so that:

$$\text{speed for } (L/D)_{max} = 1.85 \times 52 = 96 \text{ KEAS} \qquad \text{knots}$$

at which speed $C_D = 2C_{Dp}$. Knowing too that $D_p = fq$, from eq (5–35), while from eq (5–37):

$$D_p/q = f = C_{Dp}S$$
then: $$C_{Dp} = f/S = 3.5/173$$
$$= 0.0202, \text{ the parasite drag coefficient.}$$

Therefore, total drag coefficient $C_D = 2C_{Dp} = 0.0404$. Fig. 2.13 shows that at 96 KEAS the dynamic pressure, $q = 31$ lbf/ft² (1 497 N/m²), so that total drag:

$$D = C_D q S = 0.0404 \times 31 \times 173$$
$$= 216 \text{ lbf (961 N)}$$

and lift/drag, $(L/D)_{max} = 2860/216 = 13.2$ in level flight at gross weight.

Example 4

For the same aeroplane as in example 3, what will the drag be at the design cruising speed V_C?

Table 6–2 shows $V_C/V_{SO} = 3.2$ (give or take a bit) for a single-engined light aeroplane. Therefore:

$$V_C = 3.2 \times 52 = 166 \text{ KEAS}$$

From fig. 5.15c,

$$C_{Dp}/C_D = 0.89$$
$$C_D = C_{Dp}/0.89$$
$$= 1.12 \times 0.0202$$
$$= 0.0227$$

From fig. 2.13, dynamic pressure q at 166 KEAS $= 93$ lbf/ft² (4453 N/m²), so that:

$$D = C_D q S$$
$$= 0.0227 \times 93 \times 173$$
$$= 365 \text{ lbf } (1\,624 \text{ N})$$

Thrust and rated horsepower at design cruising speed (selection of engine)

This is the point at which we get our first ideas of the size of the engine. Knowing the first estimate of total drag at the design cruising speed, V_C, we may calculate the thrust horsepower, $P_t = \eta P$ from eq (2–33), where P is the rated power of the engine, BHP. The calculation requires an estimate of propeller efficiency, η, which can be made from fig. 6.15, 7.20, or 7.24b.

Example 5

If the design cruising speed and drag are 166 KEAS and 365 lbf (1 624 N) respectively, and the efficiency of a metal propeller is 80 per cent, what will be:
(a) the thrust horsepower at V_C and sea level ISA;
(b) the rated horsepower of the engine?

From fig. 6.5:

$$P_t = 186 \text{ THP } (139 \text{ kW})$$

while:

$$P = 186/0.8 = 232 \text{ BHP } (173 \text{ kW})$$

Drag estimates are always optimistic, so that we should expect the engine to be around 240 to 250 BHP (179 to 187 kW).

Example 6

If the above figures apply to the aeroplane used in previous examples, which has a wing loading at 16.5 lb/ft² (80.8 kg/m²), what would be a good state-of-the-art figure for power loading and, hence, rated BHP of a practical range of engines?

Fig. 6.6 shows that W/P at sea level might be expected to lie between about 10 and 18 lb/BHP (6.08 and 10.94 kg/kW). Fig. 6.13 suggests that the upper limit might be nearer:

$$W_O/P = 22 - 0.4 \times 16.5 = 15.4 \text{ lb/BHP } (5.7 \text{ kg/kW}), \text{ from eq (6–33)}$$

with the average around:

$$W_O/P = 19 - 0.4 \times 16.5 = 12.4 \text{ lb/BHP } (7.5 \text{ kg/kW})$$

Thus, if the gross weight is 2 860 lb (1 300 kg), then we can expect the aeroplane to have an engine which lies in the range:

$$2 860/15.4 \text{ to } 2 860/10 = 185 \text{ to } 285 \text{ BHP (138 to 213 kW)}$$

with an average around $2 860/12.4 = 230$ BHP (172 kW). Fig. 14.8 shows several engines which fall in this range, some of them turbocharged. This result corresponds with that in Example 5; and with fig. 14.6, which shows $P/W_O \approx 0.0075$:

i.e. $$P = 0.0075 \times 2 860 = 215 \text{ BHP.}$$

Second estimate of gross weight

Often we have to start with one particular engine, which means the preceding steps can be ignored, with the exception of working out the payload.

Tables 15–1 and 15–2 show rough estimates of fractional weight (percentage weight/100) of the various major items making up the gross and empty weights of an aircraft. Each item might vary by as much as ±20 per cent of its fractional weight.

In Table 15–1 the powerplant weight ratio W_P/W_O of single-engined aeroplanes is not far removed from $\frac{1}{5}$ to $\frac{1}{4}$ of the gross weight, decreasing to nearer $\frac{1}{6}$ as the aircraft become heavier and more complicated twins. We may use eq (14–9) to calculate powerplant weight ratio of a propeller-driven aeroplane. Table 14–5 is needed for the installation factor, F_P, while a crude estimate of the power/weight ratio, P/W_O, can be made from published data, or from fig. 14.6. The final term needed for the calculation is the specific weight of the engine. If engine weight and rated power are known then W_E/P can be calculated. If the weight of the engine is not known with sufficient accuracy at the initial stage, then an estimate can be made from fig. 14.8.

Having settled a powerplant weight ratio, its difference from the value suggested in table 15–1 can be added to or subtracted from the useful load ratio (minus a proportion for fuel). This gives us a revised payload weight ratio, W_{Pay}/W_O, which can be used for the second estimate of W_O.

Example 7

What will be the likely gross weight of a single-engined aeroplane to carry 715 lb (325 kg) payload, if the customer wants it to be powered by a turbocharged piston engine of 240 BHP?

For powerplant weight ratio we use:

$$W_P/W_O = F_P(W_E/P)(P/W_O) \qquad \text{eq (14–9)}$$

and assume:

$F_P = 1.3$ (from table 14–5),
$W_E/P = 1.7$ (from fig. 14.8),
$P/W_O =$ about 0.075 (from fig. 14.6), or alternatively about $\frac{1}{12}$ (i.e., 0.083) which is the 'eyeballed' average of the single-engined monoplanes with retractable gear in fig. 6.13a. Therefore, we shall assumed 0.08, which lies between.
Hence, $W_P/W_O = 1.3 \times 1.7 \times 0.08 = 0.177$, say, 0.18

The above value for powerplant weight ratio is lighter than 0.22 suggested in table 15–1. This means that we might be able to use the saving as a 'bonus' addition to the

TABLE 15-1

Fractional weight: gross weight

First rough estimate of fractional weight = percentage of gross weight/100
(Code: △ tailless: □ conventional: + canard)

Part	Hang glider Unpowered	Hang glider Powered	Man-powered	Sail-plane	Motor-glider	Military trainer	Single, piston engine Sport	Single, piston engine Cabin monoplane	Agri-cultural	Twin engine Piston	Twin engine Turbine
1 Powerplant	—	0.09△ 0.08□	0.03	—	0.15	0.23	0.28	0.22	0.20	0.20	0.18
2 Structure:	0.21△	0.19△ 0.28□	0.39□ 0.28+	0.57	0.56	0.33	0.30	0.30	0.27	0.30	0.30
3 Wing	0.3□		0.34□ 0.23+	0.28	0.28	0.14	0.13	0.14	0.12	0.12	0.12
4 Fuselage				0.26 (plus fin and rudder)	0.19	0.11	0.09	0.08	0.08	0.09	0.09
5 Tail				0.01	0.05	0.03	0.03	0.03	0.02	0.04	0.04
6 Gear			0.05	0.02	0.04	0.05	0.05	0.05	0.05	0.05	0.05
7 Controls	0.01□	0.01□	0.01		0.02	0.03	0.03	0.03	0.01 to 0.02	0.03	0.02
8 Equipment and services	0.02	0.02	0.02	0.03	0.03	0.11	0.04	0.05	0.03 to 0.04	0.07	0.08
9 Empty weight	0.24△ 0.33□	0.31△ 0.39□	0.45□ 0.34+	0.60	0.76	0.70	0.65	0.60	0.52	0.60	0.58
10 Useful or disposable load	0.76△ 0.67□	0.69△ 0.61□	0.55□ 0.66+	0.40	0.24	0.30	0.35	0.40 (fuel 0.13)	0.48	0.40 (fuel 0.16)	0.42 (fuel 0.18)
Total	1.00	1.00	1.00	1.00	1.00	1.00	1.00	1.00	1.00	1.00	1.00

TABLE 15-2

Fractional weight: empty weight

First rough estimate of fractional weight = percentage of empty weight/100
(Code: △ tailless; □ conventional; + canard)

Item	Hang glider Unpowered	Hang glider Powered	Man-powered	Sail-plane	Motor-glider	Military trainer	Single piston engine Sport	Cabin monoplane	Agri-cultural	Twin engine Piston	Turbine
1 Powerplant		0.290△ / 0.205□	0.088+ / 0.067□	—	0.197	0.329	0.431	0.367	0.385	0.333	0.310
2 Structure:	0.875△	0.613△ / 0.718□	0.824+ / 0.867□	0.950	0.737	0.471	0.462	0.500	0.519	0.5	0.517
3 Wing			0.676+ / 0.756□	0.467	0.368	0.200	0.200	0.233	0.231	0.2	0.207
4 Fuselage	0.909□			0.433	0.250	0.157	0.138	0.133	0.154	0.15	0.155
5 Tail				0.017	0.066	0.043	0.046	0.050	0.038	0.067	0.069
6 Gear			0.147+ / 0.111□	0.033	0.053	0.071	0.077	0.083	0.096	0.083	0.086
7 Controls	*0.042△ / 0.030□	*0.032△ / 0.026□	*0.029+ / 0.022□		0.026	0.043	0.046	0.050	0.019 to 0.038	0.05	0.034
8 Equipment and services	0.083△ / 0.061□	0.065△ / 0.051□	0.059+ / 0.044□	0.050	0.039	0.157	0.062	0.083	0.058 to 0.077	0.117	0.138

*Controls weight on original table 15-1 is assumed to apply to both types of aircraft.

useful load ratio, given in the table as 0.4. If the fuel weight ratio is 0.13, then the payload weight proportion is:

$$W_{Pay}/W_o = 0.4 - 0.13 = 0.27$$

Adding the powerplant weight 'bonus' of $0.22 - 0.18 = 0.04$, we have:

$$\text{new } W_{Pay}/W_o = 0.27 + 0.04 = 0.31$$

which means that $W_o =$ about $3.23 \times$ payload weight

$$= 3.23 \times 715 = 2309 \text{ lb } (1050 \text{ kg})$$

This is much lighter than the first estimate of 2860 lb (1 300 kg) in example 1, but it is still in the fair 'ballpark'. Examination of about eleven similar four-seat monoplanes, built by different manufacturers, shows them to lie between 2 315 and 3 100 lb (1 052 to 1 409 kg), with their average near 2 700 lb (1 227 kg). If we average our first and second estimates of gross weight we obtain $(2860 + 2309)/2 = 2585$ lb (1 175 kg).

It is a moot point what to do next, and much depends upon a mixture of inclination and experience. Each reader probably has a different solution, but the author is caught between the wish to be realistic, while making the sums arithmetically easy. So, we shall settle for:

$$\text{second estimate of gross weight, } W_o = 2600 \text{ lb } (1182 \text{ kg})$$

Second estimate of wing area

We follow the same procedure as before, based upon eq (15–2). Therefore, let us repeat the exercise in example 2, using the new gross weight.

Example 8

What will be the wing area of an aeroplane weight 2 600 lb (1 182 kg), designed to land in the same factored distance at sea level ISA, with the same flap arrangement, as in example 2?

The stall speed is exactly the same as originally obtained from fig. 6.22, i.e. $V_{so} = 52$ KEAS. Inserting the various values in eq (15–2):

$$\text{wing area, } S = 295 \times 2600/(1.8 \times 52^2)$$
$$= 158 \text{ ft}^2 (14.7 \text{ m}^2)$$

This result shows that the wing area has decreased in direct proportion to gross weight. This in turn will reduce wetted area and drag in the same ratio, while wing loading remains unchanged:

$$\text{i.e., } W_o/S = 2600/158 = 16.5 \text{ lb/ft}^2 (80.8 \text{ kg/m}^2)$$

Example 9

Given the results in examples 2, 3, 4, 6 and 8, what is the reduction in power loading that results from the revised gross weight?

$$\text{original power loading, } W_o/P = 2860/230 = 12.43 \text{ lb/BHP } (7.56 \text{ kg/kW})$$
$$\text{revised power loading} = 2600/240 = 10.8 \text{ lb/BHP } (6.59 \text{ kg/kW})$$

The implication of the improved power loading is that the aeroplane will fly faster and climb faster, as long as the second estimate is more accurate than the first.

Example 10

If the wing area of the aeroplane in example 2 remains fixed at 173 ft² (16.1 m²) while gross weight is reduced, what will be the factored landing distance from 50 ft?

We need to find the new stall speed and this time we shall resort to the carpet in fig. 6.23. The revised wing loading is now:

$$W_o/S = 2600/173 = 15.02 \text{ lb/ft}^2 \text{ (73.3 kg/m}^2\text{)}$$

while lift coefficient remains unchanged at $C_{Lmax} = 1.8$, so that:

$$V_{so} = \text{roughly 50 KEAS}$$

If we sketch a median line of the shaded area in fig. 6.22, the stall speed of 50 KEAS corresponds more or less with a factored landing distance of 2000 ft (610 m). The curve is rather flat and the answer lies between 1800 and 2200 ft (550 and 671 m), but *see* also examples 24 and 25.

Wing span and aspect ratio

At this point we can begin to determine the wing geometry. To do so we need to know the parasite drag coefficient, C_{Dp}, the best lift/drag ratio, $(L/D)_{max}$ for a piston-engined aeroplane, and the induced drag factor, $K' = 1/e$, all of which appeared in:

$$(L/D)_{max} \approx 8/9 \sqrt{(A/K'C_{Dp})} \qquad \text{eq (5–45a)}$$

To calculate $(L/D)_{max}$ at this early stage we first estimate the best range speed, in the same way as shown in example 3. In that example an estimate of wetted area was made around 4 times wing area. If we wish to be more accurate tables 5–5 and 5–6 enable us to make some adjustments. Note the way in which fuselage wetted area increases with changes in body section and windscreen profiles, and this is again confirmed by fig. 14.14. Thus, if the body represents about ½ the wetted area when a simple solid of revolution, the addition of a windscreen, and squareish cross-sections increases body wetted area, A_{wf}, in the ratio $2.85/2 = 1.425$, so that instead of occupying ½ of the total A_w, it grows to $1.452 \times 0.5 = 0.726$. This in turn increases A_w to $(0.5 + 0.726)/(2 \times 0.5)$ = an increase of 23 per cent, to 1.23 times the preceding value.

The upshot of this diversion is that if we are to design an aeroplane that is not too costly to produce, it must be simple and this means avoiding double curvature panels and elegant sections. But, although the effect is to keep down the cost, it increases wetted area – and this in turn reduces the lift/drag ratio.

Therefore, starting with a wing area of 158 ft² (14.7 m²), we shall assume from the above diversion and fig. 5.16 that wetted area, A_w, is something like 10 to 15 per cent higher than was expected for a cleaner design. Once we know the wetted area we look around at a number of similar aeroplanes and decide what range of aspect ratios will be most practical: less than six will not give good range, more than 8.5 results in a fairly heavy wing. We may then pick a value of induced drag factor, K', in fig. 5.18.

Aspect ratio is obtained from:

$$A \approx (4/\pi)[K'C_{Dp}(L/D)^2_{max}] \qquad \text{eq (5–46a)}$$
$$= b^2/S \qquad \text{eq (2–4)}$$

giving, wing span, $\qquad b = \sqrt{AS} \qquad \text{(15–3)}$

in which, of course, S is the wing area.

Example 11

Find the aspect ratio and span of the wing for $(L/D)_{max}$ when the gross weight and wing area of a single-engined light aeroplane are 2 600 lb (1 182 kg) and 158 ft² (14.7 m²) respectively, when $V_{so} = 50$ KEAS.

Assume total wetted area, $A_w = 1.15$ more than the average for 158 ft² wing area in fig. 5.16, for the reasons given a little earlier, i.e.,

$$A_w = \text{about } 690 \text{ ft}^2 \text{ (64.1 m}^2)$$

Again, choosing an average $C_{Dfric} = 0.006$ in fig. 5.17:

$$\text{equivalent parasite area, } f = 3.45 \text{ ft}^2 \text{ (0.32 m}^2)$$

From fig. 5.15c, speed for $(L/D)_{max} = 1.85 \times 50 = 92.5$ KEAS. As, $C_{Dp} = f/S = 3.45/158 = 0.222$ (lowish by table 5–7) then, total $C_D = 2\,C_{Dp} = 0.044$.

To find the total drag we multiply by dynamic pressure, q, at 92.5 KEAS, which is given in fig. 2.13 as 28 lb/ft² (1 390 N/m²) and by the wing area:

$$\text{total drag, } D = 0.044 \times 28 \times 195 = 866 \text{ lbf (773 N)}$$

Hence, lift/drag at 1.85 V_{so}, $(L/D)_{max} = W_o/D = 2600/195 = 13.3$. From eq (5–48) the aspect ratio is given by:

$$A = (4/\pi)[K'C_{Dfric}(A_w/S)(L/D)^2_{max}]$$

We shall pick a value of $K' = $ about 1.40 from fig. 5.18, so that:

$$\text{aspect ratio, } A = 1.27 \times 1.40 \times 0.006 \times (690/158) \times 13.3^2 = 8.24$$

While from eq (15–3), wingspan, $b = \sqrt{(8.24 \times 158)} = 36.0$ ft (11 m)

Example 12

Table 5–7 suggests that a single-engined aeroplane with retractable gear might have a parasite drag coefficient, C_{Dp}, between 0.02 and 0.03. Drag is always underestimated at this stage, so let us see what happens if we have $C_{Dp} = 0.025$ for the aeroplane in Example 11.

$$\text{total drag, } D = 2 \times 0.025 \times 28 \times 158 = 221 \text{ lbf (984 N)}$$
$$(L/D)_{max} = 2\,600/221 = 11.76$$
$$A = 1.27 \times 1.40 \times 0.006 \times (690/158) \times 11.76^2 = 6.44$$

In short, there has been a dramatic reduction in the aspect ratio of the projected wing, from 8.24 to 6.44.

The message of this calculation is that if we underestimate the drag coefficients too much, we end up concluding that a wing is needed with a higher aspect ratio than will be economical to produce and to carry around as part of the structure weight. The reason is the sensitivity of the equation to (lift/drag)². Look at eq (14–16) which told us that, among other things, wing weight varied as (aspect ratio)$^{0.45}$, i.e. roughly as $\sqrt{A}$. Thus, if we estimate the aspect ratio as 8.24 instead of 6.44, the wing will be approximately $\sqrt{(8.24/6.44)} = $ about 13 per cent heavier.

Example 13

Given the estimates in examples 11 and 12, pick an aspect ratio that is likely to be practical in these fuel-scarce times, without being too penalising in structure weight. Find the span and SMC, $\bar{c}$.

A cursory survey of a number of cantilever monoplanes with the ability to fly relatively long distances revealed aspect ratios between about 6.5 and 7.5. We shall take the average of our two calculated values, i.e.

$$A = (8.24 + 6.44)/2 \approx 7.3, \text{ say}$$

from eq (15–3), $b = \sqrt{(7.3 \times 158)} = 34$ ft (10.36 m), giving:

standard mean chord, $\bar{c} = 158/34 = 4.65$ ft (1.42 m) from eq (2–4)

First layout sketch

In chapter 9 the point was made that cockpit and cabin layout tended to be the determinants of fuselage shape. Figs. 9.2 and 9.3, together with table 9–1 enable sketches to be made of the payload-carrying volume. Fig. 9.5 shows the fuselage proportions.

The second consideration at this point is the arrangement of wing and tail surfaces. Fig. 11.13 shows the approximate proportions. Choice of tail moment arm (i.e. 2.5 to 3 $\bar{c}$ as shown in the same figure) depends upon the job that the aeroplane has to do. By implication we have so far considered a touring machine, so that it should not be too short-coupled and lively. Therefore, one should err on the side of a long arm, rather than short.

Although it would be fun to look at a tail-first aeroplane too at this point, there are so many interactions between longitudinal, directional and lateral stability, and control, that it is simpler to stick to a conventional configuration for the sake of examples.

Table 11–4 shows the proportional areas of the different surfaces, and these enable us to sketch their layout. Knowing that the tail moment arm is around 0.6 to 0.7 of the total length of the fuselage, we can then put together the body and the set of aerofoil surfaces.

We have to decide the choice of undercarriage layout: whether it should be a nosewheel or a tailwheel arrangement. Generally, for touring aeroplanes, a nosegear which keeps the fuselage attitude more or less horizontal is to be preferred (fig. 10.2). Older passengers could have difficulty clambering up the wing roots of taildraggers, before lowering themselves backwards into rear seats in a fuselage tilted about 12 deg nose-up. Different considerations apply to sporting machines (figs. 10.1 and 10.3).

As far as weight and balance are concerned, the cabin arrangement should be such that the passengers are not too far aft, otherwise there will be large moments to be trimmed out, and wide variations in stick force to manoeuvre with different seats occupied. With the payload well aft one tends to carry around uneconomically large tail surfaces, which increase the wetted area excessively, reducing the achievable lift/drag ratio. A good starting point is to locate the centre of gravity of the most rearward occupant(s) in an aeroplane with four seats no further aft than, say, 75 to 80 per cent SMC.

If an aeroplane is subsonic, and notwithstanding the dictates of fashion, it is better to mount the wings and tail surfaces more or less at right angles to the plane of symmetry and the longitudinal axis. Tailless aeroplanes involve other considerations (fig. 4.11). Swept tails, especially fins and rudders, might look fashionable, giving a misleading impression of speed, but swept hinge-lines are not a good idea. The more backward-swept the rudder hinge line the less effective is the rudder as a yaw control – while the greater is its effect as an elevator at aft **CG** and large angles of attack. On top

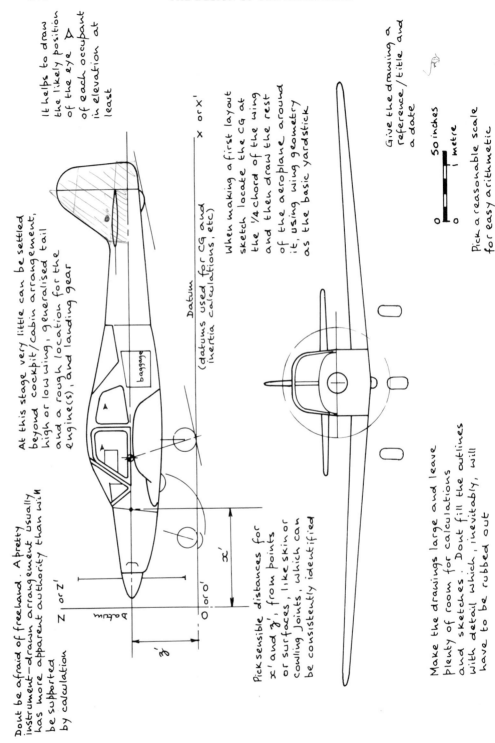

Dont be afraid of freehand. A pretty instrument-drawn arrangement usually has more apparent authority than will be supported by calculation

At this stage very little can be settled beyond cockpit/cabin arrangement, high or low wing, generalised tail and a rough location for the engine(s), and landing gear

It helps to draw the likely position of the eye ▷ of each occupant in elevation at least

Datum
(datums used for CG and inertia calculations, etc)

x or x'

When making a first layout sketch locate the CG at the ¼ chord of the wing and then draw the rest of the aeroplane around it, using wing geometry as the basic yardstick

Pick sensible distances for x' and ʒ', from points or surfaces, like skin or cowling joints, which can be consistently identified

Make the drawings large and leave plenty of room for calculations and sketches. Dont fill the outlines with detail which, inevitably, will have to be rubbed out

Give the drawing a reference/title and a date

50 inches
1 metre

Pick a reasonable scale for easy arithmetic

Fig. 15.1a   Preliminary side and front elevations of four-seat light aeroplane in

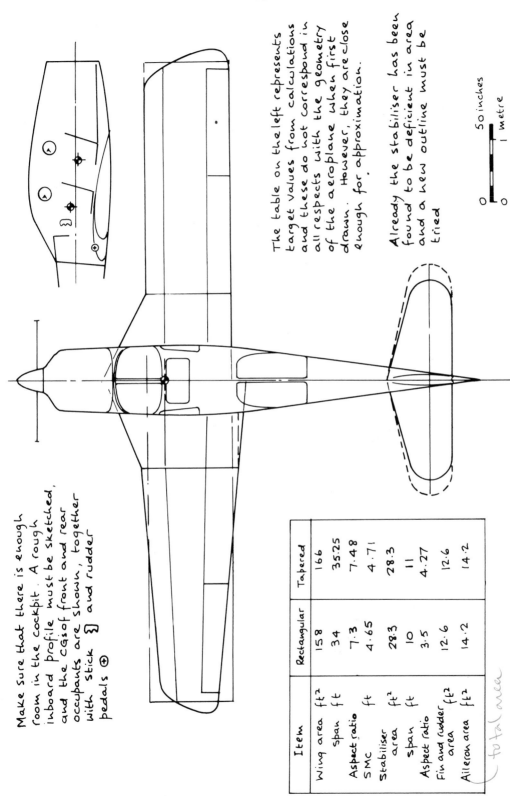

Make sure that there is enough room in the cockpit. A rough inboard profile must be sketched, and the cgs of front and rear occupants are shown, together with stick ⟨⟩ and rudder pedals ⊕

The table on the left represents target values from calculations and these do not correspond in all respects with the geometry of the aeroplane when first drawn. However, they are close enough for approximation.

Already the stabiliser has been found to be deficient in area and a new outline must be tried

Item	Rectangular	Tapered
Wing area ft²	158	166
Span ft	34	35.25
Aspect ratio	7.3	7.48
SMC ft	4.65	4.71
Stabiliser area ft²	28.3	28.3
Span ft	10	11
Aspect ratio	3.5	4.27
Fin and rudder area ft²	12.6	12.6
Aileron area ft²	14.2	14.2

(total area)

50 inches
1 metre

Fig. 15.1b Preliminary plan view and inboard profile of light aeroplane in example 14.

of which swept surfaces and hinges are structurally longer, and more complicated and costly to manufacture.

The wing section has probably not been determined at this point, but a depth of spar around 15 per cent chord, with maximum depth at 30 per cent is reasonable. Tail surfaces have thickness ratios around 9 per cent. As far as choice of wing section is concerned, do not waste too much time with theory and elaborate calculation of lift/drag ratios. Almost any section which fits the requirements of gentle stall, good $C_{Lmax,}$ low drag, low pitching moment and ample room for arranging wing spars, is good enough for our kinds of machines. The rigging angle of incidence of the wing should be that for minimum drag of the section with standard roughness: say, 3 deg.

Example 14

Use the results of examples 7 to 13 to sketch a single-engined light aeroplane with retractable gear, and a 240 BHP (179 kW) piston engine, to carry 715 lb (325 kg) payload.

This is done in fig. 15.1. The aeroplane has a number of salient features, blended with much guesswork.

The cabin has been arranged to allow room for the wing structure to pass under the seats of the four occupants, sitting side by side in tandem pairs. There is ample room for baggage behind the rear seats. From the firewall to the tailcone bulkhead is one structural unit with cutout for doors. Ideally there should be doors on both sides, but crashworthiness considerations, coupled with the need to save weight, might limit us to one door. Cabin structure (especially floor structure) should be strong enough to prevent local crumpling into and reduction of cabin volume. If there is only one door it is more convenient to locate it on the right hand side of the fuselage, away from the pilot, who can remain seated while passengers enter and leave.

The 'tadpole' shape of the fuselage in elevation is an aerodynamic gesture to reduce wetted area aft of the maximum section and, hence, frictional drag. The bulged bottom line is the result of arranging the wings to be joined at the centreline, giving a straight spar-run to the keel. This increases the volume of structure under the seats – important crashworthiness feature which helps to keep the seats intact while providing a strong keel in the event of a wheels-up landing. The flaps run from the root of each aileron to the centreline of the fuselage.

The wings could be parallel chord, or they could be tapered. The plan view shows the way in which their outlines have been built up from the basic rectangle with chord equal to SMC, and span enough to provide the required aspect ratio. Because the aspect ratio is quite high, a tapered planform is favoured, to reduce structure weight, even though it is harder and more costly to produce than one of parallel chord. The same applies to flaps and ailerons. However, a tapered wing suffers less damping in roll, so that response to aileron should be quicker than with a plank wing of the same aspect ratio, allowing slightly smaller ailerons to be used.

Wing tips are raked rearwards around 20 deg so as to reduce induced drag, by lengthening the trailing edges (*see* fig. 4.10c). The taper ratio $\lambda = \frac{1}{2}$ for the same reason (fig. 4.10b). Tips of this shape should not have the ailerons running to their ends, if high control forces are to be avoided. Wing leading edges are swept forwards inboard so as to provide fuel stowage volume forward of the wheel wells.

The wing section would be determined using the methods given in chapter 5. There would be no point in looking at sections less than 12 per cent thick, because of the lack of stowage volume for fuel and mainwheels. There could be advantages in looking at sections as thick as 18 per cent, because the calculated cruising speed is low enough.

It is unlikely that laminar flow could be achieved in service. Enough has been said earlier about such sections to make the reader think twice before expecting too much from them in this context.

We would use Schrenk's method, given in fig. 4.4, to determine the likely lift distribution along the span. Fig. 4.5 shows the way of calculating a curve of lift coefficient along the semispan: the shape being given by dividing the lift distribution by the chord at any station. Plotting the result (like fig. 4.5, middle row) we would look to see if the curve tended to approach too closely to C_{Lmax} at any point. If that happened, especially towards the wing tips, it could be necessary to alter the section locally, by introducing leading edge camber, or by changing the wing section in that region, or by washing out the wing where it occurred.

The ideal we would be aiming for would be nearly constant C_L from root to tip, and a lift distribution as near elliptical as possible.

A good example of such treatment of a wing, which has excellent range flying characteristics, is the cranked, tapered and twisted Jodel wing. Although something like the middle ⅔ of the span has a parallel chord, while the outer panels are sharply tapered and washed out, with marked undercamber of the tip sections, and dihedral only outboard of the crank, the wing is said to have near-elliptical lift distribution, with a correspondingly low lift-dependent drag.

Plate 15–1 The cranked washed-out *Jodel* wing with marked taper
outboard, has efficient range flying qualities. *Jodel D140 (Author)*

The dihedral drawn in fig. 15.1 is nominal, around 5 deg (eq (13–5)), with the wing spars running in straight lines from the centreline joint. Transport joints might be arranged to lie at points marked by the cranked leading edges.

The main wheels retract inwards between the spars. Nosegear retraction causes a problem. To find stowage room for the leg and its supporting structure requires an outline drawing of the engine and its mountings. The bottom line of the cowling could need lowering. The wheel is left protruding slightly to ease matters, a small drag penalty being offset by the advantage of having part of a wheel outside to absorb the shock of a wheels-up landing.

The **CG** is initially guessed to lie at SMC/4, approximately as shown in the side view. Two datum lines, OX and OZ (or OX′ and OZ′) have also been drawn to facilitate measurement of moment arms for calculating the actual **CG**.

As drawn, the wing trailing edge is about 2 ft (0.6 m) above the ground and an intermediate step is needed to ease entry and exit. This requires thought: a wholly retractable step, operated by the pilot, could introduce a weight penalty. A fixed step causes drag.

Cockpit glazing is a compromise between the need for a good view and strong overturn structure in the cabin roof. A direct vision panel is needed. The transparencies are by no means final at this stage.

Tail surface areas were calculated using nominal values from table 11–4.

The tapered tailplane and elevator is about 17 per cent of the tapered wing area which, on the face of it, looks reasonable. But the following checks show that we should be prepared to increase the area when tail volume coefficients have been calculated: using areas outside the lines of the fuselage, i.e. net areas:

☐ From eq (11–7) and table 11–1 the tail volume coefficient, $\overline{V}_s$, for a transport aeroplane should not be less than 0.5. With the plan forms as drawn:

$$\overline{V}_s = (S_s/S)(l_s/\overline{c})$$
$$= (28.3/158)(13.75/4.66) = 0.528, \text{ say } 0.53 \text{ (parallel chord wing)}$$
$$= (28.3/166)(13.75/4.71) = 0.498, \text{ say } 0.5 \text{ (tapered wing)}$$

Therefore, the tail area is marginal for an aeroplane which is likely to have a wide *CG* movement.

☐ If we select $\overline{V}_s = 0.6$, say, and transpose eq (11–7) for stabiliser area:

$$S_s = \overline{V}_s S/(l_s/\overline{c}) \tag{15-4}$$
$$= 0.6 \times 166/(13.75/4.71) = \text{about } 34 \text{ ft}^2 \ (3.16 \text{ m}^2)$$

The new outline is shown with a broken line. The aspect ratio is increased from 4.27 to 4.6, which improves the stabiliser lift slope, a_1.

The stabiliser is located near the top of the tailcone, leaving a good $\frac{1}{3}$ of the rudder area in relatively free air and unblanketed beneath it. To increase yaw damping, or to reduce the chance of a fin stall, we should bear in mind the possible need to add a dorsal fairing to the fin – or to add root strakes to the tailplane (table 13–3).

Fin and rudder area may be checked in two ways:

☐ From eqs (13–8) the fin volume coefficient, $\overline{V}_\zeta$ may be calculated in a similar way to that of stabiliser volume:

$$2\overline{V}_f = \overline{V}_\zeta = (S_f/S)(l_f/(b/2)) = 0.015 \text{ to } 0.06$$
$$= (12.6/158)(15/(34.0/2)) = 0.07 \text{ (parallel chord wing)}$$
$$= (12.6/166)(15/(35.25/2)) = 0.065 \text{ (tapered wing)}$$

This suggests that the fin and rudder area is adequate.

☐ Eq (13–21) gives the rudder power to prevent an incipient spin:

$$10^3 C'(S_f/S)(l_f/b) \not< 5$$

in which $C' = 0.35$ as the aeroplane has a fixed fin. Thus:

$$10^3 = 0.35 \times (12.6/158)(15/34) = 12.3 \not< 5 \text{ (parallel chord wing)}$$
$$10^3 \times 0.35 \times (12.6/166)(15/35.25) = 11.3 \not< 5 \text{ (tapered wing)}$$

so that we know that the aeroplane should not enter an incipient spin inadvertently. However, we should check the rudder volume to recover from a spin, using eq (13–23):

$$(S_s/S)(l_f/c) \not< 0.065$$

where S_s is the shaded area in fig. 13.6c. Thus:

$$(21/158)(15/4.66) = 0.43 \text{ (parallel chord wing)}$$
$$(21/166)(15/4.71) = 0.4 \text{ (tapered wing)}$$

both of which are greater than 0.065, so that there should be ample rudder volume for recovery.

So far the calculations suggest that the area of the vertical surfaces is sufficient. But we must be cautious, because there is no completely satisfactory way of making certain that the area is enough, for reasons given at the end of chapter 13. For example, if we now attempt to calculate the derivative for tail volume for positive weathercock stability, $n_{v(tail)}$, the story is slightly different:

☐ The derivative, $n_{v(tail)} = \frac{1}{2}(a_1)_\beta V_f = 0.2$ to 1.0 eq (13–13)

The lift slope $(a_1)\beta$ is given per radian in this equation, and this is obtained from fig. 4.6c after calculating the aspect ratio either by eq (13–34) or (13–34a). We shall use eq (13–34a), for purely intuitive reasons. Whether the intuition is correct or not can only be confirmed by wind tunnel results at this stage.

$$\text{fin-plus-rudder aspect ratio, } A_f = 1.55 \, f_{Af}(b_f^2/S_f) \qquad \text{eq (13–22)}$$

in which $f_{Af} = 1.0$ (fig. 13.12), $b_f = 3.75$ ft (1.14 m) and $S_f = 12.6$ ft² (1.17 m²)

i.e.
$$A_f = 1.55 \times 1.0 \times 3.75^2/12.6 = 1.73$$
$$\text{Lift slope } (a_1)_\beta = a_A = \pi \, A/2 \qquad \text{eq (4–20)}$$
$$= 3.1417 \times 1.73/2 = 2.72/\text{radian}$$

As fin-volume coefficient depends upon wing planform and, hence SMC, inserting our calculated values of $2\overline{V}_f = \overline{V}_t$ in eq (13–13):

$$n_{v(tail)} = \frac{1}{2} \times 2.72 \times 0.07 = 0.095 \text{ (parallel chord wing)}$$
$$= \frac{1}{2} \times 2.72 \times 0.065 = 0.088 \text{ (tapered wing)}$$

both of which values are slightly below the average of 0.11 in that equation. Nevertheless, both are adequately positive, showing that the aeroplane has positive directional stability.

☐ Calculation of vertical surface area and lift slope using the Royal Aeronautical Society method (Appendix A C01.01.01 and C01.01.05) for the tapered wing planform. The method takes into account side area of the body, as shown in fig. 13.11f. Although the 'span' of the fin-plus-rudder is increased, the aspect ratio of the surfaces drops from about 1.73 to 1.52. When the stabiliser location is taken into account (fig. 13.12), the effective aspect ratio rises to 1.6.

When the low wing and the height of the rear fuselage are also taken into account, the lift slope of the vertical surface is 1.81/radian, less than $(a_1)\beta = 2.72$/radian, estimated by the previous method. The additional body area may be added to the 12.6 ft² (1.17 m²) estimated previously, giving (12.6 + 5) = 17.5 ft² (1.63 m²), and this in turn increases the fin volume coefficient, $\overline{V}_{\zeta}$, to 0.09. Hence:

$$\text{new } n_{v(tail)} = \tfrac{1}{2} \times 1.81 \times 0.09 = 0.081$$

whereas the previous value was 0.088.

The last two calculations tend to suggest that the aeroplane might need a higher aspect ratio fin and rudder to improve the lift slope. Unfortunately, high aspect ratio surfaces stall at smaller angles of attack than those with lower aspect ratio. A fin stall can be delayed to larger angles of sideslip, and the lift slope can be increased, by the addition of a dorsal fin. The size and benefit due to vortex separation with yaw (like the effect shown in fig. 4.12c) cannot be determined here.

Resorting to a simple lamina like that shown in fig. 13.10, with the fin and rudder as drawn and, no dorsal, resulted in a centroid at 0.165 × fuselage length (instead of 0.175). The actual length cannot be determined properly yet, because we might need to move the engine forwards or backwards to adjust the CG. The test with the lamina tends to indicate that there might not be enough keel area and, hence, fin volume. If so, this could limit the maximum for crosswind take-off and landing.

Steps after first layout sketch

There are another ten steps to be taken, but we shall not deal with all of them here. Broadly, they are:

☐ Third estimate of gross weight based upon itemised component weights, using formulae given in chapter 14.
☐ First balance table, calculating a rough centre of gravity based upon the various component weights. The CG should come out no further aft than 0.3 SMC if the stability and control surfaces are to be reasonable.
☐ First performance estimates. These will be looked at briefly in a moment.
☐ Second layout sketch adjusting the engine, for example, to put the CG in the right place on the wing.
☐ Fourth estimate of gross weight based upon second layout.
☐ Second balance table using new component weights and moment arms.
☐ Second estimate of performance.
☐ Checks on stability and control to confirm or alter design of surfaces.
☐ Structural design (which is omitted here).
☐ Summarised feasibility study, incorporating:
  (1) final layout;
  (2) final weight and balance;
  (3) final assembly of performance data.

A quick look at performance

Although the first performance estimate is shown as the third item above, the

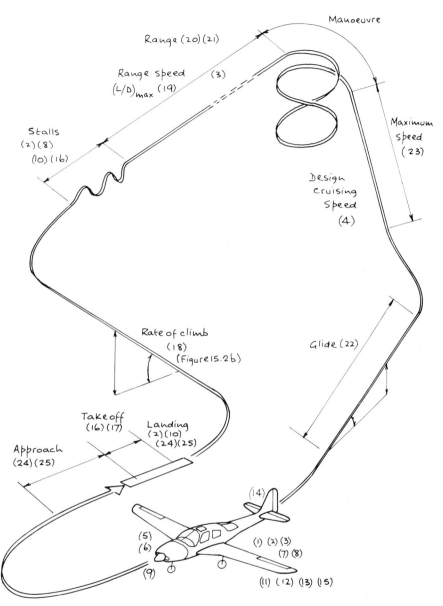

Fig. 15.2a   Some performance modes relating to configuration which may be assessed at an early stage. The numbers in brackets are the relevant examples in this chapter.

information given in chapter 6 can be used much earlier, to see if a projected aeroplane makes sense when selecting an engine, i.e. around example 5. Fig. 15.2a shows modes which might be investigated. Still concentrating upon the aeroplane we have drawn so far, its characteristics are summarised in table 15–3 – with the exception of V_{S1}, the clean stall, or minimum flying speed. This has been obtained from fig. 6.23 by assuming C_{Lmax} with gear and flap up to be about 1.4.

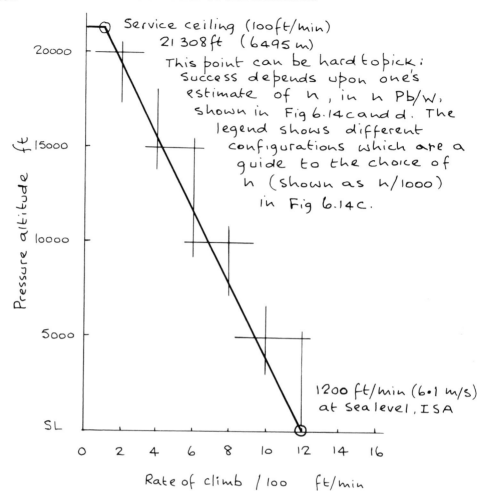

Service ceiling (100ft/min)
      21308ft (6495m)
This point can be hard to pick:
   Success depends upon one's
   estimate of n, in n Pb/W,
   shown in Fig 6.14c and d. The
   legend shows different
   configurations which are a
   guide to the choice of
   n (shown as n/1000)
   in Fig 6.14c.

1200 ft/min (6·1 m/s)
at sea level, ISA

Rate of climb / 100   ft/min

As a rough rule the rate of climb shown
will change by ±4ft/min per C° difference
from ISA. If the ambient temperature is
below ISA, engine power will be higher and
the rate of climb correspondingly faster by
the above amount. If the ambient temperature
is above ISA, power is reduced and the rate
of climb with it by the amount shown.

Fig. 15.2b   Estimation of rate of climb, ISA, with altitude in example 18.

Example 15

How does the aeroplane in example 14 compare in general with other light aircraft of a similar kind?

Fig. 6.13 shows a corridor of typical light aeroplane combinations of wing and power loading. The average line along the corridor obeys the law:

$W/P = 19 - 0.4\ W/S$, on taking the average of eqs (6–33) and (6–34)

i.e. $W_O/P = 19 - 0.4 \times 16.5 = 12.4$ (parallel chord wing)

$= 19 - 0.4 \times 15.7 = 12.7$ (tapered wing)

These are average state-of-the-art values. In both cases W_O/P, being less than the average lb/BHP, shows that the aeroplane should be a fairly lively performer with either wing.

Example 16

What will be the sea level ISA take-off distance to 50 ft (15.25 m) at gross weight for the aeroplane in table 15–3, using a dry runway?

TABLE 15–3

Data for aeroplane in example 14, fig. 15.1

Item	Plank wing	Tapered wing
Gross weight W_O lb	2600	2600
Power unit P BHP	240	240
Wing area S ft²	158	166
Wing span b ft	34	35.25
Wing aspect ratio	7.3	7.48
Parasite drag coefficient C_{Dp}	0.025	0.025
Wing loading W_O/S lb/ft²	16.5	15.7
Power loading W_O/P lb/BHP	10.8	10.8
Specific power P/W_O BHP/lb	0.093	0.093
$(W_O/S)(W_O/P)$ lb²/ft² BHP	178	170
Span loading W_O/b lb/ft	76.5	73.5
$W_O/b²$ lb/ft²	2.25	2.09
Stall speed V_{SO} KEAS	52	52
V_{S1} KEAS	60	57
(assuming $C_L = 1.4$, using fig. 6.23)		

Fig. 6.20 shows the graph to be used, after calculating take-off safety speed, V_2 which, in this case, is $1.2\ V_{S1}$:

take-off safety speed, $V_2 = 1.2 \times 60 = 72$ KEAS (parallel chord wing)

$= 1.2 \times 57 = 68.5$ KEAS (tapered wing)

The factored take-off distance varies as:

$(W_O/P)(V_2^2/1000) = 10.8 \times 72^2/1000 = 56$

i.e. take-off distance, TOD $= 1500$ ft (457 m) (parallel chord wing)

while, $(W_O/P)(V_2^2/1000) = 10.8 \times 68.5^2/1000 = 51$

i.e. TOD $= 1300$ ft (405 m) (tapered wing)

Example 17

What will be the effect upon factored take-off distance if the aeroplane in table 15–3 takes off from the grass of a typical summer airfield?

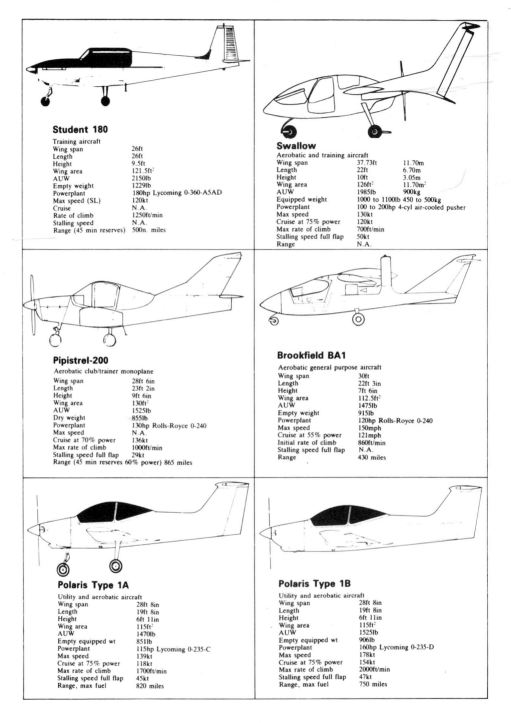

Student 180

Training aircraft

Wing span	26ft
Length	26ft
Height	9.5ft
Wing area	121.5ft²
AUW	2150lb
Empty weight	1229lb
Powerplant	180hp Lycoming 0-360-A5AD
Max speed (SL)	120kt
Cruise	N.A.
Rate of climb	1250ft/min
Stalling speed	N.A.
Range (45 min reserves)	500n. miles

Swallow

Aerobatic and training aircraft

Wing span	37.73ft	11.70m
Length	22ft	6.70m
Height	10ft	3.05m
Wing area	126ft²	11.70m²
AUW	1985lb	900kg
Equipped weight	1000 to 1100lb	450 to 500kg
Powerplant	100 to 200hp 4-cyl air-cooled pusher	
Max speed	130kt	
Cruise at 75% power	120kt	
Max rate of climb	700ft/min	
Stalling speed full flap	50kt	
Range	N.A.	

Pipistrel-200

Aerobatic club/trainer monoplane

Wing span	28ft 6in
Length	23ft 2in
Height	9ft 6in
Wing area	130ft²
AUW	1525lb
Dry weight	855lb
Powerplant	130hp Rolls-Royce 0-240
Max speed	N.A.
Cruise at 70% power	136kt
Max rate of climb	1000ft/min
Stalling speed full flap	29kt
Range (45 min reserves 60% power)	865 miles

Brookfield BA1

Aerobatic general purpose aircraft

Wing span	30ft
Length	22ft 3in
Height	7ft 6in
Wing area	112.5ft²
AUW	1475lb
Empty weight	915lb
Powerplant	120hp Rolls-Royce 0-240
Max speed	150mph
Cruise at 55% power	121mph
Initial rate of climb	860ft/min
Stalling speed full flap	N.A.
Range	430 miles

Polaris Type 1A

Utility and aerobatic aircraft

Wing span	28ft 8in
Length	19ft 8in
Height	6ft 11in
Wing area	115ft²
AUW	1470lb
Empty equipped wt	851lb
Powerplant	115hp Lycoming 0-235-C
Max speed	139kt
Cruise at 75% power	118kt
Max rate of climb	1700ft/min
Stalling speed full flap	45kt
Range, max fuel	820 miles

Polaris Type 1B

Utility and aerobatic aircraft

Wing span	28ft 8in
Length	19ft 8in
Height	6ft 11in
Wing area	115ft²
AUW	1525lb
Empty equipped wt	906lb
Powerplant	160hp Lycoming 0-235-D
Max speed	178kt
Cruise at 75% power	154kt
Max rate of climb	2000ft/min
Stalling speed full flap	47kt
Range, max fuel	750 miles

Fig. 15.3   Examples of the initial ideas of ten competitors in the *Light Aeroplane Design Competition* of the *Royal Aeronautical Society* (1978–79). They were shaped in response to a general specification like that at the beginning of chapter 9, using the guidelines of table 6–3. *By permission of the Royal Aeronautical Society.*

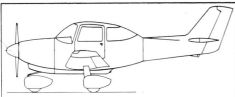

"Springbok"

Light crosscountry and training aircraft

Wing span	27.9ft	8.5m
Length	N.A.	
Height	N.A.	
Wing area	90.4ft²	8.4m²
AUW	1571lb	713kg
Empty weight	952lb	432kg
Powerplant	145hp	
Max speed		155kt
Cruise at 75% power		148kt
Stalling speed full flap		49.7kt
Range (45 min reserves, 75% power)		414n. miles

LN-11

Training aircraft

Wing span less tip tanks	25ft 5in	7.75m
Length	22ft	6.70m
Height	8ft 6in	2.60m
Wing area	104ft²	9.9m²
AUW	1600lb	700kg
Empty weight	922lb	419kg
Powerplant	100hp Continental 0-200A	
Max speed (SL)	140mph	
Cruise at 7000ft	120mph	
Rate of climb	700ft/min	
Stalling speed full flap	60mph	
Range	N.A.	

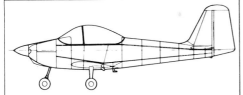

Kite 2

Trainer

Wing span	30ft
Length	23.8ft
Height	N.A.
Wing area	N.A.
AUW	1700lb
Equipped weight	N.A.
Powerplant	130hp Rolls-Royce 0-240
Max speed	N.A.
Cruise at 75% power	138mph
Max rate of climb	1000ft/min
Stalling speed full flap	N.A.
Range	620 miles

Kite 4

Cruiser and tug

Wing span	30ft
Length	24ft
Height	N.A.
Wing area	N.A.
AUW	2500lb
Equipped weight	N.A.
Powerplant	210hp Rolls-Royce I0-360
Max speed	N.A.
Cruise at 75% power	170mph
Max rate of climb	1100ft/min
Stalling speed full flap	N.A.
Range	970 miles

T.R. Brigand

Training aircraft

Wing span	26ft	7.92m
Length	23.12ft	7.05m
Height	8.12ft	2.47m
Wing area	124.5ft²	11.55m²
AUW	1700lb	771kg
Equipped weight	950lb	431kg
Powerplant	100hp Rolls-Royce 0-240A	
Max speed	159mph	138kt
Cruise at 75% power	140mph	122kt
Rate of climb (SL)	800ft/min	
Stalling speed full flap	55mph	48kt
Range (45 min reserves)	700 miles	

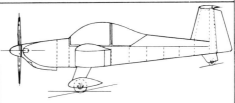

Zephyr

Training aircraft

Wing span	30ft 10in	
Length	21ft 1½in	
Height	7ft 10in	
Wing area	102ft²	
AUW	1457lb	
Equipped weight	N.A.	
Powerplant	120hp Rolls-Royce 0-240	
Max speed	137kt	
Cruise at 75% power	N.A.	
Max rate of climb	1,500ft/min	
Stalling speed full flap	44kt	
Range	N.A.	

Fig. 15.3 *contd.*

Fig. 6.17 shows the grass to be between 4 and 6 in (10 and 15 cm) long. At its longest it would probably correspond with the firm surface in fig. 6.18, which shows that at the worst the factored take-off distance at maximum weight could be doubled.

Were it necessary to take off from a summer airfield in the same distance as from one with a paved surface, the take-off weight would have to be reduced to about 0.75 W_O, i.e. by 25 to 30 per cent of gross.

Example 18

What would be the sea level rate of climb, ISA, for the aeroplane with the tapered wing in table 15–3; and what do you think might be its service ceiling?

If we transpose eq (6–35) for rate of climb, v_c, at sea level we obtain:

$$v_c = (10^5/5.25)(P/W_o - 0.03) \tag{15-5}$$
$$= 19048 \times (0.093 - 0.03)$$
$$= 1200 \text{ ft/min (6.1 m/s)}$$

A service ceiling (at which rate of climb is 100 ft/min (0.508 m/s)) may be estimated using fig. 6.14c:

First select a value of $n/1000$: with single piston engine and retractable gear a value around

$$n/1000 = 6.5$$

is reasonable. The wingspan b is 35.25 ft, giving:

$$\text{service ceiling, } n \, Pb/W_o = 6.5 \times 1000 \times 0.093 \times 35.25$$
$$= 21308 \text{ ft (6495 m)}$$

A climb graph can now be constructed, like fig. 6.14d, as shown in fig. 15.2b.

Example 19

Given a parasite drag coefficient, $C_{Dp} = 0.025$ and an induced drag factor $K' = 1.35$ for both wings in table 15–3, what $(L/D)_{max}$ might be expected for each?

From eq (5–45a):

$$(L/D)_{max} \approx 8/9\sqrt{(A/K'C_{Dp})}$$
$$= 8/9 \sqrt{[7.3/(1.35 \times 0.025)]} = 13.07 \text{ (parallel chord wing)}$$
$$= 8/9 \sqrt{[7.48/(1.35 \times 0.025)]} = 13.23 \text{ (tapered wing)}$$

Example 20

If the speed for best range occurs at 1.85 V_{so} (fig. 5.15c), and the aeroplane is fitted with a variable pitch propeller, so that propeller efficiency is 80 per cent at the engine rpm which gives a specific fuel consumption of 0.5 lb/h/BHP, what will be the range (without reserves) with each wing in table 15–3? Assume that the fuel carried is 0.13 W_O (table 15–1).

Range is given by:

$$R = 326(\eta/c')(L/D)_{max}(\Delta W_{Fuel}/W_O)$$
$$= 326 \times (0.8/0.5) \times 13.07 \times 0.13 = 886 \text{ nm (parallel chord wing)}$$
$$= 326 \times (0.8/0.5) \times 13.23 \times 0.13 = 897 \text{ nm (tapered wing)}$$

In fact this is a highly theoretical answer. At 1.85 $V_{so} = 96$ KEAS the aeroplane will be flying too slowly for the engine, which will not be developing maximum power/unit mass of fuel consumed. The specific fuel consumption will be higher than 0.5 lb/h/BHP (84 mg/J), reducing potential range.

Example 21

What benefit is the tapered wing likely to bring in terms of extra range, over the parallel chord wing?

The answer lies in the tapered wing being lighter, which allows more fuel to be carried. As the aeroplane is not aerobatic, let us assume a 3.8 g structure. We shall then use eq (14–15c) and then factor the result by the taper ratio part of eq (14–16) so as to find the reduction in structure weight. If we ignore the weight of additional fuel system to carry the extra fuel, represented by the structure weight saved, we shall be able to give a first order answer.

$$\text{wing group weight ratio, } W_W/W_O = F_W \sqrt{[N/1\,000)(W_O/b)A]/w}$$

The wings are cantilever, so that $F_W = 1$, from fig. 14.12, $N = 1.5 \times 3.8 = 5.7$, W_O/b and wing loading, w, are obtained from table 15–3.

Therefore,
$$W_W/W_O = 1 \times \sqrt{[5.7/1\,000) \times 76.5 \times 7.3]/16.5}$$
$$= 0.108 \text{ (parallel chord wing)}$$
$$= 1 \times \sqrt{[5.7/1\,000) \times 73.5 \times 7.48]/15.7}$$
$$= 0.113 \text{ (tapered wing) (unfactored for taper)}$$

We must now calculate $[(1 + 2\lambda)/(3 + 3\lambda)]^{0.27}$ for the wing in fig. 15.1, for which the value of tip chord/root chord is about $\frac{1}{2}$ (actually, the centre line chord is used). As the power 0.27 is nearly $\sqrt[4]{}$, the weight ratio of the tapered wing must have the following factor applied:

$$\frac{W_W(\text{tapered})}{W_W(\text{plank})} \approx \sqrt[4]{\frac{[(1 + 2 \times \frac{1}{2})/(3 + 3 \times \frac{1}{2})]}{(1 + 2 \times 1)/(3 + 3 \times 1)}} = 0.97$$

Therefore, the tapered wing weight ratio becomes:

$$0.97 \; W_W/W_O = 0.97 \times 0.113 = 0.11 \text{ when factored for taper}$$

The parallel chord wing of slightly lower aspect ratio is fractionally lighter by about 0.11 – 0.108 = 0.002 W_O. This is equivalent to the weight of less than one gallon of fuel, and too small to be considered.

The answer to the question is that the tapered wing could be slightly heavier than one of parallel chord, because the aspect ratio is higher, the wing loading is lower, and so is the span loading. There is no benefit from the tapered wing as drawn.

Example 22

If the throttle of the specified engine is set for zero thrust, so that the aeroplane in table 15–3 glides most efficiently, will the tapered or plank wing carry the aeroplane farther?

Eq (6–3) shows that the best glide ratio is directly proportional to $(L/D)_{max}$, so that the tapered wing, which has the highest lift/drag, enables the aircraft to glide further. The improvement over the parallel chord wing is:

$$\text{glide ratio with tapered wing} = (7.48/7.3) \times \text{glide ratio with parallel chord}$$
$$= 1.025 \text{ (2.5 per cent) farther}$$

Example 23

If the aeroplane with the parallel chord wing in table 15–3 is found to achieve only 3.05 $V_{SO} = 158$ KEAS in level flight at sea level, what is the Everling number, the total drag coefficient, C_D and parasite drag coefficient C_{Dp}, assuming the propeller efficiency is 0.8 (fig. 6.15)?

Eq (6–53) shows that:

$$\text{Everling number, } \eta / C_D = (V^3 c / 96\,000 \sqrt{\sigma})(W_O / P)/(W_O / S)$$
$$= (158^3 / 96\,000 \times 1)(10.8/(2\,600/158))$$
$$= 27 \text{ (compare with table 6–3)}$$

so that $C_D = 0.8/27 = 0.03$

At 3 V_{SO}, $C_{Dp}/C_D = 0.87$ (fig. 5.15c)

Therefore, $C_{Dp} = 0.87 \times 0.03 = 0.026$

Example 24

What will be the average landing distance of the taper-winged aeroplane in table 15–3 on a dry hard paved surface, and on a firm wet grass surface?

Surface conditions are given in table 6–6 and show that firm wet grass increases the factored landing distance by 50 per cent. The approach speed is assumed to be 1.3 V_{SO} = 68 KEAS, so that from eq (6–66):

$$\text{average landing distance} = (20/10^6) W_O \, V_{app}^2 + 900 \text{ ft}$$
$$= (20/10^6) \times 2\,600 \times 68^2 + 900$$
$$= 1\,140 \text{ ft (347 m) on a dry paved surface}$$

Landing on firm wet grass the distance is increased by 50 per cent, to 1 710 ft (521 m).

Example 25

If the aeroplane in example 24 has an electrical flap failure, will it be able to land on firm wet grass in a distance of 1 300 ft (396 m)?

This time we assume $V_{app} = 1.3 V_{S1}$, where $V_{S1} = 57$ KEAS, i.e. $V_{app} = 74$ KEAS, giving:

$$\text{average landing distance} = [(20/10^6) \times 2\,600 \times 74^2 + 900] \times 1.5$$
$$= 1\,778 \text{ ft (542 m)}$$

So, the answer is 'no', it will go through the far hedge.

More than one response to a specification

It pays to be critical with oneself when interpreting a specification, as we have just done. At each step put yourself in the position of Devil's advocate and look for snags, or better ways of solving the problem. Never take your own ideas too seriously. Seek advice from good sources.

For example, in chapter 9 we saw a shortened example of an actual specification for a light training aeroplane. This formed the basis for a light aeroplane design competition held by the *Royal Aeronautical Society*, which was announced in 1978. Fig. 15.3 shows the side views of ten submissions – ten which were short-listed by October 1979. Figs. 15.4 and 15.5 show the two seat and stretched four-seat variants of the winning *Brookfield BA1*. An enlightening exercise was the holding of a symposium for short-listed competitors, before they made their final submissions three months later.

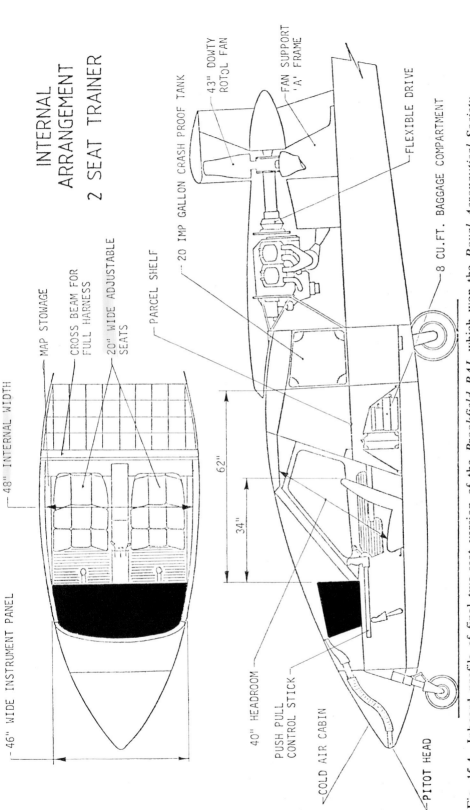

INTERNAL
ARRANGEMENT
2 SEAT TRAINER

43" DOWTY
ROTOL FAN

FAN SUPPORT
'A' FRAME

FLEXIBLE DRIVE

8 CU.FT. BAGGAGE COMPARTMENT

20 IMP GALLON CRASH PROOF TANK

PARCEL SHELF

20" WIDE ADJUSTABLE
SEATS

CROSS BEAM FOR
FULL HARNESS

MAP STOWAGE

48" INTERNAL WIDTH

46" WIDE INSTRUMENT PANEL

62"

34"

40" HEADROOM

PUSH PULL
CONTROL STICK

COLD AIR CABIN

PITOT HEAD

Fig. 15.4 Inboard profile of final two-seat version of the *Brookfield BAI*, which won the *Royal Aeronautical Society Competition (A. J. Greenhalgh)*.

There, each was able to outline his thinking, with drawings and models (where available), facing constructive criticism and observation from other competitors, and members of the Panel of Judges.

Never be afraid or ashamed to look at the ideas of others. Copy the best and improve on them when you can. Listen to pilots, no matter how inarticulate. It is said that Kurt Tank (1898–), designer of the many *Focke-Wulf* aeroplanes, including the *Fw 190* and *TA 152* fighters, used to fly around the German squadrons meeting the pilots. He was able to translate their ideas and needs onto paper and could also test his own aeroplanes, with the result that his fighters were among the best in their day. His thinking influenced designers both inside and outside Germany in the 1940s.

Listen to mechanics, engineers and operators. They are full of stories about things that go wrong and which do not pay. There is always a better way of doing something and the engineer can point this out time and again – even though he might not be able to find the best way himself. The author has never yet met a practical technician or engineer in the field who could not improve a product of someone else's imagination.

Listen to airworthiness surveyors. They are (or should be) always helpful, and their advice is free. Professional criticism is part of their job, probably because after about seven years exposure they will have seen almost everying that can (and therefore does) go wrong technically. Flight operations inspectors are valuable sources of advice and information about the things which can go wrong operationally; and so are official accident summaries and safety bulletins. Many operational failures are the result of technical failure, and the aircraft designer, whether professional or amateur, gains from such knowledge, improving the critical faculties in the process.

Juggling with centres of gravity

In general a centre of gravity is calculated by taking moments about some point or axis and summing them as follows:

$$W\bar{x} = W_1 x_1 + W_2 x_2 + \ldots + W_r x_n \qquad \text{from eq (2–64)}$$

in which $\bar{x}$ is the distance of the centre of gravity of the weight W from the O–Z axis, like that drawn in fig. 15.1, and W is the sum of the component weights, W_1 to W_n. If we now divide both sides of the equation by W, we obtain the fractional weights of the components:

$$\bar{x} = (W_1/W)x_1 + (W_2/W)x_2 + \ldots + (W_n/W)x_n \qquad (15\text{–}6)$$

In a similar way the co-ordinate of the CG about the O–X axis, $\bar{z}$, is given by:

$$\bar{z} = (W_1/W)z_1 + (W_2/W)z_2 + \ldots + (W_n/W)z_n \qquad (15\text{–}7)$$

It will be appreciated that the component weight ratios used in these two equations are exactly the same in form as have been used already in chapter 14, in which component weights were given as ratios of gross weight W_o. It follows that if one component of weight W_n, or weight ratio W_n/W, is moved through a distance $\pm\Delta x_n$, the effect upon the CG of the whole can be shown to be:

$$\Delta\bar{x} = \pm\Delta x_n(W_n/W) \qquad (15\text{–}8)$$

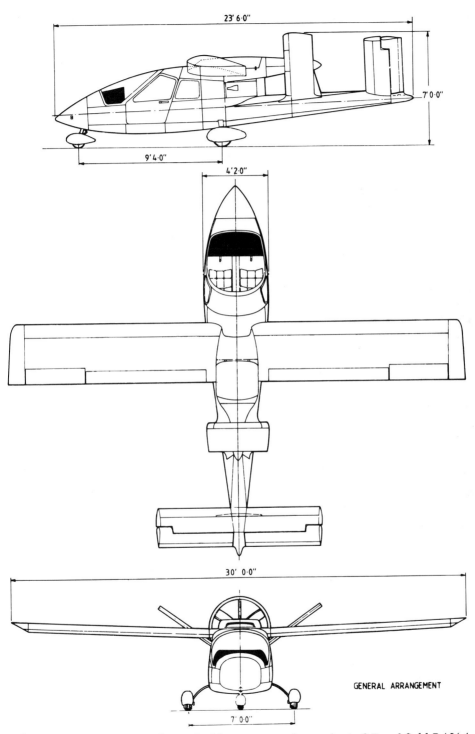

Fig. 15.5   Arrangement of stretched four-seat touring variant of *Brookfield BAI* (*A. J. Greenhalgh*).

TABLE 15–4
Guestimating CGs of major components

Major Component	Approximate ('eyeballed') CG

Fuselage structure, hulls and floats

0.4 × length from nose, or firewall

Wing group

0.4 × chord (or mean chord of bay)

Tailplane and elevator, fin and rudder

0.5 × chord

Stabilator

0.35 × chord

Powerplant

0.4 × distance from propeller to firewall

Landing gear

See Eqs (14–23), (14–24 a and b)

Fuel and other systems, equipment and services }

At the approximate centre of the main components of each

Payload   }
Fuel

Human body: about 1 ft above seat and forward of back (0.3
Fuel and payload in bulk should have CG close to tha of the aeroplane

TABLE 15-5
First estimate of **CG** using weight ratios.

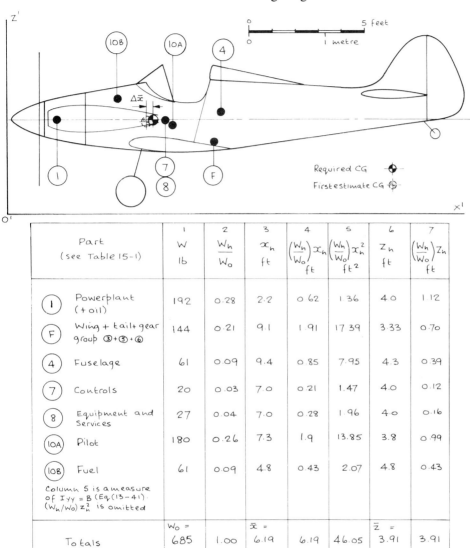

Part (see Table 15-1)	1 W lb	2 $\frac{W_n}{W_o}$	3 x_n ft	4 $\left(\frac{W_n}{W_o}\right)x_n$ ft	5 $\left(\frac{W_n}{W_o}\right)x_n^2$ ft^2	6 Z_n ft	7 $\left(\frac{W_n}{W_o}\right)Z_n$ ft
① Powerplant (+oil)	192	0.28	2.2	0.62	1.36	4.0	1.12
F Wing + tail + gear group ③+⑤+⑥	144	0.21	9.1	1.91	17.39	3.33	0.70
④ Fuselage	61	0.09	9.4	0.85	7.95	4.3	0.39
⑦ Controls	20	0.03	7.0	0.21	1.47	4.0	0.12
⑧ Equipment and Services	27	0.04	7.0	0.28	1.96	4.0	0.16
⑩A Pilot	180	0.26	7.3	1.9	13.85	3.8	0.99
⑩B Fuel	61	0.09	4.8	0.43	2.07	4.8	0.43
Column 5 is a measure of $I_{yy} = B$ (Eq (13-41). $(W_n/W_o)z_n^2$ is omitted							
Totals	$W_o =$ 685	1.00	$\bar{x} =$ 6.19	6.19	46.05	$\bar{z} =$ 3.91	3.91

In exactly the same way we can see that if there is a change in the weight (or weight ratio) of one component, by an amount ΔW_u, then the corresponding change:

$$\Delta \bar{x} = [(W_o\bar{x}_o \pm \Delta W_u x_n)/(W_o \pm W_n)] - \bar{x}_o \qquad (15\text{-}9)$$

Application to preliminary weight and balance

The first balance table is usually drawn up after the third estimate of gross weight, using formulae given in chapter 14 to calculate the various component weights. It is necessary to know where the centre of gravity of each component lies, so that we can measure the various x_n and z_n arms. Sometimes **CG**s are known, as with engines and

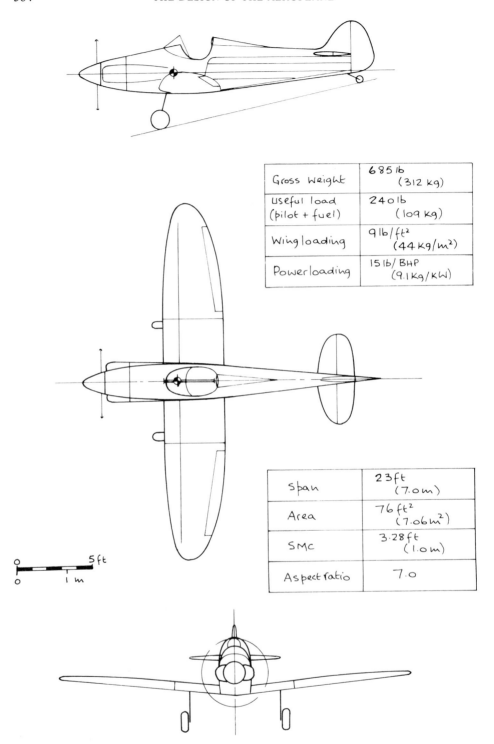

Gross Weight	685 lb (312 kg)
Useful load (pilot + fuel)	240 lb (109 kg)
Wing loading	9 lb/ft² (44 kg/m²)
Power loading	15 lb/BHP (9.1 kg/kW)

Span	23 ft (7.0 m)
Area	76 ft² (7.06 m²)
SMC	3.28 ft (1.0 m)
Aspect ratio	7.0

Fig. 15.6   Layout of a light sport aeroplane used for **CG** calculations in example 26 *et seq.*

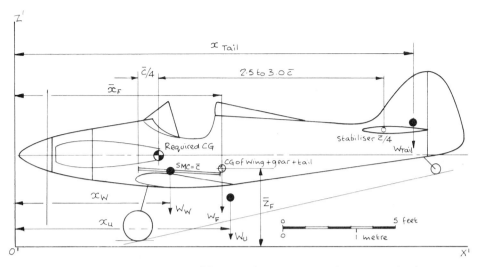

To find the location x_F of the combined centre of gravity of wing, landing gear and tail, take moments about CG datum $O\text{-}Z'$, using Eq $(15-6)$:

$$W_W\, x_W + W_U\, x_U + W_{Tail}\, x_{Tail} = (W_W + W_U + W_{Tail})\, \bar{x}_F$$

So that:
$$\bar{x}_F = \frac{W_W\, x_W + W_U\, x_U + W_{Tail}\, x_{Tail}}{W_W + W_U + W_{Tail}}$$

The same procedure is used to find $\bar{z}_F$, taking moments about axis $O\text{-}X'$.

NOTE: The standard mean chord, $\bar{c}$, is calculated separately, and is drawn at a distance above the wing root rib to account for the effect of dihedral.

Fig. 15.7 A way of finding the centre of gravity of three parts of an aeroplane (wing, undercarriage and tail) which tend to have a fixed relationship with the **CG** of the complete aircraft.

items of equipment. Often we have to 'eyeball' a **CG** which, although involving guesswork, can still be accurate enough at such an early stage.

Table 15–4 is a crude way of estimating the position of the centre of gravity of a major component, the weight ratio of which can be estimated by means of table 15–1 or table 15–2.

Earlier we saw the way of fixing the geometry of the wing and tail surfaces so that the aeroplane might be in a condition of near balance aerodynamically. We can go further, because when the **CG** is fixed, so is the undercarriage, as well as the aerofoil surfaces. If fuel is carried in the wings it too should lie close to the **CG**, to prevent the longitudinal trim changing very much as it is consumed. By arranging things in this way, the overall balance of the aeroplane will depend upon the positions of the payload and powerplant.

As an example of the method, fig. 15.6 is the first sketch of a light sport aeroplane. In fig. 15.7 the wing, tail unit and tailwheel undercarriage have been sketched, in order to find the centre of gravity of all three units together, starting with the **CG** of the aeroplane at the $\frac{1}{4}$ SMC point, working the undercarriage geometry from fig. 10.1 and its centre of gravity by means of weights based on eq (14–24a).

The undercarriage is arranged so that the tail-down attitude is slightly less than the stalling angle of the wing, with any high lift devices extended. The attitude corresponds with that for 0.9 C_{Lmax}. Tail-up the **CG** of the gear is about 0.2 × wheelbase aft of the point of contact of the mainwheels (i.e., inversely proportional to the ratio of their weights in eq (15–24a)).

Example 26

The aeroplane in fig. 15.6 has the following component weight ratios for the wing, gear and tail groups. Find their combined centre of gravity.

$$\text{landing gear, } W_U/W_O = 0.05, \; x_U = 9 \text{ ft (2.74 m)}$$
$$\text{wing group, } W_W/W_O = 0.13, \; x_W = 7 \text{ ft (2.13 m)}$$
$$\text{tail group, } W_{Tail}/W_O = 0.03, \; x_{Tail} = 17.5 \text{ ft (5.33 m)}$$

If the **CG** of all of the units lies at $\overline{x}_F$, say, aft of the O–Z datum (AOD) and their combined weight is W_F, then from fig. 15.7:

$$W_F/W_O = 0.05 + 0.13 + 0.03 = 0.21$$
$$\overline{x}_F = [(0.05 \times 9) + (0.13 \times 7) + (0.03 \times 17.5)]/0.21$$
$$= 9.19 \text{ ft (2.8 m) AOD}$$

Example 27

Using the weight ratio of the group in example 26, find the **CG** of the aeroplane in fig. 15.6. The weight ratios and moment arms of the different groups and components are given in table 15–5, while the weights and moment arms are given in table 15–6, to show the usual way of drawing up a balance table. $W_O = 685$ lb (312 kg), SMC = 3.28 ft (1.0 m), ¼ SMC = 6.4 ft AOD (1.95 m), wing area = 76 ft² (7.06 m²).

TABLE 15–6

Conventional balance table for finding the distance $\overline{x}$ (i.e., $\overline{x}_O$)

Part	Weight lb	Moment arm ft AOD	Moment lbft
1 Powerplant	192	2.2	422.4
2 Group F (wing, tail, gear)	144	9.1	1310.4
4 Fuselage	61	9.4	573.4
7 Controls	20	7.0	140
8 Equipment & services	27	7.0	189
10A Pilot	180	7.3	1314
10B Fuel	61	4.8	292.8
Total	685	$\overline{x} = 4242/685 = 6.19$	4242

$$\text{Distance from } \mathbf{CG} \text{ to } \tfrac{1}{4} \text{ SMC} = 6.19 - 6.4 = -0.21 \text{ ft (0.064 m)}$$
$$= -0.21/3.28 = -0.064 \text{ SMC}$$

Thus, the **CG** is 6.4 per cent SMC forward of the ¼ chord point, i.e.

$$\text{location of design } \mathbf{CG}, \; h = 0.25 - 0.064 = 0.186 \text{ SMC}$$

Example 28

The nose ahead of the wing quarter chord generates some lift and effectively shifts the aerodynamic centre of the wing + body forwards. Scaling from fig. 15.6, and using the method and equations accompanying fig. 11.14, find the forward shift, $-\Delta h_o$, and the new aerodynamic centre:
The formula to use is eq (11–51):

$$-\Delta h_o = 0.75(a_{nose}/aA)/[(a_{nose}/a_A) + (S/S_{nose})]$$

in which the ratio of the lift slopes of the nose and wing:

$$(a_{nose}/aA) = 0.25\ A_{nose} + 0.5\ (A_{nose}/A) \qquad \text{eq (11–52)}$$

The area of the nose + large spinner, $S_{nose} = 14$ ft², with aspect ratio

$$A_{nose} \approx 0.45.$$

Therefore, $\qquad (a_{nose}/a_A) = 0.25 \times 0.45 + 0.5(0.45/7) = 0.145$
and, $\qquad\qquad -\Delta h_o = 0.75 \times 0.145/[0.145 + (76/14)]$
$$= 0.0195,\ \text{i.e. } 0.02\ (2\ \text{per cent})$$

The new location of the aerodynamic centre, **ac** (assuming that the **ac** of the wing alone *was* at ¼ SMC), becomes:

$$h_o = 0.25 - 0.02 = 0.23\ \text{SMC}$$

This means that the centre of gravity of the aeroplane with a 180 lb (82 kg) pilot lies forwards of the aerodynamic centre of the aeroplane by an amount:

$$h_o - h = 0.23 - 0.186 = 0.044\ \text{SMC (about 4.5 per cent SMC)}$$

Example 29

Assuming that the heaviest pilot is 205 lb (93 kg) and the lightest 120 lb (55 kg), what range of **CG** movement can be expected for the light aeroplane in the above examples?

☐ *Lightweight pilot (120 lb)*
   The **CG** movement can be checked in one of two ways, either by means of eq (15–9), or as in table 15–7.

$$\Delta\bar{x} = [(W_o\bar{x}_o \pm \Delta W_n x_n)/(W_o \pm \Delta W_n)] - \bar{x}_o \qquad \text{eq (15–9)}$$

TABLE 15-7

Revised CG calculation

Item	W lb	$x : \bar{x}$ ft	Wx lbft
Gross weight, W_o	685	6.19	4242
Reduction in pilot weight, ΔW_n	−60	7.3	−438
New weight ($W_o - \Delta W_n$)	625	6.08	3804

Therefore, the **CG** has moved forward $(6.08-6.19)/3.28 = 0.033$ SMC, from 0.186 to 0.153 SMC.

☐ *Heavyweight pilot (205 lb), zero fuel:*

This time we shall use eq (15–9) inserting the following values:

$\Delta W_n = 205 - 180 = +25$ lb, $W_n = 180$ lb, $x_n = 7.3$ ft, $W_O = 685$ lb, and $\overline{x}_O = 6.19$ ft; $W_{Fuel} = 61$ lb, $x_{Fuel} = 4.8$ ft.

Thus eq (15–9) is modified by the additional term to:

$$\Delta x = [(W_O\overline{x}_O + \Delta W_n x_n - \Delta W_{Fuel}x_{Fuel})/(W_O + \Delta W_n - \Delta W_{Fuel})] - \overline{x}_O$$
$$= (4242 + 182.5 - 292.8)/649) - 6.19 = +0.18 \text{ ft}$$
$$= 0.18/3.28 = 0.055 \text{ SMC}$$

Therefore, the **CG** has moved aft from 0.186 to 0.24 SMC. Although the **CG** is within limits it would be better if it could be arranged to lie between about 0.19 and 0.28 SMC, a rearwards shift of 0.04 SMC, i.e. $0.04 \times 3.28 = 0.13$ ft (0.04 m).

Example 30

What is the easiest way of moving the **CG** of the aeroplane aft to 0.28 SMC in the previous problem?

The pilot should be arranged comfortably relative to the wing spars, so that once the seating is fixed, and the juxtaposition of the flying surfaces, we are only left with the engine. Therefore, the powerplant should be moved aft an amount $+\Delta_{xp}$, where:

$$\Delta\overline{x} = \Delta x_p(W_P/W_O) \qquad\qquad from \text{ eq (15–8)}$$

Knowing that the design **CG** must be moved aft to 0.28 SMC with a heavy pilot and fuel gone from the tank ahead of the **CG**, and that the power-plant weight-ratio is 0.28 W_O (table 15–5):

$$Shift, \ \Delta\overline{x} = (0.28 - 0.24) \text{ SMC} = 0.28 \ x_p$$
$$x_p = 0.04/0.28 = 0.143 \text{ SMC}$$
$$= 0.143 \times 3.28 = 0.47 \text{ ft (0.067 m)}$$

This means that the nose will have to be shortened by about 5.6 in (14.22 cm).

Example 31

With the aft **CG** at 0.28 SMC in the previous example, what will be the static margin K_n? Use the following data, obtained from the preceding examples and by scaling from fig. 15.6:

$$h_o = 0.23, \ h = 0.28, \ \eta_s = \text{about 70 per cent (0.7), say,}$$
$$s = b/2 = 23/2 = 11.5 \text{ ft}, \ S_s = \pi \times 1.25 \times 3 = 11.78 \text{ ft}^2 \text{ (assuming an elliptical planform),}$$
$$S = 76 \text{ ft}^2, \ \overline{c} = 3.28 \text{ ft}, \ l_s = 10 \text{ ft}, \ A = 7, \ A_s = 6^2/11.78 = 3.05,$$
$$d\epsilon/d\alpha = \text{about } 0.48 \times 1.2 \text{ (because the wing is tapered)} = 0.58,$$
$$\text{using } l_s/s = 0.87 \text{ and } h/s = \text{about 0.24 in fig. 5.13b,}$$
$$\overline{V}_s = (11.78/76)(10/3.28) = 0.47 \text{ (about mid-range in table 11–1),}$$
$$a_1/a \approx 4/5 = 0.8 \text{ in fig. 4.6c (using } A \text{ and } A_s \text{ above).}$$

Therefore, from eq (11–25):

$$\text{Static margin, } K_n = (h_o - h) + \eta_s\overline{V}(a_1/a)(1 - d\epsilon/d\alpha)$$
$$= (0.23 - 0.28) + 0.7 \times 0.47 \times 0.8 \times (1 - 0.58)$$
$$= -0.05 + 0.11 = 0.06 \text{ SMC}$$

This is larger than the recommended range in table 11–5, which suggests K_n should be

0.04 maximum. However, as stick-free stability of light aeroplanes tends to be less than stick-fixed, any adjustment should be made with caution. The physical difference between the two margins depends upon the value of (a_2b_1/a_1b_2) in eqs (11–14a) and (11–27).

Example 32

Assuming that the stick-fixed and free margins are equal to K_n in example 31, how far aft might the CG be moved to reduce the static margin to 0.04 in the previous example? What could be other consequences?

$$As \ K_n = (0.23 - h) + 0.113 = 0.04 \ SMC \ (required)$$
$$then, \ h = 0.23 + 0.113 - 0.04 = 0.30 \ SMC$$

i.e., the CG should be moved to about 30 per cent SMC, a total shift of 0.06 SMC.

This will involve the engine being moved even further aft, by $(0.06/0.04) \times 0.47$ ft = 0.705 ft (about 8.5 in). The other things we must watch are: the reduction in forward shift of the ac caused by the shorter nose; the need to check that the pilot will still have enough leg-room; and a check on the fuel space and capacity ahead of the pilot.

The problem with small-scale aeroplanes (see also Appendix C)

One of the most attractive developments in recent years is the construction of smaller (about half-scale) replicas of aeroplanes, like *Spitfire, P–51 Mustang, Focke Wulf 190* and *Chance Vought F4U–1 Corsair*. Other miniatures are more specialised, like the *BD–5* for example, and *Quickie*, both of which have appeared elsewhere in this book. Such designs represent quite courageous steps in new directions, often breaking fresh ground.

A number of problem areas are revealed when designing and building small aeroplanes, and especially replicas, both full and reduced scale:

☐ The 'square-cube law' asserts itself with small scale, as we shall see in a moment.
☐ Modern engines are often lighter, with lower specific weights than those used originally. Centres of gravity tend to migrate further aft, and this is destabilising, unless ballast is added in the nose, around engine mountings, or heavier metal propellers are used. A number of scale fighter projects with tail-dragging gear have been prone to groundlooping because of aft-wandering CG's.
☐ Control surface and wing section profiles, especially at leading and trailing edges, are inaccurate, introducing unexpectedly different handling qualities. Aileron trailing edges of a rebuilt *Hawker Hurricane* were so wrong that they caused aileron overbalance. Do remember that trailing edge profiles are sensitive, especially with lower speed aeroplanes. In fact we may say that
Subcritically (less than about *M 0.6*) the shape (slope) of rearward facing surfaces, i.e., aft of the section of maximum thickness, is crucially important.
Supercritically (when compressibility occurs) the shape (slope) of forward facing surfaces is more important than the style of those facing aft.

Plate 15–2 (Top) *War Aircraft Replicas' Focke Wulf Fw 190–A3* replica with a span of 20 ft and around 6/10 scale. The load-bearing structure is conventional, with the outside shape padded with foam and covered with fibreglass. It is flown here by Mike Searle of SBV Aero Services, Elstree, UK. The author found the aeroplane potent and twitchy. (*Gordon Bain via M. C. Searle*) (Bottom) *Thunder Wings Curtiss P40C* replica (about 9/10 scale) powered by a 300 BHP *Lightning Merlin V-12* based upon the automotive, liquid-cooled *Jaguar V-12*. The load-bearing structure is conventional wood and steel tube, with a moulded skin, like a racing car body. These replicas are comparable in size with the *Beech V35B Bonanza* (Plate 6–5 (Top)) (*Thunder Wings USA*)

☐ Control surfaces are improperly balanced and sealed, with similar adverse effects upon handling qualities.

☐ Centres of gravity wrongly placed through insufficient knowledge. For example, where should the aerodynamic centre of a triplane cellule lie? A triplane flown by the author appeared to have the **CG** about 6 in (15 cm) too far aft on a 39 in (99 cm) chord (1.4 m), and the nose had to be held down all of the time, in spite of full nose-down trim. The aeroplane looped beautifully.

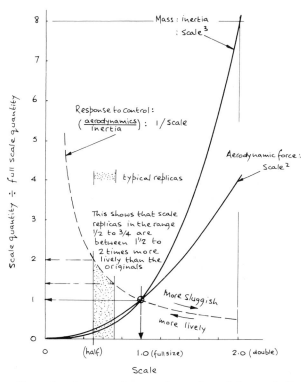

Fig. 15.8   The effect of scale upon the aerodynamic and dynamic (inertia) properties of aeroplanes. This is yet another example of the 'square-cube law'. The diagram assumes that engineering methods, construction and technology are all comparable. In practice they are probably not entirely so.

☐ Incompatibility between modern technology and methods and older technology. For example, mirror-finished cylinder bores do not trap oil as well as rougher, older surfaces. This helped to cause oiling of the plugs of a refurbished *Bristol Mercury XX* engine, giving the author three forced landings on his first three flights in a recently rebuilt *Westland Lysander*, each time the throttle was closed for stall tests.
☐ General lack of expertise and too much lost knowledge as an older generation fades away (one of the reasons for writing this book, with its accent on historic material).

Perhaps the biggest difficulty the author has met when flying very small aeroplanes is due to the square-cube law. Surface area increases in proportion to the square of size (i.e. scale) and *vice versa*, while mass and weight increase, or decrease, as its cube. The consequence is that as aeroplanes grow smaller the aerodynamics dominate the dynamics and they become so lively and quick to respond to control that they can be treacherous when flying conditions are less than ideal. The control surfaces are so small that from the point of view of pilot handling they are more 'pressure-controls' than 'movement-controls', and it becomes too easy to cause Pilot Induced Oscillations PIOs through overcontrol. The *BD–5* and *VariEze* designers have both resorted to small side-stick controls instead of the central stick, which has too much mechanical advantage. But, having said this, the authority of the control surfaces of such quick-reacting midgets usually enables a pilot who has got into trouble to get out of it – if he acts correctly.

Fig. 15.8 shows the way in which the square-cube law affects matters. Aerodynamic forces increase with surface area (length²), while mass, i.e. inertia (and weight), increases with volume (length³). If an aeroplane starts life with a particular set of dimensions and then a replica is built with a different set of dimensions, we say that the scale of the machine has been changed, such that:

$$\text{scale} = \text{new dimension}/\text{original corresponding dimension} \qquad (15\text{--}10)$$

In fig. 15.8 full scale is shown as 1.0. If we now divide 'aerodynamics' by 'inertias', which ratio is proportional to (length²/length³), the result is a measure of liveliness/sluggishness. The same result is proportional to and obtained by dividing (scale²/scale³). An asymptotic curve is produced which varies as 1/scale. Thus, as scale is reduced below 1.0 an aeroplane becomes increasingly lively. When an aircraft is scaled up it becomes more sluggish and slower to respond to control, even though control sizes have been increased in proportion.

Another problem arises from scale effect, although it usually appears in a less dramatic form. If an aeroplane is built to a smaller scale, using exactly the same wing sections, then Reynolds number decreases directly with scale. Fig. 3.10 shows that a gently humped lift curve, with good stall characteristics, can change to a 'peaky' sharp-stalling section at a lower Reynolds number. The change is accompanied by a reduction in lift slope, an overall increase in drag, and a lower lift/drag ratio. The result is that proportionally more power is needed to fly a replica than would be needed full scale, for comparable performance; and the stall could be far from docile.

Of course, as we have said already elsewhere, if scale is reduced still further the aircraft becomes uncontrollable on two counts: there is too much power and acceleration, with gyroscopic precession and other propeller effects thrown in; and the aeroplane becomes as quick as a cat in response to control.

If we want to build a replica in a smaller size, then it ought to look right. The trouble is that one cannot scale down a pilot, and it is surprising how obtrusive the subtlest hump or bump, introduced to accommodate a full-scale head or shoulders, gives away the failure of the attempt to make a replica perfect.

Many of the most interesting aeroplanes are tail-draggers – so a pilot with slowish feet is going to be straight into trouble with an aeroplane as quick as a minnow with its tail, in anything of a crosswind. Therefore, it would be unwise to choose a machine with a narrow track undercarriage. The *Spitfire* and the *Messerschmitt Bf 109* were critical in this respect and true replicas could be hard work for pilots unused to tricky ground handling.

There are several ways of tackling the problem of selecting the scale. One is to start with the cockpit area, to see what reasonably cost-effective scale will accommodate a pilot. We may alternatively start with the engine, if that is to be the determining factor (which is often the case full-scale), so that the size of the replica will be a function of power loading and wing loading. Another method, adopted by *Thunder Wings* of *Scottsdale, Arizona* is to re-contour an aeroplane so that it shares the same aerofoil sections and all basic aerodynamic characteristics with a *Beechcraft V35B*. In this way the dimensions of the replica are close to those of the *Bonanza* (span about 33 ft (10m)), and, presumably, power is in the same general range of 250 BHP to 300 BHP (187 kW to 224 kW). This method has a sound, rational appeal.

Fig. 15.8 shows the *Blackburn B–48*, or *YA1* (chosen because of certain associations) which has a number of features we might look for in a replica, and several real difficulties. The cockpit is well forward, with a deep fuselage. Although the body is

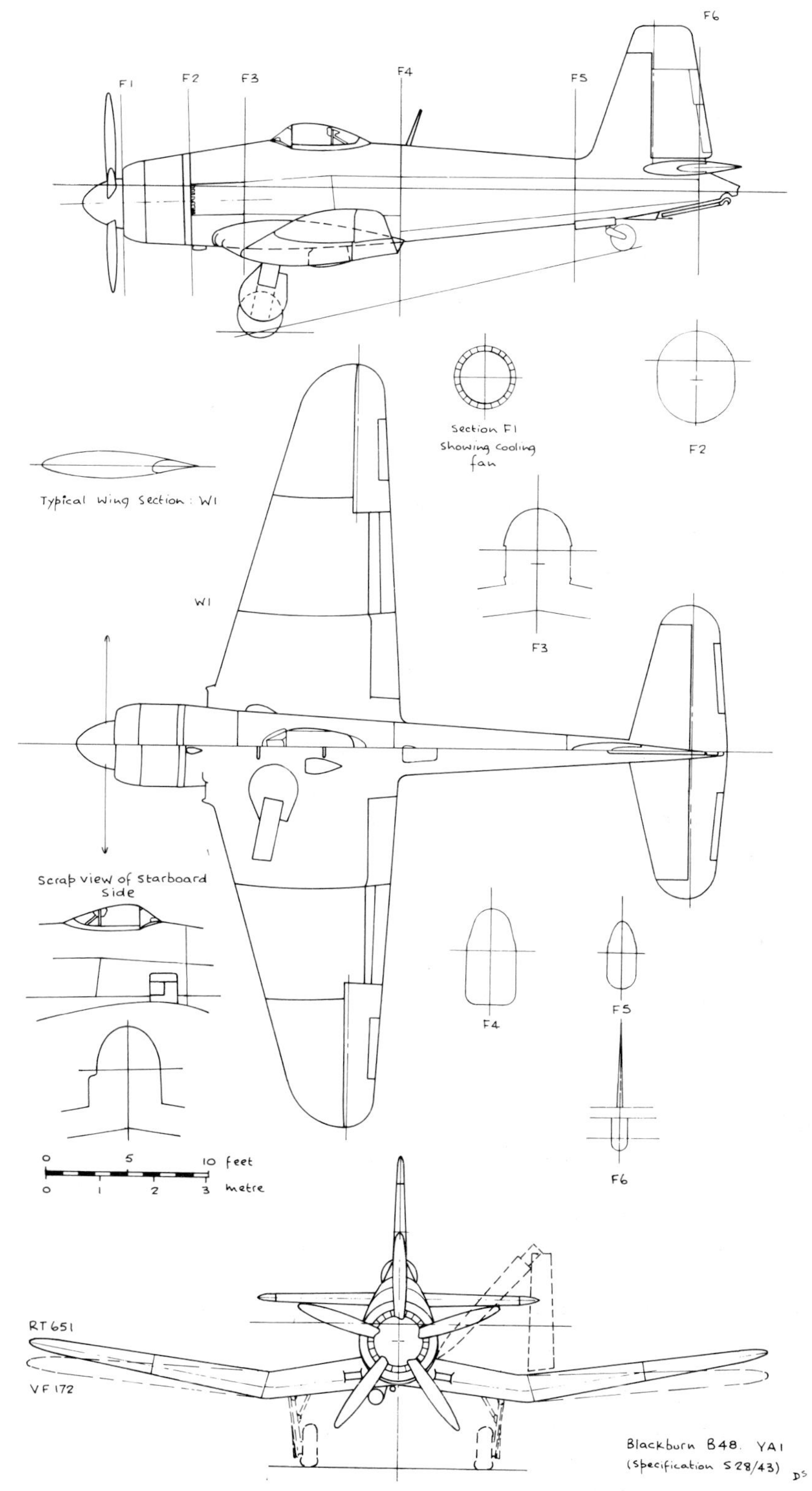
F1
F2
F3
F4
F5
F6
Section F1
Showing cooling fan
Typical Wing Section: W1
W1
Scrap view of starboard side
0
5
10 feet
0
1
2
3 metre
RT651
VF172
Blackburn B48. YA1
(Specification S28/43)
DS

Fig. 15.9 *Blackburn B-48 (YAI)*

unusually fine in plan, it should be possible to fit the pilot into the scale lines, with plenty of room above the wing centre section.

A major difficulty with the *B–48* is in the length of engine cowl available. It is most important to maintain the lines of an aeroplane as closely as possible, so that character is not lost. The distance from the intake lip to the exhaust ring was only about 42 in (1.07 m) – a benefit of a radial engine – and this is about the length of a modern flat six engine in the 250 BHP to 300 BHP range. To fit such an engine, or any engine of similar length, would require either a full-scale airframe (in which case it would have insufficient power), or special concealment of the engine contours. It is almost impossible to find an adequate radial engine today, most are well-worn, while spares are in short supply and costly. Therefore we might think about making the exhaust stub ring false and letting the rear of a flat, or in-line engine stray into the bay between sections F2 and F3 in the drawing. New exhaust outlets, which were not there on the original would have to be made in the belly.

Example 33

Given the drawing of the *B–48* in fig. 15.9, find a scale which would enable an amateur builder to make an accurate scale replica in all main external details. What would be reasonable wing and power loadings? The aeroplane should be aerobatic, and also be able to carry a scale replica torpedo. Original technical details are shown in table C–3, with application to scale B–48 in table C–4.

Plate 15–3 These photographs of the *Blackburn B-48 (YA1)*, designed as a torpedo-fighter towards the end of World War II, are typical of the research involved. Even so, many other photos were needed to draw fig. 15.9. Highlights provide important clues. Do not assume that full-scale aerofoil sections will be docile at replica Reynolds numbers – double check and get all of the advice that you can. (*British Aerospace, Brough, UK*)

Plate 15.3 – *Continued.*

Two factors should be taken into account when answering the question.

☐ Fuselage width at the cockpit should not be less than 2 ft (0.61) m) (fig. 9.3b).
☐ There should be enough space within the cowl lines to accommodate available engines.

Taking the first point, if the width of the fuselage at the cockpit is 2 ft in fig. 15.9, then the scale wingspan cannot be less than about 25 ft (7.62 m). Thus, using eq (15–10):
and 44 ft 11½ in = 44.96 ft minimum scale = 25/44.96 = 0.56
which is a rather inconvenient number to handle. If we choose the much easier 0.6, or 6/10 scale, then:

$$\text{wingspan of replica} = 0.6 \times 44.96 \text{ ft} = 27 \text{ ft}$$

while the corresponding scale of wing and other areas is $0.6^2 = 0.36$:

i.e.   scale wing area $= 0.36 \times 361.5 = 130$ ft²

The average span loading of conventionally built light aeroplanes is obtained from table 6–3, for those aircraft with aspect ratios close to that of the scale *B–48*, i.e., $27^2/130 = 5.6$. The result for the ten aeroplanes with aspect ratios between 5.4 and 6.9 is 83 lb/ft, so that:

$$\text{weight of replica} = \text{about } 83 \times 27 \text{ ft} = 2240 \text{ lb}$$
$$\text{wing loading} = 2240/130 = 17.23 \text{ lb/ft}^2$$

If the aeroplane is not built conventionally, but employs composite materials, then the weight might be reduced somewhat. However, there is no harm in being conservative at this stage. Later, we could set a weight target about 5 per cent less, say, 2130 lb (968 kg). To determine the size of powerplant we may take several routes:

☐ Using the old fashioned rule of thumb in eq (6–31) to find the range of wing loading × power loading to give good (lively) performance:

$$90 < W^2/SP < 135 \qquad\qquad \text{eq (6–31)}$$

which transposes for power loading as shown in eq (6–32), such that:

$$17.23/90 > P/W > 17.23/135$$

so that $P = 429$ BHP to 286 BHP. This will be a thirsty aeroplane if it has the bigger engine, so let us select an engine of say, 286 BHP, to see how it works out:
☐ Using fig. 6.13b, for $W/S = 17.23$ lb/ft²:
average $W/P = 19 - 0.4 \ W/S = 19 - 0.4 \times 17.23 = 12.11$ lb/BHP
so that: $P = 2240/12.11 = 185$ BHP

☐ From fig. 6.13b for the same wing loading:

power/wing area, $P/S = 1.5$ to 1.8 BHP/ft² for commercial standard light aeroplanes,
i.e. $P = 1.5 \times 130 = 195$ BHP to
$$1.8 \times 130 = 234 \text{ BHP}$$

But if we want the aeroplane to be in the racing class, we might expect:
$P/S = $ about 4 BHP/ft² = 520 BHP.
Thus, the range of engines could be:
    185 BHP for an average light aeroplane with some aerobatics,

235 to 286 BHP, fully aerobatic (international standard),
520 BHP for a 'hot rod'.

A selection of available engines falling around these values is shown in table 15-8, compiled from various published sources, with dimensions rounded up to the nearest 0.1 in (2.5 mm). Cowl surfaces should allow about 0.25 in (6 mm) minimum clearance for engine shake. There should also be room for the fingers to reach between the back of the engine and the firewall, say, 1.25 in (32 mm) minimum clearance.
Scaling the cowling we have:

length from propeller to firewall = about 33 in (0.841 m)
diameter in plan view = about 36 in (0.914 m)

Therefore, all of the engines in the table would fit within the diameter, but the IO-360-D would be tight in length. Both liquid-cooled engines would be too long for the scale distance to the exhaust ejector ring.

At this point a decision would be needed. Either the scale of the aeroplane would have to be increased to, say, 7/10, or even 3/4. Or the cowling would have to be lengthened, incorporating the bay F2 to F3 in fig. 15.9 making it no longer to scale (as wing, fuselage and tail sections might not be truly to scale either, perhaps that would not matter). Or the range of available engines should be reduced to the three *Lycoming* units.

The author's choice would be to increase the scale to 7/10 and to use one of the very smooth-running liquid-cooled automotive engines, like the *Aero-Bonner Sapphire V6*. This could be modified by the addition of an extension shaft to accommodate a multi-blade fan running within the cowling entrance, as on the original, blowing air through liquid radiators contained within the cowl lines. Additional radiator and oil-cooler area would also be available within the wing roots.

Fig. 15.10 shows an initial rough outline of the fuselage and engine installation, together with pilot, to 7/10 scale. Table 15-9 gives first estimates of a number of aircraft characteristics, including rate of climb (from fig. 6.14a), at sea level, ISA. With an engine nearer to 500 BHP, or the 700 BHP *Thunder TE495-TC700*, a variant of the replica could make a usefully cheap and cheerful ground attack aeroplane.

The weight might be on the heavy side at this stage, especially as lighter composite materials could now be used. However, there is no guarantee that the centre of gravity will appear in the right place, so that we should be prepared for some ballasting, and it is fair enough to leave the weight estimate as it is.

With a project of this kind care must be taken when attempting to settle the shape of the various sections. The original prototypes had laminar wings and glossy high speed finishes, in Royal Navy colours of the period. Highlights should come in the correct places, otherwise the impression of an otherwise careful reproduction is marred. Considerable research is needed in work of this kind.

☐ A final word of warning: beware of using original aerofoil sections without further investigation to find out if they would still be safe in smaller scale at low speed, and while manoeuvring at high g.

Aerobatic aeroplanes

There have been considerable advances in recent years in the development of aerobatic manoeuvres and the design of specialised aeroplanes, able to fly them. Table 15-10

TABLE 15-8

Engine statistics

Engine	Length from propeller base plate in	Width in	Max depth from shaft L in	Weight lb	BHP	Ref.
Air-cooled:						
Continental						
IO–360–D	35.4	31.5	14.3	328	210	15.3
Lycoming						
O–360–A	32.6	33.4	17.8	285	180	15.4
IO–360–A	32.6	34.3	12.5	323	200	
IO–360–B	32.6	33.4	16.7	300	180	
Liquid cooled:						
Aero-Bonner						
Sapphire V6	35.7	18.4	11.9	310	180	15.5
(turbocharged)					(230)	
Geschwender Aeromotive						
351 CID	56.5	23.0	Max height	600	330	15.15
460 CID	56.5	23.0	25.0	700	430	
460 CID (turbocharged)	56.5	23.0		700	600	
Javelin Aircraft Co						
Turbo-4 Ford	40.0	20.7	18.8	437 (with all accessories)	220	15.6
Thunder Engines Inc						
TE 495–TC700	46.25 (excluding turbocharger)	27.75	14.55	711.95 (with all accessories)	700	15.14
Thunder wings						
Lightning Merlin V12	46.0	23.0	?	700	300	15.19

Plate 15–4 Two crisp and effectively thoroughbred aerobatic aeroplanes for modern unlimited class aerobatics. The author found they could do everything he could think of, and probably more. (Top) Czechoslovakian *Zlin 50L* is excellent for lazy, precise manoeuvres (*James Gilbert, UK*) (Bottom) French *CAP20*, flown by Tony Bianchi (*Flight International via Tony Bianchi*). Note the symmetrical wing section of the *Zlin* (that of the *CAP20* appears to be so too) and the amount of rudder each designer has freed from adverse effects of the tailplane and elevator when spinning.

Plate 15–5 (Top) A smaller scale experimental version of a larger machine: the *Lockspeiser LDA-01*, flown by David Lockspeiser is, in effect, an airborne pick-up truck, with a wide centre of gravity range. The author found it promising, with much potential, and unusual flying qualities. (*G. R. Wrixon, the Royal Aeronautical Society*). (Bottom) *NDN Aircraft Ltd Fieldmaster* project, with an integral titanium hopper, a 750 SHP *Pratt & Whitney PT6* turboprop engine and spray nozzles built into the full-span, *Junkers*-type flaps and drooping ailerons. The aeroplane is a two-seater, like an increasing number of advanced ag-aeroplanes. (*NDN Aircraft Ltd*)

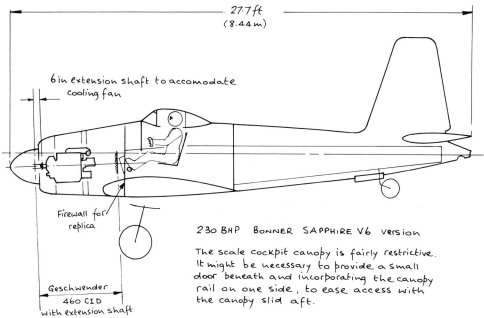

27·7 ft
(8·44 m)

6 in extension shaft to accomodate cooling fan

Firewall for replica

230 BHP BONNER SAPPHIRE V6 version

The scale cockpit canopy is fairly restrictive. It might be necessary to provide a small door beneath and incorporating the canopy rail on one side, to ease access with the canopy slid aft.

Geschwender 460 CID with extension shaft

Fig. 15.10a   Initial outline of 7/10 scale *Blackburn B-48* replica to accommodate a number of engines in the range 200 BHP to 600 BHP (149 kW to 448 kW). With the larger engines this would make a reasonably cost-effective ground attack aeroplane.

shows the basic *Aresti* system (Jose Luis de Aresti, Spanish aerobatic pilot) in which aerobatic manoeuvres are analysed in families, from 1 to 9. All erect flight (involving positive *g*) is shown as a solid line, with a circle at the start and a small vertical line at the end of each manoeuvre, o——|; while negative *g*, inverted, flight is shown with a dotted line o------|. Full rolls have arrows through the line, half rolls have only half an arrow. Flick (snap) rolls are shown as equilateral triangles, and spins as rights angled triangles; unshaded for inside, shaded for outside. Armed with the basic families it is possible to combine the manoeuvres into sequences, the most demanding of which are flown in various international aerobatic contests. The Aresti system is only the foundation of contest rules – which can modify the Aresti concept considerably.

During aerobatic contests the object is to remain within a box of airspace as shown in fig. 15.11 (refs 7.12 and 15.7). This restriction results in the requirements and limitations:

☐ High structural strength to contend with positive and negative normal accelerations around +9 and −6*g*.

☐ The ability to manoeuvre at comparatively low airspeeds (too much kinetic energy through too much speed makes it hard to stay within the box).

☐ Crisp responses to effective controls and the ability to fly erect, inverted or on the side with ease.

☐ Plenty of power per unit weight.

☐ Low wing loading (this is arguable, because it tends to spoil snap manoeuvres).

☐ Quietness.

The last requirement is added for obvious social reasons.

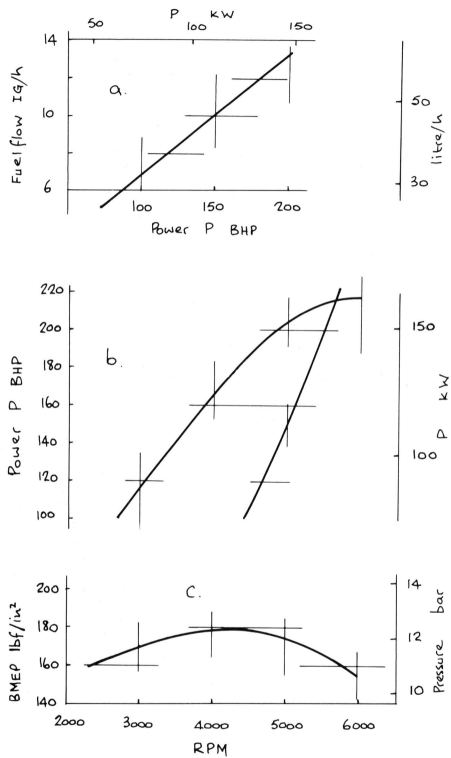

Fig. 15.10b Characteristics of the *Aero-Bonner Sapphire V6* engine.
(Ref. 15.5).

TABLE 15–9

First estimates for *Blackburn B–48* to 7/10 scale with
Aero-Bonner Sapphire V6 (180 to 230 BHP (turbocharged) engine)

Span	31.47 ft	(9.6 m)
Length	27.7	(8.44)
Wing area	177 ft^2	(16.44 m^2)
Weight (83 lb/ft)	2612 lb	(1 187 kg)
Wing loading	14.76 lb/ft^2	(72.03 kg/m^2)
Power loading	14.51 lb/BHP	(8.82 kg/kW)
(turbocharged	11.36 lb/BHP	(6.9 kg/kW))
Rate of climb	750 ft/min	(3.75 m/s)
(turbocharged	1 250 ft/min	(6.25 m/s))

To achieve these aims introduces some conflict. Aeroplanes with a lot of power and low wing loadings tend not to be efficient when cruising between displays and competitions. Very small aeroplanes are so quick in response to control that it is easy to overshoot the required altitude during a manoeuvre – in addition to which they are more boring to people on the ground who are not experts, but who have come to watch a spectacle. The author's preference is for aerobatic aeroplanes to be a reasonable size, lazy in manoeuvre, precise in response, well able to exchange potential and kinetic energy without fuss and excessive noise, and with near-identical flying qualities when either erect or inverted.

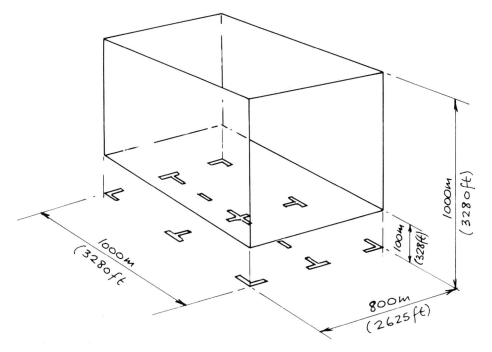

Fig. 15.11 The international competition box of air within which a sequence of aerobatic manoeuvres must be accomplished (refs. 7.12 and 15.7).

TABLE 15–10
The Aresti system of classifying aerobatic manoeuvres

Family	Key
1. Line and angle	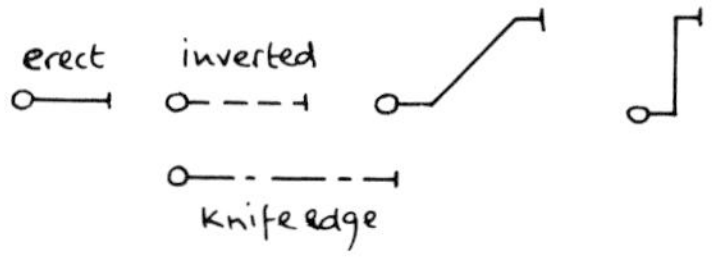 erect inverted knife edge
2. Horizontal turn	
3. Vertical turn	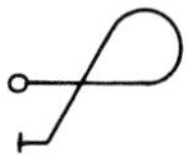
4. Spin	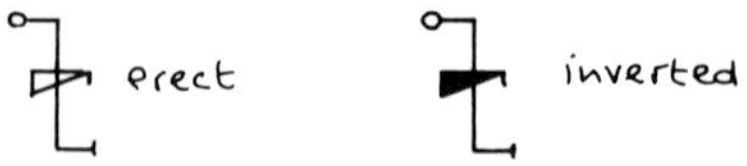 erect inverted
5 Stall turn	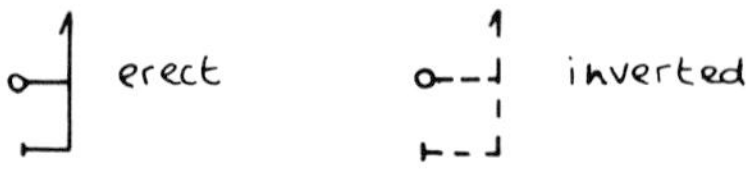 erect inverted
6. Tail slide	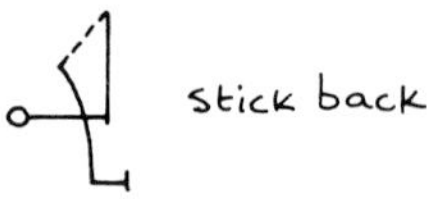 stick back
7. Loop	
8. Roll	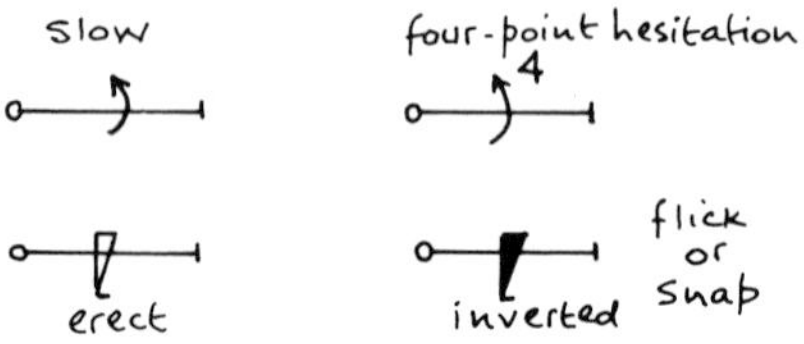 slow four-point hesitation 4 erect inverted flick or snap
9. Loop and roll	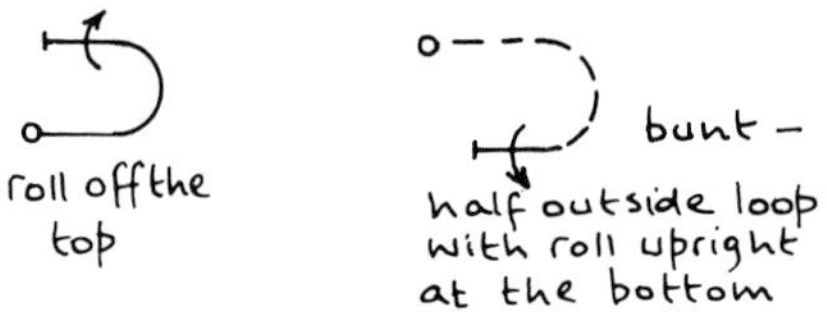 roll off the top bunt – half outside loop with roll upright at the bottom

Larger aeroplanes have the advantage that it can become possible to carry a mechanic and baggage, or spares, although this is not advocated as a necessary requirement. Nevertheless, during what display pilots call the 'silly season' through the summer one can be faced with show commitments almost anywhere within Europe, with positioning flights over continental distances, as in the USA or Australia, and the

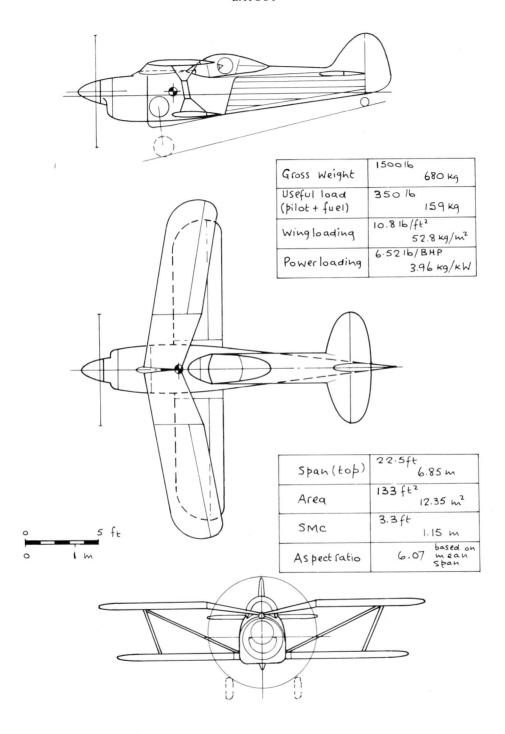

Gross weight	1500 lb 680 kg
Useful load (pilot + fuel)	350 lb 159 kg
Wing loading	10.8 lb/ft² 52.8 kg/m²
Power loading	6.52 lb/BHP 3.96 kg/kW

Span (top)	22.5 ft 6.85 m
Area	133 ft² 12.35 m²
SMC	3.3 ft 1.15 m
Aspect ratio	6.07 based on mean span

Fig. 15.12   General arrangement of biplane for championship standard aerobatics.
Tail surface areas are not finalised.

requirement is worth bearing in mind. One difficulty arising from a consideration of this kind is that a larger rather than a smaller aeroplane is inevitably heavy with a relatively high structural weight. Fuel storage can be a problem and it may be necessary to make provision for external overload tanks. There is a cut-off in rated power around 250 to 300 BHP (187 to 224 kW) in availability of suitable engines. As we are looking for power loadings as low as 5 lb/BHP up to about 7.5 lb/BHP to give flexibility in choice of manoeuvre and a margin for error, and wing loadings in the range 11 to 13 lb/ft², we are unlikely to find an aeroplane with an aerobatic weight much higher than 1 500 lb (682 kg).

Control surface areas tend to be proportionally large for precision at airspeeds well below the stall, for example in vertical climbing manoeuvres: rudder and elevator must provide adequate yawing and pitching moments in either direction when working in propwash alone, at zero TAS. Control system design must take account of reversed airflows, as when sliding backwards. Pushrods with small tolerances have much to commend them for reducing friction and backlash to a minimum, compared with cables which can become slack more easily.

Symmetrical aerofoil sections, some of unusual shape like those by Arnold Wagner in Switzerland, are needed if flight characteristics are to be the same when either erect or inverted. Dihedral of the wings tends to be almost zero, and there is usually little or no longitudinal dihedral between wing and stabiliser. Stability in the longitudinal and directional planes must not be excessive. Some aerobatic aeroplanes flown by the author have had near neutral stability about all axes. Clearly, such aeroplanes are not for novices, so that risk from lower than normal stability margins can be countered by the design of effective controls, reasonable hinge moments and sensitive 'feel', adequate aerodynamic damping – all backed up by adequate levels of inertia in pitch, roll and yaw – and an accelerometer mounted in the cockpit in full view of the pilot.

Example 34

Sketch a general arrangement drawing of an aeroplane for World championship standard aerobatics, giving reasons for its shape.

Fig. 15.12 shows a biplane with a retractable undercarriage, strut braced wings which incorporate the pre World War 2 Polish *Pulawski-type* centre-section for the top plane (Ing Zygmunt Pulawski (1901–1931)). Leading edge strakes from the tailplane run forward to the windscreen arch for two purposes. The first is to increase aerodynamic damping of the fuselage, particularly when spinning. The second is to provide a faired anchorage for canopy rails. A hood which slides and can be jettisoned rearwards is better than one opening to the side, should it be necessary to use a parachute.

The wing arrangement (which has negligible dihedral) is to give the pilot a horizontal and vertical datum relative to his eye. The trailing edge of the bottom wing is in the lateral plane of the eye. The chord of the top wing is arranged so that a tangent from the eye grazes the undersurface on a line just above the horizon in straight and level flight. Biplanes are able to use thinner wing sections than monoplanes, so that the arc of vision cut off by the wing at any moment is a minimum.

Wing sections are symmetrical with (initially) zero decalage and longitudinal dihedral. The four wing panels (i.e. minus the centre section of the top plane) are identical in all but minor details, like strut fittings and part of each top plane cut away to provide sweep. Thus, one single jig is needed for most of the wing construction. Four ailerons, increased in thickness, are provided and all can be deflected up or down simultaneously by a single flap lever (which in effect changes the datum of all four together), so that the aeroplane can be flown through a wider range of manoeuvres. Such an arrangement would also enable an aeroplane with a cambered wing section to be trimmed for a more efficient cruise (wing trailing edges slightly up).

The retractable gear, which is of the type seen on *Grumman* aeroplanes, for example in the 1930s and early 1940s, necessitates a barrel-like body to accommodate the mechanism required to provide adequate leg length and wheel track. The bay is open across the fuselage. With the gear down there could be a powerful airbrake effect from drag, useful when manoeuvring. Folding the gear away improves the cruising lift/drag ratio but, of course the weight of such gear penalises useful load and, therefore, range. Therefore, retractable gear might be useless.

The fat fuselage cross-section is sufficient to take any engine in the range 200 to 300 BHP (150 to 224 kW). The nose-shape sketched in the drawing is to accommodate a low-set engine, with a belt-drive to gear down the propeller (which has an independent shaft running in bearings mounted on top of the crank case) so reducing rpm and noise.

Table 15–11 compares the biplane with several current championship aeroplanes published in ref. 15.16. It is the least favourable in terms of power/wing area, which suggests that it would have the slowest acceleration in the group and, therefore, the lowest speed – unless the gear was up.

An alternative solution could be to reduce wing area to 121 ft² to 125 ft² (11.24m² to 11.6 m²) making wetted area and total drag coefficient smaller. We might then economise by getting rid of the retractable gear.

Example 35

Using the construction shown in fig. 2.5, find the length and locations of the standard mean chords of the top and bottom planes of the biplane used in the previous example. When found, use the standard mean chords to construct an equivalent biplane (rectangular, unswept planes).

We start by rationalising each panel into its simplest form. These are labelled $S_{T(1)}$ and $S_{T(2)}$ on the port side of the top plane, with corresponding panels $S_{T(3)}$ and $S_{T(4)}$ on the starboard side. The bottom plane is split into $S_{B(1)}$ and $S_{B(2)}$ respectively, $S_{B(2)}$ being the starboard bottom plane. The top plane must be lowered slightly to take account of the Pulawski-type arrangement of the centre-section. The distance the plane is lowered is in the ratio of $S_{T(2)}/S_{T(1)}$ times the height of the joint (between the outer panel and the centre-section panel) above the centreline location of the top plane root (where it meets the top cowling).

In the plan view of fig. 15.13 we show the construction of the two standard mean chords, $\bar{c}_T$ and $\bar{c}_B$. To arrive at the SMC of the top plane, means chords $\bar{c}_{(1)}$ and $\bar{c}_{(2)}$ were found for the panels $S_{T(1)}$ and $S_{T(2)}$. These were then projected forwards so as to form an interim plane with ends equal to $\bar{c}_{(1)}$ and $\bar{c}_{(2)}$. These had to be drawn in the correct fore and aft position, one to the other, using a line parallel with the leading edge of the top plane. The mean chord of the interim plane is the SMC of the top plane $\bar{c}_T$.

A sketch has been made of the equivalent biplane with approximately 20 deg positive stagger. This suggests that Munk's span factor k for calculating the wing span of the equivalent monoplane should be around 1.15 (from fig. 4.21a). The SMCs of the top and bottom planes are

$$\bar{c}_T = 3.3 \text{ ft } (1.01 \text{ m})$$
$$\bar{c}_B = 3.33 \text{ ft } (1.02 \text{ m})$$

and the gap

$$G = 3.5 \text{ ft } (1.07 \text{ m})$$

TABLE 15–11

Comparison of aerobatic aeroplanes

Item		Biplane Example 34	Zlin Z-50L	CAP 20L	Superstar	Pitts S-1S	Hirth Acrostar
Weight	lb	1500	1586	1433	1170	1150	1390
Power	BHP	230	260	200	200	180	220
Wingspan	ft	22.5	28.15	24.38	24	17.33	27.17
Length	ft	21.5	21.36	23.13	20	15.48	20.04
Wing area	ft^2	133	134.55	111.9	93.6	98.5	111.26
Wing loading	lb/ft^2	11.25	11.79	12.8	12.5	11.7	12.5
Power loading	lb/BHP	6.5	6.1	7.17	5.85	6.4	5.42
Wing loading × power loading (eq (6–31))	lb^2/ft^{2}BHP	73.5	71.9	91.8	73.1	74.6	67.7
Power/wing area (fig. 6.13b)	BHP/ft^2	1.73	1.93	1.79	2.14	1.82	1.97

Example 36

Find the equivalent standard mean chord and span of the monoplane by which the biplane arrangement in example 35 may be replaced for calculations. Assume that the same wing section is used for the top and bottom planes.

We start by estimating the relative lift coefficients of the top and bottom planes, using fig. 4.20 a and b. At some nominal and easily read angle of attack (say 10 deg), these indicate that:

with no stagger $p = C_{LT}/C_{LB} \approx 0.8/0.7 = 1.14$
with 30 deg stagger $p = C_{LT}/C_{LB} \approx 0.9/0.65 = 1.38$

from which we deduce that stagger of 20 deg may well produce an equivalent ratio of

$$p = C_{LT}/C_{LB} = 1.14 + (20(1.38 - 1.14)/30) = 1.3$$

The areas of the planes may be calculated by summing the area of each individual panel or, more crudely at this stage, by finding the area of each rectangular plane:

area of top plane, $S_T = b_T \bar{c}_T \approx 21.5 \times 3.3 = 71$ ft²
area of bottom plane, $S_B = b_B \bar{c}_B \approx 18.7 \times 3.33 = 62$ ft²
total wing area, $S = S_T + S_B \approx 133$ ft² (12.35 m²)

To find the height of the equivalent plane above the bottom plane we resort to eq (4-33):

$$Y = [(pS_T)/(pS_T + S_B)]G = [(1.3 \times 71)/(1.3 \times 71 + 1 \times 62)]3.25$$
$$= 1.94 \text{ ft } (0.59 \text{ m})$$

i.e. $Y = 0.6G$, which is slightly higher, by 3 per cent of the gap, than for an orthogonal biplane in eq (4-33a), where $Y/G = 4/7 = 0.57$.

The SMC of the equivalent monoplane is given by eq (4-34):

$$\bar{c} = [(p\bar{c}_T S_T + \bar{c}_B S_B)/(pS_T + S_B) = (1.3 \times 3.3 \times 71 + 3.33 \times 62)/154.3$$
$$= 3.31 \text{ ft } (1.01 \text{ m})$$

The equivalent monoplane wingspan is calculated by means of eq (4-32):

Munk's span factor, $k \approx \sqrt{[1.8 (G/b) + 1]}$

in which b is the mean span of the wings $= (21.5 + 18.7)/2 = 20.1$.

Therefore, $k \approx \sqrt{[1.8(3.25/20.1)]} + 1 = 1.136$

This value is not far from the estimate of 1.15 made at the end of example 35. Thus, the wing span of the monoplane having the same wing area and induced drag as the biplane is:

$$kb = 1.136 \times 20.1 = 22.8 \text{ ft } (6.95 \text{ m})$$

Example 37

How much larger will be the downwash angle for the biplane used in example 34 compared with a monoplane having a wing of the same area and aspect ratio?

The areas of the wings are the same, i.e.,
biplane = monoplane = 133 ft² (12.35 m²)

Aspect ratio of biplane = $2b^2/S$ eq (4–24)

$$= 2 \times 20.1^2/133 = 6.07$$

where 20.1 is the mean span of both planes. From eq (4–25):

biplane downwash/monoplane downwash = $(1 + \sigma)$

while eq (4–30) can be transposed to show:

$$1 + \sigma = 2/k^2$$
$$= 2/1.136^2 = 1.55$$

in which Munk's span factor $k = 1.136$ was calculated in example 36.

Thus, the factor $(1 + \sigma) = 1.55$ is the number by which the angle of downwash (and $d\epsilon/d\alpha$) must be multiplied when calculating static and manoeuvre margins of this particular biplane, which has the same total wing area as a monoplane with the same aspect ratio, i.e. 6.07.

Example 38

Calculate the pitching moment of the equivalent plane, C_{Mac}, if C_{MacT} and C_{MacB} are equal. Use the wing areas and chords found in example 36, and assume that $C_{MacT} = C_{MacB}$; and $\bar{c}$ is 3.31 ft.

$$C_{Mac} = \frac{C_{MacT}\bar{c}_T S_T + C_{MacB}\bar{c}_B S_B}{\bar{c}S}$$
$$= \frac{C_{MacT} \times 3.3 \times 71 + C_{MacT} \times 3.33 \times 62}{3.31 \times 133}$$
$$= (243.3 + 206.5) \, C_{MacT}/440.23 \approx C_{MacT}$$

Therefore, the pitching moment coefficient of the biplane about the aerodynamic centre of the equivalent monoplane wing will be the same, in this case, as the pitching moment of either plane.

To find the aerodynamic centre of the biplane wing, using the construction in fig. 4.19, we draw a line between the aerodynamic centres of the top and bottom planes (in this case, $\bar{c}_T/4$ and $\bar{c}_B/4$, respectively), to intercept the equivalent monoplane chord, located at 0.6 × gap above the chord line of the bottom plane. The intercept is at $\bar{c}/4$ of the equivalent monoplane. The aerodynamic centre of the biplane is located 2 per cent of this chord forward of the point of intersection, i.e. at $0.23\bar{c}$.

From here onwards we can treat the biplane as a monoplane of wing area 133 ft² and chord 3.31 ft. We estimate the lift slope of the monoplane wing as for an aspect ratio of A = 3.9 (example 36) and calculate the forward shift of the biplane-plus-body aerodynamic centre (the **ac** of the aeroplane-minus-tail) as shown in example 28 using eq (11–51) and fig. 11.14.

Fig. 15.14 summarises the various conversions of a biplane for theoretical treatment in monoplane form.

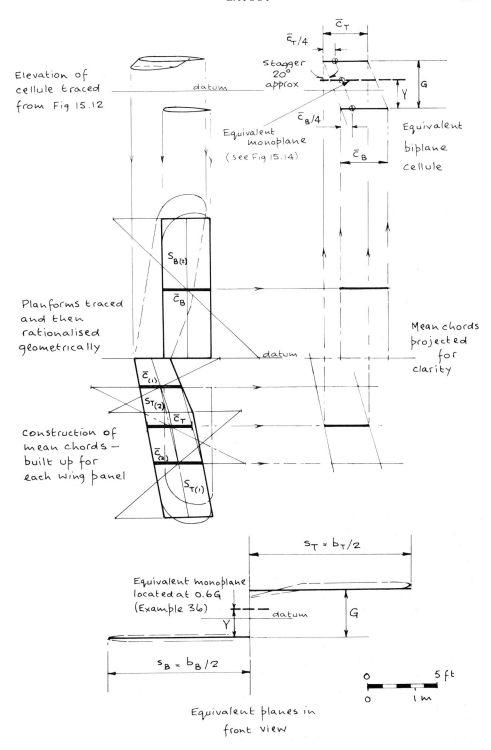

Fig. 15.13   Construction of standard mean chords and equivalent monoplane.

TABLE 15–12

Specification of *Gusty*

Item	Design	Actual
Wingspan	19.7 ft (6.0 m)	—
Length	15.42 ft (4.7 m)	—
Gross weight	725 lb (330 kg)	1000 lb (455 kg)
Wing area	84.7 ft² (7.87 m²)	—
Longitudinal dihedral	zero	zero
Engine	85 BHP (63.5 kW)	—
Power loading, W/P	8.55 lb/BHP (5.2 kg/kW)	11.76 lb/BHP (7.15 kg/kW)
Wing loading, W/S	8.55 lb/ft² (41.7 kg/m²)	11.81 lb/ft² (57.6 kg/m²)
Rate of climb (erect or inverted)	1900 ft/min (9.66 m/s)	1200 to 1400 ft/min (6.1 to 7.1 m/s)
Stall speed	48 mph (77 kph)	50 mph
Top speed	145 mph (233 kph), tested for flutter to 200 mph (322 kph)	
Turns to recover from spin (erect or inverted)	—	¼
Wing section	near symmetrical	with 6 in (15 cm) leading edge stall breaker strip added 10 in (25 cm) inboard of the tips
Vertical tail	modified *Nipper*, separate fin and rudder	enlarged area, separate fin and rudder less effective than desired
Ailerons	modified *Nipper*	
W²/SP	73 lb²/BHP ft² (217 kg²/kW m²)	139 lb²/BHP ft² (413 kg²/kW m²)

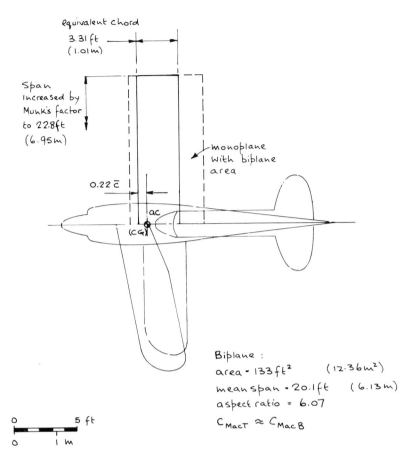

Fig. 15.14   The equivalent monoplane for biplane calculations.

Gusty

Gustave Limbach's *Gusty* represents another approach. The aeroplane was developed from the *Tipsy Nipper*, which had a Volkswagen engine. The change in elevation from the *Nipper to Gusty* is shown in fig. 15.15. The deep, cambered, basic wing section was altered to a near symmetrical section. The rigging angles were changed so that the wing and tailplane are in line, with no longitudinal dihedral. Power is by a *Continental C–85 FJ12* of 85 BHP.

General points to be noted are the changes in the aerodynamic arrangement of the surfaces; the introduction of a fin surface (*Nipper* had an all-moving rudder) and tail bracing; the considerable rudder area below the tailplane and elevator; and the tailwheel landing gear. The difference between what was planned and then actually realised is shown in table 15–12 based upon ref. 15.8. The test flight report is in ref. 15.9.

Gus Limbach summarised what he now thinks is needed for a competitive aerobatic aeroplane (ref. 15.9):

'1 The design would be based around a 180 hp (134.3 kW) *Lycoming* engine;
2 The design would be aimed for a gross weight of 1 000 lb (454.5 kg) or less;
3 The wing span should be around 26 ft (7.92 m), the length about 18 ft (5.48 m), and wing area about 120 ft² (11.15 m²).
4 Use a symmetrical airfoil with 0 deg incidence, 0 deg dihedral, with a tapered planform and keep the elevator as close in line to the wing as possible;
5 Lower the wing position from the mid-wing to increase the pilot's downward visibility;
6 Install a retractable landing gear, and if this requires going overweight, so be it;
7 Design a big comfortable cockpit;
8 Use a closed bubble canopy with good all-around visibility;
9 Employ speed brakes;
10 Find a bachelor apartment and a good divorce lawyer.'

Agricultural and other aerial work aeroplanes

Some of the most important aircraft in the world today are those needed for agricultural and other aerial work, to feed a bursting world in which many people live at a starvation level. Their tasks embrace almost everything from aerial application (i.e. spraying and dusting to spreading pesticides and fungicides) to carrying freight, fencing and fodder to hillside strips, jungle clearings and outback stations. In some cases such aeroplanes serve as rough and ready ambulances, or as passenger carriers for a workforce with bedrolls instead of cabin-baggage. Ingenuity and imagination are prime requirements of any designer turning his hand in this direction.

Such aeroplanes must be cheap and easy to maintain. There is little room for aesthetics. One way to increase their overall productivity is through utility which, in this context, means:

$$\text{Utility} = \text{versatility} + (\text{payload capacity} \times \text{block speed})$$
$$= \text{variable geometry} + \text{CTM/h} \qquad (15\text{–}11)$$

in which CTM = cost per ton mile.

Variable geometry (which costs money) may be anything from a variable pitch propeller and retractable gear to variable sweep, by way of slats, flaps and rotary wings. It can also mean the ability to change the internal configuration for different payloads (ref. 15.10). The question is what degree of variable geometry can be afforded?

In addition the designer must also think of the logistics, i.e. the whole problem of supply, repair and maintenance in support of flying operations. Fortuitously, aeroplanes are less limited by ground bearing conditions than trucks. If ground transport can get onto a strip, then so can an aeroplane.

Take aircraft needed for spraying. In the past, one tended to develop existing machines by modification for the agricultural role. Today, special aeroplanes must be designed from scratch. Hopper loads are heavy and voluminous. Designers cannot afford to waste such lost volume, and crashworthiness is vital – which is why *NDN Fieldmaster* project, in fig. 15.16 and table 15–13, incorporates a strong load-bearing stainless steel hopper. There is also room for a second occupant (either an instructor, mechanic or ground crew), which is becoming a necessary feature for such operations and training.

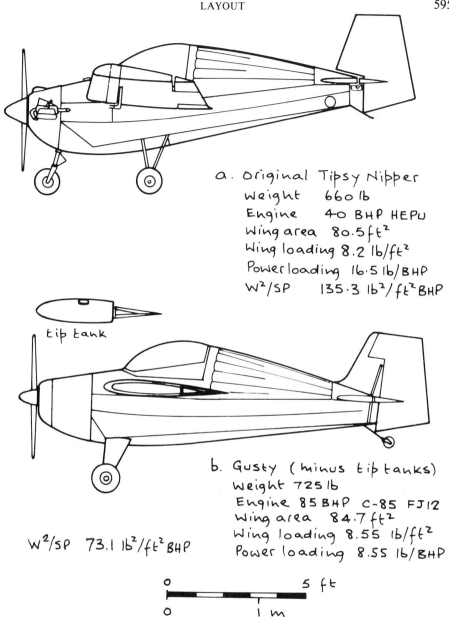

a. Original Tipsy Nipper
   Weight   660 lb
   Engine   40 BHP HEPU
   Wing area 80.5 ft²
   Wing loading 8.2 lb/ft²
   Power loading 16.5 lb/BHP
   W²/SP   135.3 lb²/ft² BHP

tip tank

b. Gusty (minus tip tanks)
   Weight 725 lb
   Engine 85 BHP C-85 FJ12
   Wing area 84.7 ft²
   Wing loading 8.55 lb/ft²
   Power loading 8.55 lb/BHP

W²/SP 73.1 lb²/ft² BHP

Fig. 15.15 Gus Limbach's conversion of a *Tipsy Nipper* into an aerobatic aeroplane which had identical flying qualities erect or inverted. With tip tanks fitted the author found *Gusty* neither knew nor cared which way up it was in any manoeuvre. Stability appeared to be neutral about all axes. The conversion is described in ref. 15.8.

Note too the undercarriage arrangement with a nosegear, and the costly turbopropeller engine. Such power-units are at least twice as expensive as piston engines, which run on costly avgas, while kerosene is more available in remote areas. Operators are begining to argue that they cannot afford to spend almost $¼m on specialised aircraft to have them damaged on take-off or landing, because of the extra skill needed to operate with tailwheel gear.

For return on investment, aircraft of this kind must have long ferry ranges: at least

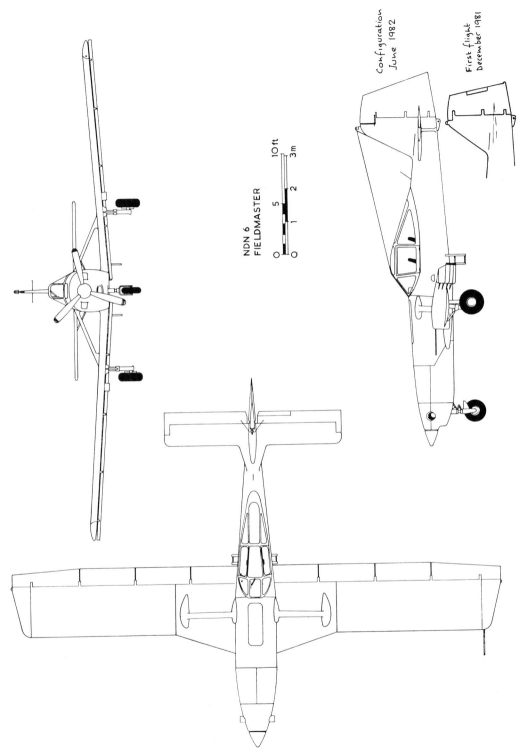

NDN 6
FIELDMASTER

10 ft

3 m

Configuration June 1982

First flight December 1981

Fig. 15.16   *NDN Fieldmaster (NDN Aircraft Ltd)*

TABLE 15–13

Project data for a number of agricultural and other aerial work aeroplanes

Item		NDN 6 Fieldmaster fig. 15.16	Biplane fig. 15.17	Biplane AGB–7–TB1 fig. 15.18a	Turbofan AGB–3–1F1 fig. 15.18b	Schapel Super Swat fig. 15.19	Project example 39
Weight	lb	10000	19600	12500 (15300)	5925 (7650)	8000	8000
Payload	lb	5500	10000	6925	3480	4118	4000
Weight fraction		0.55	0.51	0.55 (0.45)	0.58 (0.45)	0.51	0.5
Span	ft	50.25	82	70	55.17	54	49.6
Length	ft	36.17	63	47.5	41	31.7	30
Wing area	ft²	338	1400	618	380	285	308
Aspect ratio		7.5	9.6	7.9	8	10.23	8
Engine	SHP	750	2200	2 × 688	—	680	680
thrust	lbf	—	—		2040		
Wing loading	lb/ft²	29.58	14	20.2 (24.8)	20.1	28	26
Span loading	lb/ft	199	119.5 (based on sum of both spans)	108.5 (132.9) (based on sum of both spans)	107.4 (138.7)	148	161
Power loading	lb/SHP	13.3	8.9	9.1 (11.1)		11.8	11.8
Thrust loading	lb/lbf	—	—	—	2.9 (3.75)	—	—
Power/wing area	SHP/ft²	2.2	1.6	2.2	—	2.4	2.2
W²/SP	lb²/ft²SHP	394	125	184 (275)	—	330	307
Notes		To fly late 1981	—	(values for restricted gross weights in brackets)	(values for restricted gross weights in brackets)	uncertain	—

300 nm (556 km) with hopper empty. With a hopper filled with fuel some agricultural aeroplanes have transatlantic range. One finds agricultural aeroplanes flitting from northern to southern hemispheres like seasonal swallows, flown by pilots who operate as naturally without numbers as errand boys on bicycles. Designers are needed who can speak the language.

A requirement appears to be to spread loads between 0.89 to 1 000 lb/acre (1.0 to 1 120.8 kg/ha). Large parts of the world are hot, and they can be high, so that the aim should be to operate from 900 ft airstrips to 50 ft screens (274 m to 15 m) at altitudes around 5 000 ft amsl (1 524 m) in ISA to ISA +30°C. Minimum spray speed should be sufficient for a wing-over zoom to 100 ft (30 m) at the end of each run during which the airspeed should not drop to less than 1.2 V_S. Minimum spray (or swath) speed works out to be not less than about 100 KTAS. The upper limit is, say, 200 KTAS (i.e. 185 to 370 kph).

Design of wingtips with Cranfield 'Spillman sails' and Whitcomb 'winglets' now occupies research, with the object of increasing swath width to at least 1.5 times wing-span. Such devices, especially 'sails', are related aerodynamically to the pinion feathers of birds, discussed in chapter 4 and their number calculated in eq (4–20). By diffusion of the tip vortex the spray is transported laterally outboard to a greater distance.

The requirement to dump the hopper load rapidly (in the UK the present requirement is five seconds for a single-engined aeroplane and ten seconds for twins (ref. 15.11)) without encountering excessive stick forces is fraught with difficulty. When a large liquid load is dumped an aeroplane pitches nose up. The author has found it possible to run out of nose-down elevator against stick push forces of 40 lbf (182 N) or more, in an attempt to check excessive divergence. Two causes contribute:

The release of around one half of the weight makes the aeroplane leap upwards, before the angle of attack can be reduced by action of the pilot.
The fall of a large mass of water induces a downwash in the surrounding air.

Taken together, the relative airflow is caused to have a powerful downwards component. Longitudinal stability points the machine into the relative flow, pitching the nose upwards.

It follows that as structures become more efficient proportionally heavier ag loads will be carried, increasing the problem. Yet, to counter the effect by reducing longitudinal stability, or increasing control authority with quickened rate of response in pitch, could lead to reduced safety. There is a need for careful assessment and development of control surface characteristics for such aircraft – which has not been done so far. An alternative solution might be to generally introduce metering shut-off valves, so that half of the load, or enough to enable the pilot to cope with an emergency could be dumped, without loss of the lot (which could cost more than the aeroplane).

Control forces must be light enough to enable a pilot to work through a hot ten-hour day without excessive fatigue. Time spent turning, for example, when the pilot is using large control movements, can occupy 40 per cent of the total sortie time (including ferrying) i.e. some four hours in ten. But care is needed, because control forces that are too light are costly in broken aeroplanes and casualties.

Fig. 15.17 shows a study of a large cantilever biplane with a *Rolls Royce Dart* turbopropeller engine studied some years ago by the author (ref. 15.10). Technical details are shown in table 15–13. This table shows a deliberately wide spread of data to give a feel for the parameters and avenues being explored.

Figs. 15.18a and b show two NASA projects being studied.

Example 39

You are approached by someone needing an aeroplane for operations as a flying pick-up truck in Africa, South America, South East Asia, Australia and New Zealand. It must be able to carry freight, agricultural loads (with equipment for spraying, dusting or spreading), fencing, machinery and other spares. It must also be able to take off and land on unmade soft strips, or dry river beds. The terrain the aeroplane would operate from could vary from hill pasture, to savannah, desert, or hot humid jungle strips. Payload must be replaceable with fuel, for a ferry range of at least 300 nm (556 km).

First thoughts are that the aeroplane needs flexibility of a high order for exchanging payloads. Large, soft tyres will be required. As trees in primary jungle can reach 200 ft (70 m) or more the accent will be upon the need for a steep climb gradient rather than rate, so that plenty of power should be available at low-ish speed. This could point to use of a ducted propulsor instead of a free propeller. As a ducted propulsor is around 7/10 the diameter of a propeller, it might be possible to locate the powerplant out of the way of people, stones and ground vegetation.

The payload of 4000 lb (1814.4 kg) is also quite close to:

$$500 \text{ US gal (water)} = 4163 \text{ lb } (1888 \text{ kg})$$

Perhaps more usefully, because materials are pre-packaged in metric containers in many parts of the world one might aim for a payload of

$$2000 \text{ kg } (4409 \text{ lb})$$

Some of the agricultural materials are toxic, so that the pilot would need to be separated from them in a ventilated and air-conditioned cockpit. It must be possible for the pilot to evacuate the cockpit easily, with the aeroplane upright or on its back.

The engine should be able to run on tractor diesel, kerosene or gasoline.

The agricultural requirement could be summarised:

☐ To ensure an even distribution of chemical over an economically wide swath, say, 1.5 × span, which implies reshaping the wing tip vortices so that the flow around wing tips transports chemical products sideways instead of upwards.
☐ To provide utmost safety for the pilot.
☐ To avoid chemical corrosion of the structure and dangerous concentrations within control surfaces.
☐ To make the aeroplane rugged, simple and easily maintained, requiring little attention, so that flying is uninterrupted for as long as possible.

Various aeroplane shapes are sketched, but there are many conflicting demands. Fig. 15.20 shows one that satisfies some of the operational requirements for freighting and exchanging loads. The pannier may carry freight, while another version can serve as a hopper, with separate spray booms or spreader. Further, such an arrangement of payload would facilitate parachute supply in areas where landings could not be made. One conflicting demand arises from the cockpit arrangement. Many aircraft accidents are caused by hitting obstacles, so that the pilot needs a good view. So, do we put him in the nose, where he sees best and where he can leave the aeroplane whether upright or upside down? Or, do we put him somewhere else, where he will not be sandwiched between obstacle, payload and a hot engine in the back of his neck?

Most agricultural aeroplanes have the pilot located further aft. Even so, there are different points of view, as may be gathered from figs. 15.16 to 15.19. In two of the projects shown the pilot would be especially vulnerable upside down. Incidentally, experience shows the wisdom of carrying a sharp knife in the cockpit, in the event of an accident in an agricultural aircraft especially.

The size of the aeroplane depends upon the engine and the practicability of the configuration which is dependent in turn upon the diameter of the propulsor. You specify a turboprop-type engine of 680 SHP (because you have looked at *Jane's All the World's Aircraft* and that value looks about right).

How large should be the propulsor fan?

Eq (7–20c) shows that a threebladed propeller should have a diameter around:

$$d = 20^4\sqrt{P} = 20^4\sqrt{680}$$
$$= 102 \text{ in } (2.59 \text{ m})$$

Fig. 7.23 suggests that the fan duct diameter based upon eq (7–38a):

$$d_{duct} = \text{propeller diameter } d/\sqrt{2}$$
$$= 102/\sqrt{2} \approx 72 \text{ in } (1.83 \text{ m})$$

But, if we use the *Rhein-Flugzeugbau* variation: see eq (7–38b)

$$d_{duct} = d\sqrt{1.85}$$
$$= 75 \text{ in } (1.9 \text{ m})$$

Criticism of the layout

Several points of criticism stand out in fig. 15.20.

☐ The pilot is vulnerable in the nose, not only from hitting obstacles but from bird strikes. Birds tend to rise at the approach of an aeroplane, and drop to the ground -when they see helicopters (which might seem more like birds of prey?).

☐ The cranked wing, intended to shorten and lighten the fairly heavy landing gear, will be heavier than one with a straight-through spar, or one centre-line joint plus attachments. This wing has four heavy joints.

☐ The engine and propulsor are well out of the way of stones and people, but they are also hard to reach for servicing and maintenance. How do you lift out an engine and put in a new one when sitting in the open, without the equipment used by a Fixed Base Operator?

☐ The pannier is a poor shape for a hopper, even though many aeroplanes have hoppers that are long rather than high. Liquid loads slosh forwards and backwards, the heavier the load the greater the movement of the centre of gravity and the variability in stick force and longitudinal stability. Baffles are not the answer, they only reduce the rate of surge. Machines specially designed for agricultural loads (which may be heavier than the empty weight of the aeroplane) increasingly tend to have vertically mounted hoppers. This is one advantage (against a number of structural disadvantages) of the biplane in fig. 15.17. There the cranked wing, needed to give a wide gap so as to reduce interference (induced) drag, leaves room for two wing-mounted hoppers. Figs. 15.18 and 15.19 also show vertical hoppers. A hopper has also to be wedge-shaped (edge downwards) to enable the load to flow. Such a shape would reduce considerably the volume available in the hopper as sketched.

☐ There would be messy, turbulent airflows around the engine, wing centre section and propulsor, which would almost certainly degrade efficiency. Although propulsor efficiency is too easily spoilt, it is hard to calculate, because of

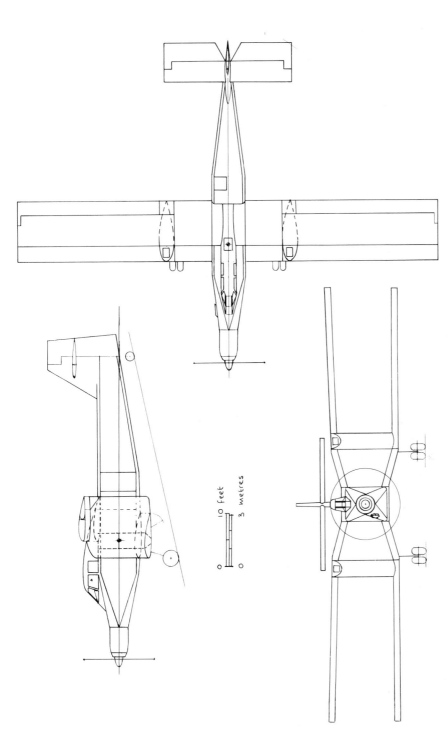

Fig. 15.17 Aerial work biplane weighing 19600 lb (8890 kg) with turbopropeller engine and two wing hoppers of 5000 lb (2268 kg) capacity each. The body has volume for freight, spares, or a ferry tank. Taper would reduce wing structure weight and improve rate of roll. The tailplane is in a poor position (*see* fig. 15.23) and would be better at the base of the fin. Background to this design was discussed in ref. 15.10.

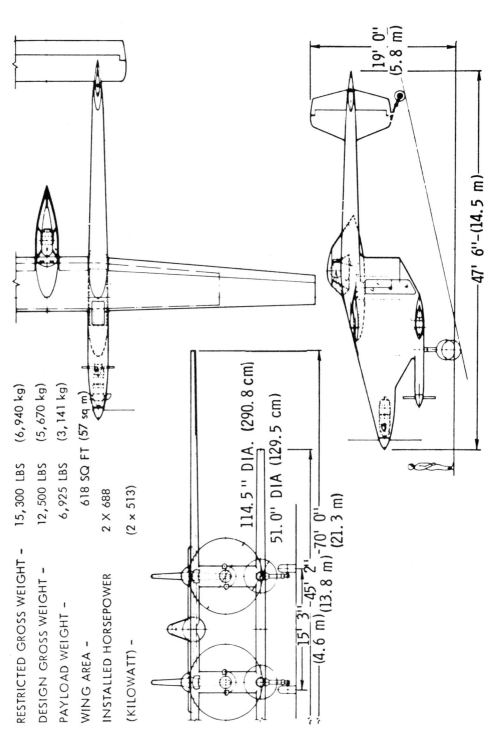

RESTRICTED GROSS WEIGHT –	15,300 LBS	(6,940 kg)
DESIGN GROSS WEIGHT –	12,500 LBS	(5,670 kg)
PAYLOAD WEIGHT –	6,925 LBS	(3,141 kg)
WING AREA –	618 SQ FT	(57 sq m)
INSTALLED HORSEPOWER	2 × 688	
(KILOWATT) –		(2 × 513)

114.5" DIA. (290.8 cm)

51.0" DIA (129.5 cm)

45' 2" -70' 0"
(13.8 m) (21.3 m)

15' 3"
(4.6 m)

Fig. 15.18 *NASA AGB-7-TBI* project (ref. 15.12).

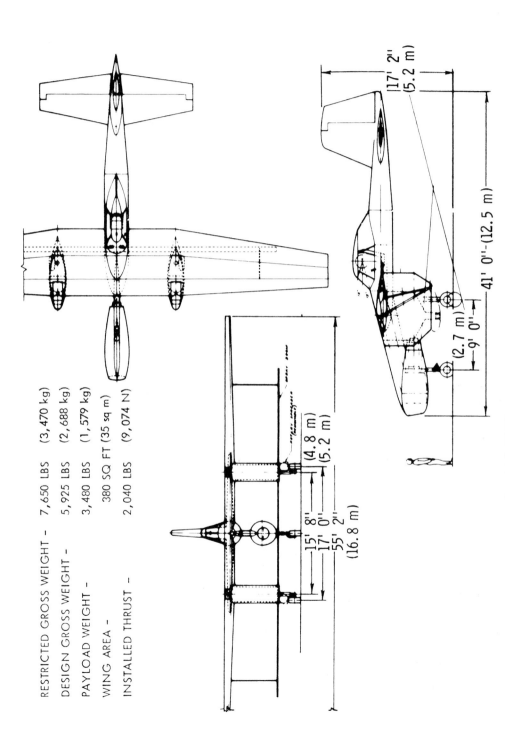

RESTRICTED GROSS WEIGHT – 7,650 LBS (3,470 kg)

DESIGN GROSS WEIGHT – 5,925 LBS (2,688 kg)

PAYLOAD WEIGHT – 3,480 LBS (1,579 kg)

WING AREA – 380 SQ FT (35 sq m)

INSTALLED THRUST – 2,040 LBS (9,074 N)

Fig. 15.19 *NASA AGB–3–IFI* project (ref. 15.12).

aerodynamic benefits bestowed by it acting somewhat as a suction pump. Thus, the flow might be improved upstream in the engine and centre section area by the fan working downstream, while the fan is made less efficient by the mess ahead of it. Drag will probably be high, to the detriment of lift/drag and range.

☐ The high thrust line will cause slightly adverse pitching effects with power (see chapter 11 and fig. 11.8).

☐ While the plank wing could be improved upon aerodynamically, its large squared tips lend themselves to the mounting of 'sails', winglets or other forms of diffuser for spreading the swath beyond the wing tips and for controlling drift. Even so, a long wing benefits structurally from some taper and there is room for refinement.

☐ The vee-tail is imponderable. It might sweeten handling qualities, reducing pilot fatigue as intended. But it might have much reduced efficiency, η_s (eq (5–24) and fig. 11.6) because of obstacles turbulating the flow ahead of it – especially when the engine is throttled back and the fan slowed. Longitudinal and directional stability might be badly degraded.

☐ It might be necessary to fit a central fin to improve directional stability, or even to resort to twin fins and rudders with a tailplane in between like the aeroplane in fig. 15.18.

☐ There could be severe structural stiffness problems around the booms and duct attachments. Somewhere in the fan shaft there would have to be a heavy universal joint, because the fan must run true in the duct. The slightest gap between fan blade tips and duct wall introduces disproportionate losses.

☐ The low set tips of the vee-tail might introduce problems in the event of inadvertent ground contact: the tips of the elevators are vulnerable.

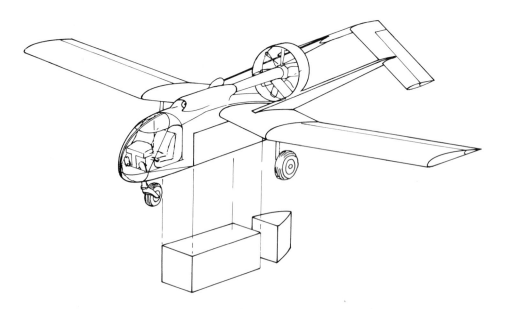

Fig. 15.20 Aerial work project for air supply (parachute delivery), freight, or spraying and dusting (see example 39).

This example has been an exercise in devil's advocacy. The criticisms are of the kind that we might use when confronted with an aeroplane that someone is trying to sell to us. They are also the sort of thoughts that pass through the minds of airworthiness engineers when someone seeks a Certificate of Airworthiness.

Handling the 'good idea'

A test pilot friend of the author, who has designed and built his own aeroplane, says that

'It seemed like a good idea at the time'

is the most useful epitaph in the world, because it applies to every aspect of the human condition and especially to aeronautics. Modern materials, methods, and technologies are now within reach of everyman and it is possible to embark on the design and construction of high performance aircraft that the amateur-builder would have thought impossible, only a decade ago.

Kits of parts with moulded skins have already appeared, based upon constructional methods employed in the manufacture of racing cars. A wide range of air cooled piston engines up to 300 BHP (224 kW) can be purchased with ease. Liquid-cooled automotive engines are being developed in the range 200 BHP to 800 BHP (149 kW to 597 kW). Small turbopropeller engines are being developed for higher powers – and turbojet engines have already begun to appear in smaller sizes. Such units tend to be costly, but they are not out of reach.

Example 40

Let us imagine that we have the facilities to build a jet aeroplane, and a garage large enough. The engine will be the French *Microturbo TRS18*, a single shaft unit, of

225 lbf thrust (100 daN)
82 lb dry weight (37 kg)
1.24 lb/h/lbf sfc (2.8 lb/h/daN)
length 22.756 in (578 mm)
width 12.047 in (306 mm)
height 13.976 in (355 mm)

(ref. manufacturer's brochure). The object is to see what sort of machine might be designed, given what we know already from this book. What might be its potential and what could be its problems?

Fig. 15.21 shows that a two seater could be designed, with a canard foreplane to shorten take-off and landing distances with a small wing and low wetted area. The weight would be around 2000 lb (907 kg), using man-made materials. Given a clean design we might achieve a value of

$$F/W_o\text{M} = 0.5 \text{ to } 0.6 \text{ in fig. } 14.7$$

□ *Design diving speed* V_D
  If we assume a mean value of $F/W_o\text{M} = 0.55$ and transpose for mach number M_c (corresponding with cruising speed V_C):
$$M_c = F/0.55 \ W_o = (2 \times 225)/(0.55 \times 2000)$$
$$= 0.41 \text{ in level flight}$$

An aerobatic aeroplane should have design diving speed V_D not less than 1.6 V_C so that corresponding Mach number in a dive:

$$M = 1.6 \times 0.41 = 0.656$$

The aeroplane may be flown as a single seater, so that the design/weight, less second occupant and supporting equipment might become:

$$2000 - 250 = 1750 \text{ lb (794 kg)}$$

This will increase the thrust/weight ratio to $F/W = 450/1750 = 0.257$ and the Mach number (assuming the same efficiency):

$$M_C = 0.257/0.55$$
$$= 0.47 \text{ in level flight, making } M = 1.6 \times 0.47 = 0.75$$

This pushes such an aeroplane well into the transonic regime.

It is a matter of choice, but the author believes that there would be such a temptation to pilots to see how fast the aeroplane would go, that it would be wise to aim for $\Delta M = 0.1$ on top of this, so that the wings and stabilising surfaces would be designed for M 0.85.

□ *Wing and canard sweep and thickness ratio*
Assuming M 0.85 to be a sensible limit fig. 4.12d shows that surfaces with sweep of 30 deg and streamwise thickness/chord of 0.1 would be reasonable corresponding with a structural thickness ratio a little under 0.12.
The first sketch shows an aircraft with a wing of 60 ft² (5.57 m²) and canard stabiliser of 9.6 ft² (0.89 m²). Wing span is 17 ft (5.18 m) so that aspect ratio $A = 17^2/60 = 4.8$.
Fig. 15.22 is a chart showing the boundary between stability and instability of swept wings. An aspect ratio of 4.8 and 30 deg sweep is on the boundary, so that when manoeuvring at high g and lift, there could be a tendency to pitch up. One palliative out of a number that could be used to inhibit pitch up is the saw tooth leading edge. This is a relatively easy device to manufacture.
The canard could be replaced with a tail, but there would be problems. Fig. 11.19 shows boundaries which should be observed. The tail would need setting low rather than high – and ground-clearances are already slight. A tail would not shorten take off and landing run.
A major problem with the aeroplane is keeping it small, light and effective, while providing adequate fuel volume. A modest operational radius of 250 nm (463 km) would result in time for a sortie of 1 hour 50 minutes which, with 10 per cent reserves (say) means enough fuel for 2 hours.
□ *Required fuel capacity*
Assuming a sortie time of 2 hours to tanks dry and lift/drag ratio around 14, from fig. 5.18,

$$\text{required thrust} = \text{drag} = 2000/14$$
$$= 143 \text{ lb}$$
$$\text{sfc} = 1.24 \text{ lb/h/lbf}$$
$$\therefore \text{required weight of fuel} = 143 \times 1.24 \times 2$$
$$= 355 \text{ lb (161 kg)}$$
$$= 43.3 \text{ Imp gal (197 litre)}$$
$$= 6.95 \text{ ft}^3$$

One modification that helps is to extend the wing forward at the root nearer to the leading edge of the air intake, as shown for the right wing in fig. 15.21. This enables a deeper wing root to be built, with more capacity where it is needed, close to the centre of gravity.

Another solution, which opens up new possibilities, because it results in a shape that is of current interest in the world at large, is to fit swept forward wings. Some of the advantages and disadvantages are shown in fig. 15.23a and b.

The possible performance that might be attained with a two seat twin jet light aeroplane which could be assembled in a smaller area than the aerobatic machine in fig. 15.12, is both exciting and disquieting. Certainly it is well within the bounds of present technology, and it could be done by careful amateur builders. But caution is needed. Shapes like the tail-first designs shown should be investigated in a wind tunnel. There would also be capabilities inherent in such designs which could put many private pilots well beyond their limits. The engines could be operated up to 30 000 ft (9.144 km). Oxygen equipment would be needed, and flight instruments of a standard that would be compatible with the performance.

We shall leave aeroplane design at this point, with a machine that could be built and operated by amateurs, but which falls into a niche for a cheap jet trainer.

Summary

A number of points can be made which extend to all designs, in one way or another:

There are no hard and fast rules about aeroplane design procedure. Every individual develops his own methods. Nevertheless, useful guidelines should always be noted and tested. A number of textbooks given in the References are rich in such guidance.

☐ Every design is a compromise and there is always room for improvement. Try to get inside the mind of the designer of the aeroplane that you want to buy, or to build.

☐ Question special features. The appearance of anything unusual in the form of stall-breaker strips, fillets, strakes, sweep, cranked surfaces, local changes in incidence, aerofoil section, and dihedral, show that a problem has been anticipated or dealt with. Always look for better solutions.

One must always talk to the operator in the field so as to build up a background of knowledge and information which is essential when attempting to draw a practical aeroplane.

☐ The same applies when buying an aeroplane, a set of plans or a kit. Seek guidance: airworthiness surveyors are useful people. They tend to be amiable critics and their advice is free. After all, people who sell aviation are just as adept at disguising flaws, faults, snags and shortfall as anyone else operating in a market place. Surveyors have seen it all.

☐ When seeking guidance, especially about amateur-built aeroplanes, it pays to go to organisations like the Experimental Aircraft Association (based in the USA, but with connections world-wide) and the Popular Flying Association in the UK. Aircraft Owner and Pilots' Associations can be commended.

☐ Read widely. Magazines like *Aviation Week, Interavia, Air et Cosmos* and *The Aviation Consumer* in the USA are comprehensively hard-hitting, so are *Flight International* and *Pilot Magazine* in the UK – and there are many other magazines too numerous to mention in other countries overseas.

☐ Old textbooks often contain information that is now overlooked or lost. The author has deliberately cast his net wide in that direction and dredged up references that deserve to be remembered, because they contain apposite, relevant information for today.

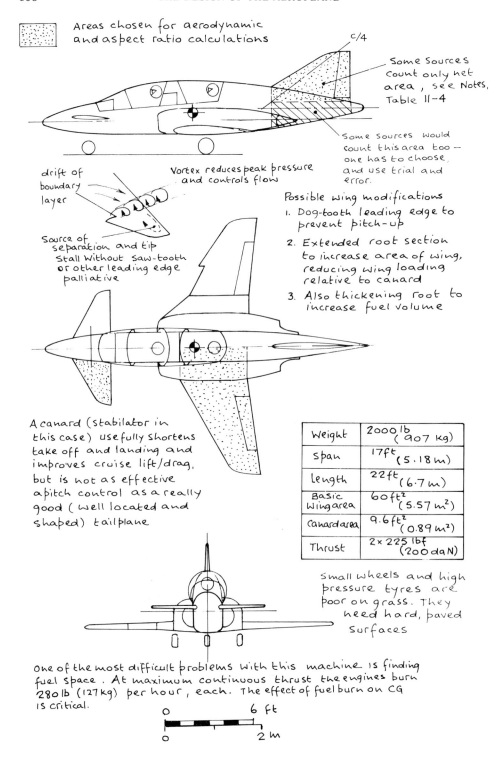

Areas chosen for aerodynamic and aspect ratio calculations

c/4

Some sources count only net area, see Notes, Table 11-4

Some sources would count this area too — one has to choose, and use trial and error.

drift of boundary layer

Vortex reduces peak pressure and controls flow

Source of separation and tip stall without saw-tooth or other leading edge palliative

Possible wing modifications
1. Dog-tooth leading edge to prevent pitch-up

2. Extended root section to increase area of wing, reducing wing loading relative to canard

3. Also thickening root to increase fuel volume

A canard (stabilator in this case) usefully shortens take off and landing and improves cruise lift/drag, but is not as effective a pitch control as a really good (well located and shaped) tailplane

Weight	2000 lb (907 kg)
Span	17 ft (5.18 m)
Length	22 ft (6.7 m)
Basic Wing area	60 ft² (5.57 m²)
Canard area	9.6 ft² (0.89 m²)
Thrust	2 × 225 lbf (200 daN)

Small wheels and high pressure tyres are poor on grass. They need hard, paved surfaces

One of the most difficult problems with this machine is finding fuel space. At maximum continuous thrust the engines burn 280 lb (127 kg) per hour, each. The effect of fuel burn on CG is critical.

0   6 ft

0   2 m

Fig. 15.21   *MO.65* amateur-built twin-jet project (*Microturbo TRS 18*).

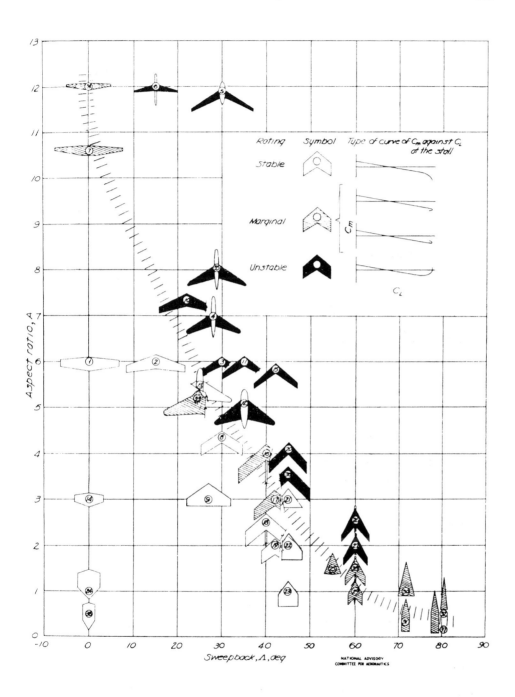

Fig. 15.22   Chart summarising the effect of aspect ratio on the pitching moment of swept-back wings at the stall (ref. 15.17).

Wing Forward sweep enables fuel volume to be arranged further forward than when the wing is swept aft. Also, the spar structure and fuselage attachments lie behind the cockpit, allowing more room for the rear occupant.

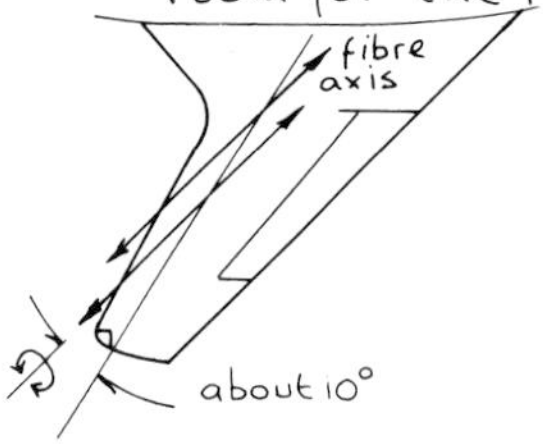

fibre axis
about 10°

Structural fibres arranged as shown ←——→ so that the wing twists about their axis, thus avoiding aeroelastic divergence caused by tip twisting nose-up to larger angle of attack under load (a common problem with earlier, conventional, forward swept structures).

Forward sweep causes a higher aerodynamic loading inboard, so that the wing roots stall first, softening the stall and reducing wing drop. A fillet at the root leading edge has a powerfully favourable effect by reducing high suction inboard. A forward-swept wing has less structural response to buffet than one swept back. Modern man-made materials assist their structural design.

Forward sweep causes marked forward shift of aerodynamic centre compared with a precisely equivalent swept-back wing. The shift, which is around 8 to 10 percent SMC of a constant (common) mean chord means that the wing must be located further aft on the fuselage. As the heaviest part of the wing is near the root, one can run into severe aft CG problems. The available static margin might be reduced by 1/6.

Wing root design of a FSW is more critical than for one swept back. A 10 percent thick rear-loaded (supercritical) wing section is used.

Canard The canard surface experiences a considerable upwash and is in danger of an early stall. Sweep has therefore been increased and span reduced slightly to increase the stalling angle of the canard. So as to reduce induced drag of the canard the trailing edge of the wing inboard has been given a slight upward reflex, offloading the smaller surface somewhat.

Downwash from the canard is favourable for the wing, bringing wing root relief (as long as the canard rides higher than the wing). Tip vortices shed by the canard can interfere adversely with the fin, at low speed and large angles of attack, especially when yawed.

Fin The fin has been made taller, with a higher aspect ratio (countered by a dorsal fillet) because of destabilising effects of tip vortices from the canard at high lift, coupled with yaw. This adjustment has shifted the aerodynamic centre and centre of pressure of the fin a little further aft, improving directional stability. A forward swept wing reduces directional stability in any case. A ventral fin-strake has been added to increase fuselage damping in yaw and to assist recovery in the event of a spin — which could be a major problem with this configuration.

Powerplant The twin engines can be mounted in an area of strong wing-fuselage structure. Flush NACA intakes improve cleanliness. NACA intakes could be fitted in the belly as an alternative, leaving the saddle-fairings free for fuel stowage. Details of a flush inlet are given in Ref 15.18.

Canopy The rake of the windshield has been reduced to cut refraction. The humped rear canopy is the result of cutting cost by making front and rear portions on the same jig. The canopy opens to starboard.

Rigging Wing tip wash-in 5° to 6° relative to root, which has an incidence of −2°. Canard has positive decalage (longitudinal dihedral) around +2° on Wing Standard chord. Wing dihedral 5°, canard 0°.

Ailerons Although highly swept they will maintain their authority to larger angles of attack than when swept back.

Fig. 15.23a Effects of forward swept wings.

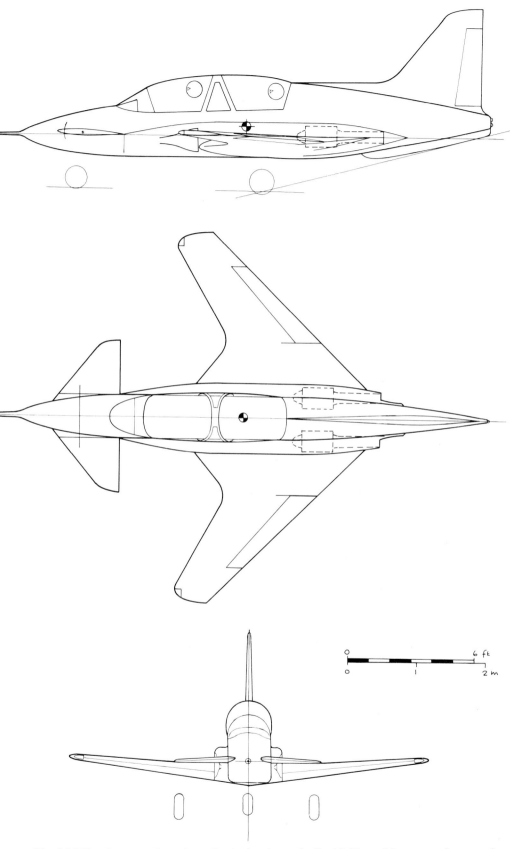

Fig. 15.23b   Improved version of twin-jet shown in fig. 15.21, making extensive use of
man-made composite materials, e.g., *Ciba-Geigy Aeroweb* and *Fibrelam*.

Finally, just because something appears in print does not mean that it is right. Keep your critical faculties sharp. Do that and you will be able to help rectify the inevitable errors which must creep into a technical work of this scope, in spite of careful editing.

References

15.1 Markowski, M. (Dec. 1979) *The Encyclopedia of Homebuilt Aircraft*. TAB Modern Aviation Series no. 2256, Blue Ridge Summit, PA 17214.

15.2 Jackson, A. J. (1968) *Blackburn Aircraft since 1909*. London: Putnam.

15.3 Specification, Continental Motors Corporation. Aircraft Engine Division, Muskegon, Michigan.

15.4 Detail Specification, Avco Lycoming Aircraft Engines. Lycoming Division, Avco Corporation, Williamsport, PA.

15.5 Bonner, H. W. Aero Bonner Company Ltd, Shoreham Airport, Shoreham-by-Sea, Sussex, England.

15.6 Blanton, D. (1980) 'Javelin Ford Engine, Replicair', **3**, no. 2. *Air Replicas International*, PO Box 2218, Durango, Colorado, 81301.

15.7 Official Rules for the Conduct of Aerobatic Contests. British Aerobatic Association c/o Artillery Mansions, 75 Victoria Street, London, SW1H 0JD.

15.8 Limbach, G. (Nov., Dec. 1966) 'Tipsy Nipper. Gusty Mk-1' ... Parts 1 and 2. *Sport Aviation*. Experimental Aircraft Association.

15.9 Limbach, G. (Apr. 1968) Testing 'Gusty', *Sport Aviation*. Experimental Aircraft Association.

15.10 Stinton, D. (1971) 'Agricultural Design Study (a heavy payload aircraft for the Tropics)', *Shell Aviation News 401*.

15.11 BCAR K4–9. Civil Aviation Authority.

15.12 Hinely, J. T. Jr and Boyles, R. Q. Jr. NASA CR–158939. *Advanced System Design Requirements for Large and Small Fixed-Wing Aerial Application Systems for Agriculture*. Langley Research Centre, Hampton, Virginia 23665.

15.13 *Flight International* (Mar. 1979) Report of Royal Aeronautical Society annual agricultural aviation symposium.

15.14 Thunder Engines Inc. (Jul. 1981) RPM, Development Company 7120, Hayvenhurst Avenue, Suite 321, Van Nuys, California 91406.

15.15 Geschwender Aeromotive. *Ford V–8 Conversion for Aircraft Application*. Geschwender Aeromotive Inc., Nebraska 68505.

15.16 Morrison, R. C. (Sep. 1978) *Aerobatic Airplanes, Participants in the IX World Aerobatic Championships*. Repla-Tech International, Inc., 48500 McKenzie Hwy, Vida, Oregon, 97488.

15.17 Shortal, J. A. and Maggin, B. (May 1946). Technical Note No. 1093. *Effect of Sweepback and Aspect Ratio on Longitudinal Stability Characteristics of Wings at Low Speeds*. National Advisory Committee for Aeronautics, Washington.

15.19 Lightning, *Merlin V–12* Thunder Wings, 7326 East Evans Road, Scottsdale, Arizona 85260.

Light and General Aviation Aerodynamics

251-259 Regent Street, London W1R 7AD. England
Telephone 01-437 4894
Telex 266168 ENDASA G

Engineering Sciences
Data Unit

Suite 916, 1511 K Street NW, Washington DC 20005 U.S.A.
Telephone (202) 638 0055
Telex 89441 KENCO WSH

LIGHT AND GENERAL AVIATION AERODYNAMICS
An Esdu DataMethod Manual

VOLUME 1

Properties of the atmosphere

77021 Properties of a standard atmosphere.

78017 True airspeed in the International Standard Atmosphere and equivalent airspeed corresponding to Mach number and pressure altitude.

Lift and pitching moment of wings, bodies and tail units

WINGS (INCLUDING WING-BODY COMBINATIONS) AND TAILPLANES

76003 Geometrical properties of cranked and straight tapered wing planforms.

W.01.01.05 Slope of lift curve for two-dimensional flow.

W.01.01.01. Lift-curve slope of swept and tapered wings.

W.01.01.04 Effect of cut-out on the slope of lift curve.

C.01.01.04 Effect of gap on slope of lift curve and slope of lift increment curve due to control surface deflection.

70011 Lift-curve slope and aerodynamic centre position of wings in inviscid subsonic flow.

76015 Aerodynamic centre of wing-fuselage combinations.

66033 Boundaries of linear characteristics of plane, symmetrical section wings at subcritical Mach numbers.

66034 The low-speed stalling characteristics of aerodynamically smooth aerofoils.

W.01.01.06 Maximum lift coefficient for various types of aerofoil sections.

80020 Average downwash at the tailplane at low angles of attack and subsonic speeds.

W.05.01.01 Kinetic pressure in the wake behind a wing.

72023 Low speed longitudinal aerodynamic characteristics of aircraft in ground effect.

BODIES

A.08.01.07 Pitching moment coefficient due to body, $(C_{mo})_b$.

TAILFINS

C.01.01.01 Lift-curve slope for single fin and rudder.
(i) Body shape merging into fin.

C.01.01.05 Lift-curve slope for single fin and rudder.
(ii) Body of circular cross-section.

C.01.01.02 Lift-curve slope for twin fins and rudders.

C.01.01.04 (see wing lift).

VOLUME 2

Lift, pitching moment and hinge moment of controls and flaps

AILERONS, ELEVATORS AND RUDDERS

C.01.01.03 Rate of change of lift coefficient with control deflection in incompressible two-dimensional flow, $(a_2)_0$.

C.01.01.04 (see wing lift – Volume 1).

C.04.01.00 Information on the use of data sheets on control hinge moments.

C.04.01.01 Rate of change of hinge-moment coefficient with incidence for a plain control in incompressible two-dimensional flow, $(b_1)_0$.

C.04.01.02 Rate of change of hinge moment coefficient with control deflection for a plain control in incompressible two-dimensional flow, $(b_2)_0$.

C.04.01.03 Effect of nose balance on two-dimensional control hinge-moment coefficients.

C.04.01.04 Effect of Irving internal balance on hinge-moment coefficient in two-dimensional flow.

C.04.01.07 Effect of horn balances on hinge-moment coefficients.

C.04.01.05 Conversion factors to hinge-moment coefficients for finite aspect ratio.

C.04.01.06 Control hinge-moment coefficient corrections for variation with span of control chord ratios and section shapes.

C.04.01.08 Control hinge-moment due to tab.

C.04.01.09 Control hinge-moments – example of procedure in computation. Combined horn and nose balance.

C.06.01.01 Control derivative L_ξ. Rolling moment due to aileron deflection.

C.08.01.01 Rate of change of pitching moment coefficient with control deflection for a plain control in incompressible two-dimensional flow, m_0.

FLAPS

75013 Information on the use of Data Items on flaps including estimation of the effects of fuselage interference.

F.01.01.08 Lift coefficient increment due to full-span slotted flaps.

F.01.01.09 Lift coefficient increment due to full-span double flap (main flap slotted).

74009 Lift coefficient increment at low speeds due to full-span split flaps.

74011 Rate of change of lift coefficient with control deflection for full-span plain controls.

74012 Conversion of lift coefficient increment due to flaps from full span to part span.

F.05.01.01 Normal force on flaps and controls.

F.08.01.01 Pitching moment coefficient increment due to flaps for unswept wings.

F.08.01.02 Increment to C_{mo} due to flaps on swept-back wings.

VOLUME 3
Drag

GENERAL

67041 Drag of fighter-type canopies at subcritical Mach numbers.

79015 Undercarriage drag prediction methods.

WINGS AND TAIL UNITS

W.02.04.00 Information on the use of Data Items in the series Wings 02.04.

W.02.04.01 Drag of a smooth flat plate at zero incidence.

W.02.04.02 Profile drag of smooth wings.

W.02.04.03 Profile drag of smooth aerofoils with straight trailing-edges at low speeds.

W.02.04.09 Limit of grain size for laminar flow over wings or bodies.

W.02.04.11 Limit of surface waviness for laminar flow over wings.

66031 Introductory sheet on subcritical lift-dependent drag of wings.

66032 Subsonic lift-dependent drag due to boundary layer of plane, symmetrical section wings.

74035 Subsonic lift-dependent drag due to the trailing vortex wake for wings without camber or twist.

72023 (see wing lift – Volume 1).

BODIES

77028 Geometrical characteristics of typical forebodies and afterbodies.

78019 Profile drag of axisymmetric bodies at zero incidence for subcritical Mach numbers.

80006 Drag increment due to rear fuselage upsweep.

FLAPS

75013 (see flap lift – Volume 2).

F.02.01.06 Profile drag coefficient increment due to full-span single-slotted flaps (Handley Page and NACA types).

74010 Low-speed drag coefficient increment at zero lift due to full-span split flaps.

F.02.01.07 Conversion factor for profile drag increment for part-span flaps.

F.02.01.08 Vortex drag coefficient of wing with part-span flap and central cut-out.

VOLUME 4
Stability derivatives

GENERAL

A.00.00.02 Dynamic stability of an aeroplane in straight flight with plane of symmetry vertical.

A.00.00.03 Longitudinal stability. Definitions and discussion of the principal terms used.

A.00.00.04 Introduction to lateral stability.

A.00.00.05 Conversion of resolutes of force and velocity and of constants of inertia for general change of axes.

A.00.00.06 Conversion of stability derivatives for a change of body axes.

67039 Introduction to the new notation for aerodynamics.

WINGS (INCLUDING WING-BODY COMBINATIONS) AND TAILPLANES

A.06.01.00 Information on the use of Data Items on the rolling moment derivatives of an aeroplane.

A.07.01.00 Information on the use of Data Items on yawing moment derivatives of an aeroplane.

80033 Contribution of wing planform to rolling moment derivative due to sideslip, $(L_v)_w$, at subsonic speeds.

A.06.01.03 Stability derivative $(L_v)_\Gamma$. Contribution of full-span dihedral to rolling moment due to sideslip.

A.06.01.09 Stability derivative $(L_v)_\Gamma$. Contribution of part-span dihedral to rolling moment due to sideslip.

73006 Effects of isolated body and wing-body interference on rolling moment due to sideslip.

80034 Effect of trailing-edge flaps on rolling moment derivative due to sideslip, $(L_v)_f$.

79006 Wing-body yawing moment and sideforce derivatives due to sideslip: N_v and Y_v.

81013 Effect of trailing-edge flaps on sideforce and yawing moment derivatives due to sideslip, $(Y_v)_f$ and $(N_v)_f$.

A.06.01.01 Stability derivative L_p. Rolling moment due to rolling for swept and tapered wings.

81014 Contribution of wing planform to derivatives of yawing moment and sideforce due to roll rate at subsonic speeds, $(N_p)_w$ and $(Y_p)_w$.

72021 Effect of wing on rolling moment due to yawing.

71017 Aero-normalised stability derivatives: effect of wing on yawing moment due to yawing.

BODIES

73006 (see wing stability derivatives).

TAILFINS

A.07.01.00 (see wing stability derivatives).

70006 Aero-normalised stability derivatives: effect of fin and rudder on rolling moments due to sideslip and yawing.

Light and General Aviation Performance

Available from *Engineering Sciences Data Unit.*(See App. A).

80032	Simplified forms of performance equations.
81026	Representation of drag in performance calculations.
EG3/1	Estimation of rate of climb.
EG3/2	The effect of small changes on rate of climb.
75018	Estimation of cruise range propeller-driven aircraft.
77015	Lost range, fuel and time due to climb and descent: propeller-driven aeroplanes.
EG8/1	Estimation of turning performance.
EG8/2	Estimation of rolling manoeuvrability.
EG5/1	Estimation of take-off distance.
EG6/0	Introduction to landing performance.
EG6/1	A first approximination to the total landing distance from 50 ft height.
EG6/2	Estimation of approach speed.
EG2/1	Effect of small changes in level speed. (Withdrawn from ESDU Performance Series but available as copies if required).
68046	Atmospheric data for performance calculations.

Treatment of Scale Quantities

All of the physical units with which we are concerned can be expressed in terms of mass, M, Length, L and time T, as shown in Table C-1.

TABLE C-1

Physical Units

Quantity	Dimensions	
Angular velocity	I/T	$= T^{-1}$
Linear velocity, V	L/T	$= LT^{-1}$
Angular acceleration	I/T^2	$= T^{-2}$
Linear acceleration	L/T^2	$= LT^{-2}$
Force (*mass × linear acceleration*)	ML/T^2	$= MLT^{-2}$
Pressure (*force/area*)	M/LT^2	$= ML^{-1}T^{-2}$
Density (*mass/volume*), ρ	M/L^3	$= ML^{-3}$
Kinematic viscosity, ν	L^2/T	$= L^2T^{-1}$

Aerodynamic (and hydrodynamic) forces can be stated in the form:

$$\text{Force} = f_1(\rho L \nu V) \tag{C-1}$$

in which f_1 is a function of density, ρ, a length, L, kinematic viscosity ν and velocity V.

But, when we are concerned with bodies in motion in fluids, like a seaplane making waves in water, with some of its surfaces moving in air; or when comparing aeroplanes manoeuvring, we must take gravity, g, into account as well. If an aircraft is moving fast enough in air, Mach number also intrudes, so that:

$$\text{Force} = \rho\, L^2 V^2 f_2 \left(\frac{VL}{\nu},\ \frac{V}{a},\ \frac{V^2}{Lg} \right) \tag{C-2}$$

where the terms in the brackets will be recognised as:

Reynolds Number, $R = cV/\nu$

in which $\bar{c}$, the standard mean chord, is also the characteristic length, L,   eq (2–11)

Mach number $M = V/a$ eq (2–51)

and the

Froude number $F = V^2/gL$ eq (2–67)

Although Froude number is usually associated with the effects of wave-making in water, it is also important in wind tunnel and free flight work when conditions are not steady. It is impossible to make Reynolds, Mach and Froude numbers constant for two similarly shaped bodies which are of different scales. Often, we have to know the effects of scale upon tests and the following useful comparisons of quantities can be made. If we express scale in terms of a number, , which is always greater than 1, then from eq (15–10):

$$\text{scale} = 1/\lambda = \lambda^{-1} \tag{C-3}$$

e.g. half scale $= 1/2$, where $\lambda = 2$

For dynamic similarity:

$$\text{Length, } L \text{ varies as scale, } 1/\lambda \text{ or } \lambda^{-1} \tag{C-4}$$
$$\text{Area, } L^2 \text{ varies as scale}^2, 1/\lambda^2 \text{ or } \lambda^{-2} \tag{C-5}$$
$$\text{Mass or Volume, } L^3 \tag{C-6}$$
$$\text{varies as scale}^3, \qquad 1/\lambda^3 \text{ or } \lambda^{-3}$$

While velocity can be shown from Froude number, V^2/Lg as:

$$V \text{ varies as } \sqrt{\text{scale}}, 1/\sqrt{\lambda} \text{ or } \lambda^{-1/2} \tag{C-7}$$

Similarly, as distance is the same as linear length L, and speed or velocity $\alpha\sqrt{L}$, then time, which is distance/speed becomes:

$$\text{Time, } T \text{ varies as } \sqrt{\text{scale}}, 1/\sqrt{\lambda} \text{ or } \lambda^{-1/2} \tag{C-8}$$

Thus, we are able to list dimensional conversions in terms of scale alone, as shown in Table C-2.

TABLE C-2

Conversion of Dimensions for Linear Scale $(1/\lambda)$

Unit	Scale Conversion	
Length L	Scale	λ^{-1}
Area L^2	Scale^2	λ^{-2}
Volume, mass, force, L^3	Scale^3	λ^{-3}
Moment L^4	Scale^4	λ^{-4}
Moment of inertia L^5	Scale^5	λ^{-5}
Linear, Velocity, Speed, V	$\sqrt{\text{Scale}}$	$\lambda^{-1/2}$
Linear acceleration L/T^2	Constant	$\lambda^\circ = 1$
Angular velocity I/T	$1/\sqrt{\text{Scale}}$	$\lambda^{1/2}$
Angular acceleration I/T^2	$1/\text{Scale}$	λ
Time, T	$\sqrt{\text{Scale}}$	$\lambda^{-1/2}$
RPM, I/T	$1/\sqrt{\text{Scale}}$	$\lambda^{1/2}$
Work L^4	Scale^4	λ^{-4}
Power $L^{7/2}$ (i.e., $L^3 \times L/\sqrt{L}$)	Scale$^{7/2}$	$\lambda^{-7/2}$
Wing loading	Scale	λ^{-1}
Powerloading	$1/\sqrt{\text{Scale}}$	$\lambda^{1/2}$

The usefulness of this result can be seen in our context when looking at a scale replica, like the *B–48* in chapter 15, example 33. Table C–3 shows technical details of original aeroplane. For a 7/10 replica to reproduce scale motions in flight, power, weight, wing

TABLE C–3

Specification and Data for *Blackburn B–48* or *YA1*

Manufacturers:	*Blackburn Aircraft Ltd*, Brough Aerodrome, East Yorkshire, England
Purpose:	One of the last piston-engined torpedo strike fighters designed for the Royal Navy and covered by Specification S28/43. Slightly smaller but similar in class to the *Douglas AD–1 Skyraider*. First flew in 1947, but never got beyond prototype stage: overtaken by gas turbine era
Power Plant:	One 2475 hp *Bristol Centaurus 59* two-row radial, with possibility of 2840 hp version
Dimensions:	Span 44 ft 11½ in (folded) 18 ft 0 in Length 39 ft 3½ in Height 14 ft 6 in Wing area 361.5 ft²
Weights:	Tare 10 513 lb Military load 2500 lb All-up 15 280 lb
Maximum Speed:	380 mph (330 knot) at 19 000 ft
Reference:	15.2 and ex-Blackburn sources

TABLE C–4

Application to Scale B–48, Chapter 15, Example 33

Item	Original	Example 33	Required for scale motions
Weight lb	15 280	2612	5241
Wing area ft²	361.5	177.13	177.13
Power BHP	2475	180	710
Wing loading lb/ft²	42.26	14.76	29.83
Power loading lb/BHP	6.17	14.51	7.38

and power loadings would have to be as shown in table C–4. The implications of the results in the table are that the 7/10 scale replica would be quicker in response to control, but much less lively in performance, so that its flight characteristics would not resemble the original with accuracy.

Index